9th Edition

2000 North American
Coins & Prices

A GUIDE TO U.S., CANADIAN AND MEXICAN COINS

Edited by David C. Harper, editor of *Numismatic News*,
World Coin News and *Bank Note Reporter*

Published by

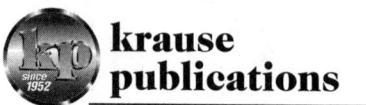

700 E. State Street • Iola, WI 54990-0001
Telephone: 715/445-2214

Please call or write for our free catalog of numismatic publications.
Our toll-free number to place an order or obtain a free catalog is 800-258-0929
or please use our regular business telephone 715-445-2214
for editorial comment and further information.

Library of Congress Catalog Number: 91-76402
ISBN: 0-87341-756-9

Printed in the United States of America

There is a reason why NGC is the world's leading certification company.

- NGC has more expert graders (7) and the world's top finalizing team (Mark Salzberg, John Maben). All of which helps us get the grade right the first time.

- NGC is known for its long-standing commitment to integrity, consistency and accuracy, which in some months rewards us with more coin submissions than all other grading services combined.

- NGC is trusted to grade virtually all of the the world's greatest rarities, most recently the Amazonian set, the 1873-CC No Arrows dime and the finest known 1799/8 Draped Bust Large Cent.

- NGC is the Official Grading Service of the American Numismatic Association.

NGC is committed to proving we deserve your trust and business every day and with every one of the 50,000-plus coins we receive each month. The more choices you have in grading services, the more important it becomes that you can trust your choice for top expertise and proven performance. That's NGC.

Contents

Preface

Providing coin collectors with accurate, independently produced pricing information on collectible coins has become a trademark of Krause Publications in its nearly 50 years of publishing. Visit our Web site at www.krause.com, or www.coincollecting.net for more information about us. We employ a full-time staff of market analysts who monitor auction results, trading on electronic networks connecting dealers across the United States and trading at major shows.

This information is compiled by our analysts and they determine what price most accurately reflects the trading that has occurred for each date and mintmark in each grade listed in *North American Coins & Prices*. By studying this information and referring back to it repeatedly, a collector can arm himself with the necessary knowledge to go out in the market and make wise purchasing decisions.

U.S. coins are the most popularly collected issues in the world. This is attributable in part to the popularity of coin collecting in the United States, but collectors in many other countries also covet collectible U.S. coins. After collecting U.S. coins for a while, many collectors in the United States branch out into issues of Canada and Mexico. These coins also enjoy a popular following in their countries of origin.

Thus, *North American Coins & Prices* brings together pricing information on all three of these countries. But this book also takes the price-guide concept a step further by providing information on the nuts and bolts of collecting coins: acquiring coins, grading them, organizing them into a collection, storing them properly and much more. Novice collectors can gain the necessary knowledge to collect coins enjoyably; veterans can pick up some pointers to add to their knowledge.

1

"A small beginning"

The U.S. Mint grew from a modest start

By Robert R. Van Ryzin

It was a "small beginning" but a significant one. In July 1792, a site for the new U.S. Mint not yet having been secured, 1,500 silver half dismes were struck on a small screw press nestled in the cellar of a Philadelphia building owned by sawmaker John Harper. Though some have since categorized these early emissions of the fledgling U.S. Mint as patterns, it is clear that first President George Washington — who is said to have deposited the silver from which the coins were struck — considered this small batch of half dismes the first official U.S. coins.

It is true that this limited coinage, the first since passage of the act establishing the Mint on April 2, 1792, pales by comparison to modern U.S. Mint presses. Today's machines can churn out up to 750 coins a minute, striking as many as four coins at a time and boasting yearly mintages in the billions. But it is also true that these first small pieces — struck from silver and stamped with a plump Liberty on the obverse and a scrawny eagle in flight on the reverse — have tremendous historical importance.

For within what Washington would declare in his 1792 address to Congress as a "small beginning" were the seeds of a monetary system that has lasted more than 200 years and has become the study and admiration of many.

Before the U.S. Mint

Collectors today can trace much of the nation's development and learn of its struggles and growth through its coinage: from a cumbersome system first proposed by Robert Morris, a Revolutionary War financier and first superintendent of finance, to the refinements tendered by Thomas Jefferson and Alexander Hamilton, which firmly placed the nation on an easily understood decimal system of coinage.

At first there was little coinage in circulation, except for foreign coins that arrived through trade or in the purses of the first settlers. Despite a dire need for coinage in the Colonies, Great Britain considered it a royal right and granted franchises sparingly. Much of the Colonial economy, therefore, revolved around barter, with food staples, crops, and goods serving as currency. Indian waupum or bead money also was used, first in the fur trade and later as a form of money for Colonial use.

Copper pieces were produced around 1616 for Sommer Islands (now Bermuda), but coinage within the American Colonies apparently didn't begin until 1652, when John Hull struck silver threepence, sixpence and shillings under authority of the General Court of Massachusetts. This coinage continued, with design changes (willow, oak and pine trees), through 1682. Most of the coins were dated 1652, apparently to avoid problems with England.

In 1658 Cecil Calvert, second Lord Baltimore, commissioned coins to be struck in England for use in Maryland. Other authorized and unauthorized coinages — including those of Mark Newby, John Holt, William Wood, and Dr. Samuel Higley — all became part of the landscape of circulating coins. In the 1780s this hodgepodge of coinage was augmented by influxes of counterfeit British halfpence and various state coinages.

In terms of the latter, the Articles of Confederation had granted individual states the right to produce copper coins. Many states found this to be appealing, and merchants in the mid-1780s traded copper coins of Vermont, Connecticut, Massachusetts, New Jersey, and New York. Not all were legal issues; various entrepreneurs used this as an invitation to strike imitation state coppers and British halfpence. Mutilated and worn foreign coins also circulated in abundance. Included among these were coins of Portugal, Great Britain and France, with the large majority of the silver arriving from Spain.

The accounting system used by the states was derived from the British system of pounds, shillings and pence. Each state was allowed to set its own rates at which foreign gold and silver coins would trade in relation to the British pound.

In 1782 Robert Morris, newly named superintendent of finance, was appointed to head a committee to determine the values and weights of the gold and silver coins in circulation. Asked simply to draw up a table of values, Morris took the opportunity to propose the establishment of a federal mint. In his Jan. 15, 1782, report (largely prepared by his assistant, Gouverneur Morris), Morris noted that the exchange rates between the states were complicated.

He observed that a farmer in New Hampshire would be hard-pressed if asked to determine the value of a bushel of wheat in South Carolina. Morris recorded that an amount of wheat worth four shillings in his home state of New Hampshire would be worth 21 shillings and eightpence under the

Robert Morris devised
a complicated plan for
a national coinage
based on a common
denominator of 1,440.

accounting system used in South Carolina.

Morris claimed these difficulties plagued not only farmers, but that "they are perplexing to most Men and troublesome to all." Morris further pressed for the adoption of an American coin to solve the problems of the need for small change and debased foreign coinages in circulation.

In essence, what he was advocating was a monometallic system based on silver. He said that gold and silver had fluctuated throughout history. Because these fluctuations resulted in the more valuable metal leaving the country, any nation that adopted a bimetallic coinage was doomed to have its gold or silver coins disappear from circulation.

Gouverneur Morris calculated the rate at which the Spanish dollar traded to the British pound in the various states. Leaving out South Carolina, because it threw off his calculations, Gouverneur Morris arrived at a common denominator of 1,440. Robert Morris, therefore, recommended a unit of value of 1/1,440, equivalent to a quarter grain of silver. He suggested the striking of a silver 100-unit coin, or cent; a silver 500-unit coin, or quint; a silver 1,000-unit coin, or mark; and two copper coins, one of eight units and the other of five units.

On Feb. 21, 1782, the Grand Committee of Congress approved the proposal and directed Morris to press forward and report with a plan to establish a mint. Morris had already done so. Apparently feeling confident that Congress would like his coinage ideas, Morris (as shown by his diary) began efforts at the physical establishment prior to his January 1782 report. He had already engaged Benjamin Dudley to acquire necessary equipment for the mint and hoped to have sample coins available to submit with his original report to Congress.

Things went awry, however.

By Dec. 12, 1782, 10 months after Congress had approved his plan, Morris still could not show any samples of his coins. He was forced, ironically, to suggest that Congress draw up a table of rates for foreign coins to be used until his report was ready. It was not until April 2, 1783, that Morris was able to note in his diary that the first of his pattern coins were being struck.

"I sent for Mr. Dudley who delivered me a piece of Silver Coin," he wrote, "being the first that has been struck as an American Coin."

He also recorded that he had urged Dudley to go ahead with production of the silver patterns.

It wasn't until April 23, 1783, that Morris was able to send his Nova Constellatio patterns to Congress and suggest that he was ready to report on establishing a mint. Apparently nothing came of Morris' efforts. Several committees looked into the matter, but nothing was accomplished. Dudley was eventually discharged as Morris' hopes dimmed.

Thomas Jefferson was the next to offer a major plan. Jefferson liked the idea of a decimal system of coinage, but disliked Morris' basic unit of value. As chairman of the Currency Committee, Jefferson reviewed Morris' plan and formulated his own ideas.

To test public reaction, Jefferson gave his "Notes on Coinage" to *The Providence Gazette, and Country Journal*, which published his plan in its July 24, 1784, issue. Jefferson disagreed with Morris' suggestion for a 1/1,440 unit of value and instead proposed a decimal coinage based on the dollar, with the lowest unit of account being the mil, or 1/1,000.

"The most easy ratio of multiplication and division is that by ten," Jefferson wrote. "Every one knows the facility of Decimal Arithmetic."

Jefferson argued that although Morris' unit would have eliminated the unwanted fraction that occurred when merchants converted British farthings to dollars, this was of little significance. After all, the original idea of establishing a mint was to get rid of foreign currencies.

Morris' unit, Jefferson said, was too cumbersome for use in normal business transactions. According to Jefferson, under Morris' plan a horse valued at 80 Spanish dollars would require a notation of six figures and would be shown as 115,200 units.

Jefferson's coinage plan suggested the striking of a dollar, or unit; half dollar, or five-tenths; a double tenth, or fifth of a dollar, equivalent to a pistereen; a tenth, equivalent to a Spanish bit; and a one-fifth copper coin, relating to the British farthing. He also wanted a gold coin of $10, corresponding to the British double guinea; and a copper one-hundredth coin, relating to the British halfpence.

In reference to his coinage denominations, Jefferson said, it was important that the coins "coincide in value with some of the known coins so nearly, that the people may by quick reference in the mind, estimate their value."

Thomas Jefferson proposed that the United States adopt a decimal system of coinage.

More than a year, however, passed without any further action on his plan or that proposed by Morris. In a letter to William Grayson, a member of the Continental Congress, Washington expressed concern for the establishment of a national coinage system, terming it "indispensibly necessary." Washington also complained of the coinage in circulation: "A man must travel with a pair of scales in his pocket, or run the risk of receiving gold at one-fourth less than it counts."

A plan at last

On May 13, 1785, the 13-member Grand Committee, to whom Jefferson's plan had been submitted, filed its report, generally favoring Jefferson's coinage system. The committee did, however, make slight alterations, including the elimination of the gold $10 coin, the addition of a gold $5 coin, and the dropping of Jefferson's double tenth, which it replaced with a quarter dollar. The committee also added a coin equal to 1/200 of a dollar (half cent). On July 6, 1785, Congress unanimously approved the Grand Committee's plan. It failed, however, to set a standard weight for the silver dollar or to order plans drawn up for a mint. These two factors led to new proposals.

On April 8, 1786, the Board of Treasury, which had been reinstated after Morris' resignation as superintendent of finance two years prior, tendered three distinct coinage proposals based on varying weights and bimetallic ratios for the silver dollar. The first of these three plans (the one passed by Congress on Aug. 8, 1786) required the silver dollar to contain 375.64 grains of pure silver. The board's proposal varied from earlier coinage plans in that it advocated a higher bimetallic ratio of 15.256-to-1 and differing charges to depositors for coining of gold and silver. It called for minting of gold $5 and $10 coins, and silver denominations of the dime, double dime, half dollar, and dollar. In copper were a cent and half cent. The proposal came during the peak of state coinages and influxes of debased coppers, which, as the board reported, were being "Imported into or manufactured in the Several States."

Concerned over the need to control state coinages and foreign coppers, the board suggested that, within nine months of passage of its proposal, the legal-tender status of all foreign coppers be repealed and that values be set at which the state coppers would circulate. The board obviously expected immediate action and ordered a supply of copper that was being stored in Boston to be brought to New York in the hope that it might soon be coined. Their hopes, however, rested on the positive and quick action of Congress, something that hadn't occurred with the other proposals and would not occur this time.

Opposition to the mint was beginning to surface. Several members of Congress expressed their belief that the supply of foreign gold and silver coins in circulation was sufficient to preclude any need for a mint. They also argued that the problem with debased coppers could be solved by contracting with private individuals to strike the nation's cents and half cents.

Several proposals were offered for a contract coinage. On April 21, 1787, the board accepted a proposal by James Jarvis to strike 300 tons of copper coin at the federal standard. Jarvis, however, delivered slightly less than 9,000 pounds of his contract. The contract was voided the following year for his failure to meet scheduled delivery times, but helped to delay further action on a mint. Concerted action on a coinage system and a mint would wait until the formation of the new government.

Alexander Hamilton, named in September 1789 to head the new Treasury, offered three different methods by which the new nation could achieve economic stability, including the funding of the national debt, establishment of the Bank of North America, and the founding of the U.S. Mint. On Jan. 21, 1791, Hamilton submitted to Congress a "Report on the Establishment of a Mint." It was compiled through his study of European economic theories and the earlier works of Morris and Jefferson, along with the 1786 report of the Board of Treasury.

Hamilton agreed with Jefferson that the dollar seemed to be best suited to serve as the basic unit, but believed it necessary to establish a proper weight and fineness for the new coin. To do so, Hamilton had several Spanish coins assayed to determine the fine weight of the Spanish dollar. He also watched the rate at which Spanish dollars traded for fine gold (24 3/4 grains per dollar) on the world market.

From his assays and observations he determined that the Spanish dollar contained 371 grains of silver. He then multiplied 24 3/4 by 15 (the gold value of silver times his suggested bimetallic ratio) and arrived at 371 1/4 as the proper fine silver weight for the new silver dollar.

In regard to his findings, Hamilton admitted that Morris had made similar assays and had arrived at a weight of 373 grains for the Spanish dollar. Hamilton attributed the discrepancy to the differing equipment used in making the assays. He failed, however, to observe that silver coins were traded in the world market at actual weight rather than the weight at time of issue. The Spanish dollar contained 376 grains of pure silver when new, 4 3/4 grains more than Hamilton's proposed silver dollar.

Hamilton also wanted a bimetallic ratio of 15-to-1, in contrast to the Board of Treasury's 15.6-to-1 ratio. Hamilton said his ratio was closer to Great Britain's, which would be important for trade, and Holland's, which would be important for repaying loans from that country.

His report suggested the striking of a gold $10; gold dollar; silver dollar; silver tenth, or disme; and copper one-hundredth and half-hundredth. Hamilton felt the last of these, the half cent, was necessary because it would enable merchants to lower their prices, which would help the poor.

Congress passed the act establishing the U.S. Mint in April 1792. It reinstated several coin denominations left out by Hamilton and dropped his gold dollar. In gold, the act authorized a $10 coin, or "eagle"; a $5 coin, or "half eagle"; and a $2.50 coin, or "quarter eagle". In silver were to be a dollar, half dollar, quarter dollar, disme, and half disme, and in copper a cent and half cent.

Though it established a sound system of U.S. coinage, the act failed to address the problem of foreign coins in circulation. It was amended in February 1793 to cancel their legal-tender status within three years of the Mint's opening.

Coinage begins

Coinage totals at the first mint were understandably low. Skilled coiners, assayers and others who could handle the mint's daily operations were in short supply in the United States. Also in want were adequate equipment and supplies of metal for coinage. Much of the former had to be built or imported. Much of the latter was also imported or salvaged from various domestic sources, including previously struck tokens and coins, and scrap metal.

Coinage began in earnest in 1793 with the striking of half cents and cents at the new mint located at Seventh Street between Market and Arch streets in Philadelphia. Silver coinage followed in 1794, with half dimes, half dollars and dollars. Gold coinage did not begin until 1795 with the minting of the first $5 and $10 coins. Silver dimes and quarters and gold $2.50

Production at the first U.S. mint, in Philadelphia, was minuscule by today's standards.

coins did not appear until 1796.

Under the bimetallic system of coinage by which gold and silver served as equal representations of the unit of value, much of the success and failure of the nation's coinage to enter and remain in circulation revolved around the supply and valuation of precious metals. One need only to gain a cursory knowledge of such movements to understand what role precious metals played in development of U.S. coinage. That role, to a large extent, determined why some coins today are rare and why some passed down from generation to generation are still plentiful and of lower value to collectors.

From the Mint's beginning, slight miscalculations in the proper weight for the silver dollar and a proper bimetallic ratio led gold and silver to disappear from circulation. The U.S. silver dollar traded at par with Spanish and Mexican dollars, but because the U.S. coin was lighter, it was doomed to export.

A depositor at the first mint could make a profit at the mint's expense by sending the coins to the West Indies. There they could be traded at par for the heavier Spanish or Mexican eight reales, which were then shipped back to the United States for recoinage. As a result, few early silver dollars entered domestic circulation; most failed to escape the melting pots.

Gold fared no better. Calculations of the bimetallic ratio by which silver traded for gold on the world market were also askew at first and were always subject to fluctuations. Gold coins either disappeared quickly after minting or never entered circulation, languishing in bank vaults. These problems led President Jefferson to halt coinage of the gold $10 and silver dollar.

The gold $10 reappeared in 1838 at a new, lower-weight standard. The silver dollar, not coined for circulation since 1803, returned in 1836 with a limited mintage. Full-scale coinage waited until 1840.

Nor was the coining of copper an easy matter for the first mint. Severe shortages of the metal led the Mint to explore various avenues of obtaining sufficient supplies for striking cents and half cents.

Witness, for example, the half-cent issues of 1795 and 1797 struck over privately issued tokens of the New York firm of Talbot, Allum & Lee because of a shortage of copper for the federal issue. Rising copper prices and continued shortages forced the Mint to lower the cent's weight from 208 grains to 168 grains in 1795.

By that same year Congress had begun to investigate the Mint. Complaints about high costs and low production had been raised. Suggestions that a contract coinage might be more suitable for the new nation surfaced again, despite bad experiences with previous attempts.

The Mint survived this and another investigation, but the problems of fluctuating metal supplies continued to plague the nation. In 1798, because of the coinage shortage, the legal-tender status of foreign coins was restored. Several more extensions were given during the 1800s, ending with the withdrawal of legal-tender status for Spanish coins in 1857.

In the 1830s great influxes of silver from foreign mints raised the value of gold in relation to silver, which made it necessary for the Mint to lower the standard weight of all gold coins in 1834. It also led to the melting of great numbers of gold coins of the old specifications.

By the 1850s discovery of gold in California had again made silver the dearer metal. All silver quickly disappeared from circulation. Congress reacted in 1853 by lowering the weight of the silver half dime, dime, quarter, and half dollar, hoping to keep silver in circulation. A new gold coin of $20 value was introduced to absorb a great amount of the gold from Western mines.

Not long after, silver was discovered in Nevada. By the mid-1870s the various mines that made up what was known as the Comstock Lode (after its colorful early proprietor, Henry P. Comstock) had hit the mother lode. Large supplies of silver from the Comstock, combined with European demonetization, caused a severe drop in its value, which continued through the close of the 19th century.

It was believed that the introduction of a heavier, 420-grain silver dollar in 1873, known as the Trade dollar, would create a market for much of the Comstock silver, bolster its price, and at the same time wrest control from Great Britain of lucrative trade with the Orient. It didn't. Large numbers of Trade dollars eventually flooded back into the United States, where they were, ironically, accepted only at a discount to the lesser-weight Morgan dollars.

The latter had been introduced in 1878 as a panacea to the severe economic problems following the Civil War. Those who proudly carried the banner of free silver contended that by taking the rich output of the Comstock mines and turning it into silver dollars, a cheaper, more plentiful form of money would become available. In its wake, they believed, would be a much needed economic recovery.

The Free Silver Movement gained its greatest support during the late 19th century when William Jennings Bryan attempted to gain the White House on a plank largely based on restoration of the free and unlimited coinage of the standard 412.5-grain silver dollar. He failed. Silver failed. Shortly thereafter the United States officially adopted a gold standard.

Silver continued to be a primary coinage metal until 1964, when rising prices led the Mint to remove it from the dime and quarter. Mintage of the silver dollar had ended in 1935. The half dollar continued to be coined through 1969 with a 40-percent-silver composition. It, too, was then debased.

Gold coinage ended in 1933 and exists today only in commemorative issues and American Eagle bullion coins with fictive face values. A clad composition of copper and nickel is now the primary coinage metal. Even the cent is no longer all copper; a copper-coated zinc composition has been used since 1982.

Precious-metal supplies were also linked to the opening of additional mints, which served the parent facility in Philadelphia. The impact of gold discoveries in the 1820s in the southern Appalachian Mountains was directly tied to the construction of branch mints in Dahlonega, Ga., and Charlotte, N.C., in 1838. These new mints struck only gold coins. New Orleans also became the site of a branch mint in the same year as Dahlonega and Charlotte. It took in some of the outflow of gold from Southern mines, but also struck silver coins.

Discovery of gold in California in the late 1840s created a gold rush, and from it sprang a great western migration. Private issues of gold coinage, often of debased quality, were prevalent, and the cost of shipping the metal eastward for coinage at Philadelphia was high. A call for an official branch mint was soon heard and heeded in 1852 with the authorization of the San Francisco Mint, which began taking deposits in 1854.

The discovery of silver in the Comstock Lode led to yet another mint. Located only a short distance via Virginia & Truckee Railroad from the fabulous Comstock Lode, the Carson City Mint began receiving bullion in early 1870. It struck only silver coins during its tenure.

Denver, also located in a mineral-rich region, became the site of an assay office in 1863 when the government purchased the Clark, Gruber & Co. private mint. It became a U.S. branch mint in 1906. In addition to the Denver and Philadelphia mints, San Francisco and a newly upgraded facility in West Point, N.Y., continue to serve as U.S. mints, but the others have left behind a rich legacy.

The collector taking a more extended journey into the history of U.S. coinage can find plenty of interesting tales — some as tall as the day is long and others factually based — all of which are part of the rich and ever-changing panoply of U.S. coinage history. There are stories of denominations that failed, great discoveries, great rarities, great collectors, and, for those with an artistic bent, a rich field of pattern coins to be explored and a wealth of much-heralded designs by famous sculptors such as Augustus Saint-Gaudens, Adolph Weinman, James Earle Fraser, and others.

For those who are drawn to the hobby by the allure of age-old relics of days gone by, or by coins handed down through the family, or even by dreams of great wealth, coin collecting has much to offer. The history of the U.S. Mint, with its small but ever so important beginning, is the starting point.

2

Making money
How coins are manufactured

By Alan Herbert

Just as printing is the process by which paper money is made, so is minting the method of manufacturing coins. The two are often confused by the public, but they are completely different.

The history of minting goes back several centuries before the birth of Christ. The Lydians are credited with making the first crude coins in the Middle East about 700 B.C., although the Chinese and Koreans trace their coinage back even further.

Some early coins were cast. That process continued in China into the 1900s, but only for low-value pieces. Here again the average person often assumes that all coins are cast, but as you will see, only a tiny fraction of a percent are — or were — actually made that way.

The methods developed by the Greeks and Romans centered on making dies that could be hammered by hand into the surface of a lump of metal, flattening it and impressing a design. Hammered coinage continued until after the end of the Middle Ages, about 1500. After that the first machines that could strike coins were invented. Today their successors can pound out 750 or more coins a minute.

From the early days when the fixed die was driven into a stump or a hole drilled in a rock, through fixing it in an anvil (the fixed die is still called the anvil die), to today's modern coin presses, the process is much the same. Force is applied to devices that impress or apply a design to a piece of material, which is transformed into a coin.

Early dies were made of wood. Then came copper, bronze, and finally iron as technology advanced. Today dies are made from exotic steels with special qualities that make them ideal for striking coins.

The history of coinage is fascinating. Interwoven into it are several familiar names: Leonardo da Vinci is credited with inventing one of the first coin presses. James Watt, English inventor of the steam engine, was the first to incorporate steam power to drive the coin presses that earlier had depended on horses or human arms.

Whether the power comes from a hand holding a hammer or a mechanical ram, and whether it comes from above, below, or the side, the process is called "striking" a coin. Modern coin presses use a variety of methods in applying brute force to a piece of metal to turn it into a coin.

Another fable that traces to casting coins is the common belief that coins are made from liquid metal or at the least are red hot when they are struck. Neither is true. A coin's design is formed by the pressure that causes the metal to cold-flow into the pattern that you see on the coins in your pocket.

There are three basic parts of the minting process: (1) the making of the planchet, which is divided into the selection and processing of the metal and the preparation of the planchets, (2) the making of the dies, and (3) the use of the dies to strike the planchets. To help you remember these three parts, think of "P", "D" and "S" for planchet, die and striking.

Choosing a metal

Many different metals have and are being used for coins. The most popular coinage metals are those commonly found and relatively cheap, so they can be used for striking low-value coins. Precious metals — like silver, gold and platinum — are still used for commemorative coins.

A good coinage metal requires certain properties. The metal must be soft enough to be easily worked yet hard enough to withstand the wear and tear of a thousand pockets, a hundred thousand transactions. Few metals have all the right properties, so coin metals usually are an alloy, or mixture of two or more metals.

Copper is a favorite coin metal, either by itself or in an alloy. Zinc, nickel, iron, and aluminum are also found in coins struck by the United States and other countries. Silver and gold have to be alloyed with some metal, usually copper, to be hard enough to withstand commercial life. The so-called "pure" coins of silver or gold are known as "bullion coins," bought and sold primarily for their precious-metal content.

The metals chosen for a coin are melted and mixed together, and either poured into ingots or blocks, or extruded from furnaces that continuously cast a long strip of the metal. The ingots are passed several times between the big rolls in a rolling mill to reduce the ingot to the thickness of the blanks needed.

Once the strip is rolled to the correct thickness, it is sent to a blanking press. A gang of blunt-end punches are driven through the sheet, producing a dozen or more blanks with each stroke. The rough blanks are then ready to be processed.

Strips of coin metal
stand ready to be cut
into "blanks."

A binful of blanks are
ready for the coin press.

Making the "blanks"

The piece of metal (occasionally some other material, so it isn't always metal) that becomes a coin is known as a "blank." This is a usually round, flat piece that usually has been punched or cut from a sheet or strip of coin metal.

Before a blank can become a coin it has to be processed, cleaned, softened, and given what is known as an "upset edge" — a raised ridge or rim around both sides. The blank then becomes a "planchet" and is ready to be struck into a coin by the dies.

First they go through what looks like a monstrous cement mixer. A huge cylinder revolves slowly as the planchets are fed in at one end and spiral their way through. This is an annealing oven, which heats the planchets to soften them. When they come out the end, they fall into a bath where they are cleaned with a diluted acid or soap solution.

As the final step, they go through the upsetting mill, the machine that puts the raised rim on the blank and turns it into a planchet, ready to be struck. In a different department the process of making the dies used to strike the coins has already begun.

Preparing the dies

For those who haven't studied metallurgy, the concept of hard metal flowing about is pretty hard to swallow, but this is actually what happens. It is basically the same process as the one used in an auto plant to turn a flat sheet of steel into a fender with multiple curves and sharp bends. The cold metal is moved about by the pressure applied.

To make the metal move into the desired design, there has to be a die. Actually there has to be two dies, because one of the laws of physics is that for every action there has to be an equal and opposite reaction. You cannot hold a piece of metal in midair and strike one side of it. Instead you make two dies, fix one, and drive the other one against it — with a piece of metal in between to accept the design from each die.

A die is a piece of hard metal, like steel, with a design on its face that helps to form a mirror image on the struck coin. Early dies were made by hand. Engravers used hand tools to laboriously cut each letter, each digit, and each owl or eagle or whatever design was being used into the face of the die. Notice that this is "into" the surface of the die. Each part of the die design is a hole or cavity of varying shape and depth.

This is because we want a mirror image on the coin, but we want it raised, or in "relief." To make a relief image on a coin, the image on the die has to be into the face of the die, or "incuse." Of course, if we want an incuse image on the coin, such as the gold $2.50 and $5 coins of 1908-1929, the design on the die face would have to be in relief.

To fully understand this, take a coin from your pocket and a piece of aluminum foil. Press the foil down over the coin design and rub it with an

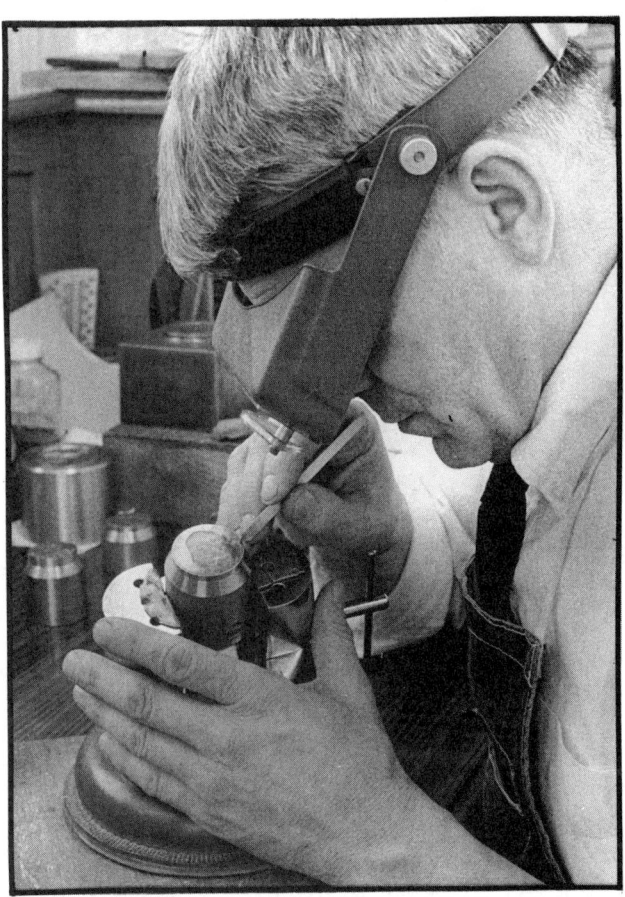

An engraver at the U.S. Mint puts the finishing touches on a die.

eraser. When you take the foil off and look at the side that was in contact with the coin, you have a perfect copy of a die. Everywhere there is a relief design on the coin there is an incuse design on your foil "die."

A galvano goes on the reducing lathe.

From sketchbook to coin

The design process begins with an artist's sketch. This is translated into a three-dimensional relief design that is hand-carved from plaster or, in recent years, from a form of plastic.

The plaster or plastic design is then transformed into a "galvano," which is an exact copy of the design that has been plated with a thin layer of copper. This is used as a template or pattern in a reducing lathe, which cuts the design into a die blank.

This die becomes the master die, from which all of the following steps descend. The process can be reversed so that the design will be cut in relief, forming a tool called a "hub," which is simply a piece of steel with the design in relief, exactly the same as the relief design on the intended coin.

To make working dies, pieces of special steel are prepared, with one end shaped with a slight cone. The die blank is softened by heating it. Then the hub is forced into the face of the die, forming the incuse, mirror-image design in the face of the die.

The process usually has to be repeated because the die metal will harden from the pressure. The die is removed, softened, and returned to the hubbing press for a second impression from the hub. As you can imagine, it takes several hundred tons per square inch to force the hub into the die. Logically, this process is called "hubbing" a die.

The advantage of hubbing a die is that thousands of working dies can be made from a single hub, each one for all practical purposes as identical as the proverbial peas in a pod. This enables, for example, U.S. mints to strike billions of one-cent coins each year, each with the identical design.

Die making has come a long way from the early days when it took a skilled engraver a full day to carve a single letter into a die. The use of punches with the digits, letters or even parts of the design on the end reduced the amount of time required for the process. Today, thanks to the use of hubs, a complete die can be finished in a matter of hours.

Striking the coin

Yesterday's die might strike only a few hundred coins. Today it is not unusual for a die to strike well over a million coins.

The coin press used to strike modern coins is a complicated piece of equipment that consists basically of a feed system to place the planchets in position for the stroke of the hammer die to form a coin. This process takes only a fraction of a second, so the press has to operate precisely to spew out the hundreds of coins that are struck every minute.

The end of the early hammered coinage came with the introduction of the collar, which often is called the "third" die. The collar is nothing more than a steel plate with a hole in it. This hole is the exact diameter of the intended coin and often is lined with carbide to prolong its life. It surrounds the lower, or fixed, die. Its sole purpose is to contain the coin metal

Rows of modern coin presses at the Philadelphia Mint turn out billions of coins a year.

A hopper is full of shiny new one-cent coins ready for shipment.

to keep it from spreading sideways under the force of the strike.

If the intended coin has serrations, or "reeds," on the edge, then the collar has the matching design. The strike forces the coin metal against the serrations in the collar, forming the reeded edge at the same time that the two dies form the front and back, or obverse and reverse, of the coin.

Lettered-edge coins are produced usually by running the planchets through an edge-lettering die, or by using a segmented collar that is forced against the edge of the planchet during the strike by hydraulic pressure.

Several hundred tons were required to drive a hub into a die. Not as much but still significant amounts of force are needed to strike coins. A cent, for example, requires about 30 tons per square inch. One of the silver dollars took 150 tons. The other denominations fall in between.

Modern coin presses apply pressure in a variety of ways. A ram, carrying the moving or "hammer" die, is forced against the planchet. Most commonly this is with the mechanical advantage of a "knuckle" or connected pieces to which pressure is applied from the side. When the joint straightens — like straightening your finger — the ram at the end of the piece is driven into the planchet.

Once the strike is complete, at the final impact of the die pair, the coin has been produced. It is officially a coin now, and it's complete and ready to be spent.

The making of proof coins

While the high-speed coining presses are turning out billions of coins for commerce, there are other presses working at much slower speeds to produce collector coins, such as "proof" coins.

Proof coins started out as special presentation pieces. They were and still are struck on specially prepared planchets with specially prepared dies. Today the definition of a proof coin also requires that it be struck two or more times.

To make a proof coin, the planchets go through much the same process, but with some special care and some extra steps. Currently all proof versions of circulating U.S. coins are struck at the San Francisco Mint, but some of the proof commemorative coins have been struck at the other mints, including West Point.

After the proof blanks are punched from the strip, they go through the annealing oven, but on a conveyor belt rather than being tumbled in the revolving drum. After cleaning and upsetting they go into a huge vibrating machine where they are mixed with steel pellets that look like tiny footballs. The movement of the steel pellets against the planchets burnishes, or smooths, the surface so any scratches and gouges the planchets pick up during processing are smoothed over.

Proof dies get an extra polishing before the hubbing process. Like all other dies, they are made at Philadelphia and shipped to the branch mints.

When the proof dies arrive at San Francisco, they are worked on by a team of specialists who use diamond dust and other polishing agents to turn the fields of the proof dies into mirrorlike surfaces. The incuse design is sandblasted to make the surface rough, producing what is known as a "frosted" design.

Because collectors like the frosted proofs, the design is periodically swabbed with acid to keep the surface rough and increase the number of frosted proofs from each die. This is a relatively recent improvement, so frosted examples of earlier proofs are considerably scarcer.

The presses that strike proof coins usually are hand-operated rather than automatic. Some of the newer presses use equipment such as vacuum suction devices to pick up the planchets, place them in the coining chamber, and then remove the struck coins. This avoids handling the pieces any more than necessary.

On a hand-operated press, the operator takes a freshly washed and dried planchet and, using tongs, places it in the collar. The ram with the die descends two or more times before the finished coin is removed from the collar and carefully stored in a box for transport to storage or the packaging line. After each strike the operator wipes the dies to make sure that lint or other particles don't stick to the dies and damage the coins as they are struck.

Proof dies are used for only a short time before being discarded. Maximum die life is usually less than 10,000 coins, varying with the size of the coin and the alloy being struck.

Keeping up with demand

The minting process has come a long way from the first metal pellets that are barely recognizable as coins. Companies that manufacture equipment used in the world's mints are constantly researching to develop new methods of producing coins.

The purpose is to strike coins at as low a cost as possible and still retain the desired beauty in the design. Modern machines and new methods help the mints keep up with demand for coins.

The important point to remember is that the coins in your pocket are made no differently from the coins in the pocket of an English schoolchild or a Spanish police officer or an Italian opera singer. Mints around the world use the same methods, same equipment, and same common coin metals, with few if any variations from the basic methods. The minting process was shrouded in secrecy for centuries, but now has become common knowledge.

For the collector, knowing exactly how coins are minted can be some of the most valuable knowledge that can be learned. It often will make the difference between accepting a coin as a valuable addition to a collection or spotting it as a fake, counterfeit, or altered coin.

Because of the improvements in the making of coins, collecting the rare misstrikes and defective coins that escape quality control has become an important segment of the numismatic hobby. For a detailed description of over 400 categories of minting varieties, see the "U.S. Minting Varieties and Errors" section in this book.

3

The thrill of the hunt

How to acquire coins for your collection

By Al Doyle

Among the many pleasures coin collecting offers is the satisfaction of acquiring that long-sought piece that fills an important hole in a set or completes a collection. Many collectors say half the fun of pursuing the hobby is the thrill of the hunt — trying to find that needed coin in the condition desired and for a good price. Following are the main sources from which collectors acquire coins.

Circulation finds

Once the most popular method of building a collection, hunting through pocket change has declined substantially since 1965, when silver dimes and quarters were replaced by clad (base-metal) coinage.

Most collectors from 1935 into the 1960s got started in numismatics by searching through circulating coinage. It was worth the effort, as scarce and interesting coins such as the 1909-S "VDB" and 1914-D Lincoln cents, Liberty and Buffalo nickels, 1916-D and 1921 Mercury dimes, and Barber and Standing Liberty quarters were often found. Hobbyists who searched bank rolls and bags obtained at face value had no downside risk, and entire date collections of Lincoln cents were obtained in this manner.

Other denominations were also pursued in the treasure hunt. One Midwestern dealer found dozens of 1939-D Jefferson nickels (worth $1 to $30 each at the time, depending on condition) by searching through change obtained from parking meters of a nearby city. Another well-known numismatist put together a complete date and mintmark set of Walking Liberty half dollars in one afternoon by searching through coins obtained at his bank. Needless to say, those days are gone forever.

What is available to pocket-change searchers today? Even the pre-1959

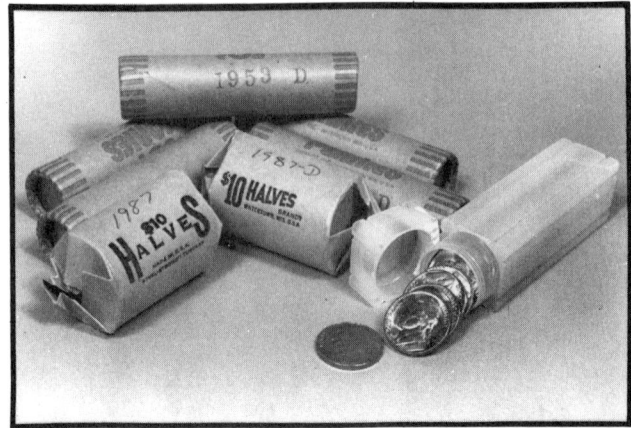

It's still possible to find collectible coins by searching large quantities of change, such as rolls.

cents, with the wheat-ears reverse, are rare sights, but some interesting coins remain undiscovered.

Jefferson nickels can provide plenty of collecting enjoyment for virtually no financial commitment. A recent sampling of five rolls (200 coins, or $10) turned up 58 different date and mintmark combinations. Some of the highlights were a 1938-S (mintage 4.1 million) in grade fine, a 1947 in very fine, and a 1953-S. Looking through Jeffersons on a regular basis should lead to building the better part of a date and mintmark set.

Half dollars are the other relatively untapped area in modern coinage. The 40-percent-silver pieces of 1965 to 1969 can sometimes be found in bank rolls. Half dollars seldom circulate, which means that older coins may be gathering dust in your local bank vault at this very moment.

Collecting Lincoln cents with the memorial reverse, from 1959 to date, makes an excellent starter set. Many of the dates can be found in circulation.

What else might turn up in pocket change? Modern proofs enter circulation from time to time, and foreign coins are found occasionally. Canadian and U.S. coins frequently cross their respective borders.

Collectors of error coins sometimes find unusual pieces in circulation. What may be scorned as a reject by the average person is a valuable item to the error and variety specialist.

Start examining your pocket change. It's an inexpensive and pleasant way to get involved in the coin hobby.

Coin shops

Most medium-sized or larger cities and suburbs have at least one coin shop within driving distance, and a surprising number of small towns also boast of having a store that caters to local numismatists. Living in or near a metropolitan area is an advantage for the coin-shop enthusiast. For example, more than 15 dealers live in or near Cincinnati, and southern California and the New York area are home to hundreds of numismatic firms.

In some ways, a coin shop is similar to a small museum. All kinds of items from early coppers to gold coinage and other collectibles such as paper currency, stock certificates, and historic curiosities can be seen. A visit to a well-stocked shop is a visual treat.

It is likely that some of those coins in the display cases will appeal to you, and that means some comparison shopping and determining the value of your favorite coin are desirable. Prices do fluctuate, although collector-oriented coins tend to maintain steadier values than coins sought by investors.

If you are a casual collector, consider a subscription to *Coins* magazine. A monthly publication, *Coins* offers articles on a wide range of topics as well as a Coin Value Guide of retail prices for U.S. coins in most grades.

Serious collectors and others who want more frequent information will find *Numismatic News* to be a timely source of knowledge. Published weekly, the *News* includes coverage of recent market trends and reports from major coin conventions. *World Coin News* is published every other week and covers non-U.S. issues. All three publications also carry display advertisements from dozens of coin dealers.

Prices are determined by supply and demand as well as the grade, or state of preservation. Grading is often described as a subjective art rather than an exact science, and it does take some study and experience to become a competent grader (see Chapter 4).

Numismatic education is a never-ending process. Getting to know an experienced dealer who is enthusiastic about his product will certainly increase your knowledge of coins. Most shops carry a wide assortment of items, but dealers (like anyone else) have their personal favorites. If you find a dealer who is especially knowledgeable about a certain series, it could be to your advantage to do business with him or her if that also happens to be your favorite area too.

Strangely enough, doing business with a dealer who does not share your particular interest could work in your favor. Learning about collectible coins is a massive undertaking, and no one knows everything. Collectors of large cents and Bust half dollars are willing to pay substantial premiums for coins that have minor differences from other specimens struck during the same year, and specialists in those areas frequently "cherrypick" rare varieties that are offered at common-date prices.

Never be embarrassed to ask questions about coins or the dealer's experience in the hobby. As the old saying goes, "There is no such thing as a dumb question." A question asked at the right time could save you plenty of grief and money.

Mail order

This is one area that generates a fair amount of emotion among collectors. Many hobbyists swear by the convenience of shopping at home; others

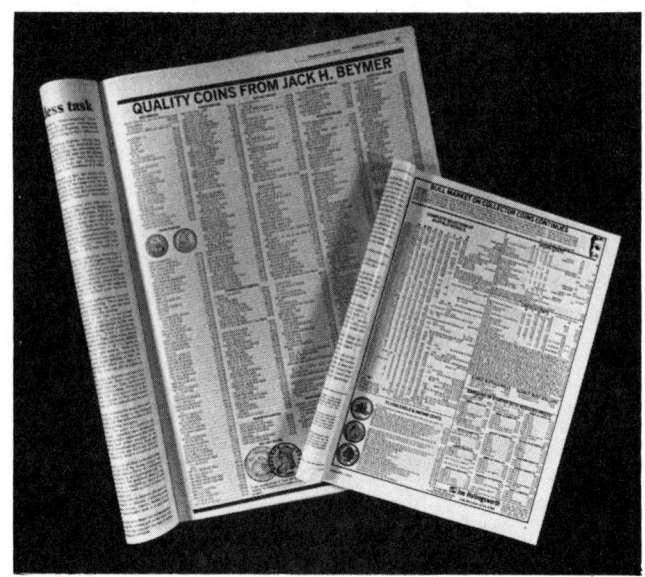

Advertisements in numismatic publications provide the convenience of shopping at home.

swear at mail-order firms that send overgraded and overpriced coins. Common sense and the same guidelines that apply to shopping for any other item should be used in selecting a mail-order coin dealer.

Look for someone who has a fair amount of experience in coins as well as enthusiasm for the hobby. Reputable dealers are willing to answer questions about their numismatic backgrounds and business practices. Word of mouth is often said to be one of the most effective forms of advertising, and it pays to ask other collectors about their favorite mail-order companies.

If several people agree that a firm provides accurately graded coins at fair prices, chances are excellent that you will also be a satisfied customer. How do you avoid being cheated? Collectors can be their own worst enemies and are often victimized by their own greed.

Take a coin that has a retail value in the $100 range in a particular grade. If that same coin is advertised at the same grade for $49.95, the savvy collector should immediately become suspicious. When a coin is offered at a price far under the going rate, remember these two sayings: "If it sounds too good to be true, it usually is," and "there is no Santa Claus in numismatics."

A dealer will generally pay $70 to $80 to acquire a popular coin with a retail value of $100. With that in mind, how can someone offer the same coin in the same grade at far less than wholesale cost? Wouldn't it be much easier to sell those coins to other dealers at a higher price and save on advertising expenses?

Obviously, the "underpriced" coins are not the same quality as their properly graded counterparts. It pays to keep up with current prices and grading standards. It is possible to find good deals at less than full retail cost, but don't expect to purchase decent coins for half price.

Does that mean all coins sold at real market prices are properly graded? Don't get complacent; overgraded coins are sometimes sold at full retail. But not everyone who sells an overgraded coin is intentionally fraudulent.

Grading standards are not carved in stone, which means that one person's MS-63 can be someone else's MS-64. Even though most dealers are extremely knowledgeable about coins, they can be fooled at times. The altered coin that a dealer bought as problem-free may be passed on to a collector in good faith, with no intention of deceit.

There is one important means of protection for consumers who buy through the mail: the return policy. Reputable firms allow buyers to return any unsatisfactory item for a full refund. The time allowed for returns varies widely from three working days to a month, but seven to ten days seems to be the most popular policy among mail-order dealers.

Most dealers list "terms of sale" in their ads. Always look for them and read them before placing your order.

If you don't like coins received through the mail for any reason, send them back within the alloted time for a full refund. Companies might extend the deadline by a day or two if you call and ask for extra time.

What happens if you don't receive a refund or cannot satisfactorily resolve a problem with a mail-order dealer? There are several options:

The first step is to file a written complaint with the advertising department of any publication in which the dealer advertises. Include copies of invoices and other documentation. The publication cannot act on verbal complaints.

Written complaints can also be filed with a local or state chapter of the Better Business Bureau as well as any hobby-related organizations (the American Numismatic Association, Professional Numismatists Guild, and so on) in which the dealer holds membership. If you do business with a reputable dealer, it is unlikely that you will ever have to endure such a drawn-out complaint process, but be ready to take the proper steps if necessary.

For those who live in rural areas or prefer to shop at home, buying coins through the mail can be a rewarding experience and a convenient way to build a collection.

Coin shows

Dozens of shows are held every weekend across the nation. These events range from simple one-day shows with 10 to 20 tables to nationally known events such as the annual American Numismatic Association convention, Florida United Numismatists convention, the three-times-a-year shows held in Long Beach, Calif., and the Central States Numismatic Society convention.

Admission to club-sponsored shows is usually free. Commercially sponsored shows oftentimes charge a small admission fee.

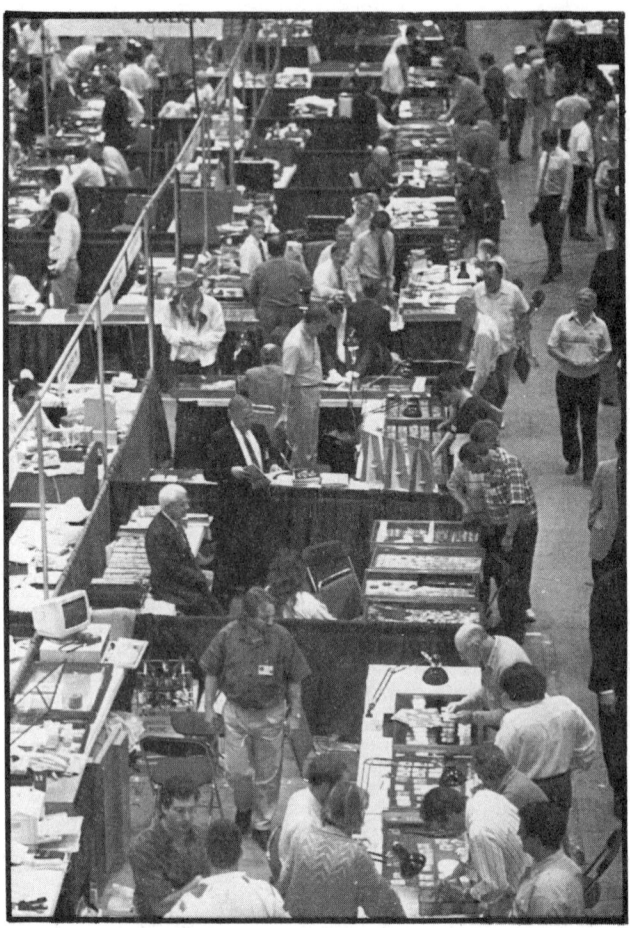

Shows big and small are held across the nation every weekend.

Somewhere between the show at the local VFW hall and Long Beach are state and regional conventions. Often sponsored by a club, these shows will have 40 to 150 dealer tables as compared to the 400 to 600 tables at a major convention. Tables at local and some regional conventions are often manned by part-time, or "vest pocket," dealers. Smaller shows tend to feature less expensive items; the larger shows will have a greater variety of scarce and expensive coins in addition to the more affordable pieces.

Major conventions will have a stunning array of merchandise ranging from coins of ancient Greece to major U.S. rarities. Even if you can't afford the expensive items, it doesn't cost anything to stroll the aisles and see some historic coins.

The big-ticket items are just part of the action at regional and major shows. A large assortment of affordable coins are available, and prices are often lower than at coin shops.

Dealers buy and sell thousands of coins among themselves at shows, and new purchases can often be had for a small markup. Good buys can sometimes be found later in the show when dealers are preparing to return home. A reasonable offer will often result in a new addition to your collection.

Speaking of offers, negotiating and dickering are as much a part of coin shows as silver dollars, but be reasonable. Tossing out an offer of $50 on a $200 coin is not shrewd; it's insulting.

If you make an offer on a coin and it is accepted, the coin is yours. Backing out of a deal is considered bad form. The coin business tends to be informal, and verbal offers carry serious weight. Your word is your bond on the bourse floor.

Purchases at a coin show do not carry a return policy. Unlike a mail-order transaction, you have ample opportunity to carefully examine the coin firsthand before making a financial commitment.

Why attend a show when you can acquire coins through the mail or from a local shop? There are many reasons to give the show circuit a try:

Conventions are an educational experience. Touring the bourse floor and talking to dealers and other collectors will increase your knowledge of numismatics, but there are other learning opportunities as well.

Many shows offer educational forums featuring speakers and presentations on various topics. These seminars cover everything from little-known specialties to advice on obtaining the best buys in a particular area of numismatics.

Exhibits will also add to your knowledge. Most medium-sized and major shows reserve a section of the bourse for collectors to display some of their holdings and compete for awards based on the educational value of their exhibit. The exhibit section offers an excellent opportunity to view something new and different.

You might be motivated to put together an exhibit yourself after a visit to a show. Keep in mind that it does not require a major collection to create a decent exhibit. Some of the most interesting displays incorporate low-priced coins and other collectibles.

Shows are excellent places to search for key-date coins and other material that may not be in stock at your local shop. Dealers do much of their shopping at shows, which should tell you something about the opportunities at a good-sized convention.

Want to introduce a friend or relative to coin collecting? Take them to a show and let them look around. Chances are excellent that the newcomer will become a fellow collector.

Looking for something different to collect? Paper money, world coins, tokens, medals, and medieval coins are often found at shows. You could find a new area of interest, and shows provide collectors with a chance to meet dealers and well-known hobbyists from across the country.

Have a game plan when you attend a show. Decide beforehand what you want to buy and how much money you plan to spend. Buying whatever looks nice will soon deplete your funds.

Coin shows offer something for everyone, so consider bringing the family. Jewelry (usually for much less than jewelry-store prices), baseball cards, antiques, and arts and crafts are also sometimes found at bourse tables.

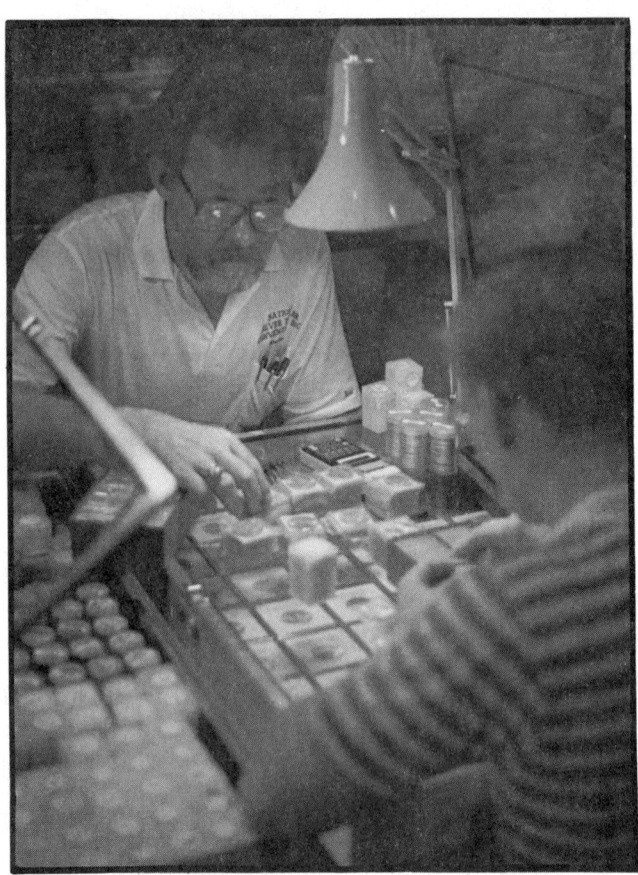

It's OK to bargain with a dealer at a show or shop, but collectors should be reasonable with their offers.

One final note on coin-show etiquette: If you don't agree with a dealer's prices or grading, do not tell him that you can buy the same coin for less at another table or call him a crook. Just move on to the next table, and enjoy the rest of the show.

Information on upcoming shows in your area can be found in *Coins* and *Numismatic News*. Shows that feature a significant number of world coins are also listed in *World Coin News*. Coin-show advertising sometimes appears in local newspapers during the week prior to a show or in the paper's free listings of community events.

Auctions

As in other collectible fields, auctions play an important role in the coin business. Prices realized at major auctions can indicate where the coin market is headed, as price fluctuations are a fact of life in numismatics. Important collections with major rarities are usually sold at auction.

However, affordable coins are often sold along with the heart-stopping pieces. A typical sale for a major auction firm will contain 1,000 to 4,000 lots, and most of those coins are not of the headline-grabbing variety.

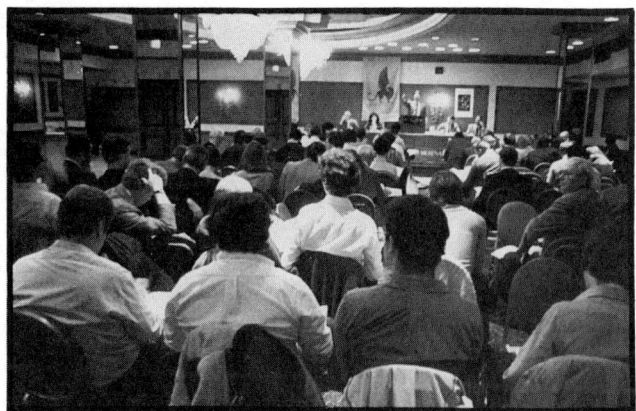

A collector doesn't have to actually attend an auction to participate in it.

The vast number of coins offered at a typical coin auction can work in favor of the collector who has a limited budget. Typical low- to medium-priced coins are often overlooked, as dealers and collectors focus on the trophy items. That may allow you to pick up some coins at reasonable prices.

How can you participate in an auction that is being held thousands of miles from your home? Catalogs are produced by auction companies for each sale, and mail bids are encouraged.

A typical auction catalog is illustrated with black and white as well as color photos of hundreds of coins. Descriptions of each lot give you an idea of the appearance of any coins that might be of interest.

If you are located near an auction site, it pays to examine your potential purchases at the pre-auction viewing session. The process is simple: Just visit the auction location (usually a major hotel or convention center) prior to the sale. The auction company sets up a room where the lots can be viewed. Long rows of tables with good lighting are provided. All you have to do is tell one of the attendants the lot numbers of the coins you want to view.

You can place written bids before you leave the premises, but it might pay to hang around for the auction and bid on coins in person. The action can be fast and furious at a major auction. Bidding increments of thousands of dollars are the rule when an expensive coin is being sold. It's an unforgettable sight to watch five or six serious competitors run up the price on a truly rare coin.

Keep several things in mind before you get involved in buying through auctions:

■ You are legally responsible to honor all winning bids placed, so plan accordingly. It is unlikely that you will win every coin on which you bid, but placing too many bids could be hazardous to your financial health.

■ Return policies vary among the major firms. Generally, floor bidders (those who personally attend the sale) do not have return privileges, as it is assumed that an adequate opportunity was provided to examine coins during the pre-auction viewing session.

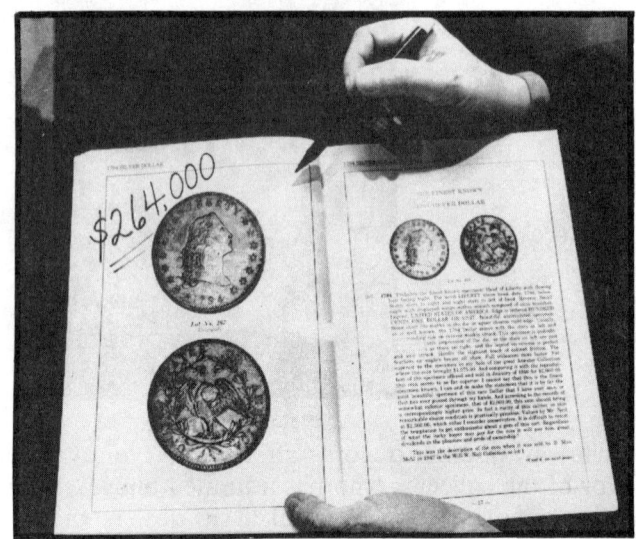

An auction catalog describes each lot offered.

One auction house does not allow any returns by mail bidders on certified coins, which are independently graded and encapsulated in a protective holder by an outside grading service. However, return privileges are the rule for all coins graded by the auction company's staff.

■ Winning bids are generally subject to a 10 percent premium, or buyer's fee. If you successfully bid $300 on a coin, your final cost will be $330 plus postage and handling. Consider the buyer's fee when deciding on bids.

Getting started in buying through auctions requires a catalog of an upcoming sale. Typically priced at $10 to $25, auction catalogs can be excellent buys even if you don't participate in the sale, as they provide a wealth of numismatic information.

Following are six major U.S. auction houses:

■ Auctions by Bowers and Merena, P.O. Box 1224, Wolfeboro, NH, 03894.

■ Butterfield-Johnson-Gillio, 220 San Bruno Ave., San Francisco, CA 94103; 7601 Sunset Blvd., Los Angeles, CA 90046.

■ Heritage Numismatic Auctions, Heritage Plaza, Highland Park Village, Dallas, TX 75205.

■ Spink America, 55 E. 59th St., Fourth Floor, New York, NY 10022.

■ Stack's, 123 W. 57th St., New York, NY 10019.

■ Superior Stamp & Coin, an A-Mark Co., 9478 W. Olympic Blvd., Beverly Hills, CA 90212.

Smaller auctions will allow you to test the bidding process before you compete at a major sale. Local firms concentrate on less expensive coins, and a typical sale for these companies ranges from 250 to 1,000 lots. Catalogs are less elaborate, but they are also inexpensive. Prices range from free to $3, and mail bids are accepted.

Among the dozens of local companies that conduct coin auctions are the following:

■ Michael Aron, P.O. Box 4388, San Clemente, CA 92674.

■ Connecticut Numismatic Auctions, P.O. Box 471, Plantsville, CT 06479.

■ Frank D'Atri Auction, 2405 Essington Road, Suite 124, Joliet, IL 60435.

■ Sonny Henry's Auction Service, 1510 Illinois Ave., Mendota, IL 61342.

Where to write for more information

Coins Magazine: 700 E. State St, Iola, WI 54990.
Numismatic News: 700 E. State St., Iola, WI 54990.
World Coin News: 700 E. State St., Iola, WI 54990.
American Numismatic Association: 818 N. Cascade Ave., Colorado Springs, CO 80903-3279.

Visit the Krause Publications Web sites
http://www.krause.com
http://www.coincollecting.net

4

The grading factor
How to classify a coin's condition

By Arlyn G. Sieber

Grading is one of the most important factors in buying and selling coins as collectibles. Unfortunately, it's also one of the most controversial. Since the early days of coin collecting in the United States, buying through the mail has been a convenient way for collectors to acquire coins. As a result, there has always been a need in numismatics for a concise way to classify the amount of wear on a coin and its condition in general.

A look back

In September 1888, Dr. George Heath, a physician in Monroe, Mich., published a four-page pamphlet titled *The American Numismatist*. Publication of subsequent issues led to the founding of the American Numismatic Association, and *The Numismatist*, as it's known today, is the association's official journal. Heath's first issues were largely devoted to selling world coins from his collection. There were no formal grades listed with the coins and their prices, but the following statement by Heath indicates that condition was a consideration for early collectors:

"The coins are in above average condition," Heath wrote, "and so confident am I that they will give satisfaction, that I agree to refund the money in any unsatisfactory sales on the return of the coins."

As coin collecting became more popular and *The Numismatist* started accepting paid advertising from others, grading became more formal. The February 1892 issue listed seven "classes" for the condition of coins (from worst to best): mutilated, poor, fair, good, fine, uncirculated, and proof. Through the years, the hobby has struggled with developing a grading sys-

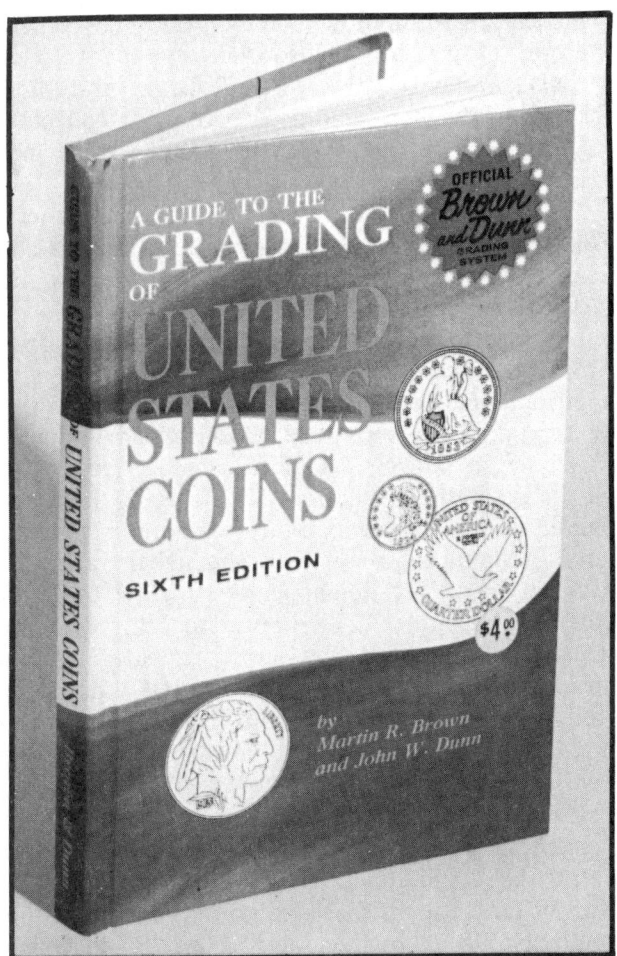

The first formal grading guide was Brown and Dunn's *A Guide to the Grading of United States Coins.*

tem that would be accepted by all and could apply to all coins. The hobby's growth was accompanied by a desire for more grades, or classifications, to more precisely define a coin's condition. The desire for more precision, however, was at odds with the basic concept of grading: to provide a *concise* method for classifying a coin's condition.

For example, even the conservatively few classifications of 1892 included fudge factors.

"To give flexibility to this classification," *The Numismatist* said, "such modification of fine, good and fair, as 'extremely,' 'very,' 'almost,' etc. are used to express slight variations from the general condition."

The debate over grading continued for decades in *The Numismatist.* A number of articles and letters prodded the ANA to write grading guidelines and endorse them as the association's official standards. Some submitted specific suggestions for terminology and accompanying standards for each grade. But grading remained a process of "instinct" gained through years of collecting or dealing experience.

A formal grading guide in book form finally appeared in 1958, but it was the work of two individuals rather than the ANA. *A Guide to the Grading of United States Coins* by Martin R. Brown and John W. Dunn was a breakthrough in the great grading debate. Now collectors had a reference that gave them specific guidelines for specific coins and could be studied and restudied at home.

The first editions of Brown and Dunn carried text only, no illustrations. For the fourth edition, in 1964, publication was assumed by Whitman Publishing Co. of Racine, Wis., and line drawings were added to illustrate the text.

The fourth edition listed six principal categories for circulated coins (from worst to best): good, very good, fine, very fine, extremely fine, and about uncirculated. But again, the desire for more precise categories was evidenced. In the book's introduction, Brown and Dunn wrote, "Dealers will sometimes advertise coins that are graded G-VG, VG-F, F-VF, VF-XF. Or the description may be ABT. G. or VG plus, etc. This means that the coin in question more than meets minimum standards for the lower grade but is not quite good enough for the higher grade."

When the fifth edition appeared, in 1969, the "New B & D Grading System" was introduced. The six principal categories for circulated coins were still intact, but variances within those categories were now designated by up to four letters: "A", "B", "C" or "D". For example, an EF-A coin was "almost about uncirculated." An EF-B was "normal extra fine" within the B & D standards. EF-C had a "normal extra fine" obverse, but the reverse was "obviously not as nice as obverse due to poor strike or excessive wear." EF-D had a "normal extra fine" reverse but a problem obverse.

But that wasn't the end. Brown and Dunn further listed 29 problem points that could appear on a coin — from No. 1 for an "edge bump" to No. 29 for "attempted re-engraving outside of the Mint." The number could be followed by the letter "O" or "R" to designate whether the problem appeared on the obverse or reverse and a Roman numeral corresponding to a clock face to designate where the problem appears on the obverse or reverse. For example, a coin described as "VG-B-9-O-X" would grade "VG-B"; the 9 designated a "single rim nick"; the "O" indicated the nick was on the obverse; and the "X" indicated it appeared at the 10 o'clock position, or upper left, of the obverse.

The authors' goal was noble — to create the perfect grading system. They again, however, fell victim to the age-old grading-system problem: Precision comes at the expense of brevity. Dealer Kurt Krueger wrote in the January 1976 issue of *The Numismatist*, ". . . under the new B & D system, the numismatist must contend with a minimum of 43,152 different grading combinations! Accuracy is apparent, but simplicity has been lost." As a result, the "new B & D system" never caught on in the marketplace.

The 1970s saw two important grading guides make their debut. The first was *Photograde* by James F. Ruddy. As the title implies, Ruddy uses photographs instead of line drawings to show how coins look in the various circulated grades. Simplicity is also a virtue of Ruddy's book. Only seven

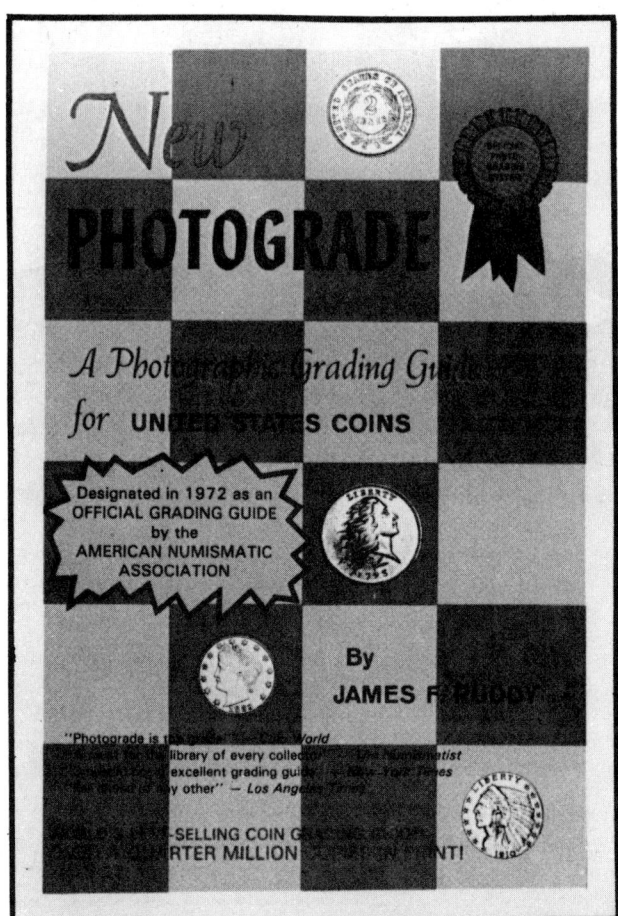

Photograde was the first widely accepted grading guide to use photos to illustrate the amount of wear on circulated coins.

circulated grades are listed (about good, good, very good, fine, very fine, extremely fine, and about uncirculated), and the designations stop there.

In 1977 the longtime call for the ANA to issue grading standards was met with the release of *Official A.N.A. Grading Standards for United States Coins*. Like Brown and Dunn, the first editions of the ANA guide used line drawings to illustrate coins in various states of wear. But instead of using adjectival descriptions, the ANA guide adopted a numerical system for designating grades.

The numerical designations were based on a system used by Dr. William H. Sheldon in his book *Early American Cents*, first published in 1949. He used a scale of 1 to 70 to designate the grades of large cents.

"On this scale," Sheldon wrote, "1 means that the coin is identifiable and not mutilated — no more than that. A 70-coin is one in flawless Mint State, exactly as it left the dies, with perfect mint color and without a blemish or nick."

(Sheldon's scale also had its pragmatic side. At the time, a No. 2 large cent was worth about twice a No. 1 coin; a No. 4 was worth about twice a

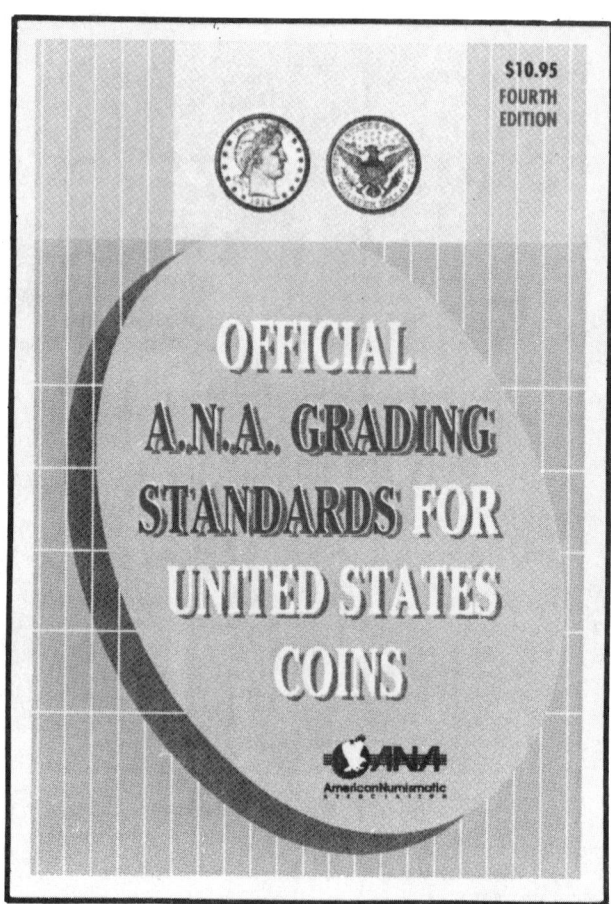

Official A.N.A. Grading Standards for United States Coins **is now in its fourth edition.**

No. 2, and so on up the scale.)

With the first edition of its grading guide, the ANA adopted the 70-point scale for grading all U.S. coins. It designated 10 categories of circulated grades: AG-3, G-4, VG-8, F-12, VF-20, VF-30, EF-40, EF-45, AU-50, and AU-55. The third edition, released in 1987, replaced the line drawings with photographs, and another circulated grade was added: AU-58. A fourth edition was released in 1991.

Grading circulated U.S. coins

Dealers today generally use either the ANA guide or *Photograde* when grading circulated coins for their inventories. (Brown and Dunn is now out of print.) Many local coin shops sell both books. Advertisers in *Numismatic News*, *Coins*, and *Coin Prices* must indicate which standards they are using in grading their coins. If the standards are not listed, they must conform to ANA standards.

Following are some general guidelines, accompanied by photos, for grading circulated U.S. coins. Grading even circulated pieces can be subjective, particularly when attempting to draw the fine line between, for example, AU-55 and AU-58. Two longtime collectors or dealers can disagree in such a case.

But by studying some combination of the following guidelines, the ANA guide, and *Photograde*, and by looking at a lot of coins at shops and shows, collectors can gain enough grading knowledge to buy circulated coins confidently from dealers and other collectors. The more you study, the more knowledge and confidence you will gain. When you decide which series of coins you want to collect, focus on the guidelines for that particular series. Read them, reread them, and then refer back to them again and again.

AU-50

Indian cent

Lincoln cent

Buffalo nickel

Jefferson nickel

Mercury dime

Standing Liberty quarter

Washington quarter

Walking Liberty half dollar

Morgan dollar

Barber coins

AU-50 (about uncirculated): Just a slight trace of wear, the result of brief exposure to circulation or light rubbing from mishandling, may be evident on the elevated design areas. These imperfections may appear as scratches or dull spots, along with bag marks or edge nicks. At least half of the original mint luster generally is still evident.

XF-40

Indian cent

Lincoln cent

Buffalo nickel

Jefferson nickel

Mercury dime

Standing Liberty quarter

Washington quarter

Walking Liberty half dollar

Morgan dollar

Barber coins

XF-40 (extremely fine): The coin must show only slight evidence of wear on the highest points of the design, particularly in the hair lines of the portrait on the obverse. The same may be said for the eagle's feathers and wreath leaves on the reverse of most U.S. coins. A trace of mint luster may still show in protected areas of the coin's surface.

VF-20

Indian cent

Lincoln cent

Buffalo nickel

Jefferson nickel

Mercury dime

Standing Liberty quarter

Washington quarter

Walking Liberty half dollar

Morgan dollar

Barber coins

VF-20 (very fine): The coin will show light wear at the fine points in the design, though they may remain sharp overall. Although the details may be slightly smoothed, all lettering and major features must remain sharp.

Indian cent: All letters in "Liberty" are complete but worn. Headdress shows considerable flatness, with flat spots on the tips of the feathers.

Lincoln cent: Hair, cheek, jaw, and bow-tie details will be worn but clearly separated, and wheat stalks on the reverse will be full with no weak spots.

Buffalo nickel: High spots on hair braid and cheek will be flat but show some detail, and a full horn will remain on the buffalo.

Jefferson nickel: Well over half of the major hair detail will remain, and the pillars on Monticello will remain well defined, with the triangular roof partially visible.

Mercury dime: Hair braid will show some detail, and three-quarters of the detail will remain in the feathers. The two diagonal bands on the fasces will show completely but will be worn smooth at the middle, with the vertical lines sharp.

Standing Liberty quarter: Rounded contour of Liberty's right leg will be flattened, as will the high point of the shield.

Washington quarter: There will be considerable wear on the hair curls, with feathers on the right and left of the eagle's breast showing clearly.

Walking Liberty half dollar: All lines of the skirt will show but will be worn on the high points. Over half the feathers on the eagle will show.

Morgan dollar: Two-thirds of the hairlines from the forehead to the ear must show. Ear should be well defined. Feathers on the eagle's breast may be worn smooth.

Barber coins: All seven letters of "Liberty" on the headband must stand out sharply. Head wreath will be well outlined from top to bottom.

F-12

Indian cent

Lincoln cent

Buffalo nickel

Jefferson nickel

Mercury dime

Standing Liberty quarter

Washington quarter

Walking Liberty half dollar

Morgan dollar

Barber coins

F-12 (fine): Coins show evidence of moderate to considerable but generally even wear on all high points, though all elements of the design and lettering remain bold. Where the word "Liberty" appears in a headband, it must be fully visible. On 20th century coins, the rim must be fully raised and sharp.

VG-8

Indian cent

Lincoln cent

Buffalo nickel

Jefferson nickel

Mercury dime

Standing Liberty quarter

Washington quarter

Walking Liberty half dollar

Morgan dollar

Barber coins

VG-8 (very good): The coin will show considerable wear, with most detail points worn nearly smooth. Where the word "Liberty" appears in a headband, at least three letters must show. On 20th century coins, the rim will start to merge with the lettering.

G-4

Indian cent

Lincoln cent

Buffalo nickel

Jefferson nickel

Mercury dime

Standing Liberty quarter

Washington quarter   **Walking Liberty half dollar**

Morgan dollar   **Barber coins**

G-4 (good): Only the basic design remains distinguishable in outline form, with all points of detail worn smooth. The word "Liberty" has disappeared, and the rims are almost merging with the lettering.

About good or fair: The coin will be identifiable by date and mint but otherwise badly worn, with only parts of the lettering showing. Such coins are of value only as fillers in a collection until a better example of the date and mintmark can be obtained. The only exceptions would be rare coins.

Grading uncirculated U.S. coins

The subjectivity of grading and the trend toward more classifications becomes more acute when venturing into uncirculated, or mint-state, coins. A minute difference between one or two grade points can mean a difference in value of hundreds or even thousands of dollars. In addition, the standards are more difficult to articulate in writing and illustrate through drawings or photographs. Thus, the possibilities for differences of opinion on one or two grade points increase in uncirculated coins.

Coins graded and encapsulated by a third-party grading service are nicknamed "slabs." The Professional Coin Grading Service graded this Saint-Gaudens gold $20 coin.

Back in Dr. George Heath's day and continuing through the 1960s, a coin was either uncirculated or it wasn't. Little distinction was made between uncirculated coins of varying condition, largely because there was little if any difference in value. When *Numismatic News* introduced its value guide in 1962 (the forerunner of today's Coin Market section in the *News*), it listed only one grade of uncirculated for Morgan dollars.

But as collectible coins increased in value and buyers of uncirculated coins became more picky, distinctions within grade uncirculated started to surface. In 1975 *Numismatic News* still listed only one uncirculated grade in Coin Market, but added this note: "Uncirculated and proof specimens in especially choice condition will also command proportionately higher premiums than these listed."

The first edition of the ANA guide listed two grades of uncirculated, MS-60 and MS-65, in addition to the theoretical but non-existent MS-70 (a flawless coin). MS-60 was described as "typical uncirculated" and MS-65 as "choice uncirculated." *Numismatic News* adopted both designations for Coin Market. In 1981, when the second edition of the ANA grading guide was released, MS-67 and MS-63 were added. In 1985 *Numismatic News* started listing six grades of uncirculated for Morgan dollars: MS-60, MS-63, MS-65, MS-65+, and MS-63 prooflike.

Then in 1986, a new entity appeared that has changed the nature of grading and trading uncirculated coins ever since. A group of dealers led by David Hall of Newport Beach, Calif., formed the Professional Coin Grading Service. For a fee, collectors could submit a coin through an authorized PCGS dealer and receive back a professional opinion of its grade.

The concept was not new; the ANA had operated an authentication service since 1972 and a grading service since 1979. A collector or dealer could submit a coin directly to the service and receive a certificate giving the service's opinion on authenticity and grade. The grading service was the source of near constant debate among dealers and ANA officials. Dealers charged that ANA graders were too young and inexperienced, and

The Numismatic Guaranty Corp. is another major grading service.

that their grading was inconsistent.

Grading stability was a problem throughout the coin business in the early 1980s, not just with the ANA service. Standards among uncirculated grades would tighten during a bear market and loosen during a bull market. As a result, a coin graded MS-65 in a bull market may have commanded only MS-63 during a bear market.

PCGS created several innovations in the grading business in response to these problems:

1. Coins could be submitted through PCGS-authorized dealers only.

2. Each coin would be graded by at least three members of a panel of "top graders," all prominent dealers in the business. (Since then, however, PCGS does not allow its graders to also deal in coins.)

3. After grading, the coin would be encapsulated in an inert, hard-plastic holder with a serial number and the grade indicated on the holder.

4. PCGS-member dealers pledged to make a market in PCGS-graded coins and honor the grades assigned.

5. In one of the most far-reaching moves, PCGS said it would use all 11 increments of uncirculated on the 70-point numerical scale: MS-60, MS-61, MS-62, MS-63, MS-64, MS-65, MS-66, MS-67, MS-68, MS-69, and MS-70.

The evolution of more uncirculated grades had reached another milestone.

Purists bemoaned the entombment of classic coins in the plastic holders and denounced the 11 uncirculated grades as implausible. Nevertheless, PCGS was an immediate commercial success. The plastic holders were nicknamed "slabs," and dealers couldn't get coins through the system fast enough.

In subsequent years, a number of similar services have appeared. Among them, one of the original PCGS "top graders," John Albanese, left PCGS to found the Numismatic Guaranty Corp. The ANA grading service succumbed to "slab mania" and introduced its own encapsulated product.

Although there are still several other reputable grading services, PCGS

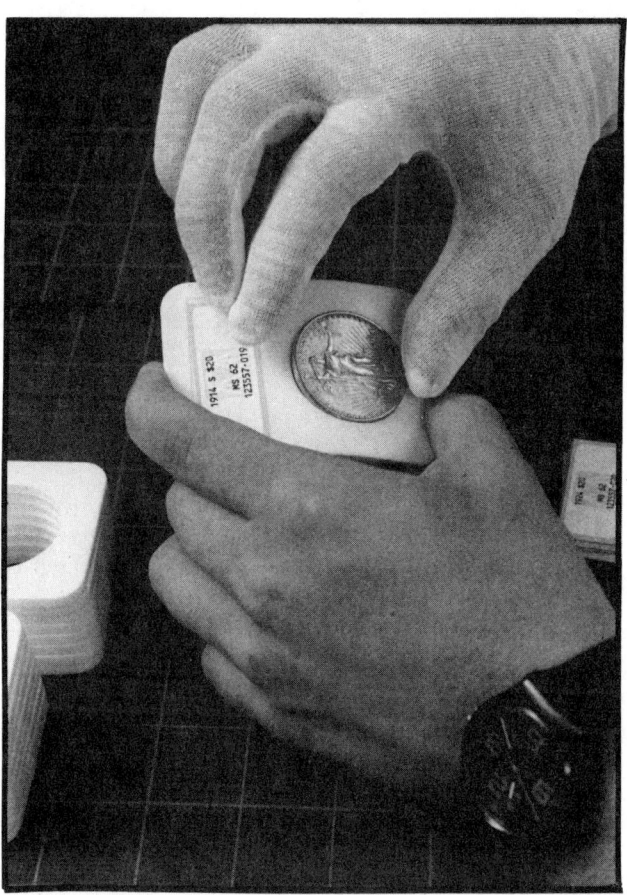

An NGC worker places
a coin in its holder after
it has been graded.

and NGC dominate market share. In 1990 the ANA sold its grading service to a private company. The association continues to authenticate coins.

How should a collector approach the buying and grading of uncirculated coins? Collecting uncirculated coins worth thousands of dollars implies a higher level of numismatic expertise by the buyer. Those buyers without that level of expertise should cut their teeth on more inexpensive coins, just as today's experienced collectors did. Inexperienced collectors can start toward that level by studying the guidelines for mint-state coins in the ANA grading guide and looking at lots of coins at shows and shops.

Study the condition and eye appeal of a coin and compare it to other coins of the same series. Then compare prices. Do the more expensive coins look better? If so, why? Start to make your own judgments concerning relationships between condition and value.

According to numismatic legend, a collector walked up to a crusty old dealer at a show one time and asked the dealer to grade a coin the collector had with him. The dealer looked at the coin and said, "I grade it a hundred dollars." Such is the bottom line to coin grading.

Grading U.S. proof coins

Because proof coins are struck by a special process (see Chapter 2), they receive their own grading designation. A coin does not start out being a proof and then become mint state if it becomes worn. Once a proof coin, always a proof coin.

In the ANA system, proof grades use the same numbers as circulated and uncirculated grades, and the amount of wear on the coin corresponds to those grades. But the number is preceded by the word "proof." For example, Proof-65, Proof-55, Proof-45, and so on. In addition, the ANA says a proof coin with many marks, scratches or other defects should be called an "impaired proof."

Grading world coins

The state of grading non-U.S. issues is similar to U.S. coin grading before Brown and Dunn. There is no detailed, illustrated guide that covers the enormous scope and variety of world coins; collectors and dealers rely on their experience in the field and knowledge of the marketplace.

The *Standard Catalog of World Coins* gives the following guidelines for grading world coins, which apply to the Canadian and Mexican value listings in this book:

In grading world coins, there are two elements to look for: (1) overall wear and (2) loss of design details, such as strands of hair, feathers on eagles, designs on coats of arms, and so on. Grade each coin by the weaker of the two sides. Age, rarity or type of coin should not be considered in grading.

Grade by the amount of overall wear and loss of detail evident in the main design on each side. On coins with a moderately small design element that is prone to early wear, grade by that design alone.

In the marketplace, adjectival grades are still used for Mexican coins. The numerical system for Canadian coins is now commonplace:

Uncirculated, MS-60: No visible signs of wear or handling, even under a 30X microscope. Bag marks may be present.

Almost uncirculated, AU-50: All detail will be visible. There will be wear on only the highest point of the coin. There will often be half or more of the original mint luster present.

Extremely fine, XF-40: About 95 percent of the original detail will be visible. Or, on a coin with a design that has no inner detail to wear down, there will be light wear over nearly the entire coin. If a small design is used as the grading area, about 90 percent of the original detail will be visible. This latter rule stems from the logic that a smaller amount of detail needs to be present because a small area is being used to grade the whole coin.

Very fine, VF-20: About 75 percent of the original detail will be visible. Or, on a coin with no inner detail, there will be moderate wear over the entire coin. Corners of letters and numbers may be weak. A small grading area will have about 60 percent of the original detail.

Fine, F-12: About 50 percent of the original detail will be visible. Or, on a coin with no inner detail, there will be fairly heavy wear over the entire coin. Sides of letters will be weak. A typically uncleaned coin will often appear dirty or dull. A small grading area will have just under 50 percent of the original detail.

Very good, VG-8: About 25 percent of the original detail will be visible. There will be heavy wear on the entire coin.

Good, G-4: Design will be clearly outlined but with substantial wear. Some of the larger detail may be visible. The rim may have a few weak spots of wear.

About good, AG-3: Typically only a silhouette of a large design will be visible. The rim will be worn down into the letters, if any.

Where to write for more information

Official A.N.A. Grading Standards for United States Coins: Whitman Coin Products, 10101 Science Drive, Sturtevant, WI 53177.

Photograde: Bowers and Merena Galleries, Inc., Books Dept., Box 1224, Wolfeboro, NH 03894.

Professional Coin Grading Service: P.O. Box 9458, Newport Beach, CA 92658.

Numismatic Guaranty Corp: P.O. Box 1776, Parsippany, NJ 07054.

Independent Coin Grading Co.: 7901 E. Belleview Ave., Suite 50, Englewood, CO 80111.

American Numismatic Association Authentication Bureau: 818 N. Cascade Ave., Colorado Springs, CO 80903-3279.

Visit the Krause Publications Web sites
http://www.krause.com
http://www.coincollecting.net

5

Get a map

How to organize a collection

By David C. Harper

Do you have a jar full of old coins? Did a favorite relative give you a few silver dollars over the years? Or did you just come across something unusual that you set aside?

All three circumstances make good beginnings for collecting coins. It may surprise you, but this is how just about everybody starts in the hobby. It is a rare collector who decides to start down the hobby road without first having come into a few coins one way or another.

What these random groupings lack is organization. It is organization that makes a collection. But think about it another way: Organization is the map that tells you where you can go in coin collecting and how you can get there.

Have you ever been at a large fair or a huge office building and seen the maps that say "you are here"? Did you ever consider that, over time, thousands of other people have stood on the same spot? This is true in numismatics also. Figuratively, you are standing on the same spot on which the writers of this book stood at some point in their lives.

At a fair, the map helps you consider various ways of seeing all the sights. In coin collecting, too, there are different ways to organize a collection. The method you choose helps you see the hobby sights you want to see.

It should be something that suits you. Remember, do what you want to do. See what you want to see. But don't be afraid to make a mistake; there aren't any. Just as one can easily retrace steps at a fair, one can turn around and head in another direction in the coin-collecting hobby. Besides, when you start off for any given point, often you see something along the way that was unplanned but more interesting. That's numismatics.

There are two major ways to organize a collection: by type, and by date and mintmark. These approaches work in basically the same fashion for coins of the United States, Canada and Mexico. Naturally, there are differences. But to establish the concepts, let's focus first on U.S. coins.

United States

Let's take collecting by type first. Look at your jar of coins, or take the change out of your pocket. You find Abraham Lincoln and the Lincoln Memorial on current cents. You find Thomas Jefferson and his home, Monticello, on the nickel. Franklin D. Roosevelt and a torch share the dime. George Washington and an eagle appear on the quarter. John F. Kennedy and the presidential seal are featured on the half dollar.

Each design is called a "type." If you took one of each and put the five coins in a holder, you would have a type set of the coins that are currently being produced for circulation by the U.S. Mint.

With just these five coins, you can study various metallic compositions. You can evaluate their states of preservation and assign a grade to each. You can learn about the artists who designed the coins, and you can learn of the times in which these designs were created.

As you might have guessed, many different coin types have been used in the United States over the years. You may remember seeing some of them circulating. These designs reflect the hopes and aspirations of people over time. Putting all of them together forms a wonderful numismatic mosaic of American history.

George Washington did not mandate that his image appear on the quarter. Quite the contrary. He would have been horrified. When he was president, he headed off those individuals in Congress who thought the leader of the country should have his image on its coins. Washington said it smacked of monarchy and would have nothing of it.

Almost a century and a half later, during the bicentennial of Washington's birth in 1932, a nation searching for its roots during troubled economic times decided that it needed his portrait on its coins as a reminder of his great accomplishments and as reassurance that this nation was the same place it had been in more prosperous days.

In its broadest definition, collecting coins by type requires that you obtain an example of every design that was struck by the U.S. Mint since it was founded in 1792. That's a tall order. You would be looking for denominations like the half cent, two-cent piece, three-cent piece, and 20-cent piece, which have not been produced in over a century. You would be looking for gold coins ranging in face value from $1 to $50.

But even more important than odd-sounding denominations or high face values is the question of rarity. Some of the pieces in this two-century type set are rare and expensive. That's why type collectors often divide the challenge into more digestible units.

Type collecting can be divided into 18th, 19th and 20th century units. Starting type collectors can focus on 20th century coin designs, which are easily obtainable. The fun and satisfaction of putting the 20th century set together then creates the momentum to continue backward in time.

In the process of putting a 20th century type set together, one is also learning how to grade, learning hobby jargon, and discovering how to obtain coins from dealers, the U.S. Mint, and other collectors. All of this knowledge is then refined as the collector increases the challenge to himself.

This book is designed to help. How many dollar types were struck in the 20th century? Turn to the U.S. price-guide section and check it out. We see the Morgan dollar, Peace dollar, Eisenhower dollar, and Anthony dollar. Hobbyists could also add the Ike dollar with the Bicentennial design of 1976 and the silver American Eagle bullion coin struck since 1986. One can also find out their approximate retail prices from the listings.

The beauty of type collecting is that one can choose the most inexpensive example of each type. There is no need to select a 1903-O Morgan when the 1921 will do just as well. With the 20th century type set, hobbyists can dodge some truly big-league prices.

As a collector's hobby confidence grows, he can tailor goals to fit his desires. He can take the road less traveled if that is what suits him. Type sets can be divided by denomination. You can choose two centuries of one-cent coins. You can take just obsolete denominations or copper, silver or gold denominations.

You can even collect by size. Perhaps you would like to collect all coin types larger than 30 millimeters or all coins smaller than 20 millimeters. Many find this freedom of choice stimulating.

Type collecting has proven itself to be enduringly popular over the years. It provides a maximum amount of design variety while allowing collectors to set their own level of challenge.

The second popular method of collecting is by date and mintmark. What this means, quite simply, is that a collector picks a given type — Jefferson nickels, for example — and then goes after an example of every year, every mintmark, and every type of manufacture that was used with the Jefferson design.

Looking at this method of collecting brings up the subject of mintmarks. The "U.S. Mint" is about as specific as most non-collectors get in describing the government agency that provides everyday coins. Behind that label are the various production facilities that actually do the work.

In two centuries of U.S. coinage, there have been eight such facilities. Four are still in operation. Those eight in alphabetical order are Carson City, Nev., which used a "CC" mintmark to identify its work; Charlotte, N.C. ("C"); Dahlonega, Ga. ("D"); Denver (also uses a "D," but it opened long after the Dahlonega Mint closed, so there was never any confusion); New Orleans ("O"); Philadelphia (because it was the primary mint, it used no mintmark for much of its history, but currently uses a "P"); San Francisco ("S"); and West Point, N.Y. ("W").

A basic type set of 20th century dollar coins would consist of (from top), a Morgan type, Peace type, Eisenhower type, and Anthony type.

A person contemplating the collecting of Jefferson nickels by date and mintmark will find that three mints produced them: San Francisco, Denver and Philadelphia. Because the first two are branch mints serving smaller populations, their output has tended over time to be smaller than that of Philadelphia. This fact, repeated in other series, has helped give mintmarks quite an allure to collectors. It provides one of the major attractions in collecting coins by date and mintmark.

The key date for Jeffersons is the 1950-D when using mintages as a guide. In that year, production was just 2.6 million pieces. Because collectors of the time were aware of the coin's low mintage, many examples were saved. As a result, prices are reasonable.

Jefferson nickels have been produced at the (from top) Philadelphia, Denver and San Francisco mints. Note the Denver and San Francisco mintmarks to the right of Monticello.

The wartime nickels of 1942-45 marked the first time a "P" mintmark, for Philadelphia, was used.

The Depression-era 1939-D comes in as the most valuable regular-issue Jefferson nickel despite a mintage of 3.5 million — almost 1 million more than the 1950-D. The reason: Fewer were saved for later generations of coin collectors.

Date and mintmark collecting teaches hobbyists to use mintage figures as a guide but to take them with a grain of salt. Rarity, after all, is determined by the number of surviving coins, not the number initially created.

The Jefferson series is a good one to collect by date and mintmark, because the mintmarks have moved around, grown in size, and expanded in number.

When the series was first introduced, the Jefferson nickel was produced at the three mints previously mentioned. In 1942, because of a diversion of certain metals to wartime use, the coin's alloy of 75 percent copper and 25 percent nickel was changed. The new alloy was 35 percent silver, 56 percent copper, and 9 percent manganese.

To denote the change, the mintmarks were moved and greatly enlarged. The pre-1942 mintmarks were small and located to the right of Monticello; the wartime mintmarks were enlarged and placed over the dome. What's more, for the first time in American history, the Philadelphia Mint used a mintmark ("P").

The war's end restored the alloy and mintmarks to their previous status. The "P" disappeared. This lasted until the 1960s, when a national coin shortage saw all mintmarks removed for three years (1965-1967) and then returned, but in a different location. Mintmarks were placed on the obverse, to the right of Jefferson's portrait near the date in 1968. In 1980 the "P" came back in a smaller form and is still used.

Another consideration arises with date and mintmark collecting: Should the hobbyist include proof coins in the set? This can be argued both ways. Suffice to say that anyone who has the desire to add proof coins to the set will have a larger one. It is not necessary nor is it discouraged.

Some of the first proof coins to carry mintmarks were Jefferson nickels. When proof coins were made in 1968 after lapsing from 1965 to 1967, production occurred at San Francisco instead of Philadelphia. The "S" mintmark was placed on the proof coins of that year, including the Jefferson nickel, to denote the change. Since that time, mintmarks used on proof

In 1968 mintmarks reappeared on U.S. coins and production of proof coins resumed, this time at the San Francisco Mint. On the nickels, the mintmark moved from the reverse to the obverse below the date.

examples of various denominations have included the "P", "D", "S", and "W".

For all of the mintmark history that is embodied in the Jefferson series, prices are reasonable. For a first attempt at collecting coins by date and mintmark, it provides excellent background for going on to the more expensive and difficult types. After all, if you are ever going to get used to the proper handling of a coin, it is far better to experiment on a low-cost coin than a high-value rarity.

As one progresses in date and mintmark collecting and type collecting, it is important to remember that all of the coins should be of similar states of preservation. Sets look slapdash if one coin is VG and another is MS-65 and still another is VF. Take a look at the prices of all the coins in the series before you get too far, figure out what you can afford, and then stick to that grade or range of grades.

Sure, there is a time-honored practice of filling a spot with any old example until a better one comes along. That is how we got the term "filler." But if you get a few placeholders, don't stop there. By assembling a set of uniform quality, you end up with a more aesthetically pleasing collection.

The date and mintmark method used to be the overwhelmingly dominant form of collecting. It still has many adherents. Give it a try if you think it sounds right for you.

Before we leave the discussion of collecting U.S. coins, it should be pointed out that the two major methods of organizing a collection are simply guidelines. They are no hard-and-fast rules that must be followed without question. Collecting should be satisfying to the hobbyist. It should never be just one more item in the daily grind. Take the elements of these collecting approaches that you like or invent your own.

It should also be pointed out that U.S. coinage history does not start with 1792 nor do all of the coins struck since that time conform precisely to the two major organizational approaches. But these two areas are good places to start.

There are coins and tokens from the American Colonial period (1607-1776) that are just as fascinating and collectible as regular U.S. Mint issues. There are federal issues struck before the Mint was actually established. See the Colonial price-guide section in this book.

There are special coins called commemoratives, which have been struck by the U.S. Mint since 1892 to celebrate some aspect of American history or a contemporary event. They are not intended for circulation. There was a long interruption between 1954 and 1982, but currently numerous commemoratives are being offered for sale directly to collectors by the Mint.

Collecting commemoratives has always been considered something separate from collecting regular U.S. coinage. It is, however, organized the same way. Commemoratives can be collected by date and mintmark or by type.

Current commemoratives can be purchased from the U.S. Mint. To get on its mailing list, write U.S. Mint, Customer Service Center, 10001 Aerospace Drive, Lanham MD 20706. Once on the list, hobbyists will get the various solicitations for not only commemoratives, but regular proof sets and mint sets and American Eagle bullion coinage.

Buying coins from the Mint can be considered a hobby pursuit in its own right. Some collectors let the Mint organize their holdings for them. They buy complete sets and put them away. They never buy anything from anywhere else.

Admittedly, this is a passive form of collecting, but there are individuals around the world who enjoy collecting at this level without ever really going any deeper. They like acquiring every new issue as it comes off the Mint's presses.

Once done, there is a certain knowledge that one has all the examples of the current year. Obviously, too, collectors by date and mintmark of the current types would have to buy the new coins each year, but, of course, they do not stop there.

Varieties and errors make up another area. Under this heading come the coins the Mint did not intend to make. There are all kinds of errors. Many of them are inexpensive. Check out the U.S. Minting Varieties and Errors section in the price guide. If you want to pursue it further, there are specialty books that deal with the topic in more detail.

Canada

Starting point for the national coinage of Canada is popularly fixed at 1858. In that year a large cent was first produced for use in Upper and Lower Canada (Ontario and Quebec). These pieces were intended to supplant local copper coinage, which in turn had been attempts to give various regions a medium of exchange.

What was circulating in Canada at the time was a hodgepodge of world issues. The large cent predates a unified national government by nine years, but it is considered the beginning of national issues nevertheless.

There are many similarities between the United States and Canada and their respective monetary systems. Both continent-sized nations thought in terms of taming the frontier, new settlements, and growth. Both came to use the dollar as the unit of account because of the pervasiveness of the Spanish milled dollar in trade. For each, the dollar divides into 100 cents.

Canadian coins have depicted (from top) Queen Victoria, King Edward VII, King George V, King George VI, and Queen Elizabeth II.

However, Canada had a far longer colonial history. Many of its residents resisted the tide that carried the United States to independence and worked to preserve their loyalties to the British crown. As a result, Canada was firmly a part of the British Empire. So even today with its constitution (the British North America Act transferred from Westminster to Ottawa in 1982), parliamentary democracy, and a national consciousness perhaps best symbolized by the maple leaf, Canada retains a loyalty to the crown in the person of Queen Elizabeth II of the United Kingdom. Canada is a member of the British Commonwealth of Nations.

The effect of this on coins is obvious. Current issues carry the queen's effigy. How Canada got its coins in the past was also influenced. The fledgling U.S. government set about creating its own mint as one of its earliest goals, despite that better-quality pieces could be purchased abroad at lower cost. Canada found that ties to mints located in England were logical and comfortable.

The Royal Canadian Mint was not established until 1908, when it was called the Ottawa branch of the British Royal Mint, and it was not given its present name until 1931. Both events are within living memory. Canadian coins, therefore, have a unique mixture of qualities. They are tantalizingly familiar to U.S. citizens yet distinctly different.

The coinage of a monarchy brings its own logic to the organization of a collection. Type collecting is delineated by the monarch. United Canada has had six. The first was Queen Victoria, whose image appeared on those large cents of 1858. Her reign began in 1837 and lasted until 1901.

She was followed by Edward VII, 1901-1910; George V, 1910-1936; Edward VIII, 1936; George VI, 1936-1952; and Queen Elizabeth II, 1952-present. All but Edward VIII had coins struck for circulation in Canada. The collectible monarchs, therefore, number five, but the longer reigns inspired changes of portraits over time to show the aging process at work. Legends also changed. When George VI ceased being emperor of India, Canada's coins were modified to recognize the change.

Like U.S. coins, sizes and alloys were altered to meet new demands placed on the coinage. However, the separateness of each nation might best be summed up this way: Though the United States abolished its large cent in 1857, Canada's was just getting under way in 1858. The United States put an end to the silver dollar in 1935, the very year Canada finally got its series going.

And Canada, the nickel-mining giant, used a small-sized silver five-cent coin until 1921, almost 50 years after the half dime was abolished in the United States. But whereas the Civil War was the major cause of the emergence of modern U.S. coinage as specified by the Coinage Act of 1873, World War I influenced the alterations that made Canada's coins what they are today.

It might be assumed that change in the monarch also signaled a change in the reverse designs of the various denominations. A check of the Canadian price guide section shows this is not necessarily the case. Current designs paired with Queen Elizabeth II basically date back to the beginning of her father's reign. The familiar maple-leaf cent, beaver five-cent piece, schooner 10-cent, caribou 25-cent, and coat-of-arms 50-cent have been running for over 50 years. Significant changes were made to the 50-cent coin in 1959, but the reverse design remains the coat of arms.

So where does that leave type collectors? It puts them in a situation similar to categorizing the various eagles on U.S. coins. They can be universalists and accept the broadest definitions of type, or they can narrow the bands to whatever degree suits them best.

By checking the price-guide section, date and mintmark collectors will quickly note that their method of organization more or less turns into collecting by date. Though currently there are three mints in Canada — Hull, Quebec; Ottawa, Ontario; and Winnipeg, Manitoba — they don't use mintmarks. Historically, few mintmarks were employed.

Ottawa used a "C" on gold sovereigns of 1908-1919 and on some exported colonial issues. The private Heaton Mint in Birmingham, England, used an "H" on coins it supplied to Canada from 1871 to 1907.

But the coins supplied to Canada by the British Royal Mint and later by its Ottawa branch did not carry any identifying mark. Collectors who confine their activities to the more recent issues need never think about a mintmark.

It would be easy to slant a presentation on Canadian issues to stress similarities or differences to U.S. issues. One should remember that the monetary structures of each evolved independently, but each was always having an impact on the other.

Common events, such as World War II, had a similar impact. For example, the Canadian five-cent coin changed in much the same way as the U.S. nickel. In Canada, nickel was removed and replaced first by a tombac (brass) alloy and then by chromium-plated steel. Peace brought with it a return to the prewar composition.

To see an example of differences between the United States and Canada, take the Canadian approach to the worldwide trend of removing silver from coinage. Canada made its move in 1968, three years after the United States. Instead of choosing a copper-nickel alloy as a substitute for silver, Canada looked to its own vast natural resources and employed pure nickel.

Canada also seems more comfortable with its coinage than the United States. Whereas the United States often feared confusion and counterfeiting from making the least little changes in its coins, Canada has long embraced coinage to communicate national events, celebrations and culture. Its silver-dollar series actually began as a celebration of George V's 25 years on the throne.

Succeeding years saw additional commemorative $1 designs interspersed with the regular voyageur design. When the centennial of national confederation was observed in 1967, all of the denominations were altered for one year. The United States only reluctantly tried out the idea on three of its denominations for the nation's Bicentennial.

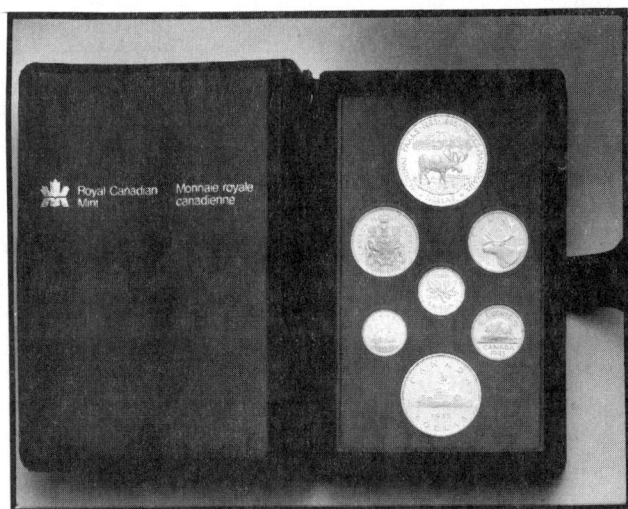

Like the U.S. Mint, the Royal Canadian Mint offers sets of coins in a variety of finishes to the collector market.

Ultimately, Canada began an annual commemorative dollar series in 1971. It issued coins for the 1976 Montreal Olympic Games and again in 1988 for the Calgary Olympic Games. Bullion coins were created to market its gold, silver and platinum output. A commemorative series of gold $100 coins was also undertaken. Canada, too, issues special proof, prooflike and specimen sets, similar to the United States.

Hobbyists who would like to be informed of new issues should write Royal Canadian Mint, P.O. Box 457, Station A, Ontario K1A 8V5, Canada. The mint also maintains special toll-free lines. In the United States, hobbyists may telephone the Royal Canadian Mint at 1-800-268-6468. In Canada, the number is 1-800-267-1871. You can get on the mailing list by using these numbers and you can buy currently available coins.

When collecting Canada, another thing to remember is the importance varieties play in the nation's various series. Certainly, a type collector has no need to dwell on this information, but the date and mintmark collector may puzzle over the many extra identifying abbreviations in the price guide for certain coins. These varieties should not be confused with the U.S. variety-and-error category.

Here the varieties are not mistakes; they are deliberately created and issued variations of the standard design. We see voyageur dollars on which the number of water lines changes. Other dollars count the number of beads.

These differences are minor. Though they were deliberately done to meet varying mint needs, they were not intended to be set apart in the public mind. The hobby, however, likes to look at things under a microscope.

Some varieties were indeed intended to be deliberately and noticeably different. An example of this occurs with 1947-dated issues. A maple leaf was placed on the 1947-dated cent through 50-cent issues. This indicated the coin was struck after George VI lost his title of emperor of India, as proclaimed in the Latin legend, but that the design had not yet been altered to reflect this. All of these varieties are considered integral parts of the Canadian series, and they are listed as such.

Do not construe any of this to mean there is no collecting of varieties and errors of the type common in the United States. There is. Collecting Royal Canadian Mint mistakes is just as active, just as interesting, and just as rewarding. After all, mint errors are universal. The methods of manufacture are the same. So the mistakes can be classified in the same manner.

Canada's numismatic listings also include items from various provinces issued before they were part of the confederation. The largest portion of this section is devoted to Newfoundland, because it retained a separate status far longer than the other provinces — until 1949 in fact.

Advice given to collectors of U.S. coins also applies to collectors of Canadian coins: Do what interests you. Do what you can afford. Create sets of uniform grade.

The rules of rarity transcend national boundaries. The only thing to keep in mind is the relative size of the collecting population. Because Canada has only a tenth of the U.S. population, it stands to reason that the number of collectors in that nation is but a fraction of the U.S. number. A mintage that seems to indicate scarcity for a U.S. coin, therefore, could indicate something quite common in Canada.

Don't forget that mintage is just a guide. The same factors that caused loss of available specimens or preserved unusually large quantities were at work in Canada, too.

Mexico

Coinage produced in Mexico dates to the establishment of a mint in Mexico City in 1536, over 250 years before a federal mint was set up in the United States and more than 300 years before Canada circulated its own coins. The output of those extra centuries alone would make organizing a Mexican coin collection more challenging than a collection of U.S. or Canadian coins. But there are numerous other factors involved.

You say you like the kings and queens on Canada's coins? Mexico has kings, too — nearly 300 years' worth, plus a couple of emperors. You say the ideals of liberty embodied by the great men and women on U.S. coins is more your cup of tea? Mexico's coins also feature men and women committed to liberty.

In addition, Mexico is the crossroads of civilizations and empires. The great pyramid-building society of southern Mexico and Central America met its end at the hands of the Spanish conquistadors led initially by Hernando Cortez. The great Aztec empire was looted and overturned in 1519-1521 in the name of Spain.

The great natural resources of the area then supported successive Spanish kings in their grand dreams of dominating Europe. Through the doors

One thousand of these equaled one new peso as 1993 began.

of the Mexico City Mint and later facilities scattered about the country passed legendary quantities of silver. Even today the country ranks at the top of the list of silver producers.

But while Spain could dominate Mexico for a long time, the basic ideals of liberty and human dignity eventually motivated the people to throw off the foreign yoke. Unfortunately, victory was often neither complete nor wisely led. And in more recent years, the scourge of inflation has exacted a high toll on the currency itself. The numismatic consequences of a long history punctuated by periods of turmoil are an abundance of denominations, metals and types.

It is tempting for a would-be collector of Mexican coins to forget about anything that happened in the country prior to its monetary reform of 1905. By starting at that point, a hobbyist can happily overlook anything other than a decimal monetary system in which 100 centavos equal 1 peso. That system is as modern as any. The coins' striking quality is high. Legends are easy to read and understand, and the variety of issues is wide but not overwhelming.

There always is a certain logic to begin the collecting of any country with recent issues. The costs of learning are minimized, and as one becomes comfortable, a level of confidence can be built up sufficient to prompt diving further into the past.

The issues of 1905 to date also more easily fit into the mold of type collecting and collecting by date and mintmark. To take type collecting, for example, let's look at the peso. In 1905 it was a silver-dollar-sized coin with a silver-dollar-sized quantity of bullion in it, 0.786 ounces. In 1918 it was reduced to 0.4663 ounces; in 1920, 0.3856 ounces; in 1947, 0.2250 ounces; 1950, 0.1285 ounces; 1957, 0.0514 ounces; and in 1970 silver was eliminated completely in favor of a copper-nickel alloy.

At almost every one of those steps, the design changed, too. After sinking to 3,300 to the U.S. dollar, monetary reform dropped three zeroes in 1993. The new peso, equal to 1,000 old ones, is now 9.3 to the U.S. dollar.

By beginning with 1905, a date and mintmark collector misses out on issues of the various branch mints that were located around the country. Regular issues were all struck in Mexico City. Yearly output was reasonably regular for the various denominations, so date sets are extensive.

There have been rumblings since the early 1980s that Mexico would

Mexico also strikes commemorative coins for the collector market. They are available through private firms in the United States.

abandon the peso because of its greatly reduced value. The government, however, has been working hard to retain it. So far it has succeeded.

One thing the government cannot do, however, is turn the clock back to a time when the fractional denominations of 1, 2, 5, 10, 20, 25, and 50 centavos had sufficient face value to circulate. However, it is stimulating to assemble sets because they offer a range of rarities. They are neither so expensive that it would prevent a collector from acquiring them at some point, but neither are they so common that you can walk into a shop, write a check, and come away with all of the 20th century sets complete. Check out the price guide section and see.

Gold in the post-1905 era is basically so much bullion. There are some scarcer pieces and some strikingly beautiful designs, such as the centenario, a gold 50-peso coin containing 1.2 ounces of bullion. It was first struck in 1921 to mark 100 years of independence. Because Mexico actively restruck its gold coins, however, it is virtually impossible to tell an original issue from the newer version.

The result is a retail price structure based on metallic content. Gold, however, does not conjure up the images that silver does. Silver is the magic word for Mexico. That, of course, means the peso.

The modern Mexico City Mint also strikes commemoratives and collector sets from time to time. These are generally marketed to collectors through private firms, details of which are published in hobby newspapers like *World Coin News*. Mexico, like the United States and Canada, also issues gold and silver bullion coins.

These also are marketed through arrangements with private firms. Interestingly, Mexico's many gold-coin restrikes were the bullion coins of their day. They had the advantage of ready identification, and they were legally tradable according to gold-coin regulations that existed in the United States from 1933 through 1974.

It is appropriate that we conclude discussion of the modern period on the concept of bullion, because bullion is at the root of Mexico's numismatic history. That is a period to which we now turn.

When Cortez toppled the Aztec Empire, for a time the wealth returning to Spain was merely that taken by the victors from the vanquished. But the business of permanently administering a vast area in the name of the Spanish king, exploiting its natural resources, and funneling the proceeds to Spain quite soon involved the establishment of a mint in Mexico City. This was undertaken in 1536, just 15 years after the end of Aztec dominion.

At first, the authorized coins were low denominations: silver quarter, half, 1, 2, 3, and 4 reales, and copper 2 and 4 maravedis. To understand their face values and how they related to each other, let's take the common reference point of a silver dollar. The silver dollar is 8 reales, and you might recognize the nickname for the denomination of "piece of eight" from pirate lore. The eighth part, the silver real, was divided into 34 copper maravedis. That means the 8 reales was worth 272 copper maravedis.

The copper coinage was hated and soon abolished, not to reappear until 1814. The silver coins were fine as far as they went. When the mines of Mexico began producing undreamed of quantities of metal, however, it was the 8 reales that took center stage. This occurred after 1572. The piece of eight became the standard form for shipping silver back to Spain.

Mexico City's output was prodigious. Minting standards were crude. All denominations produced are called "cobs," because they are basically little more than irregular-looking lumps of metal on which bits and pieces of design can be seen. The only constant was weight, fineness, and the appearance of assayer's initials (which guaranteed the weight and fineness). Not showing those initials was cause for severe punishment.

Designs showed the arms of the monarch on one side, a cross on the other, appropriate legends, and an indication of denomination. The period of cob issues lasted until 1732. Rulers of the period start with Charles and Johanna, 1516-1556; Philip II, 1556-1598; Philip III, 1598-1621; Philip IV, 1621-1665; Charles II, 1665-1700; Philip V, 1700-1724 and 1724-1746; and Luis I, 1724.

Modern mint machinery began turning out coins in 1732. Quality was similar to today. The arms design was continued. It was not until 1772 that the monarch's portrait began appearing. The honor of this numismatic debut belongs to Charles III. Kings of this period are Ferdinand VI, 1746-1759; Charles III, 1760-1788; Charles IV, 1788-1808; and Ferdinand VII, 1808-1821. The *Standard Catalog of Mexican Coins* by Colin R. Bruce II and Dr. George W. Vogt is recommended to those who want to study this period in greater depth.

The revolutionary period begins in 1810, when a parish priest, Miguel Hidalgo y Costilla, issued the call for independence. The first attempts to achieve this were violently suppressed. Hidalgo was executed, but independence did come in 1821.

With revolt against central authority came a dispersal of the right to strike coins. Mexico City continued as the major facility, but other operations began. The list of these over the next century is lengthy. Mintmarks and assayer initials proliferated.

The old colonial coinage standard survived the period. The 8 reales and its parts carried on. A slight reduction in bullion content had been ordered by the king in 1760, but otherwise things continued as they were. Gold was coined during the colonial period beginning in 1679 based on an 8-escudo piece, which divided into eighths just like the 8 reales. Gold, however, was not as important as silver.

Mexico's first emperor came shortly after independence. He was a leader in the struggle that set Mexico free from Spain. Augustin de Iturbide, originally an officer in the service of Spain, was proclaimed emperor in 1822. He abdicated in 1823 and was executed in 1824.

The second emperor had a reign almost as short as the first. Maximilian I, emperor only because he had a French army to secure the throne, reigned from 1863 to 1867. He was shot by a firing squad when the French left.

He is remembered numismatically because he decided to decimalize the coinage. The centavo and peso were born. Soon afterward, the republic was re-established. Further monetary changes were minor thereafter until 1905.

Collectors focusing on Mexico can devote much time to the study of the quasi-official issues of rebels during the periods of instability. They can look at hacienda tokens, which were issued by large farms or ranches that employed hundreds or thousands of people. Or they can pick whichever period in Mexico's history that fascinates them most. Whatever collectors of Mexico eventually settle on, they will find it rewarding.

Where to write for more information

World Coin News: 700 E. State St., Iola, WI 54990.

6

Caring for coins

How to store and preserve your collection

By Alan Herbert

From the day you acquire your first collectible coin, you have to consider where and how to store your collection. Often a shoebox or a small cardboard or plastic box of some kind will be the principal storage point as you start to gather coins, even before they can be considered a collection. Sooner or later you will outgrow that first box and need to think seriously about what to do with your coins to protect and preserve them.

All too often security takes precedence over preservation. We're more worried that the kids will dip into the coins for candy or ice cream or that burglars will somehow learn about your "valuable" collection and pay a visit. It often isn't until years later when you suddenly notice that your once beautiful coins are now dingy and dull, with spots and fingerprints all over them, that preservation becomes a primary consideration.

Learning good storage habits should be one of the first things to do right along with acquiring those first coins. There are a multitude of storage products on the market that are intended for more or less specific situations, so learning which to use and how to use them is vital to the health of your collection. Most if not all of the products mentioned here should be available at your nearest coin shop or hobby store.

Safe storage methods

The common impulse is to use what's available around the house; never allow that impulse to control your collecting. Plastic wrap, aluminum foil, cardboard, stationery envelopes, and other common household products are not designed for coin storage and never should be used for your collec-

Two-by-two cardboard holders are a common form of short-term, inexpensive coin storage.

Many dealers sell coins in 2-by-2 plastic "flips," but they should not be used for long-term storage.

tion. The same goes for soaps and cleansers found around the home.

There are specific products that have been designed, tested and found safe to use for coins. These are the media your collection deserves. The slight added expense will pay a thousand dividends years from now when you sell your collection or pass it on to your heirs.

The most common storage media are 2-inch by 2-inch cardboard holders with Mylar windows, 2-by-2 plastic "flips," coin tubes, hard-plastic holders, coin boards, and coin albums.

The 2-by-2 cardboard holders are the cheapest and most commonly used storage method. They are usually folded and stapled around the coin. They are intended for short-term general storage. They are not airtight or watertight, and staples driven too close to the coin can ruin it.

The 2-by-2 plastic flips come in good and bad varieties. The old, usually soft flips are made of plastics that contain polyvinylchloride, a chemical found in many plastics. Over time it breaks down into substances that put a green slime on your coins, which attacks the surface and ruins them.

The good flips are made of Mylar, but they are brittle and prone to splitting. So they should not be used to mail coins or when the coins are moved about frequently. Mylar flips, too, are for short-term general storage.

Coin tubes are often used for bulk storage, but there is a proper technique to placing the coins in the tube.

Often you will find coins in PVC holders when you buy them from a dealer. Remove them immediately and put them in some better storage medium.

Coin tubes come in clear and cloudy, or translucent, plastic. These are made of an inert plastic that will not harm your coins. Tubes are intended for bulk, medium- to long-term storage, with one caution: Use care when inserting the coins. Merely dropping one coin onto another in a tube can damage both coins. The best technique is to make a stack or pile of the coins, then slide the pile carefully into the tube while holding it at an angle.

Hard-plastic holders are the elite items for storing your collection. There are a number of varieties, some of which come in three parts that are screwed together. Some come in two pieces that fit together. Some of these are airtight and watertight. They are more expensive, but they deserve to be used for any really valuable coins in your collection.

Coins processed by the third-party grading services come in hard-plastic holders, most of which are at least semiairtight. The hard-plastic holders used by the U.S. Mint for proof sets since 1968 are not airtight, so coins should be watched carefully for signs of problems. In recent years these holders have been improved, but you should check your proof sets periodically.

Any stored coins should be checked regularly, at least twice a year. Check coins for signs of spotting or discoloration. Check the storage media for any signs of deterioration, rust, mildew, or other problems.

The older mint sets and proof sets — issued from 1955 to 1964 — come in soft-plastic envelopes that are not intended for long-term storage. Coins

Hard-plastic holders are the top of the line in coin storage.

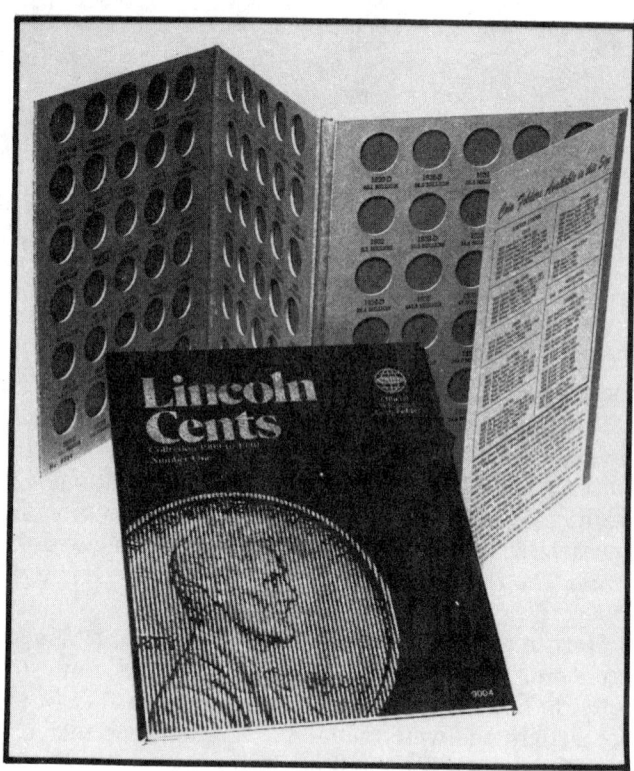

Coin folders are a low-cost and attractive way to store inexpensive circulated coins.

in these envelopes should be put in better storage media for the long term. In recent years the Mint has switched to an inert, stiffer plastic for the mint sets. This plastic is safe.

A coin folder is frequently the first piece of equipment the beginning collector buys. It is simply a piece of cardboard with holes to hold the coins. The holder folds up for storage. It is intended for inexpensive circulated coins only.

They give no protection from contamination or fingerprints. Worn coins will often fall out of the holes, which leads some novice collectors to tape the coins in the album. This is another example of misuse of a household

Coin albums also provide attractive storage for inexpensive circulated coins.

product; tape can permanently damage a coin's surface.

Pride of ownership and the desire to show off a collection are the moving forces behind the sale of thousands of coin albums. They should also be used for inexpensive circulated coins only, with a couple of exceptions.

Some albums are merely coin boards mounted between covers. Others have pages with sliding plastic strips on both sides of the page so both sides of the coin can be seen.

The open-face albums are subject to fingerprints and contamination. Sneezing on your coins can do as much damage as gouging them with a knife. The slides will rub on your coins, damaging the high points of the design over time. These two types of albums should never be used for expensive uncirculated or proof coins, although they are fine for circulated coins that you want to display.

Fairly new on the market are albums designed for coins in inert, airtight holders. This allows you to display your coins and still keep them safe from handling and contact with the atmosphere.

One more storage medium that deserves mention is the clear-plastic notebook page that has pockets for 2-by-2 holders or flips. Here again there are good and bad. Most old pocket sheets contain PVC, so they cannot be used to hold coins in non-airtight holders because the gases will migrate into the holders and damage the coins. The newer Mylar pages are brittle but will not generate damaging gases or liquids.

When buying storage media, make sure the dealer guarantees that his products are safe for coins. Many of the old albums, flips and pocket pages are still around, especially at flea markets. If you are in doubt, don't buy.

There are also thin, two-piece, inert plastic holders that many collectors use to protect coins put in flips or 2-by-2 cardboard holders, especially to protect them from moving about against the holder and getting scratched. They are virtually airtight, so they do offer some protection.

Coins need to be protected from burglars. A box under the bed or in the closet offers no protection. If you must keep coins at home, a good, fireproof safe is a must. Otherwise, rent a safe-deposit box at a bank, but read the fine print on your box contract to make sure a coin collection is covered.

Most homeowner's insurance policies will not cover a coin collection or will cover only a fraction of its value. Special riders are expensive, but if you keep most of your coins at the bank, this will cut costs. For details, consult your insurance agent. The American Numismatic Association also offers collection insurance.

Where to store coins is often a problem. The commonest solution is to put them in the attic or basement. Those are the two worst places for your collection. Attics are notoriously hot. Heat can damage almost any storage media, and if there is the slightest hint of PVC, you've got trouble.

Basements are equally bad. They can flood, and humidity is high. Mildew can attack holders and other material stored with your coins.

So what's left? Ideally coins should be treated like a family member. They should be stored in some part of the house where temperature and humidity are relatively constant year round. If it's comfortable for you, it's probably much more comfortable for your coins than the basement or attic.

Protecting coins from humidity is always a good idea, even in areas where it is not a major health problem. For your coins, too much dampness can become a serious problem, often before you realize it. A good solution is to get several good-sized packets of silica gel and store them with your coins in your safe or a container of some kind that will isolate them from the general climate in the home.

To clean or not to clean

Before you store your coins, you should be aware that coins are like dishes: They should never be put away dirty. Ah, but you've probably already heard or read that you should never clean a coin. If you haven't, I'll say it now: Never clean a coin.

OK, so there are exceptions, but be careful of those exceptions and for good reason. Ignoring the exceptions can be excruciatingly and embarassingly expensive.

Coins get dirty, just like anything else. The impulse is to shine them up — polish them to a brilliance that will dazzle the viewer. If you've already succumbed to the temptation to clean even a single coin, stand up, kick yourself, then sit back down and read on. The one exception is loose dirt, grease, oil, or something similar, and there are even exceptions to that rule.

Use a neutral solvent to dissolve the grease and oils that usually coat uncirculated coins as they come from the mint. Follow the instructions on the container exactly, and if the directions say to use the product outdoors, they mean it.

For circulated coins, lighter fluid will often dissolve the accumulated "gunk" that sticks to them, but I don't recommend it for uncirculated coins, especially copper alloy coins. Air dry the coins; don't rub or wipe them. Even the softest cloth or paper towel can pick up sharp-edged particles that will ruin a coin's surface. Proof coins are clean when they are packaged, so this should not be necessary and should be done only as a last resort if they have somehow picked up oil in handling.

Using dips, household cleansers, metal polish, and even soap can permanently damage a coin. Avoid acid-based cleaners at all costs. They work by eating away the coin's surface to remove the embedded dirt or discoloration. Cleaning a coin with any of these products will sharply reduce its collectible value. To put it simply, collectors do not want cleaned coins, so they are heavily discounted.

One of the reasons for this is that once a coin has been cleaned, it will discolor much more quickly, requiring fresh cleaning. Each time it is cleaned, the surface is further dulled, reducing the coin's appeal and reducing its value.

Obviously this advice applies especially to uncirculated and proof coins, but it applies to any coin that is or has the potential to become valuable. But if you clean it, its career ends right there.

There are products specifically designed for removing the green PVC slime from coins. They do not contain acid, so they are safe. They will stop but cannot reverse the damage that the PVC has already done to the coin. Read the label, and use exactly as directed.

I frequently am asked about ultrasonic cleaners. They fall under the same heading as the various cleaning products I've described. In other words, the apparatus should not be used for uncirculated, proof, or other valuable coins. If you do use one, do one coin at a time so there is no chance for the vibration to rub two coins together. Change or filter the cleaning solution frequently to keep abrasive particles from coming in contact with the vibrating coin.

Like anything else, cleaning can be carried to an extreme, so I'll give you one horror story of just such a mistake: Years ago I had a collector fly several hundred miles to bring his collection for me to sell for him. When he laid out the coins on the table, I was shocked to discover that the hundreds of coins had all been harshly cleaned.

When I questioned him he calmly recounted that he had decided that the coins needed cleaning, so he dumped them all into a rock tumbler and left it on for several hours. It ruined all his coins, reducing them to face value. With his passion for cleanliness he had destroyed several thousand dollars worth of collectible value, plus air fare, a rental car, and a motel bill.

The key to a long-term collection that might appreciate in value is to learn what not to do to your coins and what care they need to survive years of waiting in the wings. Learning to protect your coins with the best available storage methods and media is a key first step toward enjoying your collection for years to come.

Where to write for more information

American Numismatic Association: 818 N. Cascade Ave., Colorado Springs, CO 80903-3279.

7

The profit motive

Some comments on coins as investments

By Robert E. Wilhite

When gold and silver bullion prices reached all-time highs in 1980, prices for many U.S. gold and silver coins hit record highs too. Double-digit inflation prompted many investors to seek refuge in tangible assets. Companies touting coins as investments popped up all over. Many of those investors, however, became disenchanted when coin prices crashed along with precious-metals prices just a few months later.

Also, as mentioned in Chapter 4, grading standards for uncirculated coins were loose during the boom, but tightened during the bust in these pre-slab days. Investors who bought coins billed as MS-65 or higher during the boom tried to sell during the bust and oftentimes were offered only MS-63 or lower money.

The investment aspect of coins was not new in 1980. Articles in early coin publications often addressed the subject. Those collectors who fancy themselves as traditionalists generally scorn the thought of coins as investments. To them, the reasons to collect coins are the joy and educational benefits of pursuing a hobby.

In reality, though, few collectors purchase coins with the expectation that they will go down in value. There is no guarantee that their coins will increase in value, but collectors who do their homework before buying help their chances. They check the value guides – such as those appearing in *Numismatic News*, *Coins* and *Coin Prices* – and shop their local dealers, shows and advertisements in the aforementioned publications to try to get the best value for their money.

There are many financial success stories in numismatics, as evidenced by auction results. Some common themes keep reappearing in profiles of the people whose collections have provided major sales: These people collected coins over a long time – 10, 20, 30 years or more – and they knew their stuff. They knew what was rare and what was common and they knew the going rates for each. They formed collections of coins; they didn't just accumulate a mishmash of pieces.

Many had an advantage from the beginning: They were wealthy and could afford some of the top rarities. But their methods carry lessons for collectors of all means.

The financial failure stories also have common themes: There are coin sellers who operate on the fringe of numismatics and prey upon people who know nothing about coins. A slick salesman calls on the telephone and overstates the rarity of the coins he has for sale. He sells them for several times what they could be purchased for from a mainstream numismatic dealer. Several years later the buyer takes them to a mainstream dealer and finds out his coins are worth a fraction of what he paid for them. A person who studies coins and the market for them before jumping in, however, avoids such a scenario.

The value guide for U.S. coins in this book includes charts showing the price performance of selected key dates. As can be seen, coins are subject to price fluctuations just like any investment that carries risk. Some coins experienced a great increase in value in the early 1980s and then dropped toward the middle of the decade. Others have been less volatile, showing little if any fluctuation over the time studied.

Generally the volatile areas are the more popularly collected coins in high grades – series like Morgan dollars, Walking Liberty half dollars, and some gold coins. The less volatile areas usually have a smaller universe of collectors – series like the early silver and copper coins, and obsolete denominations (3 cents and 20 cents, for example).

In the latter case, the rarity of these coins sometimes works against them. To have a successful promotion, a dealer selling coins as investments needs a certain quantity to fill all his orders. The earlier issues are usually not available in the quantities needed for a profitable promotion. Demand for these earlier issues comes mostly from a relatively small but avid group of collectors, and as a result, they're less subject to sharp price fluctuations.

In 1979 *Numismatic News* began publishing a weekly Coin Market Index. The index charted the composite performance of the market's more expensive coins, similar to the stock market's Dow Jones Industrial Average. It provided a means for comparing the state of the market at various points in the index's 19-year history.

A chart of the index from 1979 to 1997 shows a number of peaks and valleys in the market. After its inception in May 1979, the index jumped over 4,000 points to 6,062 on July 5, 1980, during the precious metals boom. It then crashed to 3,540 on Sept. 11, 1982. Over the next six years the index enjoyed a steady climb to 6,311 on Sept. 27, 1988.

Shortly thereafter, several Wall Street investment firms announced that they would offer limited partnerships that invested in coins. This set off speculation that coins would increase in value because of the new

COIN MARKET INDEX
Numismatic News

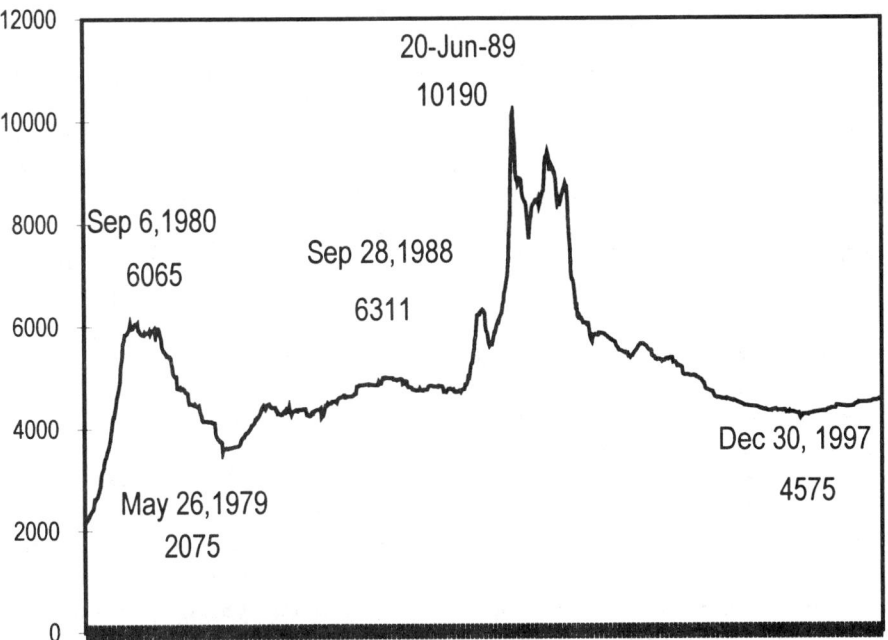

demand. The index climbed to an all-time high of 10,190 on June 18, 1989, but when the demand did not turn out to be great enough to support the widespread speculation, the index crashed to 6,160 on Dec. 18, 1990. It enjoyed a bit of a spurt early in 1991, before dropping steadily to close the year at 5482. The index recovered slightly in the first two quarters of 1992, but then went basically sideways. It closed 1997 at 4575. At that point, it was abolished.

The Coin Market section of *Numismatic News* was redesigned as 1998 began. Its frequency was changed from weekly to monthly. The index was eliminated as part of this redesign.

Why? Well, in 1979, the Coin Market Index was established to answer the question: How is the market doing? There were no other indexes then. Those were exciting times. The market seemed to go straight up. The past seven or eight years have seen much less dramatic swings. The graph is flat. You need months or years to see any real movement recorded.

Who wants to see a flat graph in an era when a booming stock market has accustomed people to 20 percent and 30 percent annual returns? That does not mean certain coins are not doing well, even rapidly increasing in price, but you have to search a little bit to find them. But when you add them to every other coin, you get the flat graph.

Collectors who are interested in graphs can find them all over nowadays, but the savvy investor needs to ask a question when these many graphs are examined. That question is: Did the maker of the graph simply take advantage of hindsight and use the top-performing 50, 100 or 200 coins of the previous 10, 20 or 30 years? It is easy to make the coin market look like a rocket when you do that.

While it existed, the lesson the index taught is: To be a successful coin investor, think like a collector. That means forming a set of coins (see Chapter 5) and holding for the long term – 10, 15, 20 years or more. You will get some slowpokes this way, but you will also more likely buy the future top performers. This approach is also fun and interesting.

Investors who bought high-grade, investment coins at the June 18, 1989, peak, are hurting right now, but maybe they won't be in 10 years. Those who bought in May 1979 and didn't sell on June 18, 1989, probably wish they had, but they're still ahead of prices from 20 years ago. The collecting approach means you have fun while you hold your coins through these lengthy periods.

There is no guarantee that high-grade coins will continue to increase in value over time, but market history shows that the odds favor those collectors who stick it out for the long term. Remember, too, that the index was slanted toward high-grade coins. Because the index is down from its peak, it does not mean that every coin decreased in value. In fact, as high-grade investment coins experienced a slump in 1991, some traditional collectible series such as Indian cents, Lincoln cents, and Buffalo nickels – saw a resurgence of trading activity.

Whether your motivation for buying collectible coins is purely invest-ment or purely collecting pleasure or something in between, keep good records of your purchases. You'll need them after you sell your coins for figuring your gain or loss on your taxes. Record the date of purchase, seller and purchase price. To make sure your records are adequate, consult a certified public accountant.

Also, advise your heirs on the disposal of your collection in the event of your death. Make sure they know where your records are stored, approxi-mately how much your collection is worth and possible purchasers of your coins.

8

Join the club
Coin collecting has lots of organizations

By David C. Harper

More than 150 years ago, Alexis de Tocqueville noted in his *Democracy in America* the penchant of people in the United States to create and voluntarily join public groups for a multitude of purposes. This urge to join carries over into coin collecting.

Whether it be a national organization or local coin club, groups have been organized in the United States, Canada and Mexico to help collectors enhance their hobby knowledge and enjoyment. They serve as clearing-houses for new information, maintain libraries, and bring collectors together in meetings to share their hobby experiences with each other. Clubs are so well defined that collectors can find one to serve any activity level and any degree of personal interaction with other collectors.

At the extreme, you can join a national organization by mail, spend a hobby lifetime utilizing its services, and yet never leave the privacy and comfort of home. At the other end, some areas offer such a multitude of clubs that you can find a meeting to attend on many nights of the week.

There are many ways to find a club. Some hobbyists inquire at the local coin shop to identify the organization nearest them. *Numismatic News* publishes news about clubs. Also, watch your local newspaper for listings of community events.

How does a collector match his needs with an appropriate club? The closest thing to a one-stop shopping place for an answer is the American Numismatic Association.

It is the United States' national coin-collecting organization and was granted a perpetual charter by Congress with a mission of education. It can be reached at 818 N. Cascade Ave., Colorado Springs, CO 80903-3279. It offers a wide array of personal hobby services, and its benefits cross national boundaries. In fact, when it was founded in 1891, it was expected that Canadians and Mexicans would be just as likely to join as U.S. citizens.

The most obvious benefit to an ANA member is a subscription to *The Numismatist*, the association's monthly magazine. In it you find news, historical features, membership information, and advertisements placed by dealers who are ready to fill every collector's want list.

More than 30,000 titles are available in the ANA library, and you don't have to walk into the ANA building to check them out. Any member anywhere can do that by mail. The ANA has called upon renowned numismatic authorities to create a correspondence course, which distills into 29 separate readings information that has taken many people a lifetime to learn. There are ANA educational seminars held in Colorado Springs and other sites across the United States.

The ANA sponsors two conventions annually. The early spring convention is usually held in March at locations across the country, selected and announced well in advance. The summer convention, which is so huge that it's billed as the "World's Fair of Money," is a tradition that dates back almost to the organization's founding.

Members also are offered a variety of optional services, ranging from coin-collection insurance to credit cards and car rental discounts. And if you do go to Colorado Springs, the ANA maintains its Money Museum at its headquarters. In it are some of the rarest and most famous coins in history.

Joining the ANA is easy. The membership fee is $35 the first year and $29 thereafter. Members over 65 years old get a $4 discount, and junior members (those under 18) are charged $11.

Beyond simply belonging to the ANA, though, are the doors that open to members. If you want to find a regional, state or local club, you can get help from the ANA. The important thing to remember is that you set your own level of involvement. If your profession is so hectic that you don't need another meeting to go to, the ANA is the place for you. If your hours are so regular that joining in the fun and camaraderie of a local club is just what you are looking for, the ANA can help you find that, too.

And just because the American Numismatic Association has "American" in its name, it doesn't mean that members are focused only on U.S. coins. Far from it. It is more accurate to say that if a coin was struck at any time anywhere in the world in the last 2,600 years, there are ANA members who collect it.

The ANA, if it connotes any exclusivity at all, is basically a regional designation based on where its members live. The farther one gets from the United States, the longer correspondence takes and the greater the possibility of a language barrier between the ANA staff and a potential member. It is therefore not surprising to find that 27,000 members are predominantly located in the United States.

The Canadian Numismatic Association dates to 1950. It publishes *The Canadian Numismatic Journal*, published 11 times a year, and it also sponsors an annual convention. Membership is considerably smaller than the ANA's, in line with the population difference between the United States and Canada. Membership fee is $33 a year. The mailing address is Executive Secretary, Canadian Numismatic Association, P.O. Box 226, Barrie, Ontario L4M 4T2, Canada.

The Sociedad Numismatica de Mexico A.C. was established in 1952. Basically, it oversees an annual convention in Mexico City. It may be contacted through its U.S. representative at 102 E. Main St., Homer, MI 49245. A related group at the same address is the U.S. Mexican Numismatic Society.

That covers the national hobby umbrella groups. There are many more organizations of a national character that have somewhat narrower poses. Among these is the American Numismatic Society in New York City. It is older than the ANA, having been established in 1858. It also maintains a superb museum of U.S. and world coins, and a world-class library. Emphasis in the ANS is on scholarly research.

Numismatics would be nothing if it were not for its research pioneers. If that is what appeals to you, you can write the ANS at Broadway and 155th St., New York, NY 10032, for information regarding its structure and various classes of membership.

Other national organizations focus on specific collectible areas, such as Seated Liberty coinage or tokens and medals. These are popular and active. Many are member organizations of the ANA and hold meetings in conjunction with the ANA's conventions.

Coin dealers have organizations of their own. The Professional Numismatists Guild Inc. maintains high standards of membership qualification and conduct. Members are a who's who of the commercial sector of the hobby. All are ready to serve you in furthering your collecting goals. For a membership roster, contact Robert Brueggeman, Executive Director, 3950 Concordia Lane, Fallbrook, CA 92028.

This brief review merely puts you on the threshold of the organized numismatic world. It is up to you to open that door or walk away. Over the years, many collectors have found membership to be the most rewarding aspect of the hobby. They have benefited from working with others with a common interest to further their own knowledge and advance their collecting goals in an environment of mutual support and friendship.

9

Worried about Y2K?

Concern pushes up silver coin prices

By David C. Kranz

What potential does the Year 2000 computer glitch have for affecting numismatics? It may seem a curious issue to address in a coin guide with the date 2000 on its cover, for quite honestly Y2K worries may become instantly laughable on the morning of Jan. 1, 2000, but throughout 1999 the "what ifs" held sway as people considered how to prepare for the unknown. Many of these people included coins in their preparations, driving up prices for common silver coins.

The root of the Y2K computer problem is easy to understand. As a matter of convenience and as a method of conserving computer memory, programmers often used just two digits to indicate the year, for example, 67 for 1967, 79 for 1979 and so on. Potential problems arise with 00, which could be interpreted as 1900 instead of 2000. Different programs and computers would react differently to this input, some working just fine, some failing to operate, others perhaps setting into motion undesirable processes that could range from individual annoyances to massive disasters. So much has been said about the scary scenarios to which we may wake on Jan. 1, 2000, that it has been difficult to separate realistic concerns from overblown paranoia.

Certainly, however, it is true that institutions have become increasingly computer dependent, particularly in the past 20 years. Communications networks, accounting procedures and thousands of business and governmental functions worldwide – including banking, utilities, telephones and, it may be assumed, high-tech national defense systems – involve computers. Work has been done to evaluate as best as can be determined what the possible outcomes of Y2K computer errors are and how to avoid them. Many dollars have been spent to eliminate Y2K problems. But "what if ..." persists.

The essence of the Y2K problem is simple; it's the looming uncertainties – and how people will react – that feed the worries. That's where coins come in.

In times of unease and anxiety, traditional stores of value like gold and silver are often given increased precedence. With the addition of the Y2K fears, concerned individuals are steering clear of valuables that require

Buyers worried about Y2k bid up the price of Eagles and other silver coins.

computers for their trade, use or storage. Gold, silver and other precious metals have received extra attention.

Are people buying thousand-ounce bars of silver and unliftable hunks of gold? No. If you should need to buy 10 gallons of gasoline from the survivalist down the street and you lug out a silver bar worth over $5,000 to pay, it'll probably take some quick maneuvering to get out of the deal at a reasonable cost. More practical for such situations is a smaller measured unit that can be used in a post-disaster transaction.

People have picked up on bullion coinage. Sales of the United States' gold and silver American Eagle coins increased dramatically though the first portion of 1999. These coins are all one ounce or smaller, making them more suitable for individual transactions as well as easily portable. And their purity and metal content are specified and consistent – in a post-disaster situation that allows for a precious metal barter system, payments in genuine gold American Eagles will probably trump payment in, say, a gold necklace of undetermined purity.

The smallest gold American Eagle received the most attention. 127,500 ounces of the tenth-ounce gold Eagles were sold between Jan. 1, 1999, and April 12, 1999, compared with only 15,000 ounces of that size sold January through April 1998. Another avenue for pursuing bullion, one which held appeal in late 1998 and early 1999, has been to gather once-circulating coinage that contains silver. Mass quantities of low-grade U.S. quarters, half dollars and dimes from before 1965, back when those coins were 90 percent silver, were subject to incredible speculation in 1999. Should they be necessary, these coins could be doled out in small amounts. Their value is a function of the price of silver bullion and the fluctuating demand for bags at any given time.

The market value of bags containing $1,000 in face value of 90 percent silver coins escalated to far above the normal trading levels as Y2K fears presented themselves. At the end of July 1998, when silver was priced at $5.63 per ounce, the trading value of a $1,000 bag of 90 percent silver was $4,010 and the value of the silver in the coins, called the melt value, was $4,025. Thus, dealers were paying $15 less than melt value for these bags. In late October 1998, when silver was at $5.07 per ounce, the same bags were trading for $4,060 when the melt value was $3,625. Dealers were paying $435 over melt value. In March 1999 when silver was $5.50 per troy ounce, the dealer buying price was $4,700, over a melt value of $3,933 (a difference of over $750). But by mid-May 1999 the trend had cooled. With silver at $5.45, meaning a melt value of $3,897, dealers were buying at $4,100, a premium of only $203 over melt value.

One of the psychological comforts of hoarding silver circulating coinage is that, if all's well and Y2K ends well, the coins are still worth their $1,000 face value at minimum even if the silver price drops out of the bottom. No one has predicted that the silver price will fall so far, so any loss of value would more likely be much less. The premium paid to set aside bags of old silver coins, just in case, has been promoted as an insurance cost, a price paid to gain a sense of security. Governments also took steps to provide a sense of security.

The U.S. Federal Reserve announced in late 1998 that it was working with the Bureau of Engraving and Printing to increase the amount of paper money that would be available in circulation by $40 billion, a move based on the likelihood that lots of people would be hoarding larger-than-normal stashes of cash outside of their computer-dependent banks. The estimate was about $500 hoarded per household. There is about $400 billion in paper money circulating, so about a 10 percent increase in available "emergency" cash was planned.

Since $20 and $100 notes are most likely to be set aside by the average person, Y2K may be creating paper money collecting opportunities. The Fed's currency supply boost will increase the number of newly designed Series 1996 $20, $50 and $100 notes relative to the number of old-design notes. If Y2K fizzles into nothing, the Fed will be removing notes from circulation to return to a regular supply level. My bet is that notes of the older designs will be targeted for removal over the Series 1996 notes, making the older notes tougher to find – with the possible effect of upping prices for high-quality older $20s, $50s and $100s.

The effect of Y2K on the numismatic collector market is impossible to predict, not knowing what problems may arise. If Y2K proves a major disaster, collecting will recede from the forefront as people look to stabilize their situations. If it involves only some minor annoyances – some localized accounting errors, brief telephone outages and the like – the effects on coin prices will be nil.

Many people think that all the Y2K concern is overblown. They see it as a promotional gimmick for charlatans who want to play off of people's fears to sell generators, bottled water and bullion. What happens to numismatics in 2000? Most likely, thousands of collectors will complete their 20th century type sets and set aside 1999- and 2000-dated coins for their grandchildren. The United States will try out a new dollar coin. People who bought up bullion just in case will be trying to unload it for as much as they can get. And the numismatic market will roll on.

10

New dollar in 2000

Sacagawea replaces Susan B. Anthony

By Maureen Woon

America will have a new dollar coin in the year 2000. It is the product of a very long approval process.

Choosing an image for a coin that best represents America – its greatness and its future – is no easy task. Lady Liberty is an obvious choice. So are presidents and other prominent Americans. But the U.S. Treasury's selection of a not-so-obvious choice, the Native American heroine Sacagawea, inspired both acclaim and attack.

The new dollar coin is the work of Rep. Michael Castle, R-Del. He convinced Congress to authorize it in late 1997, a move that ended nearly a decade of stiff congressional resistance to any new dollar coin following the failure of the Susan B. Anthony dollar to circulate widely. His legislation, signed into law, attempted to address what were thought to be the many failures of the Anthony dollar. One thing it did not do was specify who should be on the coin.

To correct the problems of the SBA dollar, the law authorizing the new coin specified that it will be a golden color with a distinctively unreeded edge, but it will be the same size as the SBA in order to fit into existing coin slots. The next hurdle was the adoption of a suitable design.

A Dollar Coin Design Advisory Committee, formed under former Treasury Secretary Robert E. Rubin's guidance, recommended in June 1998 that the new coin should depict the image of Sacagawea, a Shoshone interpreter who contributed to the success of the 1804-1806 Lewis and Clark expedition to the Pacific Ocean.

Sacagawea was captured by the Hidatsa tribe when she was 11 years old and later sold to a French-Canadian trapper, Toussaint Charbonneau. Sacagawea and Charbonneau were hired by Lewis and Clark to make contact with the Shoshones, who lived in the Rocky Mountains at the source of the Missouri River, near present day Idaho, to buy horses. Sacagawea not only provided invaluable interpreting skills, she taught the explorers to forage roots and plants for food, rescued relevant journals from a capsized boat and, most importantly, served as a peace symbol for the mission. Sacagawea did all this while she was pregnant and later

The new dollar coin shows Sacagawea and her infant son on obverse and a soaring eagle on reverse.

The Fine Arts Commission liked the eagle on the rock design better.

toting an infant. In this regard, Mint Director Philip Diehl explained in an editorial at the convening of the DCDAC, his endorsement of the Committee's choice: "The story of Sacagawea is rich with the symbols and values that make our nation great. It is fitting and proper that after almost 200 years, we repay this national debt in the coin of the realm Sacagawea helped create." (*www.usmint.gov/dollarcoin/editorial-saca.cfm*, June 24, 1998).

After 23 artists submitted more than 121 designs, the Mint selected three obverses and four reverses for the consideration of members of the Commission of Fine Arts in December 1998. Proposed designs were posted on the Mint's Web site. Glenna Goodacre, the sculptor of the Women's Vietnam Veterans Memorial statue, designed all three finalist obverses using a 22-year-old Shoshone college student as her model. The three contenders included Design #97, which featured a relief profile of Sacagawea with her chin tilted upwards in hope; Design #99, a three-quarter portrait of Sacagawea with her baby slung on her back, her face showing strength, dignity and leadership; and Design #123, another three-quarter pose of Sacagawea without her baby, looking back toward those she was leading.

Reverse designs submitted included Design #15 depicting an eagle in shining mountains; Design #35, a soaring American Bald Eagle flying over Sacagawea's birthplace; Design #36, an American Bald Eagle unfurling its wings and holding an olive branch and Design #117, showing a standing eagle.

Design #99 of the obverse and reverse Design #36 were the recommended choices of the Commission of Fine Arts. That particular obverse design showed Sacagawea with her infant son, Jean Baptiste. It drew criticism from several feminist groups who argue that too many women were typecast in conventional roles as mothers, daughters, or wives. The recommended reverse showed an eagle sitting on a rock on which appeared Native American petroglyphs. Then four months passed as tensions built in the collector community about what the Treasury secretary would choose.

On May 4, 1999, a crowd gathered at the White House to witness the U.S. Treasury's unveiling of the Sacagawea coin. The ceremony, presided over by First Lady Hillary Rodham Clinton, honored Native Americans and their contribution to the country. Mrs. Clinton together with Treasury Secretary Robert E. Rubin, Mint Director Philip N. Diehl and several prominent members of Native Indian communities, revealed the final designs for the coin.

Sacagawea and the baby, Design #99, was, indeed, selected. The reverse chosen was a surprise. It was Thomas D. Rogers Sr.'s soaring American Bald Eagle, Design #35. The soaring eagle is surrounded by 17 stars and the legend, UNITED STATES OF AMERICA.

Once the design was chosen, the critical issue became the alloy. How do you get the golden color to keep the coin from being confused with the quarter as occurred in 1978 with the Anthony dollar? The Mint was still working on the answer as this book went to press. The alloy had yet to be determined. According to the Coin Coalition, an organization formed in 1987 and represented by James C. Benfield to lobby for a new dollar coin, the metallic content of the coin would include less nickel and more copper than the standard copper-nickel clad alloy of dimes, quarters and halves, which would give the coin a golden appearance. Will the golden appearance and the smooth edge be enough? In terms of diameter, thickness and weight, the new Sacagawea dollar will retain the specifications of the SBA. This is to ensure that existing vending machines do not have to be retrofitted to accept the new coin.

Although the Coin Coalition recommended the gradual phasing out of the dollar note, Congress was adamant that the success of the new dollar coin was not dependent on the abolition of the Federal Reserve Note. A poll taken of the American public indicated that the dollar note is still desired as a circulating medium. "We reject the notion that [the new dollar] coin will be a failure if it does not completely replace the paper currency," said Diehl. The relationship of the bank note and dollar coin is no small matter; the Coin Coalition estimates that, because coins remain in circulation much longer than bank notes (30 years compared to 18 months), the federal government could save at least $456 million per year over a 30-year period if the bank note were phased out entirely.

The next crucial question will be the time line for releasing the new Sacagawea coin. The Mint said 1999-dated SBA dollars will be struck to tide the country over until the new dollar is ready. That gives collectors one last shot at a coin they love to hate. Once the alloy question is settled, production of the Sacagawea coins was expected to begin in the later part of 1999, and the Mint targeted the spring of the year 2000 for its introduction. Are you ready?

11

Hot bets?

Consider these for the new millennium

By David C. Harper

If you believe the world ends with Y2K, Jan. 1, 2000, and you stocked up on gold and silver bullion coins, don't read this chapter.

What happens after Y2K? There is a new century and a new millennium to face. Where will the hobby go? At some point, even if there are massive computer glitches as the new millennium dawns, they will be sorted out and there will be a hobby in place with a bright future.

Fads and worries aside, the fundamental factors that influence coin prices will remain the same for the next 100 years as they have for the past 100. Rarity, condition and demand from collectors will rule the pricing roost.

Rarity is the factor that tells you whether there is one of something or one million. Condition tells you if the coin is visually desirable, its state of preservation. This helps in the sorting process. Condition plays very little role in the value of a one-of-a-kind coin. But find the top coin out of a one-million mintage and you would expect the top price in that group of coins to be paid for the top-condition coin.

Demand from collectors is a little trickier. Hypothetically, a one-of-a-kind coin would have little value if no collector wanted it and one million examples of the same design would have a high and rising value if two million collectors were jostling with each other to get them.

Demand is the least stable element in this three-factor determination of coin value. Some series turn hot and prices soar. Some cool off and prices plunge. Rarity doesn't change (with a few exceptions). Condition doesn't either, unless a coin is not properly protected. But demand can fluctuate widely.

The doubled-die 1972 cent above left is a classic American rarity. The 1982 No-P dime is less so, but still scarce. The prices of both may rise in the next millennium.

Morgan silver dollar prices plunged after 1989. It wasn't their rarity that changed. It wasn't their condition that deteriorated. It simply seemed to be higher prices that turned off enough collectors to reduce overall demand for Morgans, but two years from now demand could came back strong and prices could soar again as they did in the 1980s.

The key to informed collector behavior is to buy when the rest of the hobby wants to sell and to sell when the rest of the hobby is buying. That is the thinking behind this Lucky Half Dozen coin list for the start of the new millennium. There is no one-of-a-kind coin on the list. All readers of this chapter can buy them from the nation's coin dealers, but all listed pieces have some element of scarcity. Top condition is available and demand for the most part is not at the peak of the hobby cycle.

1972 doubled-die cent: It is priced at $145 in XF-40 and $400 in MS-65 condition. Those are pretty good values, until you compare them to the 1955 doubled die numbers, which are three to five times higher. I think the values of the two will move closer together over time.

Rarity of the 1972 doubled die is difficult to evaluate. Estimates of 25,000 coins come up against a possibility that the Mint could have struck 600,000 to one million of them, because that was the average die life in 1972. Nobody knows for sure just how long the die with the doubling on it was used to strike cents. We will never know. Only the market value is an indication of just how rare the hobby thinks the 1972 doubled die is at any given time.

The 1982 No-P dime: It is valued at $220 in MS-65 and $115 in MS-60. It is a coin that passing time should reward.

First a word of explanation. All dimes minted at Philadelphia before 1980 do not have a mintmark on them. From 1980 on, all dimes minted at Philadelphia are supposed to have a "P" mintmark on them. What makes this 1982 dime scarce is it has no mintmark when it is supposed to have one. That makes it easy to identify.

The problem with this rarity is virtually the whole supply of 6,000 to 25,000 ended up in very few hands. Concentration of supply has always been the enemy of price appreciation, so as the years pass and the coins get more widely dispersed, the fundamental rarity should begin to be more strongly felt on prices.

1983-P quarter: This coin could be a loser for all eternity. It has little going for it in any obvious sense. It is a clad coin from an era that worshipped silver. Its mintage is almost 677 million pieces, so it is not rare in the classic sense. It is not an error of any kind.

What could possibly put this coin on the Lucky Half Dozen list? Well, it was released in 1983. It was a recession year. It was also a year in which no uncirculated coin sets were produced by the Mint. That makes for an interesting possibility. People save fewer coins during a recession, so that means fewer uncirculateds survived. The hobby has no 1983 sets to raid for uncirculated versions, so the question is: just how many exist in uncirculated condition?

The current price of rolls of this date may have an answer. A 40-coin roll of uncirculated coins ($10 face value) is priced at $250. That's 25 times face for a clad quarter! Putting a few of these coins away for the future is probably a good idea.

1992 quarter-ounce gold Eagle: People who like precious metals will feel warm toward this gold American Eagle coin. The possibility of price gains for this coin is largely dependent on where the price of gold bullion goes, but this is the first year this coin didn't express its date in Roman numerals. That should mean something. The 21st century will reveal what that will be. It is currently trading at basically the price of an ordinary gold quarter-ounce bullion coin.

1996 silver American Eagle: This is the 11th year of this series. It is priced basically at the same cost as every other date, but with a mintage of 3,603,386, it is scarcer than the others. If collectors start collecting these coins by date and mintmark, rarity will start pushing this price higher than the more common years.

1997 platinum American Eagle: Americans aren't used to platinum coinage. Before this was struck, platinum was unknown in regular U.S. coinage. The next century should see American collectors getting more familiar with platinum. With familiarity will come a greater willingness to collect it and that should impact the price in a favorable way. If that doesn't happen, it is still a convenient way to invest in a precious metal.

There you have them, the Lucky Half Dozen coins. Some are made of precious metal. Some are base metal. Some are already respected rarities. All have stories to tell. Will collectors of the next century think more highly of them and bid up their prices? There is a good chance they will.

12

Collect on the Web

Internet gives hobbyists new options
By Timothy Rolands

The successful coin collector relies on a variety of resources to provide access to the coins he pursues as well as information about them. In recent years a new resource has become available that does both – the Internet.

The Internet offers coin collectors a number of benefits based on enhanced communications. Internet communications are generally faster, farther reaching and more robust than other means of personal communications. You can exchange not only words but sounds, images, video and more.

E-mail and discussion groups advance the way collectors communicate with one another. With e-mail, you can communicate with collectors from around the world at lightning speeds, getting answers to questions or making plans within minutes. Discussion groups provide a centralized online community where you can meet other collectors, trade coins, discuss hobby news and events, or simply talk about coins.

Speedier communications alone can be a big help to the coin collecting community, but the World Wide Web offers even more benefits.

Although the earliest incarnation of the Internet dates back to 1969, the World Wide Web as we know it did not exist until 1992. It's only in the last few years that the Web has really come of age. Today there are Web sites dedicated to any kind of hobby one could imagine, and coin collecting is no exception.

With Web browser software such as Netscape Navigator or Microsoft Internet Explorer – both free and often included with your operating system – you can take advantage of the Internet and find out what all the hoopla is about. Keep up with the latest versions of your browser software, and you can enjoy all the bells and whistles the Web has to offer.

The most useful Web sites for collectors include online auction sites, organization sites, dealer and grading services sites and a selection of useful government sites. In the following paragraphs the URLs, or addresses, for selected Web sites appear in parentheses.

Auction sites like eBay (www.ebay.com) and Teletrade (www.teletrade.com) allow collectors to read about or view coin lots and to bid on them over the Internet. For example, eBay, which touts itself as the world's largest personal online trading community, lists a variety of U.S. and world coins with current prices and the dates when each item's auction closes. Each listing is linked to a page with expanded information on the selected item, including the seller, a picture if available, payment and shipping information and a place for the user to enter a bid. A collector looking for that elusive coin can call up the eBay Web site, search for the coin he wants, read about the particular coin being offered, perhaps view a picture of it and place a bid on it, all within minutes from anywhere on the continent.

Collectors can also learn more about national and local numismatic organizations on the Web. The American Numismatic Association (www.money.org) is a good place to start. Its Web site provides information about the organization's history and mission and even includes a membership form for joining. It also hosts a number of smaller member clubs from all over the United States. The American Numismatic Society also has a large Web site with in-depth numismatic information.

A growing number of coin dealers large and small are establishing a presence on the Web as well. SilverTowne (www.silvertowne.com), for example, greets visitors with daily and weekly specials and features a character named Prospector Pete, who comments on different areas within the site. Other dealers, too, like David Lawrence Rare Coins (www.davidlawrence.com) and Eagle Numismatics (www.coinmaven.com) have Web sites. Using a search engine like Yahoo (www.yahoo.com), you can search for dealers in your area or with a particular specialty.

Many grading services also have Web sites. At the Web site for Numismatic Guaranty Corp. (www.ngccoin.com), you can learn more about NGC services, see a list of authorized NGC member/dealers or visit the gallery, where NGC displays coins from world-renowned collections. If you don't find what you're looking for, you can fill out a form to ask a specific question or comment on the Web site.

One of the most important Web sites for any coin collector is that of the U.S. Mint (www.usmint.gov). The Mint's Web site not only provides current information about new coins and numismatic products, but also about the minting process and the history of the Mint, not to mention interesting "Fun Facts" about coins. The Mint's online catalog allows you to browse various numismatic products and make purchases. You may even find numismatic products from the Mint that are only available through its online catalog.

The Mint is actively testing the limits of the Web and exploring new possibilities. When the announcement of the new Sacagawea dollar coin was made at the White House in May 1999, the Mint offered a live Webcast of the event at its Web site. Using a special browser plug-in, visitors were able to watch and listen in as First Lady Hillary Clinton and Treasury Secretary Robert E. Rubin unveiled the design.

Other useful government Web sites include the U.S. Bureau of

The following Web sites may be worth visiting as you begin to explore numismatics on the World Wide Web. This list is not intended to be a complete and final list. There are a number of good sites out there that are not mentioned here, because space is limited.

U.S. Mint at www.usmint.gov
Bureau of Engraving and Printing at www.moneyfactory.com
Numismatists Online at www.Numismatists.com
Royal Canadian Mint at www.rcmint.ca
Mexican Mint at www.cmonedam.com.mx/cmm
eBay at www.ebay.com
Teletrade at www.teletrade.com
CollectIt.net at www.collectit.net
American Numismatic Association at www.money.org
American Numismatic Society at www.amnumsoc2.org
Eagle Numismatics at www.coinmaven.com
David Lawrence Rare Coins at www.davidlawrence.com/
Coast to Coast Coins at www.coastcoin.com
Numismatic Guaranty Corp. at www.ngccoin.com
Independent Coin Grading Co. at www.icgcoin.com
Thomas Legislative Server at thomas.loc.gov
Coin Universe at www.coin-universe.com
Heritage Rare Coins at www.heritagecoin.com
Krause Publications Coin Division at www.coincollecting.net
Internet Encyclopedia and Price Guide of U.S. Coins at www.coin-facts.com.

Engraving and Printing (www.moneyfactory.com), where you can learn more about paper money, and THOMAS (thomas.loc.gov), a site where you can look in on current legislation, including commemorative coin bills. It's not only the U.S. government that offers coin-centric Web sites. The Royal Canadian Mint (www.rcmint.ca) and the Mexican Mint (www.cmonedam.com.mx/cmm) both have informative Web sites.

Where there are so many benefits and opportunities, there are also drawbacks and potential pitfalls.

While the Internet is capable of spreading information faster than any other mode of communication, the integrity of that information is no better or worse than in any other exchange. False information spreads just as quickly as true information, and the responsible Web surfer must learn to tell the difference. Collectors should look for trusted sites as reliable sources of information and should pay close attention to sources. In many ways, it's no different than going to a library to do research in books. The researcher consults a variety of works and weighs the credibility of authors and publishers. A numismatic Web surfer must do the same. Consult more than one site and carefully consider the credibility of the site itself or of its webmaster.

There you have it – the online world of coin collecting charged with numismatic knowledge. In the coming years, the Internet promises to establish its presence in every walk of life. The ancient hobby of coin collecting is making the most of the new technology.

Glossary of coin terms

Adjustment marks: Marks made by use of a file to correct the weight of overweight coinage planchets prior to striking. Adjusting the weight of planchets was a common practice at the first U.S. mint in Philadelphia and was often carried out by women hired to weigh planchets and do any necessary filing.

Altered coin: A coin that has been changed after it left the mint. Such changes are often to the date or mintmark of a common coin in an attempt to increase its value by passing to an unsuspecting buyer as a rare date or mint.

Alloy: A metal or mixture of metals added to the primary metal in the coinage composition, often as a means of facilitating hardness during striking. For example, most U.S. silver coins contain an alloy of 10-percent copper.

Anneal: To heat in order to soften. In the minting process planchets are annealed prior to striking.

Authentication: The act of determining whether a coin, medal, token or other related item is a genuine product of the issuing authority.

Bag marks: Scrapes and impairments to a coin's surface obtained after minting by contact with other coins. The term originates from the storage of coins in bags, but such marks can occur as coins leave the presses and enter hoppers. A larger coin is more susceptible to marks, which affect its grade and, therefore, its value.

Base metal: A metal with low intrinsic value.

Beading: A form of design around the edge of a coin. Beading once served a functional purpose of deterring clipping or shaving parts of the metal by those looking to make a profit and then return the debased coin to circulation.

Blank: Often used in reference to the coinage planchet or disc of metal from which the actual coin is struck. Planchets or blanks are punched out of a sheet of metal by what is known as a blanking press.

Business strike: A coin produced for circulation.

Beading

Cast copy: A copy of a coin or medal made by a casting process in which molds are used to produce the finished product. Casting imparts a different surface texture to the finished product than striking and often leaves traces of a seam where the molds came together.

Center dot: A raised dot at the center of a coin caused by use of a compass to aid the engraver in the circular positioning of die devices, such as stars, letters and dates. Center dots are prevalent on early U.S. coinage.

Chop mark

Chop mark: A mark used by Oriental merchants as a means of guaranteeing the silver content of coins paid out. The merchants' chop marks, or stamped insignia, often obliterated the original design of the host coin. U.S. Trade dollars, struck from 1873 through 1878 and intended for use in trade with China, are sometimes found bearing multiple marks.

Clash marks: Marks impressed in the coinage dies when they come together without a planchet between them. Such marks will affect coins struck subsequently by causing portions of the obverse design to appear in raised form on the reverse, and vice versa.

Clipping: The practice of shaving or cutting small pieces of metal from a coin in circulation. Clipping was prevalent in Colonial times as a means of surreptitiously extracting precious metal from a coin before placing it back into circulation. The introduction of beading and a raised border helped to alleviate the problem.

Coin alignment: U.S. coins are normally struck with an alignment by which, when a coin is held by the top and bottom edge and rotated from side-to-side, the reverse will appear upside down.

Collar: A ring-shaped die between which the obverse and reverse coinage dies are held during striking. The collar contains the outward flow during striking and can be used to produce edge reeding.

Commemorative: A coin issued to honor a special event or person. U.S. commemoratives are generally produced for sale to collectors and are not placed in circulation.

Copy: A replica of an original issue. Copies often vary in quality and metallic composition to the original. Since passage of the Hobby Protection Act (Public Law 93-167) of Nov. 29, 1973, it has been illegal to produce or import copies of coins or other numismatic items that are not clearly and permanently marked with the word "Copy."

Counterfeit: A coin or medal or other numismatic item made fraudulently, either for entry into circulation or sale to collectors.

Denticles: The toothlike pattern found around a coin's obverse or reverse border.

Die: A cylindrical piece of metal containing an incuse image that imparts a raised image when stamped into a planchet.

Die crack: A crack that develops in a coinage die after extensive usage, or if the die is defective or is used to strike harder metals. Die cracks, which often run through border lettering, appear as raised lines on the finished coin.

Device: The principal design element.

Double eagle: Name adopted by the Act of March 3, 1849, for the gold coin valued at 20 units or $20.

Rim

Field

Mintmark

Exergue

Obverse

Legend

Reverse

Eagle: Name adopted by the Coinage Act of 1792 for a gold coin valued at 10 units or $10.

Edge: The cylindrical surface of a coin between the two sides. The edge can be plain, reeded, ornamented, or lettered.

Electrotype: A copy of a coin, medal or token made by electroplating.

Exergue: The lower segment of a coin, below the main design, generally separated by a line and often containing the date, designer initials and mintmark.

Face value: The nominal legal-tender value assigned to a given coin by the governing authority.

Fasces: A Roman symbol of authority consisting of a bound bundle of rods and an ax.

Field: The flat area of a coin's obverse or reverse, devoid of devices or inscriptions.

Galvano: A reproduction of a proposed design from an artist's original model produced in plaster or other substance and then electroplated with metal. The galvano is then used in a reducing lathe to make a die or hub.

Glory: A heraldic term for stars, rays or other devices placed as if in the sky or luminous.

Grading: The largely subjective practice of providing a numerical or adjectival ranking of the condition of a coin, token or medal. The grade is often a major determinant of value.

Gresham's law: The name for the observation made by Sir Thomas Gresham, 16th century English financier, that when two coins with the same face value but different intrinsic values are in circulation at the same time, the one with the lesser intrinsic value will remain in circulation while the other is hoarded.

Half eagle: Name adopted by the Coinage Act of 1792 for a gold coin valued at five units or $5.

Hub: A piece of die steel showing the coinage devices in relief. The hub is used to produce a die that, in contrast, has the relief details incuse. The die is then used to produce the final coin, which looks much the same as the hub. Hubs may be reused to make new dies.

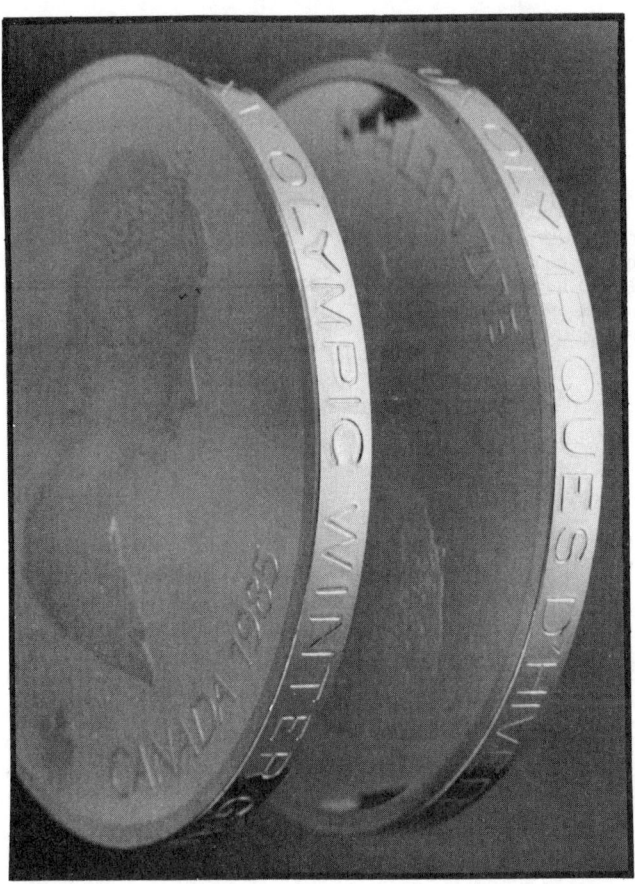

These Canadian Olympic commemoratives have lettered edges.

Legend: A coin's principal lettering, generally shown along its outer perimeter.

Lettered edge: Incuse or raised lettering on a coin's edge.

Matte proof: A proof coin on which the surface is granular or dull. On U.S. coins this type of surface was used on proofs of the early 20th century. The process has since been abandoned.

Magician's coin: A term sometimes used to describe a coin with two heads or two tails. Such a coin is impossible in normal production, and all are products made outside the Mint as novelty pieces.

Medal: Made to commemorate an event or person. Medals differ from coins in that a medal is not legal tender and, in general, is not produced with the intent of circulating as money.

A medal usually commemorates an event but has no monetary value. It can be issued by a private entity or a government.

Medal alignment: Medals are generally struck with the coinage dies facing the same direction during striking. When held by the top and bottom edge and rotated from side-to-side, a piece struck in this manner will show both the obverse and reverse right side up.

Mintage: The total number of coins struck during a given time frame, generally one year.

Mintmark: A letter or other marking on a coin's surface to identify the mint at which the coin was struck.

Mule: The combination of two coinage dies not intended for use together.

Numismatics: The science, study or collecting of coins, tokens, medals, paper money, and related items.

Obverse: The front or "heads" side of a coin, medal or token.

Overdate: Variety produced when one or more digits of the date are re-engraved over an old date on a die at the Mint, generally to save on dies or correct an error. Portions of the old date can still be seen under the new one.

Overmintmark: Variety created at the Mint when a different mintmark is punched over an already existing mintmark, generally done to make a coinage die already punched for one mint usable at another. Portions of the old mintmark can still be seen under the new one.

Overstrike: A coin, token or medal struck over another coin, token or medal.

Pattern: A trial strike of a proposed coin design, issued by the Mint or authorized agent of a governing authority. Patterns can be in a variety of metals, thicknesses and sizes.

This U.S. Trade dollar has a reeded edge.

Phrygian cap: A close-fitting, egg-shell-shaped hat placed on the head of a freed slave when Rome was in its ascendancy. Hung from a pole, it was a popular symbol of freedom during the French Revolution and in 18th century United States.

Planchet: A disc of metal or other material on which the image of the dies are impressed, resulting in a finished coin. Also sometimes called a blank.

Proof: A coin struck twice or more from specially polished dies and polished planchets. Modern proofs are prepared with a mirror finish. Early 20th century proofs were prepared with a matte surface.

Prooflike: A prooflike coin exhibits some of the characteristics of a proof despite having been struck by regular production processes. Many Morgan dollars are found with prooflike surfaces. The field will have a mirror background similar to that of a proof, and design details are frosted like some proofs.

Quarter eagle: Name adopted by the Coinage Act of 1792 for a gold coin valued at 2.5 units or $2.50.

Reeding: Serrated (toothlike) ornamentation applied to the coin's edge during striking.

Relief: The portion of a design raised above the surface of a coin, medal or token.

A token is issued by a private entity and can be redeemed for its face value in trade or service.

Restrike: A coin, medal or token produced from original dies at a later date, often with the purpose of sale to collectors.

Reverse: The backside or "tails" side of a coin, medal or token, opposite from the principal figure of the design or obverse.

Rim: The raised area bordering the edge and surrounding the field.

Series: The complete group of coins of the same denomination and design and representing all issuing mints.

Token: A privately issued piece, generally in metal, with a represented value in trade or offer of service. Tokens are also produced for advertising purposes.

Type coin: A coin from a given series representing the basic design. A type coin is collected as an example of a particular design rather than for its date and mintmark.

Variety: Any coin noticeably different in dies from another of the same design, date and mint. Overdates and overmintmarks are examples of varieties.

Wire edge: Created when coinage metal flows between the coinage die and collar, producing a thin flange of coin metal at the outside edge or edges of a coin.

PRICING SECTION

Introduction to pricing

The following value guide is divided into six sections:

1. Colonial coins, issued prior to the establishment of the United States.
2. U.S. issues of 1792.
3. U.S. issues of 1793-present.
4. U.S. minting varieties and errors.
5. Canadian coins.
6. Mexican coins.

Value listings

Values listed in the following price guide are average retail prices. These are the approximate prices collectors can expect to pay when purchasing coins from dealers. They are not offers to buy or sell. The pricing section should be considered a guide only; actual selling prices will vary.

The values were compiled by Krause Publications' independent staff of market analysts. They derived the values listed by monitoring auction results, business on electronic dealer trading networks, and business at major shows, and in consultation with a panel of dealers. For rare coins, when only a few specimens of a particular date and mintmark are known, a confirmed transaction may occur only once every several years. In those instances, the most recent auction result is listed.

Grading

Values are listed for coins in various states of preservation, or grades. Standards used in determining grades for U.S. coins are those set by the American Numismatic Association. See Chapter 4 for more on grading.

Dates and mintmarks

The dates listed are the individual dates that appear on each coin. The letter that follows the date is the mintmark and indicates where the coin was struck: "C" — Charlotte, N.C. (1838-1861); "CC" — Carson City, Nev. (1870-1893); "D" — Dahlonega, Ga. (1838-1861), and Denver (1906-present); "O" — New Orleans (1838-1909); "P" — Philadelphia (1793-present); "S" — San Francisco (1854-present); and "W" — West Point, N.Y. (1984-present). Coins without mintmarks were struck at Philadelphia.

A slash mark in a date indicates an overdate. This means a new date was engraved on a die over an old date. For example, if the date is listed as "1899/8," an 1898 die had a 9 engraved over the last 8 in the date. Portions of the old numeral are still visible on the coin.

A slash mark in a mintmark listing indicates an overmintmark (example: "1922-P/D"). The same process as above occurred, but this time a new mintmark was engraved over an old.

See the "U.S. Minting Varieties and Errors" section for more information on overdates and overmintmarks.

Price charts

Pricing data for the selected charts in the U.S. section were taken from the January issues of "Coin Prices" for the years indicated.

Mexican coin mintages

Quantities minted of each date are indicated when that information is available, generally stated in millions and rounded off to the nearest 10,000 pieces. The following mintage conversion formulas are used:

10,000,000 — 10,000.
1,000,000 — 1.000.
100,000 — .100.
10,000 — .010.
9,999 — 9,999.
1,000 — 1,000.
842 — 842 pcs. (pieces).
27 — 27 pcs.

Precious-metal content

Throughout this book precious-metal content is indicated in troy ounces. One troy ounce equals 480 grains, or 31.103 grams.

Abbreviations

AGW. Actual gold weight.

APW. Actual platinum weight.

ASW. Actual silver weight.

BV. Bullion value. This indicates the coin's current value is based on the amount of its precious-metal content and the current price for that metal.

Est. Indicates the exact mintage is not known and the figure listed is an estimate.

G. Grams.

Inc. Abv. Indicates the mintage for the date and mintmark listed is included in the previous listing.

KM#. In the Canadian and Mexican price sections, indicates "Krause-Mishler number." This sequential cataloging numbering system originated with the "Standard Catalog of World Coins" by Chester L. Krause and Clifford Mishler, and provides collectors with a means for identifying world issues.

Leg. Legend.

Mkt value. Market value.

MM. Millimeters.

Obv. Obverse.

P/L. Indicates "prooflike," a type of finish used on some Canadian coins.

Rev. Reverse.

Spec. Indicates "specimen," a type of finish used on some Canadian coins.

Colonial coins

MASSACHUSETTS
"New England" Coinage

NE/III THREEPENCE

Date
(1652)

Only two examples known

NE/VI SIXPENCE

(1652)   Garrett 75,000.

Only seven examples known

NE/XII SHILLING

Date	AG	Good	VG	Fine	VF
(1652)	1250.	3500.	5500.	11,000.	25,000.

WILLOW TREE COINAGE

THREEPENCE

1652

Only three examples known

SIXPENCE

1652	3500.	7500.	10,000.	15,000.	20,000.

SHILLING

Date	AG	Good	VG	Fine	VF
1652	4000.	10,000.	12,500.	18,000.	25,000.

OAK TREE COINAGE

TWOPENCE

	AG	Good	VG	Fine	VF
1662	150.00	300.00	500.00	750.00	1650.

THREEPENCE

	AG	Good	VG	Fine	VF
1652 (two types of legends)	200.00	400.00	600.00	900.00	2000.

SIXPENCE

	AG	Good	VG	Fine	VF
1652 (three types of legends)	250.00	450.00	750.00	1200.	2500

SHILLING

Date	AG	Good	VG	Fine	VF
1652 (two types of legends)	175.00	300.00	500.00	775.00	1750.

PINE TREE COINAGE

THREEPENCE

Date	AG	Good	VG	Fine	VF
1652 tree w/o berries	150.00	300.00	375.00	550.00	1000.

1652 tree w/berries (two types of legends)	165.00	325.00	425.00	600.00	1150.

SIXPENCE

1652 tree w/o berries ("Spiney Tree")	525.00	900.00	1400.	1800.	2650.

1652 tree w/berries	150.00	300.00	450.00	650.00	1200.

SHILLING, Large Planchet

Date	AG	Good	VG	Fine	VF
1652 (many varieties; some very rare)	160.00	350.00	525.00	775.00	1650.

Small Planchet, Large Dies
1652 (struck w/large dies. All examples are thought to be contemporary fabrications.)

Small Planchet, Small Dies

Date	AG	Good	VG	Fine	VF
1652 (many varieties; some very rare)	150.00	220.00	320.00	625.00	1350.

MARYLAND

LORD BALTIMORE'S COINAGE

PENNY (Denarium)

Date	AG	Good	VG	Fine	VF
(1659)				Only four examples known	

FOURPENCE (Groat)

Date	Good	VG	Fine	VF	XF
(1659) large bust and shield	1000.	1750.	3500.	5000.	9500.
(1659) small bust and shield	Norweb 26,400.				Unique

SIXPENCE

	Good	VG	Fine	VF	XF
(1659) small bust	800.00	1250.	2200.	4500.	8000.

Known in two other rare small bust varieties, plus two rare large bust varieties.

SHILLING

Date	Good	VG	Fine	VF	XF
(1659) varieties, one very rare	900.00	1500.	2750.	4800.	8500.

NEW JERSEY
St. Patrick or Mark Newby Coinage

FARTHING

Date	AG	Good	VG	Fine	VF
(1682) also rare varieties	20.00	40.00	65.00	145.00	285.00
(1682) struck of silver	350.00	550.00	1150.	1650.	2750.

HALFPENNY

Date					
(1682)	50.00	80.00	150.00	285.00	550.00

COINAGE OF WILLIAM WOOD
"Rosa Americana" Coinage

HALFPENNY

Date	Good	VG	Fine	VF	XF
1722 D.G. REX	40.00	60.00	95.00	200.00	475.00

Date	Good	VG	Fine	VF	XF
1722 DIE GRATIA REX (Several varieties)	30.00	50.00	85.00	150.00	325.00

	Good	VG	Fine	VF	XF
1722 VTILE DVLCI	—	—	1045.	—	—

Date	Good	VG	Fine	VF	XF
1723 Crowned Rose	35.00	55.00	90.00	165.00	375.00

Date	Good	VG	Fine	VF	XF
1723 Uncrowned Rose	—	750.00	1350.	2250.	—

PENNY

	Good	VG	Fine	VF	XF
1722 UTILE DULCI (Several Varieties)	30.00	50.00	85.00	145.00	285.00

Date	Good	VG	Fine	VF	XF
1722 VTILE DVLCI (Several Varieties)	30.00	50.00	90.00	155.00	300.00

Also known in two rare pattern types w/long hair ribbons, one w/V's for U's on obverse.

	Good	VG	Fine	VF	XF
1723 (several varieties)	30.00	50.00	85.00	145.00	285.00

Date	Good	VG	Fine	VF	XF
1724 (Pattern)				Only two examples known	

(1724) undated	Norweb 2,035.			Only five examples known	
1727 Pattern, George II				Only two examples known	

TWOPENCE

	Good	VG	Fine	VF	XF
(1722) Undated, motto w/scroll	60.00	100.00	190.00	300.00	500.00

Date	Good	VG	Fine	VF	XF
(1722) w/o scroll				Only three examples known	

Date	Good	VG	Fine	VF	XF
1722 dated, period after REX	40.00	60.00	90.00	180.00	400.00
1722 w/o period	40.00	60.00	90.00	180.00	400.00

Date	Good	VG	Fine	VF	XF
1723 (several varieties)	30.00	55.00	85.00	165.00	350.00

1724 Patterns; two types	ex-Garrett 5,775.	Both extremely rare

Date	Good	VG	Fine	VF	XF
1733 Pattern	Norweb 19,800.			Only four examples known	

HIBERNIA COINAGE

FARTHING

Date	Good	VG	Fine	VF	XF
1722 Pattern	50.00	125.00	220.00	325.00	700.00
1723 D:G:REX. (1722 obverse)	40.00	60.00	90.00	150.00	300.00

1723 DEI. GRATIA. REX.	20.00	40.00	65.00	90.00	165.00
1723 Silver	—	—	—	800.00	1600.
1723 Silver	—	—	—	Proof	2700.
1724	25.00	45.00	75.00	125.00	200.00

HALFPENNY

1722 harp left, head right	15.00	35.00	60.00	125.00	250.00

1722 harp left, head right (pattern)	—	—	1800.	2350.	3200.

Date	Good	VG	Fine	VF	XF
1722 harp right	15.00	35.00	60.00	125.00	250.00
1722 legend DEII error	90.00	180.00	300.00	500.00	750.00
1723/22 three varieties	20.00	40.00	90.00	165.00	275.00

	Good	VG	Fine	VF	XF
1723 many varieties	15.00	25.00	40.00	80.00	165.00
1723 large head, rare, generally mint state only. Probably a pattern.					Rare

	Good	VG	Fine	VF	XF
1724 varieties	15.00	35.00	60.00	125.00	265.00
1724 continuous legend over head	65.00	150.00	300.00	475.00	750.00

PITT TOKENS

FARTHING

Date	Good	VG	Fine	VF	XF
1766	—	—	1250.	2500.	5000.

HALFPENNY

Date	Good	VG	Fine	VF	XF
1766	65.00	125.00	250.00	475.00	975.00

STATES OF THE CONFEDERATION
CONNECTICUT

Date	Good	VG	Fine	VF	XF
1785 bust left	120.00	160.00	275.00	400.00	750.00

	Good	VG	Fine	VF	XF
1785 African head	45.00	85.00	200.00	375.00	1450.

Date	Good	VG	Fine	VF	XF
1785 bust left	120.00	160.00	275.00	400.00	750.00

Small Mailed Bust Right					
1786 ETLIB INDE	35.00	55.00	85.00	165.00	400.00
1786 INDE ET LIB	55.00	75.00	115.00	225.00	465.00

Date	Good	VG	Fine	VF	XF
1786 large mailed bust right	50.00	90.00	165.00	350.00	825.00
1786 Mailed bust left	30.00	50.00	90.00	185.00	465.00

Date	Good	VG	Fine	VF	XF
1786 Hercules head	40.00	75.00	125.00	285.00	550.00
1786 draped bust	35.00	65.00	120.00	265.00	500.00
1787 small head, ETLIB INDE	40.00	90.00	150.00	275.00	550.00
1787 small head, INDE ET LIB	135.00	175.00	265.00	400.00	850.00
1787 medium bust, two rev. legend types	80.00	140.00	200.00	325.00	575.00

Date	Good	VG	Fine	VF	XF
1787 Muttonhead variety	50.00	120.00	250.00	600.00	1350.
(Extremely rare with legend: INDE ET LIB)					

Date	Good	VG	Fine	VF	XF
1787 Mailed bust left	35.00	60.00	110.00	125.00	350.00
1787 Perfect date, legend: IN DE ET	65.00	85.00	135.00	250.00	585.00

1787 Laughing head	25.00	45.00	85.00	190.00	525.00
1787 Horned bust	25.00	40.00	70.00	165.00	450.00
1787/8 IND ET LIB	40.00	75.00	130.00	250.00	600.00
1787/1887 INDE ET LIB	30.00	50.00	90.00	190.00	500.00
1787 CONNECT/INDE ET LIB	37.50	60.00	115.00	200.00	525.00

Also two additional scarce reverse legend types.

1787 Draped bust, many varieties	20.00	40.00	80.00	135.00	275.00
1787 AUCIORI variety	25.00	45.00	95.00	220.00	545.00
1787 AUCTOPI variety	30.00	60.00	120.00	240.00	575.00
1787 AUCTOBI variety	25.00	45.00	90.00	200.00	525.00
1787 CONNFC variety	20.00	40.00	85.00	170.00	440.00
1787 CONNLC variety	30.00	60.00	125.00	250.00	550.00
1787 FNDE variety	25.00	45.00	90.00	180.00	465.00
1787 ETLIR variety	25.00	45.00	90.00	180.00	465.00
1787 ETIIB variety	30.00	50.00	100.00	200.00	525.00

Date	Good	VG	Fine	VF	XF
1788 mailed bust right	25.00	45.00	85.00	185.00	425.00
1788 small mailed bust right	125.00	250.00	500.00	1000.	2400.

Date	Good	VG	Fine	VF	XF
1788 mailed bust left	25.00	50.00	100.00	200.00	500.00

Date	Good	VG	Fine	VF	XF
1788 legend: CONNLC	25.00	40.00	75.00	165.00	375.00
1788 draped bust left, INDE ET LIB	20.00	35.00	55.00	125.00	285.00
1788 similar, INDLET LIB	30.00	55.00	75.00	135.00	300.00
1788 similar, CONNLC/INDE ET LIB	35.00	60.00	90.00	175.00	400.00
1788 similar, CONNLC/INDL ET LIB	35.00	60.00	90.00	175.00	400.00

MASSACHUSETTS

HALFPENNY
Garrett 40,000.

1776   Unique

PENNY

Date	Good	VG	Fine	VF	XF
1776					Unique

HALF CENT

	Good	VG	Fine	VF	XF
1787 (varieties-some rare)	50.00	75.00	140.00	320.00	800.00
1788 (two varieties-one rare)	55.00	90.00	150.00	330.00	825.00

CENT

	Good	VG	Fine	VF	XF
1787 arrows in right talon	Ex-Bushnell-Brand 8800. Garrett 5500.				Rare

Date	Good	VG	Fine	VF	XF
1787 arrows in left talon	40.00	65.00	110.00	285.00	750.00

Date	Good	VG	Fine	VF	XF
1787 "Horned Eagle" die break	45.00	70.00	125.00	300.00	750.00

Date	Good	VG	Fine	VF	XF
1788 w/o period after Massachusetts	45.00	70.00	130.00	320.00	800.00
1788 period, normal S's	45.00	70.00	100.00	275.00	775.00

	Good	VG	Fine	VF	XF
1788 period, S's like 8's	35.00	60.00	100.00	275.00	775.00

NEW HAMPSHIRE

Date	Good	VG	Fine	VF	XF
1776		Garrett 13,000.			Extremely Rare

NEW JERSEY

Date	Good	VG	Fine	VF	XF
(1786) Washington obverse	Garrett 50,000. Only three examples known Steinberg 12,650.				

1786 Eagle obv.
1786 Wash. obv., eagle rev.

Garrett 37,500.   Unique
Only two examples known

Date	Good	VG	Fine	VF	XF
1786 Immunis Columbia obv.		Rescigno AU 33,000. Steinberg VF 11,000.			Extremely Rare

1786 Immunis Columbia/eagle   Only three examples known

1786 date below draw bar   Garrett 52,000.   Extremely Rare

Date	Good	VG	Fine	VF	XF
1786 large horse head, date below plow, no coulter on plow	125.00	250.00	425.00	950.00	3200.
1786 narrow shield, straight beam	35.00	60.00	145.00	325.00	1000.

Date	Good	VG	Fine	VF	XF
1786 wide shield, curved beam (varieties)	45.00	75.00	155.00	325.00	1000.
1786 bridle variety (die break) (other rev. varieties)	50.00	80.00	165.00	350.00	1000.
1787 small planchet, plain shield (varieties)	30.00	50.00	90.00	175.00	400.00
1787 small planchet, shield heavily outlined	30.00	50.00	90.00	175.00	400.00
1787 "serpent head" variety	55.00	85.00	200.00	350.00	1000.
1787 large planchet, plain shield (varieties)	30.00	50.00	90.00	185.00	475.00

Date	Good	VG	Fine	VF	XF
1787 "PLURIBS" variety	50.00	100.00	175.00	450.00	925.00
1788 horse's head right (varieties)	30.00	60.00	100.00	225.00	550.00

1788 fox before rev. legend (varieties)	50.00	100.00	200.00	475.00	1000.

1788 horse's head left (varieties)	100.00	200.00	350.00	700.00	1750.

NEW YORK

Date	Good	VG	Fine	VF	XF
1786 NON VI VIRTUTE VICI	2000.	3500.	6000.	11,500.	—

Date	Good	VG	Fine	VF	XF
1787 Obv.: Eagle on globe faces left	600.00	925.00	1650.	4750.	9500.

Date	Good	VG	Fine	VF	XF
1787 Obv.: Eagle on globe faces left	600.00	925.00	1500.	3750.	8800.

| 1787 Rev.: Large eagle, arrows in right talon | Norweb 18,700. | | | Only two examples known | |

| 1787 George Clinton | 3500. | 5500. | 8500. | 19,500. | — |

| 1787 Indian/N.Y. arms | 2000. | 4000. | 6500. | 10,500. | 21,500. |

Date	Good	VG	Fine	VF	XF
1787 Indian/eagle on globe	3000.	6000.	10,000.	20,000.	30,000.

Date	Good	VG	Fine	VF	XF
1787 IMMUNIS COLUMBIA	200.00	325.00	450.00	800.00	2450.

Date	Good	VG	Fine	VF	XF
1787 NOVA EBORAC/Rev: Figure seated right	75.00	125.00	250.00	400.00	850.00

	Good	VG	Fine	VF	XF
1787 Rev: Figure seated left	50.00	85.00	170.00	275.00	550.00

Date	Good	VG	Fine	VF	XF
1787 NOVA EBORAC/Obv: Small head, star above.	600.00	1750.	3000.	4500.	6500.

	Good	VG	Fine	VF	XF
1787 NOVA EBORAC/Obv: Large head, two quatrefoils left	300.00	400.00	650.00	1150.	2450.

MACHIN'S MILL COPPERS

Date	Good	VG	Fine	VF	XF
	35.00	65.00	140.00	275.00	750.00

Crude, lightweight imitations of the British Halfpenny were struck at Machin's Mill in large quantities bearing the obverse legends: GEORGIVS II REX, GEORGIVS III REX, and GEORGIUS III REX, with the BRITANNIA reverse, and dates of: 1747, 1771, 1772, 1774, 1775, 1776, 1777, 1778, 1784, 1785, 1786, 1787 and 1788. Other dates may exist. There are many different mulings. These pieces, which have plain crosses in the shield of Britannia, are not to be confused with the very common British made imitations, which usually have outlined crosses in the shield. Some varieties are very rare.

Vermont

Date	Good	VG	Fine	VF	XF
(1785) IMMUNE COLUMBIA	1750.	2650.	3750.	—	—
1785 VERMONTIS	125.00	220.00	500.00	900.00	3750.
1785 VERMONTS	125.00	200.00	400.00	750.00	3250.
1786 VERMONTENSIUM	125.00	200.00	400.00	750.00	3250.

Date	Good	VG	Fine	VF	XF
1786 AUCTORI:VERMON:/baby head	125.00	220.00	500.00	900.00	4500.

1786 VERMON:AUCTORI:/head left	75.00	145.00	275.00	600.00	2250.
1787 bust left					Extremely Rare

1787 bust right, several varieties	45.00	85.00	175.00	400.00	1250.

1787 BRITANNIA mule	40.00	60.00	120.00	275.00	950.00

Date	Good	VG	Fine	VF	XF
1788 Rev: INDE ET LIB, several varieties	45.00	85.00	185.00	450.00	1350.
1788 "C" backwards in AUCTORI					Extremely Rare
1788 ET LIB INDE	120.00	225.00	350.00	700.00	—
1788 GEORGE III REX mule	120.00	275.00	425.00	950.00	1850.

FEDERAL ISSUES OF THE CONFEDERATION
THE CONTINENTAL DOLLAR

Date	VG	Fine	VF	XF	Unc
1776 CURRENCY, Pewter	1850.	3000.	4750.	8250.	16,500.
1776 CURRENCY, EG FECIT, Pewter	1750.	2850.	4250.	7750.	15,500.
1776 CURRENCY, EG FECIT, Silver				Only two examples known	
1776 CURRENCY, Pewter				Extremely rare	
1776 CURRENCY, Pewter, floral cross		Norweb 50,600.		Three recorded	
		Johnson 25,300.			

Date	VG	Fine	VF	XF	Unc
1776 CURENCY, Pewter	1650.	2750.	3750.	7150.	15,500.
1776 CURENCY, Brass (2 varieties)	—	—	12,000.	15,500.	—
1776 CURENCY, Silver		Romano 99,000.			Unique

NOVA CONSTELLATIO COPPERS

Date	Good	VG	Fine	VF	XF
1783 CONSTELLATIO, pointed rays, small US	25.00	50.00	75.00	200.00	400.00

Date	Good	VG	Fine	VF	XF
1783 CONSTELLATIO, pointed rays, large US	25.00	50.00	75.00	200.00	400.00

	Good	VG	Fine	VF	XF
1783 CONSTELATIO, blunt rays	28.00	55.00	100.00	250.00	550.00

	Good	VG	Fine	VF	XF
1785 CONSTELLATIO, blunt rays	28.00	55.00	100.00	250.00	550.00

Date	Good	VG	Fine	VF	XF
1785 CONSTELLATIO, pointed rays	35.00	75.00	125.00	275.00	600.00
1786 Similar, contemporary circulating counterfeit					Extremely Rare

NOVA CONSTELLATIO SILVER

BIT - 100

Date	Good	VG	Fine	VF	XF
1783 leaf edge			Garrett 97,500.		2 known
1783 plain edge		Stack's auction, May 1991, 72,500			Unique

QUINT - 500

Date	Good	VG	Fine	VF	XF
1783 Type 1			Garrett 165,000.		Unique

1783 Type 2			Garrett 55,000.		Unique

MARK - 1000

Date	Good	VG	Fine	VF	XF
1783			Garrett 190,000.		Unique

IMMUNE COLUMBIA COPPERS

Date	Good	VG	Fine	VF	XF
1785 CONSTELLATIO, Copper	—	—	—	—	13,750.
1785 CONSTELLATIO, Silver	—	—	—	—	17,600.

1785 CONSTELLATIO, Copper, extra star in border			Caldwell 4675.	—	—

Date	Good	VG	Fine	VF	XF
1785 CONSTELATIO, Copper, blunt rays	Norweb 22,000.			Only two examples known	
1785 CONSTELATIO, Gold				Unique	

	Good	VG	Fine	VF	XF
1785 George III obv.	1250.	1850.	2250.	5000.	9000.
1785 Vermon obv.	1000.	1650.	2000.	4750.	8500.

CONFEDERATIO COPPERS

Date	Good	VG	Fine	VF	XF
1785 small circle of stars	—	—	—	8800.	16,500.

1785 large circle of stars   Extremely Rare

NOTE: The Confederatio dies were struck in combination with thirteen other dies of the period. All surviving examples of these combinations are extremely rare.

FUGIO CENTS

Date	Good	VG	Fine	VF	XF
1787 club rays, round ends	55.00	110.00	235.00	475.00	950.00
1787 club rays, concave ends	500.00	1000.	2000.	4000.	—
1787 similar, FUCIO error	550.00	1200.	2250.	4850.	—

Date	Good	VG	Fine	VF	XF
1787 pointed rays, UNITED above, STATES below	200.00	500.00	900.00	1350.	3000.
1787 similar, UNITED STATES, at sides of ring	45.00	90.00	175.00	275.00	600.00
1787 similar, STATES UNITED at sides of ring	55.00	110.00	200.00	300.00	650.00
1787 similar, 8-pointed stars on ring	65.00	120.00	220.00	350.00	700.00
1787 similar, raised rims on ring, large lettering in center	70.00	130.00	250.00	425.00	800.00
1787 Obv: No cinquefoils. Cross after date. Rev: UNITED STATES	100.00	200.00	400.00	550.00	1000.
1787 Same obv., Rev: STATES UNITED	125.00	225.00	450.00	750.00	1400.
1787 Same obv. Rev: Raised rims on ring	—	—	—	2600.	—

1787 Same obv. Rev. w/rays and AMERICAN CONGRESS   Norweb 63,800.   Extremely Rare

New Haven Restrikes (1858) Brass		Unc 385.00
Copper		385.00
Silver		1250.
Gold	Norweb 1430. (holed)	Only two examples known

COLONIAL TOKENS
THE NEW YORKE TOKEN

Date	Good	VG	Fine	VF	XF
C.1700 Brass	1250.	2750.	4000.	6500.	—
White Metal				Only four examples known	

AMERICAN PLANTATIONS

Date	Good	VG	Fine	VF	XF
1/24th REAL					
(1688) leg: ET HIB REX	125.00	165.00	220.00	300.00	450.00
(1828) restrike, two obv. dies rider's head left of "B" in leg.	65.00	100.00	150.00	225.00	325.00
(1688) rev, horizontal 4	300.00	400.00	500.00	650.00	1350.
(1688) leg: ET HB REX					Unc 6000.
(1688) rev, Arms of Scotland left, Ireland right	750.00	1250.	2000.	2500.	—

ELEPHANT TOKENS

Date	Good	VG	Fine	VF	XF
(1664) thick planchet	80.00	100.00	165.00	325.00	650.00
(1664) thin planchet	100.00	150.00	225.00	450.00	850.00
(1664) diagonals tie shield	140.00	200.00	350.00	650.00	1275.
(1664) sword right side of shield			Norweb 1320.	Only three examples known	

	Good	VG	Fine	VF	XF
(1684) leg: LON DON	300.00	500.00	1000.	1450.	2750.

Date	Good	VG	Fine	VF	XF
1694 NEW ENGLAND			Norweb 25,300.	Only two examples known	

| 1694 CAROLINA (PROPRIETERS) | | Norweb 35,200. | Only five examples known |

Date	Good	VG	Fine	VF	XF
1694 CAROLINA (PROPRIETORS, O over E)	1100.	1700. Norweb 17,600.	2750.	5500.	11,000.

GLOUCESTER TOKEN

Date	Good	VG	Fine	VF	XF
(1714)	Garrett 36,000.			Only two examples known	

HIGLEY OR GRANBY COPPERS

Date	Good	VG	Fine	VF	XF
1737 THE VALVE OF THREE PENCE/ CONNECTICVT				Garrett 16,000.	
1737 THE VALVE OF THREE PENCE/ I AM GOOD COPPER	ex-Norweb 6875.			Only two examples known	

Date	Good	VG	Fine	VF	XF
1737 VALUE ME AS YOU PLEASE/I AM GOOD COPPER	8500.	10,500.	12,500.	—	—
1737 Similar except leg: VALVE				Only two examples known	

(1737) Broad axe rev.	Garrett 45,000.				
1739 Similar	Eliasberg 12,650.				
	Oechsner 9900.				
	Steinberg (holed) 4400.			Only five examples known	

(1737) THE WHEELE GOES ROUND/ J CUT MY WAY THROUGH	Roper 60,500.		Unique

HIBERNIA-VOCE POPULI COPPERS

FARTHING

1760 large letters	125.00	250.00	400.00	600.00	1350.
1760 small letters		Norweb 5940.			Extremely Rare

HALFPENNY

1700 date is error	ex-Roper 575. Norweb 577.50				Extremely Rare
1760 varieties	30.00	50.00	90.00	140.00	285.00

Date	Good	VG	Fine	VF	XF
1760 leg. VOOE POPULI	35.00	60.00	110.00	170.00	400.00

VIRGINIA HALFPENNY

Date	VG	Fine	VF	XF	Unc
1773 small 7's in date, struck on Irish halfpenny planchets				Proof	3500.
1773 period after GEORGIVS varieties w/7 to 8 strings in harp	25.00	50.00	90.00	170.00	440.00
1773 w/o period after GEORGIVS Varieties w/6,7 or 8 strings in harp	30.00	60.00	135.00	200.00	500.00

NOTE: 1773 w/o period 8 harp strings, dot on cross variety Unc. ex-Steinberg 2600.

1774 so-called "Shilling" Silver Proofs   Garrett 23,000. Only six examples known

EARLY AMERICAN TOKENS
RHODE ISLAND SHIP TOKENS

Date	Good	VG	Fine	VF	XF
1779 w/o wreath below ship, Brass or Copper	150.00	250.00	500.00	950.00	1450.
1779 w/o wreath below ship, Pewter	—	—	800.00	1650.	3700.

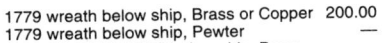

	Good	VG	Fine	VF	XF
1779 wreath below ship, Brass or Copper	200.00	300.00	550.00	975.00	1500.
1779 wreath below ship, Pewter	—	—	1000.	2000.	4000.
1779 "VLUGTENDE" below ship, Brass			Garrett 16,000.		Unique

NORTH AMERICAN TOKEN

Date	VG	Fine	VF	XF	Unc
1781 Halfpenny	25.00	75.00	145.00	350.00	700.00

CHALMERS' SILVER TOKENS

THREEPENCE

Date	Good	VG	Fine	VF	XF
1783	500.00	1000.	1450.	2250.	4000.

SIXPENCE

Date	Good	VG	Fine	VF	XF
1783 small date (unique in trial piece exists.)	700.00	1500.	2200.	4750.	12,000.
1783 large date	550.00	1200.	1850.	2850.	9000.

SHILLING

Date	Good	VG	Fine	VF	XF
1783 birds w/long worm	300.00	475.00	900.00	1800.	4500.
1783 birds w/short worm	225.00	400.00	825.00	1650.	4250.

Date	Good	VG	Fine	VF	XF
1783 rings and stars rev.	Garrett 75,000.			Only four examples known	

THE BAR "CENT"

Date	Good	VG	Fine	VF	XF
(1785)	150.00	250.00	650.00	1000.	1850.

AUCTORI PLEBIS TOKEN

Date	Good	VG	Fine	VF	XF
1787	40.00	70.00	145.00	285.00	450.00

BRASHER'S DOUBLOONS

1787 E.B. on wing   Garrett 725,000.   Only six examples known

Date	Good	VG	Fine	VF	XF
1787 EB on breast	Garrett 625,000.				Unique

THE MOTT TOKEN

Date	Good	VG	Fine	VF	XF
1789 thin planchet	60.00	120.00	200.00	350.00	700.00
1789 thick planchet (weight generally about 170 grs.)	50.00	100.00	175.00	300.00	600.00
1789 fully engrailed edge	85.00	160.00	325.00	600.00	1200.

(Specimens of the above struck with perfect dies are scarcer and generally command higher prices.)

ALBANY CHURCH PENNY

Date	VG	Fine	VF	XF	Unc
(1790) w/o "D" above CHURCH	2500.	5200.	11,500.	—	Five known
(1790) w/"D" above CHURCH	2000.	3200.	7000.	—	Rare

STANDISH BARRY THREEPENCE

Date	Good	VG	Fine	VF	XF
1790	1200.	1850.	2750.	4500.	9500.

KENTUCKY TOKEN

Date	VG	Fine	VF	XF	Unc
(c.1793) plain edge	40.00	60.00	85.00	225.00	450.00
Engrailed edge	125.00	200.00	325.00	725.00	1750.
Lettered edges:					
PAYABLE AT BEDWORTH	—	—	—	1980.	Unique
PAYABLE AT LANCASTER	45.00	65.00	100.00	275.00	700.00
PAYABLE AT I.FIELDING					Unique
PAYABLE AT W. PARKERS	—	—	1800.	—	Unique
Branch w/two leaves on edge					Unique

TALBOT ALLUM & LEE CENTS

With NEW YORK above ship

Date	Good	VG	Fine	VF	XF
1794 edge: PAYABLE AT THE STORE OF	40.00	65.00	145.00	245.00	650.00
1794 edge: plain		Only four examples known		2860.	—
(Size of ampersand varies on obv. and rev. dies.)					

Without NEW YORK

	Good	VG	Fine	VF	XF
1794 edge: PAYABLE AT THE STORE OF	300.00	600.00	900.00	1750.	3500.

Date	VG	Fine	VF	XF	Unc
1795 edge: WE PROMISE TO PAY THE BEARER ONE CENT	25.00	50.00	120.00	220.00	575.00
1795 edge: CURRENT EVERYWHERE					Unique
1795 edge: olive leaf		Norweb 4400.			Unique
1795 plain edge					Two known
1795 edge: Cambridge Bedford Huntingdon.X.X.			Norweb 3960.		Unique

FRANKLIN PRESS TOKEN

1794 plain edge	55.00	85.00	175.00	265.00	575.00

MYDDELTON TOKENS

Date	VG	Fine	VF	XF	Unc
1796 Copper				Proof	6500.
1796 Silver				Proof	5500.

COPPER COMPANY OF UPPER CANADA

1796 Copper/Copper Company rev.	Proof	3750.

CASTORLAND "HALF DOLLAR"

Date	Good	VG	Fine	VF	XF
1796 Silver, reeded edge					3200.
1796 Copper, reeded edge	Only three examples known				1650.
1796 Brass, reeded edge					Unique
1796 Copper, plain edge, thin planchet	Norweb 467.50				Unique
1796 Silver, same dies, reeded edge, thin planchet restrick				Proof	325.00
1796 Silver, same but ARGENT on plain edge				Proof	60.00
1796 Copper, same restrike on thin planchet				Proof	285.00
1796 Copper, same but CUIVRE on plain edge				Proof	40.00

Modern restrikes with large and small lettering on the rev. have been produced in Gold, Silver, Copper and Bronze. Original dies distinguished by wavy die breaks about the upper right corner of pot on the rev.

NEW YORK THEATRE TOKEN

Date	VG	Fine	VF	XF	Unc
(ca.1796)	250.00	850.00	1750.	2750.	6000.

WASHINGTON PIECES

Date	Good	VG	Fine	VF	XF
1783 GEORGIVS TRIUMPHO	35.00	55.00	145.00	250.00	650.00

	Good	VG	Fine	VF	XF
1783 large military bust, several varieties	12.00	20.00	45.00	110.00	240.00
1783 small military bust, plain edge	18.00	25.00	50.00	120.00	260.00

NOTE: One Proof is known. Value $12,500.

	Good	VG	Fine	VF	XF
1783 similar, engrailed edge	30.00	45.00	65.00	175.00	300.00

Date	Good	VG	Fine	VF	XF
1783 draped bust, no button on drapery, small letter	15.00	30.00	50.00	110.00	245.00
1783 draped bust, button on drapery, large letter	25.00	40.00	60.00	160.00	285.00
1783 similar, copper restrike, large modern lettering, plain edge				Proof	500.00
1783 similar but engrailed edge				Proof	375.00
1783 similar, bronzed				Proof	250.00
1783 similar,Silver				Proof	1000.
1783 similar, Gold				Only two examples known	

Date	Good	VG	Fine	VF	XF
1783 UNITY STATES	15.00	30.00	50.00	100.00	225.00

	Good	VG	Fine	VF	XF
(1783) double head cent	15.00	30.00	50.00	100.00	225.00

1784 ugly head	Roper 14,850.	3 known Copper, 1 White Metal

Date	Good	VG	Fine	VF	XF
1791 LIVERPOOL HALFPENNY	450.00	550.00	850.00	1760.	—

Date	Good	VG	Fine	VF	XF
1791 small eagle cent	60.00	125.00	250.00	325.00	600.00

Date	VG	Fine	VF	XF	Unc
1791 large eagle cent	60.00	125.00	250.00	325.00	600.00

Date	Good	VG	Fine	VF	XF
1792 "Half Dollar" Copper, lettered edge	Roper 2860.			Only two examples known	
1792 similar, plain edge				Only three examples known	
1792 similar, Silver, lettered edge	Roper 35,200.				Rare
1792 similar, plain edge					Rare
1792 similar, Gold					Unique

Date	VG	Fine	VF	XF	Unc
1792 WASHINGTON PRESIDENT cent, plain edge	Steinberg 12,650.				
	1450.	3250.	5000.	7500.	—
	Garrett 15,500.				
1792 similar, lettered edge est.	2250.	4500.	7500.	12,500.	—

Date	Good	VG	Fine	VF	XF
(1792) BORN VIRGINIA, varieties	450.00	850.00	1450.	2750.	6500.
Silver, lettered edge				Only two examples known	
Silver, plain edge	Roper 16,500.			Only four examples known	
Mule, heraldic eagle 1792 half dollar rev.				Only three examples known	

Date	Good	VG	Fine	VF	XF
1792 Half dollar, Silver, small eagle, plain edge	7000.	9000.	12,500.	20,000.	37,500.
1792 Half Dollar, similar, circle and squares, ornamented edge				Only five examples known	
1792 half dollar, similar, Copper	Garrett 34,000.			Roper 24,200.	Rare
1792 half dollar, Copper, plain edge	1450.	2250.	4500.	—	—
	Garrett 32,000.				
1792 Half Dollar, Silver, twin olive leaves on edge					Unique

Date	Good	VG	Fine	VF	XF
1792 Half Dollar, Silver, large heraldic eagle	Garrett 16,500.				Unique

		Proof	
1792 Roman head cent		Proof	12,500.

1793 Ship Halfpenny, lettered edge	30.00	60.00	100.00	200.00	475.00
1793 Ship Halfpenny, plain edge		Two to five examples known		1300.	—

Date	VG	Fine	VF	XF	Unc
1795 "Grate" Halfpenny, large coat buttons, reeded edge	30.00	60.00	110.00	220.00	550.00
1795 similar, lettered edge	180.00	250.00	320.00	650.00	1250.
1795 similar, small coat buttons, reeded edge	60.00	100.00	180.00	400.00	850.00

	VG	Fine	VF	XF	Unc
1795 LIBERTY AND SECURITY Halfpenny, plain edge	60.00	100.00	150.00	375.00	850.00
1795 similar, edge lettered: PAYABLE AT LONDON etc.	30.00	60.00	125.00	275.00	600.00
1795 similar, edge lettered: BIRMINGHAM etc.	35.00	65.00	135.00	285.00	650.00
1795 similar, edge lettered: AN ASYLUM etc.	50.00	80.00	200.00	400.00	850.00
1795 similar, edge lettered: PAYABLE AT LIVERPOOL etc.					Unique
1795 similar, edge lettered: PAYABLE AT LONDON-LIVERPOOL					Unique

	VG	Fine	VF	XF	Unc
(1795) LIBERTY AND SECURITY penny, lettered edge	65.00	125.00	200.00	450.00	1150.
(1795) similar, plain edge					Extremely Rare
(1795) similar, engine turned borders		ex-Garrett 2750.			Very Rare
1795 similar to halfpenny w/date on rev.		Roper 6600.			Very Rare

Date	VG	Fine	VF	XF	Unc
(ca.1795) small success medal, plain or reeded edge	85.00	150.00	300.00	500.00	1000.
(c.1795) large success medal, plain or reeded edge	75.00	125.00	250.00	450.00	950.00

Date	VG	Fine	VF	XF	Unc
(1795) NORTH WALES Halfpenny, plain edge	75.00	120.00	200.00	400.00	1250.
(1795) similar, lettered edge	325.00	450.00	725.00	1400.	2950.
(1795) four stars at bottom of rev.	600.00	1250.	2250.	4000.	—

Issues of 1792

HALF DISME

Date	Good	VG	Fine	VF	XF
1792	2000.	3500.	6500.	8500.	16,500.
1792 copper, (Unique)	—	—	—	—	—

DISME

Date
1792 silver   3 known
1792 Copper, (2 reeded edge,
  about 10 plain right   Garrett 54,000

SILVER-CENTER CENT

1792 Silver center (about 8 known)   Norweb, MS-60,143,000
1792 no silver center
  (copper or billon, 4 known   Norweb, EF-40, 35,200

BIRCH CENT

Date
1792 Copper known with plain and two types of
  lettered edges, about 15 known combined   Garrett 200,000
1792 "G.W.Pt." on reverse below wreath tie
  white metal, unique   Garrett 90,000

WRIGHT QUARTER

Date	Good	Fine	VF
1792 Copper, reeded edge (2 known)			
1792 White metal, die trial		Garrett	12,000

Half cents

Liberty Cap

Head facing left

Designer: Adam Eckfeldt. **Size:** 22 millimeters. **Weight:** 6.74 grams. **Composition:** 100% copper.

Date	Mintage	G-4	VG-8	F-12	VF-20	XF-40	MS-60
1793	35,334	1400.	2000.	3000.	5000.	11,000.	35,000.

Head facing right

Designers: Robert Scot (1794) and John Smith Gardner (1795). **Size:** 23.5 millimeters. **Weight:** 6.74 grams (1794-1795) and 5.44 grams (1795-1797). **Composition:** 100% copper. **Notes:** The "lettered edge" varieties have "Two Hundred for a Dollar" inscribed around the edge. The "pole" varieties have a pole, upon which the cap is hanging, resting on Liberty's shoulder. The "punctuated date" varieties have a comma after the 1 in the date. The 1797 "1 above 1" variety has a second 1 above the 1 in the date.

Date	Mintage	G-4	VG-8	F-12	VF-20	XF-40	MS-60
1794	81,600	265.	500.	750.	1500.	3250.	18,000.
1795 lettered edge, pole	25,600	245.	450.	700.	1250.	3500.	15,000.
1795 plain edge, no pole	109,000	175.	325.	525.	1100.	3000.	15,000.
1795 lettered edge, punctuated date	Inc. Ab.	250.	450.	750.	1200.	3500.	18,500.
1795 plain edge, punctuated date	Inc. Ab.	210.	335.	625.	1100.	2500.	25,000.
1796 pole	5,090	6300.	9000.	13,000.	19,000.	27,500.	—
1796 no pole	1,390	20,000.	30,000.	45,000.	85,000.	—	—
1797 pl. edge	119,215	265.	425.	750.	1700.	4500.	25,000.
1797 let. edge	Inc. Ab.	700.	1300.	2750.	6000.	20,000.	—
1797 1 above 1	Inc. Ab.	160.	300.	450.	975.	3000.	15,000.
1797 gripped edge	Inc. Ab.	9000.	15,000.	—	—	—	—

Draped Bust

Stems

Stemless

Designer: Robert Scot. **Size:** 23.5 millimeters. **Weight:** 5.44 grams. **Composition:** 100% copper. **Notes:** The wreath on the reverse was redesigned slightly in 1802, resulting in "reverse of 1800" and "reverse of 1802" varieties. The "stems" varieties have stems extending from the wreath above and on both sides of the fraction on the reverse. On the "crosslet 4" variety, a serif appears at the far right of the crossbar on the 4 in the date. The "spiked chin" variety appears to have a spike extending from Liberty's chin, the result of a damaged die. Varieties of the 1805 strikes are distinguished by the size of the 5 in the date. Varieties of the 1806 strikes are distinguished by the size of the 6 in the date.

Date	Mintage	G-4	VG-8	F-12	VF-20	XF-40	MS-60
1800	211,530	40.00	60.00	85.00	150.	450.	1800.
1802/0 rev. 1800	14,366	12,000.	19,500.	27,500.	—	—	—
1802/0 rev. 1802	Inc. Ab.	600.	975.	2350.	4750.	9800.	—
1803	97,900	33.00	48.00	100.	225.	800.	6500.
1804 plain 4, stemless wreath	1,055,312	30.00	38.00	50.00	80.00	250.	1200.
1804 plain 4, stems	Inc. Ab.	40.00	75.00	140.	250.	1500.	12,000.
1804 crosslet 4, stemless	Inc. Ab.	30.00	45.00	75.00	110.	350.	1250.
1804 crosslet 4, stems	Inc. Ab.	30.00	40.00	65.00	100.	325.	1100.
1804 spiked chin	Inc.Ab.	30.00	45.00	70.00	100.	300.	1050.
1805 small 5, stemless	814,464	30.00	42.00	65.00	105.	350.	2750.
1805 small 5, stems	Inc. Ab.	700.	1250.	2250.	4250.	12,500.	—
1805 large 5, stems	Inc. Ab.	30.00	49.00	70.00	110.	350.	2500.
1806 small 6, stems	356,000	150.	300.	450.	900.	2500.	—
1806 small 6, stemless	Inc. Ab.	29.00	40.00	50.00	70.00	195.	1250.
1806 large 6, stems	Inc. Ab.	28.00	40.00	50.00	70.00	225.	1050.
1807	476,000	28.00	45.00	65.00	110.	400.	3000.
1808/7	400,000	150.	275.	550.	1000.	5000.	25,000.
1808	Inc. Ab.	29.00	40.00	60.00	150.	750.	4500.

Classic Head

Designer: John Reich. **Size:** 23.5 millimeters. **Weight:** 5.44 grams. **Composition:** 100% copper. **Notes:** Restrikes listed were produced privately in the mid-1800s. The two varieties of the 1831 restrikes are distinguished by the size of the berries in the wreath on the reverse. The 1828 strikes have either 12 or 13 stars on the obverse.

Date	Mintage	G-4	VG-8	F-12	VF-20	XF-40	MS-60
1809/6	1,154,572	28.00	40.00	45.00	60.00	175.	850.
1809	Inc. Ab.	28.00	40.00	50.00	75.00	200.	750.
1809 circle in 0	—	32.00	45.00	65.00	100.	350.	2000.
1810	215,000	34.00	45.00	75.00	140.	600.	3000.
1811	63,140	110.	200.	500.	1250.	3500.	—

1825 Half Cent
Grade F-12

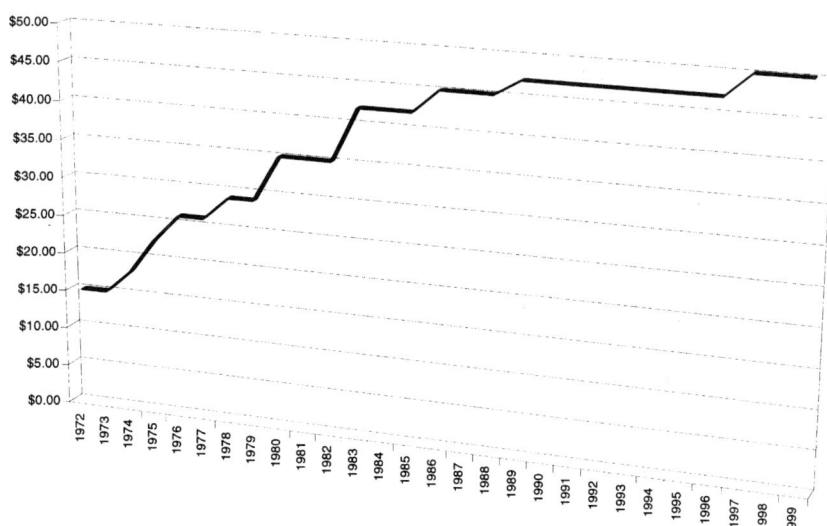

■ Retail Price

Source: COIN PRICES

Date	Mintage	G-4	VG-8	F-12	VF-20	XF-40	MS-60
1811 restrike, reverse of 1802, uncirculated						—	25,000.
1825	63,000	29.00	37.00	50.00	75.00	200.	850.
1826	234,000	27.00	35.00	40.00	60.00	125.	600.
1828 13 stars	606,000	27.00	30.00	35.00	50.00	85.00	300.
1828 12 stars	Inc. Ab.	30.00	33.00	40.00	60.00	225.	850.
1829	487,000	27.00	30.00	35.00	50.00	125.	475.
1831 original	2,200	—	—	4900.	5600.	7700.	—
1831 1st restrike, lg. berries, reverse of 1836, proof						—	6000.
1831 2nd restrike, sm. berries, reverse of 1840, proof						—	20,000.
1832	154,000	27.00	30.00	35.00	55.00	90.00	300.
1833	120,000	27.00	30.00	35.00	45.00	80.00	250.
1834	141,000	27.00	30.00	35.00	45.00	80.00	250.
1835	398,000	27.00	30.00	35.00	45.00	80.00	250.
1836 original	—	—		Proof only	—	—	5000.
1836 restrike, reverse of 1840, proof only						—	18,000.

Coronet

Designer: Christian Gobrecht. **Size:** 23 millimeters. **Weight:** 5.44 grams. **Composition:** 100% copper. **Notes:** 1840-1848 strikes, both originals and restrikes, are known in proof only; mintages are unknown. The small-date varieties of the 1849, both originals and restrikes, are known in proof only. Restrikes were produced clandestinely by Philadelphia Mint personnel in the mid-1800s.

Date	Mintage	G-4	VG-8	F-12	VF-20	XF-40	MS-60	Prf-60
1840 original	—	—	—	—	Proof only	—	—	3800.
1840 1st restrike	—	—	—	—	Proof only	—	—	3500.
1840 2nd restrike	—	—	—	—	Proof only	—	—	3200.
1841 original	—	—	—	—	Proof only	—	—	3800.
1841 1st restrike	—	—	—	—	Proof only	—	—	3500.
1841 2nd restrike	—	—	—	—	Proof only	—	—	3000.
1842 original	—	—	—	—	Proof only	—	—	3800.
1842 1st restrike	—	—	—	—	Proof only	—	—	3500.
1842 2nd restrike	—	—	—	—	Proof only	—	—	3200.
1843 original	—	—	—	—	Proof only	—	—	3800.
1843 1st restrike	—	—	—	—	Proof only	—	—	3500.
1843 2nd restrike	—	—	—	—	Proof only	—	—	3200.
1844 original	—	—	—	—	Proof only	—	—	3800.
1844 1st restrike	—	—	—	—	Proof only	—	—	3500.
1844 2nd restrike	—	—	—	—	Proof only	—	—	3200.
1845 original	—	—	—	—	Proof only	—	—	3800.
1845 1st restrike	—	—	—	—	Proof only	—	—	3500.
1845 2nd restrike	—	—	—	—	Proof only	—	—	3200.
1846 original	—	—	—	—	Proof only	—	—	3800.
1846 1st restrike	—	—	—	—	Proof only	—	—	3500.
1846 2nd restrike	—	—	—	—	Proof only	—	—	3200.
1847 original	—	—	—	—	Proof only	—	—	3800.
1847 1st restrike	—	—	—	—	Proof only	—	—	10,000.
1847 2nd restrike	—	—	—	—	Proof only	—	—	3200.
1848 original	—	—	—	—	Proof only	—	—	3800.
1848 1st restrike	—	—	—	—	Proof only	—	—	3500.
1848 2nd restrike	—	—	—	—	Proof only	—	—	3200.
1849 original, small date			—	—	Proof only	—	—	3800.
1849 1st restrike small date			—	—	Proof only	—	—	3200.

Date	Mintage	G-4	VG-8	F-12	VF-20	XF-40	MS-60
1849 lg. date	39,864	35.00	40.00	45.00	60.00	150.	600.
1850	39,812	33.00	38.00	45.00	60.00	200.	750.
1851	147,672	23.00	28.00	35.00	50.00	70.00	200.
1852 original	—	—		—	Proof only	—	35,000.
1852 1st restrike	—	—		—	Proof only	—	3500.
1852 2nd restrike	—	—		—	Proof only	—	5000.
1853	129,694	24.00	29.00	35.00	45.00	65.00	195.
1854	55,358	25.00	32.00	35.00	45.00	65.00	195.
1855	56,500	25.00	32.00	35.00	45.00	65.00	195.
1856	40,430	30.00	38.00	44.00	52.00	90.00	275.
1857	35,180	45.00	52.00	65.00	80.00	140.	350.

LARGE CENTS
Flowing Hair

Chain reverse

Designer: Henry Voigt. **Size:** 26-27 millimeters. **Weight:** 13.48 grams. **Composition:** 100% copper.

Date	Mintage	G-4	VG-8	F-12	VF-20	XF-40	MS-60
1793 chain	36,103	2400.	3750.	5500.	11,000.	17,500.	63,000.

Wreath reverse

Designer: Adam Eckfeldt. **Size:** 26-28 millimeters. **Weight:** 13.48 grams. **Composition:** 100% copper.

Date	Mintage	G-4	VG-8	F-12	VF-20	XF-40	MS-60
1793 wreath	63,353	980.	1200.	2650.	4000.	7000.	23,000.

Liberty Cap

Designers: Joseph Wright (1793-1795) and John Smith Gardner (1795-1796). **Size:** 29 millimeters. **Weight:** 13.48 grams (1793-1795) and 10.89 grams (1795-1796). **Notes:** The heavier pieces were struck on thicker planchets. The Liberty design on the obverse was revised slightly in 1794, but the 1793 design was used on some 1794 strikes. The 1795 "lettered edge" variety has "One Hundred for a Dollar" and a leaf inscribed on the edge.

Date	Mintage	G-4	VG-8	F-12	VF-20	XF-40	MS-60
1793 cap	11,056	3000.	3950.	5850.	20,000.	30,000.	—
1794	918,521	165.	250.	460.	850.	2450.	—
1794 head '93	Inc. Ab.	900.	1800.	3000.	5900.	10,000.	—
1795	501,500	130.	240.	375.	630.	1750.	3500.
1795 lettered edge, "One Cent" high in wreath							
	37,000	160.	310.	525.	1150.	2900.	5750.
1796 Lib. Cap	109,825	145.	260.	700.	1500.	3100.	6100.

Draped Bust

Designer: Robert Scot. **Size:** 29 millimeters. **Weight:** 10.98 grams. **Composition:** 100% copper. **Notes:** The "stemless" variety does not have stems extending from the wreath above and on both sides of the fraction on the reverse. The 1801 "3 errors" variety has the fraction on the reverse reading "1/000", has only one stem extending from the wreath above and on both sides of the fraction on the reverse, and "United" in "United States of America" appears as "linited."

Date	Mintage	G-4	VG-8	F-12	VF-20	XF-40	MS-60
1796	363,375	160.	225.	550.	1400.	3100.	—
1797	897,510	49.00	100.	160.	335.	1150.	3300.
1797 stemless	Inc. Ab.	125.	210.	385.	910.	3200.	—
1798	1,841,745	48.00	85.00	130.	385.	975.	3100.
1798/7	Inc. Ab.	91.00	180.	310.	1050.	3900.	—
1799	42,540	1900.	3500.	5250.	15,000.	27,500.	—
1800	2,822,175	37.00	65.00	115.	350.	1250.	—
1801	1,362,837	36.00	65.00	125.	280.	1000.	—
1801 3 errors	Inc. Ab.	85.00	175.	900.	1750.	5500.	—
1802	3,435,100	34.00	55.00	110.	225.	775.	2250.
1803	2,471,353	34.00	55.00	110.	225.	775.	2250.
1804	96,500	850.	1100.	1500.	2550.	7000.	—
1805	941,116	35.00	55.00	125.	300.	875.	2450.
1806	348,000	39.00	95.00	135.	350.	1100.	4700.
1807	727,221	31.00	53.00	110.	225.	775.	2250.

1804 Cent
Grade F-12

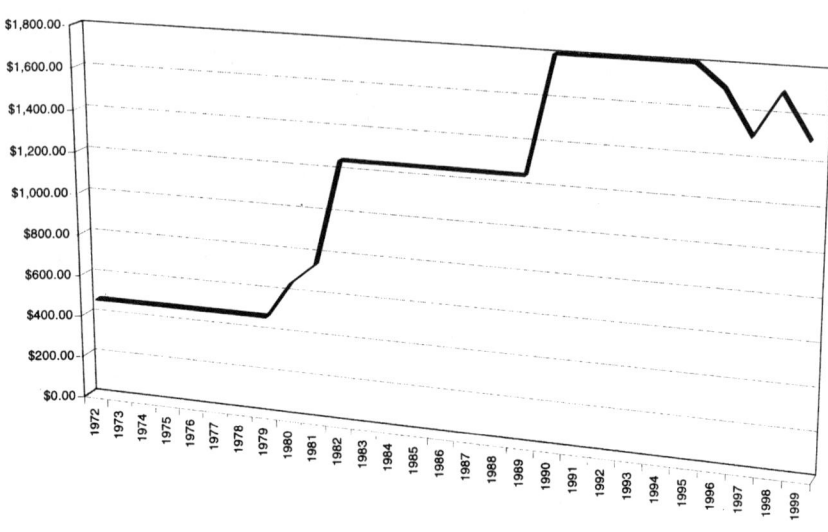

■ Retail Price

Source: COIN PRICES

Classic Head

Designer: John Reich. **Size:** 29 millimeters. **Weight:** 10.89 grams. **Composition:** 100% copper.

Date	Mintage	G-4	VG-8	F-12	VF-20	XF-40	MS-60
1808	1,109,000	35.00	75.00	175.	425.	1200.	3600.
1809	222,867	60.00	140.	350.	1300.	2650.	6300.
1810	1,458,500	36.00	75.00	210.	600.	1100.	3850.
1811	218,025	65.00	120.	315.	875.	1300.	7000.
1811/10	Inc. Ab.	70.00	130.	340.	900.	1400.	—
1812	1,075,500	36.00	65.00	180.	525.	975.	2800.
1813	418,000	55.00	115.	665.	1100.	1400.	—
1814	357,830	36.00	65.00	180.	530.	975.	2800.

Coronet Type

Designer: Robert Scot. **Size:** 28-29 millimeters. **Weight:** 10.89 grams. **Composition:** 100% copper. **Notes:** The 1817 strikes have either 13 or 15 stars on the obverse.

Date	Mintage	G-4	VG-8	F-12	VF-20	XF-40	MS-60
1816	2,820,982	14.00	17.00	28.00	84.00	175.	420.
1817 13 stars	3,948,400	12.50	15.00	24.00	56.00	120.	275.
1817 15 stars	Inc. Ab.	16.00	25.00	45.00	125.00	350.	1550.
1818	3,167,000	12.50	16.00	24.00	56.00	125.	250.
1819	2,671,000	12.50	14.00	23.00	63.00	120.	275.
1820	4,407,550	12.50	17.00	23.00	63.00	120.	275.
1821	389,000	28.00	49.00	185.	550.	2000.	6650.
1822	2,072,339	12.50	15.00	32.00	84.00	195.	575.
1823	Inc. 1824	60.00	110.	275.	625.	2750.	—
1823/22	Inc. 1824	49.00	95.00	240.	600.	2450.	—
1823 Restrike	—	300.	400.	450.	500.	550.	700.
1824	1,262,000	14.00	23.00	38.00	145.	350.	625.
1824/22	Inc. Ab.	17.00	25.00	56.00	225.	975.	—
1825	1,461,100	13.00	16.00	35.00	110.	300.	840.
1826	1,517,425	12.50	16.00	26.00	84.00	175.	700.
1826/25	Inc. Ab.	16.00	24.00	60.00	175.	700.	1800.
1827	2,357,732	12.50	15.00	23.00	75.00	135.	385.
1828	2,260,624	12.50	14.00	26.00	84.00	175.	425.
1829	1,414,500	12.50	14.00	22.00	100.	140.	425.
1830	1,711,500	12.50	14.00	22.00	70.00	135.	385.
1831	3,359,260	12.50	14.00	22.00	63.00	125.	315.
1832	2,362,000	12.50	14.00	22.00	63.00	125.	315.
1833	2,739,000	12.50	14.00	22.00	56.00	120.	265.
1834	1,855,100	12.50	14.00	22.00	56.00	140.	250.
1835	3,878,400	12.50	14.00	22.00	56.00	91.00	225.
1836	2,111,000	13.00	15.00	23.00	57.00	105.	250.

Braided Hair

Designer: Christian Gobrecht. **Size:** 27.5 millimeters. **Weight:** 10.89 grams. **Composition:** 100% copper. **Notes:** 1840 and 1842 strikes have either small or large dates, with little difference in value. 1855 and 1856 strikes have either slanting or upright 5s in the date, with little difference in value. A slightly larger Liberty head and larger reverse lettering were used beginning in 1843. One 1843 variety uses the old obverse with the new reverse.

Date	Mintage	G-4	VG-8	F-12	VF-20	XF-40	MS-60
1837	5,558,300	12.50	14.00	22.00	51.00	91.00	300.
1838	6,370,200	12.50	14.00	22.00	51.00	91.00	225.
1839	3,128,661	12.50	14.00	22.00	51.00	105.	350.
1839/36	Inc. Ab.	325.	500.	840.	1850.	4750.	—
1840	2,462,700	11.00	14.00	17.00	38.00	70.00	475.
1841	1,597,367	13.00	15.00	18.00	40.00	75.00	440.
1842	2,383,390	11.00	14.00	17.00	38.00	70.00	425.
1843	2,425,342	11.00	14.00	17.00	38.00	75.00	445.
1843 obverse 1842 with reverse of 1844							
	Inc. Ab.	12.00	15.00	21.00	38.00	80.00	350.

Date	Mintage	G-4	VG-8	F-12	VF-20	XF-40	MS-60
1844	2,398,752	9.00	14.00	14.00	22.00	54.00	215.
1844/81	Inc. Ab.	14.00	25.00	40.00	65.00	200.	600.
1845	3,894,804	9.00	12.00	14.00	19.50	44.00	225.
1846	4,120,800	9.00	12.00	14.00	19.50	44.00	225.
1847	6,183,669	9.00	12.00	14.00	19.50	44.00	160.
1848	6,415,799	9.00	12.00	14.00	19.50	44.00	160.
1849	4,178,500	9.00	12.00	14.00	28.00	60.00	275.
1850	4,426,844	9.00	12.00	14.00	19.50	44.00	160.
1851	9,889,707	9.00	12.00	14.00	19.50	41.00	160.
1851/81	Inc. Ab.	15.00	19.00	35.00	60.00	100.	500.
1852	5,063,094	9.00	12.00	14.00	19.50	41.00	160.
1853	6,641,131	9.00	12.00	14.00	19.50	41.00	160.
1854	4,236,156	9.00	12.00	14.00	19.50	41.00	160.
1855	1,574,829	12.00	14.00	17.00	21.00	45.00	170.
1856	2,690,463	11.00	13.00	15.00	16.00	40.00	160.
1857	333,456	42.00	52.00	60.00	70.00	90.00	250.

Small cents

FLYING EAGLE CENTS

Large letters;   Small letters;
"AM" connected   "AM" separated

Designer: James B. Longacre. **Size:** 19 millimeters. **Weight:** 4.67 grams. **Composition:** 88% copper, 12% nickel. **Notes:** On the large-letter variety of 1858, the "A" and "M" in "America" are connected at their bases; on the small-letter variety, the two letters are separated.

Date	Mintage	G-4	VG-8	F-12	VF-20	XF-40	AU-50	MS-60	MS-65	Prf-65
1856	Est. 2,500	4000.	4250.	4550.	5250.	5750.	6150.	7500.	30,000.	18,250.
1857	17,450,000	15.00	17.00	25.00	36.00	95.00	135.	225.	3000.	25,000.
1858/7	—	90.00	110.	130.	170.	300.	400.	—	—	—
1858 LL	24,600,000	16.00	18.00	27.00	38.00	100.	155.	240.	3000.	19,000.
1858 SL	Inc. Ab.	15.00	17.00	25.00	38.00	100.	150.	240.	3000.	25,000.

INDIAN HEAD CENTS

1859   1860-1909   1864 "L"

Copper-nickel composition

Designer: James B. Longacre. **Size:** 19 millimeters. **Weight:** 4.67 grams. **Composition:** 88% copper, 12% nickel.

Date	Mintage	G-4	VG-8	F-12	VF-20	XF-40	AU-50	MS-60	MS-65	Prf-65
1859	36,400,000	9.00	11.00	15.00	35.00	75.00	135.	200.	2500.	5500.
1860	20,566,000	6.50	9.50	12.00	17.50	45.00	75.00	130.	850.	3500.
1861	10,100,000	16.00	22.00	29.00	39.00	75.00	140.	170.	850.	6500.
1862	28,075,000	6.00	8.50	11.50	18.00	29.00	53.00	80.00	750.	2200.
1863	49,840,000	5.50	7.00	9.00	12.50	25.00	47.50	65.00	850.	2800.
1864	13,740,000	14.00	18.00	25.00	32.00	50.00	75.00	125.	1250.	3000.

PRICING SECTION

1857 Cent
Grade XF-40

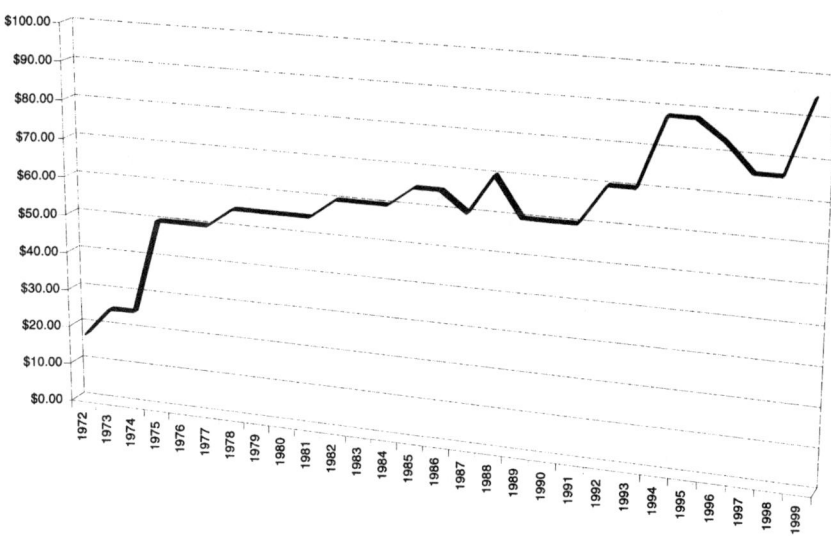

■ Retail Price

Source: COIN PRICES

Bronze composition

Weight: 3.11 grams. **Composition:** 95% copper, 5% tin and zinc. **Notes:** The 1864 "L" variety has the designer's initial in Liberty's hair to the right of her neck.

Date	Mintage	G-4	VG-8	F-12	VF-20	XF-40	AU-50	MS-60	MS-65	Prf-65
1864	39,233,714	6.50	10.00	17.50	27.50	47.00	55.00	75.00	315.	9300.
1864 L	Inc. Ab.	38.50	55.00	85.00	115.	175.	225.	275.	1350.	50,000.
1865	35,429,286	6.50	9.00	16.00	20.00	35.00	50.00	77.00	400.	1750.
1866	9,826,500	34.00	40.00	55.00	80.00	150.	185.	230.	1100.	850.
1867	9,821,000	34.00	40.00	56.00	90.00	145.	185.	235.	1100.	925.
1868	10,266,500	29.00	35.00	50.00	80.00	135.	175.	225.	900.	925.
1869/9	6,420,000	95.00	125.	200.	265.	300.	365.	400.	1550.	—
1869	Inc. Ab.	42.00	70.00	160.	210.	260.	325.	380.	1425.	1050.
1870	5,275,000	36.00	62.00	140.	210.	260.	325.	375.	1425.	1075.
1871	3,929,500	42.00	62.00	190.	240.	300.	375.	425.	2500.	1100.
1872	4,042,000	65.00	85.00	240.	260.	325.	400.	485.	3500.	1075.
1873	11,676,500	15.50	25.00	39.00	49.00	130.	145.	185.	1100.	750.
1874	14,187,500	13.00	21.00	32.00	44.00	85.00	120.	150.	725.	775.
1875	13,528,000	13.00	17.00	39.00	44.00	81.00	115.	150.	900.	1500.
1876	7,944,000	24.00	32.00	45.00	60.00	130.	155.	190.	1100.	750.
1877	852,500	435.	510.	675.	925.	1300.	1700.	2100.	7500.	4500.
1878	5,799,850	24.00	32.00	50.00	70.00	125.	170.	190.	900.	450.
1879	16,231,200	6.00	9.50	18.00	35.00	59.00	69.00	75.00	350.	425.
1880	38,964,955	2.75	4.50	6.50	10.00	27.00	42.00	70.00	325.	410.
1881	39,211,575	2.75	4.00	6.50	9.00	20.00	30.00	40.00	275.	400.
1882	38,581,100	2.75	4.00	6.00	9.75	20.00	31.00	40.00	265.	400.
1883	45,589,109	2.50	3.50	5.00	8.50	20.00	30.00	40.00	255.	400.
1884	23,261,742	3.00	4.00	7.00	12.00	27.00	35.00	65.00	550.	400.
1885	11,765,384	5.50	8.00	13.50	25.00	52.00	65.00	95.00	750.	400.
1886	17,654,290	3.25	7.50	19.00	39.00	95.00	110.	130.	1150.	450.
1887	45,226,483	1.60	2.25	5.00	7.50	22.00	30.00	45.00	350.	440.
1888	37,494,414	1.60	2.25	5.00	7.50	22.00	30.00	45.00	900.	450.
1889	48,869,361	1.40	2.25	4.00	7.00	13.	25.00	45.	350.	425.
1890	57,182,854	1.40	1.85	2.60	5.00	11.50	24.00	45.00	350.	500.
1891	47,072,350	1.40	1.85	2.60	5.00	11.50	24.00	43.00	300.	475.
1892	37,649,832	1.40	1.95	3.50	5.50	12.50	26.00	37.00	265.	475.
1893	46,642,195	1.40	1.75	2.60	5.00	11.50	24.00	35.00	265.	525.
1894	16,752,132	2.50	3.95	10.00	15.00	37.00	49.00	65.00	350.	500.
1895	38,343,636	1.40	1.75	2.50	5.00	12.50	22.50	35.00	195.	450.

1864-L Indian Cent
Grade F-12

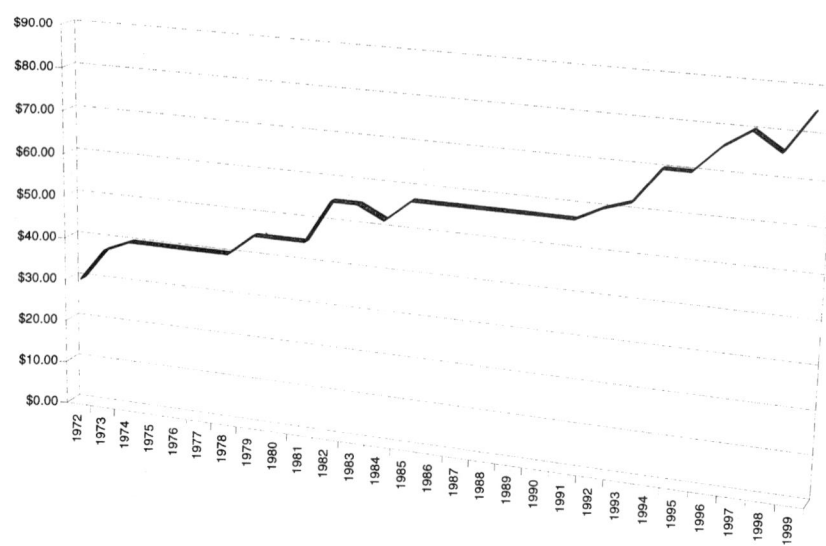

■ Retail Price

Source: COIN PRICES

Date	Mintage	G-4	VG-8	F-12	VF-20	XF-40	AU-50	MS-60	MS-65	Prf-65
1896	39,057,293	1.40	1.75	2.50	5.00	12.00	23.00	36.00	200.	400.
1897	50,466,330	1.35	1.75	2.50	4.00	9.50	22.00	35.00	175.	430.
1898	49,823,079	1.30	1.75	2.50	4.00	10.00	17.00	30.00	175.	425.
1899	53,600,031	1.30	1.50	2.30	4.00	10.00	17.00	30.00	135.	390.
1900	66,833,764	1.30	1.40	2.25	3.00	7.50	16.00	26.00	125.	390.
1901	79,611,143	1.30	1.40	1.75	2.75	7.50	15.00	25.00	135.	390.
1902	87,376,722	1.30	1.40	1.75	2.75	7.50	15.00	25.00	135.	390.
1903	85,094,493	1.30	1.40	1.75	2.75	7.50	15.00	25.00	135.	400.
1904	61,328,015	1.30	1.40	1.75	2.75	7.50	15.00	25.00	135.	435.
1905	80,719,163	1.30	1.40	1.75	2.75	7.50	15.00	25.00	135.	435.
1906	96,022,255	1.30	1.40	1.70	2.75	7.50	15.00	25.00	135.	390.
1907	108,138,618	1.30	1.40	1.70	2.75	7.50	15.00	25.00	135.	470.
1908	32,327,987	1.30	1.75	2.25	3.00	8.00	15.00	25.00	135.	375.
1908S	1,115,000	36.00	40.00	46.00	52.00	80.00	130.	195.	600.	—
1909	14,370,645	2.50	3.00	4.00	5.75	17.50	26.00	35.00	135.	425.
1909S	309,000	240.	275.	300.	345.	380.	430.	485.	1450.	—

Lincoln

"V.D.B."

Wheat reverse, bronze composition

Designer: Victor D. Brenner. **Size:** 19 millimeters. **Weight:** 3.11 grams. **Composition:** 95% copper, 5% tin and zinc. **Notes:** The 1909 "V.D.B." varieties have the designer's initials inscribed at the 6 o'clock position on the reverse. Later in 1909 the initials were removed until 1918, when they were placed on the obverse.

1914-D Cent
Grade F-12

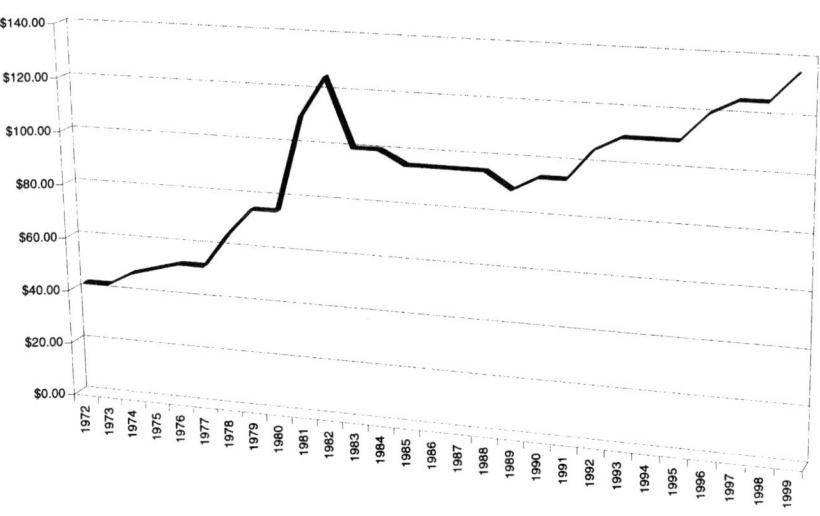

■ Retail Price

Source: **COIN PRICES**

Date	Mintage	G-4	VG-8	F-12	VF-20	XF-40	AU-50	MS-60	MS-65	Prf-65
1909	72,702,618	1.00	1.10	1.50	1.75	2.75	6.75	14.00	70.00	490.
1909VDB	27,995,000	2.50	2.60	2.75	2.90	4.25	6.00	9.00	43.00	3100.
1909S	1,825,000	38.00	43.00	52.00	68.00	95.00	110.	120.	425.	—
1909SVDB	484,000	350.	395.	435.	470.	510.	560.	660.	2250.	—
1910	146,801,218	.20	.25	.35	.60	2.50	6.00	14.50	75.00	470.
1910S	6,045,000	6.00	7.00	8.50	12.00	23.00	45.00	60.00	250.	—
1911	101,177,787	.25	.40	.75	1.95	4.50	7.50	18.00	125.	470.
1911D	12,672,000	4.50	5.00	7.00	12.00	35.00	55.00	72.00	750.	—
1911S	4,026,000	15.00	16.00	18.50	22.00	46.00	75.00	135.	1050.	—
1912	68,153,060	1.25	1.40	2.00	4.50	11.00	14.50	30.00	190.	625.
1912D	10,411,000	4.75	5.25	7.00	16.00	41.00	65.00	125.	790.	—
1912S	4,431,000	10.50	13.00	14.50	18.50	40.00	63.00	95.00	1200.	—
1913	76,532,352	.45	.60	1.60	3.50	13.00	17.00	29.00	190.	470.
1913D	15,804,000	2.25	2.40	3.50	8.00	26.00	50.00	80.00	925.	—
1913S	6,101,000	5.00	6.00	7.50	13.50	34.00	60.00	120.	1700.	—
1914	75,238,432	.35	.65	1.50	3.75	10.00	26.00	40.00	225.	500.
1914D	1,193,000	85.00	105.	135.	195.	450.	690.	1000.	7250.	—
1914S	4,137,000	10.00	11.00	13.00	20.00	42.50	95.00	195.	6500.	—
1915	29,092,120	1.10	1.20	4.00	12.00	44.00	65.00	80.00	475.	490.
1915D	22,050,000	1.10	1.20	2.00	3.50	12.00	25.00	49.00	450.	—
1915S	4,833,000	6.50	7.50	9.00	12.50	35.00	60.00	125.	2150.	—
1916	131,833,677	.15	.20	.45	1.25	4.00	6.50	12.00	100.	1250.
1916D	35,956,000	.35	.50	1.20	2.50	9.50	19.50	50.00	1350.	—
1916S	22,510,000	1.00	1.25	1.60	2.75	9.50	19.00	60.00	3000.	—
1917	196,429,785	.15	.20	.40	1.00	4.00	7.00	13.00	100.	—
1917D	55,120,000	.30	.40	1.00	2.50	9.00	17.00	55.00	850.	—
1917S	32,620,000	.45	.55	1.00	2.25	8.00	18.00	55.00	1800.	—
1918	288,104,634	.15	.20	.35	.90	4.00	7.00	12.00	165.	—
1918D	47,830,000	.30	.60	1.00	2.50	8.50	18.00	55.00	1050.	—
1918S	34,680,000	.35	.55	1.00	2.00	8.00	22.00	55.00	3900.	—
1919	392,021,000	.15	.20	.40	.65	2.00	5.00	9.00	75.00	—
1919D	57,154,000	.30	.40	.65	2.00	7.50	17.50	43.00	775.	—
1919S	139,760,000	.15	.25	1.25	1.50	3.50	13.50	33.00	1850.	—
1920	310,165,000	.15	.20	.30	.65	2.50	5.50	10.00	75.00	—
1920D	49,280,000	.25	.35	.95	2.50	8.75	17.00	50.00	680.	—
1920S	46,220,000	.25	.30	1.25	1.75	7.00	23.00	75.00	4200.	—
1921	39,157,000	.25	.35	.60	1.25	5.50	16.50	35.00	115.	—
1921S	15,274,000	1.00	1.10	1.75	3.75	16.50	60.00	85.00	3200.	—
1922D	7,160,000	7.00	8.50	10.00	12.50	23.00	42.00	65.00	600.	—
1922	Inc. Ab.	300.	350.	415.	540.	1250.	2500.	5200.	60,000.	—
1923	74,723,000	.20	.30	.40	1.25	4.50	7.00	11.50	185.	—

Date	Mintage	G-4	VG-8	F-12	VF-20	XF-40	AU-50	MS-60	MS-65	Prf-65
1923S	8,700,000	1.60	2.00	3.50	5.50	23.00	65.00	170.	2600.	—
1924	75,178,000	.20	.25	.45	1.25	4.50	10.00	20.00	100.	—
1924D	2,520,000	8.50	10.00	12.50	22.00	60.00	130.	225.	3700.	—
1924S	11,696,000	.85	1.10	2.00	3.00	12.00	50.00	95.00	5300.	—
1925	139,949,000	.20	.25	.40	1.00	3.00	6.00	9.00	70.00	—
1925D	22,580,000	.35	.70	1.00	2.00	9.00	22.50	45.00	1050.	—
1925S	26,380,000	.25	.35	.80	1.25	8.50	17.50	55.00	4450.	—
1926	157,088,000	.15	.20	.30	.80	2.00	5.50	8.00	45.00	—
1926D	28,020,000	.20	.40	.70	1.50	6.50	15.00	50.00	1200.	—
1926S	4,550,000	2.75	3.25	5.00	6.00	12.00	50.00	95.00	9500.	—
1927	144,440,000	.15	.20	.30	.80	2.00	5.00	8.00	85.00	—
1927D	27,170,000	.20	.25	.60	1.25	4.00	12.50	48.00	950.	—
1927S	14,276,000	.80	.95	1.50	3.00	10.00	18.00	60.00	2800.	—
1928	134,116,000	.15	.20	.30	.80	2.00	5.00	8.00	75.00	—
1928D	31,170,000	.20	.25	.50	1.00	3.50	10.00	25.00	375.	—
1928S	17,266,000	.60	.75	1.10	1.75	4.00	12.00	52.00	1150.	—
1929	185,262,000	.15	.20	.30	.80	1.50	5.00	6.00	70.00	—
1929D	41,730,000	.15	.20	.45	.90	3.50	7.50	15.00	170.	—
1929S	50,148,000	.15	.20	.35	.75	2.50	4.50	11.00	115.	—
1930	157,415,000	.10	.15	.20	.50	1.75	3.00	5.50	35.00	—
1930D	40,100,000	.15	.20	.45	.75	2.50	5.00	12.00	75.00	—
1930S	24,286,000	.20	.25	.35	.80	1.60	3.00	7.00	38.00	—
1931	19,396,000	.50	.60	1.00	1.35	2.00	7.00	16.50	80.00	—
1931D	4,480,000	2.75	3.00	3.25	4.00	8.50	34.00	46.00	450.	—
1931S	866,000	34.00	35.00	40.00	42.00	44.00	49.00	59.00	250.	—
1932	9,062,000	1.50	1.80	2.25	2.50	3.50	9.50	17.00	60.00	—
1932D	10,500,000	1.00	1.25	1.40	1.50	2.75	7.00	14.00	57.00	—
1933	14,360,000	.90	1.15	1.50	1.90	3.50	9.00	16.00	59.00	—
1933D	6,200,000	1.75	2.25	3.00	3.20	5.00	11.00	16.00	50.00	—
1934	219,080,000	—	.15	.20	.25	.75	1.50	3.00	20.00	—
1934D	28,446,000	.15	.20	.25	.45	1.50	5.00	15.00	45.00	—
1935	245,338,000	—	.10	.15	.25	.75	1.00	1.50	20.00	—
1935D	11100.00	—	.15	.20	.30	.95	2.50	4.50	9.00	—
1935S	38,702,000	.10	.20	.30	.40	1.00	3.00	10.00	44.00	—
1936	309,637,569	—	.10	.15	.25	.75	1.00	1.50	6.00	825.
1936D	40,620,000	—	.10	.15	.25	.75	1.50	2.50	8.00	—
1936S	29,130,000	.10	.15	.25	.35	.85	1.75	2.50	8.00	—
1937	309,179,320	—	.10	.15	.20	.70	.90	1.50	7.00	120.
1937D	50,430,000	—	.10	.15	.25	.70	1.00	2.25	9.00	—
1937S	34,500,000	—	.10	.15	.25	.60	1.25	1.75	8.00	—
1938	156,696,734	—	.10	.15	.20	.50	1.00	1.60	5.75	85.00
1938D	20,010,000	.20	.25	.35	.45	.75	1.50	2.50	8.00	—
1938S	15,180,000	.30	.35	.50	.70	.90	1.25	2.25	8.00	—
1939	316,479,520	—	.10	.15	.20	.30	.50	1.00	5.50	75.00
1939D	15,160,000	.30	.30	.35	.60	.85	1.90	2.25	8.00	—
1939S	52,070,000	—	.15	.20	.25	.45	.90	1.35	8.50	—
1940	586,825,872	—	.15	.20	.25	.30	.45	.95	5.50	65.00
1940D	81,390,000	—	.15	.20	.25	.35	.50	1.00	5.50	—
1940S	112,940,000	—	.15	.20	.25	.40	.75	1.00	5.50	—
1941	887,039,100	—	—	.10	.15	.25	.40	.85	5.50	65.00
1941D	128,700,000	—	—	.15	.20	.25	1.00	2.00	8.00	—
1941S	92,360,000	—	—	.15	.20	.25	1.25	2.25	11.00	—
1942	657,828,600	—	—	.10	.15	.20	.25	.50	4.50	70.00
1942D	206,698,000	—	—	.10	.15	.20	.30	.50	5.75	—
1942S	85,590,000	—	—	.10	.20	.30	1.50	3.50	14.00	—

Steel composition

Weight: 2.7 grams. **Composition:** steel coated with zinc.

Date	Mintage	G-4	VG-8	F-12	VF-20	XF-40	AU-50	MS-60	MS-65	Prf-65
1943	684,628,670	—	—	.25	.30	.50	.70	.85	4.50	—
1943D	217,660,000	—	—	.25	.35	.60	.65	1.00	6.00	—
1943S	191,550,000	—	.30	.35	.40	.70	1.00	1.75	8.50	—

Copper-zinc composition

Weight: 3.11 grams. **Composition:** 95% copper, 5% zinc. **Notes:** The 1955 "doubled die" has distinct doubling of the date and lettering on the obverse.

Date	Mintage	XF-40	MS-60	Prf-65	Date	Mintage	XF-40	MS-60	Prf-65
1944	1,435,400,000	.20	.50	—	1946S	198,100,000	.20	.50	—
1944D	430,578,000	.20	.45	—	1947	190,555,000	.20	.60	—
1944D/S	—	150.	375.	—	1947D	194,750,000	.20	.40	—
1944S	282,760,000	.20	.45	—	1947S	99,000,000	.20	.55	—
1945	1,040,515,000	.20	.60	—	1948	317,570,000	.20	.50	—
1945D	226,268,000	.20	.70	—	1948D	172,637,000	.20	.45	—
1945S	181,770,000	.20	.45	—	1948S	81,735,000	.20	.65	—
1946	991,655,000	.20	.35	—	1949	217,775,000	.20	.75	—
1946D	315,690,000	.20	.50	—	1949D	153,132,000	.20	.50	—

Date	Mintage	XF-40	MS-60	Prf-65
1949S	64,290,000	.25	1.00	—
1950	272,686,386	.20	.50	35.00
1950D	334,950,000	.20	.50	—
1950S	118,505,000	.20	.80	—
1951	295,633,500	.20	.90	30.00
1951D	625,355,000	.10	.50	—
1951S	136,010,000	.15	.75	—
1952	186,856,980	.10	.50	25.00
1952D	746,130,000	.10	.50	—
1952S	137,800,004	.15	1.00	—
1953	256,883,800	.10	.50	27.00
1953D	700,515,000	.10	.50	—
1953S	181,835,000	.15	.45	—

Date	Mintage	XF-40	MS-60	Prf-65
1954	71,873,350	.15	.75	15.00
1954D	251,552,500	.10	.35	—
1954S	96,190,000	.15	.35	—
1955	330,958,000	.10	.30	11.50
1955 doubled die	—	550.	1250.	—
1955D	563,257,500	.10	.30	—
1955S	44,610,000	.25	.60	—
1956	421,414,384	—	.30	2.50
1956D	1,098,201,100	—	.30	—
1957	283,787,952	—	.30	1.75
1957D	1,051,342,000	—	.30	—
1958	253,400,652	—	.30	2.50
1958D	800,953,300	—	.30	—

Lincoln Memorial reverse

Reverse designer: Frank Gasparro. **Weight:** 3.11 grams (1959-82) and 2.5 grams (1982-present). **Composition:** 95% copper, 5% tin and zinc (1959-62); 95% copper, 5% zinc (1962-82); and 97.6% zinc, 2.4% copper (1982-present). **Notes:** The dates were modified in 1960, 1970 and 1982, resulting in large-date and small-date varieties for those years. The 1972 "doubled die" shows doubling of "In God We Trust." The 1979-S Type II proof has a clearer mintmark than the Type I proof. Some 1982 cents have the predominantly copper composition; others have the predominantly zinc composition. They can be distinguished by weight. The 1983 "doubled die reverse" shows doubling of "United States of America." The 1984 "doubled die" shows doubling of Lincoln's ear on the obverse.

Date	Mintage	XF-40	MS-65	Prf-65
1959	610,864,291	—	.50	1.50
1959D	1,279,760,000	—	.50	—
1960 small date	588,096,602	1.50	2.50	16.00
1960 large date	Inc. Ab.	—	.30	1.00
1960D small date	1,580,884,000	—	.50	—
1960D large date	Inc. Ab.	—	.30	—
1961	756,373,244	—	.30	.90
1961D	1,753,266,700	—	.30	—
1962	609,263,019	—	.30	.90
1962D	1,793,148,400	—	.30	—
1963	757,185,645	—	.30	.90
1963D	1,774,020,400	—	.30	—
1964	2,652,525,762	—	.30	.90
1964D	3,799,071,500	—	.30	—
1965	1,497,224,900	—	.30	—
1966	2,188,147,783	—	.30	—
1967	3,048,667,100	—	.30	—
1968	1,707,880,970	—	.30	—
1968D	2,886,269,600	—	.40	—
1968S	261,311,510	—	.40	.80
1969	1,136,910,000	—	.60	—
1969D	4,002,832,200	—	.40	—
1969S	547,309,631	—	.40	.80
1970	1,898,315,000	—	.40	—
1970D	2,891,438,900	—	.40	—
1970S	693,192,814	—	.40	.80
1970S small date	—	—	45.00	55.00
1971	1,919,490,000	—	.35	—
1971D	2,911,045,600	—	.40	—
1971S	528,354,192	—	.20	.80
1972	2,933,255,000	—	.20	—
1972 doubled die	—	145.	400.	—
1972D	2,665,071,400	—	.20	—
1972S	380,200,104	—	.20	.90
1973	3,728,245,000	—	.15	—
1973D	3,549,576,588	—	.15	—
1973S	319,937,634	—	.20	.80
1974	4,232,140,523	—	.15	—
1974D	4,235,098,000	—	.15	—
1974S	412,039,228	—	.20	.75
1975	5,451,476,142	—	.15	—
1975D	4,505,245,300	—	.15	—
1975S	(2,845,450)	—	—	5.50
1976	4,674,292,426	—	.20	—
1976D	4,221,592,455	—	.20	—
1976S	(4,149,730)	—	—	4.50
1977	4,469,930,000	—	.20	—

Date	Mintage	XF-40	MS-65	Prf-65
1977D	4,149,062,300	—	.20	—
1977S	(3,251,152)	—	—	4.00
1978	5,558,605,000	—	.20	—
1978D	4,280,233,400	—	.20	—
1978S	(3,127,781)	—	—	3.00
1979	6,018,515,000	—	.20	—
1979D	4,139,357,254	—	.20	—
1979S T-I	(3,677,175)	—	—	3.00
1979S T-II	(Inc. Ab.)	—	—	4.00
1980	7,414,705,000	—	.20	—
1980D	5,140,098,660	—	.20	—
1980S	(3,554,806)	—	—	2.25
1981	7,491,750,000	—	.20	—
1981D	5,373,235,677	—	.20	—
1981S T-I	(4,063,083)	—	—	3.00
1981S T-II	(Inc. Ab.)	—	—	50.00
1982 copper lg.dt.	10,712,525,000	—	.20	—
1982 copper sm.dt.		—	.20	—
1982 zinc lg.dt.		—	.50	—
1982 zinc sm.dt.		—	1.00	—
1982D copper lg.dt.	6,012,979,368	—	.20	—
1982D zinc lg.dt.		—	.30	—
1982D zinc sm.dt.		—	.20	—
1982S	(3,857,479)	—	—	3.00
1983	7,752,355,000	—	.20	—
1983 doubled die	—	—	400.	—
1983D	6,467,199,428	—	.20	—
1983S	(3,279,126)	—	—	4.50
1984	8,151,079,000	—	.20	—
1984 doubled die	—	—	275.	—
1984D	5,569,238,906	—	.70	—
1984S	(3,065,110)	—	—	3.50
1985	5,648,489,887	—	.25	—
1985D	5,287,399,926	—	.20	—
1985S	(3,362,821)	—	—	4.50
1986	4,491,395,493	—	.70	—
1986D	4,442,866,698	—	.20	—
1986S	(3,010,497)	—	—	7.50
1987	4,682,466,931	—	.20	—
1987D	4,879,389,514	—	.20	—
1987S	(4,227,728)	—	—	4.00
1988	6,092,810,000	—	.20	—
1988D	5,253,740,443	—	.20	—
1988S	(3,262,948)	—	—	2.75
1989	7,261,535,000	—	.20	—
1989D	5,345,467,111	—	.20	—
1989S	(3,220,194)	—	—	2.75
1990	6,851,765,000	—	.20	—
1990D	4,922,894,533	—	.20	—

1955 doubled die

1972 doubled die

1983 doubled die

Small date

Large date

Large date

Small date

Large date

Small date

Date	Mintage	XF-40	MS-65	Prf-65
1990S	(3,299,559)	—	—	5.75
1990 no S	—	—	—	1250.
1991	5,165,940,000	—	.20	—
1991D	4,158,442,076	—	.20	—
1991S	(2,867,787)	—	—	7.50
1992	4,648,905,000	—	.20	—
1992D	4,448,673,300	—	.20	—
1992S	(4,176,560)	—	—	6.50
1993	5,684,705,000	—	.25	—
1993D	6,426,650,571	—	.25	—
1993S	(3,394,792)	—	—	9.50
1994	6,500,850,000	—	.20	—
1994D	7,131,765,000	—	.20	—
1994S	(3,269,923)	—	—	8.00
1995	6,411,440,000	—	.20	—

Date	Mintage	XF-40	MS-65	Prf-65
1995 doubled die	—	—	35.00	—
1995D	7,128,560,000	—	.15	—
1995S	—	—	—	9.50
1996	6,612,465,000	—	.15	—
1996D	6,510,795,000	—	.15	—
1996S	—	—	—	6.50
1997	4,622,800,000	—	.15	—
1997D	4,576,555,000	—	.15	—
1997S	(1,975,000)	—	—	7.00
1998	—	—	.15	—
1998D	—	—	.15	—
1998S	—	—	—	5.50
1999	—	—	.15	—
1999D	—	—	.15	—
1999S	—	—	—	—

PRICING SECTION

Two-cent

Small motto

Large motto

Designer: James B. Longacre. **Size:** 23 millimeters. **Weight:** 6.22 grams. **Composition:** 95% copper, 5% tin and zinc. **Notes:** The motto "In God We Trust" was modified in 1864, resulting in small-motto and large-motto varieties for that year.

Date	Mintage	G-4	VG-8	F-12	VF-20	XF-40	AU-50	MS-60	MS-65	Prf-65
1864 SM	19,847,500.	60.00	75.00	100.	150.	260.	325.	500.	1350.	45,000.
1864 LM	Inc. Ab.	9.50	11.00	18.00	23.00	33.00	55.00	70.00	420.	1400.
1865	13,640,000	9.50	11.00	18.00	24.00	33.00	59.00	70.00	460.	900.
1866	3,177,000	10.00	13.00	18.00	26.00	33.00	59.00	70.00	550.	900.
1867	2,938,750	11.00	13.00	18.00	25.00	33.00	60.00	95.00	500.	900.
1868	2,803,750	11.00	13.00	18.00	25.00	36.00	70.00	120.	550.	900.
1869	1,546,000	11.00	14.00	18.00	30.00	40.00	80.00	120.	550.	900.
1870	861,250	12.00	13.00	25.00	37.00	64.00	90.00	185.	600.	900.
1871	721,250	13.00	16.00	27.00	40.00	75.00	115.	175.	600.	900.
1872	65,000	90.00	130.	175.	250.	380.	550.	775.	2400.	925.
1873	Est. 1100		Proof only	900.	925.	950.	975.	—	—	1700.

Silver three-cent

Type I

Designer: James B. Longacre. **Size:** 14 millimeters. **Weight:** 0.8 grams. **Composition:** 75% silver (0.0193 ounces), 25% copper. **Notes:** The Type I design has no outlines in the star.

Date	Mintage	G-4	VG-8	F-12	VF-20	XF-40	AU-50	MS-60	MS-65	Prf-65
1851	5,447,400	15.00	17.00	25.00	30.00	65.00	125.	145.	1000.	—
1851O	720,000	19.00	24.00	40.00	56.00	130.	210.	280.	2000.	—
1852	18,663,500	15.00	17.00	25.00	30.00	65.00	125.	145.	1000.	—
1853	11,400,000	15.00	17.00	25.00	30.00	65.00	125.	145.	1000.	—

Type II

Weight: 0.75 grams. **Composition:** 90% silver (0.0218 ounces), 10% copper. **Notes:** The Type II design has three lines outlining the star.

1851-O Silver Three-Cent Piece
Grade XF-40

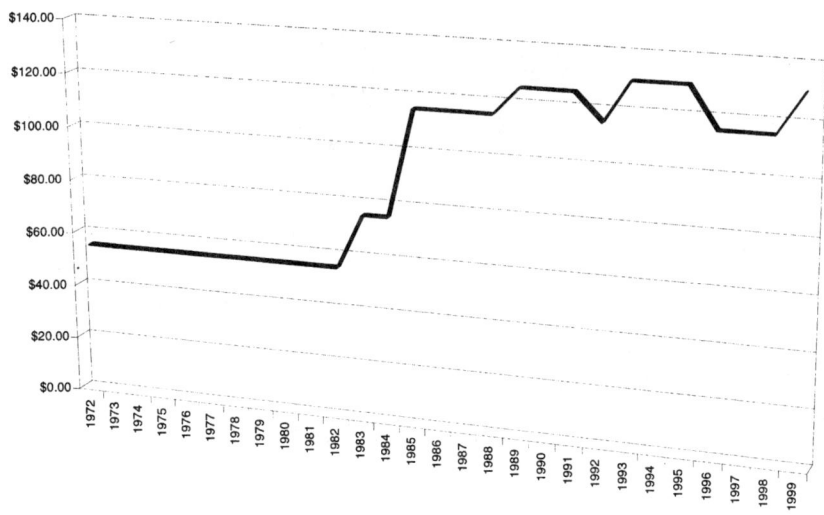

Source: COIN PRICES

Date	Mintage	G-4	VG-8	F-12	VF-20	XF-40	AU-50	MS-60	MS-65	Prf-65
1854	671,000	17.00	19.00	26.00	40.00	95.00	215.	315.	2750.	20,500.
1855	139,000	21.00	32.00	48.00	85.00	145.	265.	460.	8650.	13,500.
1856	1,458,000	17.00	19.00	26.00	44.00	85.00	170.	260.	4100.	13,500.
1857	1,042,000	17.00	19.00	27.00	43.00	85.00	230.	275.	2750.	12,500.
1858	1,604,000	17.00	19.00	26.00	40.00	85.00	170.	240.	3200.	6200.

Type III

Notes: The Type III design has two lines outlining the star.

Date	Mintage	G-4	VG-8	F-12	VF-20	XF-40	AU-50	MS-60	MS-65	Prf-65
1859	365,000	16.00	19.00	26.00	38.00	65.00	125.	150.	1050.	2100.
1860	287,000	17.00	19.00	26.00	38.00	68.00	125.	150.	1050.	4000.
1861	498,000	16.00	19.00	26.00	35.00	65.00	125.	150.	1050.	1900.
1862	343,550	17.00	20.00	26.00	45.00	65.00	125.	150.	1050.	1500.
1863	21,460	260.	285.	295.	315.	350.	440.	600.	1925.	1500.
1864	12,470	260.	285.	295.	315.	350.	440.	565.	1500.	1350.
1865	8,500	310.	335.	360.	385.	410.	450.	595.	1400.	1250.
1866	22,725	260.	285.	295.	315.	350.	385.	565.	1625.	1200.
1867	4,625	310.	335.	360.	385.	410.	450.	595.	2400.	1200.
1868	4,100	310.	335.	360.	385.	410.	450.	595.	4800.	1300.
1869	5,100	310.	335.	360.	385.	410.	450.	595.	1400.	1400.
1870	4,000	310.	335.	360.	385.	410.	440.	750.	4600.	1275.
1871	4,360	310.	375.	410.	420.	435.	460.	600.	1450.	1275.
1872	1,950	335.	360.	385.	430.	460.	575.	690.	4600.	1275.
1873	600		Proof only	600.	675.	700.	730.	—	—	1400.

Nickel three-cent

Designer: James B. Longacre. **Size:** 17.9 millimeters. **Weight:** 1.94 grams. **Composition:** 75% copper, 25% nickel.

Date	Mintage	G-4	VG-8	F-12	VF-20	XF-40	AU-50	MS-60	MS-65	Prf-65
1865	11,382,000	9.50	10.50	11.50	14.50	20.00	45.00	83.00	750.	4300.
1866	4,801,000	9.50	10.50	11.50	14.50	20.00	45.00	83.00	750.	1300.
1867	3,915,000	9.50	10.50	11.50	14.50	20.00	45.00	83.00	750.	1200.
1868	3,252,000	9.50	10.50	11.50	14.50	20.00	45.00	83.00	750.	1300.
1869	1,604,000	10.00	11.00	12.00	14.50	20.00	47.50	100.	750.	850.
1870	1,335,000	10.00	11.50	13.50	17.50	23.00	47.50	110.	765.	1175.
1871	604,000	10.00	11.50	12.00	15.00	23.00	48.00	115.	760.	950.
1872	862,000	10.00	11.50	12.50	15.00	20.00	45.00	120.	1150.	850.
1873	1,173,000	10.00	12.00	13.00	15.50	22.00	45.00	115.	1250.	825.
1874	790,000	10.00	12.00	13.00	15.00	20.00	50.00	120.	1150.	750.
1875	228,000	10.00	12.00	13.50	17.00	30.00	65.00	150.	750.	1500.
1876	162,000	10.50	14.50	17.00	25.00	38.00	90.00	175.	1800.	875.
1877	Est. 900		Proof only	900.	950.	1000.	1050.	—	—	1800.
1878	2,350		Proof only	445.	455.	475.	485.	—	—	650.
1879	41,200	45.00	52.00	62.00	70.00	80.00	120.	240.	800.	540.
1880	24,955	63.00	75.00	90.00	100.	125.	150.	265.	725.	535.
1881	1,080,575	9.50	10.50	11.50	14.50	20.00	45.00	83.00	725.	550.
1882	25,300	68.00	75.00	84.00	95.00	115.	140.	250.	1000.	525.
1883	10,609	130.	145.	175.	200.	240.	260.	375.	3550.	535.
1884	5,642	290.	330.	400.	415.	430.	450.	525.	4450.	545.
1885	4,790	350.	380.	425.	460.	500.	600.	725.	1950.	675.
1886	4,290		Proof only	—	275.	325.	350.	—	—	490.
1887/6	7,961		Proof only	—	325.	360.	400.	—	—	625.
1887	Inc. Ab.	230.	250.	270.	285.	330.	375.	440.	975.	800.
1888	41,083	36.00	43.00	48.00	52.00	65.00	110.	235.	775.	550.
1889	21,561	63.00	70.00	85.00	100.	115.	135.	260.	850.	550.

Half dimes

Flowing Hair

Designer: Robert Scot. **Size:** 16.5 millimeters. **Weight:** 1.35 grams. **Composition:** 89.24% silver (0.0388 ounces), 10.76% copper.

Date	Mintage	G-4	VG-8	F-12	VF-20	XF-40	MS-60
1794	86,416	750.	875.	1150.	1750.	2950.	6700.
1795	Inc. Ab.	540.	2750.	900.	1200.	2200.	4500.

Draped Bust

Small-eagle reverse

Designer: Robert Scot. **Size:** 16.5 millimeters. **Weight:** 1.35 grams. **Composition:** 89.24% silver (0.0388 ounces), 10.76% copper. **Notes:** Some 1796 strikes have "Liberty" spelled as "Libekty." The 1797 strikes have either 13, 15 or 16 stars on the obverse.

Date	Mintage	G-4	VG-8	F-12	VF-20	XF-40	MS-60
1796	10,230	750.	850.	1175.	1950.	3250.	6500.
1796 "Liberty"	Inc. Ab.	750.	850.	1200.	1950.	3350.	6750.
1796/5	Inc. Ab.	1000.	1475.	2250.	5250.	8500.	14,250.
1797 13 stars	44,527	950.	1175.	1575.	2650.	4250.	8250.
1797 15 stars	Inc. Ab.	670.	925.	1350.	2150.	3650.	5650.
1797 16 stars	Inc. Ab.	850.	1000.	1400.	2200.	3950.	5800.

Heraldic-eagle reverse

Notes: Some 1800 strikes have "Liberty" spelled as "Likerty."

Date	Mintage	G-4	VG-8	F-12	VF-20	XF-40	MS-60
1800	24,000	625.	700.	1050.	1400.	2400.	5050.
1800 "Libekty"	Inc. Ab.	675.	750.	1100.	1500.	2600.	5050.
1801	33,910	700.	800.	1075.	1500.	2650.	10,000.
1802	13,010	9500.	13,500.	20,000.	35,000.	60,000.	—
1803	37,850	625.	700.	1050.	1400.	2400.	5050.
1805	15,600	725.	825.	1125.	1550.	2750.	—

Liberty Cap

Designer: William Kneass. **Size:** 15.5 millimeters. **Weight:** 1.35 grams. **Composition:** 89.24% silver (0.0388 ounces), 10.76% copper. **Notes:** Design modifications in 1835, 1836 and 1837 resulted in variety combinations with large and small dates, and large and small "5C." inscriptions on the reverse.

Date	Mintage	G-4	VG-8	F-12	VF-20	XF-40	AU-50	MS-60	MS-65
1829	1,230,000	15.00	25.00	29.00	50.00	125.	225.	270.	2850.
1830	1,240,000	15.00	25.00	29.00	50.00	125.	225.	270.	2850.
1831	1,242,700	15.00	25.00	29.00	50.00	125.	225.	270.	2850.
1832	965,000	15.00	25.00	29.00	50.00	125.	300.	450.	7000.
1833	1,370,000	15.00	25.00	29.00	50.00	125.	230.	325.	3500.
1834	1,480,000	15.00	25.00	29.00	50.00	125.	225.	270.	2850.
1835 lg.dt., lg. 5C.	2,760,000	15.00	25.00	29.00	50.00	125.	240.	270.	2850.
1835 lg.dt., sm. 5C.	Inc. Ab.	15.00	25.00	29.00	50.00	125.	220.	270.	2850.

1802 Half Dime
Grade F-12

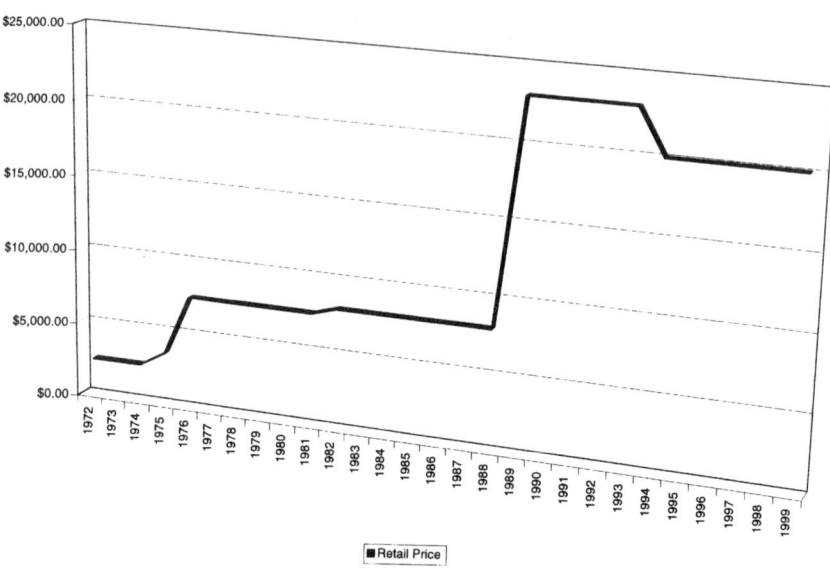

Source: COIN PRICES

Date	Mintage	G-4	VG-8	F-12	VF-20	XF-40	AU-50	MS-60	MS-65
1835 sm.dt., lg. 5C.									
	Inc. Ab.	15.00	25.00	29.00	50.00	125.	225.	270.	2850.
1835 sm.dt., sm. 5C.									
	Inc. Ab.	15.00	25.00	29.00	50.00	125.	225.	270.	2850.
1836 lg. 5C.	1,900,000	15.00	25.00	29.00	50.00	125.	225.	270.	2850.
1836 sm. 5C.	Inc. Ab.	15.00	25.00	29.00	50.00	125.	225.	270.	2850.
1837 lg. 5C.	2,276,000	15.00	25.00	29.00	50.00	125.	225.	270.	2850.
1837 sm. 5C.	Inc. Ab.	25.00	40.00	50.00	80.00	160.	350.	1250.	8500.

Seated Liberty

No stars around rim

Designer: Christian Gobrecht. **Size:** 15.5 millimeters. **Weight:** 1.34 grams. **Composition:** 90% silver (0.0388 ounces), 10% copper. **Notes:** A design modification in 1837 resulted in small-date and large-date varieties for that year.

Date	Mintage	G-4	VG-8	F-12	VF-20	XF-40	AU-50	MS-60	MS-65
1837 sm. dt.	Inc. Ab.	25.00	35.00	53.00	100.	210.	375.	600.	3400.
1837 lg. dt.	Inc. Ab.	25.00	35.00	53.00	100.	210.	375.	600.	3400.
1838O	70,000	70.00	110.	225.	400.	750.	1450.	—	—

1846 Half Dime Grade XF-40

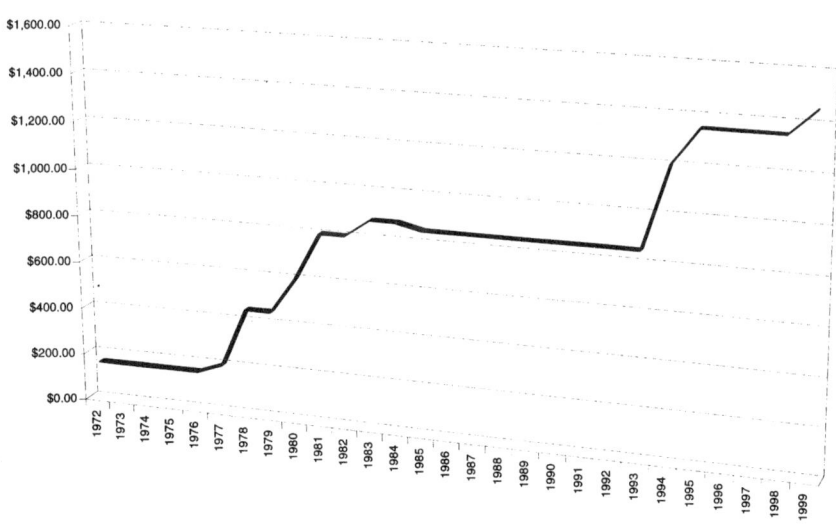

■ Retail Price

Source: COIN PRICES

Stars around rim

Notes: The two varieties of 1838 are distinguished by the size of the stars on the obverse. The 1839-O with reverse of 1838-O was struck from rusted reverse dies. The result is a bumpy surface on this variety's reverse.

Date	Mintage	G-4	VG-8	F-12	VF-20	XF-40	AU-50	MS-60	MS-65
1838 lg.stars	2,255,000	9.25	9.50	12.50	25.00	65.00	150.	240.	1900.
1838 sm.stars	Inc. Ab.	20.00	30.00	50.00	125.	225.	285.	750.	4150.
1839	1,069,150	9.50	11.00	13.00	29.00	70.00	150.	240.	1900.
1839O	1,034,039	10.00	12.00	16.00	31.00	75.00	200.	350.	2000.
1839O rev. 1838O	—	375.	575.	750.	1200.	2250.	3500.	—	—
1840	1,344,085	9.25	9.50	13.00	21.00	65.00	140.	225.	1800.
1840O	935,000	10.00	15.00	24.00	50.00	85.00	225.	600.	10,500.

Drapery added to Liberty

Notes: In 1840 drapery was added to Liberty's left elbow. Varieties for the 1848 Philadelphia strikes are distinguished by the size of the numerals in the date.

Date	Mintage	G-4	VG-8	F-12	VF-20	XF-40	AU-50	MS-60	MS-65
1840	Inc. Ab.	20.00	32.50	50.00	75.00	150.	250.	700.	6500.
1840O	Inc. Ab.	30.00	50.00	80.00	125.	325.	950.	—	—
1841	1,150,000	9.25	9.50	12.00	22.00	55.00	90.00	130.	1150.
1841O	815,000	10.00	15.00	22.50	40.00	85.00	200.	650.	—
1842	815,000	9.25	9.50	12.00	22.00	55.00	90.00	130.	1150.
1842O	350,000	28.00	40.00	65.00	185.	600.	1500.	—	—
1843	1,165,000	9.25	9.50	12.00	18.00	41.00	95.00	130.	1150.
1844	430,000	10.00	12.00	14.00	24.00	60.00	110.	165.	1150.
1844O	220,000	60.00	95.00	175.	350.	950.	2200.	—	—
1845	1,564,000	9.25	9.50	12.00	22.00	44.00	95.00	130.	1150.
1845/1845	Inc. Ab.	9.25	9.50	12.00	22.00	44.00	95.00	130.	1150.
1846	27,000	225.	325.	450.	700.	1450.	3000.	—	—
1847	1,274,000	9.25	9.50	12.00	18.00	55.00	95.00	130.	1150.
1848 med. date	668,000	9.50	10.00	12.00	32.00	60.00	125.	225.	2250.
1848 lg. date	Inc. Ab.	15.00	20.00	30.00	50.00	100.	225.	425.	2250.
1848O	600,000	12.00	17.50	25.00	43.00	90.00	225.	450.	2250.
1849/8	1,309,000	12.00	17.50	25.00	45.00	100.	180.	375.	1800.
1849/6	Inc. Ab.	10.00	14.00	20.00	35.00	75.00	175.	350.	1800.
1849	Inc. Ab.	9.25	9.50	12.00	18.00	45.00	95.00	250.	1500.
1849O	140,000	22.00	40.00	75.00	145.	450.	800.	1775.	16,000.
1850	955,000	9.25	9.50	12.00	18.00	41.00	115.	150.	1500.
1850O	690,000	11.00	16.00	22.50	50.00	100.	350.	800.	4000.
1851	781,000	9.25	9.50	12.00	18.00	50.00	110.	150.	1500.
1851O	860,000	10.00	15.00	25.00	35.00	75.00	165.	600.	2250.
1852	1,000,500	9.25	9.50	12.50	18.00	41.00	100.	130.	1150.
1852O	260,000	23.00	35.00	60.00	100.	275.	675.	1200.	—
1853	135,000	30.00	40.00	60.00	90.00	185.	350.	600.	8500.
1853O	160,000	135.	190.	275.	550.	1200.	3000.	—	—

Arrows at date

Weight: 1.24 grams. **Composition:** 90% silver (0.0362 ounces), 10% copper.

Date	Mintage	G-4	VG-8	F-12	VF-20	XF-40	AU-50	MS-60	MS-65	Prf-65
1853	13,210,020	7.50	8.00	12.50	17.00	50.00	100.	160.	2000.	20,000.
1853O	2,200,000	9.25	9.50	15.00	35.00	75.00	125.	325.	—	—
1854	5,740,000	8.00	9.00	12.50	17.00	50.00	135.	250.	4550.	20,000.
1854O	1,560,000	9.50	10.00	12.50	25.00	60.00	175.	700.	—	—
1855	1,750,000	9.50	10.00	12.50	20.00	55.00	135.	250.	5000.	20,000.
1855O	600,000	15.00	20.00	25.00	55.00	125.	325.	1000.	—	—

Arrows at date removed

Notes: On the 1858/inverted date variety, the date was engraved into the die upside down and then re-engraved right side up. Another 1858 variety has the date doubled.

Date	Mintage	G-4	VG-8	F-12	VF-20	XF-40	AU-50	MS-60	MS-65	Prf-65
1856	4,880,000	9.50	10.00	12.50	18.00	41.00	90.00	200.	1550.	22,500.
1856O	1,100,000	9.50	10.00	12.50	27.00	70.00	200.	600.	—	—
1857	7,280,000	8.00	9.00	12.50	15.00	45.00	90.00	200.	1550.	5000.
1857O	1,380,000	9.50	11.50	13.00	25.00	65.00	200.	450.	—	—
1858	3,500,000	9.25	9.50	12.50	18.00	45.00	75.00	145.	1550.	9000.
1858 inverted date										
	Inc. Ab.	30.00	40.00	65.00	115.	200.	325.	500.	—	—
1858 doubled date										
	Inc. Ab.	45.00	60.00	90.00	175.	285.	425.	700.	—	—
1858O	1,660,000	9.50	11.50	14.00	26.00	65.00	190.	265.	—	—
1859	340,000	9.50	12.00	15.00	33.00	85.00	145.	225.	1550.	5000.
1859O	560,000	9.25	10.00	13.00	30.00	80.00	175.	350.	—	—

Transitional patterns

Notes: These non-circulation pieces were struck as experiments in transferring the legend "United States of America" from the reverse to the obverse.

Date	Mintage	G-4	VG-8	F-12	VF-20	XF-40	AU-50	MS-60	MS-65	Prf-65
1859 obverse of 1859, reverse 1860						—	—	—	—	17,500.
1860 obverse of 1859, reverse 1860						—	—	4000.	8500.	—

Obverse legend

Notes: In 1860 the legend "United States of America" replaced the stars on the obverse.

Date	Mintage	G-4	VG-8	F-12	VF-20	XF-40	AU-50	MS-60	MS-65	Prf-65
1860	799,000	10.00	12.00	15.00	25.00	45.00	70.00	145.	1150.	2150.
1860O	1,060,000	9.00	10.00	15.00	30.00	55.00	85.00	350.	3550.	—
1861	3,361,000	8.00	9.50	12.50	14.00	28.00	57.00	145.	1150.	1650.
1861/0	Inc. Ab.	20.00	30.00	50.00	90.00	150.	275.	450.	—	—
1862	1,492,550	8.00	9.50	12.50	16.00	30.00	57.00	145.	1150.	1650.
1863	18,460	135.	165.	200.	260.	375.	500.	650.	1500.	1400.
1863S	100,000	18.00	25.00	35.00	65.00	125.	250.	900.	—	—
1864	48,470	275.	315.	375.	500.	625.	700.	950.	2750.	1500.
1864S	90,000	32.00	45.00	65.00	95.00	200.	425.	850.	—	—
1865	13,500	275.	300.	345.	425.	500.	700.	900.	2500.	1400.
1865S	120,000	22.00	28.00	37.00	60.00	110.	300.	900.	—	—
1866	10,725	215.	250.	300.	450.	525.	600.	1000.	2400.	1400.
1866S	120,000	19.00	24.00	29.00	50.00	115.	300.	800.	6000.	—
1867	8,625	350.	400.	475.	550.	625.	765.	975.	2750.	1500.
1867S	120,000	19.00	27.00	40.00	60.00	115.	300.	825.	—	—
1868	89,200	30.00	60.00	95.00	135.	195.	300.	475.	2400.	1400.
1868S	280,000	9.50	15.00	20.00	30.00	60.00	150.	325.	—	—
1869	208,600	10.00	15.00	30.00	40.00	75.00	125.	235.	4900.	1650.
1869S	230,000	10.00	14.00	20.00	33.00	60.00	150.	325.	—	—
1870	536,600	9.50	10.00	12.50	17.00	35.00	125.	175.	1200.	1650.
1870S			Unique, Superior Galleries, July 1986, B.U., $253,000.							
1871	1,873,960	9.25	9.50	12.50	14.00	28.00	65.00	150.	1100.	1650.
1871S	161,000	16.00	22.00	30.00	55.00	95.00	135.	350.	3200.	—
1872	2,947,950	8.00	9.00	12.50	14.00	25.00	65.00	150.	1100.	1650.
1872S mint mark in wreath	837,000	10.00	15.00	20.00	30.00	45.00	65.00	155.	1100.	—
1872S mint mark below wreath	Inc. Ab.	10.00	15.00	20.00	30.00	35.00	65.00	150.	1100.	—
1873	712,600	10.00	12.00	15.00	24.00	40.00	70.00	200.	1500.	3500.
1873S	324,000	15.00	19.00	22.00	40.00	60.00	90.00	250.	1750.	—

Nickel five-cent

Shield

With rays   Without rays

Designer: James B. Longacre. **Size:** 20.5 millimeters. **Weight:** 5 grams. **Composition:** 75% copper, 25% nickel. **Notes:** In 1867 the rays between the stars on the reverse were eliminated, resulting in varieties with and without rays for that year.

Date	Mintage	G-4	VG-8	F-12	VF-20	XF-40	AU-50	MS-60	MS-65	Prf-65
1866	14,742,500	15.00	18.00	22.00	35.00	95.00	140.	225.	2100.	3400.
1867 w/rays	2,019,000	16.00	19.00	25.00	38.00	125.	185.	290.	2900.	75,000.
1867 w/o rays	28,890,500	10.00	11.00	15.00	17.50	34.00	55.00	90.00	600.	2300.
1868	28,817,000	10.00	11.00	15.00	17.50	34.00	55.00	90.00	600.	1150.
1869	16,395,000	10.00	12.00	15.00	18.00	35.00	55.00	90.00	600.	940.
1870	4,806,000	11.00	13.00	17.50	20.00	38.00	60.00	100.	800.	1075.
1871	561,000	30.00	40.00	50.00	65.00	120.	165.	260.	1200.	900.
1872	6,036,000	11.00	13.00	17.00	23.00	40.00	65.00	115.	850.	700.
1873	4,550,000	11.00	14.00	18.00	30.00	40.00	67.50	125.	900.	675.
1874	3,538,000	11.00	14.00	25.00	30.00	55.00	70.00	125.	850.	950.
1875	2,097,000	14.00	16.00	30.00	40.00	65.00	85.00	150.	1900.	1650.
1876	2,530,000	13.00	15.00	25.00	35.00	57.50	80.00	125.	825.	850.
1877	Est. 900		Proof only	—	1100.	1150.	1200.	—	—	2000.
1878	2,350		Proof only	500.	540.	580.	600.	—	—	700.
1879	29,100	245.	285.	345.	390.	440.	455.	600.	1500.	700.
1880	19,995	275.	375.	370.	430.	470.	495.	540.	4400.	650.
1881	72,375	140.	165.	220.	240.	330.	365.	535.	1200.	550.
1882	11,476,600	10.00	12.00	15.00	17.50	35.00	59.00	90.00	625.	625.
1883	1,456,919	11.00	13.00	15.00	19.00	35.00	59.00	90.00	625.	625.
1883/2	—	65.00	88.00	130.	165.	235.	300.	415.	2950.	—

Liberty

With "Cents"   No "Cents"

Designer: Charles E. Barber. **Size:** 21.2 millimeters. **Weight:** 5 grams. **Composition:** 75% copper, 25% nickel. **Notes:** In 1883 the word "Cents" was added to the reverse, resulting in varieties with "Cents" and without "Cents" for that year.

Date	Mintage	G-4	VG-8	F-12	VF-20	XF-40	AU-50	MS-60	MS-65	Prf-65
1883 NC	5,479,519	3.75	4.25	4.75	5.50	7.50	12.00	29.00	250.	1150.
1883 WC	16,032,983	9.00	11.00	14.00	24.00	40.00	65.00	90.00	485.	550.
1884	11,273,942	12.00	15.00	18.50	25.00	42.00	75.00	125.	750.	525.
1885	1,476,490	260.	280.	350.	425.	600.	695.	800.	2200.	860.
1886	3,330,290	80.00	110.	150.	205.	280.	370.	485.	2150.	525.
1887	15,263,652	7.50	11.00	18.50	24.00	43.00	65.00	95.00	540.	520.
1888	10,720,483	13.00	17.00	25.00	45.00	70.00	91.00	170.	750.	515.
1889	15,881,361	5.50	8.50	17.00	20.00	39.00	65.00	94.00	525.	535.
1890	16,259,272	5.50	10.00	17.00	21.00	38.00	67.00	100.	850.	595.
1891	16,834,350	5.00	7.00	13.00	19.00	38.00	65.00	94.00	850.	525.
1892	11,699,642	5.00	7.25	14.00	19.50	39.00	68.00	120.	775.	520.
1893	13,370,195	4.00	5.00	12.50	18.50	35.00	65.00	95.00	700.	525.
1894	5,413,132	7.50	12.00	50.00	75.00	140.	155.	200.	800.	535.
1895	9,979,884	3.00	4.00	15.00	22.50	40.00	65.00	120.	875.	600.
1896	8,842,920	5.50	9.00	19.50	28.00	44.00	75.00	120.	1050.	575.
1897	20,428,735	2.00	3.00	7.50	12.50	25.00	50.00	80.00	740.	490.
1898	12,532,087	2.00	3.50	7.50	13.00	33.00	55.00	90.00	700.	490.
1899	26,029,031	1.35	1.75	5.50	10.00	21.00	47.50	80.00	480.	490.
1900	27,255,995	1.20	1.65	5.00	9.00	19.00	52.00	65.00	480.	490.
1901	26,480,213	1.20	2.25	5.50	8.50	20.00	40.00	60.00	480.	450.
1902	31,480,579	1.20	2.25	4.25	8.00	19.00	40.00	60.00	480.	450.
1903	28,006,725	1.20	2.35	4.25	8.00	20.00	40.00	60.00	480.	450.
1904	21,404,984	1.20	1.50	4.25	9.00	21.00	40.00	60.00	480.	590.
1905	29,827,276	1.20	1.40	4.00	7.75	19.00	40.00	60.00	480.	490.
1906	38,613,725	1.20	1.40	4.00	7.75	20.00	40.00	60.00	490.	490.
1907	39,214,800	1.20	1.40	4.00	7.50	19.00	39.00	60.00	550.	550.
1908	22,686,177	1.20	1.40	4.50	8.00	20.00	38.00	60.00	600.	450.
1909	11,590,526	1.50	2.50	5.00	9.00	23.00	40.00	75.00	600.	490.
1910	30,169,353	1.20	1.40	4.00	7.50	19.00	40.00	60.00	550.	490.
1911	39,559,372	1.20	1.40	4.00	7.50	19.00	38.00	60.00	480.	490.
1912	26,236,714	1.20	1.40	4.00	7.50	19.00	38.00	60.00	480.	490.
1912D	8,474,000	1.40	1.75	6.00	18.00	48.00	125.	225.	900.	—
1912S	238,000	43.00	57.00	85.00	225.	450.	650.	800.	2250.	—

1913 Only 5 known, Eliasberg Sale, May 1996, Prf, $1,485,000.

1884 Nickel Five-Cent
Grade F-12

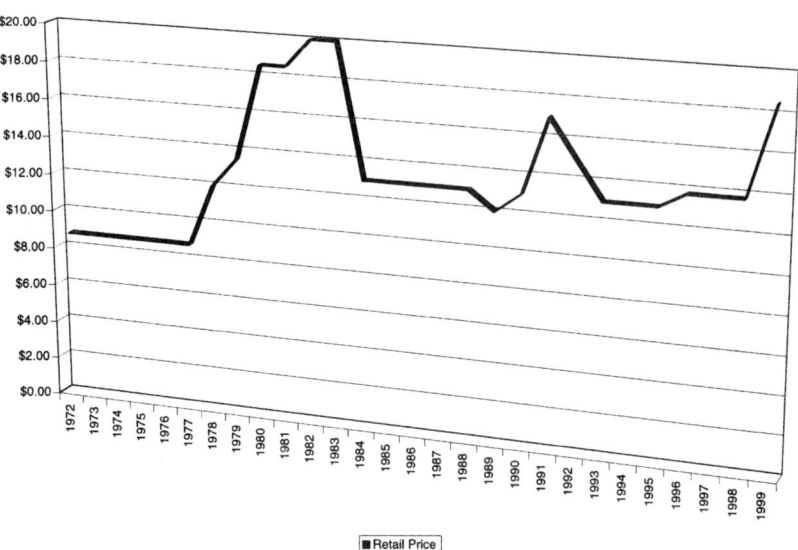

■ Retail Price

Source: COIN PRICES

BUFFALO NICKELS

Mound type

Designer: James Earle Fraser. **Size:** 21.2 millimeters. **Weight:** 5 grams. **Composition:** 75% copper, 25% nickel.

Date	Mintage	G-4	VG-8	F-12	VF-20	XF-40	AU-50	MS-60	MS-65	Prf-65
1913	30,993,520	5.50	6.00	6.50	8.00	14.00	21.00	32.00	110.	2000.
1913D	5,337,000	8.75	10.50	12.50	16.00	25.00	40.00	50.00	215.	—
1913S	2,105,000	15.00	17.00	22.00	30.00	45.00	59.00	65.00	600.	—

Line type

Notes: In 1913 the reverse design was modified so the ground under the buffalo was represented as a line rather than a mound. On the 1937-D 3-legged variety, the buffalo's right front leg is missing, the result of a damaged die.

1921-S Nickel
Grade F-12

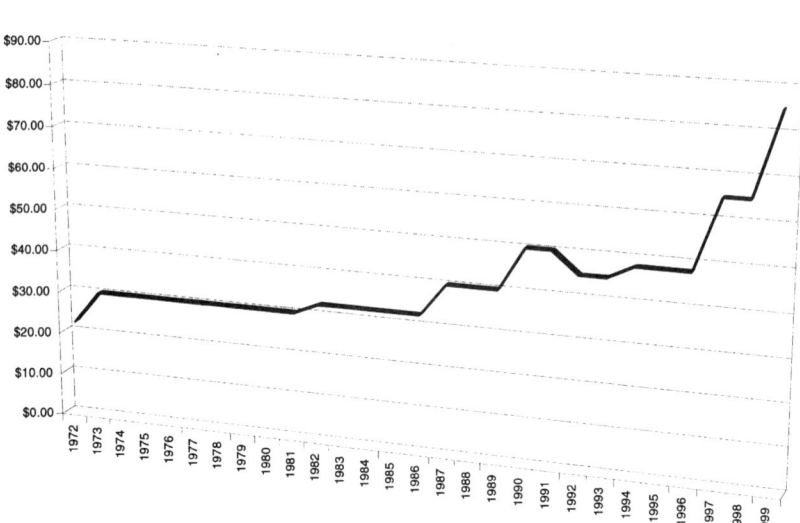

■ Retail Price

Source: COIN PRICES

Date	Mintage	G-4	VG-8	F-12	VF-20	XF-40	AU-50	MS-60	MS-65	Prf-65
1913	29,858,700	6.50	7.50	9.00	11.00	15.00	23.00	32.50	275.	1400.
1913D	4,156,000	49.00	60.00	70.00	80.00	90.00	110.	155.	800.	—
1913S	1,209,000	100.	140.	170.	185.	210.	260.	325.	2700.	—
1914	20,665,738	9.50	11.00	12.50	20.00	25.00	35.00	45.00	340.	1300.
1914D	3,912,000	45.00	55.00	70.00	80.00	120.	140.	195.	1400.	—
1914S	3,470,000	9.50	12.00	20.00	28.00	45.00	75.00	130.	1650.	—
1915	20,987,270	4.75	5.50	7.00	10.50	17.50	35.00	45.00	250.	1250.
1915D	7,569,500	12.50	15.50	29.00	39.00	70.00	90.00	190.	1850.	—
1915S	1,505,000	16.00	25.00	59.50	85.00	160.	260.	450.	2150.	—
1916	63,498,066	2.50	2.75	3.50	5.50	11.00	20.00	39.00	260.	2200.
1916/16	Inc. Ab.	1700.	3350.	5000.	8000.	11,500.	17,000.	28,000.	100,000.	—
1916D	13,333,000	8.50	11.00	16.50	28.00	58.00	80.00	130.	1600.	—
1916S	11,860,000	5.00	8.00	13.50	25.00	55.00	80.00	155.	2200.	—
1917	51,424,029	2.40	3.00	5.00	9.00	17.50	35.00	48.00	475.	—
1917D	9,910,800	9.00	14.00	30.00	65.00	100.	160.	280.	2750.	—
1917S	4,193,000	10.00	15.00	33.00	70.00	120.	250.	340.	2900.	—
1918	32,086,314	1.90	3.25	5.50	12.50	28.00	45.00	85.00	1300.	—

1918/17-D

Date	Mintage	G-4	VG-8	F-12	VF-20	XF-40	AU-50	MS-60	MS-65	Prf-65
1918/17D	8,362,314	390.	600.	1050.	2150.	4900.	8950.	13,000.	215,000.	—
1918D	Inc. Ab.	9.00	13.50	33.00	80.00	160.	255.	340.	4000.	—
1918S	4,882,000	9.00	16.00	30.00	79.00	160.	250.	390.	25,000.	—
1919	60,868,000	1.30	1.60	2.50	6.50	15.00	35.00	45.00	440.	—
1919D	8,006,000	10.00	16.50	38.00	89.00	175.	295.	475.	4400.	—
1919S	7,521,000	5.50	13.00	30.00	80.00	190.	310.	440.	10,000.	—
1920	63,093,000	1.00	1.50	2.25	7.00	15.00	35.00	45.00	650.	—
1920D	9,418,000	6.50	16.00	35.00	85.00	240.	300.	420.	4200.	—
1920S	9,689,000	3.50	6.50	18.50	75.00	175.	275.	360.	15,750.	—

Date	Mintage	G-4	VG-8	F-12	VF-20	XF-40	AU-50	MS-60	MS-65	Prf-65
1921	10,663,000	2.00	3.00	4.50	17.50	40.00	57.50	100.	620.	—
1921S	1,557,000	27.50	49.50	85.00	395.	725.	950.	1350.	5300.	—
1923	35,715,000	1.40	1.75	3.00	7.50	15.00	30.00	43.00	475.	—
1923S	6,142,000	3.00	6.00	16.50	90.00	250.	300.	385.	7500.	—
1924	21,620,000	1.25	1.90	3.00	8.00	20.00	35.00	62.00	600.	—
1924D	5,258,000	3.50	6.00	17.50	65.00	180.	250.	315.	3200.	—
1924S	1,437,000	7.00	16.00	69.50	400.	1100.	1375.	1850.	7600.	—
1925	35,565,100	2.25	2.50	3.50	8.00	15.00	36.00	40.00	500.	—
1925D	4,450,000	8.00	17.00	39.50	80.00	165.	245.	340.	3200.	—
1925S	6,256,000	3.00	9.00	17.50	69.00	175.	250.	340.	32,000.	—
1926	44,693,000	.75	.95	1.50	6.00	14.50	25.00	35.00	150.	—
1926D	5,638,000	4.00	9.50	29.00	85.00	160.	210.	240.	3050.	—
1926S	970,000	10.00	18.00	50.00	325.	700.	1350.	2650.	36,500.	—
1927	37,981,000	.80	1.00	1.50	5.00	12.50	25.00	30.00	190.	—
1927D	5,730,000	2.00	4.90	8.00	30.00	80.00	125.	160.	4000.	—
1927S	3,430,000	1.35	2.00	4.60	25.00	80.00	160.	450.	14,000.	—
1928	23,411,000	1.10	1.25	1.50	7.00	15.00	30.00	35.00	240.	—
1928D	6,436,000	1.35	2.50	6.00	17.50	35.00	45.00	49.00	600.	—
1928S	6,936,000	1.35	1.50	2.75	10.00	25.00	100.	200.	3500.	—
1929	36,446,000	.80	1.00	1.50	7.00	13.00	25.00	34.00	270.	—
1929D	8,370,000	1.25	1.25	2.00	8.00	35.00	45.00	55.00	1450.	—
1929S	7,754,000	.80	.90	1.25	3.00	12.00	30.00	45.00	375.	—
1930	22,849,000	.75	.85	1.50	4.00	9.00	20.00	27.00	125.	—
1930S	5,435,000	.85	1.00	2.00	4.00	10.00	30.00	43.00	450.	—
1931S	1,200,000	4.00	4.25	4.75	6.50	18.50	33.00	43.00	200.	—
1934	20,213,003	.70	.75	1.00	5.00	10.00	19.00	25.00	325.	—
1934D	7,480,000	.80	1.00	1.85	7.50	18.50	35.00	42.00	1000.	—
1935	58,264,000	.65	.80	1.00	2.75	4.50	9.50	17.00	100.	—
1935D	12,092,000	.70	.90	2.00	6.00	18.00	35.00	40.00	350.	—
1935S	10,300,000	.70	.80	1.00	2.90	5.50	15.00	30.00	150.	—
1936	119,001,420	.65	.75	.85	1.60	3.50	8.50	14.00	90.00	900.
1936D	24,814,000	.65	.75	.85	2.00	5.50	12.50	19.00	105.	—
1936S	14,930,000	.70	.75	.85	2.00	3.50	12.00	19.00	95.00	—
1937	79,485,769	.65	.75	.85	1.60	3.50	8.50	14.00	45.00	750.
1937D	17,826,000	.65	.75	.85	1.75	3.75	9.50	14.00	60.00	—
1937D 3 Leg.	Inc. Ab.	160.	225.	250.	295.	375.	575.	1150.	15,500.	—

1937-D three-legged

Date	Mintage	G-4	VG-8	F-12	VF-20	XF-40	AU-50	MS-60	MS-65	Prf-65
1937S	5,635,000	.80	.90	1.00	1.90	3.75	9.00	14.00	55.00	—
1938D	7,020,000	1.40	1.50	1.75	3.00	4.50	9.00	13.00	35.00	—
1938 D/D	—	2.25	4.25	5.75	10.00	14.00	17.00	19.00	60.00	—
1938D/S	Inc. Ab.	6.00	8.00	10.00	15.00	19.00	32.00	40.00	165.	—

Jefferson

Prewar composition

Designer: Felix Schlag. **Size:** 21.2 millimeters. **Weight:** 5 grams. **Composition:** 75% copper, 25% nickel. **Notes:** Some 1939 strikes have doubling of the word "Monticello" on the reverse.

PRICING SECTION

Date	Mintage	G-4	VG-8	F-12	VF-20	XF-40	MS-60	MS-65	Prf-65
1938	19,515,365	—	.25	.40	.80	1.25	3.50	7.00	60.00
1938D	5,376,000	.60	.90	1.00	1.25	1.75	4.25	8.00	—
1938S	4,105,000	1.25	1.35	1.50	1.75	2.25	3.75	8.50	—
1939	120,627,535	—	—	.20	.25	.30	1.75	3.50	55.00
1939 Doubled Monticello	—	—	20.00	30.00	45.00	75.00	200.	—	—
1939D	3,514,000	2.50	3.00	3.50	5.00	10.00	36.00	55.00	—
1939S	6,630,000	.40	.45	.60	1.50	2.75	13.00	30.00	—
1940	176,499,158	—	—	—	—	.25	1.00	1.25	53.00
1940D	43,540,000	—	—	.20	.30	.40	2.50	2.75	—
1940S	39,690,000	—	—	.20	.25	.50	2.75	5.00	—
1941	203,283,720	—	—	—	—	.20	.90	2.00	50.00
1941D	53,432,000	—	—	.20	.30	.50	2.50	5.00	—
1941S	43,445,000	—	—	.20	.30	.50	3.75	6.75	—
1942	49,818,600	—	—	—	—	.40	4.50	8.50	46.00
1942D	13,938,000	—	.30	.40	.60	2.00	17.00	35.00	—

Wartime composition

Composition: 56% copper, 35% silver (0.0563 ounces), 9% manganese. **Notes:** Wartime-composition nickels have a large mintmark above Monticello on the reverse.

Date	Mintage	G-4	VG-8	F-12	VF-20	XF-40	MS-60	MS-65	Prf-65
1942P	57,900,600	.40	.65	.85	1.00	1.75	7.00	12.50	85.00
1942S	32,900,000	.45	.70	1.00	1.10	1.75	5.00	8.50	—
1943P	271,165,000	.35	.50	.85	1.00	1.50	3.50	6.50	—
1943/2P	Inc. Ab.	20.00	30.00	45.00	60.00	75.00	250.	550.	—
1943D	15,294,000	.75	.90	1.20	1.50	1.75	2.75	5.50	—
1943S	104,060,000	.35	.55	.70	1.00	1.50	3.25	5.75	—
1944P	119,150,000	.35	.50	.70	1.00	1.50	4.50	8.50	—
1944D	32,309,000	.40	.60	.80	1.00	1.75	5.00	9.50	—
1944S	21,640,000	.40	.60	.80	1.15	1.75	3.50	7.00	—
1945P	119,408,100	.30	.50	.70	1.00	1.50	3.50	7.00	—
1945D	37,158,000	.40	.55	.75	1.00	1.50	3.50	7.00	—
1945S	58,939,000	.35	.50	.70	.80	.90	2.00	5.00	—

Prewar composition resumed

Notes: The 1979-S Type II proof has a clearer mintmark than the Type I.

Date	Mintage	G-4	VG-8	F-12	VF-20	XF-40	MS-60	MS-65	Prf-65
1946	161,116,000	—	—	—	.20	.25	.40	.75	—
1946D	45,292,200	—	—	—	.25	.35	.75	1.25	—
1946S	13,560,000	—	—	—	.30	.40	.50	1.00	—
1947	95,000,000	—	—	—	.20	.25	.75	2.00	—
1947D	37,822,000	—	—	—	.20	.30	.90	2.00	—
1947S	24,720,000	—	—	—	.20	.25	.70	2.00	—
1948	89,348,000	—	—	—	.20	.25	.40	1.50	—
1948D	44,734,000	—	—	—	.25	.35	1.20	2.75	—
1948S	11,300,000	—	—	—	.25	.50	1.00	2.25	—
1949	60,652,000	—	—	—	.25	.30	.80	2.50	—
1949D	36,498,000	—	—	—	.30	.40	1.00	2.50	—
1949D/S	Inc. Ab.	—	—	30.00	40.00	65.00	170.	325.	—
1949S	9,716,000	—	.25	.35	.45	.90	1.50	3.50	—
1950	9,847,386	—	.20	.30	.35	.75	1.50	3.50	33.00
1950D	2,630,030	—	5.00	5.15	5.25	5.50	6.50	9.00	—
1951	28,609,500	—	—	—	.40	.50	1.10	2.50	26.00
1951D	20,460,000	—	.25	.30	.40	.50	1.00	2.00	—
1951S	7,776,000	—	.30	.40	.50	1.10	1.75	4.00	—
1952	64,069,980	—	—	—	.20	.25	.85	3.00	26.00
1952D	30,638,000	—	—	—	.30	.45	1.50	3.50	—
1952S	20,572,000	—	—	—	.20	.25	.75	3.50	—
1953	46,772,800	—	—	—	.20	.25	.40	1.50	27.00
1953D	59,878,600	—	—	—	.20	.25	.40	1.50	—
1953S	19,210,900	—	—	—	.20	.25	.50	2.50	—
1954	47,917,350	—	—	—	—	—	.35	1.50	16.00
1954D	117,136,560	—	—	—	—	—	.35	1.00	—
1954S	29,384,000	—	—	—	—	.20	.35	2.50	—
1954S/D	Inc. Ab.	—	—	5.00	8.00	14.00	22.00	65.00	—
1955	8,266,200	—	.25	.35	.40	.45	.75	2.00	12.00
1955D	74,464,100	—	—	—	—	—	.30	1.00	—
1955D/S	Inc. Ab.	—	—	5.00	8.50	13.00	33.00	65.00	—
1956	35,885,384	—	—	—	—	—	.30	.70	2.50

Date	Mintage	G-4	VG-8	F-12	VF-20	XF-40	MS-60	MS-65	Prf-65
1956D	67,222,940	—	—	—	—	—	.25	.60	—
1957	39,655,952	—	—	—	—	—	.25	.60	1.50
1957D	136,828,900	—	—	—	—	—	.25	.60	—
1958	17,963,652	—	—	—	.15	.20	.30	.65	2.50
1958D	168,249,120	—	—	—	—	—	.25	.60	—

Date	Mintage	MS-65	Prf-65	Date	Mintage	MS-65	Prf-65
1959	28,397,291	.65	1.25	1981D	364,801,843	.40	—
1959D	160,738,240	.55	—	1981S T-I	—	—	2.00
1960	57,107,602	.55	1.00	1981S T-II	—	—	2.00
1960D	192,582,180	.55	—	1982P	292,355,000	2.50	—
1961	76,668,244	.55	.70	1982D	373,726,544	2.50	—
1961D	229,342,760	.55	—	1982S	—	—	3.00
1962	100,602,019	.55	.70	1983P	561,615,000	3.00	—
1962D	280,195,720	.55	—	1983D	536,726,276	2.00	—
1963	178,851,645	.55	.70	1983S	—	—	3.50
1963D	276,829,460	.55	—	1984P	746,769,000	3.00	—
1964	1,028,622,762	.55	.70	1984D	517,675,146	.85	—
1964D	1,787,297,160	.50	—	1984S	—	—	5.00
1965	136,131,380	.50	—	1985P	647,114,962	.75	—
1966	156,208,283	.50	—	1985D	459,747,446	.75	—
1967	107,325,800	.50	—	1985S	—	—	3.50
1968	None minted	—	—	1986P	536,883,483	1.00	—
1968D	91,227,880	.50	—	1986D	361,819,140	2.00	—
1968S	103,437,510	.50	.60	1986S	—	—	6.50
1969	None minted	—	—	1987P	371,499,481	.75	—
1969D	202,807,500	.50	—	1987D	410,590,604	.75	—
1969S	123,099,631	.50	.60	1987S	—	—	3.50
1970	None minted	—	—	1988P	771,360,000	.75	—
1970D	515,485,380	.50	—	1988D	663,771,652	.75	—
1970S	241,464,814	.50	.60	1988S	—	—	4.50
1971	106,884,000	1.25	—	1989P	898,812,000	.75	—
1971D	316,144,800	.50	—	1989D	570,842,474	.75	—
1971S	—	—	1.50	1989S	—	—	3.25
1972	202,036,000	.50	—	1990P	661,636,000	.75	—
1972D	351,694,600	.50	—	1990D	663,938,503	.75	—
1972S	—	—	1.50	1990S	—	—	4.75
1973	384,396,000	.50	—	1991P	614,104,000	.75	—
1973D	261,405,000	.50	—	1991D	436,496,678	.75	—
1973S	—	—	1.60	1991S	(2,867,787)	—	5.50
1974	601,752,000	.50	—	1992P	399,552,000	1.10	—
1974D	277,373,000	.50	—	1992D	450,565,113	.75	—
1974S	—	—	2.00	1992S	(4,176,560)	—	4.00
1975	181,772,000	.75	—	1993P	412,076,000	.75	—
1975D	401,875,300	.50	—	1993D	406,084,135	.75	—
1975S	—	—	2.25	1993S	(3,394,792)	—	4.00
1976	367,124,000	.75	—	1994P	722,160,000	.75	—
1976D	563,964,147	.60	—	1994D	715,762,110	.75	—
1976S	—	—	2.00	1994S	(3,269,923)	—	4.50
1977	585,376,000	.40	—	1995P	774,156,000	.75	—
1977D	297,313,460	.55	—	1995D	888,112,000	.85	—
1977S	—	—	2.75	1995S	—	—	6.50
1978	391,308,000	.40	—	1996P	829,332,000	.75	—
1978D	313,092,780	.40	—	1996D	817,736,000	.75	—
1978S	—	—	1.75	1996S	—	—	3.00
1979	463,188,000	.40	—	1997P	470,972,000	.75	—
1979D	325,867,672	.40	—	1997D	466,640,000	.80	—
1979S T-I	—	—	1.50	1997S	(1,975,000)	—	4.75
1979S T-II	—	—	1.75	1998P	—	.80	—
1980P	593,004,000	.40	—	1998D	—	.80	—
1980D	502,323,448	.40	—	1998S	—	—	4.75
1980S	—	—	1.60	1999	—	.80	—
1981P	657,504,000	.40	—	1999D	—	.80	—
				1999S	—	—	—

Dimes

Draped Bust

Small-eagle reverse

Designer: Robert Scot. **Size:** 19 millimeters. **Weight:** 2.7 grams. **Composition:** 89.24% silver (0.0775 ounces), 10.76% copper. **Notes:** The 1797 strikes have either 13 or 16 stars on the obverse.

Date	Mintage	G-4	VG-8	F-12	VF-20	XF-40	MS-60
1796	22,135	1000.	1450.	1900.	3000.	5000.	6750.
1797 13 stars	25,261	1200.	1800.	2100.	3450.	5500.	7500.
1797 16 stars	Inc. Ab.	1150.	1750.	2100.	3250.	5250.	7300.

Heraldic-eagle reverse

Notes: The 1798 overdates have either 13 or 16 stars on the obverse. Varieties of the regular 1798 strikes are distinguished by the size of the 8 in the date. The 1804 strikes have either 13 or 14 stars on the obverse. The 1805 strikes have either 4 or 5 berries on the olive branch held by the eagle.

Date	Mintage	G-4	VG-8	F-12	VF-20	XF-40	MS-60
1798	27,550	450.	560.	750.	1125.	1975.	6000.
1798/97 13 stars	Inc. Ab.	2250.	3000.	5000.	7500.	11,500.	—
1798/97 16 stars	Inc. Ab.	475.	650.	950.	1800.	2775.	6000.
1798 small 8	Inc. Ab.	900.	1200.	1650.	2800.	4400.	—
1800	21,760	450.	560.	750.	1125.	1975.	5400.
1801	34,640	450.	560.	875.	1375.	3200.	—
1802	10,975	500.	850.	1200.	2200.	4200.	—
1803	33,040	450.	560.	750.	1125.	1975.	5500.
1804 13 stars	8,265	1000.	1400.	2100.	4400.	7500.	—
1804 14 stars	Inc. Ab.	1200.	1700.	2750.	4750.	8000.	—
1805 4 berries	120,780	375.	525.	725.	950.	1800.	4050.
1805 5 berries	Inc. Ab.	650.	800.	1000.	1500.	2500.	4200.
1807	165,000	375.	525.	725.	975.	1800.	4050.

1809 Dime
Grade F-12

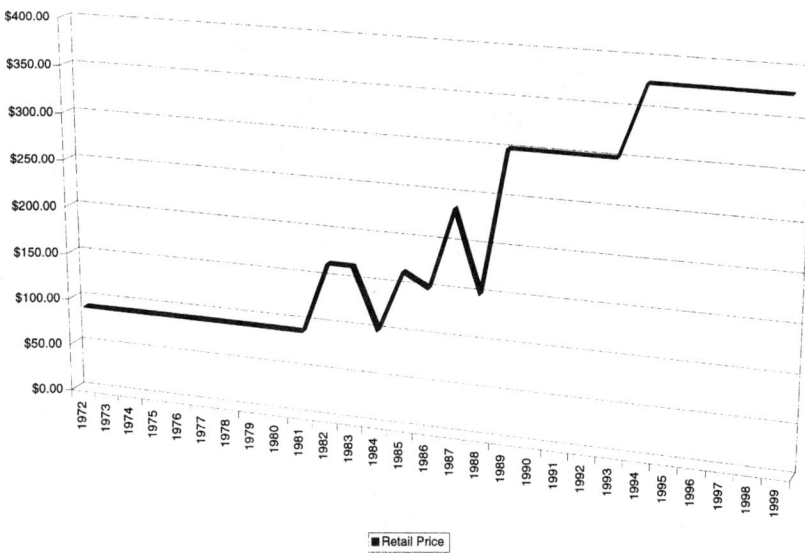

Retail Price

Source: COIN PRICES

Liberty Cap

Designer: John Reich. **Size:** 18.8 millimeters. **Weight:** 2.7 grams. **Composition:** 89.24% silver (0.0775 ounces), 10.76% copper. **Notes:** Varieties of the 1814, 1821 and 1828 strikes are distinguished by the size of the numerals in the dates. The 1820 varieties are distinguished by the size of the 0 in the date. The 1823 overdates have either large "E's" or small "E's" in "United States of America" on the reverse.

Date	Mintage	G-4	VG-8	F-12	VF-20	XF-40	AU-50	MS-60	MS-65
1809	51,065	100.	200.	375.	650.	925.	2500.	4200.	22,500.
1811/9	65,180	90.00	165.	240.	425.	750.	1500.	4000.	22,500.
1814 sm. dt.	421,500	40.00	60.00	90.00	210.	450.	700.	800.	8000.
1814 lg. dt.	Inc.Ab.	17.50	26.00	44.00	115.	350.	625.	800.	8000.
1820 lg. O	942,587	17.00	24.00	35.00	105.	330.	625.	800.	8000.
1820 sm. O	Inc.Ab.	22.00	45.00	65.00	175.	425.	725.	975.	8000.
1821 lg. dt.	1,186,512	16.00	23.00	38.00	105.	330.	625.	800.	8000.
1821 sm. dt.	Inc.Ab.	18.50	25.00	45.00	125.	370.	625.	800.	8000.
1822	100,000	300.	450.	800.	1450.	2500.	4450.	6000.	—
1823/22 lg.E's	440,000	15.00	22.00	40.00	110.	300.	625.	800.	8000.
1823/22 sm.E's	Inc.Ab.	15.00	22.00	40.00	110.	300.	625.	800.	8000.
1824/22	Undetermined	30.00	48.00	90.00	325.	525.	1275.	2500.	—
1825	510,000	20.00	27.00	40.00	145.	375.	775.	1250.	8000.
1827	1,215,000	15.00	22.00	35.00	95.00	300.	775.	1000.	8000.
1828 lg.dt.	125,000	75.00	95.00	135.	265.	650.	900.	2600.	—

Reduced size

Size: 18.5 millimeters. **Notes:** The three varieties of 1829 strikes and two varieties of 1830 strikes are distinguished by the size of "10C." on the reverse. On the 1833 "high 3" variety, the last 3 in the date is higher than the first 3. The two varieties of the 1834 strikes are distinguished by the size of the 4 in the date.

Date	Mintage	G-4	VG-8	F-12	VF-20	XF-40	AU-50	MS-60	MS-65
1828 sm.dt.	Inc. Ab.	30.00	45.00	75.00	195.	475.	775.	1750.	—
1829 very lg.10C.	770,000	35.00	45.00	85.00	150.	375.	600.	1500.	—
1829 lg.10C.		25.00	35.00	52.00	105.	285.	475.	725.	8000.
1829 med.10C.	Inc. Ab.	17.50	25.00	35.00	85.00	265.	425.	625.	8000.
1829 sm.10C.	Inc. Ab.	14.00	17.00	22.00	60.00	185.	415.	625.	8000.
1829 curl base 2		3200.	3950.	7500.	—	—	—	—	—
1830 lg.10C.	510,000	14.00	17.00	22.00	60.00	185.	415.	625.	8000.
1830 sm.10C.	Inc. Ab.	15.00	19.00	25.00	63.00	200.	415.	625.	8000.
1830/29	Inc. Ab.	20.00	25.00	50.00	100.	240.	500.	1000.	—
1831	771,350	14.00	17.00	22.00	60.00	185.	350.	600.	5050.
1832	522,500	14.00	17.00	22.00	60.00	185.	350.	600.	5050.
1833	485,000	15.00	18.00	23.00	62.00	190.	350.	600.	5050.
1834	635,000	14.00	17.00	22.00	60.00	185.	350.	600.	5050.
1835	1,410,000	14.00	17.00	22.00	60.00	185.	350.	600.	5050.
1836	1,190,000	14.00	17.00	22.00	60.00	185.	350.	600.	5050.
1837	1,042,000	14.00	17.00	22.00	60.00	185.	350.	625.	5050.

Seated Liberty

No stars

Designer: Christian Gobrecht. **Size:** 17.9 millimeters. **Weight:** 2.67 grams. **Composition:** 90% silver (0.0773 ounces), 10% copper. **Notes:** The two 1837 varieties are distinguished by the size of the numerals in the date.

Date	Mintage	G-4	VG-8	F-12	VF-20	XF-40	AU-50	MS-60	MS-65
1837 sm.date	Inc. Ab.	29.00	40.00	75.00	275.	550.	750.	1100.	6500.
1837 lg.date	Inc. Ab.	29.00	40.00	75.00	275.	550.	750.	1100.	6500.
1838O	406,034	35.00	45.00	90.00	300.	725.	1250.	3500.	21,000.

Stars around rim

Notes: The two 1838 varieties are distinguished by the size of the stars on the obverse. The 1838 "partial drapery" variety has drapery on Liberty's left elbow. The 1839-O with reverse of 1838-O variety was struck from rusted dies. This variety has a bumpy surface on the reverse.

Date	Mintage	G-4	VG-8	F-12	VF-20	XF-40	AU-50	MS-60	MS-65
1838 sm.stars	1,992,500	20.00	30.00	45.00	75.00	175.	300.	950.	—
1838 lg.stars	Inc. Ab.	9.00	11.00	15.00	25.00	60.00	170.	575.	8500.
1838 partial drapery									
	Inc. Ab.	30.00	45.00	60.00	125.	195.	325.	550.	—
1839	1,053,115	9.00	15.00	17.50	35.00	70.00	170.	265.	2500.
1839O	1,323,000	8.75	12.00	20.00	40.00	85.00	300.	1250.	—
1839O rev. 1838O	—	145.	200.	350.	550.	950.	—	—	—
1840	1,358,580	9.00	15.00	20.00	30.00	60.00	170.	300.	2500.
1840O	1,175,000	12.50	22.00	40.00	70.00	125.	295.	975.	—

Drapery added to Liberty

Notes: In 1840 drapery was added to Liberty's left elbow.

Date	Mintage	G-4	VG-8	F-12	VF-20	XF-40	AU-50	MS-60	MS-65
1840	Inc. Ab.	30.00	45.00	85.00	165.	275.	1250.	—	—
1841	1,622,500	10.00	13.00	16.00	25.00	45.00	175.	260.	2550.
1841O	2,007,500	9.00	11.00	15.00	28.00	60.00	250.	1500.	—
1842	1,887,500	8.75	9.50	10.00	17.00	45.00	175.	260.	2550.
1842O	2,020,000	10.00	18.00	30.00	75.00	225.	1350.	2900.	—
1843	1,370,000	8.75	9.25	10.00	17.00	45.00	175.	260.	2550.
1843/1843	—	9.00	12.00	18.00	30.00	75.00	200.	295.	—
1843O	150,000	35.00	65.00	125.	250.	700.	2000.	—	—
1844	72,500	275.	350.	550.	800.	1450.	2200.	3000.	—
1845	1,755,000	8.75	9.25	10.00	19.00	45.00	120.	260.	2550.
1845O	230,000	19.00	35.00	60.00	165.	475.	1200.	—	—
1846	31,300	100.	135.	200.	295.	850.	2000.	—	—
1847	245,000	17.50	25.00	35.00	60.00	125.	350.	950.	—
1848	451,500	12.00	15.00	22.00	40.00	75.00	185.00	750.	7050.
1849	839,000	10.00	13.00	18.00	28.00	55.00	140.00	500.	7050.

Date	Mintage	G-4	VG-8	F-12	VF-20	XF-40	AU-50	MS-60	MS-65
1849O	300,000	15.00	22.00	35.00	85.00	275.	950.	—	—
1850	1,931,500	8.75	9.25	10.00	25.00	60.00	120.	260.	2550.
1850O	510,000	10.00	14.00	28.00	60.00	160.	400.	1250.	—
1851	1,026,500	8.75	9.25	10.00	19.00	60.00	120.	325.	—
1851O	400,000	10.00	15.00	30.00	75.00	175.	450.	1500.	—
1852	1,535,500	8.75	9.25	10.00	15.00	50.00	120.	290.	2550.
1852O	430,000	16.00	22.00	39.00	100.	195.	425.	1800.	—
1853	95,000	70.00	90.00	110.	180.	300.	450.	800.	—

Arrows at date

Weight: 2.49 grams. **Composition:** 90% silver (0.0721 ounces), 10% copper.

Date	Mintage	G-4	VG-8	F-12	VF-20	XF-40	AU-50	MS-60	MS-65	Prf-65
1853	12,078,010	8.00	9.00	10.00	14.00	45.00	125.	330.	2500.	31,500.
1853O	1,100,000	10.00	13.00	20.00	45.00	145.	400.	900.	—	—
1854	4,470,000	8.75	9.25	10.00	14.00	45.00	125.	330.	2500.	31,500.
1854O	1,770,000	9.00	9.50	11.00	25.00	75.00	175.	600.	—	—
1855	2,075,000	8.75	9.25	10.00	15.00	48.00	170.	350.	3800.	31,500.

Arrows at date removed

Notes: The two 1856 varieties are distinguished by the size of the numerals in the date.

Date	Mintage	G-4	VG-8	F-12	VF-20	XF-40	AU-50	MS-60	MS-65	Prf-65
1856 sm. dt.	5,780,000	8.75	9.25	10.00	12.50	32.00	115.	250.	7050.	38,000.
1856 lg. dt.	Inc. Ab.	10.00	12.00	15.00	25.00	65.00	175.	475.	—	—
1856O	1,180,000	9.00	15.00	20.00	35.00	85.00	200.	500.	—	—
1856S	70,000	145.	170.	250.	425.	900.	1750.	—	—	—
1857	5,580,000	8.75	9.25	11.25	13.00	32.00	100.	260.	2500.	3400.
1857O	1,540,000	9.00	10.00	12.00	25.00	65.00	200.	350.	—	—
1858	1,540,000	10.00	14.00	20.00	35.00	55.00	145.	260.	2500.	3400.
1858O	290,000	15.00	19.00	35.00	70.00	125.	275.	800.	—	—
1858S	60,000	110.	150.	200.	325.	675.	1400.	—	—	—
1859	430,000	11.00	15.00	20.00	40.00	60.00	140.	350.	—	3400.
1859O	480,000	9.00	11.00	19.00	35.00	70.00	225.	550.	—	—
1859S	60,000	125.	160.	250.	425.	1000.	2000.	—	—	—
1860S	140,000	28.00	36.00	48.00	100.	275.	800.	—	—	—

Transitional patterns

Notes: These non-circulation strikes were struck as experiments in transferring the legend "United States of America" from the reverse to the obverse.

Date	Mintage	G-4	VG-8	F-12	VF-20	XF-40	AU-50	MS-60	MS-65	Prf-65
1859 obverse of 1859, reverse of 1860					—	—	—	—	—	25,000.

1866-S Dime
Grade F-12

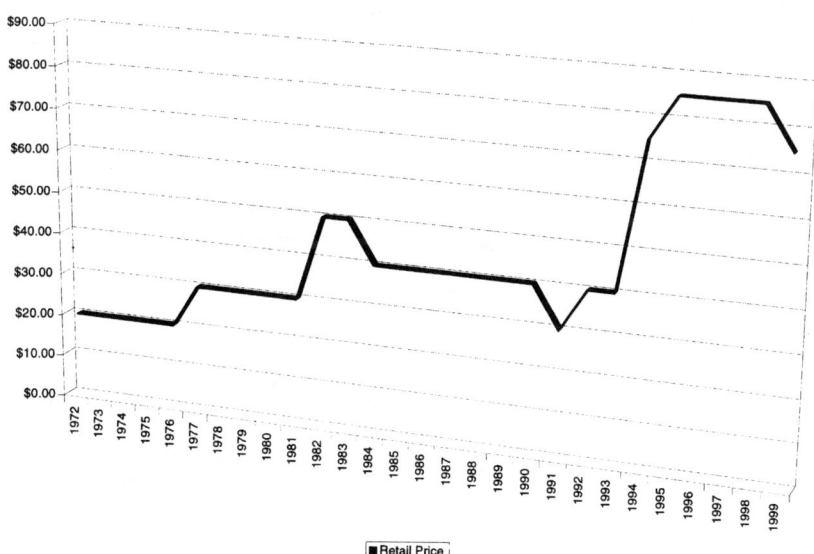

Retail Price

Source: COIN PRICES

Obverse legend

Notes: In 1860 the legend ''United States of America'' replaced the stars on the obverse. The 1873 ''closed-3'' and ''open-3'' varieties are distinguished by the amount of space between the upper left and lower left serifs of the 3 in the date.

Date	Mintage	G-4	VG-8	F-12	VF-20	XF-40	AU-50	MS-60	MS-65	Prf-65
1860	607,000	17.50	25.00	35.00	45.00	65.00	125.	275.	—	1400.
1860O	40,000	300.	425.	600.	1150.	2500.	4200.	6000.	—	—
1861	1,884,000	8.75	10.00	13.00	18.00	35.00	65.00	125.	—	1400.
1861S	172,500	45.00	80.00	125.	225.	375.	900.	—	—	—
1862	847,550	10.00	13.00	19.00	25.00	45.00	65.00	150.	—	1400.
1862S	180,750	35.00	52.00	95.00	175.	300.	775.	—	—	—
1863	14,460	250.	375.	500.	600.	750.	900.	1200.	—	1400.
1863S	157,500	30.00	35.00	55.00	90.00	275.	550.	1200.	—	—
1864	11,470	250.	325.	400.	500.	600.	775.	1650.	—	1400.
1864S	230,000	24.00	30.00	40.00	80.00	225.	425.	1200.	—	—
1865	10,500	275.	350.	450.	550.	675.	1050.	1250.	—	1400.
1865S	175,000	35.00	45.00	60.00	100.	250.	700.	—	—	—
1866	8,725	300.	375.	575.	675.	800.	1200.	1800.	—	1750.
1866S	135,000	35.00	45.00	75.00	145.	325.	675.	1900.	—	—
1867	6,625	425.	575.	800.	900.	1150.	1300.	1600.	—	1750.
1867S	140,000	35.00	45.00	70.00	125.	275.	575.	1200.	—	—
1868	464,000	10.00	12.00	20.00	31.00	70.00	175.	300.	—	1400.
1868S	260,000	15.00	20.00	30.00	60.00	115.	285.	600.	—	—
1869	256,600	12.00	16.00	30.00	55.00	115.	200.	600.	—	1400.
1869S	450,000	12.00	17.00	25.00	38.00	65.00	150.	400.	—	—
1870	471,000	11.00	14.00	19.00	32.00	70.00	135.	300.	—	1400.
1870S	50,000	215.	280.	375.	450.	575.	850.	2000.	—	—
1871	907,710	11.00	15.00	20.00	28.00	45.00	130.	300.	—	1400.
1871CC	20,100	800.	1150.	1950.	3500.	6750.	10,500.	—	—	—

Date	Mintage	G-4	VG-8	F-12	VF-20	XF-40	AU-50	MS-60	MS-65	Prf-65
1871S	320,000	35.00	55.00	75.00	115.	175.	350.	900.	—	—
1872	2,396,450	8.75	9.50	11.00	18.00	31.00	95.00	175.	—	1400.
1872CC	35,480	350.	525.	850.	1750.	3000.	4750.	—	—	—
1872S	190,000	40.00	50.00	70.00	125.	215.	450.	1100.	—	—
1873 closed 3	1,568,600	9.00	11.00	14.00	27.00	50.00	100.	200.	—	1400.
1873 open 3	Inc. Ab.	15.00	18.00	30.00	48.00	100.	225.	650.	—	—
1873CC	12,400				Eliasberg Sale, May 1996, MS-65 $550,000					

Arrows at date

Weight: 2.5 grams. **Composition:** 90% silver (0.0724 ounces), 10% copper.

Date	Mintage	G-4	VG-8	F-12	VF-20	XF-40	AU-50	MS-60	MS-65	Prf-65
1873	2,378,500	8.75	13.00	25.00	50.00	150.	350.	500.	4500.	4500.
1873CC	18,791	750.	975.	1850.	3750.	5750.	9750.	—	—	—
1873S	455,000	15.00	20.00	28.00	60.00	180.	320.	1500.	—	—
1874	2,940,700	8.75	13.00	17.50	50.00	150.	315.	500.	4500.	4500.
1874CC	10,817	2950.	4500.	6500.	9750.	17,500.	—	—	—	—
1874S	240,000	32.00	36.00	60.00	125.	250.	450.	1500.	—	—

Arrows at date removed

Notes: On the 1876-CC doubled-obverse variety, doubling appears in the words "of America" in the legend.

Date	Mintage	G-4	VG-8	F-12	VF-20	XF-40	AU-50	MS-60	MS-65	Prf-65
1875	10,350,700	8.75	9.25	10.00	12.00	22.00	60.00	125.	2250.	4600.
1875CC mint mark in wreath	4,645,000	8.75	9.50	11.00	18.00	3750.	90.00	160.	2700.	—
1875CC mint mark under wreath	Inc. Ab.	10.00	15.00	22.50	37.50	65.00	165.	235.	3000.	—
1875S mint mark in wreath	9,070,000	12.00	17.50	28.00	43.00	65.00	125.	225.	3100.	—
1875S mint mark under wreath	Inc. Ab.	10.00	14.00	17.50	25.00	35.00	70.00	125.	1100.	—
1876	11,461,150	8.75	9.25	11.00	12.00	24.00	60.00	110.	1100.	1200.
1876CC	8,270,000	8.75	9.25	11.00	18.00	30.00	60.00	175.	—	—
1876CC (doubled obverse)	Inc. Ab.	12.00	20.00	32.00	95.00	225.	400.	700.	—	—
1876S	10,420,000	10.00	13.00	15.00	20.00	35.00	85.00	165.	1100.	—
1877	7,310,510	8.75	9.25	9.75	13.00	23.00	60.00	110.	1100.	1200.
1877CC	7,700,000	8.75	9.25	10.75	18.00	35.00	75.00	175.	—	—
1877S	2,340,000	12.00	16.00	18.00	27.00	50.00	105.	225.	—	—
1878	1,678,800	9.00	9.50	10.00	18.00	30.00	60.00	110.	1100.	1200.
1878CC	200,000	50.00	75.00	110.	165.	275.	450.	775.	3900.	—
1879	15,100	165.	200.	250.	275.	350.	475.	675.	1750.	1500.
1880	37,335	120.	140.	175.	210.	250.	325.	450.	1750.	1500.
1881	24,975	145.	175.	200.	250.	325.	425.	650.	2500.	1600.
1882	3,911,100	8.75	9.25	11.00	12.00	24.00	60.00	110.	1100.	1200.
1883	7,675,712	8.75	9.25	11.00	12.00	24.00	60.00	110.	1100.	1200.
1884	3,366,380	8.75	9.25	11.00	12.00	24.00	60.00	110.	1100.	1200.
1884S	564,969	18.00	20.00	33.00	60.00	125.	200.	500.	—	—
1885	2,533,427	8.75	9.25	10.75	12.00	24.00	60.00	110.	1100.	1200.
1885S	43,690	350.	475.	725.	1400.	2450.	2950.	3750.	—	—
1886	6,377,570	8.75	9.25	10.00	12.00	22.00	60.00	110.	1100.	1200.
1886S	206,524	40.00	55.00	85.00	135.	200.	275.	600.	—	—
1887	11,283,939	8.75	9.25	10.00	12.00	22.00	60.00	110.	1100.	1200.
1887S	4,454,450	9.00	12.00	16.00	22.00	38.00	80.00	110.	1100.	—
1888	5,496,487	8.75	9.25	10.00	12.00	22.00	60.00	110.	1100.	1200.
1888S	1,720,000	10.00	13.00	17.00	25.00	40.00	95.00	200.	—	—
1889	7,380,711	8.75	9.25	10.00	12.00	22.00	60.00	110.	1100.	1200.

Date	Mintage	G-4	VG-8	F-12	VF-20	XF-40	AU-50	MS-60	MS-65	Prf-65
1889S	972,678	14.00	18.00	25.00	35.00	70.00	150.	475.	4500.	—
1890	9,911,541	8.75	9.25	10.00	12.00	22.00	60.00	110.	1100.	1200.
1890S	1,423,076	11.00	14.00	20.00	57.50	85.00	155.	400.	4900.	—
1890S/S	Inc. Ab.	25.00	30.00	40.00	85.00	135.	250.	—	—	—
1891	15,310,600	8.75	9.25	10.00	12.00	22.00	60.00	110.	1100.	1200.
1891O	4,540,000	9.00	9.75	11.00	13.00	24.00	70.00	175.	1750.	—
1891O/horz. O										
	Inc. Ab.	65.00	95.00	125.	175.	225.	400.	—	—	—
1891S	3,196,116	10.00	12.00	18.00	35.00	55.00	135.	225.	1650.	—

Barber

Designer: Charles E. Barber. **Size:** 17.9 millimeters. **Weight:** 2.5 grams. **Composition:** 90% silver (0.0724 ounces), 10% copper.

Date	Mintage	G-4	VG-8	F-12	VF-20	XF-40	AU-50	MS-60	MS-65	Prf-65
1892	12,121,245	2.50	5.00	14.00	19.50	22.00	55.00	90.00	540.	1450.
1892O	3,841,700	5.85	11.50	27.00	38.00	45.00	72.00	145.	1200.	—
1892S	990,710	35.00	69.00	140.	170.	210.	230.	350.	2500.	—
1893	3,340,792	5.50	10.50	17.50	21.00	32.00	72.00	145.	810.	1450.
1893O	1,760,000	16.50	30.00	90.00	110.	135.	155.	260.	2900.	—
1893S	2,491,401	7.75	19.00	25.00	30.00	49.00	110.	230.	3600.	—
1894	1,330,972	10.00	24.00	84.00	110.	130.	155.	250.	1110.	1450.
1894O	720,000	39.00	78.00	160.	205.	290.	600.	1100.	8400.	—
1894S	24				Eliasberg Sale, May 1996, Prf-64 $451,000.				—	—
1895	690,880	55.00	85.00	200.	400.	450.	500.	600.	2400.	2000.
1895O	440,000	225.	300.	690.	950.	1825.	2500.	2800.	10,000.	—
1895S	1,120,000	26.00	40.00	105.	145.	175.	230.	440.	6300.	—
1896	2,000,762	8.00	19.00	44.00	58.00	74.00	100.	145.	1320.	1450.
1896O	610,000	50.00	95.00	215.	285.	380.	600.	755.	6000.	—
1896S	575,056	60.00	100.	220.	240.	295.	440.	695.	3500.	—
1897	10,869,264	2.25	2.75	5.85	8.50	23.00	68.00	110.	700.	1450.
1897O	666,000	43.00	74.00	225.	280.	345.	505.	755.	4150.	—
1897S	1,342,844	12.00	25.00	72.00	83.00	140.	200.	390.	3500.	—
1898	16,320,735	1.45	1.95	6.50	9.00	20.00	50.00	91.00	540.	1450.
1898O	2,130,000	5.50	12.00	60.00	91.00	130.	195.	425.	3500.	—
1898S	1,702,507	4.50	8.50	22.00	31.00	52.00	110.	325.	3800.	—
1899	19,580,846	1.45	1.75	5.85	8.50	20.00	52.00	91.00	540.	1450.
1899O	2,650,000	4.50	9.75	58.00	78.00	115.	200.	360.	4800.	—
1899S	1,867,493	4.75	9.75	16.50	20.00	35.00	85.00	295.	3500.	—
1900	17,600,912	1.50	2.10	6.00	8.50	20.00	52.00	91.00	900.	1450.
1900O	2,010,000	8.00	17.00	78.00	125.	190.	325.	520.	6000.	—
1900S	5,168,270	2.75	3.60	8.50	11.00	21.00	72.00	165.	1675.	—
1901	18,860,478	1.45	1.65	5.25	7.75	20.00	45.00	100.	1170.	1450.
1901O	5,620,000	2.75	4.50	12.00	18.00	42.00	115.	360.	2900.	—
1901S	593,022	39.00	64.00	280.	315.	380.	565.	790.	5000.	—
1902	21,380,777	1.30	1.75	4.50	6.75	21.00	52.00	91.00	540.	1450.
1902O	4,500,000	2.50	6.50	13.00	20.00	41.00	105.	325.	3350.	—
1902S	2,070,000	5.50	11.00	44.00	58.00	84.00	145.	325.	3600.	—
1903	19,500,755	1.30	1.75	4.50	7.15	20.00	52.00	91.00	1150.	1450.
1903O	8,180,000	2.00	3.00	8.75	13.00	26.00	91.00	240.	5050.	—
1903S	613,300	38.00	66.00	320.	415.	680.	855.	1050.	3800.	—
1904	14,601,027	1.30	1.75	5.50	9.00	20.00	52.00	105.	2100.	1450.
1904S	800,000	25.00	41.00	120.	155.	225.	430.	565.	4700.	—
1905	14,552,350	1.30	1.75	4.00	6.50	19.00	52.00	91.00	540.	1450.
1905O	3,400,000	2.50	5.75	30.00	43.00	58.00	105.	230.	2050.	—
1905S	6,855,199	2.25	4.75	7.75	16.50	30.00	72.00	210.	725.	—
1906	19,958,406	1.30	1.75	3.50	6.50	21.00	52.00	91.00	540.	1450.
1906D	4,060,000	2.25	3.75	9.00	14.00	27.00	72.00	155.	1950.	—
1906O	2,610,000	4.50	5.85	41.00	57.00	78.00	125.	180.	1250.	—
1906S	3,136,640	2.50	4.75	10.00	18.00	36.00	91.00	230.	1200.	—
1907	22,220,575	1.30	1.60	3.50	6.50	21.00	52.00	91.00	540.	1450.
1907D	4,080,000	2.75	4.75	9.00	15.00	32.00	91.00	260.	3550.	—
1907O	5,058,000	1.75	3.00	25.00	37.00	52.00	72.00	200.	1100.	—
1907S	3,178,470	2.25	5.00	9.75	18.00	41.00	100.	325.	2300.	—
1908	10,600,545	1.30	1.75	3.50	6.50	18.00	52.00	91.00	540.	1450.
1908D	7,490,000	1.75	2.25	6.50	9.50	26.00	59.00	125.	960.	—
1908O	1,789,000	2.75	5.50	39.00	52.00	72.00	130.	260.	1860.	—
1908S	3,220,000	2.75	4.50	9.00	14.00	32.00	145.	260.	2300.	—
1909	10,240,650	1.75	2.25	3.50	6.50	18.00	52.00	91.00	540.	1700.
1909D	954,000	3.25	9.00	58.00	85.00	105.	195.	390.	2300.	—

PRICING SECTION

1901-S Dime
Grade F-12

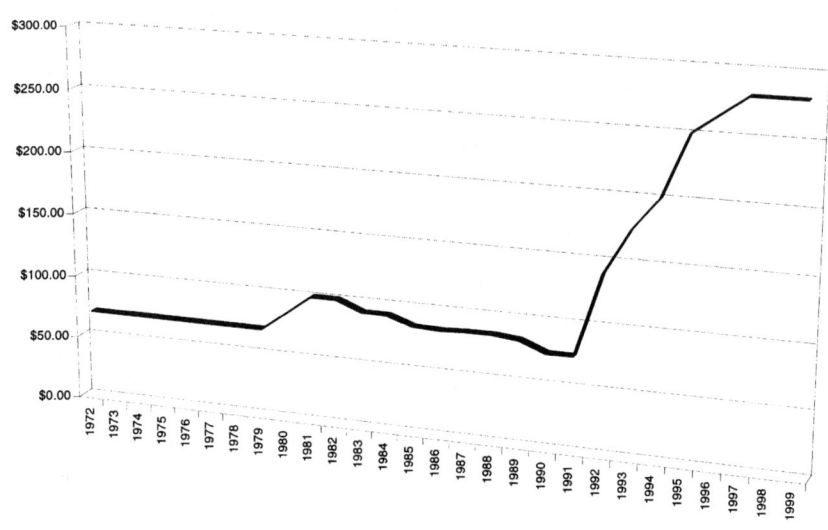

■ Retail Price

Source: COIN PRICES

Date	Mintage	G-4	VG-8	F-12	VF-20	XF-40	AU-50	MS-60	MS-65	Prf-65
1909O	2,287,000	2.75	5.00	8.50	15.00	27.00	91.00	180.	1250.	—
1909S	1,000,000	4.00	11.00	78.00	110.	145.	295.	470.	3000.	—
1910	11,520,551	1.30	2.25	5.75	10.50	20.00	52.00	91.00	540.	1450.
1910D	3,490,000	2.75	4.75	7.75	15.00	34.00	91.00	195.	1800.	—
1910S	1,240,000	3.00	7.00	49.00	62.00	88.00	150.	350.	1925.	—
1911	18,870,543	1.30	1.75	3.00	6.50	18.00	52.00	91.00	540.	1700.
1911D	11,209,000	1.30	1.75	3.75	7.50	20.00	52.00	91.00	685.	—
1911S	3,520,000	1.75	2.75	7.75	15.00	31.00	85.00	145.	725.	—
1912	19,350,700	1.30	1.75	2.75	6.50	20.00	52.00	91.00	540.	1700.
1912D	11,760,000	1.30	1.75	3.75	7.50	18.00	52.00	91.00	720.	—
1912S	3,420,000	1.75	2.75	6.50	10.00	26.00	85.00	150.	1150.	—
1913	19,760,622	1.50	1.75	2.75	6.50	20.00	52.00	91.00	540.	1450.
1913S	510,000	8.00	13.00	67.00	100.	175.	260.	390.	1100.	—
1914	17,360,655	1.50	1.75	3.50	6.50	18.00	52.00	91.00	540.	1700.
1914D	11,908,000	1.50	1.75	3.50	6.75	18.00	52.00	91.00	540.	—
1914S	2,100,000	1.80	2.40	6.50	10.00	31.00	72.00	145.	1250.	—
1915	5,620,450	1.50	1.75	3.90	7.00	20.00	52.00	91.00	540.	2000.
1915S	960,000	2.40	4.40	29.00	39.00	52.00	125.	235.	1775.	—
1916	18,490,000	1.30	1.75	3.75	6.75	21.00	52.00	91.00	540.	—
1916S	5,820,000	1.50	2.25	4.75	6.50	20.00	52.00	91.00	780.	—

Mercury

Designer: Adolph A. Weinman. **Size:** 17.9 millimeters. **Weight:** 2.5 grams. **Composition:** 90% silver (0.0724 ounces), 10% copper. **Notes:** ''-65FSB'' values are for coins with fully split and rounded horizontal bands around the fasces on the reverse. The 1945-S ''micro'' variety has a smaller mintmark than the normal variety.

1916-D Dime
Grade F-12

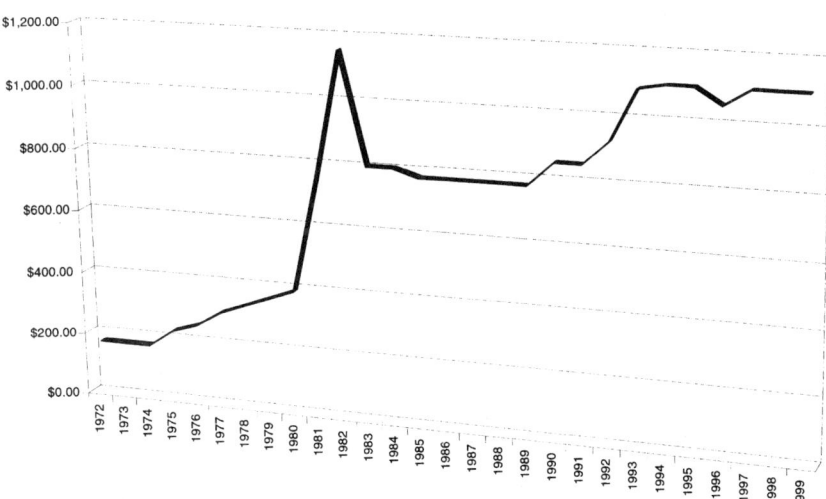

■ Retail Price

Source: **COIN PRICES**

Date	Mintage	G-4	VG-8	F-12	VF-20	XF-40	MS-60	MS-65	-65FSB	Prf-65
1916	22,180,080	2.25	3.50	4.75	7.25	11.00	25.00	90.00	110.	—
1916D	264,000	475.	700.	1100.	1550.	2450.	4900.	18,000.	35,000.	—
1916S	10,450,000	3.50	4.50	5.75	9.75	16.50	34.00	195.	450.	—
1917	55,230,000	1.00	2.10	2.75	5.50	8.00	28.00	150.	340.	—
1917D	9,402,000	3.50	5.25	8.00	16.00	38.00	125.	1825.	5700.	—
1917S	27,330,000	1.25	2.35	3.25	6.00	9.50	49.00	585.	1690.	—
1918	26,680,000	1.50	3.00	4.25	11.00	25.00	70.00	390.	675.	—
1918D	22,674,800	2.25	3.00	4.00	9.50	23.00	105.	2200.	9750.	—
1918S	19,300,000	2.00	2.50	3.50	6.50	14.00	85.00	975.	6500.	—
1919	35,740,000	1.00	2.25	3.25	5.50	8.00	35.00	360.	550.	—
1919D	9,939,000	3.00	4.25	6.00	15.00	39.00	140.	1800.	18,000.	—
1919S	8,850,000	2.50	3.60	5.00	13.00	29.00	175.	1100.	10,500.	—
1920	59,030,000	1.00	2.10	2.75	5.00	7.00	27.00	230.	365.	—
1920D	19,171,000	2.25	3.25	4.25	7.00	15.00	100.	1250.	3050.	—
1920S	13,820,000	2.00	2.80	4.00	6.50	13.50	70.00	1175.	4875.	—
1921	1,230,000	20.00	32.00	70.00	160.	440.	945.	2850.	4000.	—
1921D	1,080,000	38.00	53.00	100.	210.	475.	1000.	2650.	5100.	—
1923	50,130,000	.90	1.40	2.25	4.25	7.00	25.00	115.	195.	—
1923S	6,440,000	2.25	3.50	4.25	11.00	29.00	135.	1500.	4000.	—
1924	24,010,000	1.00	1.60	2.75	5.00	9.00	38.00	170.	480.	—
1924D	6,810,000	2.25	3.25	5.50	10.00	29.00	155.	1275.	3300.	—
1924S	7,120,000	2.00	3.00	4.00	8.00	29.00	155.	1550.	10,500.	—
1925	25,610,000	1.00	1.60	2.75	4.25	7.50	28.00	195.	535.	
1925D	5,117,000	4.00	6.00	8.50	25.00	85.00	260.	1700.	5300.	—
1925S	5,850,000	2.00	2.80	4.00	8.00	30.00	140.	2200.	4250.	—
1926	32,160,000	1.00	1.50	2.25	4.25	6.50	28.00	235.	560.	—
1926D	6,828,000	1.95	3.00	4.00	7.50	15.00	70.00	550.	2400.	—
1926S	1,520,000	6.00	9.50	15.00	34.00	190.	770.	3000.	4950.	—
1927	28,080,000	1.00	1.50	2.25	4.25	6.50	21.00	180.	325.	—
1927D	4,812,000	2.75	3.75	5.00	12.00	42.00	175.	1200.	8500.	—
1927S	4,770,000	1.90	2.65	3.75	5.50	11.00	240.	1625.	4550.	—
1928	19,480,000	1.00	1.50	2.25	4.25	6.50	21.00	115.	250.	—
1928D	4,161,000	3.00	4.25	6.00	15.00	30.00	135.	910.	2500.	—
1928S	7,400,000	1.75	2.35	3.25	5.00	12.00	70.00	495.	1500.	—
1929	25,970,000	1.00	1.40	2.35	3.75	5.00	19.50	58.00	180.	—
1929D	5,034,000	2.00	3.00	4.00	6.00	10.00	28.00	85.00	130.	—
1929S	4,730,000	1.65	1.90	2.25	4.25	5.50	34.00	120.	310.	—
1930	6,770,000	1.50	1.80	2.25	4.25	5.50	22.00	130.	275.	—
1930S	1,843,000	3.50	4.25	5.00	7.50	13.00	70.00	135.	260.	—
1931	3,150,000	2.60	3.00	3.75	5.00	11.00	35.00	155.	440.	—
1931D	1,260,000	6.00	8.00	11.00	18.00	30.00	77.00	210.	290.	—
1931S	1,800,000	3.50	4.00	5.00	7.50	13.00	63.00	210.	1900.	—

Date	Mintage	G-4	VG-8	F-12	VF-20	XF-40	MS-60	MS-65	-65FSB	Prf-65
1934	24,080,000	1.00	1.45	1.75	3.00	5.00	15.00	32.00	100.	—
1934D	6,772,000	1.60	2.10	2.75	4.00	8.00	32.00	62.00	250.	—
1935	58,830,000	.80	1.00	1.50	2.15	4.25	11.00	30.00	45.00	—
1935D	10,477,000	1.50	2.00	3.00	4.75	9.25	32.00	60.00	425.	—
1935S	15,840,000	1.35	1.50	1.75	3.00	5.50	24.00	33.00	265.	—
1936	87,504,130	.80	1.00	1.50	2.25	3.50	8.50	24.00	60.00	875.
1936D	16,132,000	1.25	1.50	2.00	3.25	6.75	22.00	42.00	210.	—
1936S	9,210,000	1.25	1.50	1.75	2.75	4.75	17.00	28.00	50.00	—
1937	56,865,756	.80	1.00	1.50	2.00	3.25	10.00	24.00	36.00	300.
1937D	14,146,000	1.25	1.50	1.90	3.00	5.50	21.00	41.00	100.	—
1937S	9,740,000	1.25	1.50	1.90	3.00	5.50	18.00	31.00	160.	—
1938	22,198,728	.80	1.00	1.50	2.25	3.50	14.00	23.00	51.00	215.
1938D	5,537,000	1.75	2.00	2.25	3.75	6.00	15.00	26.00	41.00	—
1938S	8,090,000	1.35	1.55	1.85	2.35	3.75	16.00	31.00	110.	—
1939	67,749,321	.80	1.00	1.50	2.00	3.25	10.00	25.00	150.	210.
1939D	24,394,000	1.25	1.45	1.75	2.25	3.50	12.50	24.00	36.00	—
1939S	10,540,000	1.55	1.75	2.00	2.50	4.25	24.00	35.00	340.	—
1940	65,361,827	.60	.70	.90	1.10	2.50	6.50	23.00	33.00	185.
1940D	21,198,000	.60	.70	.90	1.10	1.50	8.50	23.00	33.00	—
1940S	21,560,000	.60	.70	.90	1.10	1.50	8.50	23.00	43.00	—
1941	175,106,557	.60	.70	.90	1.10	1.50	5.50	19.00	23.00	160.
1941D	45,634,000	.60	.70	.90	1.10	1.50	8.00	21.00	23.00	—
1941S	43,090,000	.60	.70	.90	1.10	1.50	10.00	19.00	30.00	—

Fully split bands

1942/41

1942/41-D

Date	Mintage	G-4	VG-8	F-12	VF-20	XF-40	MS-60	MS-65	-65FSB	Prf-65
1942	205,432,329	.60	.70	.90	1.10	1.50	5.50	20.00	36.00	160.
1942/41	Inc. Ab.	230.	280.	300.	320.	350.	1450.	6300.	9350.	—
1942D	60,740,000	.60	.70	.90	1.10	1.50	8.50	23.00	30.00	—
1942/41D	Inc. Ab.	260.	300.	320.	375.	490.	1600.	4850.	7300.	—
1942S	49,300,000	.60	.70	.90	1.10	1.50	10.00	23.00	61.00	—
1943	191,710,000	.60	.70	.90	1.10	1.50	6.50	19.00	23.00	—
1943D	71,949,000	.60	.70	.90	1.10	1.50	8.50	24.00	26.00	—
1943S	60,400,000	.60	.70	.90	1.10	1.50	10.00	20.00	32.00	—
1944	231,410,000	.60	.70	.90	1.10	1.50	5.50	20.00	39.00	—
1944D	62,224,000	.60	.70	.90	1.10	1.50	8.50	20.00	27.00	—
1944S	49,490,000	.60	.70	.90	1.10	1.50	10.00	20.00	30.00	—
1945	159,130,000	.60	.70	.90	1.10	1.50	5.50	22.00	3125.	—
1945D	40,245,000	.60	.70	.90	1.10	1.50	8.00	20.00	29.00	—
1945S	41,920,000	.60	.70	.90	1.10	1.50	8.50	20.00	85.00	—
1945S micro	Inc. Ab.	1.00	1.25	1.50	3.00	4.25	17.00	52.00	450.	—

Roosevelt

Reverse mintmark
(1946-64)

Obverse mintmark
(1968-present)

Silver composition

Designer: John R. Sinnock. **Size:** 17.9 millimeters. **Weight:** 2.5 grams. **Composition:** 90% silver (0.0724 ounces), 10% copper.

Date	Mintage	G-4	VG-8	F-12	VF-20	XF-40	AU-50	MS-60	MS-65	Prf-65
1946	225,250,000	—	—	—	.50	.65	.95	1.05	2.50	—
1946D	61,043,500	—	—	—	.50	.65	1.10	1.25	4.50	—
1946S	27,900,000	—	—	—	.50	.65	1.10	2.00	5.25	—
1947	121,520,000	—	—	—	.50	.65	.95	1.00	4.75	—
1947D	46,835,000	—	—	—	.50	.95	1.20	1.40	10.00	—
1947S	34,840,000	—	—	—	.50	.95	1.10	1.35	5.50	—
1948	74,950,000	—	—	—	.50	.95	1.10	1.75	11.00	—
1948D	52,841,000	—	—	—	.50	1.20	1.50	2.00	10.00	—
1948S	35,520,000	—	—	—	.50	.95	1.10	1.35	9.00	—
1949	30,940,000	—	—	—	1.00	1.50	4.50	6.00	29.00	—
1949D	26,034,000	—	—	.60	.80	1.25	2.00	3.50	12.50	—
1949S	13,510,000	—	1.00	1.25	1.50	2.75	7.50	9.00	55.00	—
1950	50,181,500	—	—	—	.50	.95	1.10	1.35	4.60	37.00
1950D	46,803,000	—	—	—	.50	.65	.95	1.00	4.60	—
1950S	20,440,000	—	.85	1.00	1.10	1.25	5.00	7.00	35.00	—
1951	102,937,602	—	—	—	.50	.85	1.00	1.10	3.30	26.00
1951D	56,529,000	—	—	—	.50	.65	.95	1.00	3.50	—
1951S	31,630,000	—	—	—	1.00	1.05	2.75	3.25	24.00	—
1952	99,122,073	—	—	—	.50	.95	1.10	1.20	3.30	29.00
1952D	122,100,000	—	—	—	.50	.65	.95	1.00	3.80	—
1952S	44,419,500	—	—	—	1.00	1.05	1.10	1.35	7.00	—
1953	53,618,920	—	—	—	.50	.65	1.00	1.10	3.60	24.00
1953D	136,433,000	—	—	—	.50	.65	.95	1.00	3.50	—
1953S	39,180,000	—	—	—	.50	.95	1.10	2.00	2.75	—
1954	114,243,503	—	—	—	.50	.75	.90	1.00	2.15	11.00
1954D	106,397,000	—	—	—	.50	.65	.95	1.00	2.15	—
1954S	22,860,000	—	—	—	.50	.65	.80	.90	2.20	—
1955	12,828,381	—	—	—	.70	.80	.85	.95	3.00	15.00
1955D	13,959,000	—	—	—	.65	.75	.80	.90	2.25	—
1955S	18,510,000	—	—	—	.65	.75	.80	.90	2.00	—
1956	109,309,384	—	—	—	.50	.65	.80	.90	2.00	2.50
1956D	108,015,100	—	—	—	.50	.65	.80	.90	1.65	—
1957	161,407,952	—	—	—	.50	.65	.80	.90	1.60	1.50
1957D	113,354,330	—	—	—	.50	.65	.80	.90	3.00	—
1958	32,785,652	—	—	—	.50	.65	.80	.90	1.80	2.00
1958D	136,564,600	—	—	—	.50	.65	.80	.90	1.50	—
1959	86,929,291	—	—	—	.50	.65	.80	.90	1.50	1.50
1959D	164,919,790	—	—	—	.50	.65	.80	.90	1.35	—
1960	72,081,602	—	—	—	.50	.65	.80	.90	1.40	1.40
1960D	200,160,400	—	—	—	.50	.65	.80	.90	1.35	—
1961	96,758,244	—	—	—	.50	.65	.80	.90	1.35	1.10
1961D	209,146,550	—	—	—	.50	.65	.80	.90	1.35	—
1962	75,668,019	—	—	—	.50	.65	.80	.90	1.35	1.10
1962D	334,948,380	—	—	—	.50	.65	.80	.90	1.35	—
1963	126,725,645	—	—	—	.50	.65	.80	.90	1.35	1.10
1963D	421,476,530	—	—	—	.50	.65	.80	.90	1.35	—
1964	933,310,762	—	—	—	.50	.65	.80	.90	1.35	1.00
1964D	1,357,517,180	—	—	—	.50	.65	.80	.90	1.35	—

Clad composition

Weight: 2.27 grams. **Composition:** clad layers of 75% copper and 25% nickel, bonded to a pure-copper core. **Notes:** The 1979-S Type II proof has a clearer mintmark than the Type I. On the 1982 no-mintmark variety, the mintmark was inadvertently left off.

Date	Mintage	G-4	F-12	VF-20	XF-40	AU-50	MS-60	MS-65	Prf-65
1965	1,652,140,570	—	—	—	—	—	—	.75	—
1966	1,382,734,540	—	—	—	—	—	—	.65	—
1967	2,244,007,320	—	—	—	—	—	—	.65	—
1968	424,470,000	—	—	—	—	—	—	.60	—
1968D	480,748,280	—	—	—	—	—	—	.60	—
1968S	—	—	—	—	—	—	—	—	.65
1969	145,790,000	—	—	—	—	—	—	.75	—
1969D	563,323,870	—	—	—	—	—	—	.75	—
1969S	—	—	—	—	—	—	—	—	.65
1970	345,570,000	—	—	—	—	—	—	.60	—
1970D	754,942,100	—	—	—	—	—	—	.60	—
1970S	—	—	—	—	—	—	—	—	.65
1971	162,690,000	—	—	—	—	—	—	.75	—
1971D	377,914,240	—	—	—	—	—	—	.60	—
1971S	—	—	—	—	—	—	—	—	.80
1972	431,540,000	—	—	—	—	—	—	.60	—
1972D	330,290,000	—	—	—	—	—	—	.60	—
1972S	—	—	—	—	—	—	—	—	.80
1973	315,670,000	—	—	—	—	—	—	.60	—
1973D	455,032,426	—	—	—	—	—	—	.50	—
1973S	—	—	—	—	—	—	—	—	.60
1974	470,248,000	—	—	—	—	—	—	.50	—
1974D	571,083,000	—	—	—	—	—	—	.50	—
1974S	—	—	—	—	—	—	—	—	1.25
1975	585,673,900	—	—	—	—	—	—	.60	—
1975D	313,705,300	—	—	—	—	—	—	.50	—
1975S	—	—	—	—	—	—	—	—	.60
1976	568,760,000	—	—	—	—	—	—	.60	—
1976D	695,222,774	—	—	—	—	—	—	.60	—
1976S	—	—	—	—	—	—	—	—	.75
1977	796,930,000	—	—	—	—	—	—	.50	—

PRICING SECTION

Date	Mintage	G-4	F-12	VF-20	XF-40	AU-50	MS-60	MS-65	Prf-65
1977D	376,607,228	—	—	—	—	—	—	.50	—
1977S	—	—	—	—	—	—	—	—	.60
1978	663,980,000	—	—	—	—	—	—	.50	—
1978D	282,847,540	—	—	—	—	—	—	.50	—
1978S	—	—	—	—	—	—	—	—	.60
1979	315,440,000	—	—	—	—	—	—	.50	—
1979D	390,921,184	—	—	—	—	—	—	.50	—
1979S T-I	—	—	—	—	—	—	—	—	.55
1979S T-II	—	—	—	—	—	—	—	—	1.25
1980P	735,170,000	—	—	—	—	—	—	.50	—
1980D	719,354,321 ·	—	—	—	—	—	—	.50	—
1980S	—	—	—	—	—	—	—	—	.50
1981P	676,650,000	—	—	—	—	—	—	.50	—
1981D	712,284,143	—	—	—	—	—	—	.50	—
1981S T-I	—	—	—	—	—	—	—	—	.50
1981S T-II	—	—	—	—	—	—	—	—	4.00
1982P	519,475,000	—	—	—	—	—	—	1.50	—
1982 no mint mark		—	—	—	—	85.00	115.	220.	—
1982D	542,713,584	—	—	—	—	—	—	.60	—
1982S	—	—	—	—	—	—	—	—	.65
1983P	647,025,000	—	—	—	—	—	—	.75	—
1983D	730,129,224	—	—	—	—	—	—	.70	—
1983S	—	—	—	—	—	—	—	—	1.10
1984P	856,669,000	—	—	—	—	—	—	.50	—
1984D	704,803,976	—	—	—	—	—	—	.60	—
1984S	—	—	—	—	—	—	—	—	1.60
1985P	705,200,962	—	—	—	—	—	—	.60	—
1985D	587,979,970	—	—	—	—	—	—	.55	—
1985S	—	—	—	—	—	—	—	—	1.10
1986P	682,649,693	—	—	—	—	—	—	.70	—
1986D	473,326,970	—	—	—	—	—	—	.75	—
1986S	—	—	—	—	—	—	—	—	2.00
1987P	762,709,481	—	—	—	—	—	—	.50	—
1987D	653,203,402	—	—	—	—	—	—	.50	—
1987S	—	—	—	—	—	—	—	—	1.25
1988P	1,030,550,000	—	—	—	—	—	—	.50	—
1988D	962,385,488	—	—	—	—	—	—	.50	—
1988S	—	—	—	—	—	—	—	—	1.50
1989P	1,298,400,000	—	—	—	—	—	—	.50	—
1989D	896,535,597	—	—	—	—	—	—	.50	—
1989S	—	—	—	—	—	—	—	—	1.45
1990P	1,034,340,000	—	—	—	—	—	—	.50	—
1990D	839,995,824	—	—	—	—	—	—	.50	—
1990S	—	—	—	—	—	—	—	—	2.75
1991P	927,220,000	—	—	—	—	—	—	.50	—
1991D	601,241,114	—	—	—	—	—	—	.50	—
1991S	—	—	—	—	—	—	—	—	3.25
1992P	593,500,000	—	—	—	—	—	—	.50	—
1992D	616,273,932	—	—	—	—	—	—	.50	—
1992S	(2,858,981)	—	—	—	—	—	—	—	3.40
1992S	Silver proof	—	—	—	—	—	—	—	3.25
1993P	766,180,000	—	—	—	—	—	—	.50	—
1993D	750,110,166	—	—	—	—	—	—	.50	—
1993S	—	—	—	—	—	—	—	—	2.85
1993S	Silver proof	—	—	—	—	—	—	—	4.00
1994P	1,189,000,000	—	—	—	—	—	—	.50	—
1994D	1,303,268,110	—	—	—	—	—	—	.50	—
1994S	—	—	—	—	—	—	—	—	2.60
1994S	Silver proof	—	—	—	—	—	—	—	3.75
1995P	1,125,500,000	—	—	—	—	—	—	.50	—
1995D	1,274,890,000	—	—	—	—	—	—	.50	—
1995S	—	—	—	—	—	—	—	—	2.60
1995S	Silver proof	—	—	—	—	—	—	—	3.75
1996P	1,421,163,000	—	—	—	—	—	—	.50	—
1996D	1,400,300,000	—	—	—	—	—	—	.50	—
1996W	—	—	—	—	—	—	6.00	7.00	—
1996S	—	—	—	—	—	—	—	—	2.50
1996S	Silver proof	—	—	—	—	—	—	—	3.50
1997P	991,640,000	—	—	—	—	—	—	.50	—
1997D	979,810,000	—	—	—	—	—	—	.50	—
1997S	—	—	—	—	—	—	—	—	3.50
1997S	Silver proof	—	—	—	—	—	—	—	3.50
1998P	—	—	—	—	—	—	—	.50	—
1998D	—	—	—	—	—	—	—	.50	—
1998S	—	—	—	—	—	—	—	—	3.50
1998S	Silver proof	—	—	—	—	—	—	—	3.50
1999	—	—	—	—	—	—	—	.50	—
1999D	—	—	—	—	—	—	—	.50	—
1999S	—	—	—	—	—	—	—	—	—
1999S	Silver proof	—	—	—	—	—	—	—	—

20-cent

Designer: William Barber. **Size:** 22 millimeters. **Weight:** 5 grams. **Composition:** 90% silver (0.1447 ounces), 10% copper.

Date	Mintage	G-4	VG-8	F-12	VF-20	XF-40	AU-50	MS-60	MS-65	Prf-65
1875	39,700	65.00	75.00	90.00	120.	180.	325.	600.	6000.	9500.
1875S	1,155,000	45.00	50.00	70.00	100.	160.	300.	475.	4900.	—
1875CC	133,290	50.00	60.00	95.00	150.	265.	475.	630.	8200.	—
1876	15,900	110.	125.	150.	200.	315.	500.	650.	6000.	7500.
1876CC	10,000			Eliasberg sale, Apr. 1997, MS-65, $148,500.					—	—
1877	510		Proof only	—	1500.	1700.	1850.	—	—	7500.
1878	600		Proof only	—	1300.	1400.	1500.	—	—	7600.

1876 20-Cent
Grade F-12

Source: COIN PRICES

1804 Quarter
Grade XF-40

Source: COIN PRICES

Quarters

Draped Bust

Small-eagle reverse

Designer: Robert Scot. **Size:** 27.5 millimeters. **Weight:** 6.74 grams. **Composition:** 89.24% silver (0.1935 ounces), 10.76% copper.

Date	Mintage	G-4	VG-8	F-12	VF-20	XF-40	AU-50	MS-60	MS-65
1796	6,146	4350.	6000.	9150.	14,000.	17,000.	19,000.	28,000.	125,000.

Heraldic-eagle reverse

Date	Mintage	G-4	VG-8	F-12	VF-20	XF-40	AU-50	MS-60	MS-65
1804	6,738	1000.	1475.	2750.	4750.	9750.	22,500.	40,000.	116,000.
1805	121,394	210.	300.	450.	850.	2900.	3500.	5850.	46,500.
1806	206,124	225.	285.	425.	800.	2900.	3500.	5850.	46,500.
1806/5	Inc. Ab.	235.	315.	495.	950.	2900.	4350.	5850.	46,500.
1807	220,643	210.	300.	450.	850.	2900.	3500.	5850.	46,500.

Liberty Cap

Designer: John Reich. **Size:** 27 millimeters. **Weight:** 6.74 grams. **Composition:** 89.24% silver (0.1935 ounces), 10.76% copper. **Notes:** Varieties of the 1819 strikes are distinguished by the size of the 9 in the date. Varieties of the 1820 strikes are distinguished by the size of the 0 in the date. One 1822 variety and one 1828 variety have "25" engraved over "50" in the denomination. The 1827 restrikes were produced privately using dies sold as scrap by the U.S. Mint.

Date	Mintage	G-4	VG-8	F-12	VF-20	XF-40	AU-50	MS-60	MS-65
1815	89,235	60.00	80.00	125.	335.	850.	2000.	3100.	22,000.
1818	361,174	40.00	60.00	90.00	275.	675.	1300.	1550.	12,500.
1818/15	Inc. Ab.	60.00	75.00	110.	315.	800.	2000.	3100.	22,000.
1819 sm.9	144,000	55.00	70.00	100.	300.	700.	1350.	1550.	12,500.
1819 lg.9	Inc. Ab.	55.00	70.00	100.	300.	700.	1350.	1550.	12,500.
1820 sm.O	127,444	60.00	75.00	110.	315.	700.	1500.	3000.	12,500.
1820 lg.O	Inc. Ab.	50.00	65.00	100.	275.	675.	1300.	1550.	12,500.
1821	216,851	50.00	65.00	100.	275.	675.	1300.	1550.	12,500.
1822	64,080	75.00	90.00	130.	400.	975.	1400.	1550.	12,500.
1822 25/50C.	I.A.	2500.	3500.	4750.	7250.	9750.	12,500.	17,500.	45,000.
1823/22	17,800	12,500.	17,500.	22,500.	27,500.	44,000.	—	—	—
				Superior, Aug. 1990, proof, $62,500.					
1824/2	Unrecorded	100.	140.	200.	575.	1250.	1950.	5000.	—
1825/22	168,000	100.	165.	285.	575.	1250.	1850.	2450.	—
1825/23	Inc. Ab.	50.00	65.00	100.	275.	725.	1200.	1700.	10,500.
1825/24	Inc. Ab.	60.00	75.00	115.	325.	825.	1400.	1900.	11,500.
1827 original	4,000				Eliasberg, Apr. 1997, VF-20, $39,600.			—	—
1827 restrike	I.A.				Eliasberg, Apr. 1997, Prf-65, $77,000.			—	—
1828	102,000	50.00	65.00	95.00	275.	650.	1500.	1900.	12,500.
1828 25/50C.	I.A.	165.	205.	350.	650.	1350.	3000.	8000.	—

No motto

Designer: William Kneass. **Size:** 24.3 millimeters. **Notes:** In 1831 the motto "E Pluribus Unum" was removed from the reverse. Varieties of the 1831 strikes are distinguished by the size of the lettering on the reverse.

Date	Mintage	G-4	VG-8	F-12	VF-20	XF-40	AU-50	MS-60	MS-65
1831 sm. let.	398,000	45.00	50.00	60.00	90.00	240.	750.	900.	13,000.
1831 lg.let.	Inc. Ab.	45.00	50.00	60.00	90.00	240.	750.	900.	13,000.
1832	320,000	45.00	50.00	60.00	90.00	240.	750.	900.	13,000.
1833	156,000	48.00	60.00	80.00	120.	325.	800.	1275.	17,000.
1834	286,000	45.00	50.00	60.00	90.00	240.	750.	900.	13,000.
1835	1,952,000	45.00	50.00	60.00	90.00	240.	750.	900.	13,000.
1836	472,000	45.00	50.00	60.00	90.00	240.	750.	900.	13,000.
1837	252,400	47.00	53.00	64.00	95.00	250.	750.	900.	13,000.
1838	832,000	45.00	50.00	60.00	90.00	240.	750.	900.	13,000.

Seated Liberty

No drapery

Designer: Christian Gobrecht. **Size:** 24.3 millimeters. **Weight:** 6.68 grams. **Composition:** 90% silver (0.1934 ounces), 10% copper.

Date	Mintage	G-4	VG-8	F-12	VF-20	XF-40	AU-50	MS-60	MS-65
1838	Inc. Ab.	15.00	22.00	27.00	55.00	195.	475.	1050.	—
1839	491,146	14.00	20.00	27.00	52.00	195.	450.	1050.	25,000.
1840O	425,200	13.00	19.00	27.00	60.00	300.	400.	1050.	25,000.

Drapery added to Liberty

Notes: In 1840 drapery was added to Liberty's left elbow. Two varieties for 1842 and 1842-O are distinguished by the size of the numerals in the date. 1852 obverse dies were used to strike the 1853 no-arrows variety, with the 2 being recut to form a 3.

Date	Mintage	G-4	VG-8	F-12	VF-20	XF-40	AU-50	MS-60	MS-65
1840	188,127	30.00	40.00	55.00	75.00	180.	350.	750.	—
1840O	Inc. Ab.	20.00	30.00	50.00	110.	185.	500.	1150.	—
1841	120,000	45.00	60.00	80.00	135.	225.	385.	800.	—
1841O	452,000	12.50	24.00	40.00	70.00	185.	300.	800.	—
1842 sm. dt.	88,000				Eliasberg, Apr. 1997, Prf-63, $66,000.				—
1842 lg. dt.	Inc. Ab.	95.00	145.	170.	275.	475.	950.	2700.	—
1842O sm. dt.	769,000	375.	500.	850.	1750.	3750.	—	—	—
1842O lg. dt.	Inc. Ab.	13.50	16.00	30.00	60.00	245.	800.	—	—
1843	645,600	12.50	16.00	25.00	45.00	80.00	175.	290.	3500.
1843O	968,000	20.00	33.00	53.00	175.	375.	1250.	—	—
1844	421,200	12.50	16.00	25.00	43.00	80.00	185.	290.	3500.
1844O	740,000	12.50	21.00	38.00	55.00	175.	375.	1200.	—
1845	922,000	12.50	15.00	25.00	40.00	75.00	185.	450.	3500.
1846	510,000	15.00	25.00	37.50	65.00	115.	245.	485.	3500.
1847	734,000	12.50	15.00	25.00	45.00	75.00	190.	425.	3500.
1847O	368,000	22.00	40.00	80.00	110.	285.	850.	—	—
1848	146,000	35.00	48.00	70.00	130.	275.	425.	1175.	—
1849	340,000	16.00	22.00	40.00	70.00	100.	375.	1000.	—
1849O	Unrecorded	375.	545.	1175.	1675.	3000.	7000.	—	—
1850	190,800	30.00	45.00	55.00	95.00	175.	325.	1000.	—
1850O	412,000	17.50	30.00	45.00	85.00	225.	750.	1100.	—
1851	160,000	35.00	50.00	75.00	135.	225.	400.	1000.	—
1851O	88,000	175.	265.	325.	575.	1000.	2600.	—	—
1852	177,060	37.50	47.50	75.00	135.	185.	400.	900.	—
1852O	96,000	165.	255.	300.	550.	900.	2750.	—	—
1853 recut date	44,200	350.	475.	675.	925.	1200.	1750.	3250.	—

Arrows at date, reverse rays

Weight: 6.22 grams. **Composition:** 90% silver (0.18 ounces), 10% copper.

Date	Mintage	G-4	VG-8	F-12	VF-20	XF-40	AU-50	MS-60	MS-65	Prf-65
1853 rays	15,210,020	12.50	16.00	24.00	38.00	160.	295.	900.	17,500.	—
1853/4	Inc. Ab.	30.00	47.50	75.00	165.	300.	950.	2750.	—	—
1853O rays	1,332,000	14.00	20.00	30.00	75.00	275.	1500.	3000.	—	—

Reverse rays removed

Notes: The 1854-O "huge O" variety has an oversized mintmark.

Date	Mintage	G-4	VG-8	F-12	VF-20	XF-40	AU-50	MS-60	MS-65	Prf-65
1854	12,380,000	12.50	16.00	22.00	32.00	75.00	225.	410.	7100.	15,000.
1854O	1,484,000	14.00	20.00	28.00	45.00	120.	300.	1500.	—	—
1854O huge O	Inc. Ab.	100.	165.	245.	375.	775.	—	—	—	—
1855	2,857,000	12.50	16.00	22.00	24.00	80.00	285.	410.	7100.	15,000.
1855O	176,000	35.00	55.00	90.00	275.	750.	1750.	3750.	—	—
1855S	396,400	25.00	45.00	65.00	145.	375.	1250.	1750.	—	—

Arrows at date removed

1856-S Quarter
Grade F-12

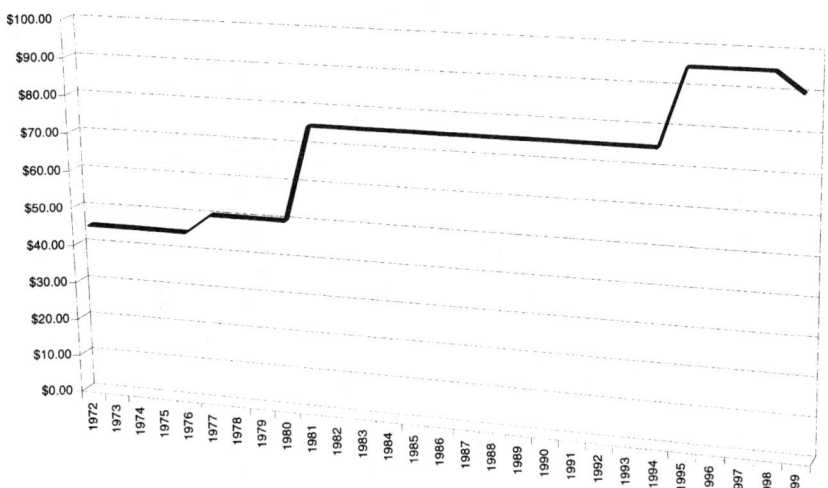

■ Retail Price

Source: **COIN PRICES**

Date	Mintage	G-4	VG-8	F-12	VF-20	XF-40	AU-50	MS-60	MS-65	Prf-65
1856	7,264,000	12.50	15.00	22.00	32.00	58.00	145.	325.	3500.	15,000.
1856O	968,000	13.00	16.00	26.00	40.00	110.	485.	1250.	—	—
1856S	286,000	45.00	65.00	90.00	195.	450.	1275.	—	—	—
1856S/S	Inc. Ab.	55.00	80.00	135.	285.	650.	1875.	—	—	—
1857	9,644,000	12.50	15.00	22.00	28.00	50.00	145.	290.	3000.	15,000.
1857O	1,180,000	13.00	17.00	27.00	40.00	80.00	275.	1075.	—	—
1857S	82,000	105.	140.	185.	275.	575.	1050.	3250.	—	—
1858	7,368,000	12.50	15.00	22.00	28.00	50.00	190.	290.	3000.	11,500.
1858O	520,000	18.00	25.00	45.00	65.00	135.	425.	1250.	—	—
1858S	121,000	45.00	70.00	120.	275.	675.	1650.	—	—	—
1859	1,344,000	14.00	15.00	23.00	30.00	63.00	190.	700.	—	7000.
1859O	260,000	18.00	25.00	35.00	50.00	90.00	450.	900.	—	—
1859S	80,000	90.00	125.	175.	275.	675.	7000.	—	—	—
1860	805,400	12.50	15.00	23.00	30.00	64.00	155.	900.	11,500.	4000.
1860O	388,000	14.00	19.00	35.00	50.00	95.00	225.	1450.	—	—
1860S	56,000	165.	245.	350.	625.	2750.	9000.	—	—	—
1861	4,854,600	12.50	14.00	22.00	28.00	45.00	190.	290.	3000.	4000.
1861S	96,000	60.00	80.00	165.	295.	775.	5250.	—	—	—
1862	932,550	10.00	15.00	24.00	35.00	60.00	175.	290.	3000.	4000.
1862S	67,000	55.00	70.00	140.	245.	650.	1775.	2750.	—	—
1863	192,060	25.00	40.00	60.00	95.00	225.	325.	750.	—	7000.
1864	94,070	50.00	60.00	90.00	125.	275.	450.	925.	11,500.	7000.
1864S	20,000	250.	375.	575.	1200.	2500.	3750.	—	—	—
1865	59,300	55.00	70.00	95.00	120.	250.	375.	875.	11,500.	7000.
1865S	41,000	85.00	125.	165.	275.	575.	1250.	2000.	—	—
1866	—	Unique	—	—	—	—	—	—	—	—

Motto above eagle

Notes: In 1866 the motto "In God We Trust" was added to the reverse. The 1873 closed-3 and open-3 varieties are distinguished by the amount of space between the upper left and lower left serifs in the 3.

Date	Mintage	G-4	VG-8	F-12	VF-20	XF-40	AU-50	MS-60	MS-65	Prf-65
1866	17,525	275.	395.	450.	595.	795.	1500.	2250.	—	6750.
1866S	28,000	200.	290.	450.	725.	1250.	1800.	—	—	—
1867	20,625	175.	225.	295.	375.	475.	625.	1300.	—	6750.
1867S	48,000	145.	210.	295.	375.	750.	1750.	3000.	—	—
1868	30,000	105.	155.	200.	255.	375.	525.	1200.	—	6750.
1868S	96,000	50.00	70.00	135.	245.	575.	1250.	2300.	—	—
1869	16,600	215.	260.	340.	425.	575.	950.	1400.	—	6750.
1869S	76,000	60.00	95.00	165.	300.	625.	1575.	—	—	—
1870	87,400	40.00	48.00	80.00	135.	250.	325.	1000.	—	6550.
1870CC	8,340	3200.	4250.	5750.	9500.	15,500.	—	—	—	—
1871	119,160	30.00	40.00	55.00	115.	185.	425.	1000.	—	6550.
1871CC	10,890	1700.	2750.	3750.	6500.	11,500.	25,000.	—	—	—
1871S	30,900	275.	375.	425.	625.	975.	1750.	3000.	—	—
1872	182,950	30.00	40.00	50.00	100.	155.	445.	1250.	—	4050.
1872CC	22,850	400.	625.	1050.	2250.	3750.	7500.	—	—	—
1872S	83,000	900.	1475.	1950.	2500.	3850.	6750.	—	—	—
1873 clsd.3	212,600	175.	265.	325.	525.	775.	1250.	—	—	8000.
1873 open 3	Inc. Ab.	30.00	37.50	55.00	95.00	175.	325.	750.	—	—
1873CC	4,000	Eliasberg, Apr. 1997, MS-62, $187,000.							—	—

Arrows at date

Weight: 6.25 grams. **Composition:** 90% silver (0.1809 ounces), 10% copper.

Date	Mintage	G-4	VG-8	F-12	VF-20	XF-40	AU-50	MS-60	MS-65	Prf-65
1873	1,271,700	12.50	16.00	31.00	50.00	190.	380.	700.	3500.	5500.
1873CC	12,462	1500.	2950.	4500.	9250.	13,500.	—	—	—	—
1873S	156,000	25.00	35.00	70.00	145.	275.	600.	1100.	—	—
1874	471,900	16.00	24.00	38.00	75.00	200.	400.	750.	3500.	5500.
1874S	392,000	18.50	28.00	40.00	110.	195.	400.	725.	—	—

Arrows at date removed

Notes: The 1876-CC fine-reeding variety has a more finely reeded edge.

Date	Mintage	G-4	VG-8	F-12	VF-20	XF-40	AU-50	MS-60	MS-65	Prf-65
1875	4,293,500	12.00	15.00	22.00	28.00	70.00	115.	350.	1450.	1650.
1875CC	140,000	50.00	80.00	145.	295.	575.	775.	1400.	—	—
1875S	680,000	22.00	30.00	50.00	80.00	165.	300.	575.	—	—
1876	17,817,150	12.00	15.00	22.00	28.00	70.00	115.	350.	1450.	1650.
1876CC	4,944,000	14.00	17.00	25.00	40.00	85.00	235.	425.	3900.	—
1876CC fine reeding										
Inc. Ab.		13.00	16.00	24.00	35.00	70.00	210.	375.	—	—
1876S	8,596,000	12.00	15.00	22.00	28.00	70.00	115.	225.	1450.	—
1877	10,911,710	12.00	15.00	22.00	28.00	70.00	115.	225.	1450.	1650.
1877CC	4,192,000	12.00	16.00	25.00	35.00	70.00	200.	375.	—	—
1877S	8,996,000	12.00	15.00	22.00	28.00	70.00	115.	220.	1450.	—
1877/horz. S	Inc. Ab.	32.00	48.00	65.00	100.	225.	375.	650.	—	—
1878	2,260,800	12.00	15.00	25.00	40.00	70.00	165.	360.	4100.	1650.
1878CC	996,000	16.00	25.00	38.00	55.00	100.	215.	425.	4100.	—
1878S	140,000	100.	140.	260.	325.	650.	950.	1750.	—	—
1879	14,700	145.	170.	215.	285.	345.	410.	525.	—	1650.
1880	14,955	155.	170.	215.	285.	345.	410.	525.	—	1650.
1881	12,975	145.	170.	215.	285.	345.	410.	525.	—	1650.
1882	16,300	160.	185.	225.	295.	355.	450.	600.	—	1650.
1883	15,439	160.	195.	225.	295.	355.	450.	600.	—	1650.
1884	8,875	200.	245.	300.	375.	475.	550.	650.	—	1650.
1885	14,530	170.	190.	245.	285.	345.	415.	600.	—	1650.
1886	5,886	375.	425.	450.	540.	675.	850.	1000.	—	1650.
1887	10,710	245.	295.	345.	400.	475.	550.	650.	—	1650.
1888	10,833	185.	205.	245.	295.	375.	475.	600.	—	1650.
1888S	1,216,000	13.00	15.00	22.00	30.00	70.00	135.	225.	1450.	—
1889	12,711	170.	200.	235.	285.	360.	450.	600.	—	1650.
1890	80,590	50.00	55.00	80.00	110.	185.	275.	400.	—	1650.
1891	3,920,600	12.00	15.00	22.00	30.00	70.00	150.	225.	1450.	1650.
1891O	68,000	125.	165.	260.	475.	875.	—	—	—	—
1891S	2,216,000	12.00	15.00	25.00	45.00	85.00	185.	350.	4400.	—

Barber

Designer: Charles E. Barber. **Size:** 24.3 millimeters. **Weight:** 6.25 grams. **Composition:** 90% silver (0.1809 ounces), 10% copper.

Date	Mintage	G-4	VG-8	F-12	VF-20	XF-40	AU-50	MS-60	MS-65	Prf-65
1892	8,237,245	3.75	4.50	19.50	30.00	65.00	115.	175.	1300.	1600.
1892O	2,640,000	5.75	8.50	24.00	35.00	72.00	145.	275.	1350.	—
1892S	964,079	13.00	30.00	62.00	80.00	125.	260.	390.	6300.	—
1893	5,484,838	3.50	6.50	21.00	30.00	65.00	115.	205.	1700.	1600.

PRICING SECTION

Date	Mintage	G-4	VG-8	F-12	VF-20	XF-40	AU-50	MS-60	MS-65	Prf-65
18930	3,396,000	5.00	7.50	25.00	40.00	72.00	145.	260.	1800.	—
1893S	1,454,535	9.00	13.00	34.00	55.00	100.	260.	390.	7100.	—
1894	3,432,972	4.50	5.75	23.00	32.00	75.00	120.	205.	1275.	1600.
18940	2,852,000	5.50	9.00	33.00	39.00	75.00	180.	310.	3000.	—
1894S	2,648,821	5.75	7.50	28.00	39.00	75.00	165.	310.	4100.	—
1895	4,440,880	4.75	5.75	22.00	30.00	65.00	120.	205.	1700.	1600.
18950	2,816,000	5.00	8.00	35.00	45.00	82.00	215.	360.	2800.	—
1895S	1,764,681	6.50	11.00	40.00	55.00	75.00	210.	345.	3500.	—
1896	3,874,762	5.00	5.75	24.00	30.00	65.00	120.	220.	1550.	1600.
18960	1,484,000	7.50	14.00	65.00	180.	320.	620.	845.	8100.	—
1896S	188,039	260.	415.	590.	870.	1900.	2900.	4150.	15,000.	—
1897	8,140,731	3.50	6.00	22.00	35.00	65.00	115.	175.	1300.	1600.
18970	1,414,800	7.75	15.00	75.00	175.	310.	550.	775.	3700.	—
1897S	542,229	18.00	50.00	175.	250.	375.	600.	900.	6300.	—
1898	11,100,735	3.20	5.00	19.00	30.00	65.00	110.	175.	1300.	1600.
18980	1,868,000	6.75	15.00	55.00	75.00	155.	315.	490.	8600.	—
1898S	1,020,592	5.00	12.50	30.00	44.00	65.00	175.	345.	5200.	—
1899	12,624,846	3.20	5.00	19.00	30.00	65.00	110.	170.	1300.	2200.
18990	2,644,000	4.75	12.00	30.00	36.00	85.00	240.	370.	5200.	—
1899S	708,000	9.00	22.00	47.00	58.00	75.00	195.	345.	3350.	—
1900	10,016,912	3.50	5.50	19.00	30.00	65.00	110.	170.	1300.	2200.
19000	3,416,000	6.50	14.00	60.00	75.00	95.00	240.	390.	3700.	—
1900S	1,858,585	5.75	9.00	36.00	48.00	65.00	110.	300.	5800.	—
1901	8,892,813	5.75	6.75	20.00	32.00	65.00	110.	170.	1900.	1900.
19010	1,612,000	17.00	35.00	85.00	150.	275.	585.	750.	5750.	—
1901S	72,664	1750.	2800.	4500.	6500.	9500.	9650.	12,600.	40,500.	—
1902	12,197,744	3.25	4.25	19.00	30.00	65.00	110.	170.	1300.	2275.
19020	4,748,000	4.75	8.50	35.00	54.00	100.	190.	360.	5700.	—
1902S	1,524,612	7.50	15.00	38.00	54.00	115.	190.	360.	3600.	—
1903	9,670,064	3.25	4.25	21.00	30.00	65.00	110.	170.	2600.	1600.
19030	3,500,000	5.50	7.50	38.00	48.00	78.00	200.	275.	6800.	—
1903S	1,036,000	8.00	20.00	40.00	55.00	91.00	235.	360.	2100.	—
1904	9,588,813	3.25	5.00	21.00	30.00	65.00	110.	170.	1550.	1600.
19040	2,456,000	6.00	11.00	48.00	70.00	160.	325.	675.	2750.	—
1905	4,968,250	3.75	5.00	24.00	35.00	65.00	110.	205.	1675.	1600.
19050	1,230,000	6.00	10.00	36.00	75.00	130.	340.	450.	5700.	—
1905S	1,884,000	5.00	9.00	36.00	48.00	83.00	185.	295.	4100.	—
1906	3,656,435	3.50	5.00	21.00	30.00	65.00	110.	170.	1300.	1600.
1906D	3,280,000	4.00	5.25	28.00	39.00	65.00	150.	210.	3600.	—

1896-S Quarter
Grade F-12

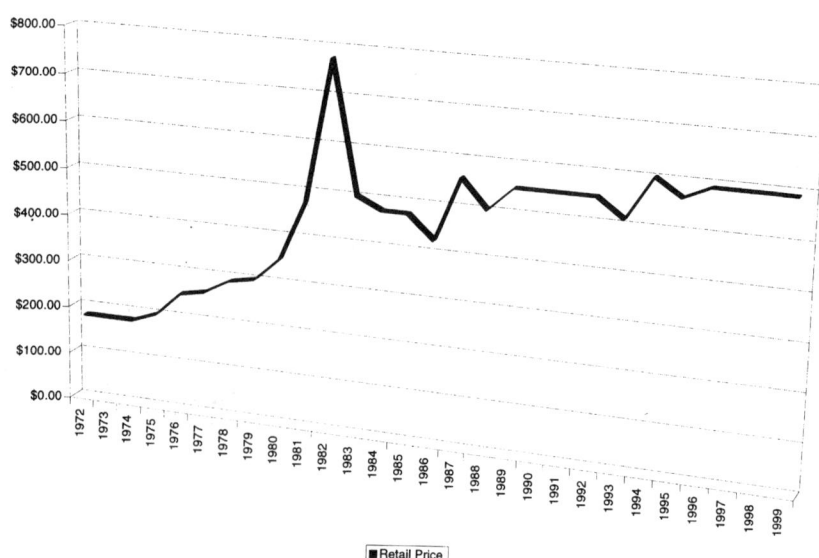

■ Retail Price

Source: COIN PRICES

PRICING SECTION

1913-S Quarter
Grade XF-40

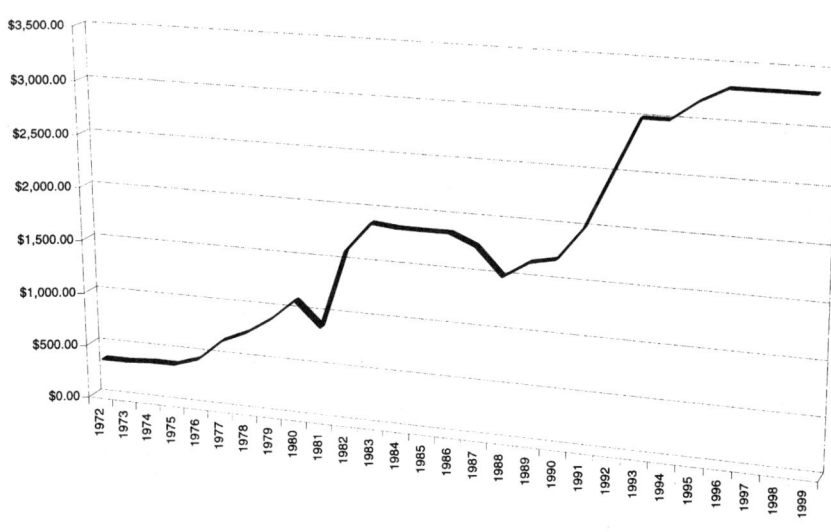

■ Retail Price

Source: COIN PRICES

Date	Mintage	G-4	VG-8	F-12	VF-20	XF-40	AU-50	MS-60	MS-65	Prf-65
1906O	2,056,000	4.25	5.25	32.00	39.00	77.00	180.	250.	1350.	—
1907	7,192,575	3.25	4.00	19.00	30.00	65.00	110.	170.	1300.	1600.
1907D	2,484,000	4.50	5.50	25.00	40.00	75.00	170.	295.	2650.	—
1907O	4,560,000	3.25	4.50	21.00	39.00	65.00	130.	235.	2750.	—
1907S	1,360,000	5.75	8.00	40.00	50.00	100.	200.	360.	3600.	—
1908	4,232,545	3.00	4.25	19.00	30.00	65.00	110.	205.	1300.	4050.
1908D	5,788,000	3.50	4.75	19.00	30.00	70.00	110.	215.	1500.	—
1908O	6,244,000	3.50	4.75	19.00	30.00	70.00	110.	205.	1300.	—
1908S	784,000	10.00	22.00	64.00	100.	215.	390.	650.	7200.	—
1909	9,268,650	2.75	4.00	19.00	30.00	65.00	110.	170.	1300.	1600.
1909D	5,114,000	3.00	4.50	19.00	30.00	65.00	165.	215.	1800.	—
1909O	712,000	10.00	24.00	75.00	125.	225.	360.	650.	7800.	—
1909S	1,348,000	3.50	5.50	28.00	36.00	65.00	175.	275.	3000.	—
1910	2,244,551	3.75	4.50	23.00	31.00	65.00	120.	175.	1425.	1600.
1910D	1,500,000	4.50	6.50	41.00	55.00	75.00	180.	280.	1400.	—
1911	3,720,543	3.25	4.00	30.00	21.00	72.00	110.	170.	1350.	1600.
1911D	933,600	5.00	8.00	65.00	125.	260.	425.	585.	5000.	—
1911S	988,000	5.00	8.50	45.00	75.00	115.	210.	295.	1425.	—
1912	4,400,700	3.25	4.00	19.00	30.00	65.00	110.	170.	1300.	1600.
1912S	708,000	6.00	8.00	43.00	51.00	90.00	210.	345.	3000.	—
1913	484,613	8.00	14.00	65.00	130.	370.	520.	1000.	4700.	2500.
1913D	1,450,800	5.50	6.50	30.00	42.00	70.00	145.	250.	1325.	—
1913S	40,000	415.	665.	1900.	2500.	3300.	4050.	4650.	10,000.	—
1914	6,244,610	3.25	4.00	16.00	30.00	65.00	110.	170.	1300.	2200.
1914D	3,046,000	3.25	4.00	17.00	29.00	65.00	110.	170.	1300.	—
1914S	264,000	50.00	75.00	130.	180.	370.	565.	865.	3250.	—
1915	3,480,450	3.25	4.00	17.00	28.00	65.00	110.	170.	1300.	2500.
1915D	3,694,000	3.25	4.00	17.00	28.00	65.00	110.	170.	1300.	—
1915S	704,000	4.00	6.00	28.00	36.00	88.00	180.	225.	1400.	—
1916	1,788,000	3.75	4.50	18.00	30.00	70.00	115.	170.	1300.	—
1916D	6,540,800	3.25	4.00	16.00	28.00	68.00	110.	170.	1300.	—

Standing Liberty

Type I

Designer: Hermon A. MacNeil. **Size:** 24.3 millimeters. **Weight:** 6.25 grams. **Composition:** 90% silver (0.1809 ounces), 10% copper. **Notes:** "MS-65FH" values are for coins that have full detail on Liberty's head.

Date	Mintage	G-4	VG-8	F-12	VF-20	XF-40	AU-50	MS-60	MS-65	-65FH
1916	52,000	1450.	1900.	2150.	2950.	3300.	4350.	5500.	17,500.	24,000.
1917	8,792,000	14.50	18.00	28.00	44.00	59.00	115.	175.	850.	1300.
1917D	1,509,200	16.50	20.00	27.00	55.00	85.00	140.	235.	975.	1600.
1917S	1,952,000	18.00	23.00	29.00	64.00	135.	190.	310.	1700.	2350.

Type II

Notes: In 1917 the obverse design was modified to cover Liberty's bare right breast. On the reverse, three stars were added below the eagle.

Date	Mintage	G-4	VG-8	F-12	VF-20	XF-40	AU-50	MS-60	MS-65	-65FH
1917	13,880,000	13.50	17.00	21.00	26.00	48.00	75.00	125.	550.	900.
1917D	6,224,400	25.00	33.00	49.00	63.00	92.00	120.	175.	1450.	3500.
1917S	5,522,000	20.00	27.50	38.00	55.00	75.00	105.	175.	1100.	3500.
1918	14,240,000	14.00	18.00	22.00	33.00	47.00	78.00	150.	650.	1550.
1918D	7,380,000	28.00	34.00	43.00	65.00	95.00	140.	225.	1500.	5500.
1918S	11,072,000	15.00	21.00	28.00	35.00	45.00	89.00	190.	1500.	19,500.
1918/17S	Inc.Ab.	1200.	1450.	1950.	2800.	4900.	8950.	14,500.	85,000.	—
1919	11,324,000	29.00	35.00	43.00	53.00	67.50	95.00	150.	615.	1175.
1919D	1,944,000	68.00	100.	135.	190.	315.	495.	750.	2200.	24,000.
1919S	1,836,000	68.00	100.	135.	260.	380.	550.	895.	3000.	31,000.
1920	27,860,000	15.00	17.00	20.00	24.00	35.00	69.00	125.	500.	1700.
1920D	3,586,400	45.00	58.00	79.00	95.00	125.	180.	225.	1950.	5900.
1920S	6,380,000	17.00	22.00	28.00	39.00	59.00	92.50	250.	2300.	35,000.
1921	1,916,000	75.00	110.	145.	180.	280.	330.	450.	1650.	4000.
1923	9,716,000	15.00	17.00	22.00	28.00	40.00	65.00	125.	500.	3900.
1923S	1,360,000	145.	185.	250.	350.	450.	530.	695.	1975.	3750.
1924	10,920,000	16.00	18.00	24.00	28.00	35.00	65.00	125.	450.	1575.
1924D	3,112,000	38.00	43.00	51.00	73.00	95.00	135.	150.	465.	4900.
1924S	2,860,000	24.00	28.00	34.00	39.00	88.00	175.	350.	1975.	5900.
1925	12,280,000	2.50	3.00	6.30	15.00	25.00	59.00	110.	475.	850.
1926	11,316,000	2.50	3.00	6.30	15.00	26.00	57.00	110.	450.	1900.
1926D	1,716,000	6.50	9.00	14.00	29.00	65.00	95.00	110.	525.	30,000.
1926S	2,700,000	3.00	4.00	13.00	29.00	95.00	220.	350.	2100.	28,000.
1927	11,912,000	2.50	3.00	6.30	15.00	25.00	57.50	110.	450.	800.
1927D	976,400	7.00	12.00	19.00	45.00	95.00	120.	150.	450.	3500.
1927S	396,000	9.00	20.00	52.00	170.	1050.	3000.	3450.	9250.	110,000.
1928	6,336,000	2.50	3.00	6.30	15.00	25.00	57.50	110.	450.	1425.
1928D	1,627,600	4.00	6.00	8.00	23.00	39.00	83.00	145.	410.	7500.
1928S	2,644,000	3.50	4.25	6.75	15.00	33.00	68.00	135.	450.	750.
1929	11,140,000	3.50	4.00	6.30	15.00	30.00	50.00	110.	440.	675.
1929D	1,358,000	4.50	8.00	11.00	18.00	35.00	67.50	135.	480.	7500.
1929S	1,764,000	3.50	4.75	6.30	15.00	30.00	58.00	120.	430.	695.
1930	5,632,000	3.50	4.00	6.50	15.00	26.00	52.50	110.	450.	650.
1930S	1,556,000	3.50	4.25	6.30	15.00	30.00	59.50	115.	550.	995.

Washington

Reverse mintmark
(1932-1964)

Silver composition

Designer: John Flanagan. **Size:** 24.3 millimeters. **Weight:** 6.25 grams. **Composition:** 90% silver (0.1809 ounces), 10% copper.

Date	Mintage	G-4	VG-8	F-12	VF-20	XF-40	AU-50	MS-60	MS-65	Prf-65
1932	5,404,000	3.50	4.50	5.00	7.50	9.00	13.00	21.00	195.	—
1932D	436,800	34.00	40.00	48.00	60.00	150.	325.	490.	5400.	—
1932S	408,000	38.00	40.00	42.00	45.00	72.00	175.	290.	2800.	—
1934	31,912,052	1.75	2.25	2.50	2.75	3.50	8.00	22.00	65.00	—
1934D	3,527,200	3.50	5.25	6.50	8.50	19.00	75.00	195.	1125.	—
1935	32,484,000	1.75	2.25	2.50	2.75	5.75	7.50	23.00	59.00	—
1935D	5,780,000	2.00	4.00	5.50	9.50	18.00	75.00	225.00	635.	—
1935S	5,660,000	2.00	3.00	4.50	5.00	15.00	32.00	66.00	180.	—
1936	41,303,837	1.75	2.25	2.50	2.75	6.00	7.50	20.00	52.00	1150.
1936D	5,374,000	2.80	3.50	4.50	15.00	42.00	165.	350.	650.	—
1936S	3,828,000	2.25	3.00	4.00	7.00	12.00	40.00	63.00	130.	—
1937	19,701,542	1.75	2.25	3.25	4.50	6.00	15.00	22.00	72.00	425.
1937D	7,189,600	1.80	3.00	4.00	5.50	12.00	28.00	44.00	78.00	—
1937S	1,652,000	2.00	3.50	5.50	12.00	21.00	68.00	110.	190.	—
1938	9,480,045	2.25	3.75	4.50	7.50	15.00	28.00	61.00	130.	260.
1938S	2,832,000	2.80	4.50	5.50	8.00	15.00	34.00	59.00	130.	—
1939	33,548,795	1.75	2.25	2.50	2.75	5.50	7.50	16.00	52.00	215.
1939D	7,092,000	2.00	2.50	3.75	4.50	7.50	16.00	35.00	72.00	—

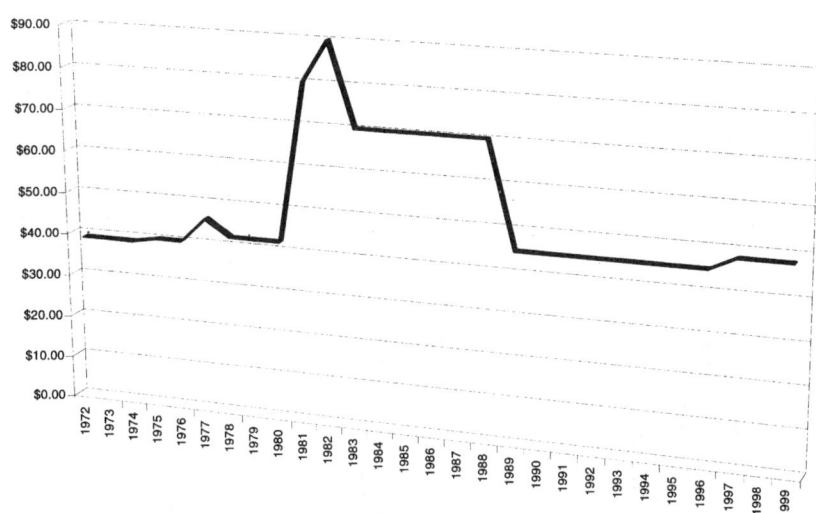

1932-D Quarter
Grade F-12

■ Retail Price

Source: COIN PRICES

Date	Mintage	G-4	VG-8	F-12	VF-20	XF-40	AU-50	MS-60	MS-65	Prf-65
1939S	2,628,000	3.25	3.50	4.50	6.50	14.00	36.00	62.00	125.	—
1940	35,715,246	1.50	2.25	3.00	3.25	4.50	8.25	15.00	42.00	225.
1940D	2,797,600	1.75	2.50	7.00	9.00	18.00	47.00	70.00	125.	—
1940S	8,244,000	1.75	2.50	4.25	5.00	7.00	12.00	16.00	44.00	—
1941	79,047,287	—	—	1.50	2.00	3.25	4.50	7.50	33.00	155.
1941D	16,714,800	—	—	1.50	2.00	3.25	6.50	30.00	50.00	—
1941S	16,080,000	—	—	1.50	2.00	3.25	6.50	20.00	70.00	—
1942	102,117,123	—	—	1.50	2.00	2.75	3.50	4.50	31.00	165.
1942D	17,487,200	—	—	1.50	2.00	3.25	7.00	11.00	36.00	—
1942S	19,384,000	—	—	1.50	2.00	4.50	17.00	50.00	100.	—
1943	99,700,000	—	—	1.50	2.00	2.25	2.75	5.00	36.00	—
1943D	16,095,600	—	—	1.50	2.00	3.25	10.00	17.50	39.00	—
1943S	21,700,000	—	—	1.50	2.00	5.50	11.50	26.00	43.00	—
1944	104,956,000	—	—	1.50	2.00	3.25	3.75	4.50	36.00	—
1944D	14,600,800	—	—	1.50	2.00	3.25	5.00	9.00	36.00	—
1944S	12,560,000	—	—	1.50	2.00	3.25	5.50	11.00	37.00	—
1945	74,372,000	—	—	1.50	2.00	3.25	4.00	5.00	36.00	—
1945D	12,341,600	—	—	1.50	2.00	3.25	5.00	7.50	36.00	—
1945S	17,004,001	—	—	1.50	2.00	3.25	4.50	6.00	36.00	—
1946	53,436,000	—	—	1.50	2.00	2.25	2.50	4.75	34.00	—
1946D	9,072,800	—	—	1.50	2.00	2.25	2.75	5.00	35.00	—
1946S	4,204,000	—	—	2.00	2.25	2.50	2.75	4.00	36.00	—
1947	22,556,000	—	—	1.50	2.00	3.00	4.50	6.50	35.00	—
1947D	15,338,400	—	—	1.50	2.00	3.00	4.00	5.00	36.00	—
1947S	5,532,000	—	—	1.50	2.00	2.25	2.50	5.00	35.00	—
1948	35,196,000	—	—	1.50	2.00	2.25	2.50	4.00	34.00	—
1948D	16,766,800	—	—	1.50	2.00	2.25	2.50	5.00	35.00	—
1948S	15,960,000	—	—	1.50	2.00	3.25	3.60	5.00	36.00	—
1949	9,312,000	—	—	1.50	2.50	3.50	14.00	19.00	36.00	—
1949D	10,068,400	—	—	1.50	2.00	4.00	5.00	9.00	42.00	—
1950	24,971,512	—	—	1.50	2.00	3.00	3.75	5.00	8.00	60.00
1950D	21,075,600	—	—	1.50	2.00	2.75	3.00	4.50	26.00	—
1950D/S	Inc. Ab.	21.00	25.00	36.00	60.00	150.	210.	275.	650.	—
1950S	10,284,004	—	—	1.50	2.50	3.25	5.75	7.25	20.00	—
1950S/D	Inc. Ab.	21.00	25.00	36.00	60.00	190.	315.	425.	715.	—
1951	43,505,602	—	—	1.40	1.75	2.00	2.25	4.75	16.00	46.00
1951D	35,354,800	—	—	1.40	1.75	2.00	2.25	3.25	20.00	—
1951S	9,048,000	—	—	1.40	1.75	4.25	8.25	15.00	20.00	—
1952	38,862,073	—	—	1.40	1.75	2.00	2.25	3.00	16.00	33.00
1952D	49,795,200	—	—	1.40	1.75	2.00	2.25	3.25	16.00	—
1952S	13,707,800	—	—	1.40	2.00	2.50	5.25	10.00	20.00	—
1953	18,664,920	—	—	1.40	1.75	2.00	2.50	3.25	20.00	26.00
1953D	56,112,400	—	—	—	1.25	1.50	1.75	2.25	16.00	—
1953S	14,016,000	—	—	1.40	1.75	2.25	2.75	4.00	16.00	—
1954	54,645,503	—	—	—	—	1.40	1.50	2.00	24.00	12.00
1954D	42,305,500	—	—	—	—	1.75	2.00	2.00	20.00	—
1954S	11,834,722	—	—	—	1.50	1.75	2.00	2.00	16.00	—
1955	18,558,381	—	—	—	1.50	1.75	2.00	2.00	13.00	12.00
1955D	3,182,400	—	—	—	1.75	2.00	2.75	3.00	16.00	—
1956	44,813,384	—	—	—	—	1.75	2.00	2.00	13.00	6.50
1956D	32,334,500	—	—	—	—	2.00	2.25	2.50	13.00	—
1957	47,779,952	—	—	—	—	1.40	2.00	2.75	16.00	3.50
1957D	77,924,160	—	—	—	—	1.40	1.75	2.00	16.00	—
1958	7,235,652	—	—	—	—	1.40	2.00	2.50	16.00	6.00
1958D	78,124,900	—	—	—	—	1.40	1.75	2.00	13.00	—
1959	25,533,291	—	—	—	—	1.40	1.75	2.00	13.00	4.25
1959D	62,054,232	—	—	—	—	1.40	1.75	2.00	13.00	—
1960	30,855,602	—	—	—	—	1.40	1.75	2.75	11.00	3.75
1960D	63,000,324	—	—	—	—	1.40	1.75	2.00	11.00	—
1961	40,064,244	—	—	—	—	1.40	1.50	1.75	13.00	3.50
1961D	83,656,928	—	—	—	—	1.40	1.50	1.75	13.00	—
1962	39,374,019	—	—	—	—	1.40	1.50	1.75	11.00	3.50
1962D	127,554,756	—	—	—	—	1.40	1.50	1.75	9.00	—
1963	77,391,645	—	—	—	—	1.40	1.50	1.75	9.00	3.50
1963D	135,288,184	—	—	—	—	1.40	1.50	1.75	9.00	—
1964	564,341,347	—	—	—	—	1.40	1.50	1.75	6.50	3.50
1964D	704,135,528	—	—	—	—	1.40	1.50	1.75	6.50	—

Clad composition

Weight: 5.67 grams. **Composition:** clad layers of 75% copper and 25% nickel bonded to a pure-copper core.

Date	Mintage	MS-65	Prf-65	Date	Mintage	MS-65	Prf-65
1965	1,819,717,540	1.60	—	1971	109,284,000	1.00	—
1966	821,101,500	1.60	—	1971D	258,634,428	.70	—
1967	1,524,031,848	2.00	—	1971S	—	—	.95
1968	220,731,500	1.60	—	1972	215,048,000	1.00	—
1968D	101,534,000	2.00	—	1972D	311,067,732	1.00	—
1968S	—	—	1.00	1972S	—	—	.95
1969	176,212,000	2.00	—	1973	346,924,000	1.00	—
1969D	114,372,000	2.25	—	1973D	232,977,400	1.00	—
1969S	—	—	1.00	1973S	—	—	.95
1970	136,420,000	1.00	—	1974	801,456,000	1.00	—
1970D	417,341,364	1.00	—	1974D	353,160,300	1.00	—
1970S	—	—	.95	1974S	—	—	1.40

Obverse mintmark (1968-present)

Bicentennial reverse, clad composition

Reverse designer: Jack L. Ahr.

Date	Mintage	G-4	VG-8	F-12	VF-20	XF-40	MS-60	MS-65	Prf-65
1976	809,784,016	—	—	—	—	—	—	1.20	—
1976D	860,118,839	—	—	—	—	—	—	1.20	—
1976S	—	—	—	—	—	—	—	—	.90

Bicentennial reverse, silver composition

Weight: 5.75 grams. **Composition:** clad layers of 80% silver and 20% copper bonded to a core of 20.9% silver and 79.1% copper (0.0739 total ounces of silver).

Date	Mintage	G-4	VG-8	F-12	VF-20	XF-40	MS-60	MS-65	Prf-65
1976S silver	11,000,000	—	—	—	—	—	—	2.00	1.95

Regular design resumed, clad composition

Notes: The 1979-S Type II proof has a clearer mintmark than the Type I.

Date	Mintage	MS-65	Prf-65	Date	Mintage	MS-65	Prf-65
1977	468,556,000	1.00	—	1989P	512,868,000	1.00	—
1977D	258,898,212	1.00	—	1989D	896,535,597	1.00	—
1977S	—	—	.95	1989S	—	—	1.35
1978	521,452,000	1.00	—	1990P	613,792,000	1.00	—
1978D	287,373,152	1.00	—	1990D	927,638,181	1.00	—
1978S	—	—	.95	1990S	—	—	3.60
1979	515,708,000	1.00	—	1991P	570,968,000	1.00	—
1979D	489,789,780	1.00	—	1991D	630,966,693	1.00	—
1979S T-I	—	—	.95	1991S	(2,867,787)	—	5.00
1979S T-II	—	—	1.45	1992P	384,764,000	1.00	—
1980P	635,832,000	1.00	—	1992D	389,777,107	1.00	—
1980D	518,327,487	1.00	—	1992S	(2,858,981)	—	4.00
1980S	—	—	.95	1992S	Silver proof	—	4.00
1981P	601,716,000	1.00	—	1993P	639,276,000	1.00	—
1981D	575,722,833	1.00	—	1993D	645,476,128	1.00	—
1981S T-I	—	—	.95	1993S	(2,633,439)	—	4.75
1981S T-II	—	—	3.00	1993S	Silver proof	—	5.00
1982P	500,931,000	2.00	—	1994P	825,600,000	1.00	—
1982D	480,042,788	2.00	—	1994D	880,034,110	1.00	—
1982S	—	—	2.25	1994S	(2,484,594)	—	3.25
1983P	673,535,000	4.00	—	1994S	Silver proof	—	4.50
1983D	617,806,446	3.50	—	1995P	1,004,336,000	1.00	—
1983S	—	—	1.75	1995D	1,103,216,000	1.00	—
1984P	676,545,000	1.75	—	1995S	(2,010,384)	—	3.00
1984D	546,483,064	2.00	—	1995S	Silver proof	—	4.75
1984S	—	—	1.60	1996P	925,040,000	1.00	—
1985P	775,818,962	2.50	—	1996D	906,868,000	1.00	—
1985D	519,962,888	3.25	—	1996S	—	—	3.00
1985S	—	—	1.25	1996S	Silver proof	—	4.75
1986P	551,199,333	4.00	—	1997P	595,740,000	1.00	—
1986D	504,298,660	2.75	—	1997D	599,680,000	1.00	—
1986S	—	—	2.00	1997S	(1,975,000)	—	3.00
1987P	582,499,481	1.00	—	1997S	Silver proof	—	4.75
1987D	655,594,696	1.00	—	1998P	—	1.00	—
1987S	—	—	1.10	1998D	—	1.00	—
1988P	562,052,000	1.50	—	1998S	—	—	3.00
1988D	596,810,688	1.20	—	1998S	Silver proof	—	4.75
1988S	—	—	1.25				

50 States Commemorative Quarters

Delaware

Date	Mintage	MS-63	MS-65	Prf-65
1999P	—	.75	1.00	—
1999D	—	.75	1.00	—
1999S	—	—	—	—
1999S Silver	—	—	—	—

Pennsylvania

Date	Mintage	MS-63	MS-65	Prf-65
1999P	—	.75	1.00	—
1999D	—	.75	1.00	—
1999S	—	—	—	—
1999S Silver	—	—	—	—

New Jersey

Date	Mintage	MS-63	MS-65	Prf-65
1999P	—	.75	1.00	—
1999D	—	.75	1.00	—
1999S	—	—	—	—
1999S Silver	—	—	—	—

Georgia

Date	Mintage	MS-63	MS-65	Prf-65
1999P	—	.75	1.00	—
1999D	—	.75	1.00	—
1999S	—	—	—	—
1999S Silver	—	—	—	—

Connecticut

Date	Mintage	MS-63	MS-65	Prf-65
1999P	—	—	—	—
1999D	—	—	—	—
1999S	—	—	—	—
1999S Silver	—	—	—	—

Massachusetts

Date	Mintage	MS-63	MS-65	Prf-65
2000P	—	—	—	—
2000D	—	—	—	—
2000S	—	—	—	—
2000S Silver	—	—	—	—

Maryland

Date	Mintage	MS-63	MS-65	Prf-65
2000P	—	—	—	—
2000D	—	—	—	—
2000S	—	—	—	—
2000S Silver	—	—	—	—

South Carolina

Date	Mintage	MS-63	MS-65	Prf-65
2000P	—	—	—	—
2000D	—	—	—	—
2000S	—	—	—	—
2000S Silver	—	—	—	—

New Hampshire

Date	Mintage	MS-63	MS-65	Prf-65
2000P	—	—	—	—
2000D	—	—	—	—
2000S	—	—	—	—
2000S Silver	—	—	—	—

Virginia

Date	Mintage	MS-63	MS-65	Prf-65
2000P	—	—	—	—
2000D	—	—	—	—
2000S	—	—	—	—
2000S Silver	—	—	—	—

Half dollars

Flowing Hair

Designer: Robert Scot. **Size:** 32.5 millimeters. **Weight:** 13.48 grams. **Composition:** 89.24% silver (0.3869 ounces), 10.76% copper. **Notes:** The 1795 "recut date" variety had the date cut into the dies twice, so both sets of numbers are visible on the coin. The 1795 "3 leaves" variety has three leaves under each of the eagle's wings on the reverse.

Date	Mintage	G-4	VG-8	F-12	VF-20	XF-40	MS-60
1794	23,464	1150.	1750.	2650.	3700.	8000.	55,000.
1795	299,680	450.	625.	850.	1550.	4750.	15,000.
1795 recut date	Inc. Ab.	550.	650.	950.	2200.	6500.	18,000.
1795 3 leaves	Inc. Ab.	800.	1450.	2000.	3750.	9500.	—

1797 Half Dollar
Grade F-12

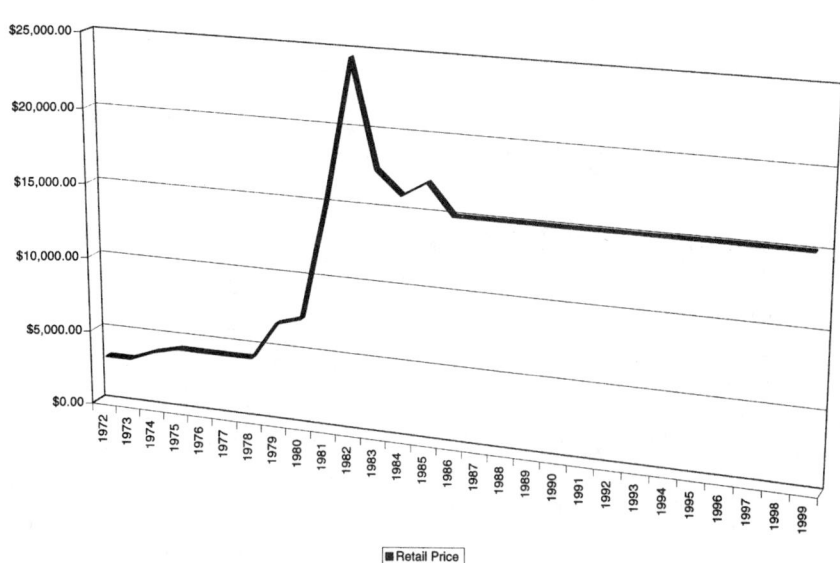

■ Retail Price

Source: COIN PRICES

Draped Bust Half Dollars

Small-eagle reverse

Designer: Robert Scot. **Size:** 32.5 millimeters. **Weight:** 13.48 grams. **Composition:** 89.24% silver (0.3869 ounces), 10.76% copper. **Notes:** The 1796 strikes have either 15 or 16 stars on the obverse.

Date	Mintage	G-4	VG-8	F-12	VF-20	XF-40	MS-60
1796 15 stars	3,918	9750.	11,500.	15,000.	25,000.	37,500.	100,000.
1796 16 stars	Inc. Ab.	10,000.	12,000.	17,000.	27,000.	39,000.	120,000.
1797	Inc. Ab.	9500.	11,500.	15,000.	24,000.	37,500.	100,000.

Heraldic Eagle Introduced

Notes: The two varieties of the 1803 strikes are distinguished by the size of the 3 in the date. The several varieties of the 1806 strikes are distinguished by the style of 6 in the date, size of the stars on the obverse, and whether the stem of the olive branch held by the reverse eagle extends through the claw.

Date	Mintage	G-4	VG-8	F-12	VF-20	XF-40	MS-60
1801	30,289	225.	300.	550.	825.	1850.	25,000.
1802	29,890	175.	240.	440.	775.	1700.	25,000.
1803 sm. 3	188,234	150.	170.	285.	450.	900.	7500.
1803 lg. 3	Inc. Ab.	125.	150.	200.	350.	750.	6000.
1805	211,722	125.	150.	200.	350.	800.	6500.
1805/4	Inc. Ab.	140.	200.	300.	500.	1200.	8750.
1806 round top 6, large stars							
	839,576	125.	140.	180.	350.	675.	6000.
1806 round top 6, small stars							
	Inc. Ab.	125.	140.	180.	375.	675.	6250.
1806 knobbed 6, stem not through claw							
	—	—	35,000.	45,000.	70,000.	95,000.	—
1806 pointed top 6, stem not through claw							
	Inc. Ab.	115.	130.	160.	290.	550.	5000.
1806 pointed top 6, stem through claw							
	Inc. Ab.	120.	135.	175.	300.	600.	5750.
1806/5	Inc. Ab.	125.	160.	210.	350.	675.	6500.
1806/inverted 6	Inc. Ab.	200.	250.	475.	750.	1500.	10,000.
1807	301,076	120.	135.	175.	300.	600.	5750.

Liberty Cap

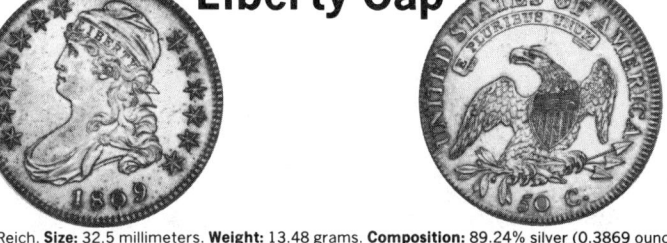

Designer: John Reich. **Size:** 32.5 millimeters. **Weight:** 13.48 grams. **Composition:** 89.24% silver (0.3869 ounces), 10.76% copper. **Notes:** There are three varieties of the 1807 strikes. Two are distinguished by the size of the stars on the obverse. The third was struck from a reverse die that had a 5 cut over a 2 in the "50C." denomination. Two varieties of the 1811 are distinguished by the size of the 8 in the date. A third has a period between the 8 and second 1 in the date. One variety of the 1817 has a period between the 1 and 7 in the date. Two varieties of the 1819/18 overdate are distinguished by the size of the 9 in the date. Two varieties of the 1820 are distinguished by the size of the date. On the 1823 varieties, the "broken 3" appears to be almost separated in the middle of the 3 in the date; the "patched 3" has the error repaired; the "ugly 3" has portions of its detail missing. The 1827 "curled-2" and "square-2" varieties are distinguished by the numeral's base — either curled or square. Among the 1828 varieties, "knobbed 2" and "no knob" refers to whether the upper left serif of the digit is rounded. The 1830 varieties are distinguished by the size of the 0 in the date. The four 1834 varieties are distinguished by the sizes of the stars, date and letters in the inscriptions. The 1836 "50/00" variety was struck from a reverse die that had "50" recut over "00" in the denomination.

Date	Mintage	G-4	VG-8	F-12	VF-20	XF-40	AU-50	MS-60	MS-65
1807 sm. stars	750,500	65.00	90.00	175.	325.	800.	3500.	5900.	40,000.
1807 lg. stars	Inc. Ab.	50.00	80.00	150.	300.	750.	3000.	5500.	—
1807 50/20 C.	Inc. Ab.	45.00	60.00	75.00	165.	400.	1500.	4000.	30,000.
1807 bearded goddess									
	—	300.	500.	675.	1175.	2750.	7500.	—	—
1808	1,368,600	37.50	42.50	53.00	90.00	185.	600.	1800.	11,000.
1808/7	Inc. Ab.	40.00	50.00	60.00	125.	200.	750.	1750.	15,000.
1809	1,405,810	36.00	42.50	55.00	85.00	185.	550.	1600.	15,000.
1810	1,276,276	34.50	38.00	46.00	90.00	170.	500.	1750.	15,000.
1811 sm. 8	1,203,644	32.00	37.50	45.00	60.00	110.	450.	750.	7500.
1811 lg. 8	Inc. Ab.	32.50	38.00	50.00	70.00	140.	500.	900.	8500.
1811 dt. 18.11	Inc. Ab.	40.00	47.00	72.00	135.	275.	650.	1500.	12,000.
1812	1,628,059	32.50	37.50	45.00	60.00	105.	375.	775.	7500.
1812/1 sm. 8	Inc. Ab.	42.50	50.00	75.00	110.	250.	800.	2000.	12,000.
1812/1 lg. 8	Inc. Ab.	1275.	1875.	2450.	3750.	6000.	17,500.	—	—
1813	1,241,903	32.50	37.50	45.00	70.00	125.	450.	1250.	11,000.
1813 50/UNI reverse									
	1,241,903	40.00	70.00	100.	195.	325.	775.	1750.	12,000.
1814	1,039,075	34.50	38.00	45.00	60.00	125.	500.	1350.	9000.
1814/3	Inc. Ab.	40.00	60.00	95.00	145.	295.	650.	1200.	10,000.
1815/2	47,150	700.	850.	1150.	1500.	2200.	4000.	9000.	50,000.
1817	1,215,567	31.50	33.00	40.00	60.00	100.	350.	750.	8500.
1817/3	Inc. Ab.	70.00	105.	165.	275.	500.	1350.	3150.	25,000.
1817/4		50,000.	60,000.	85,000.	145,000.	200,000.	—	—	—
1817 dt. 181.7	Inc. Ab.	37.00	47.00	60.00	100.	175.	500.	1200.	10,000.
1818	1,960,322	31.50	33.00	40.00	60.00	100.	350.	800.	8500.
1818/7	Inc. Ab.	35.00	40.00	55.00	85.00	165.	600.	1250.	11,000.
1819	2,208,000	31.50	33.00	40.00	60.00	100.	350.	800.	8500.
1819/8 sm. 9	Inc. Ab.	31.50	33.00	40.00	70.00	130.	450.	1100.	9500.
1819/8 lg. 9	Inc. Ab.	31.50	33.00	40.00	70.00	120.	400.	1000.	9000.
1820 sm. dt.	751,122	40.00	55.00	80.00	145.	250.	650.	1400.	10,000.
1820 lg. dt.	Inc. Ab.	37.00	50.00	68.00	120.	220.	500.	1200.	10,000.
1820/19	Inc. Ab.	40.00	53.00	75.00	130.	240.	700.	1400.	12,000.
1821	1,305,797	33.00	35.00	40.00	70.00	95.00	500.	950.	9750.
1822	1,559,573	32.00	34.00	40.00	55.00	85.00	300.	700.	7250.
1822/1	Inc. Ab.	40.00	49.00	60.00	125.	235.	475.	950.	11,000.
1823	1,694,200	31.50	33.00	40.00	50.00	85.00	290.	750.	7500.
1823 broken 3	Inc. Ab.	43.00	63.00	90.00	160.	275.	750.	1300.	12,000.
1823 patched 3	Inc. Ab.	38.00	53.00	78.00	125.	200.	450.	880.	8000.
1823 ugly 3	Inc. Ab.	40.00	58.00	83.00	145.	235.	650.	1200.	11,000.
1824	3,504,954	31.00	33.00	40.00	47.00	80.00	225.	575.	7500.
1824/21	Inc. Ab.	35.00	40.00	55.00	65.00	130.	380.	950.	7900.
1824/various dates									
	Inc. Ab.	35.00	45.00	70.00	145.	265.	475.	975.	12,000.
1825	2,943,166	31.50	33.00	40.00	50.00	77.00	210.	500.	7000.
1826	4,004,180	31.50	33.00	40.00	50.00	77.00	210.	500.	7000.
1827 curled 2	5,493,400	33.00	45.00	58.00	85.00	165.	325.	700.	7750.
1827 square 2	Inc. Ab.	31.50	33.00	40.00	45.00	77.00	250.	650.	7500.
1827/6	Inc. Ab.	35.00	40.00	43.00	60.00	125.	325.	850.	9000.
1828 curled base 2, no knob									
	3,075,200	33.00	36.00	40.00	55.00	90.00	275.	650.	7000.
1828 curled base 2, knobbed 2									
	Inc. Ab.	35.00	40.00	50.00	65.00	100.	300.	700.	7250.
1828 small 8s, square base 2, large letters									
	Inc. Ab.	27.50	33.00	36.00	43.00	80.00	210.	550.	6250.
1828 small 8s, square base 2, small letters									
	Inc. Ab.	45.00	58.00	100.	185.	275.	700.	1200.	9500.

Date	Mintage	G-4	VG-8	F-12	VF-20	XF-40	AU-50	MS-60	MS-65
1828 large 8s, square base 2									
	Inc. Ab.	33.00	37.00	43.00	55.00	95.00	325.	750.	8000.
1829	3,712,156	27.50	33.00	36.00	43.00	77.00	210.	500.	9000.
1829/7	Inc. Ab.	35.00	40.00	60.00	85.00	165.	250.	800.	—
1830 small 0 in date									
	4,764,800	27.50	33.00	36.00	43.00	77.00	210.	500.	6500.
1830 large 0 in date									
	Inc. Ab.	27.50	33.00	36.00	43.00	77.00	210.	500.	6500.
1831	5,873,660	27.50	33.00	36.00	43.00	77.00	210.	500.	6500.
1832 sm. lt.	4,797,000	27.50	33.00	36.00	43.00	77.00	210.	500.	6500.
1832 lg. let.	Inc. Ab.	30.00	45.00	58.00	85.00	145.	300.	650.	7500.
1833	5,206,000	27.50	33.00	36.00	43.00	77.00	210.	500.	6500.
1834 small date, large stars, small letters									
	6,412,004	27.50	33.00	36.00	43.00	77.00	210.	500.	6500.
1834 small date, small stars, small letters									
	Inc. Ab.	27.50	33.00	36.00	43.00	77.00	210.	500.	6500.
1834 large date, small letters									
	Inc. Ab.	27.50	33.00	36.00	43.00	77.00	210.	500.	6500.
1834 large date, large letters									
	Inc. Ab.	27.50	33.00	36.00	43.00	77.00	210.	500.	6500.
1835	5,352,006	27.50	33.00	36.00	43.00	77.00	275.	600.	9000.
1836	6,545,000	27.50	33.00	36.00	43.00	77.00	210.	500.	6500.
1836 50/00	Inc. Ab.	55.00	80.00	105.	185.	275.	600.	1300.	—

Reeded Edge - 50 Cents On Reverse

Designer: Christian Gobrecht. **Size:** 30 millimeters. **Weight:** 13.36 grams. **Composition:** 90% silver (0.3867 ounces), 10% copper.

Date	Mintage	G-4	VG-8	F-12	VF-20	XF-40	AU-50	MS-60	MS-65
1836	1,200	575.	675.	875.	1150.	1875.	3000.	5000.	22,500.
1837	3,629,820	32.00	38.00	43.00	60.00	115.	325.	750.	12,500.

Half Dol. On Reverse

Date	Mintage	G-4	VG-8	F-12	VF-20	XF-40	AU-50	MS-60	MS-65
1838	3,546,000	32.00	38.00	43.00	60.00	125.	475.	825.	14,000.
1838O Proof only	Est. 20	—	—	—	—	45,000.	75,000.	90,000.	200,000.
1839	1,392,976	32.00	38.00	41.00	60.00	125.	365.	900.	16,000.
1839O	178,976	115.	145.	195.	280.	500.	1200.	2500.	17,500.

Seated Liberty

Designer: Christian Gobrecht. **Size:** 30.6 millimeters. **Weight:** 13.36 grams. **Composition:** 90% silver (0.3867 ounces), 10% copper. **Notes:** Some 1839 strikes have drapery extending from Liberty's left elbow. One variety of the 1840 strikes has smaller lettering; another used the old reverse of 1838. Varieties of 1842 and 1846 are distinguished by the size of the numerals in the date.

Date	Mintage	G-4	VG-8	F-12	VF-20	XF-40	AU-50	MS-60	MS-65
1839 no drapery from elbow									
	Inc. Ab.	38.00	65.00	110.	250.	725.	1500.	2350.	107 K
1839 drapery	Inc. Ab.	20.00	28.00	40.00	75.00	145.	265.	450.	—

Date	Mintage	G-4	VG-8	F-12	VF-20	XF-40	AU-50	MS-60	MS-65
1840 sm. let.	1,435,008	16.50	24.00	30.00	60.00	110.	350.	575.	8250.
1840 rev. 1838	Inc. Ab.	115.	165.	215.	325.	500.	1200.	2500.	—
1840O	855,100	17.00	29.00	45.00	80.00	125.	300.	585.	—
1841	310,000	35.00	45.00	80.00	140.	265.	425.	1300.	—
1841O	401,000	17.00	29.00	45.00	85.00	150.	240.	875.	—
1842 sm. date	2,012,764	27.00	37.00	55.00	95.00	165.	325.	1300.	12,000.
1842 lg. date	Inc. Ab.	16.00	24.00	39.00	50.00	75.00	120.	1250.	12,000.
1842O sm. date	957,000	575.	800.	1400.	2250.	4000.	—	—	—
1842O lg. date	Inc. Ab.	22.00	29.00	48.00	115.	225.	750.	1750.	—
1843	3,844,000	16.00	24.00	39.00	50.00	80.00	180.	350.	4500.
1843O	2,268,000	16.00	24.00	39.00	55.00	90.00	250.	550.	—
1844	1,766,000	16.00	24.00	39.00	50.00	85.00	180.	350.	4500.
1844O	2,005,000	16.00	24.00	39.00	55.00	80.00	195.	525.	—
1844/1844O	Inc. Ab.	425.	650.	1000.	1375.	2300.	4900.	—	—
1845	589,000	30.00	40.00	50.00	90.00	170.	340.	900.	—
1845O	2,094,000	16.00	24.00	39.00	45.00	100.	240.	550.	—
1845O no drapery									
	Inc. Ab.	25.00	35.00	65.00	115.	185.	375.	750.	—
1846 med. dt.	2,210,000	16.00	24.00	39.00	50.00	70.00	175.	500.	9000.
1846 tall dt.	Inc. Ab.	22.00	30.00	60.00	85.00	145.	250.	650.	12,000.
1846/horiz. 6	Inc. Ab.	140.	215.	250.	375.	550.	1000.	2500.	—
1846O med.dt.	2,304,000	16.00	24.00	39.00	45.00	100.	225.	550.	12,000.
1846O tall dt.	Inc. Ab.	125.	245.	325.	575.	950.	2000.	3600.	—
1847/1846	1,156,000	2000.	2750.	3200.	4250.	6500.	—	—	—
1847	Inc. Ab.	20.00	30.00	45.00	60.00	90.00	190.	480.	9000.
1847O	2,584,000	16.00	25.00	39.00	50.00	95.00	250.	640.	7000.
1848	580,000	35.00	55.00	75.00	135.	240.	475.	1400.	9000.
1848O	3,180,000	18.00	25.00	40.00	50.00	95.00	285.	750.	9000.
1849	1,252,000	22.00	35.00	50.00	85.00	150.	365.	1250.	9000.
1849O	2,310,000	16.00	25.00	40.00	60.00	115.	250.	650.	9000.
1850	227,000	225.	275.	340.	400.	575.	875.	1500.	—

1855-S Half Dollar
Grade XF-40

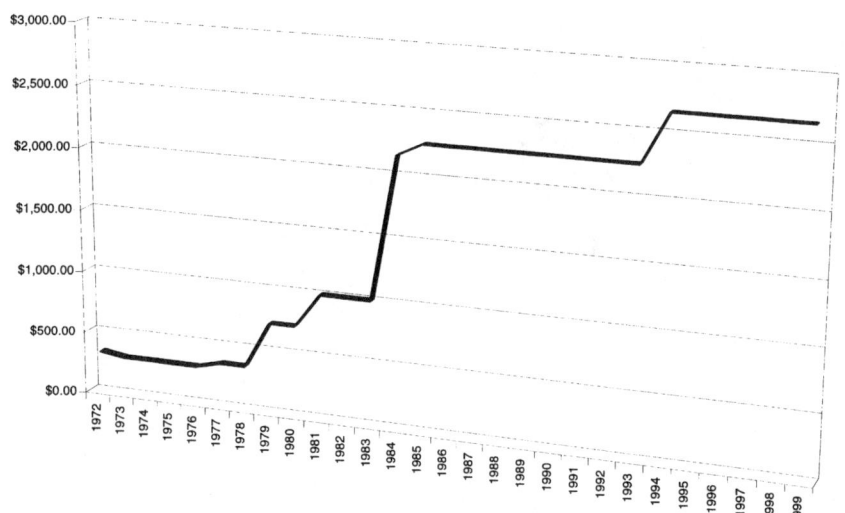

Source: COIN PRICES

Date	Mintage	G-4	VG-8	F-12	VF-20	XF-40	AU-50	MS-60	MS-65
1850O	2,456,000	16.00	25.00	45.00	60.00	125.	250.	650.	9000.
1851	200,750	285.	325.	425.	525.	650.	800.	1800.	—
1851O	402,000	37.00	45.00	75.00	105.	175.	300.	610.	9000.
1852	77,130	300.	375.	485.	600.	800.	1050.	1450.	—
1852O	144,000	60.00	90.00	150.	325.	525.	975.	1850.	—
1853O	Unrecorded			Eliasberg Sale, 1997, VG-8, $154,000.					

Arrows At Date

Weight: 12.44 grams. **Composition:** 90% silver (0.36 ounces), 10% copper.

Date	Mintage	G-4	VG-8	F-12	VF-20	XF-40	AU-50	MS-60	MS-65	Prf-65
1853 rays on reverse										
	3,532,708	16.50	27.00	40.00	90.00	250.	505.	1700.	21,500.	—
1853O rays on reverse										
	1,328,000	19.00	31.00	44.00	110.	290.	700.	2100.	21,500.	—

Reverse rays removed

Date	Mintage	G-4	VG-8	F-12	VF-20	XF-40	AU-50	MS-60	MS-65	Prf-65
1854	2,982,000	16.00	22.00	33.00	50.00	100.	270.	675.	8000.	—
1854O	5,240,000	16.00	22.00	33.00	50.00	100.	265.	500.	8000.	—
1855	759,500	23.00	30.00	40.00	60.00	150.	325.	1200.	8000.	22,500.
1855/4	Inc. Ab.	35.00	60.00	80.00	125.	225.	400.	1500.	—	—
1855O	3,688,000	16.00	22.00	33.00	50.00	100.	270.	650.	8000.	—
1855S	129,950	275.	400.	650.	1300.	2650.	6000.	—	—	—

Arrows At Date Removed

Date	Mintage	G-4	VG-8	F-12	VF-20	XF-40	AU-50	MS-60	MS-65	Prf-65
1856	938,000	19.00	25.00	32.00	47.50	90.00	150.	350.	6500.	12,500.
1856O	2,658,000	16.00	21.00	28.00	45.00	82.00	150.	450.	12,500.	—
1856S	211,000	50.00	70.00	115.	220.	450.	1250.	2500.	19,000.	—
1857	1,988,000	16.00	18.00	28.00	45.00	82.00	150.	350.	5150.	12,500.
1857O	818,000	18.00	21.00	25.00	55.00	100.	250.	850.	12,500.	—
1857S	158,000	75.00	95.00	145.	285.	575.	800.	2400.	19,000.	—
1858	4,226,000	16.00	18.00	35.00	60.00	80.00	150.	350.	6500.	12,500.
1858O	7,294,000	16.00	17.00	35.00	45.00	70.00	150.	450.	12,500.	—

Date	Mintage	G-4	VG-8	F-12	VF-20	XF-40	AU-50	MS-60	MS-65	Prf-65
1858S	476,000	20.00	30.00	48.00	90.00	175.	400.	950.	12,500.	—
1859	748,000	16.50	27.00	42.00	55.00	90.00	200.	650.	6600.	5500.
1859O	2,834,000	16.00	25.00	40.00	50.00	85.00	150.	450.	6500.	—
1859S	566,000	20.00	38.00	55.00	85.00	215.	375.	750.	12,500.	—
1860	303,700	25.00	35.00	47.50	75.00	120.	350.	1000.	6500.	5500.
1860O	1,290,000	16.00	20.00	35.00	45.00	76.00	160.	450.	5150.	—
1860S	472,000	20.00	30.00	50.00	75.00	130.	245.	850.	12,500.	—
1861	2,888,400	16.00	23.00	35.00	45.00	70.00	150.	410.	5150.	5500.
1861O	2,532,633	16.00	25.00	40.00	50.00	85.00	150.	450.	5150.	—
1861S	939,500	17.00	28.00	42.50	60.00	100.	195.	975.	9500.	—
1862	253,550	24.00	32.00	50.00	95.00	150.	265.	750.	5150.	5500.
1862S	1,352,000	16.00	27.00	39.00	60.00	90.00	175.	450.	9000.	—
1863	503,660	20.00	28.00	40.00	70.00	130.	250.	750.	5150.	5500.
1863S	916,000	16.00	25.00	39.00	50.00	80.00	150.	410.	9000.	—
1864	379,570	24.00	32.00	55.00	85.00	160.	200.	750.	5150.	5500.
1864S	658,000	18.00	23.00	45.00	60.00	115.	275.	675.	9000.	—
1865	511,900	25.00	32.00	49.00	80.00	125.	240.	750.	5150.	5500.
1865S	675,000	17.00	23.00	39.00	50.00	85.00	160.	450.	9000.	—
1866	—	—	—	—	Proof, unique		—	—	—	—
1866S	60,000	75.00	110.	165.	325.	795.	1500.	5000.	—	—

Motto Above Eagle

Notes: In 1866 the motto "In God We Trust" was added to the reverse. The "closed-3" and "open-3" varieties are distinguished by the amount of space between the upper left and lower left serifs of the 3.

Date	Mintage	G-4	VG-8	F-12	VF-20	XF-40	AU-50	MS-60	MS-65	Prf-65
1866	745,625	16.00	27.00	45.00	65.00	90.00	155.	350.	4800.	3750.
1866S	994,000	16.00	24.00	40.00	58.00	95.00	275.	650.	5000.	—
1867	449,925	25.00	35.00	55.00	85.00	145.	240.	350.	4800.	3750.
1867S	1,196,000	16.00	24.00	40.00	50.00	75.00	155.	350.	7000.	—
1868	418,200	35.00	49.00	75.00	135.	225.	300.	525.	7100.	3750.
1868S	1,160,000	16.00	24.00	39.00	50.00	105.	165.	350.	7000.	—
1869	795,900	18.00	24.00	39.00	45.00	85.00	160.	385.	4600.	3750.
1869S	656,000	16.00	27.00	39.00	50.00	100.	175.	600.	7000.	—
1870	634,900	18.00	27.00	39.00	65.00	100.	160.	475.	7000.	3750.
1870CC	54,617	500.	800.	1300.	2650.	4500.	—	—	—	—
1870S	1,004,000	18.00	29.00	45.00	70.00	110.	275.	575.	7000.	—
1871	1,204,560	16.00	24.00	39.00	50.00	70.00	155.	350.	7000.	3750.
1871CC	153,950	135.	180.	295.	485.	950.	2000.	3500.	9150.	—
1871S	2,178,000	16.00	24.00	39.00	50.00	69.00	155.	400.	7000.	—
1872	881,550	16.00	24.00	39.00	55.00	75.00	160.	430.	2850.	3750.
1872CC	272,000	50.00	85.00	190.	300.	650.	1700.	2500.	8800.	—
1872S	580,000	23.00	28.00	55.00	85.00	170.	375.	975.	7000.	—
1873 closed 3	801,800	19.00	24.00	38.00	90.00	125.	235.	500.	4500.	3750.
1873 open 3	Inc. Ab.	2200.	2700.	4100.	5500.	7500.	—	—	—	—
1873CC	122,500	140.	185.	275.	575.	1250.	2500.	4100.	9000.	3750.

1873S no arrows, 5,000 minted, no specimens known to survive.

Arrows At Date

Weight: 12.5 grams. **Composition:** 90% silver (0.3618 ounces), 10% copper.

Date	Mintage	G-4	VG-8	F-12	VF-20	XF-40	AU-50	MS-60	MS-65	Prf-65
1873	1,815,700	16.50	25.00	36.00	85.00	225.	530.	950.	15,000.	9000.
1873CC	214,560	135.	160.	250.	550.	1350.	2250.	4500.	—	—
1873S	233,000	60.00	80.00	110.	225.	475.	725.	1600.	15,000.	—
1874	2,360,300	16.50	25.00	36.00	85.00	225.	530.	950.	15,000.	9000.
1874CC	59,000	250.	350.	525.	975.	1850.	2900.	4500.	14,000.	—
1874S	394,000	25.00	35.00	55.00	135.	275.	575.	1700.	15,000.	—

Arrows At Date Removed

Date	Mintage	G-4	VG-8	F-12	VF-20	XF-40	AU-50	MS-60	MS-65	Prf-65
1875	6,027,500	15.00	24.00	29.00	40.00	60.00	120.	425.	3500.	3200.
1875CC	1,008,000	18.00	34.00	53.00	95.00	185.	300.	540.	5450.	—
1875S	3,200,000	15.00	24.00	29.00	42.00	70.00	135.	340.	2700.	—
1876	8,419,150	15.00	24.00	32.00	40.00	60.00	135.	340.	5300.	3200.
1876CC	1,956,000	17.00	30.00	48.00	85.00	175.	275.	560.	4200.	—
1876S	4,528,000	15.00	24.00	32.00	40.00	70.00	145.	340.	2700.	—
1877	8,304,510	15.00	24.00	29.00	40.00	65.00	145.	340.	2700.	3750.
1877CC	1,420,000	17.00	33.00	43.00	75.00	145.	275.	630.	3250.	—
1877S	5,356,000	15.00	24.00	29.00	40.00	65.00	145.	340.	2700.	—
1878	1,378,400	20.00	28.00	36.00	55.00	115.	170.	425.	3650.	3200.
1878CC	62,000	285.	365.	475.	850.	1350.	2300.	4000.	—	—
1878S	12,000	8500.	11,000.	14,000.	17,500.	21,000.	24,500.	30,000.	—	—
1879	5,900	200.	220.	290.	350.	400.	475.	700.	2900.	3250.
1880	9,755	190.	210.	240.	310.	375.	475.	700.	2900.	3250.
1881	10,975	170.	195.	240.	300.	365.	465.	700.	2900.	3250.

1878-S Half Dollar
Grade F-12

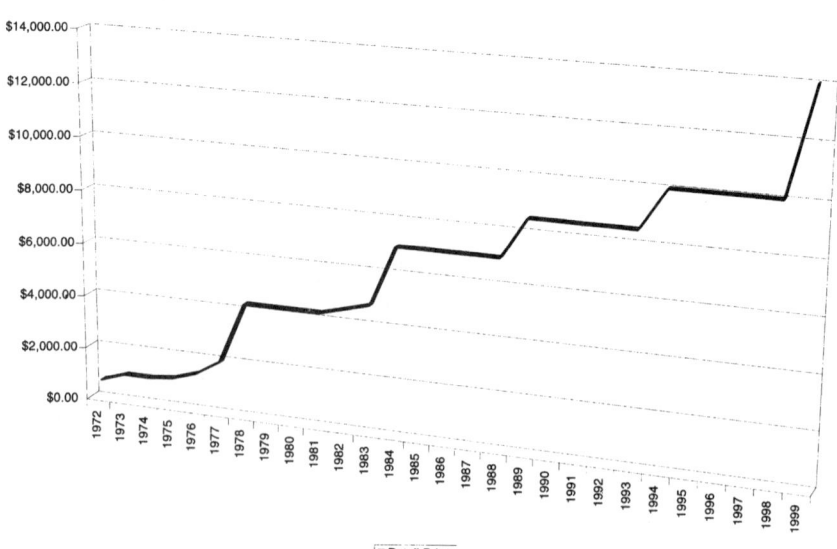

■ Retail Price

Source: COIN PRICES

Date	Mintage	G-4	VG-8	F-12	VF-20	XF-40	AU-50	MS-60	MS-65	Prf-65
1882	5,500	250.	270.	310.	390.	470.	550.	850.	3600.	3250.
1883	9,039	180.	210.	240.	290.	375.	475.	750.	2900.	3250.
1884	5,275	275.	300.	365.	425.	475.	550.	800.	2900.	3250.
1885	6,130	245.	265.	300.	360.	435.	525.	800.	2900.	3250.
1886	5,886	295.	345.	410.	450.	495.	600.	850.	4800.	3250.
1887	5,710	325.	385.	450.	550.	650.	750.	900.	2900.	3250.
1888	12,833	190.	210.	250.	310.	390.	440.	700.	2900.	3250.
1889	12,711	175.	200.	235.	300.	375.	425.	700.	2900.	3250.
1890	12,590	175.	200.	235.	300.	375.	425.	700.	3250.	3250.
1891	200,600	40.00	50.00	60.00	90.00	140.	290.	500.	3250.	3250.

BARBER HALVES

Designer: Charles E. Barber. **Size:** 30.6 millimeters. **Weight:** 12.5 grams. **Composition:** 90% silver (0.3618 ounces), 10% copper.

Date	Mintage	G-4	VG-8	F-12	VF-20	XF-40	AU-50	MS-60	MS-65	Prf-65
1892	935,245	19.00	26.00	48.00	90.00	180.	260.	390.	2600.	3300.
1892O	390,000	165.	190.	230.	285.	405.	425.	820.	5500.	—
1892 micro o	—	1500.	3450.	4250.	5750.	9500.	16,500.	—	55,000.	—
1892S	1,029,028	170.	195.	235.	295.	380.	565.	855.	9900.	—
1893	1,826,792	13.50	20.00	45.00	80.00	150.	310.	500.	4125.	3300.
1893O	1,389,000	23.00	34.00	70.00	125.	275.	370.	520.	16,500.	—
1893S	740,000	75.00	95.00	175.	285.	400.	505.	1100.	12,500.	—
1894	1,148,972	18.00	33.00	68.00	100.	215.	350.	520.	3125.	3300.
1894O	2,138,000	13.00	19.00	63.00	95.00	235.	340.	500.	4500.	—
1894S	4,048,690	12.00	18.00	48.00	80.00	200.	340.	440.	9600.	—
1895	1,835,218	9.00	15.00	50.00	85.00	165.	310.	560.	3850.	3300.
1895O	1,766,000	12.50	22.00	55.00	100.	230.	360.	560.	6000.	—
1895S	1,108,086	20.00	28.00	75.00	140.	260.	360.	540.	7800.	—
1896	950,762	16.00	23.00	55.00	90.00	200.	325.	535.	5400.	3400.
1896O	924,000	20.00	28.00	90.00	145.	345.	620.	1150.	17,600.	—
1896S	1,140,948	65.00	80.00	125.	200.	350.	540.	1100.	8800.	—
1897	2,480,731	8.00	10.00	30.00	75.00	130.	310.	435.	4675.	3300.
1897O	632,000	60.00	90.00	350.	650.	850.	1150.	1450.	4950.	—
1897S	933,900	110.	125.	260.	400.	630.	945.	1250.	8000.	—
1898	2,956,735	6.75	8.00	28.00	71.00	135.	300.	390.	2600.	3300.
1898O	874,000	18.00	35.00	100.	160.	360.	495.	800.	10,450.	—
1898S	2,358,550	10.00	17.00	42.00	86.00	200.	350.	800.	12,000.	—
1899	5,538,846	6.75	8.00	26.00	71.00	135.	300.	390.	5225.	3900.
1899O	1,724,000	8.00	13.00	45.00	90.00	210.	360.	585.	6100.	—
1899S	1,686,411	13.00	22.00	54.00	88.00	190.	340.	585.	6600.	—
1900	4,762,912	6.00	7.75	28.00	71.00	130.	300.	390.	2600.	3300.
1900O	2,744,000	7.00	9.00	40.00	90.00	250.	310.	750.	14,500.	—
1900S	2,560,322	8.00	12.00	42.00	95.00	190.	310.	625.	9600.	—
1901	4,268,813	6.00	7.75	28.00	71.00	130.	300.	390.	4200.	3500.
1901O	1,124,000	8.00	13.00	53.00	115.	285.	450.	1250.	14,500.	—
1901S	847,044	17.00	28.00	110.	225.	500.	880.	1400.	12,500.	—
1902	4,922,777	5.85	7.75	28.00	71.00	130.	260.	390.	3400.	3700.
1902O	2,526,000	6.50	11.00	38.00	77.00	190.	350.	690.	9900.	—
1902S	1,460,670	8.00	13.00	48.00	87.00	200.	360.	585.	5500.	—
1903	2,278,755	7.50	10.00	37.00	78.00	165.	325.	500.	8000.	3825.
1903O	2,100,000	7.00	12.00	43.00	75.00	180.	325.	690.	9000.	—
1903S	1,920,772	7.00	12.00	43.00	75.00	210.	365.	565.	5900.	—
1904	2,992,670	5.85	8.00	28.00	71.00	130.	300.	390.	4200.	4100.
1904O	1,117,600	9.00	17.00	50.00	110.	300.	500.	1000.	9600.	—
1904S	553,038	16.00	27.00	135.00	325.	625.	950.	1800.	14,000.	—
1905	662,727	12.00	19.00	52.00	78.00	195.	300.	540.	5400.	3900.
1905O	505,000	15.00	29.00	80.00	130.	240.	415.	715.	6000.	—
1905S	2,494,000	6.75	11.00	38.00	79.00	190.	345.	550.	9000.	—
1906	2,638,675	5.50	7.50	27.00	71.00	130.	300.	390.	3400.	3300.
1906D	4,028,000	5.50	7.50	27.00	71.00	140.	300.	390.	4100.	—
1906O	2,446,000	5.50	7.50	35.00	74.00	165.	300.	585.	5400.	—
1906S	1,740,154	6.75	12.00	42.00	80.00	190.	300.	565.	5650.	—
1907	2,598,575	5.50	6.75	26.00	75.00	130.	300.	400.	2600.	4000.
1907D	3,856,000	5.50	8.25	27.00	75.00	150.	300.	390.	2600.	—
1907O	3,946,000	5.50	8.25	27.00	71.00	150.	300.	490.	3400.	—
1907S	1,250,000	6.50	12.00	73.00	125.00	300.	450.	850.	10,750.	—
1908	1,354,545	5.75	8.00	31.00	74.00	150.	300.	390.	3250.	4000.
1908D	3,280,000	5.50	7.50	28.00	71.00	145.	300.	480.	2600.	—
1908O	5,360,000	5.50	7.50	28.00	71.00	150.	300.	480.	2600.	—

Date	Mintage	G-4	VG-8	F-12	VF-20	XF-40	AU-50	MS-60	MS-65	Prf-65
1908S	1,644,828	7.00	13.00	42.00	82.00	190.	340.	750.	5200.	—
1909	2,368,650	5.50	7.50	26.00	60.00	130.	260.	390.	2600.	4000.
1909O	925,400	8.50	12.00	45.00	84.00	260.	475.	700.	4750.	—
1909S	1,764,000	5.75	8.50	28.00	71.00	175.	330.	550.	3350.	—
1910	418,551	10.00	15.00	64.00	115.	260.	415.	585.	3850.	4250.
1910S	1,948,000	5.50	8.25	28.00	71.00	175.	325.	625.	4300.	—
1911	1,406,543	5.50	6.75	28.00	60.00	130.	300.	390.	2600.	3300.
1911D	695,080	6.50	11.00	39.00	82.00	180.	260.	540.	2600.	—
1911S	1,272,000	5.50	8.25	31.00	74.00	165.	320.	550.	4900.	—
1912	1,550,700	5.50	7.50	26.00	60.00	150.	320.	390.	3700.	4000.
1912D	2,300,800	5.50	8.25	26.00	71.00	130.	300.	425.	2600.	—
1912S	1,370,000	5.50	8.25	29.00	71.00	165.	320.	500.	5300.	—
1913	188,627	20.00	25.00	100.	175.	345.	630.	880.	3800.	3800.
1913D	534,000	7.00	10.00	35.00	73.00	175.	285.	495.	4550.	—
1913S	604,000	7.50	11.00	44.00	80.00	190.	350.	585.	4000.	—
1914	124,610	30.00	45.00	160.	295.	460.	730.	915.	9200.	4300.
1914S	992,000	6.50	9.00	34.00	71.00	175.	345.	550.	3400.	—
1915	138,450	20.00	29.00	90.00	190.	350.	665.	945.	4550.	4250.
1915D	1,170,400	5.50	7.00	27.00	71.00	135.	260.	390.	2600.	—
1915S	1,604,000	5.50	7.00	27.00	71.00	145.	260.	470.	2600.	—

WALKING LIBERTY HALVES

Obverse mintmark

Mintmark on obverse

Designer: Adolph A. Weinman. **Size:** 30.6 millimeters. **Weight:** 12.5 grams. **Composition:** 90% silver (0.3618 ounces), 10% copper.

Date	Mintage	G-4	VG-8	F-12	VF-20	XF-40	AU-50	MS-60	MS-65	Prf-65
1916	608,000	25.00	29.00	57.00	120.	160.	210.	235.	1425.	—
1916D	1,014,400	19.00	21.00	30.00	70.00	145.	180.	260.	1800.	—
1916S	508,000	65.00	81.00	125.	285.	525.	600.	770.	4900.	—
1917D	765,400	12.00	18.00	39.00	84.00	165.	210.	550.	6500.	—
1917S	952,000	15.00	25.00	55.00	235.	665.	800.	1825.	19,000.	—

Reverse mintmark

Mintmark on reverse

Date	Mintage	G-4	VG-8	F-12	VF-20	XF-40	AU-50	MS-60	MS-65	Prf-65
1917	12,292,000	4.00	7.00	10.50	20.00	35.00	63.00	100.	875.	—
1917D	1,940,000	8.50	11.00	21.00	59.00	230.	380.	650.	20,500.	—
1917S	5,554,000	5.00	8.00	13.50	25.00	55.00	120.	280.	9750.	—
1918	6,634,000	5.00	9.00	17.00	45.00	145.	245.	410.	3500.	—
1918D	3,853,040	8.00	9.50	22.00	51.00	155.	350.	750.	18,500.	—
1918S	10,282,000	5.00	8.00	14.00	27.00	56.00	135.	330.	14,250.	—
1919	962,000	10.50	15.00	30.00	140.	400.	595.	915.	4675.	—
1919D	1,165,000	9.50	12.00	48.00	150.	540.	875.	2600	97,500.	—
1919S	1,552,000	8.50	10.00	30.00	135.	650.	1650.	2100.	11,000.	—
1920	6,372,000	5.00	8.00	11.00	23.00	56.00	91.00	220.	6800.	—
1920D	1,551,000	9.00	11.00	25.00	135.	350.	665.	1075.	9100.	—
1920S	4,624,000	5.00	8.00	14.00	45.00	160.	350.	650.	8050.	—
1921	246,000	73.00	105.	175.	540.	1350.	2500.	2850.	10,350.	—
1921D	208,000	115.	145.	230.	660.	2500.	2950.	3700.	11,000.	—
1921S	548,000	20.00	24.00	57.00	500.	5000.	6150.	8200.	60,000.	—
1923S	2,178,000	8.50	10.00	24.00	42.00	210.	525.	1100.	12,250.	—
1927S	2,392,000	5.00	7.75	11.00	25.00	90.00	265.	650.	8700.	—

1923-S Half Dollar
Grade XF-40

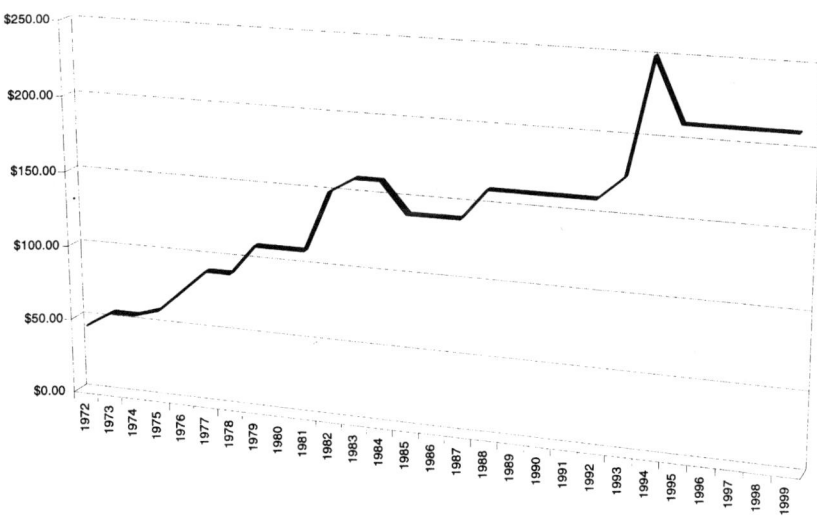

■ Retail Price

Source: COIN PRICES

Date	Mintage	G-4	VG-8	F-12	VF-20	XF-40	AU-50	MS-60	MS-65	Prf-65
1928S	1,940,000	5.00	7.25	12.50	30.00	90.00	250.	650.	4700.	—
1929D	1,001,200	6.25	8.00	14.00	35.00	80.00	155.	260.	2100.	—
1929S	1,902,000	4.00	6.75	10.00	16.00	68.00	170.	310.	2465.	—
1933S	1,786,000	5.00	7.00	10.00	11.50	45.00	170.	470.	3375.	—
1934	6,964,000	2.65	2.80	2.95	4.50	11.00	26.50	48.00	290.	—
1934D	2,361,400	3.25	4.00	5.50	7.50	25.00	56.00	125.	975.	—
1934S	3,652,000	3.00	3.50	4.50	6.00	25.00	77.00	250.	2700.	—
1935	9,162,000	2.65	2.80	2.95	4.50	9.00	22.00	44.00	265.	—
1935D	3,003,800	3.25	4.00	5.50	7.50	25.00	56.00	115.	1250.	—
1935S	3,854,000	3.10	3.50	4.50	5.50	25.00	70.00	125.	2000.	—
1936	12,617,901	2.50	2.80	3.50	4.50	9.00	21.00	36.00	130.	3250.
1936D	4,252,400	2.95	3.50	4.50	5.50	17.00	47.00	71.00	365.	—
1936S	3,884,000	3.00	3.50	4.50	5.50	17.00	50.00	115.	520.	—
1937	9,527,728	2.65	2.80	3.50	4.50	9.00	21.00	36.00	195.	850.
1937D	1,676,000	5.00	6.00	8.00	11.00	28.00	91.00	160.	500.	—
1937S	2,090,000	4.00	5.00	6.00	8.00	18.00	63.00	115.	515.	—
1938	4,118,152	3.00	3.50	4.50	6.50	11.00	42.00	65.00	260.	580.
1938D	491,600	22.00	25.00	28.00	34.00	90.00	240.	380.	915.	—
1939	6,820,808	2.65	2.80	3.50	4.50	10.00	21.00	39.00	140.	525.
1939D	4,267,800	2.95	3.50	4.50	5.50	10.50	24.00	39.00	140.	—
1939S	2,552,000	4.00	5.00	6.00	8.75	12.50	46.00	99.00	215.	—
1940	9,167,279	2.25	2.40	3.00	5.50	9.00	11.00	32.00	105.	450.
1940S	4,550,000	2.25	2.40	3.00	5.50	10.00	18.00	35.00	415.	—
1941	24,207,412	2.25	2.40	3.00	4.50	7.00	7.75	23.00	100.	375.
1941D	11,248,400	2.25	2.40	3.00	4.50	6.00	14.00	40.00	115.	—
1941S	8,098,000	2.25	2.40	3.00	4.75	7.00	24.00	71.00	1150.	—
1942	47,839,120	2.25	2.40	3.00	4.50	5.50	7.75	23.00	100.	375.
1942D	10,973,800	2.25	2.40	3.00	4.50	6.00	17.00	44.00	195.	—
1942S	12,708,000	2.25	2.40	3.00	4.75	7.00	21.00	34.00	415.	—
1943	53,190,000	2.25	2.40	3.00	4.50	5.50	7.75	23.00	100.	—
1943D	11,346,000	2.25	2.40	3.00	4.50	6.00	20.00	47.00	150.	—
1943S	13,450,000	2.25	2.40	3.00	4.75	6.00	21.00	33.00	325.	—
1944	28,206,000	2.25	2.40	3.00	4.50	5.50	7.75	32.00	105.	—
1944D	9,769,000	2.25	2.40	3.00	4.50	6.00	17.00	36.00	105.	—
1944S	8,904,000	2.25	2.40	3.00	4.75	6.25	21.00	36.00	605.	—
1945	31,502,000	2.25	2.40	3.00	4.50	5.50	7.75	23.00	100.	—
1945D	9,966,800	2.25	2.40	3.00	4.50	6.00	14.00	35.00	105.	—
1945S	10,156,000	2.25	2.40	3.00	4.75	6.00	17.00	34.00	145.	—
1946	12,118,000	2.25	2.40	3.00	4.50	5.50	12.50	32.00	130.	—
1946D	2,151,000	4.50	4.75	6.00	8.75	9.50	18.00	34.00	100.	—
1946S	3,724,000	2.65	2.80	3.50	5.00	5.50	15.00	33.00	105.	—
1947	4,094,000	2.65	3.15	3.50	5.00	7.00	18.00	34.00	170.	—
1947D	3,900,600	2.65	2.80	3.50	5.00	7.00	18.00	34.00	105.	—

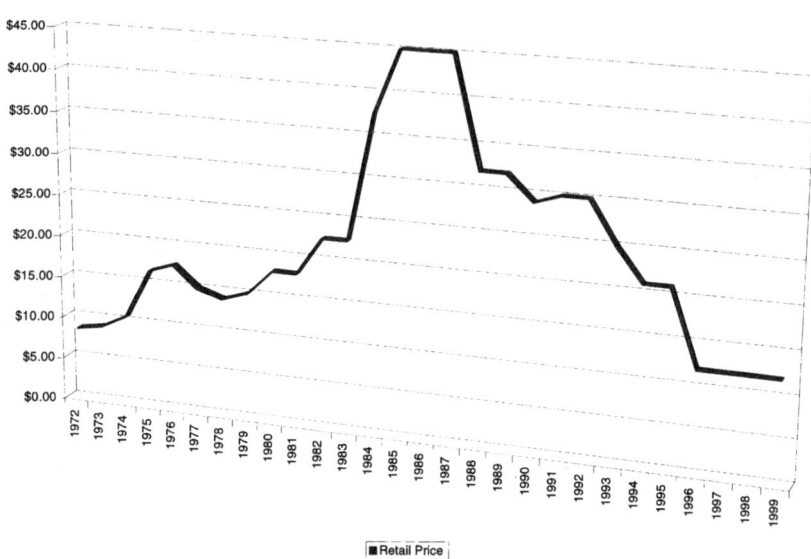

1953 Half Dollar
Grade MS-60

■ Retail Price

Source: COIN PRICES

FRANKLIN HALVES

Designer: John R. Sinnock. **Size:** 30.6 millimeters. **Weight:** 12.5 grams. **Composition:** 90% silver (0.3618 ounces), 10% copper. **Notes:** "MS-65FBL" values are for coins with full lines across the bell on the reverse.

Date	Mintage	G-4	VG-8	F-12	VF-20	XF-40	AU-50	MS-60	MS-65	-65FBL	-65CAM
1948	3,006,814	—	3.00	3.50	3.75	4.00	5.00	13.75	90.00	205.	—
1948D	122600.	—	3.00	3.25	3.50	3.75	5.00	9.50	195.	295.	—
1949	5,614,000	—	3.00	3.25	3.50	4.00	10.00	28.00	150.	290.	—
1949D	4,120,600	—	3.00	3.50	3.75	4.00	13.00	29.00	1050.	2200.	—
1949S	3,744,000	—	3.50	4.75	6.25	8.00	21.00	48.00	210.	725.	—
1950	7,793,509	—	—	3.00	3.50	6.00	7.00	20.00	150.	295.	3700.
1950D	8,031,600	—	—	3.00	3.50	6.50	7.75	16.00	575.	1050.	—
1951	16,859,602	—	—	3.00	3.50	4.00	4.50	8.75	95.00	335.	2200.
1951D	9,475,200	—	—	3.00	4.25	5.00	11.50	19.00	300.	500.	—
1951S	13,696,000	—	—	2.75	3.00	3.50	10.00	18.00	125.	695.	—
1952	21,274,073	—	—	2.50	2.75	3.00	4.00	7.00	90.00	290.	1100.
1952D	25,395,600	—	—	2.50	2.75	3.00	4.00	6.25	250.	400.	—
1952S	5,526,000	—	—	2.50	3.25	3.75	17.00	33.00	135.	975.	—
1953	2,796,920	3.00	3.00	3.25	3.50	5.00	10.00	12.00	275.	950.	475.
1953D	20,900,400	—	—	2.25	3.50	4.00	4.25	6.00	250.	400.	—
1953S	4,148,000	—	—	2.60	4.25	4.75	8.50	11.00	70.00	7500.	—
1954	13,421,503	—	—	2.25	3.50	3.75	4.00	5.50	85.00	275.	225.
1954D	25,445,580	—	—	2.25	3.25	3.50	4.00	4.75	165.	250.	—

Date	Mintage	G-4	VG-8	F-12	VF-20	XF-40	AU-50	MS-60	MS-65	-65FBL	-65CAM
1954S	4,993,400	—	—	2.25	3.75	4.00	4.25	6.50	60.00	425.	—
1955	2,876,381	—	—	5.25	5.50	5.75	6.00	6.50	75.00	150.	175.
1956	4,701,384	—	—	2.50	3.00	3.50	4.25	5.00	50.00	120.	65.00
1957	6,361,952	—	—	2.50	2.75	3.00	3.75	4.00	50.00	120.	125.
1957D	19,966,850	—	—	—	2.10	2.25	2.50	3.50	50.00	105.	—
1958	4,917,652	—	—	2.25	2.50	2.75	3.00	3.75	50.00	135.	200.
1958D	23,962,412	—	—	—	2.25	2.50	2.75	3.25	50.00	105.	—
1959	7,349,291	—	—	—	2.25	2.50	2.75	3.75	150.	295.	400.
1959D	13,053,750	—	—	—	2.25	2.50	2.75	3.75	150.	275.	—
1960	7,715,602	—	—	—	2.25	2.50	2.75	2.80	175.	400.	75.00
1960D	18,215,812	—	—	—	2.25	2.50	2.75	3.50	750.	1450.	—
1961	11,318,244	—	—	—	2.25	2.50	2.75	3.25	275.	1550.	75.00
1961D	20,276,442	—	—	—	2.25	2.50	2.75	3.25	450.	1000.	—
1962	12,932,019	—	—	—	2.25	2.50	2.75	3.00	290.	2250.	50.00
1962D	35,473,281	—	—	—	2.25	2.50	2.75	3.00	400.	1000.	—
1963	25,239,645	—	—	—	—	2.50	2.75	3.00	90.00	925.	50.00
1963D	67,069,292	—	—	—	—	2.50	2.75	3.00	90.00	250.	—

Kennedy

Reverse mintmark
(1964)

Obverse mintmark
(1968-present)

90% silver composition

Designers: Gilroy Roberts and Frank Gasparro. **Size:** 30.6 millimeters. **Weight:** 12.5 grams. **Composition:** 90% silver (0.3618 ounces), 10% copper.

Date	Mintage	G-4	VG-8	F-12	VF-20	XF-40	MS-60	MS-65	Prf-65
1964	277,254,766	—	—	—	—	—	2.50	3.50	8.00
1964D	156,205,446	—	—	—	—	—	2.50	3.50	—

40% silver composition

Weight: 11.5 grams. **Composition:** clad layers of 80% silver and 20% copper bonded to a core of 20.9% silver and 79.1% copper (0.148 total ounces of silver).

Date	Mintage	G-4	VG-8	F-12	VF-20	XF-40	MS-60	MS-65	Prf-65
1965	65,879,366	—	—	—	—	—	1.25	2.50	—
1966	108,984,932	—	—	—	—	—	1.20	2.40	—
1967	295,046,978	—	—	—	—	—	1.00	2.25	—
1968D	246,951,930	—	—	—	—	—	1.00	2.25	—
1968S	3,041,506	—	—	—	—	—	—	—	3.50
1969D	129,881,800	—	—	—	—	—	1.00	2.00	—
1969S	2,934,631	—	—	—	—	—	—	—	3.50
1970D	2,150,000	—	—	—	—	—	9.00	13.50	—
1970S	2,632,810	—	—	—	—	—	—	—	7.50

Clad composition

Weight: 11.34 grams. **Composition:** clad layers of 75% copper and 25% nickel bonded to a pure-copper core.

Date	Mintage	G-4	VG-8	F-12	VF-20	XF-40	MS-60	MS-65	Prf-65
1971	155,640,000	—	—	—	—	—	1.50	2.50	—
1971D	302,097,424	—	—	—	—	—	1.00	1.50	—
1971S	3,244,183	—	—	—	—	—	—	—	2.75
1972	153,180,000	—	—	—	—	—	1.00	1.75	—
1972D	141,890,000	—	—	—	—	—	1.00	1.75	—
1972S	3,267,667	—	—	—	—	—	—	—	2.50
1973	64,964,000	—	—	—	—	—	1.35	2.50	—
1973D	83,171,400	—	—	—	—	—	—	2.50	—
1973S		—	—	—	—	—	—	—	1.75
1974	201,596,000	—	—	—	—	—	1.00	2.00	—
1974D	79,066,300	—	—	—	—	—	1.20	2.00	—
1974S	—	—	—	—	—	—	—	—	3.00

Bicentennial design, clad composition

Reverse designer: Seth Huntington.

Date	Mintage	G-4	VG-8	F-12	VF-20	XF-40	MS-60	MS-65	Prf-65
1976	234,308,000	—	—	—	—	—	1.00	1.50	—
1976D	287,565,248	—	—	—	—	—	1.00	1.50	—
1976S	—	—	—	—	—	—	—	—	1.25

Bicentennial design, silver composition

Weight: 11.5 grams. **Composition:** 40% silver (0.148 ounces), 60% copper.

Date	Mintage	G-4	VG-8	F-12	VF-20	XF-40	MS-60	MS-65	Prf-65
1976S silver	11,000,000	—	—	—	—	—	—	6.00	5.75

Regular design resumed, clad composition

Notes: 1979-S Type II proof has a clearer mintmark than the Type I.

Date	Mintage	G-4	VG-8	F-12	VF-20	XF-40	MS-60	MS-65	Prf-65
1977	43,598,000	—	—	—	—	—	1.25	1.75	—
1977D	31,449,106	—	—	—	—	—	1.25	1.75	—
1978	14,350,000	—	—	—	—	—	1.25	1.75	—
1978D	13,765,799	—	—	—	—	—	1.50	2.00	—
1978S	Proof only	—	—	—	—	—	—	Proof only	1.75
1979	68,312,000	—	—	—	—	—	—	1.50	—
1979D	15,815,422	—	—	—	—	—	—	1.25	—
1979S T-I	—	—	—	—	—	—	—	—	2.00
1979S T-II	—	—	—	—	—	—	—	—	14.00
1980P	44,134,000	—	—	—	—	—	—	1.75	—
1980D	33,456,449	—	—	—	—	—	—	2.00	—
1980S	—	—	—	—	—	—	—	—	1.25
1981P	29,544,000	—	—	—	—	—	—	2.00	—
1981D	27,839,533	—	—	—	—	—	—	2.00	—
1981S T-I	—	—	—	—	—	—	—	—	1.25
1981S T-II	—	—	—	—	—	—	—	—	14.50
1982P	10,819,000	—	—	—	—	—	—	1.50	—
1982D	13,140,102	—	—	—	—	—	—	2.00	—
1982S	—	—	—	—	—	—	—	—	3.50
1983P	34,139,000	—	—	—	—	—	—	1.50	—
1983D	32,472,244	—	—	—	—	—	—	1.50	—
1983S	—	—	—	—	—	—	—	—	3.00
1984P	26,029,000	—	—	—	—	—	—	1.50	—
1984D	26,262,158	—	—	—	—	—	—	1.50	—
1984S	—	—	—	—	—	—	—	—	6.50
1985P	18,706,962	—	—	—	—	—	—	1.50	—
1985D	19,814,034	—	—	—	—	—	—	1.50	—
1985S	—	—	—	—	—	—	—	—	4.50
1986P	13,107,633	—	—	—	—	—	—	3.50	—
1986D	15,336,145	—	—	—	—	—	—	2.75	—
1986S	—	—	—	—	—	—	—	—	15.00
1987P	2,890,758	—	—	—	—	—	—	4.50	—
1987D	2,890,758	—	—	—	—	—	—	5.00	—
1987S	—	—	—	—	—	—	—	—	3.50
1988P	13,626,000	—	—	—	—	—	—	2.50	—
1988D	12,000,096	—	—	—	—	—	—	2.50	—
1988S	—	—	—	—	—	—	—	—	7.25
1989P	24,542,000	—	—	—	—	—	—	2.50	—
1989D	23,000,216	—	—	—	—	—	—	2.50	—
1989S	—	—	—	—	—	—	—	—	3.50
1990P	22,780,000	—	—	—	—	—	—	1.50	—
1990D	20,096,242	—	—	—	—	—	—	1.50	—
1990S	—	—	—	—	—	—	—	—	9.75

Date	Mintage	G-4	VG-8	F-12	VF-20	XF-40	MS-60	MS-65	Prf-65
1991P	14,874,000	—	—	—	—	—	—	1.50	—
1991D	15,054,678	—	—	—	—	—	—	1.50	—
1991S	(2,867,787)	—	—	—	—	—	—	—	15.00
1992P	17,628,000	—	—	—	—	—	—	1.50	—
1992D	17,000,106	—	—	—	—	—	—	1.50	—
1992S	(2,858,981)	—	—	—	—	—	—	—	16.00
1992S	Silver proof	—	—	—	—	—	—	—	13.50
1993P	15,510,000	—	—	—	—	—	—	1.50	—
1993D	15,000,006	—	—	—	—	—	—	1.50	—
1993S	(2,633,439)	—	—	—	—	—	—	—	14.00
1993S	Silver proof	—	—	—	—	—	—	—	14.75
1994P	23,718,000	—	—	—	—	—	—	1.50	—
1994D	23,828,110	—	—	—	—	—	—	1.50	—
1994S	(2,484,594)	—	—	—	—	—	—	—	9.75
1994S	Silver proof	—	—	—	—	—	—	—	13.00
1995P	26,496,000	—	—	—	—	—	—	1.50	—
1995D	26,288,000	—	—	—	—	—	—	1.50	—
1995S	(2,010,384)	—	—	—	—	—	—	—	13.00
1995S	Silver proof	—	—	—	—	—	—	—	13.00
1996P	24,442,000	—	—	—	—	—	—	1.50	—
1996D	24,744,000	—	—	—	—	—	—	1.50	—
1996S	—	—	—	—	—	—	—	—	13.00
1996S	Silver proof	—	—	—	—	—	—	—	13.00
1997P	20,882,000	—	—	—	—	—	—	1.50	—
1997D	19,876,000	—	—	—	—	—	—	1.50	—
1997S	(1,975,000)	—	—	—	—	—	—	—	13.00
1997S	Silver proof	—	—	—	—	—	—	—	13.00
1998P	—	—	—	—	—	—	—	1.50	—
1998D	—	—	—	—	—	—	—	1.50	—
1998S	—	—	—	—	—	—	—	—	5.00
1998S	Silver proof	—	—	—	—	—	—	—	13.00
1998S	Matte finish	—	—	—	—	—	—	150.00	—
1999P	—	—	—	—	—	—	—	1.50	—
1999D	—	—	—	—	—	—	—	1.50	—
1999S	—	—	—	—	—	—	—	—	—
1999S	Silver proof	—	—	—	—	—	—	—	—

Silver dollars

Flowing Hair Silver Dollars

Designer: Robert Scot. **Size:** 39-40 millimeters. **Weight:** 26.96 grams. **Composition:** 89.24% silver (0.7737 ounces), 10.76% copper. **Notes:** The two 1795 varieties have either two or three leaves under each of the eagle's wings on the reverse.

Date	Mintage	G-4	VG-8	F-12	VF-20	XF-40	MS-60
1794	1,758	10,000.	13,500.	18,500.	27,500.	42,500.	—
1795 2 leaves	203,033	800.	900.	1500.	2200.	4400.	40,000.
1795 3 leaves	Inc. Ab.	800.	900.	1500.	2200.	4400.	40,000.

Draped Bust Silver Dollars

Small Eagle

Designer: Robert Scot. **Size:** 39-40 millimeters. **Weight:** 26.96 grams. **Composition:** 89.24% silver (0.7737 ounces), 10.76% copper. **Notes:** The 1796 varieties are distinguished by the size of the numerals in the date and letters in "United States of America." The 1797 varieties are distinguished by the number of stars to the left and right of the word "Liberty" and by the size of the letters in "United States of America." The 1798 varieties have either 13 or 15 stars on the obverse.

Date	Mintage	G-4	VG-8	F-12	VF-20	XF-40	MS-60
1795	Inc. Ab.	600.	800.	1070.	1825.	3750.	17,000.
1796 small date, small letters	72,920	625.	800.	1150.	1950.	3650.	16,000.
1796 small date, large letters	Inc. Ab.	625.	775.	1100.	1450.	3400.	16,000.
1796 large date, small letters	Inc. Ab.	575.	765.	1050.	1400.	3300.	16,000.
1797 9 stars left, 7 stars right, small letters	7,776	1500.	2000.	2750.	4500.	8450.	22,000.
1797 9 stars left, 7 stars right, large letters	Inc. Ab.	585.	775.	1050.	1400.	3300.	16,000.
1797 10 stars left, 6 stars right	Inc. Ab.	585.	775.	1050.	1400.	3300.	16,000.
1798 13 stars	327,536	900.	1150.	1450.	2400.	4500.	18,000.
1798 15 stars	Inc. Ab.	1100.	1600.	2100.	3150.	6900.	18,000.

Heraldic Eagle

1794 Silver Dollar
Grade XF-40

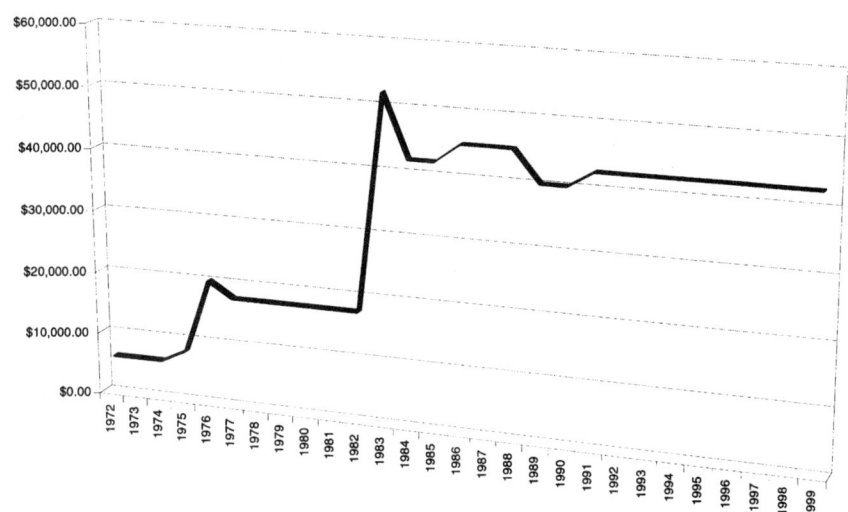

Source: COIN PRICES

Notes: The 1798 "knob 9" variety has a serif on the lower left of the 9 in the date. The 1798 varieties are distinguished by the number of arrows held by the eagle on the reverse and the number of berries on the olive branch. On the 1798 "high 8" variety, the 8 in the date is higher than the other numerals. The 1799 varieties are distinguished by the number and positioning of the stars on the obverse and by the size of the berries in the olive branch on the reverse. On the 1799 "irregular date" variety, the first 9 in the date is smaller than the other numerals. Some varieties of the 1800 strikes had letters in the legend cut twice into the dies; as the dies became worn, the letters were touched up. On the 1800 "very wide date, low 8" variety, the spacing between the numerals in the date is wider than other varieties, and the 8 is lower than the other numerals. The 1800 "small berries" variety refers to the size of the berries in the olive branch on the reverse. The 1800 "12 arrows" and "10 arrows" varieties refer to the number of arrows held by the eagle. The 1800 "Americai" variety appears to have the faint outline of an "I" after "America" in the reverse legend. The "close" and "wide" varieties of 1802 refer to the amount of space between the numerals in the date. For the 1802 "perfect date" varieties, all numerals in the date are of the same size. The 1803 large-3 and small-3 varieties are distinguished by the size of the 3 in the date.

Date	Mintage	G-4	VG-8	F-12	VF-20	XF-40	MS-60
1798 knob 9	Inc. Ab.	375.	450.	575.	850.	1675.	9600.
1798 10 arrows	Inc. Ab.	350.	440.	550.	700.	1300.	9600.
1798 4 berries	Inc. Ab.	350.	440.	550.	700.	1300.	9600.
1798 5 berries, 12 arrows							
	Inc. Ab.	350.	440.	550.	700.	1300.	9600.
1798 high 8	Inc. Ab.	350.	440.	550.	700.	1300.	9600.
1798 13 arrows	Inc. Ab.	350.	440.	550.	700.	1300.	9600.
1799/98 13 star reverse							
	423,515	350.	440.	550.	700.	1300.	15,000.
1799/98 15 star reverse							
	Inc. Ab.	400.	500.	850.	1150.	2000.	15,000.
1799 irregular date, 13 star reverse							
	Inc. Ab.	350.	440.	550.	700.	1300.	9600.
1799 irregular date, 15 star reverse							
	Inc. Ab.	350.	425.	550.	700.	1300.	9600.
1799 perfect date, 7 and 6 star obverse, no berries							
	Inc. Ab.	350.	425.	550.	700.	1300.	9600.
1799 perfect date, 7 and 6 star obverse, small berries							
	Inc. Ab.	350.	425.	550.	700.	1300.	9600.
1799 perfect date, 7 and 6 star obverse, medium large berries	Inc. Ab.	350.	425.	550.	700.	1300.	9600.
1799 perfect date, 7 and 6 star obverse, extra large berries	Inc. Ab.	350.	440.	550.	700.	1300.	9600.
1799 8 stars left, 5 stars right on obverse							
	Inc. Ab.	425.	500.	800.	1100.	2000.	9600.
1800 "R" in "Liberty" double cut							
	220,920	350.	440.	550.	700.	1300.	9600.
1800 first "T" in "States" double cut							
	Inc. Ab.	350.	440.	550.	700.	1300.	9600.
1800 both letters double cut							
	Inc. Ab.	350.	440.	550.	700.	1300.	9600.
1800 "T" in "United" double cut							
	Inc. Ab.	350.	440.	550.	700.	1300.	9600.
1800 very wide date, low 8							
	Inc. Ab.	350.	440.	550.	700.	1300.	9600.
1800 sm. berries	Inc. Ab.	350.	440.	550.	700.	1300.	9600.
1800 dot date	Inc. Ab.	350.	440.	550.	700.	1300.	9600.
1800 12 arrows	Inc. Ab.	350.	440.	550.	700.	1300.	9600.
1800 10 arrows	Inc. Ab.	350.	440.	550.	700.	1300.	9600.
1800 "Americai"	Inc. Ab.	360.	440.	550.	700.	1500.	9600.
1801	54,454	400.	475.	600.	850.	1900.	10,000.
1801	Unrecorded		Proof restrike, rare				
1802/1 close	Inc. Ab.	360.	450.	550.	850.	1600.	9600.
1802/1 wide	Inc. Ab.	360.	450.	550.	850.	1600.	9600.
1802 close, perfect date							
	Inc. Ab.	375.	450.	600.	875.	1650.	7500.
1802 wide, perfect date							
	Inc. Ab.	375.	450.	600.	875.	1650.	9600.
1802	Unrecorded		Proof restrike, rare				
1803 lg. 3	85,634	360.	440.	600.	850.	1575.	9600.
1803 sm. 3	Inc. Ab.	395.	475.	675.	975.	1850.	7500.
1803	Unrecorded		Proof restrike, rare				
1804	15 known	—			Eliasberg Sale, Apr. 1997, Prf-63, $1,825,000.		

GOBRECHT PATTERNS

Designer: Christian Gobrecht. **Size:** 38.1 millimeters. **Weight:** 26.73 grams. **Composition:** 90% silver (0.7736 ounces), 10% copper. **Notes:** Several obverse and reverse combinations exist, as described. Restrikes were produced by the U.S. Mint between 1855 and 1860.

Date	Mintage	VF-20	XF-40	AU-50	Prf-60
1836 "C. Gobrecht F." below base. Rev: eagle flying left amid stars. Plain edge.	—	—	—	—	—
1836 Obv: same as above. Rev: eagle flying in plain field. Plain edge.	—	—	—	—	—

Date	Mintage	VF-20	XF-40	AU-50	Prf-60
1836 "C. Gobrecht F." on base. Rev: eagle flying left amid stars. Plain edge.	—	2500.	3750.	4750.	7500.
1836 Same as above, reeded edge.	—	—	—	—	—
1836 Obv: same as above. Rev: eagle flying in plain field. Plain edge.	—	—	—	—	10,000.

Obverse stars   Reverse stars

Date	Mintage	VF-20	XF-40	AU-50	Prf-60
1838 Similar obv., designer's name omitted, stars added around border. Rev: eagle flying left in plain field. Reeded edge.	—	8750.	12,500.	—	—
1838 Same as above. Plain edge. Restrikes only.	3 known	—	—	—	—
1838 Obv: same as above. Rev: eagle flying left amid stars. Plain edge. Restrikes only.	2 known	—	—	—	—
1839 Obv: same as above. Rev: eagle in plain field. Reeded edge. Also known with plain edge and plain edge with eagle amid stars.	—	—	6500.	—	15,000.

LIBERTY SEATED DOLLARS

No motto

Designer: Christian Gobrecht. **Size:** 38.1 millimeters. **Weight:** 26.73 grams. **Composition:** 90% silver (0.7736 ounces), 10% copper.

Date	Mintage	G-4	VG-8	F-12	VF-20	XF-40	AU-50	MS-60	MS-65	Prf-65
1840	61,005	160.	180.	225.	300.	525.	750.	1600.	—	—
1841	173,000	100.	130.	180.	220.	375.	575.	1300.	24,000.	—
1842	184,618	100.	120.	175.	220.	300.	550.	1100.	24,000.	—
1843	165,100	100.	120.	175.	220.	300.	550.	1400.	24,000.	—
1844	20,000	180.	245.	300.	425.	625.	800.	3000.	—	—
1845	24,500	175.	235.	250.	350.	550.	750.	2000.	—	—
1846	110,600	100.	120.	175.	220.	275.	500.	1400.	24,000.	—
1846O	59,000	110.	140.	210.	285.	475.	1400.	4000.	—	—
1847	140,750	100.	120.	175.	220.	300.	650.	950.	15,000.	—
1848	15,000	250.	290.	400.	525.	700.	1400.	2050.	—	—
1849	62,600	110.	140.	190.	240.	350.	700.	1600.	—	—
1850	7,500	600.	650.	750.	900.	1100.	1975.	3500.	—	—
1850O	40,000	220.	260.	350.	650.	1400.	3200.	5000.	—	—
1851	1,300	—	—	8000.	9500.	13,500.	21,500.	—	—	—
1852	1,100	—	—	6500.	7500.	11,500.	21,500.	—	—	—
1853	46,110	175.	225.	270.	375.	575.	800.	1300.	—	—

Date	Mintage	G-4	VG-8	F-12	VF-20	XF-40	AU-50	MS-60	MS-65	Prf-65
1854	33,140	1000.	1200.	1500.	2250.	3900.	4850.	7000.	—	—
1855	26,000	800.	1000.	1300.	1900.	2650.	4500.	9000.	—	—
1856	63,500	400.	500.	575.	650.	975.	1650.	2250.	—	—
1857	94,000	375.	475.	550.	900.	1500.	1900.	3000.	—	—
1858	Est. 200		Proof only	—	4200.	5500.	6250.	9000.	—	—
1859	256,500	200.	250.	350.	450.	700.	1000.	2500.	15,000.	13,500.
1859O	360,000	100.	110.	175.	210.	265.	500.	950.	15,000.	—
1859S	20,000	225.	275.	400.	600.	1350.	3000.	—	—	—
1860	218,930	140.	180.	230.	300.	475.	600.	1300.	15,000.	13,500.
1860O	515,000	100.	110.	175.	210.	265.	500.	900.	15,000.	—
1861	78,500	440.	500.	600.	800.	1250.	1400.	3000.	—	13,500.
1862	12,090	450.	525.	625.	850.	1250.	1750.	3200.	—	13,500.
1863	27,660	285.	340.	450.	500.	800.	1350.	2750.	—	13,500.
1864	31,170	220.	265.	315.	425.	675.	1300.	2900.	—	13,500.
1865	47,000	195.	245.	290.	400.	625.	1250.	2750.	—	13,500.
1866	2 known without motto									

Motto added on reverse

Notes: In 1866 the motto "In God We Trust" was added to the reverse above the eagle.

Date	Mintage	G-4	VG-8	F-12	VF-20	XF-40	AU-50	MS-60	MS-65	Prf-65
1866	49,625	150.	200.	250.	350.	550.	900.	1600.	28,500.	7000.
1867	47,525	170.	250.	300.	415.	600.	1000.	1800.	28,500.	7000.
1868	162,700	140.	190.	225.	350.	525.	900.	1700.	28,500.	7000.
1869	424,300	115.	150.	200.	325.	500.	800.	2000.	28,500.	7000.
1870	416,000	100.	135.	175.	225.	325.	600.	1500.	28,500.	7000.
1870CC	12,462	200.	245.	325.	500.	1050.	2475.	5750.	—	—
1870S	Unrecorded			Eliasberg Sale, Apr. 1997, EF-45 to AU-50, $264,000.					—	—
1871	1,074,760	90.00	95.00	165.	210.	315.	550.	900.	24,000.	7000.
1871CC	1,376	1800.	2350.	3750.	5750.	8950.	18,500.	—	—	—
1872	1,106,450	90.00	95.00	165.	210.	315.	550.	1250.	24,000.	7000.
1872CC	3,150	900.	1250.	1600.	2575.	4250.	8500.	15,000.	—	—
1872S	9,000	175.	225.	400.	575.	1100.	3000.	10,000.	—	—
1873	293,600	130.	150.	200.	250.	350.	600.	1350.	28,500.	7000.
1873CC	2,300	3250.	4750.	6500.	9500.	17,500.	35,000.	47,500.	—	—
1873S	700			None known to exist				—	—	—

TRADE DOLLARS

Designer: William Barber. **Size:** 38.1 millimeters. **Weight:** 27.22 grams. **Composition:** 90% silver (0.7878 ounces), 10% copper.

1875 Trade Dollar
Grade F-12

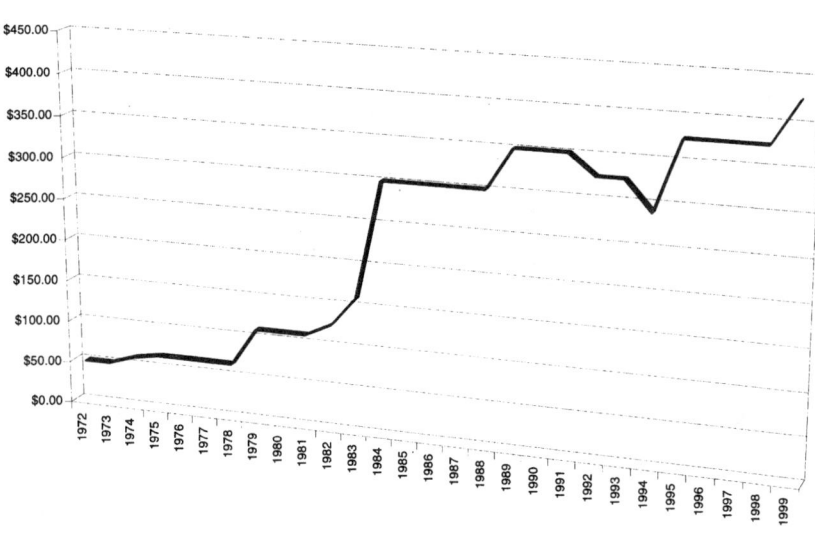

■ Retail Price

Source: **COIN PRICES**

Date	Mintage	G-4	VG-8	F-12	VF-20	XF-40	AU-50	MS-60	MS-65	Prf-65
1873	397,500	100.	110.	125.	165.	250.	325.	1000.	12,000.	12,000.
1873CC	124,500	150.	175.	225.	450.	700.	1200.	2100.	80,000.	—
1873S	703,000	130.	145.	160.	180.	260.	375.	1200.	25,000.	—
1874	987,800	110.	120.	140.	175.	240.	340.	700.	15,000.	12,000.
1874CC	1,373,200	80.00	90.00	105.	165.	240.	350.	1000.	40,000.	—
1874S	2,549,000	70.00	80.00	95.00	120.	165.	250.	675.	30,000.	—
1875	218,900	295.	350.	425.	525.	675.	800.	1850.	13,000.	6500.
1875CC	1,573,700	80.00	90.00	105.	130.	200.	375.	900.	40,000.	—
1875S	4,487,000	60.00	70.00	85.00	100.	120.	210.	500.	7000.	—
1875S/CC	Inc.Ab.	275.	325.	400.	525.	695.	1100.	1900.	—	—
1876	456,150	70.00	80.00	100.	125.	165.	400.	675.	7500.	6500.
1876CC	509,000	110.00	125.00	150.	200.	325.	450.	2100.	75,000.	—
1876S	5,227,000	60.00	70.00	85.00	100.	120.	210.	475.	10,000.	—
1877	3,039,710	60.00	70.00	85.00	105.	130.	210.	525.	16,000.	19,000.
1877CC	534,000	130.	150.	175.	245.	350.	600.	1275.	70,000.	—
1877S	9,519,000	60.00	70.00	85.00	100.	120.	210.	475.	8000.	—
1878	900		Proof only	—	1100.	1250.	1500.	—	—	22,000.
1878CC	97,000	425.	525.	675.	850.	1750.	2100.	5500.	67,500.	—
1878S	4,162,000	60.00	70.00	85.00	100.	120.	210.	475.	7000.	—
1879	1,541		Proof only	—	900.	950.	1100.		—	22,000.
1880	1,987		Proof only	—	900.	950.	1100.		—	19,500.
1881	960		Proof only	—	950.	1000.	1250.		—	20,000.
1882	1,097		Proof only	—	950.	1000.	1250.		—	20,000.
1883	979		Proof only	—	1100.	1200.	1400.		—	20,000.
1884	10		Proof only			Eliasberg, Apr. 1997, Prf-66, $396,000.				—
1885	5		Proof only			Eliasberg, Apr. 1997, Prf-65, $907,500.				—

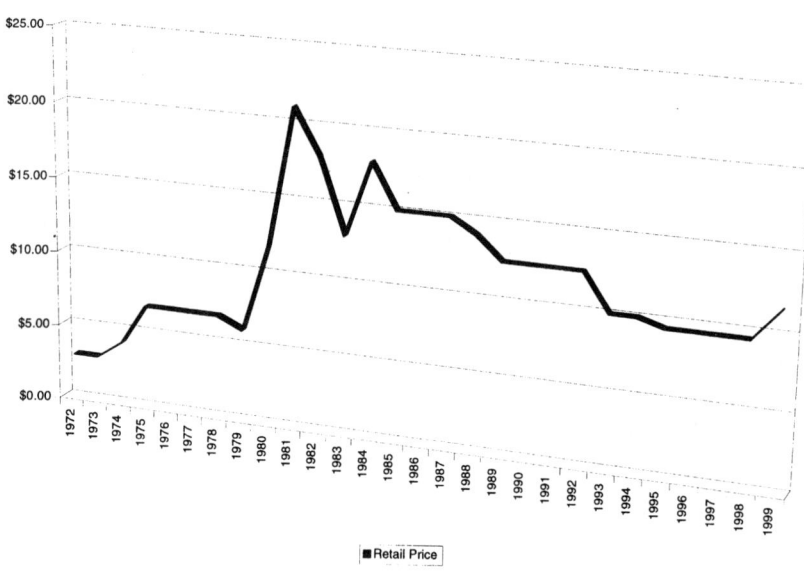

1889-O Silver Dollar
Grade F-12

■ Retail Price

Source: **COIN PRICES**

MORGAN DOLLARS

Reverse of 1879   7 over 8 tail feathers

Designer: George T. Morgan. **Size:** 38.1 millimeters. **Weight:** 26.73 grams. **Composition:** 90% silver (0.7736 ounces), 10% copper. **Notes:** "65DMPL" values are for coins grading MS-65 with deep-mirror prooflike surfaces. The 1878 "8 tail feathers" and "7 tail feathers" varieties are distinguished by the number of feathers in the eagle's tail. On the "reverse of 1878" varieties, the top of the top feather in the arrows held by the eagle is straight across and the eagle's breast is concave. On the "reverse of 1878 varieties," the top of the top feather in the arrows held by the eagle is slanted and the eagle's breast is convex. The 1890-CC "tail-bar variety" has a bar extending from the arrow feathers to the wreath on the reverse, the result of a die gouge.

Date	Mintage	VG-8	F-12	VF-20	XF-40	AU-50	MS-60	MS-63	MS-64	MS-65	65DMPL	Prf-65
1878 8 tail feathers												
	750,000	12.50	14.00	17.50	21.00	37.00	88.00	135.	240.	1450.	6300.	6250.
1878 7 tail feathers, reverse of 1878												
	Inc. Ab.	12.50	13.00	15.00	16.00	22.50	45.00	76.00	190.	1500.	5350.	5350.
1878 7 tail feathers, reverse of 1879												
	Inc. Ab.	12.50	13.00	15.00	17.50	25.00	38.00	120.	315.	2600.	8800.	55,000.
1878 7 over 8 tail feathers												
	9,759,550	12.50	14.00	19.00	28.00	44.00	100.	145.	330.	2650.	14,500.	—
1878CC	2,212,000	38.00	39.00	42.00	46.00	70.00	120.	145.	240.	1200.	3150.	—
1878S	9,744,000	12.50	13.50	14.00	15.00	18.00	32.00	45.00	66.00	225.	2200.	—
1879	14,807,100	12.00	12.50	13.00	14.00	17.00	25.00	50.00	110.	1000.	6950.	5500.
1879CC	756,000	44.00	76.00	117.	365.	790.	1500.	3550.	5350.	17,500.	50,000.	—
1879O	2,887,000	12.00	12.50	13.00	14.00	19.00	50.00	150.	365.	3300.	16,500.	—
1879S reverse of 1878												
	9,110,000	12.00	13.50	15.00	17.00	30.00	83.00	360.	1500.	7250.	22,000.	—
1879S reverse of 1879												
	9,110,000	12.00	12.50	13.50	14.00	17.00	24.00	32.00	57.00	120.	400.	—
1880	12,601,335	12.00	12.50	13.50	14.00	17.00	22.00	50.00	91.00	900.	3450.	5500.
1880CC reverse of 1878												
	591,000	41.00	58.00	76.00	95.00	130.	230.	310.	630.	2500.	11,000.	—
1880CC reverse of 1879												
	591,000	41.00	58.00	76.00	95.00	130.	225.	230.	300.	850.	3000.	—
1880O	5,305,000	12.00	12.50	13.00	13.50	17.00	43.00	285.	1650.	16,000.	70,000.	—
1880S	8,900,000	12.00	12.50	13.50	15.00	17.00	24.00	28.00	59.00	130.	410.	—
1881	9,163,975	12.00	12.50	13.00	13.50	17.00	22.00	35.00	85.00	900.	13,750.	5500.
1881CC	296,000	85.00	110.	120.	130.	140.	215.	225.	280.	650.	1400.	—
1881O	5,708,000	12.00	12.50	13.00	13.50	17.00	22.00	31.00	140.	1850.	15,000.	—
1881S	12,760,000	12.00	12.50	13.50	14.00	16.00	24.00	32.00	59.00	130.	410.	—
1882	11,101,100	12.00	12.50	13.00	13.50	16.00	22.00	31.00	63.00	480.	4400.	5500.
1882CC	1,133,000	38.00	39.00	40.00	50.00	53.00	88.00	100.	110.	380.	630.	—
1882O	6,090,000	12.00	12.50	13.00	13.50	16.00	22.00	29.00	66.00	800.	4200.	—
1882S	9,250,000	12.00	12.50	13.00	14.00	16.00	24.00	32.00	59.00	130.	1100.	—
1883	12,291,039	12.00	12.50	13.00	13.50	17.00	15.00	22.00	29.00	60.00	150.	760.	5500.
1883CC	1,204,000	38.00	39.00	40.00	45.00	50.00	88.00	95.00	112.	340.	575.	—
1883O	8,725,000	12.00	12.50	13.00	13.50	16.00	22.00	31.00	59.00	130.	500.	—
1883S	6,250,000	12.00	13.50	14.00	23.00	110.	365.	1600.	5300.	24,500.	94,500.	—
1884	14,070,875	12.00	12.50	13.00	13.50	15.50	22.00	31.00	71.00	250.	2200.	5500.
1884CC	1,136,000	40.00	42.00	45.00	49.00	51.00	87.00	95.00	110.	330.	730.	—
1884O	9,730,000	12.00	12.50	13.00	13.50	16.00	22.00	31.00	59.00	130.	500.	—
1884S	3,200,000	12.00	13.50	14.50	33.00	200.	3400.	24,500.	69,500.	150,000.	—	—
1885	17,787,767	12.00	12.50	13.00	13.50	16.00	22.00	31.00	59.00	130.	570.	5500.
1885CC	228,000	160.	170.	175.	180.	190.	250.	260.	320.	850.	1250.	—
1885O	9,185,000	12.00	12.50	13.00	13.50	16.00	22.00	31.00	59.00	130.	490.	—
1885S	1,497,000	12.00	13.50	14.00	19.00	44.00	97.00	190.	400.	2400.	16,500.	—
1886	19,963,886	12.00	12.50	13.00	13.50	16.00	22.00	29.00	59.00	130.	500.	5500.
1886O	10,710,000	12.00	12.50	13.00	13.50	76.00	285.	3000.	9200.	235,000.	—	—
1886S	750,000	15.00	19.00	28.00	41.00	61.00	140.	265.	650.	3300.	16,500.	—
1887	20,290,710	12.00	12.50	13.00	13.50	16.00	22.00	31.00	59.00	130.	480.	5500.
1887O	11,550,000	12.00	12.50	13.00	13.50	21.00	41.00	105.	290.	4900.	8500.	—
1887S	1,771,000	12.00	13.50	15.00	16.00	31.00	57.00	175.	500.	3400.	25,000.	—
1888	19,183,833	12.00	12.50	13.00	13.50	16.00	22.00	28.00	60.00	190.	2350.	5500.
1888O	12,150,000	12.00	12.50	13.00	13.50	16.00	22.00	31.00	63.00	640.	1600.	—
1888S	657,000	15.00	20.00	27.00	34.00	61.00	140.	265.	650.	4400.	10,500.	—
1889	21,726,811	12.00	12.50	13.00	13.50	16.00	22.00	31.00	63.00	340.	2950.	5500.
1889CC	350,000	200.	265.	465.	1050.	2700.	6600.	16,000.	25,000.	280,000.	—	—
1889O	11,875,000	12.00	12.50	13.00	13.50	29.00	91.00	240.	670.	5650.	14,500.	—
1889S	700,000	13.00	17.50	22.00	30.00	48.00	125.	205.	320.	1750.	7550.	—
1890	16,802,590	12.00	12.50	13.00	13.50	16.00	22.00	31.00	150.	4100.	12,500.	5500.
1890CC	2,309,041	38.00	39.00	41.00	51.00	88.00	285.	390.	825.	8050.	8200.	—
1890CC tail bar												
	Inc. Ab.	38.00	39.00	41.00	51.00	88.00	285.	390.	825.	8050.	8200.	—
1890O	10,701,000	12.00	12.50	13.00	13.50	23.00	31.00	76.00	210.	2450.	7550.	—
1890S	8,230,373	12.00	13.50	14.00	15.00	19.00	39.00	91.00	180.	1050.	8200.	—
1891	8,694,206	12.00	12.50	13.00	13.50	23.00	38.00	135.	690.	7550.	19,000.	5500.
1891CC	1,618,000	38.00	39.00	41.00	50.00	86.00	295.	320.	650.	3300.	20,000.	—
1891O	7,954,529	12.00	12.50	13.00	13.50	33.00	76.00	240.	650.	6500.	21,500.	—
1891S	5,296,000	12.00	13.50	15.00	16.00	22.00	39.00	94.00	220.	1700.	7550.	—
1892	1,037,245	12.00	12.50	13.00	23.00	57.00	120.	280.	660.	3600.	15,750.	5500.
1892CC	1,352,000	40.00	50.00	69.00	110.	210.	390.	800.	1400.	8800.	19,000.	—
1892O	2,744,000	12.00	12.50	13.00	17.00	53.00	95.00	225.	600.	7300.	27,000.	—
1892S	1,200,000	13.00	18.00	39.00	150.	2150.	14,000.	51,500.	79,000.	94,500.	157,500.	—
1893	378,792	58.00	70.00	83.00	125.	185.	330.	790.	1400.	7200.	38,000.	5500.
1893CC	677,000	82.00	100.	200.	490.	750.	1170.	4650.	9450.	53,500.	88,000.	—
1893O	300,000	63.00	88.00	115.	190.	490.	1250.	6050.	14,750.	150,000.	285,000.	—
1893S	100,000	915.	1250.	1775.	4150.	12,750.	44,000.	69,500.	150,000.	285,000.	—	—
1894	110,972	245.	285.	315.	365.	550.	900.	3550.	6050.	18,500.	—	5500.
1894O	1,723,000	14.00	18.00	28.00	48.00	125.	480.	3800.	7550.	45,500.	56,500.	—
1894S	1,260,000	22.00	34.00	50.00	100.	200.	415.	770.	1600.	5850.	19,000.	—
1895	12,880 Proof only	11,250.	13,750.	16,000.	17,500.	—	—	—	—	—	—	32,000.
1895O	450,000	95.00	110.	150.	250.	730.	10,000.	36,500.	69,500.	215,000.	—	—
1895S	400,000	125.	165.	215.	435.	670.	1250.	3650.	6850.	19,000.	40,500.	—
1896	9,967,762	12.00	12.50	13.00	13.50	16.00	22.00	32.00	63.00	160.	630.	5500.
1896O	4,900,000	12.00	12.50	15.00	16.50	115.	650.	7700.	34,500.	157,500.	—	—
1896S	5,000,000	12.00	18.00	42.00	145.	380.	680.	1500.	3150.	8800.	25,000.	—
1897	2,822,731	12.00	12.50	13.00	13.50	16.00	22.00	28.00	63.00	250.	3000.	5500.

1897-O Dollar
Grade MS-60

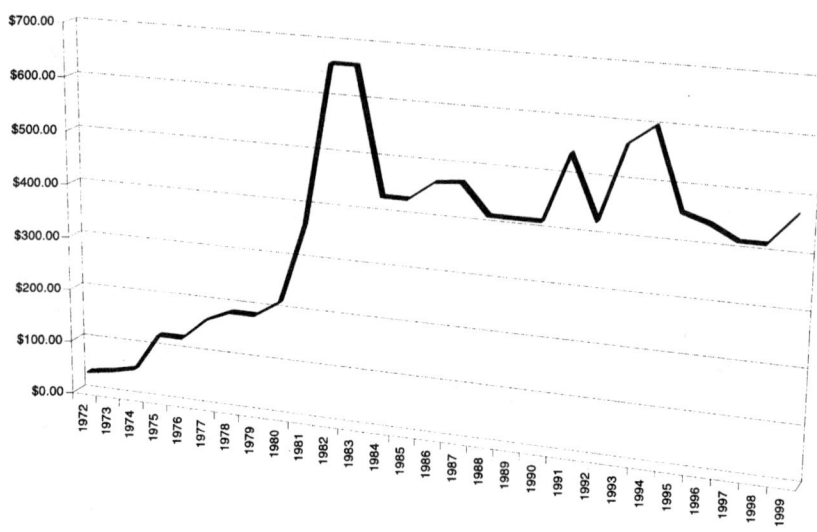

■ Retail Price

Source: COIN PRICES

Date	Mintage	VG-8	F-12	VF-20	XF-40	AU-50	MS-60	MS-63	MS-64	MS-65	65DMPL	Prf-65
1897O	4,004,000	12.00	12.50	14.00	20.00	100.	470.	4900.	17,000.	45,500.	52,500.	—
1897S	5,825,000	12.00	12.50	14.00	15.00	22.00	42.00	81.00	120.	615.	2000.	—
1898	5,884,735	12.00	12.50	14.00	15.00	16.00	22.00	32.00	66.00	220.	1150.	5500.
1898O	4,440,000	13.50	14.00	14.50	15.00	17.00	25.00	32.00	59.00	130.	480.	—
1898S	4,102,000	13.00	14.00	15.00	25.00	57.00	155.	250.	500.	2150.	11,250.	—
1899	330,846	20.00	28.00	33.00	46.00	57.00	83.00	120.	180.	650.	2250.	5500.
1899O	12,290,000	12.00	12.50	13.00	13.50	16.00	22.00	31.00	59.00	130.	825.	—
1899S	2,562,000	12.00	14.00	20.00	28.00	67.00	160.	250.	470.	1850.	8600.	—
1900	8,880,938	12.00	12.50	13.00	13.50	16.00	22.00	29.00	59.00	190.	11,000.	5500.
1900O	12,590,000	12.00	12.50	13.00	13.50	17.00	25.00	29.00	59.00	130.	3150.	—
1900O/CC	Inc. Ab.	17.50	21.00	32.00	44.00	110.	170.	315.	520.	1640.	18,000.	—
1900S	3,540,000	12.00	14.00	16.50	29.00	47.00	115.	190.	330.	925.	9450.	—
1901	6,962,813	14.00	17.00	25.00	51.00	220.	1500.	16,000.	50,500.	189,000.	—	8100.
1901O	13,320,000	12.00	12.50	13.00	13.50	16.00	22.00	32.00	59.00	190.	3800.	—
1901S	2,284,000	12.00	15.00	24.00	44.00	115.	265.	480.	850.	4150.	12,500.	—
1902	7,994,777	12.00	12.50	13.00	13.50	19.00	32.00	81.00	130.	550.	15,750.	5750.
1902O	8,636,000	12.00	12.50	13.00	13.50	16.00	22.00	29.00	59.00	150.	3600.	—
1902S	1,530,000	23.00	34.00	76.00	82.00	110.	190.	280.	550.	3150.	15,000.	—
1903	4,652,755	12.50	14.00	15.00	16.50	19.00	32.00	53.00	73.00	210.	9150.	5500.
1903O	4,450,000	115.	120.	125.	135.	160.	225.	240.	250.	475.	5050.	—
1903S	1,241,000	14.00	23.00	63.00	250.	1075.	2750.	4450.	5250.	7450.	35,000.	—
1904	2,788,650	12.00	12.50	13.00	14.00	30.00	57.00	160.	540.	4200.	38,000.	5500.
1904O	1138250.	12.00	12.50	13.00	14.00	16.00	22.00	29.00	59.00	130.	550.	—
1904S	2,304,000	13.00	20.00	38.00	175.	475.	950.	2000.	2900.	6300.	19,000.	—
1921	44,690,000	11.00	11.50	12.00	13.00	14.00	18.00	21.00	25.00	150.	8800.	—
1921D	20,345,000	11.00	11.50	12.00	13.00	14.00	32.00	34.00	66.00	300.	15,000.	—
1921S	21,695,000	11.00	11.50	12.00	13.00	14.00	22.00	49.00	140.	1750.	22,000.	—

1903-O Dollar
Grade MS-60

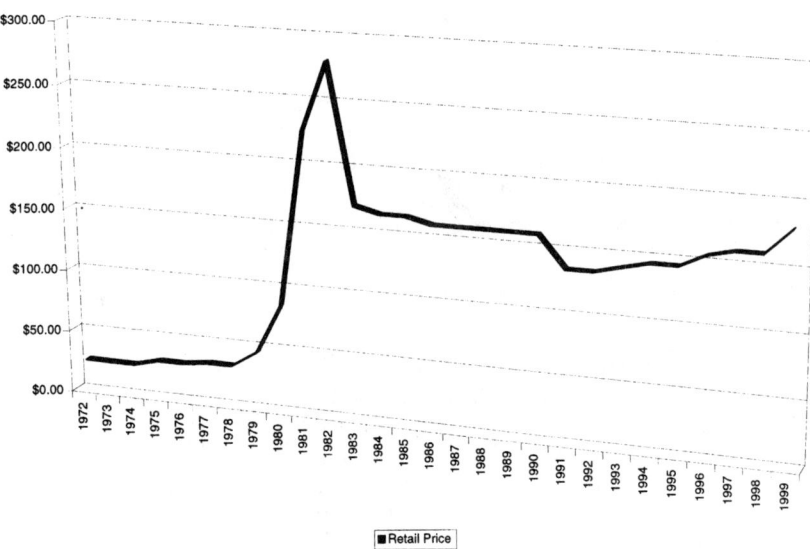

■ Retail Price

Source: COIN PRICES

1921 Silver Dollar
Grade MS-60

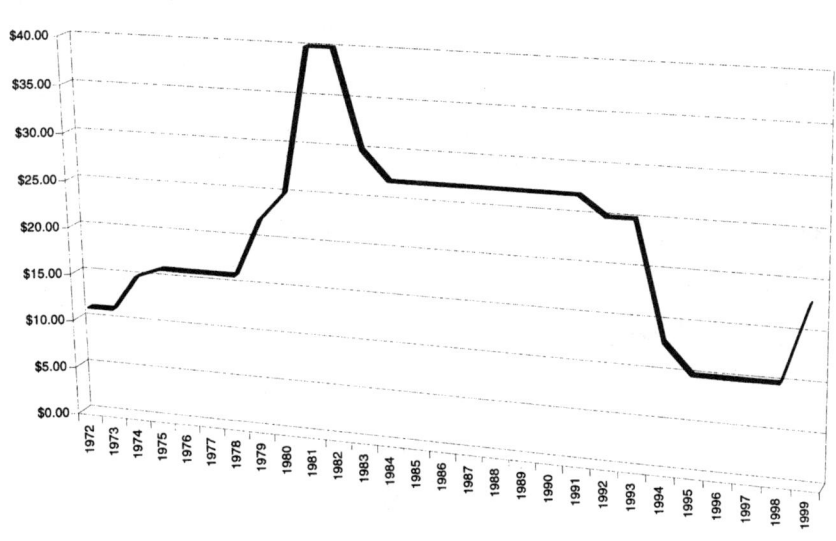

■ Retail Price

Source: COIN PRICES

PRICING SECTION

PEACE DOLLARS

Designer: Anthony de Francisci. **Size:** 38.1 millimeters. **Weight:** 26.73 grams. **Composition:** 90% silver (0.7736 ounces), 10% copper.

Date	Mintage	G-4	VG-8	F-12	VF-20	XF-40	AU-50	MS-60	MS-63	MS-64	MS-65
1921	1,006,473	16.00	35.00	38.00	40.00	50.00	76.00	135.	195.	450.	2750.
1922	51,737,000	8.00	11.00	11.25	11.50	12.00	13.00	15.00	20.00	59.00	155.
1922D	15,063,000	8.00	11.00	11.25	11.50	12.00	13.00	18.00	29.00	66.00	315.
1922S	17,475,000	8.00	11.00	11.00	11.50	12.00	13.00	18.00	53.00	245.	2400.
1923	30,800,000	8.00	11.00	11.00	11.50	12.00	13.00	15.00	20.00	59.00	155.
1923D	6,811,000	8.00	11.00	11.00	11.50	12.00	14.00	32.00	91.00	240.	1050.
1923S	19,020,000	8.00	11.00	11.00	11.50	12.00	13.00	18.00	57.00	190.	7500.
1924	11,811,000	8.00	11.00	11.25	11.50	12.00	13.00	15.00	20.00	59.00	160.
1924S	1,728,000	9.00	11.00	13.00	14.00	20.00	48.00	160.	350.	1250.	8500.
1925	10,198,000	8.00	11.00	11.25	11.50	12.00	13.00	17.00	21.00	59.00	160.
1925S	1,610,000	8.50	11.00	11.25	11.50	13.50	25.00	56.00	125.	650.	21,000.
1926	1,939,000	8.00	11.00	11.25	11.50	12.00	15.00	21.00	43.00	85.00	315.
1926D	2,348,700	8.00	11.00	11.25	11.50	12.00	25.00	50.00	120.	240.	750.
1926S	6,980,000	8.00	11.00	11.25	11.50	12.00	17.00	32.00	69.00	160.	900.

1927-S Dollar
Grade MS-60

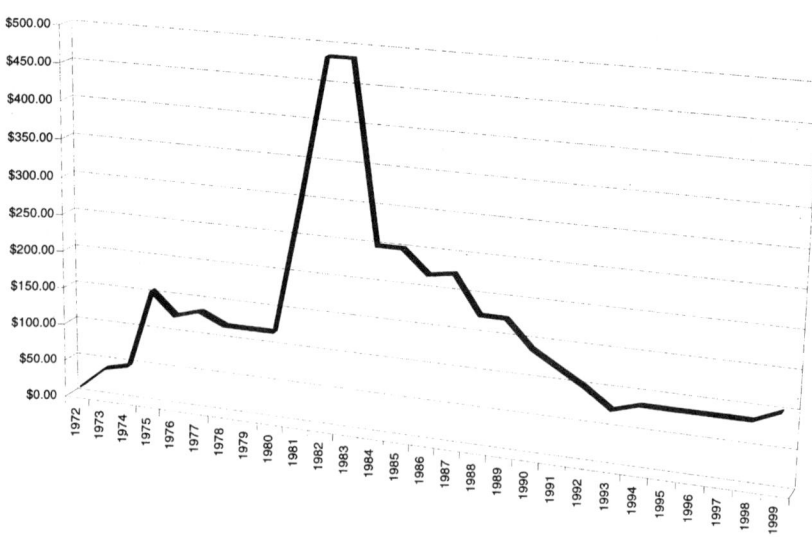

Retail Price

Source: COIN PRICES

Date	Mintage	G-4	VG-8	F-12	VF-20	XF-40	AU-50	MS-60	MS-63	MS-64	MS-65
1927	848,000	11.00	12.50	14.00	16.50	25.00	32.00	53.00	105.	240.	2600.
1927D	1,268,900	8.00	12.50	14.00	17.00	22.00	63.00	125.	215.	540.	5350.
1927S	866,000	10.00	12.50	14.00	17.00	24.00	63.00	105.	225.	700.	9450.
1928	360,649	75.00	110.	120.	125.	140.	160.	215.	290.	700.	3150.
1928S	1,632,000	8.00	13.00	14.00	18.00	20.00	35.00	100.	285.	1300.	22,000.
1934	954,057	9.00	13.00	14.00	18.00	20.00	32.00	70.00	120.	265.	1200.
1934D	1,569,500	8.00	12.00	12.50	15.00	18.00	32.00	70.00	190.	500.	2100.
1934S	1,011,000	9.00	13.00	15.00	50.00	125.	440.	1000.	2500.	4150.	7000.
1935	1,576,000	8.00	11.50	12.50	13.50	15.00	22.00	49.00	81.00	155.	600.
1935S	1,964,000	8.00	11.50	12.50	13.50	20.00	63.00	120.	250.	440.	1100.

Clad dollars

EISENHOWER DOLLARS

Designer: Frank Gasparro. **Size:** 38.1 millimeters. **Weight:** 24.59 grams (silver issues) and 22.68 grams (copper-nickel issues). **Clad composition:** 75% copper and 25% nickel bonded to a pure copper core. **Silver clad composition:** clad layers of 80% silver and 20% copper bonded to a core of 20.9% silver and 79.1% copper (0.3161 total ounces of silver).

Date	Mintage	(Proof)	MS-63	Prf-65
1971	47,799,000	—	2.50	—
1971D	68,587,424	—	2.50	—
1971S silver	6,868,530	(4,265,234)	4.60	5.00
1972	75,890,000	—	2.25	—
1972D	92,548,511	—	2.25	—
1972S silver	2,193,056	(1,811,631)	5.00	5.75
1973	2,000,056	—	3.50	—
1973D	2,000,000	—	3.50	—
1973S silver	1,833,140	(1,005,617)	5.00	17.00
1973S clad	—	2,769,624	—	5.50
1974	27,366,000	—	2.25	—
1974D	35,466,000	—	2.25	—
1974S silver	1,720,000	(1,306,579)	5.25	8.50
1974S clad	—	(2,617,350)	—	5.50

Type I Bicentennial reverse   Type II Bicentennial reverse

Bicentennial design

Reverse designer: Dennis R. Williams. **Notes:** In 1976 the lettering on the reverse was changed to thinner letters, resulting in Type I and Type II varieties for that year.

Date	Mintage	(Proof)	MS-63	Prf-65
1976 Type I	117,337,000	—	3.25	—
1976 Type II	Inc. Ab.	—	2.00	—
1976D Type I	103,228,274	—	3.25	—
1976D Type II	Inc. Ab.	—	2.00	—
1976S cld Type I	—	(2,909,369)	—	5.60
1976S cld Type II	—	(4,149,730)	—	5.50
1976S silver	11,000,000	(4,000,000)	10.00	10.00

Regular design resumed

Date	Mintage	(Proof)	MS-63	Prf-65
1977	12,596,000	—	3.25	—
1977D	32,983,006	—	2.25	—
1977S clad	—	(3,251,152)	—	5.50
1978	25,702,000	—	2.25	—
1978D	33,012,890	—	3.30	—
1978S clad	—	(3,127,788)	—	5.50

ANTHONY DOLLARS

Designer: Frank Gasparro. **Size:** 26.5 millimeters. **Weight:** 8.1 grams. **Composition:** clad layers of 75% copper and 25% nickel bonded to a pure copper core. **Notes:** The 1979-S and 1981-S Type II coins have a clearer mintmark than the Type I varieties for those years.

Date	Mintage	MS-63
1979P	360,222,000	1.30
1979P Near Date	Inc. Ab.	4.00
1979D	288,015,744	1.30
1979S	109,576,000	1.60
1979S Prf. Type I	3,677,175	4.50
1979S Prf. Type II	—	69.00
1980P	27,610,000	1.40
1980D	41,628,708	1.30

Date	Mintage	MS-63
1980S	20,422,000	1.30
1980S Prf.	3,547,030	4.50
1981P	3,000,000	3.75
1981D	3,250,000	3.50
1981S	3,492,000	3.50
1981S Prf.Type I	4,063,083	5.50
1981S Prf. Type II		110.

At left is the Sacagawea dollar, expected to enter circulation in the spring of 2000. Its golden color and plain edge are meant to set it apart from other circulating coins. As this book goes to press, there is also the possibility that 1999 Anthony dollars will be struck.

Type coins

Notes: Values listed are for the most common dates of each design type in grades MS-64 and proof-64. The -64 grade is relatively new. Except for Morgan dollars, Peace dollars and commemoratives, there is little history among other issues to support MS-64 and proof-64 values, other than as type coins. Among copper coins, the "red" and "brown" designations refer to coins that still retain their original color (red) and those that have toned over time (brown).

Description	MS-64	Proof-64
Draped Bust half cents (red & brown)	4250.	—
Classic Head half cents (red & brown)	770.	—
Braided Hair half cents (red & brown)	630.	—
Draped Bust large cents (red & brown)	8800.	—
Classic Head large cents (red & brown)	11,500.	—
Coronet large cents (red & brown)	650.	—
Braided Hair large cents (red & brown)	330.	—
Flying Eagle cents	975.	11,350.
Indian Head cents, 1859 copper-nickel	850.	3000.
Indian Head cents, 1860-1864 copper-nickel	240.	1100.
Indian Head cents, bronze (red & brown)	78.00	250.
Two-cent (red & brown)	240.	550.
Nickel three-cent	240.	350.
Silver three-cent, Type I	415.	—
Silver three-cent, Type II	1400.	4000.
Silver three-cent, Type III	400.	600.
Flowing Hair half dimes	12,000.	—
Draped Bust half dimes, small eagle	26,500.	—
Draped Bust half dimes, heraldic eagle	13,000.	—
Liberty Cap half dimes	1150.	—
Seated Liberty half dimes, no stars	1400.	—
Seated Liberty half dimes, no drapery	610.	—
Seated Liberty half dimes, stars around rim	550.	1800.
Seated Liberty half dimes, with arrows	595.	—
Seated Liberty half dimes, obverse legend	375.	650.
Shield nickels, with rays	650.	2350.
Shield nickels, no rays	240.	350.
Liberty nickels, no "Cents"	63.00	400.
Liberty nickels, with "Cents"	170.	250.
Buffalo nickels, Type I	50.00	900.
Buffalo nickels, Type II	—	—
Jefferson nickels, wartime	—	75.00
Draped Bust dimes, small eagle	22,000.	—
Draped Bust dimes, heraldic eagle	12,500.	—
Liberty Cap dimes, 1809-1827 (large size)	3700.	—
Liberty Cap dimes, 1828-1837 (reduced size)	2400.	—
Seated Liberty dimes, no stars	3650.	—
Seated Liberty dimes, no drapery	1050.	—
Seated Liberty dimes, stars around rim	1050.	1800.
Seated Liberty dimes, 1853-1855 with arrows	385.	600.
Seated Liberty dimes, obverse legend	350.	550.
Seated Liberty dimes, 1873-1874 with arrows	2200.	2050.
Barber dimes	200.	600.
Mercury dimes	—	125.
Twenty-cent	1800.	3300.
Draped Bust quarters, heraldic eagle	20,000.	—
Liberty Cap quarters, 1815-1828 (large size)	5600.	—
Liberty Cap quarters, 1831-1838 (reduced size)	4650.	—
Seated Liberty quarters, no drapery	8050.	—
Seated Liberty quarters, no motto	1150.	2000.
Seated Liberty quarters, arrows and rays	4850.	—
Seated Liberty quarters, 1854-1855, with arrows	2550.	—
Seated Liberty quarters, with motto	825.	900.
Seated Liberty quarters, 1873-1874, with arrows	2750.	3200.
Barber quarters	525.	850.
Standing Liberty quarters, Type I, full head	350.	—
Standing Liberty quarters, Type II	250.	—
Standing Liberty quarters, Type II, full head	285.	—
Flowing Hair half dollars	82,000.	—
Draped Bust half dollars, heraldic eagle	23,500.	—
Liberty Cap half dollars	3000.	—
Liberty Cap half dollars, reeded edge	4500.	—
Seated Liberty half dollars, no drapery	38,000.	—
Seated Liberty half dollars, no motto	2200.	2200.
Seated Liberty half dollars, arrows and rays	7450.	—
Seated Liberty half dollars, 1854-1855, with arrows	2700.	—
Seated Liberty half dollars, with motto	1150.	1200.
Seated Liberty half dollars, 1873-1874, with arrows	4000.	3200.
Barber half dollars	1150.	1400.
Walking Liberty half dollars	—	310.
Draped Bust dollars, small eagle	86,500.	—
Draped Bust dollars, heraldic eagle	36,500.	—
Seated Liberty dollars, no motto	6150.	6000.
Seated Liberty dollars, with motto	6300.	5500.
Morgan dollars	—	3000.
Trade dollars	3000.	3600.

Gold dollars
Liberty Head

Designer: James B. Longacre. **Size:** 13 millimeters. **Weight:** 1.672 grams. **Composition:** 90% gold (0.0484 ounces), 10% copper. **Notes:** On the "closed wreath" varieties of 1849, the wreath on the reverse extends closer to the numeral 1.

Date	Mintage	F-12	VF-20	XF-40	AU-50	MS-60
1849 open wreath	688,567	110.	120.	165.	185.	650.
1849 closed wreath	Inc. Ab.	110.	120.	165.	175.	375.
1849C closed wreath	11,634	275.	425.	750.	1500.	4500.
1849C open wreath	Inc. Ab.				Extremely Rare	—
1849D open wreath	21,588	285.	410.	800.	1100.	3125.
1849O open wreath	215,000	135.	165.	210.	325.	700.
1850	481,953	120.	135.	167.	190.	380.
1850C	6,966	390.	585.	950.	2200.	6000.
1850D	8,382	350.	550.	1150.	1950.	6100.
1850O	14,000	195.	260.	370.	775.	2750.
1851	3,317,671	120.	135.	165.	175.	275.
1851C	41,267	275.	410.	650.	950.	2300.
1851D	9,882	275.	400.	750.	1600.	3650.
1851O	290,000	150.	175.	195.	250.	690.
1852	2,045,351	100.	120.	165.	190.	255.
1852C	9,434	275.	450.	750.	1200.	3400.
1852D	6,360	315.	600.	1150.	1400.	5500.
1852O	140,000	120.	150.	210.	295.	1000.
1853	4,076,051	115.	130.	165.	190.	255.
1853C	11,515	240.	475.	1200.	1650.	5000.
1853D	6,583	325.	675.	950.	2100.	6250.
1853O	290,000	140.	160.	195.	220.	500.
1854	736,709	115.	150.	170.	195.	265.
1854D	2,935	530.	860.	1850.	5000.	15,000.
1854S	14,632	260.	300.	440.	650.	1800.

Small Indian Head

Designer: James B. Longacre. **Size:** 15 millimeters. **Weight:** 1.672 grams. **Composition:** 90% gold (0.0484 ounces), 10% copper.

Date	Mintage	F-12	VF-20	XF-40	AU-50	MS-60
1854	902,736	210.	265.	340.	440.	2400.
1855	758,269	210.	265.	340.	440.	2400.
1855C	9,803	625.	950.	2650.	5000.	9000.
1855D	1,811	1400.	2300.	4500.	6900.	19,000.
1855O	55,000	350.	550.	800.	950.	5500.
1856S	24,600	390.	650.	1100.	1700.	6900.

Large Indian Head

Designer: James B. Longacre. **Size:** 15 millimeters. **Weight:** 1.672 grams. **Composition:** 90% gold (0.0484 ounces), 10% copper. **Notes:** The 1856 varieties are distinguished by whether the 5 in the date is slanted or upright. The 1873 varieties are distinguished by the amount of space between the upper left and lower left serifs in the 3.

Date	Mintage	F-12	VF-20	XF-40	AU-50	MS-60	Prf-65
1856 upright 5	1,762,936	130.	160.	195.	325.	475.	—
1856 slanted 5	Inc. Ab.	120.	140.	170.	190.	300.	—
1856D	1,460	2250.	3500.	5500.	8500.	22,000.	—
1857	774,789	120.	140.	170.	190.	300.	—
1857C	13,280	350.	500.	1000.	2300.	9400.	—
1857D	3,533	275.	825.	1650.	2900.	11,000.	—
1857S	10,000	260.	500.	600.	1000.	5650.	—
1858	117,995	120.	140.	170.	190.	300.	19,000.
1858D	3,477	375.	775.	1300.	1900.	7250.	—
1858S	10,000	280.	375.	500.	1350.	6250.	—
1859	168,244	120.	140.	160.	190.	300.	12,000.
1859C	5,235	300.	500.	1250.	2500.	10,000.	—
1859D	4,952	475.	780.	1150.	2000.	7200.	—
1859S	15,000	225.	250.	480.	1000.	5500.	—
1860	36,668	120.	140.	170.	190.	375.	16,000.
1860D	1,566	1700.	2500.	3800.	5750.	25,000.	—
1860S	13,000	200.	325.	475.	700.	2500.	—
1861	527,499	120.	140.	170.	190.	3000.	16,000.
1861D	Unrecorded	4300.	6000.	8500.	14,000.	32,500.	—
1862	1,361,390	110.	120.	155.	175.	280.	18,000.
1863	6,250	360.	450.	875.	1700.	4000.	16,500.
1864	5,950	285.	370.	475.	750.	900.	—
1865	3,725	285.	370.	585.	750.	1600.	16,500.
1866	7,130	290.	380.	450.	700.	1000.	16,500.
1867	5,250	345.	440.	550.	750.	1200.	18,000.
1868	10,525	260.	295.	400.	585.	1100.	—
1869	5,925	325.	360.	520.	800.	1100.	—
1870	6,335	260.	285.	500.	775.	1050.	19,500.
1870S	3,000	350.	475.	800.	1400.	2400.	—
1871	3,930	260.	285.	440.	525.	750.	—
1872	3,530	285.	315.	480.	575.	900.	20,500.
1873 closed 3	125,125	325.	425.	700.	1000.	2000.	—
1873 open 3	Inc. Ab.	110.	120.	160.	190.	280.	—
1874	198,820	110.	120.	160.	190.	280.	—
1875	420	1800.	2500.	3600.	4500.	5700.	45,000.
1876	3,245	220.	250.	360.	475.	890.	17,500.
1877	3,920	150.	175.	350.	480.	800.	24,000.
1878	3,020	180.	215.	365.	470.	850.	18,000.
1879	3,030	165.	190.	300.	400.	700.	18,000.
1880	1,636	145.	160.	200.	235.	450.	18,000.
1881	7,707	145.	160.	200.	235.	450.	15,500.
1882	5,125	160.	175.	210.	235.	350.	9750.
1883	11,007	145.	165.	200.	235.	300.	9750.
1884	6,236	140.	160.	190.	230.	300.	9750.
1885	12,261	145.	160.	200.	235.	300.	9750.
1886	6,016	145.	165.	200.	235.	300.	9750.
1887	8,543	145.	165.	200.	235.	300.	9750.
1888	16,580	145.	165.	200.	235.	300.	9750.
1889	30,729	145.	165.	200.	235.	300.	9750.

Gold $2.50 (Quarter Eagle)

Liberty Cap

Designer: Robert Scot. **Size:** 20 millimeters. **Weight:** 4.37 grams. **Composition:** 91.67% gold (0.1289 ounces), 8.33% copper. **Notes:** The 1796 ''no-stars'' variety does not have stars on the obverse. The 1804 varieties are distinguished by the number of stars on the obverse.

Date	Mintage	F-12	VF-20	XF-40	MS-60
1796 no stars	963	9500.	21,000.	31,000.	150,000.
1796 stars	432	8500.	12,000.	20,000.	105,000.
1797	427	8500.	10,000.	12,500.	120,000.
1798	1,094	3500.	5000.	7750.	22,500.
1802/1	3,035	3000.	4250.	5000.	20,000.
1804 13-star reverse	3,327	16,000.	25,000.	55,000.	155,000.
1804 14-star reverse	Inc. Ab.	3250.	4250.	5750.	21,000.
1805	1,781	3000.	4500.	5400.	22,500.
1806/4	1,616	3000.	4500.	5000.	22,500.
1806/5	Inc. Ab.	6500.	12,500.	22,000.	110,000.
1807	6,812	2800.	4000.	5000.	20,000.

Turban Head

Designer: John Reich. **Sizes:** 20 millimeters (1808), 18.5 millimeters (1821-1827), and 18.2 millimeters (1829-1834). **Weight:** 4.37 grams. **Composition:** 91.67% gold (0.1289 ounces), 8.33% copper.

Date	Mintage	F-12	VF-20	XF-40	MS-60
1808	2,710	9000.	12,500.	22,000.	45,000.
1821	6,448	3250.	3500.	4500.	16,250.
1824/21	2,600	3000.	3600.	4250.	15,000.
1825	4,434	3000.	3600.	4250.	12,500.
1826/25	760	3500.	4600.	5500.	35,000.
1827	2,800	3600.	4500.	5000.	18,500.
1829	3,403	3000.	3250.	4000.	9500.
1830	4,540	3000.	3250.	4250.	9250.
1831	4,520	3000.	3250.	4250.	9500.
1832	4,400	3000.	3250.	4250.	9500.
1833	4,160	3000.	3500.	4250.	9750.
1834	4,000	6750.	10,000.	19,500.	55,000.

Classic Head

Designer: William Kneass. **Size:** 18.2 millimeters. **Weight:** 4.18 grams. **Composition:** 89.92% gold (0.1209 ounces), 10.08% copper.

Date	Mintage	VF-20	XF-40	AU-50	MS-60	MS-65
1834	112,234	300.	550.	700.	2000.	25,000.
1835	131,402	265.	400.	700.	2000.	25,000.
1836	547,986	255.	375.	565.	1500.	25,000.
1837	45,080	265.	425.	700.	2850.	25,000.
1838	47,030	265.	425.	700.	2400.	25,000.
1838C	7,880	1000.	2500.	6500.	20,000.	—
1839	27,021	265.	600.	1800.	4000.	25,000.
1839C	18,140	775.	1800.	8000.	16,000.	—
1839D	13,674	1200.	2250.	5000.	24,000.	—
1839O	17,781	500.	1100.	1650.	5000.	—

Coronet Head

Designer: Christian Gobrecht. **Size:** 18 millimeters. **Weight:** 4.18 grams. **Composition:** 90% gold (0.121 ounces), 10% copper. **Notes:** Varieties for 1843 are distinguished by the size of the numerals in the date. One 1848 variety has "Cal." inscribed on the reverse, indicating it was made from California gold. The 1873 "closed-3" and "open-3" varieties are distinguished by the amount of space between the upper left and lower left serifs in the 3 in the date.

Date	Mintage	F-12	VF-20	XF-40	AU-50	MS-60	Prf-65
1840	18,859	180.	245.	700.	1625.	7500.	—
1840C	12,822	325.	600.	1250.	5000.	15,000.	—
1840D	3,532	500.	2000.	4100.	9500.	28,000.	—
1840O	33,580	225.	250.	900.	1800.	7500.	—
1841	—	—	—	27,500.	50,000.	—	—
1841C	10,281	275.	550.	1250.	3250.	9600.	—
1841D	4,164	600.	1200.	2600.	9000.	18,750.	—
1842	2,823	350.	850.	3000.	6250.	15,500.	—
1842C	6,729	525.	1200.	2600.	7500.	11,000.	—
1842D	4,643	700.	1500.	2900.	8250.	18,500.	—
1842O	19,800	375.	375.	1500.	2900.	14,500.	—
1843	100,546	200.	225.	250.	375.	1750.	—
1843C sm. dt.	26,064	1000.	2500.	5500.	8500.	21,000.	—
1843C lg. dt.	Inc. Ab.	500.	600.	900.	3500.	8000.	—
1843D	36,209	400.	650.	1100.	2000.	7900.	—
1843O sm. dt.	288,002	200.	225.	325.	450.	1250.	—
1843O lg. dt.	76,000	250.	350.	450.	1750.	3125.	—
1844	6,784	200.	400.	850.	2500.	6800.	—
1844C	11,622	375.	675.	1550.	6500.	17,000.	—
1844D	17,332	325.	625.	1200.	2000.	7200.	—
1845	91,051	200.	250.	290.	350.	1100.	—
1845D	19,460	325.	650.	1125.	2500.	8500.	—
1845O	4,000	750.	750.	1900.	5600.	15,000.	—
1846	21,598	300.	400.	725.	1350.	6500.	—
1846C	4,808	550.	1000.	2000.	7500.	20,000.	—
1846D	19,303	450.	750.	1200.	2400.	8500.	—
1846O	66,000	200.	300.	525.	1150.	5000.	—
1847	29,814	200.	275.	400.	700.	3500.	—
1847C	23,226	300.	600.	1000.	2000.	5600.	—
1847D	15,784	300.	600.	1000.	2000.	7500.	—
1847O	124,000	200.	275.	425.	1150.	3000.	—
1848	7,497	350.	625.	1000.	1750.	8250.	—

1848 "Cal."

Date	Mintage	F-12	VF-20	XF-40	AU-50	MS-60	Prf-65
1848 "Cal."	1,389	7000.	9500.	15,000.	22,500.	35,000.	—
1848C	16,788	400.	650.	1200.	2250.	10,000.	—
1848D	13,771	400.	600.	1200.	2000.	8750.	—
1849	23,294	175.	280.	500.	800.	2200.	—
1849C	10,220	400.	700.	1750.	4750.	20,000.	—
1849D	10,945	400.	700.	1200.	2750.	16,000.	—
1850	252,923	175.	200.	225.	500.	1250.	—
1850C	9,148	275.	600.	1400.	3250.	16,000.	—
1850D	12,148	350.	700.	1200.	2500.	14,000.	—
1850O	84,000	200.	300.	575.	1400.	5500.	—
1851	1,372,748	115.	125.	170.	200.	350.	—
1851C	14,923	375.	675.	1500.	4000.	16,500.	—
1851D	11,264	275.	650.	1300.	3450.	12,000.	—
1851O	148,000	200.	250.	350.	1000.	5000.	—
1852	1,159,681	115.	125.	170.	180.	350.	—
1852C	9,772	350.	625.	1550.	3500.	17,000.	—
1852D	4,078	450.	1000.	2750.	5250.	18,000.	—
1852O	140,000	200.	250.	300.	975.	5500.	—
1853	1,404,668	115.	125.	180.	200.	350.	—
1853D	3,178	500.	1350.	2650.	4500.	17,000.	—
1854	596,258	175.	185.	210.	250.	375.	—
1854C	7,295	250.	625.	1650.	5000.	17,500.	—
1854D	1,760	1800.	2700.	6000.	12,500.	21,000.	—
1854O	153,000	200.	250.	300.	650.	1700.	—
1854S	246	15,000.	19,000.	37,500.	62,500.	—	—

Date	Mintage	F-12	VF-20	XF-40	AU-50	MS-60	Prf-65
1855	235,480	175.	185.	180.	225.	400.	—
1855C	3,677	500.	1300.	2850.	5000.	19,000.	—
1855D	1,123	2000.	4000.	8000.	18,500.	31,000.	—
1856	384,240	125.	150.	180.	200.	350.	—
1856C	7,913	500.	850.	2000.	4500.	17,500.	—
1856D	874	4000.	6000.	13,000.	19,000.	42,000.	—
1856O	21,100	200.	250.	715.	1500.	7000.	—
1856S	71,120	200.	250.	435.	900.	4800.	—
1857	214,130	175.	185.	210.	250.	390.	—
1857D	2,364	565.	1000.	2000.	4000.	13,000.	—
1857O	34,000	160.	180.	350.	1500.	5600.	—
1857S	69,200	150.	180.	400.	1100.	6250.	—
1858	47,377	135.	150.	225.	400.	1600.	—
1858C	9,056	350.	600.	1300.	2500.	10,000.	—
1859	39,444	150.	180.	300.	500.	1350.	—
1859D	2,244	600.	1350.	3000.	5000.	25,000.	—
1859S	15,200	200.	500.	1200.	3000.	8500.	—
1860	22,675	200.	250.	300.	600.	1250.	19,000.
1860C	7,469	350.	850.	1400.	4500.	21,000.	—
1860S	35,600	200.	300.	700.	1500.	4400.	—
1861	1,283,878	115.	125.	170.	200.	325.	20,000.
1861S	24,000	200.	350.	950.	3000.	6600.	—
1862	98,543	200.	250.	300.	550.	1250.	20,000.
1862/1	Inc. Ab.	650.	1000.	2150.	3500.	8750.	—
1862S	8,000	650.	950.	2500.	5950.	15,500.	—
1863S	10,800	400.	600.	1500.	2800.	6700.	—
1864	2,874	2500.	5400.	13,500.	26,000.	65,000.	22,500.
1865	1,545	2000.	4325.	8500.	20,000.	45,000.	32,000.
1865S	23,376	200.	225.	630.	2000.	4500.	—
1866	3,110	550.	1200.	5000.	11,000.	20,000.	29,500.
1866S	38,960	200.	300.	975.	2600.	8750.	—
1867	3,250	225.	360.	840.	1700.	5500.	29,500.
1867S	28,000	200.	250.	875.	2400.	5600.	—
1868	3,625	200.	300.	500.	1000.	2500.	—
1868S	34,000	200.	250.	500.	1500.	5000.	—
1869	4,345	200.	250.	500.	850.	2800.	24,500.
1869S	29,500	200.	250.	600.	1200.	4500.	—
1870	4,555	210.	275.	550.	1000.	3800.	32,500.
1870S	16,000	200.	285.	350.	1300.	5500.	—
1871	5,350	210.	275.	350.	900.	2400.	32,500.
1871S	22,000	225.	285.	350.	800.	3000.	—
1872	3,030	225.	360.	825.	2000.	8000.	30,000.
1872S	18,000	225.	285.	500.	1375.	4300.	—
1873 closed 3	178,025	125.	175.	200.	230.	560.	24,000.
1873 open 3	Inc. Ab.	125.	160.	225.	250.	325.	—
1873S	27,000	200.	250.	575.	1100.	2500.	—
1874	3,940	200.	250.	500.	1000.	2500.	28,000.
1875	420	1500.	3600.	5250.	9000.	16,000.	—
1875S	11,600	200.	250.	400.	800.	4500.	—
1876	4,221	175.	230.	625.	900.	3400.	24,500.
1876S	5,000	210.	250.	600.	1200.	3600.	—
1877	1,652	325.	450.	600.	900.	3000.	32,500.
1877S	35,400	125.	180.	210.	250.	650.	—
1878	286,260	125.	130.	180.	210.	300.	34,000.
1878S	178,000	125.	150.	180.	225.	425.	—
1879	88,990	125.	130.	180.	210.	300.	24,500.
1879S	43,500	125.	130.	165.	500.	1350.	—
1880	2,996	215.	250.	350.	600.	1200.	26,000.
1881	691	700.	1350.	2750.	5000.	8600.	27,500.
1882	4,067	125.	225.	300.	350.	800.	18,000.
1883	2,002	125.	225.	400.	800.	2000.	18,000.
1884	2,023	125.	225.	400.	625.	1550.	20,000.
1885	887	500.	800.	1500.	2500.	4650.	18,000.
1886	4,088	125.	210.	300.	550.	1400.	19,500.
1887	6,282	125.	190.	225.	500.	1000.	16,000.
1888	16,098	125.	190.	225.	260.	350.	21,000.
1889	17,648	125.	190.	250.	275.	450.	21,000.
1890	8,813	125.	190.	200.	250.	475.	16,000.
1891	11,040	125.	190.	250.	275.	450.	17,500.
1892	2,545	135.	195.	200.	450.	950.	17,000.
1893	30,106	125.	130.	200.	260.	400.	13,000.
1894	4,122	125.	130.	200.	325.	650.	13,000.
1895	6,199	125.	130.	200.	270.	325.	13,000.
1896	19,202	125.	130.	180.	210.	300.	13,000.
1897	29,904	125.	130.	180.	210.	275.	13,000.
1898	24,165	125.	130.	180.	210.	275.	13,000.
1899	27,350	125.	130.	180.	210.	275.	13,000.
1900	67,205	125.	130.	180.	210.	275.	13,000.
1901	91,322	125.	130.	180.	210.	275.	13,000.
1902	133,733	125.	130.	180.	210.	275.	13,000.
1903	201,257	125.	130.	180.	210.	275.	13,000.

Date	Mintage	F-12	VF-20	XF-40	AU-50	MS-60	Prf-65
1904	160,960	125.	130.	180.	210.	275.	13,000.
1905	217,944	125.	130.	180.	210.	275.	13,000.
1906	176,490	125.	130.	180.	210.	275.	13,000.
1907	336,448	125.	130.	180.	210.	275.	13,000.

1911-D $2.50 Gold
Grade MS-60

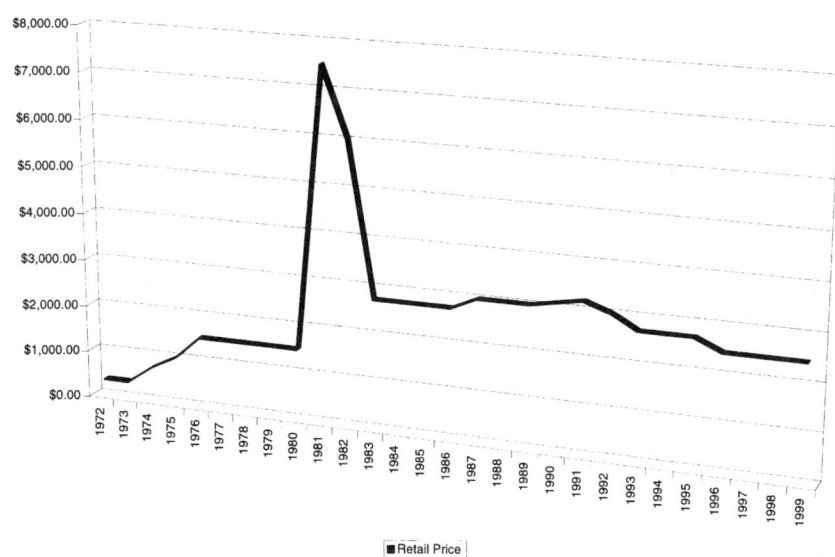

■ Retail Price

Source: COIN PRICES

Indian Head

Designer: Bela Lyon Pratt. **Size:** 18 millimeters. **Weight:** 4.18 grams. **Composition:** 90% gold (0.121 ounces), 10% copper.

Date	Mintage	VF-20	XF-40	AU-50	MS-60	MS-63	MS-65	Prf-65
1908	565,057	135.	175.	185.	210.	870.	2700.	15,000.
1909	441,899	135.	175.	185.	260.	930.	2700.	21,000.
1910	492,682	135.	175.	185.	255.	960.	5200.	18,000.
1911	704,191	135.	175.	185.	260.	600.	2700.	15,000.
1911D	55,680	700.	950.	1250.	2450.	7800.	36,000.	—
1912	616,197	135.	175.	185.	265.	960.	5200.	15,000.
1913	722,165	135.	175.	185.	270.	600.	2700.	15,000.
1914	240,117	135.	175.	210.	430.	2200.	13,750.	18,000.
1914D	448,000	135.	175.	185.	265.	1175.	19,000.	—
1915	606,100	135.	175.	185.	210.	600.	2700.	18,000.
1925D	578,000	135.	175.	185.	210.	600.	2700.	—
1926	446,000	135.	175.	185.	210.	600.	2700.	—
1927	388,000	135.	175.	185.	210.	600.	2700.	—
1928	416,000	135.	175.	185.	210.	600.	2700.	—
1929	532,000	135.	175.	185.	210.	600.	4800.	—

Gold $3

Designer: James B. Longacre. **Size:** 20.5 millimeters. **Weight:** 5.015 grams. **Composition:** 90% gold (0.1452 ounces), 10% copper. **Notes:** The 1873 "closed-3" and "open-3" varieties are distinguished by the amount of space between the upper left and lower left serifs of the 3 in the date.

Date	Mintage	F-12	VF-20	XF-40	AU-50	MS-60	Prf-65
1854	138,618	400.	575.	625.	765.	1450.	35,000.
1854D	1,120	4500.	7250.	13,500.	23,500.	47,000.	—
1854O	24,000	450.	475.	750.	2000.	4300.	—
1855	50,555	425.	475.	600.	765.	1450.	—
1855S	6,600	650.	1000.	1750.	4750.	20,000.	—
1856	26,010	425.	600.	690.	900.	2250.	—
1856S	34,500	500.	760.	900.	1800.	8250.	—
1857	20,891	425.	600.	690.	1100.	3000.	35,000.
1857S	14,000	650.	1000.	1800.	4000.	16,000.	—
1858	2,133	625.	800.	1050.	2000.	4900.	35,000.
1859	15,638	425.	600.	675.	765.	2250.	35,000.
1860	7,155	425.	700.	850.	1000.	2500.	35,000.
1860S	7,000	525.	760.	1800.	5000.	10,000.	—
1861	6,072	550.	760.	1000.	1500.	3000.	35,000.
1862	5,785	525.	760.	900.	1300.	3200.	35,000.
1863	5,039	550.	700.	850.	1450.	3400.	35,000.
1864	2,680	600.	760.	1150.	2400.	4000.	35,000.
1865	1,165	700.	800.	1600.	3750.	6000.	35,000.
1866	4,030	600.	700.	950.	1275.	3000.	35,000.
1867	2,650	600.	700.	950.	1275.	3000.	35,000.
1868	4,875	600.	700.	900.	1275.	3000.	35,000.
1869	2,525	600.	700.	1000.	1275.	3500.	35,000.
1870	3,535	600.	700.	1000.	1350.	3800.	35,000.
1870S	Unique			Private Sale, 1992 XF-40 $1,500,000.			
1871	1,330	600.	750.	1200.	1500.	3400.	35,000.
1872	2,030	600.	700.	1200.	1800.	2900.	35,000.
1873 open 3	25			Proof only	—		—
1873 closed 3	Unknown	—	4000.	6500.	7000.	23,000.	—
1874	41,820	400.	550.	600.	750.	1700.	35,000.
1875	20			Proof only			175,000.
1876	45			10,000.	12,000.		65,000.
1877	1,488	700.	1100.	2750.	4400.	7500.	35,000.
1878	82,324	400.	550.	625.	730.	1650.	30,000.
1879	3,030	475.	650.	850.	1250.	2250.	30,000.
1880	1,036	550.	750.	1200.	1800.	2250.	30,000.
1881	554	600.	1000.	2100.	3500.	4250.	32,000.
1882	1,576	550.	700.	1250.	1600.	2200.	30,000.
1883	989	700.	700.	1250.	1750.	2300.	32,000.
1884	1,106	550.	900.	1500.	1850.	2250.	30,000.
1885	910	550.	900.	1500.	2000.	2750.	32,000.
1886	1,142	550.	825.	1400.	2000.	3000.	30,000.
1887	6,160	525.	625.	800.	1000.	2300.	30,000.
1888	5,291	525.	625.	800.	1000.	2300.	30,000.
1889	2,429	525.	625.	800.	1000.	2300.	30,000.

Gold $4 (Stella)

Flowing Hair   **Coiled Hair**

Designers: Charles E. Barber (Flowing Hair type) and George T. Morgan (Coiled Hair type). **Notes:** These are patterns, rather than coins struck for circulation. Examples in other metals also exist; values listed here are only for those struck in gold.

Date	Type	Mintage	VF-20	XF-40	AU-50	Prf-65
1879	Flowing Hair	415	—	—	—	62,000.
Impaired Proofs		—	10,000.	13,500.	33,000.	—
1879	Coiled Hair	10	—	—	—	500,000.
1880	Flowing Hair	15	—	—	—	225,000.
1880	Coiled Hair	10	—	—	—	500,000.

Gold $5 (Half Eagle)

Liberty Cap

Small eagle   Heraldic eagle

Designer: Robert Scot. **Size:** 25 millimeters. **Weight:** 8.75 grams. **Composition:** 91.67% gold (0.258 ounces), 8.33% copper. **Notes:** From 1795 through 1798, varieties exist with either a "small eagle" or a "large (heraldic) eagle" on the reverse. After 1798, only the heraldic eagle was used. Two 1797 varieties are distinguished by the number of stars on the obverse. 1798 varieties are distinguished by the size of the 8 in the date and the number of stars on the reverse. 1804 varieties are distinguished by the size of the 8 in the date. 1806 varieties are distinguished by whether the top of the 6 has a serif.

Date	Mintage	F-12	VF-20	XF-40	MS-60
1795 sm. eagle	8,707	5250.	7250.	10,000.	35,000.
1795 lg. eagle	Inc. Ab.	6500.	7500.	15,000.	85,000.
1796/95 sm. eagle	6,196	6000.	9100.	14,000.	—
1797/95 lg. eagle	3,609	5000.	7000.	15,000.	130,000.
1797 15 stars, sm. eagle	Inc. Ab.	7500.	10,000.	25,000.	85,000.
1797 16 stars, sm. eagle	Inc. Ab.	7000.	9000.	24,000.	75,000.
1798 sm.eagle	7 known	—	—	95,000.	—
1798 lg. eagle, sm. 8	24,867	1500.	1850.	3700.	10,500.
1798 lg. eagle, lg. 8, 13-star reverse					
	Inc. Ab.	1200.	1850.	3000.	13,000.
1798 lg. eagle, lg. 8, 14-star reverse					
	Inc. Ab.	1600.	2300.	6000.	24,000.
1799	7,451	1300.	1600.	3000.	12,500.
1800	37,628	1150.	1550.	2450.	6000.
1802/1	53,176	1150.	1550.	2450.	6000.
1803/2	33,506	1150.	1550.	2450.	6000.
1804 sm. 8	30,475	1150.	1550.	2450.	6850.
1804 lg. 8	Inc. Ab.	1150.	1550.	2450.	7300.
1805	33,183	1150.	1550.	2450.	6000.
1806 pointed 6	64,093	1150.	1550.	2600.	6250.
1806 round 6	Inc. Ab.	1150.	1550.	2450.	5000.
1807	32,488	1150.	1550.	2450.	5200.

Turban Head

Capped draped bust

Designer: John Reich. **Size:** 25 millimeters. **Weight:** 8.75 grams. **Composition:** 91.67% gold (0.258 ounces), 8.33% copper. **Notes:** The 1810 varieties are distinguished by the size of the numerals in the date and the size of the 5 in the "5D." on the reverse. The 1811 varieties are distinguished by the size of the 5 in the "5D." on the reverse.

Date	Mintage	F-12	VF-20	XF-40	MS-60
1807	51,605	1250.	1650.	2150.	6000.
1808	55,578	1250.	1650.	2150.	6000.
1808/7	Inc. Ab.	1400.	1550.	2400.	9500.
1809/8	33,875	1250.	1500.	2150.	6000.
1810 sm. date, sm. 5	100,287	—	20,000.	35,000.	85,000.
1810 sm. dt., lg. 5	Inc. Ab.	1300.	1650.	2400.	6000.
1810 lg. dt., sm. 5	Inc. Ab.	14,000.	25,000.	40,000.	100,000.
1810 lg. dt., lg. 5	Inc. Ab.	1250.	1400.	2000.	5750.
1811 sm. 5	99,581	1250.	1400.	2000.	5000.
1811 lg. 5	Inc. Ab.	1150.	1350.	2000.	5000.
1812	58,087	1000.	1350.	2000.	5250.

Capped head

Notes: 1820 varieties are distinguished by whether the 2 in the date has a curved base or square base, and by the size of the letters in the reverse inscriptions. 1832 varieties are distinguished by whether the 2 in the date has a curved base or square base and by the number of stars on the reverse. 1834 varieties are distinguished by whether the 4 has a serif at its far right.

Date	Mintage	F-12	VF-20	XF-40	MS-60
1813	95,428	1300.	1500.	2250.	5600.
1814/13	15,454	1600.	2000.	4000.	8000.
1815	635			Private sale Jan. 1994, MS-61, $150,000.	
1818	48,588	1500.	1900.	2850.	8500.
1819	51,723	6250.	12,500.	22,000.	37,500.
1820 curved base 2, sm. letters	263,806	1500.	1900.	3200.	9400.
1820 curved base 2, lg. letters	Inc. Ab.	1500.	1900.	4500.	40,000.
1820 sq. base 2	Inc. Ab.	1500.	1900.	3200.	9400.
1821	34,641	2200.	8000.	13,000.	30,000.
1822	(3 known) 17,796			Private Sale 1993, VF-30, $1,000,000.	
1823	14,485	1600.	2000.	3700.	14,500.
1824	17,340	4500.	8750.	13,000.	27,500.
1825/21	29,060	4500.	6750.	11,000.	26,500.
1825/24	I.A.			Bowers & Merena, Mar. 1989, XF,$148,500.	
1826	18,069	2750.	6000.	7100.	19,000.
1827	24,913	—	—	—	32,500.
1828/7	28,029			Bowers & Merena, Jun. 1989, XF, $20,900.	
1828	Inc. Ab.	4250.	6500.	12,500.	48,000.
1829 lg. plan.	57,442			Superior, July 1985, MS-65, $104,500.	
1829 sm. plan.	Inc. Ab.			Private Sale, 1992 (XF-45), $89,000.	
1830 sm. "5D."	126,351	3500.	5000.	6500.	12,000.
1830 lg. "5D."	Inc. Ab.	3500.	5000.	7000.	12,500.
1831	140,594	3500.	5100.	6500.	16,000.
1832 curved base 2, 12-stars	157,487	—	Rare	—	—

Date	Mintage	F-12	VF-20	XF-40	MS-60
1832 square base 2, 13 stars	Inc. Ab.	1800.	2000.	3000.	12,000.
1833	193,630	3500.	5000.	6250.	15,500.
1834 plain 4	50,141	3500.	5000.	6250.	17,000.
1834 crosslet 4	Inc. Ab.	4000.	6000.	7750.	20,000.

Classic Head

Designer: William Kneass. **Size:** 22.5 millimeters. **Weight:** 8.36 grams. **Composition:** 89.92% gold (0.2418 ounces), 10.08% copper. **Notes:** 1834 varieties are distinguished by whether the 4 has a serif at its far right.

Date	Mintage	VF-20	XF-40	AU-50	MS-60	MS-65
1834 plain 4	658,028	250.	375.	700.	1900.	48,000.
1834 crosslet 4	Inc. Ab.	1150.	2375.	5250.	15,000.	—
1835	371,534	250.	375.	900.	2900.	62,000.
1836	553,147	250.	375.	700.	1900.	62,000.
1837	207,121	325.	525.	925.	3500.	62,000.
1838	286,588	250.	375.	900.	3250.	62,000.
1838C	17,179	1550.	4250.	9500.	30,000.	—
1838D	20,583	1450.	3500.	7000.	25,000.	—

Coronet Head

No motto

Designer: Christian Gobrecht. **Size:** 21.6 millimeters. **Weight:** 8.359 grams. **Composition:** 90% gold (0.242 ounces), 10% copper. **Notes:** Varieties for the 1842 Philadelphia strikes are distinguished by the size of the letters in the reverse inscriptions. Varieties for the 1842-C and -D strikes are distinguished by the size of the numerals in the date. Varieties for the 1843-O strikes are distinguished by the size of the letters in the reverse inscriptions.

Date	Mintage	F-12	VF-20	XF-40	MS-60	Prf-65
1839	118,143	200.	250.	435.	3500.	—
1839/8 curved date	Inc. Ab.	200.	300.	600.	1750.	—
1839C	17,205	450.	950.	1300.	20,000.	—
1839D	18,939	400.	800.	1700.	15,000.	—
1840	137,382	190.	225.	350.	4100.	—
1840C	18,992	400.	700.	1650.	23,000.	—
1840D	22,896	400.	700.	1500.	16,000.	—
1840O	40,120	200.	325.	700.	9500.	—
1841	15,833	200.	375.	850.	5600.	—
1841C	21,467	300.	675.	1450.	12,000.	—
1841D	30,495	325.	600.	1250.	11,000.	—
1841O	50		2 known	—	—	—
1842 sm. let.	27,578	150.	300.	1300.	12,500.	—
1842 lg. let.	Inc. Ab.	350.	700.	2000.	13,500.	—
1842C sm. dt.	28,184	2000.	6500.	25,000.	100,000.	—
1842C lg. dt.	Inc. Ab.	350.	750.	1500.	11,250.	—
1842D sm. dt.	59,608	350.	650.	1250.	14,000.	—
1842D lg. dt.	Inc. Ab.	1250.	2250.	6000.	37,500.	—
1842O	16,400	350.	1000.	5000.	24,000.	—
1843	611,205	150.	200.	215.	2200.	—
1843C	44,201	350.	600.	1400.	10,000.	—
1843D	98,452	350.	550.	1000.	8000.	—
1843O sm. let.	19,075	325.	550.	1400.	20,000.	—
1843O lg. let.	82,000	200.	325.	900.	11,250.	—
1844	340,330	150.	200.	250.	2100.	—

1852-C $5 Gold
Grade MS-60

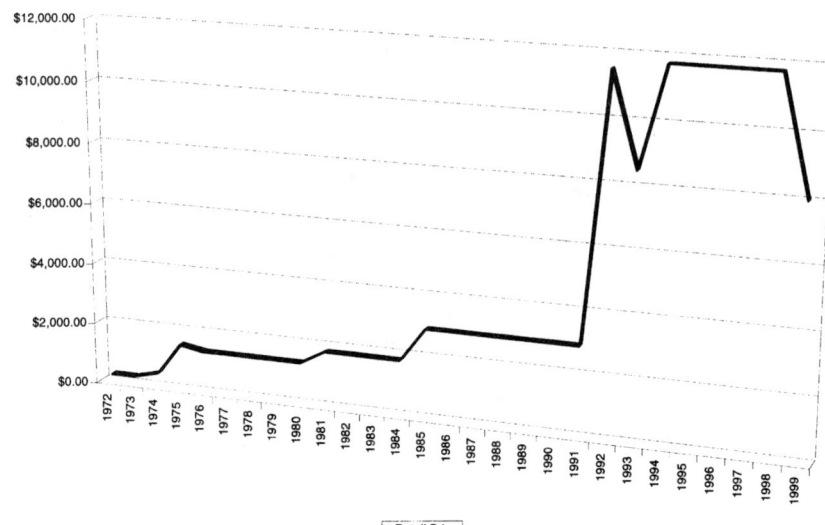

■ Retail Price

Source: COIN PRICES

Date	Mintage	F-12	VF-20	XF-40	MS-60	Prf-65
1844C	23,631	300.	725.	2700.	18,500.	—
1844D	88,982	375.	550.	1050.	12,000.	—
1844O	364,600	200.	225.	600.	5000.	—
1845	417,099	150.	200.	215.	2750.	—
1845D	90,629	360.	850.	1850.	12,500.	—
1845O	41,000	200.	350.	1100.	12,000.	—
1846	395,942	150.	200.	235.	3000.	—
1846C	12,995	425.	900.	2500.	22,500.	—
1846D	80,294	400.	550.	1350.	9250.	—
1846O	58,000	200.	350.	1450.	12,750.	—
1847	915,981	150.	200.	215.	1000.	—
1847C	84,151	375.	575.	1450.	16,500.	—
1847D	64,405	400.	500.	1100.	9000.	—
1847O	12,000	475.	2300.	10,500.	29,000.	—
1848	260,775	150.	200.	250.	1200.	—
1848C	64,472	400.	650.	1600.	15,000.	—
1848D	47,465	400.	500.	1500.	13,000.	—
1849	133,070	150.	200.	300.	2700.	—
1849C	64,823	350.	500.	1100.	11,500.	—
1849D	39,036	350.	700.	1350.	14,500.	—
1850	64,491	200.	350.	550.	3500.	—
1850C	63,591	325.	550.	1100.	13,000.	—
1850D	43,984	350.	500.	1500.	20,000.	—
1851	377,505	150.	200.	215.	2800.	—
1851C	49,176	325.	600.	1100.	14,000.	—
1851D	62,710	350.	525.	1375.	15,000.	—
1851O	41,000	325.	650.	1500.	15,000.	—
1852	573,901	150.	200.	215.	1000.	—
1852C	72,574	350.	550.	1100.	8000.	—
1852D	91,584	350.	500.	1000.	8750.	—
1853	305,770	150.	215.	235.	2250.	—
1853C	65,571	350.	525.	1000.	8000.	—
1853D	89,678	350.	500.	900.	7500.	—
1854	160,675	160.	200.	500.	3000.	—
1854C	39,283	400.	600.	1600.	16,500.	—
1854D	56,413	350.	500.	1000.	10,000.	—
1854O	46,000	250.	300.	500.	6800.	—
1855	117,098	160.	200.	250.	2400.	—
1855C	39,788	350.	625.	1750.	13,500.	—
1855D	22,432	400.	600.	1500.	19,000.	—

Date	Mintage	F-12	VF-20	XF-40	MS-60	Prf-65
1855O	11,100	350.	700.	2900.	20,000.	—
1855S	61,000	200.	425.	1100.	15,000.	—
1856	197,990	175.	310.	340.	2000.	—
1856C	28,457	350.	600.	1300.	11,500.	—
1856D	19,786	400.	600.	1300.	11,000.	—
1856O	10,000	400.	800.	2800.	22,000.	—
1856S	105,100	190.	300.	800.	6600.	—
1857	98,188	160.	200.	250.	3000.	—
1857C	31,360	300.	600.	1300.	13,000.	—
1857D	17,046	300.	600.	1250.	14,500.	—
1857O	13,000	300.	700.	2000.	20,000.	—
1857S	87,000	200.	300.	700.	8000.	—
1858	15,136	200.	275.	800.	5250.	70,000.
1858C	38,856	375.	800.	1250.	14,000.	—
1858D	15,362	300.	600.	1200.	12,000.	—
1858S	18,600	350.	650.	2600.	25,000.	—
1859	16,814	200.	275.	600.	6500.	—
1859C	31,847	300.	525.	1400.	15,000.	—
1859D	10,366	400.	725.	2000.	13,000.	—
1859S	13,220	450.	1250.	4750.	31,000.	—
1860	19,825	200.	300.	600.	3500.	—
1860C	14,813	350.	800.	2000.	13,500.	—
1860D	14,635	300.	800.	1800.	13,500.	—
1860S	21,200	450.	1200.	2800.	23,000.	—
1861	688,150	150.	200.	215.	1000.	—
1861C	6,879	700.	1500.	3400.	25,000.	—
1861D	1,597	2500.	4000.	7000.	34,000.	—
1861S	18,000	450.	1100.	4500.	33,000.	—
1862	4,465	450.	750.	2500.	19,000.	—
1862S	9,500	1400.	4500.	10,500.	56,000.	—
1863	2,472	500.	1150.	3450.	23,000.	—
1863S	17,000	425.	1200.	4750.	32,500.	—
1864	4,220	400.	600.	2100.	13,500.	—
1864S	3,888	2200.	6750.	15,000.	50,000.	—
1865	1,295	600.	1200.	3150.	22,000.	—
1865S	27,612	425.	1200.	3600.	15,000.	—
1866S	9,000	600.	1600.	6000.	30,000.	—

With motto

Notes: In 1866 the motto "In God We Trust" was added above the eagle on the reverse. The 1873 "closed-3" and "open-3" varieties are distinguished by the amount of space between the upper left and lower left serifs of the 3 in the date.

Date	Mintage	VF-20	XF-40	AU-50	MS-60	MS-65	Prf-65
1866	6,730	725.	1800.	4400.	12,500.	—	35,000.
1866S	34,920	1350.	4500.	8500.	25,000.	—	—
1867	6,920	550.	2500.	4000.	8000.	—	35,000.
1867S	29,000	1600.	5000.	10,000.	25,000.	—	—
1868	5,725	650.	1800.	4000.	10,000.	—	35,000.
1868S	52,000	500.	2400.	7200.	20,000.	—	—
1869	1,785	875.	2300.	5000.	21,000.	—	35,000.
1869S	31,000	375.	2400.	8500.	24,000.	—	—
1870	4,035	700.	2800.	4500.	17,500.	—	35,000.
1870CC	7,675	4400.	9500.	20,000.	40,000.	—	—
1870S	17,000	1200.	4000.	11,500.	26,000.	—	—
1871	3,230	875.	2150.	6500.	22,000.	—	35,000.
1871CC	20,770	975.	3000.	8000	28,000.	—	—
1871S	25,000	550.	2000.	3250.	17,500.	—	—
1872	1,690	750.	2000.	4700.	15,000.	—	35,000.
1872CC	16,980	850.	3500.	14,000.	20,000.	—	—
1872S	36,400	525.	1850.	3550.	10,000.	—	—
1873 closed 3	49,305	225.	250.	625.	1250.	—	35,000.
1873 open 3	63,200	225.	250.	625.	2800.	—	—
1873CC	7,416	2200.	6500.	15,500.	28,500.	—	—
1873S	31,000	875.	2700.	5000.	20,000.	—	—
1874	3,508	625.	2200.	5000.	16,500.	—	35,000.
1874CC	21,198	675.	1750.	5500.	12,000.	—	—
1874S	16,000	725.	3750.	9000.	20,000.	—	—
1875	220	45,000.	55,000.	96,000.	—	—	110,000.
1875CC	11,828	1500.	5400.	13,000.	31,500.	—	—

Date	Mintage	VF-20	XF-40	AU-50	MS-60	MS-65	Prf-65
1875S	9,000	950.	3300.	7900.	23,500.	—	—
1876	1,477	1000.	2600.	5300.	11,250.	47,000.	35,000.
1876CC	6,887	1500.	5750.	9500.	20,000.	—	—
1876S	4,000	1700.	5000.	12,750.	28,000.	—	—
1877	1,152	800.	2400.	4500.	12,000.	—	35,000.
1877CC	8,680	1000.	3300.	8000.	18,000.	—	—
1877S	26,700	325.	900.	3600.	8300.	—	—
1878	131,740	175.	225.	250.	375.	—	35,000.
1878CC	9,054	3500.	9000.	20,000.	34,000.	—	—
1878S	144,700	175.	220.	250.	500.	—	—
1879	301,950	175.	210.	225.	250.	11,000.	20,000.
1879CC	17,281	350.	1300.	3000.	6250.	—	—
1879S	426,200	200.	275.	325.	975.	—	—
1880	3,166,436	175.	210.	215.	250.	—	20,000.
1880CC	51,017	350.	875.	2000.	7500.	—	—
1880S	1,348,900	175.	210.	215.	240.	—	—
1881	5,708,802	175.	210.	215.	240.	7000.	20,000.
1881/80	Inc. Ab.	350.	600.	750.	1500.	—	—
1881CC	13,886	500.	1500.	4150.	9000.	—	—
1881S	969,000	175.	210.	215.	240.	—	—
1882	2,514,568	165.	175.	180.	235.	7000.	20,000.
1882CC	82,817	375.	650.	1500.	5000.	—	—
1882S	969,000	175.	210.	220.	250.	—	—
1883	233,461	175.	210.	225.	550.	7000.	20,000.
1883CC	12,958	375.	800.	3500.	12,000.	—	—
1883S	83,200	195.	225.	330.	1150.	—	—
1884	191,078	175.	210.	260.	1250.	—	20,000.
1884CC	16,402	450.	825.	4250.	13,500.	—	—
1884S	177,000	175.	210.	225.	325.	—	—
1885	601,506	175.	210.	215.	240.	—	20,000.
1885S	1,211,500	175.	210.	215.	250.	7000.	—
1886	388,432	175.	210.	225.	375.	—	20,000.
1886S	3,268,000	175.	210.	215.	240.	—	—
1887	87	Proof only		—	—	—	140,000.
1887S	1,912,000	175.	210.	215.	240.	—	—
1888	18,296	175.	250.	300.	530.	—	20,000.
1888S	293,900	190.	275.	340.	1700.	—	—
1889	7,565	260.	440.	530.	1125.	—	20,000.
1890	4,328	250.	400.	875.	2000.	—	20,000.
1890CC	53,800	300.	400.	550.	1250.	—	—
1891	61,413	175.	235.	250.	775.	7500.	20,000.
1891CC	208,000	250.	375.	500.	850.	29,500.	—
1892	753,572	175.	210.	220.	240.	—	20,000.
1892CC	82,968	300.	600.	700.	1550.	—	—
1892O	10,000	600.	1250.	2250.	4700.	—	—
1892S	298,400	175.	225.	325.	725.	—	—
1893	1,528,197	175.	210.	220.	240.	5600.	20,000.
1893CC	60,000	300.	400.	625.	2000.	4400.	—
1893O	110,000	200.	300.	400.	2000.	—	—
1893S	224,000	180.	225.	250.	290.	7500.	—
1894	957,955	175.	220.	235.	300.	4750.	20,000.
1894O	16,600	195.	350.	475.	1125.	—	—
1894S	55,900	275.	350.	850.	3750.	7500.	—
1895	1,345,936	175.	210.	215.	240.	4750.	20,000.
1895S	112,000	190.	275.	400.	2900.	20,000.	—
1896	59,063	185.	225.	225.	350.	7500.	20,000.
1896S	155,400	225.	275.	600.	1200.	—	—
1897	867,883	175.	210.	215.	240.	4750.	20,000.
1897S	354,000	185.	190.	250.	940.	—	—
1898	633,495	175.	210.	215.	240.	4400.	20,000.
1898S	1,397,400	175.	210.	215.	240.	4400.	—
1899	1,710,729	175.	210.	215.	240.	4400.	20,000.
1899S	1,545,000	175.	210.	215.	240.	4400.	—
1900	1,405,730	175.	210.	215.	240.	4400.	20,000.
1900S	329,000	185.	225.	300.	700.	5000.	—
1901	616,040	175.	210.	215.	240.	4400.	12,500.
1901S	3,648,000	175.	210.	215.	240.	4400.	—
1902	172,562	175.	210.	215.	240.	4400.	12,500.
1902S	939,000	175.	210.	215.	240.	4400.	—
1903	227,024	175.	210.	215.	240.	4400.	15,000.
1903S	1,855,000	175.	210.	215.	240.	4400.	—
1904	392,136	175.	210.	215.	240.	4400.	12,500.
1904S	97,000	195.	225.	300.	800.	11,000.	—
1905	302,308	175.	210.	215.	240.	7200.	12,500.
1905S	880,700	175.	225.	260.	900.	4400.	—
1906	348,820	175.	210.	215.	240.	4400.	12,500.
1906D	320,000	175.	210.	215.	240.	4400.	—
1906S	598,000	175.	210.	215.	275.	4400.	—
1907	626,192	175.	210.	215.	240.	4400.	20,000.
1907D	888,000	175.	210.	215.	240.	4400.	—
1908	421,874	175.	210.	215.	240.	4400.	—

Indian Head

Designer: Bela Lyon Pratt. **Size:** 21.6 millimeters. **Weight:** 8.359 grams. **Composition:** 90% gold (0.242 ounces), 10% copper.

Date	Mintage	VF-20	XF-40	AU-50	MS-60	MS-63	MS-65	Prf-65
1908	578,012	190.	225.	240.	280.	1400.	12,500.	21,500.
1908D	148,000	190.	225.	240.	280.	1400.	27,000.	—
1908S	82,000	225.	450.	540.	1100.	2600.	12,500.	—
1909	627,138	190.	225.	240.	325.	1400.	12,500.	26,500.
1909D	3,423,560	190.	225.	240.	280.	1400.	12,500.	—
1909O	34,200	600.	900.	1600.	5400.	30,000.	210,000.	—
1909S	297,200	215.	235.	275.	1175.	6600.	31,000.	—
1910	604,250	190.	225.	240.	280.	1700.	18,000.	23,000.
1910D	193,600	190.	225.	240.	350.	1700.	51,000.	—
1910S	770,200	190.	240.	260.	875.	7200.	49,000.	—
1911	915,139	190.	225.	240.	280.	1700.	12,500.	21,500.
1911D	72,500	350.	475.	600.	2850.	13,500.	130,000.	—
1911S	1,416,000	190.	240.	250.	425.	2900.	42,000.	—
1912	790,144	190.	225.	240.	280.	1700.	17,500.	21,500.
1912S	392,000	215.	240.	250.	1450.	9500.	74,000.	—
1913	916,099	190.	225.	240.	280.	1700.	14,500.	25,000.
1913S	408,000	250.	270.	340.	1200.	10,500.	115,000.	—
1914	247,125	190.	225.	240.	335.	1700.	14,500.	21,500.
1914D	247,000	190.	225.	240.	360.	1700.	42,000.	—
1914S	263,000	215.	235.	255.	1200.	8200.	57,000.	—
1915	588,075	190.	225.	240.	280.	1400.	12,500.	33,000.
1915S	164,000	300.	325.	425.	1850.	11,500.	75,000.	—
1916S	240,000	190.	250.	275.	515.	1700.	19,000.	—
1929	662,000	2000.	3500.	4200.	5400.	7500.	31,000.	—

Gold $10 (Eagle)

Liberty Cap

Small eagle

Designer: Robert Scot. **Size:** 33 millimeters. **Weight:** 17.5 grams. **Composition:** 91.67% gold (0.5159 ounces), 8.33% copper.

Date	Mintage	F-12	VF-20	XF-40	MS-60
1795 13 leaves	5,583	6000.	8500.	11,000.	39,500.
1795 9 leaves	Inc. Ab.	17,000.	35,000.	50,000.	—
1796	4,146	6000.	9500.	11,000.	50,000.
1797 sm. eagle	3,615	7500.	12,500.	25,000.	—

Heraldic eagle

Notes: The 1798/97 varieties are distinguished by the positioning of the stars on the obverse.

Date	Mintage	F-12	VF-20	XF-40	MS-60
1797 lg. eagle	10,940	2500.	3500.	5000.	14,000.
1798/97, 9 stars left, 4 right	900	4500.	8000.	20,000.	70,000.
1798/97, 7 stars left, 6 right	842	15,000.	27,500.	57,500.	—
1799	37,449	2400.	3000.	4500.	8500.
1800	5,999	2400.	3250.	5000.	13,750.
1801	44,344	2400.	3000.	4000.	11,000.
1803	15,017	2600.	3250.	4000.	11,000.
1804	3,757	3750.	4200.	6000.	18,000.

Coronet Head

Old-style head, no motto

Designer: Christian Gobrecht. **Size:** 27 millimeters. **Weight:** 16.718 grams. **Composition:** 90% gold (0.4839 ounces), 10% copper.

Date	Mintage	F-12	VF-20	XF-40	MS-60	Prf-65
1838	7,200	650.	1175.	2900.	21,000.	—
1839 lg. lts.	38,248	600.	1175.	1950.	17,500.	—

New-style head, no motto

Notes: The 1842 varieties are distinguished by the size of the numerals in the date.

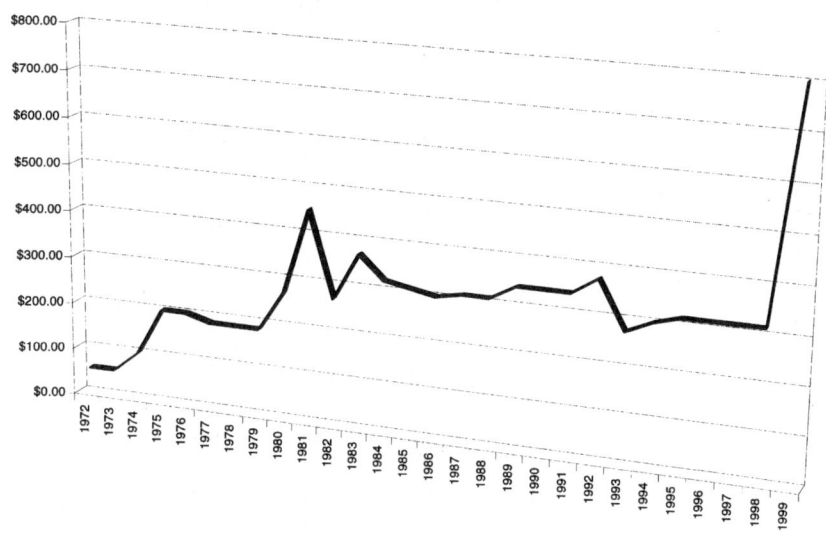

Date	Mintage	F-12	VF-20	XF-40	MS-60	Prf-65
1839 sm. lts.	Inc. Ab.	700.	1600.	5500.	—	—
1840	47,338	380.	425.	750.	9000.	—
1841	63,131	380.	415.	650.	8000.	—
1841O	2,500	850.	2450.	5400.	29,000.	—
1842 sm. dt.	81,507	380.	425.	1200.	35,000.	—
1842 lg. dt.	Inc. Ab.	380.	415.	750.	8750.	—
1842O	27,400	250.	395.	700.	12,500.	—
1843	75,462	380.	415.	700.	13.00	—
1843O	175,162	380.	415.	600.	8000.	—
1844	6,361	475.	1300.	2900.	16,000.	—
1844O	118,700	380.	425.	600.	11,000.	—
1845	26,153	380.	750.	950.	16,000.	—
1845O	47,500	350.	490.	625.	12,500.	—
1846	20,095	500.	900.	1275.	22,000.	—
1846O	81,780	350.	490.	975.	10,500.	—
1847	862,258	240.	310.	350.	3750.	—
1847O	571,500	250.	325.	400.	5000.	—
1848	145,484	300.	350.	400.	5500.	—
1848O	38,850	400.	600.	1400.	16,000.	—
1849	653,618	240.	310.	360.	3900.	—
1849O	23,900	500.	800.	3000.	21,000.	—
1850	291,451	240.	310.	325.	3500.	—
1850O	57,500	350.	400.	600.	11,250.	—
1851	176,328	300.	325.	525.	9500.	—
1851O	263,000	280.	325.	550.	5750.	—
1852	263,106	330.	425.	525.	3500.	—
1852O	18,000	500.	700.	1200.	22,500.	—
1853	201,253	240.	310.	800.	3500.	—
1853O	51,000	350.	400.	575.	8750.	—
1854	54,250	350.	400.	700.	6000.	—
1854O sm. dt.	52,500	225.	400.	1000.	12,000.	—
1854O lg. dt.	Inc. Ab.	375.	600.	2250.	—	—
1854S	123,826	280.	300.	575.	11,000.	—
1855	121,701	240.	310.	350.	3500.	—
1855O	18,000	350.	600.	2000.	15,000.	—
1855S	9,000	850.	1900.	4250.	31,000.	—
1856	60,490	300.	330.	360.	4800.	—
1856O	14,500	400.	600.	2000.	15,500.	—
1856S	68,000	330.	380.	625.	10,000.	—
1857	16,606	330.	380.	1000.	12,000.	—
1857O	5,500	700.	1000.	2000.	18,750.	—
1857S	26,000	380.	525.	800.	7750.	—
1858	2,521	2500.	5000.	8000.	33,000.	—
1858O	20,000	330.	380.	850.	12,000.	—

1853 $10 Gold
Grade XF-40

Source: COIN PRICES

Date	Mintage	F-12	VF-20	XF-40	MS-60	Prf-65
1858S	11,800	750.	2150.	3250.	31,000.	—
1859	16,093	330.	380.	825.	11,500.	—
1859O	2,300	1275.	3500.	9000.	49,000.	—
1859S	7,000	900.	2000.	4500.	43,500.	—
1860	15,105	330.	380.	800.	8100.	—
1860O	11,100	400.	575.	1000.	12,500.	—
1860S	5,000	750.	2700.	6000.	43,500.	—
1861	113,233	280.	310.	350.	2750.	—
1861S	15,500	675.	1900.	2750.	34,000.	—
1862	10,995	350.	475.	1000.	11,250.	—
1862S	12,500	700.	1950.	3000.	37,500.	—
1863	1,248	2000.	3650.	9000.	50,000.	—
1863S	10,000	725.	1700.	3500.	26,000.	—
1864	3,580	800.	1900.	3000.	16,750.	—
1864S	2,500	2750.	5800.	11,500.	50,000.	—
1865	4,005	750.	2150.	3500.	34,000.	—
1865S	16,700	1450.	5000.	14,500.	48,500.	—
1865S/inverted 186	—	—	2500.	6000.	49,000.	—
1866S	8,500	1300.	3000.	3600.	47,500.	—

New-style head, with motto

Notes: In 1866 the motto "In God We Trust" was added above the eagle on the reverse. The 1873 "closed-3" and "open-3" varieties are distinguished by the amount of space between the upper left and lower left serifs of the 3 in the date.

Date	Mintage	VF-20	XF-40	AU-50	MS-60	MS-65	Prf-65
1866	3,780	750.	3000.	6750.	15,500.	—	60,000.
1866S	11,500	1750.	3900.	9500.	24,000.	—	—
1867	3,140	1750.	4500.	10,500.	28,000.	—	60,000.
1867S	9,000	2600.	8500.	20,000.	43,500.	—	—
1868	10,655	600.	1800.	5750.	15,000.	—	60,000.
1868S	13,500	1250.	2000.	3500.	25,000.	—	—
1869	1,855	1750.	3000.	5600.	33,500.	—	65,000.
1869S	6,430	1800.	3200.	5400.	28,500.	—	—
1870	4,025	750.	1450.	2125.	16,500.	—	60,000.
1870CC	5,908	7000.	19,000.	32,500.	68,500.	—	—
1870S	8,000	2000.	3250.	7250.	34,000.	—	—
1871	1,820	1600.	2875.	3750.	20,000.	—	60,000.
1871CC	8,085	2250.	6000.	15,000.	43,500.	—	—
1871S	16,500	1750.	4700.	8000.	27,500.	—	—
1872	1,650	2500.	3900.	12,500.	25,000.	—	60,000.
1872CC	4,600	2500.	10,000.	25,000.	60,000.	—	—
1872S	17,300	530.	1000.	2000.	25,000.	—	—
1873 closed 3	825	4200.	14,000.	28,000.	46,500.	—	60,000.
1873CC	4,543	2700.	12,000.	27,000.	46,500.	—	—
1873S	12,000	1600.	5000.	9000.	31,250.	—	—
1874	53,160	310.	350.	550.	2450.	—	60,000.
1874CC	16,767	875.	2900.	7200.	23,500.	—	—
1874S	10,000	1700.	3375.	6900.	43,500.	—	—
1875	120				Akers, Aug. 1990, proof, $115,000.		—
1875CC	7,715	3500.	9000.	20,000.	53,000.	—	—
1876	732	3000.	6750.	12,500.	55,000.	—	50,000.
1876CC	4,696	3000.	10,000.	19,000.	50,000.	—	—
1876S	5,000	2100.	4000.	12,000.	40,000.	—	—
1877	817	3500.	9000.	16,000.	43,500.	—	40,000.
1877CC	3,332	2400.	4550.	8750.	37,500.	—	—
1877S	17,000	500.	6750.	2300.	24,000.	—	—
1878	73,800	305.	350.	450.	1000.	—	50,000.
1878CC	3,244	3500.	8000.	17,000.	40,000.	—	—
1878S	26,100	450.	715.	1625.	21,000.	—	—
1879	384,770	305.	310.	375.	850.	—	40,000.
1879CC	1,762	5000.	12,500.	26,000.	43,500.	—	—
1879O	1,500	2200.	3800.	11,000.	32,000.	—	—
1879S	224,000	310.	360.	425.	1700.	—	—
1880	1,644,876	305.	310.	350.	400.	—	40,000.
1880CC	11,190	425.	675.	2200.	7500.	—	—
1880O	9,200	400.	600.	900.	7500.	—	—
1880S	506,250	305.	310.	400.	600.	—	—
1881	3,877,260	305.	310.	350.	375.	—	40,000.
1881CC	24,015	400.	550.	1300.	7500.	—	—
1881O	8,350	400.	875.	3000.	8000.	—	—

Date	Mintage	VF-20	XF-40	AU-50	MS-60	MS-65	Prf-65
1881S	970,000	305.	310.	350.	450.	—	—
1882	2,324,480	305.	310.	350.	375.	—	40,000.
1882CC	6,764	475.	1800.	5250.	10,000.	—	—
1882O	10,820	400.	850.	2500.	5000.	—	—
1882S	132,000	305.	310.	350.	1100.	13,500.	—
1883	208,740	305.	310.	375.	450.	6500.	40,000.
1883CC	12,000	400.	850.	3000.	9250.	—	—
1883O	800	3200.	8500.	17,000.	37,500.	—	—
1883S	38,000	310.	375.	450.	900.	13,500.	—
1884	76,905	310.	325.	400.	715.	13,500.	86,000.
1884CC	9,925	525.	1300.	4000.	10,000.	—	—
1884S	124,250	305.	310.	375.	425.	—	—
1885	253,527	305.	310.	350.	425.	6500.	40,000.
1885S	228,000	305.	310.	350.	375.	6500.	—
1886	236,160	305.	310.	350.	395.	6500.	40,000.
1886S	826,000	305.	310.	350.	375.	6500.	—
1887	53,680	310.	325.	475.	750.	50,000.	40,000.
1887S	817,000	305.	310.	350.	425.	6500.	—
1888	132,996	315.	325.	365.	565.	50,000.	40,000.
1888O	21,335	305.	310.	350.	750.	—	—
1888S	648,700	305.	310.	350.	375.	6500.	—
1889	4,485	400.	500.	1000.	2000.	—	40,000.
1889S	425,400	305.	310.	350.	375.	6500.	—
1890	58,043	305.	315.	425.	650.	13,500.	40,000.
1890CC	17,500	375.	450.	600.	2000.	—	—
1891	91,868	305.	310.	350.	375.	13,500.	40,000.
1891CC	103,732	325.	350.	550.	650.	—	—
1892	797,552	305.	310.	350.	375.	6500.	40,000.
1892CC	40,000	375.	450.	500.	2150.	—	—
1892O	28,688	305.	310.	350.	375.	—	—
1892S	115,500	305.	310.	350.	400.	13,500.	—
1893	1,840,895	305.	310.	350.	375.	4350.	40,000.
1893CC	14,000	305.	600.	1400.	4750.	—	—
1893O	17,000	305.	310.	350.	675.	—	—
1893S	141,350	305.	310.	350.	425.	13,500.	—
1894	2,470,778	305.	310.	350.	375.	4850.	40,000.
1894O	107,500	305.	300.	375.	900.	13,500.	—
1894S	25,000	305.	475.	1200.	4500.	13,500.	—
1895	567,826	305.	310.	360.	400.	6500.	40,000.
1895O	98,000	305.	310.	350.	650.	13,500.	—
1895S	49,000	305.	400.	1250.	4000.	40,000.	—
1896	76,348	305.	310.	350.	375.	6500.	40,000.
1896S	123,750	305.	350.	1000.	2750.	—	—
1897	1,000,159	305.	310.	350.	375.	5000.	40,000.
1897O	42,500	305.	310.	375.	500.	11,000.	—
1897S	234,750	305.	325.	500.	850.	6500.	—
1898	812,197	305.	310.	350.	375.	6500.	40,000.
1898S	473,600	305.	310.	360.	450.	6500.	—
1899	1,262,305	305.	310.	350.	375.	4350.	40,000.
1899O	37,047	310.	315.	375.	950.	13,500.	—
1899S	841,000	305.	310.	375.	400.	6500.	—
1900	293,960	305.	310.	350.	375.	6500.	40,000.
1900S	81,000	310.	330.	400.	815.	12,500.	—
1901	1,718,825	305.	310.	350.	375.	4350.	40,000.
1901O	72,041	310.	325.	400.	450.	13,500.	—
1901S	2,812,750	305.	310.	350.	375.	4500.	—
1902	82,513	305.	310.	350.	375.	12,500.	40,000.
1902S	469,500	305.	310.	350.	375.	6500.	—
1903	125,926	305.	325.	385.	425.	6500.	40,000.
1903O	112,771	305.	310.	375.	400.	6500.	—
1903S	538,000	305.	310.	350.	375.	6500.	—
1904	162,038	305.	310.	350.	375.	6500.	40,000.
1904O	108,950	305.	310.	375.	400.	6500.	—
1905	201,078	305.	310.	350.	375.	6500.	40,000.
1905S	369,250	305.	350.	425.	1300.	6500.	—
1906	165,497	305.	310.	350.	375.	6500.	40,000.
1906D	981,000	305.	310.	350.	375.	6500.	—
1906O	86,895	305.	325.	350.	750.	13,500.	—
1906S	457,000	305.	310.	325.	675.	6500.	—
1907	1,203,973	305.	310.	350.	375.	4350.	40,000.
1907D	1,030,000	305.	310.	350.	375.	4350.	—
1907S	210,500	305.	325.	375.	600.	6500.	—

Indian Head

No motto

Designer: Augustus Saint-Gaudens. **Size:** 27 millimeters. **Weight:** 16.718 grams. **Composition:** 90% gold (0.4839 ounces), 10% copper. **Notes:** 1907 varieties are distinguished by whether the edge is rolled or wired, and whether the legend "E Pluribus Unum" has periods between each word.

Date	Mintage	VF-20	XF-40	AU-50	MS-60	MS-63	MS-65	Prf-65
1907 wire edge, periods before & after leg.								
	500	—	4500.	—	7800.	11,500.	36,000.	—
1907 same, without stars on edge								
		—	Unique	—	—	—	—	—
1907 rolled edge, periods								
	42	—	—	—	21,500.	34,000.	60,000.	—
1907 without periods								
	239,406	430.	450.	475.	490.	1750.	6000.	27,500.
1908 without motto								
	33,500	480.	525.	600.	780.	2500.	11,500.	—
1908D without motto								
	210,000	430.	440.	500.	720.	5650.	36,000.	—

1933 $10 Gold
Grade MS-60

■ Retail Price

With motto

Notes: In 1908 the motto "In God We Trust" was added on the reverse to the left of the eagle.

Date	Mintage	VF-20	XF-40	AU-50	MS-60	MS-63	MS-65	Prf-65
1908	341,486	300.	325.	350.	490.	1125.	6000.	27,500.
1908D	836,500	300.	325.	480.	650.	2800.	21,500.	—
1908S	59,850	300.	325.	600.	1450.	4800.	18,000.	—
1909	184,863	300.	325.	350.	510.	1400.	9000.	41,000.
1909D	121,540	300.	325.	350.	750.	2350.	42,000.	—
1909S	292,350	300.	325.	350.	590.	2050.	9600.	—
1910	318,704	300.	325.	350.	480.	930.	6000.	33,000.
1910D	2,356,640	300.	325.	350.	480.	925.	5150.	—
1910S	811,000	300.	325.	350.	725.	3100.	48,000.	—
1911	505,595	300.	325.	350.	490.	975.	5150.	35,000.
1911D	30,100	300.	550.	750.	3850.	11,000.	90,000.	—
1911S	51,000	300.	460.	650.	990.	3250.	8400.	—
1912	405,083	300.	325.	350.	480.	1050.	5500.	33,500.
1912S	300,000	300.	325.	350.	675.	2100.	45,000.	—
1913	442,071	300.	325.	350.	490.	1100.	5150.	36,000.
1913S	66,000	300.	650.	800.	3250.	20,000.	162,000.	—
1914	151,050	300.	325.	350.	500.	985.	6000.	30,000.
1914D	343,500	300.	325.	350.	510.	1100.	9000.	—
1914S	208,000	300.	325.	350.	750.	2900.	39,500.	—
1915	351,075	300.	325.	350.	500.	1100.	5150.	36,000.
1915S	59,000	300.	550.	600.	2500.	7800.	73,000.	—
1916S	138,500	300.	385.	400.	660.	2150.	12,000.	—
1920S	126,500	6500.	7500.	8000.	15,000.	33,000.	120,000.	—
1926	1,014,000	300.	325.	350.	400.	800.	4000.	—
1930S	96,000	3500.	5000.	7500.	8300.	9000.	23,500.	—
1932	4,463,000	300.	325.	350.	400.	800.	4000.	—
1933	312,500	—	—	—	—	264,000.	340,000.	—

Gold $20 (Double Eagle)

Coronet Head

"Twenty D.," no motto

Designer: James B. Longacre. **Size:** 34 millimeters. **Weight:** 33.436 grams. **Composition:** 90% gold (0.9677 ounces), 10% copper. **Notes:** In 1861 the reverse was redesigned by Anthony C. Paquet, but it was withdrawn soon after its release. The letters in the inscriptions on the Paquet-reverse variety are taller than those on the regular reverse.

Date	Mintage	VF-20	XF-40	AU-50	MS-60	MS-65	Prf-65
1849	1		Unique, in Smithsonion collection			—	—
1850	1,170,261	600.	625.	1000.	3125.	—	—
1850O	141,000	780.	1250.	3000.	15,000.	—	—
1851	2,087,155	600.	625.	950.	2300.	—	—
1851O	315,000	715.	810.	1825.	11,500.	—	—
1852	2,053,026	600.	625.	950.	3000.	—	—
1852O	190,000	685.	815.	1775.	12,000.	—	—
1853	1,261,326	600.	625.	950.	4850.	—	—
1853O	71,000	700.	1000.	2900.	20,000.	—	—
1854	757,899	600.	625.	950.	5500.	—	—
1854O	3,250	17,500.	52,000.	—	—	—	—
1854S	141,468	700.	880.	1025.	2000.	34,000.	—
1855	364,666	600.	625.	1050.	6250.	34,000.	—
1855O	8,000	3000.	6000.	14,750.	54,000.	—	—
1855S	879,675	600.	625.	1000.	9100.	—	—
1856	329,878	600.	715.	1050.	8450.	—	—
1856O	2,250	19,000.	30,000.	60,000.	—	—	—
1856S	1,189,750	545.	560.	700.	3650.	—	—
1857	439,375	600.	625.	950.	3800.	—	—
1857O	30,000	1075.	1850.	3650.	14,000.	—	—
1857S	970,500	600.	625.	950.	2600.	—	—
1858	211,714	835.	1075.	1300.	4950.	—	—
1858O	35,250	1175.	1950.	6000.	15,500.	—	—
1858S	846,710	600.	625.	975.	8100.	—	—
1859	43,597	975.	2600.	4250.	37,500.	—	—
1859O	9,100	3150.	6800.	12,500.	37,500.	—	—
1859S	636,445	600.	625.	1000.	4200.	—	—
1860	577,670	600.	625.	950.	3900.	—	—
1860O	6,600	3450.	6250.	14,000.	37,500.	—	—
1860S	544,950	600.	625.	1050.	5850.	—	—
1861	2,976,453	545.	560.	700.	2750.	—	—

Paquet reverse

Date	Mintage	VF-20	XF-40	AU-50	MS-60	MS-65	Prf-65
1861 Paquet rev.	Inc. Ab.						
			Bowers & Merena, Nov. 1988, MS-67, $660,000.				—
1861O	17,741	1500.	3550.	7000.	18,000.	—	—
1861S	768,000	600.	625.	1050.	7500.	—	—
1861S Paquet rev.	Inc. Ab.	5850.	11,000.	20,000.	59,000.	—	—
1862	92,133	910.	1600.	2750.	14,750.	—	—
1862S	854,173	600.	625.	1375.	8000.	—	—
1863	142,790	600.	750.	1625.	12,500.	—	—
1863S	966,570	600.	625.	1050.	6350.	—	—
1864	204,285	600.	950.	1650.	10,500.	—	—
1864S	793,660	600.	560.	1575.	8850.	—	—
1865	351,200	600.	700.	700.	5750.	—	—
1865S	1,042,500	545.	700.	1125.	7150.	—	—
1866S	Inc. Below	1850.	3750.	7750.	25,000.	—	—

"Twenty D.," with motto

Notes: In 1866 the motto "In God We Trust" was added to the reverse above the eagle. The 1873 "closed-3" and "open-3" varieties are distinguished by the amount of space between the upper left and lower left serif in the 3 in the date.

Date	Mintage	VF-20	XF-40	AU-50	MS-60	MS-65	Prf-65
1866	698,775	685.	780.	1175.	4700.	—	—
1866S	842,250	665.	850.	1575.	11,250.	—	—
1867	251,065	625.	650.	800.	1300.	—	—
1867S	920,750	615.	650.	1500.	13,250.	—	—
1868	98,600	850.	1125.	1950.	7500.	—	—
1868S	837,500	625.	675.	975.	8450.	—	—
1869	175,155	725.	810.	875.	4950.	—	—
1869S	686,750	625.	665.	875.	3900.	—	—
1870	155,185	775.	885.	1650.	8450.	—	—
1870CC	3,789	35,000.	65,000.	80,000.	125,000.	—	—
1870S	982,000	625.	640.	835.	5200.	—	—
1871	80,150	750.	910.	1400.	3650.	—	—
1871CC	17,387	3000.	4700.	10,500.	35,000.	—	—
1871S	928,000	625.	665.	765.	3450.	—	—
1872	251,880	625.	650.	750.	2600.	—	—
1872CC	26,900	1150.	1500.	4950.	18,500.	—	—
1872S	780,000	535.	540.	550.	2750.	—	—
1873 closed 3	Est. 208,925	625.	750.	1150.	2200.	—	—
1873 open 3	Est. 1,500,900	535.	540.	550.	675.	—	—
1873CC	22,410	850.	1700.	3900.	21,500.	—	—
1873S	1,040,600	625.	650.	750.	1500.	—	—
1874	366,800	625.	650.	715.	1075.	—	—
1874CC	115,085	685.	780.	1075.	7800.	—	—
1874S	1,214,000	535.	540.	550.	1250.	—	—
1875	295,740	535.	540.	550.	675.	—	—
1875CC	111,151	665.	780.	950.	1825.	—	—
1875S	1,230,000	535.	540.	550.	675.	—	—
1876	583,905	535.	540.	550.	675.	—	—
1876CC	138,441	690.	775.	1150.	3250.	—	—
1876S	1,597,000	560.	575.	615.	715.	—	—

"Twenty Dollars"

Notes: In 1877 the denomination on the reverse was changed to read "Twenty Dollars" instead of "Twenty D."

Date	Mintage	VF-20	XF-40	AU-50	MS-60	MS-65	Prf-65
1877	397,670	595.	600.	665.	700.	—	—
1877CC	42,565	730.	975.	1575.	12,500.	—	—
1877S	1,735,000	530.	595.	605.	660.	—	—
1878	543,645	585.	600.	625.	675.	—	—
1878CC	13,180	975.	1300.	3400.	18,000.	—	—
1878S	1,739,000	530.	585.	600.	690.	—	—
1879	207,630	650.	665.	685.	910.	—	—
1879CC	10,708	1050.	1650.	4500.	18,500.	—	—
1879O	2,325	3250.	4700.	13,000.	25,000.	—	—
1879S	1,223,800	530.	585.	600.	1250.	—	—
1880	51,456	530.	600.	800.	3200.	—	—
1880S	836,000	530.	625.	650.	1125.	—	—
1881	2,260	4050.	6800.	13,000.	45,000.	—	65,000.
1881S	727,000	530.	585.	650.	900.	—	—
1882	630	7800.	15,000.	24,000.	50,000.	—	75,000.
1882CC	39,140	730.	780.	1050.	6500.	—	—
1882S	1,125,000	530.	580.	600.	715.	—	—
1883	92	—	—	—	—	—	—
1883CC	59,962	715.	775.	950.	3100.	—	—
1883S	1,189,000	500.	580.	600.	665.	—	—
1884	71			Stacks, Nov. 1989, proof, $71,500.			
1884CC	81,139	650.	775.	975.	2600.	—	—
1884S	916,000	500.	580.	600.	650.	—	—
1885	828	7400.	9100.	11,500.	32,500.	—	—
1885CC	9,450	1025.	1600.	3800.	11,500.	—	—
1885S	683,500	500.	585.	625.	650.	—	—
1886	1,106	8800.	11,000.	20,000.	43,000.	—	65,000.
1887	121	—	—	—	—	—	65,000.
1887S	283,000	500.	585.	615.	750.	—	—
1888	226,266	500.	575.	600.	675.	—	—
1888S	859,600	500.	525.	545.	650.	—	—
1889	44,111	575.	600.	625.	750.	—	78,000.

1907-S $20 Gold
Grade VF-20

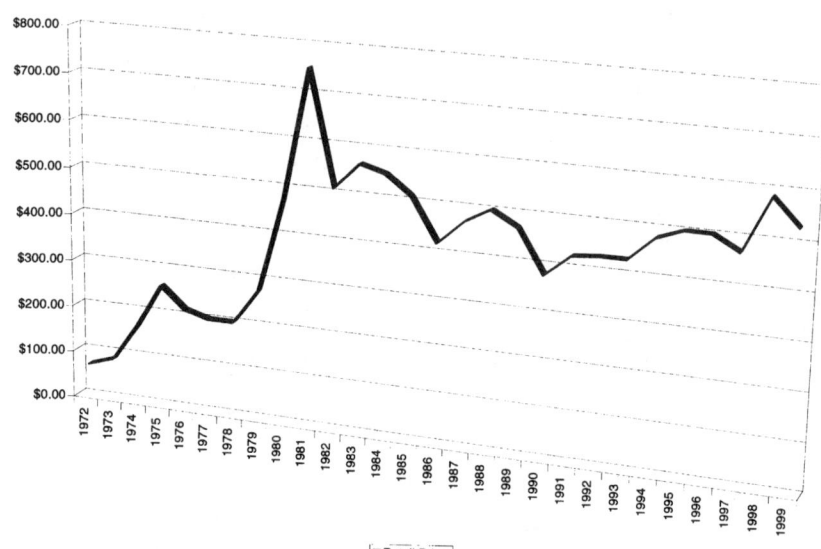

■ Retail Price

Source: COIN PRICES

Date	Mintage	VF-20	XF-40	AU-50	MS-60	MS-65	Prf-65
1889CC	30,945	795.	875.	1300.	3900.	—	—
1889S	774,700	500.	525.	545.	665.	—	—
1890	75,995	540.	550.	560.	665.	—	—
1890CC	91,209	675.	775.	1050.	2600.	—	—
1890S	802,750	500.	525.	545.	665.	—	—
1891	1,442	3600.	5500.	8250.	27,000.	—	—
1891CC	5,000	1900.	2900.	5500.	14,000.	—	—
1891S	1,288,125	500.	525.	545.	580.	—	—
1892	4,523	1200.	1600.	2900.	5900.	—	—
1892CC	27,265	745.	810.	1250.	2900.	—	—
1892S	930,150	530.	535.	545.	580.	—	—
1893	344,339	530.	535.	545.	580.	—	—
1893CC	18,402	815.	875.	1175.	2100.	—	—
1893S	996,175	500.	525.	545.	580.	—	—
1894	1,368,990	500.	525.	545.	580.	—	67,500.
1894S	1,048,550	500.	525.	545.	580.	—	—
1895	1,114,656	500.	525.	545.	580.	—	—
1895S	1,143,500	500.	525.	545.	580.	7200.	—
1896	792,663	500.	525.	545.	580.	—	67,500.
1896S	1,403,925	500.	525.	545.	580.	—	—
1897	1,383,261	500.	525.	545.	580.	—	67,500.
1897S	1,470,250	500.	525.	545.	580.	—	—
1898	170,470	500.	525.	545.	650.	—	67,500.
1898S	2,575,175	500.	525.	545.	580.	7800.	—
1899	1,669,384	500.	525.	545.	580.	7800.	67,500.
1899S	2,010,300	500.	525.	545.	580.	—	—
1900	1,874,584	500.	525.	545.	580.	5400.	67,500.
1900S	2,459,500	500.	525.	545.	580.	7200.	—
1901	111,526	500.	525.	545.	580.	7000.	—
1901S	1,596,000	500.	525.	650.	665.	—	—
1902	31,254	500.	525.	625.	975.	7200.	—
1902S	1,753,625	500.	525.	545.	580.	—	—
1903	287,428	500.	525.	545.	580.	4700.	62,000.
1903S	954,000	500.	525.	545.	580.	7200.	—
1904	6,256,797	500.	525.	545.	580.	3200.	67,500.
1904S	5,134,175	500.	525.	545.	580.	5550.	—
1905	59,011	500.	620.	650.	1200.	—	—
1905S	1,813,000	500.	575.	620.	635.	—	—
1906	69,690	500.	600.	615.	625.	6000.	67,500.
1906D	620,250	500.	525.	545.	580.	—	—
1906S	2,065,750	500.	525.	545.	580.	—	—
1907	1,451,864	500.	525.	545.	580.	9100.	—
1907D	842,250	500.	525.	545.	580.	3200.	—
1907S	2,165,800	500.	525.	545.	580.	—	—

1908-D $20 Gold
Grade MS-60

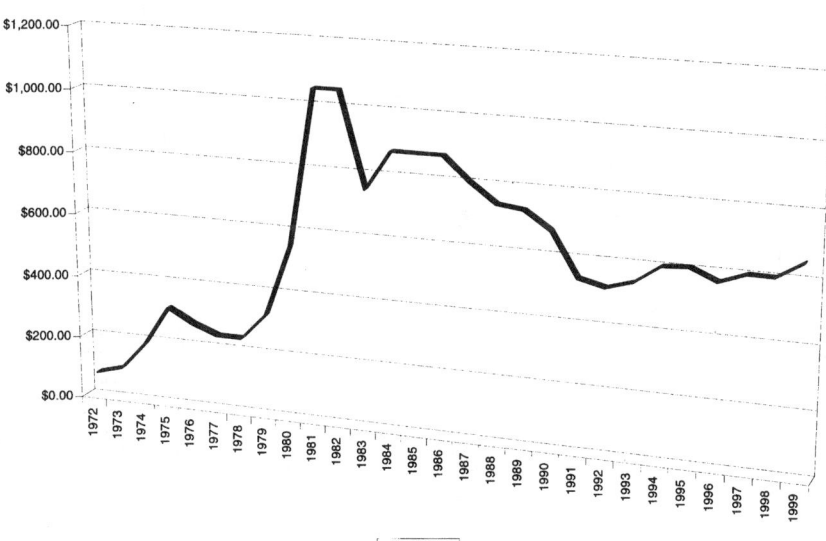

■ Retail Price

Source: COIN PRICES

Saint-Gaudens

No motto

Designer: Augustus Saint-Gaudens. **Size:** 34 millimeters. **Weight:** 33.436 grams. **Composition:** 90% gold (0.9677 ounces), 10% copper. **Notes:** The "Roman numerals" varieties for 1907 use Roman numerals for the date instead of Arabic numerals. The lettered-edge varieties have "E Pluribus Unum" on the edge, with stars between the words.

Date	Mintage	VF-20	XF-40	AU-50	MS-60	MS-63	MS-65	Prf-65
1907 extremely high relief, plain edge		—	—	—			Unique	
1907 extremely high relief, lettered edge								
Unrecorded		Prf-68 Private sale 1990 $1,500,000.					—	—
1907 high relief, Roman numerals, plain edge						Unique - AU55 $150,000		
1907 high relief, Roman numerals, wire rim								
11,250	2500.	4000.	4800.	7100.	11,000.	28,000.		
1907 high relief, Roman numerals, flat rim								
Inc. Ab.	3000.	4200.	5000.	7200.	11,000.	28,000.		—
1907 large letters on edge		—	—	—	—	Unique		—
1907 small letters on edge								
361,667	540.	615.	625.	650.	815.	2900.		—
1908	4,271,551	500.	525.	550.	575.	660.	1450.	—
1908D	663,750	500.	525.	565.	600.	815.	17,000.	—

With motto

Notes: In 1908 the motto "In God We Trust" was added at the bottom of the reverse.

Date	Mintage	VF-20	XF-40	AU-50	MS-60	MS-63	MS-65	Prf-65
1908	156,359	535.	575.	585.	685.	1125.	19,500.	40,500.
1908D	349,500	500.	525.	550.	650.	830.	3900.	—
1908S	22,000	650.	1125.	1500.	3900.	10,500.	36,500.	—
1909/8	161,282	550.	640.	650.	1300.	5850.	45,500.	—
1909	Inc. Ab.	550.	615.	640.	875.	3150.	48,000.	58,000.
1909D	52,500	575.	685.	775.	1250.	3250.	36,000.	—
1909S	2,774,925	500.	525.	550.	575.	810.	4800.	—
1910	482,167	500.	525.	550.	575.	750.	5850.	58,000.
1910D	429,000	500.	525.	550.	575.·	750.	2750.	—
1910S	2,128,250	550.	625.	640.	650.	850.	12,000.	—
1911	197,350	550.	625.	640.	650.	1175.	13,750.	41,000.
1911D	846,500	500.	525.	550.	575.	685.	1600.	—
1911S	775,750	535.	540.	550.	575.	715.	4700.	—
1912	149,824	550.	600.	615.	700.	1250.	17,000.	36,000.
1913	168,838	550.	585.	600.	690.	1825.	22,500.	52,000.
1913D	393,500	500.	525.	550.	575.	880.	4600.	—
1913S	34,000	575.	715.	815.	1150.	3450.	39,500.	—
1914	95,320	500.	600.	625.	685.	1375.	13,750.	40,000.
1914D	453,000	500.	525.	550.	575.	730.	2350.	—
1914S	1,498,000	500.	525.	550.	575.	700.	2100.	—
1915	152,050	500.	525.	550.	680.	1450.	16,000.	52,000.
1915S	567,500	500.	525.	550.	575.	715.	2025.	—
1916S	796,000	500.	525.	550.	615.	710.	1900.	—
1920	228,250	500.	525.	550.	575.	780.	32,500.	—
1920S	558,000	4500.	8450.	15,000.	22,500.	62,000.	90,000.	—
1921	528,500	7200.	11,000.	12,500.	35,500.	61,000.	150,000.	—
1922	1,375,500	500.	525.	550.	575.	600.	3600.	—
1922S	2,658,000	500.	650.	715.	885.	1575.	36,000.	—
1923	566,000	500.	525.	550.	575.	600.	5850.	—
1923D	1,702,250	500.	525.	550.	575.	600.	1500.	—
1924	4,323,500	500.	525.	550.	575.	600.	1300.	—
1924D	3,049,500	700.	1150.	1350.	1800.	4950.	48,000.	—
1924S	2,927,500	700.	1050.	1175.	2200.	4950.	45,000.	—
1925	2,831,750	500.	525.	550.	575.	600.	1200.	—
1925D	2,938,500	875.	1300.	1800.	3000.	6800.	54,000.	—
1925S	3,776,500	875.	1250.	1625.	5200.	19,500.	75,000.	—
1926	816,750	500.	525.	550.	575.	600.	1400.	—
1926D	481,000	1250.	1950.	2400.	6150.	19,500.	57,500.	—
1926S	2,041,500	700.	1150.	1300.	1700.	3150.	36,000.	—
1927	2,946,750	500.	525.	550.	575.	600.	1200.	—
1927D	180,000	—	—	150,000.	265,000.	—	577,500.	—
1927S	3,107,000	2000.	3900.	4550.	11,750.	25,000.	90,000.	—
1928	8,816,000	500.	525.	550.	575.	600.	1200.	—
1929	1,779,750	4000.	6850.	7500.	9100.	13,000.	68,500.	—
1930S	74,000	6000.	9450.	10,500.	18,000.	45,500.	126,500.	—
1931	2,938,250	4250.	9100.	10,000.	13,000.	26,000.	66,000.	—
1931D	106,500	5500.	8450.	9100.	14,250.	23,000.	80,000.	—
1932	1,101,750	7000.	10,000.	11,750.	15,600.	22,500.	60,500.	—
1933	445,500			None placed in circulation			—	—

Proof sets

Notes: Proof sets have been sold off and on by the U.S. Mint since 1858. Listings here are for sets from what is commonly called the modern era, since 1936. Values for earlier individual proof coins are included in the regular date listings. Sets were not offered in years not listed. Since 1968, proof versions of circulating U.S. coins have been produced at the San Francisco Mint; before that they were produced at the Philadelphia Mint. In 1942 the five-cent coin was struck in two compositions. Some proof sets for that year contain only one type (five-coin set); others contain both types. Two types of packaging were used in 1955: a box and sealed Pliofilm packets. The 1960 large-date and small-date sets are distinguished by the size of the date on the cent. Some 1968 sets are missing the mintmark on the dime, the result of an error in the preparation of an obverse die. The 1970 large-date and small-date sets are distinguished by the size of the date on the cent. Some 1970 sets are missing the mintmark on the dime, the result of an error in the preparation of an obverse die. Some 1971 sets are missing the mintmark on the five-cent piece, the result of an error in the preparation of an obverse die. The 1976 three-piece set contains the quarter, half dollar and dollar with the Bicentennial designs. The 1979 and 1981 Type II sets have clearer mintmarks than the Type I sets for those years. Some 1983 sets are missing the mintmark on the dime, the result of an error in the preparation of an obverse die. Prestige sets contain the five regular-issue coins plus a commemorative silver dollar from that year: 1983, Olympics; 1984, Olympics; 1986, Statue of Liberty; 1987, Constitution Bicentennial; 1988, Olympics; 1989, Congress Bicentennial; 1990, Eisenhower; and 1991, Mount Rushmore. The 1992 prestige set contains the Olympic silver dollar and half dollar from that year.

Date	Sets Sold	Issue Price	Value
1936	3,837	1.89	3700.
1937	5,542	1.89	1950.
1938	8,045	1.89	760.
1939	8,795	1.89	910.
1940	11,246	1.89	680.
1941	15,287	1.89	590.
1942 6 coins	21,120	1.89	640.
1942 5 coins	Inc. Ab.	1.89	600.
1950	51,386	2.10	415.
1951	57,500	2.10	330.
1952	81,980	2.10	170.
1953	128,800	2.10	120.
1954	233,300	2.10	69.00
1955 box	378,200	2.10	63.00
1955 flat pack	Inc. Ab.	2.10	88.00
1956	669,384	2.10	31.00
1957	1,247,952	2.10	12.50
1958	875,652	2.10	26.50
1959	1,149,291	2.10	16.00
1960 large date	1,691,602	2.10	11.00
1960 small date	Inc. Ab.	2.10	23.00
1961	3,028,244	2.10	8.40
1962	3,218,019	2.10	8.40
1963	3,075,645	2.10	8.40
1964	3,950,762	2.10	8.40
1968S	3,041,509	5.00	4.25
1968 S no mint mark dime	—	5.00	7500.
1969S	2,934,631	5.00	4.25
1970S large date	2,632,810	5.00	10.00
1970S small date	Inc. Ab.	5.00	55.00
1970S no mint mark dime	Est. 2,200	5.00	365.
1971S	3,224,138	5.00	4.90
1971S no mint mark nickel	Est. 1,655	5.00	630.
1972S	3,267,667	5.00	5.50
1973S	2,769,624	7.00	9.75

PRICING SECTION

Date	Sets Sold	Issue Price	Value
1974S	2,617,350	7.00	10.00
1975S	2,909,369	7.00	9.50
1976S 3 coins	3,998,621	12.00	15.00
1976S	4,149,730	7.00	8.00
1977S	3,251,152	9.00	8.50
1978S	3,127,788	9.00	9.25
1979S Type I	3,677,175	9.00	7.80
1979S Type II	Inc.Ab.	9.00	84.00
1980S	3,547,030	10.00	6.25
1981S Type I	4,063,083	11.00	8.50
1981S Type II	—	11.00	210.
1982S	3,857,479	11.00	4.30
1983S Prestige set	140,361	59.00	90.00
1983S	3,138,765	11.00	5.40
1983S no mint mark dime	—	11.00	340.
1984S Prestige set	316,680	59.00	21.00
1984S	2,748,430	11.00	7.50
1985S	3,362,821	11.00	5.00
1986S Prestige set	599,317	48.50	21.00
1986S	2,411,180	11.00	11.00
1987S	3,972,233	11.00	5.50
1987S Prestige set	435,495	45.00	21.00
1988S	3,031,287	11.00	6.50
1988S Prestige set	231,661	45.00	31.00
1989S	3,009,107	11.00	5.50
1989S Prestige set	211,087	45.00	32.00
1990S	2,793,433	11.00	7.00
1990S no S 1¢	3,555	11.00	1200.
1990S Prestige set	506,126	45.00	21.00
1990S no S 1¢ Prestige set	—	45.00	1200.
1991S	2,610,833	11.00	14.00
1991S Prestige set	256,954	59.00	45.00
1992S	2,675,618	12.50	10.00
1992S Prestige set	183,285	59.00	39.00
1992S Silver	1,009,585	21.00	12.50
1992S Silver premier	308,055	37.00	14.00
1993S	2,337,819	12.50	24.00
1993S Prestige set	224,045	57.00	36.00
1993S Silver	570,213	21.00	32.00
1993S Silver premier	191,140	37.00	32.00
1994S	2,308,701	12.50	12.50
1994S Prestige Set	175,893	57.00	50.00
1994S Silver	636,009	21.00	41.00
1994S Silver premier	149,320	37.50	41.00
1995S	2,010,384	12.50	39.00
1995S Silver	—	21.00	42.00
1995S Prestige Set	107,112	57.00	100.
1995S Silver premier	—	37.00	42.00
1996S	1,695,244	12.50	8.50
1996S Silver	—	21.00	32.00
1996S Prestige set	55,000	57.00	140.
1996S Silver premier	—	37.00	36.00
1997S	1,975,000	12.50	32.00
1997S Silver	—	21.00	35.00
1997S Prestige set	—	57.00	225.
1997S Silver premier	—	37.00	35.00
1998S	—	12.50	20.00
1998S Silver	—	21.00	29.00
1998S Silver premier	—	37.00	45.00

1952 Proof Set

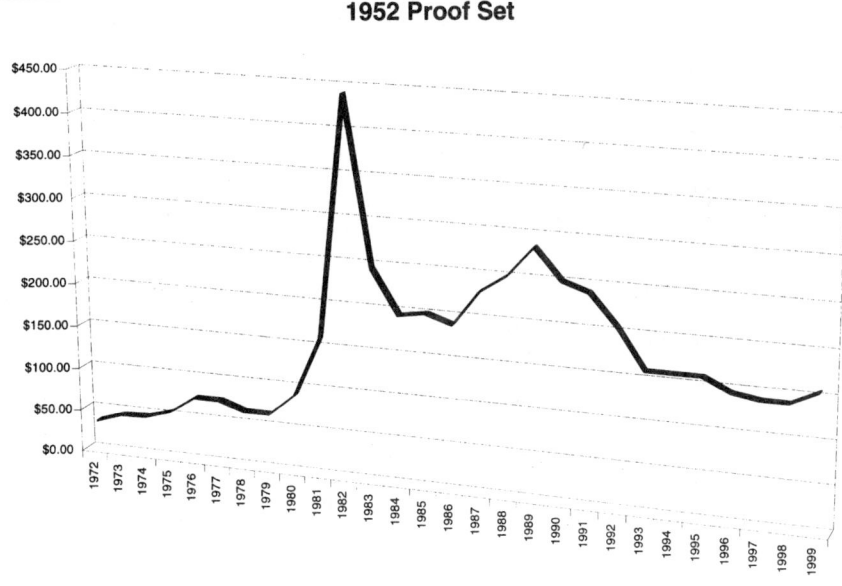

■ Retail Price

Source: COIN PRICES

Mint sets

WITH D AND P MINT MARKS

Notes: Mint, or uncirculated, sets contain one uncirculated coin of each denomination from each mint produced for circulation that year. Values listed here are only for those sets packaged and marketed by the U.S. Mint. Sets were not offered in years not listed. In years when the Mint did not offer the sets, some private companies packaged and marketed uncirculated sets. Mint sets from 1947 through 1958 contain two examples of each coin mounted in cardboard holders, which caused the coins to tarnish. Beginning in 1959, the sets have been packaged in sealed Pliofilm packets and include only one specimen of each non-commemorative coin authorized for that year. Listings for 1965, 1966 and 1967 are for "special mint sets," which were of higher quality than regular mint sets and were prooflike. The 1965 sets were packaged in Pliofilm; the '66 and '67 sets in plastic cases. The 1970 large-date and small-date varieties are distinguished by the size of the date on the cent. The 1976 three-piece set contains the quarter, half dollar and dollar with the Bicentennial design. The 1971 and 1972 sets do not include a dollar coin; the 1979 set does not include an S-mintmarked dollar.

Date	Sets Sold	Issue Price	Value
1947	Est. 5,000	4.87	595.
1948	Est. 6,000	4.92	225.
1949	Est. 5,200	5.45	400.
1950	None issued	—	—
1951	8,654	6.75	370.
1952	11,499	6.14	295.
1953	15,538	6.14	230.
1954	25,599	6.19	115.
1955	49,656	3.57	81.00
1956	45,475	3.34	76.00
1957	32,324	4.40	105.
1958	50,314	4.43	88.00
1959	187,000	2.40	21.00
1960	260,485	2.40	19.00
1961	223,704	2.40	28.00
1962	385,285	2.40	11.00
1963	606,612	2.40	11.00
1964	1,008,108	2.40	10.00
1965 SMS*	2,360,000	4.00	3.25
1966 SMS*	2,261,583	4.00	3.25
1967 SMS*	1,863,344	4.00	4.50
1968	2,105,128	2.50	2.25
1969	1,817,392	2.50	4.60
1970 large date	2,038,134	2.50	10.00
1970 small date	Inc. Ab.	2.50	37.00
1971	2,193,396	3.50	3.25
1972	2,750,000	3.50	2.60
1973	1,767,691	6.00	8.70
1974	1,975,981	6.00	6.70
1975	1,921,488	6.00	8.40
1976 3 coins	4,908,319	9.00	13.50
1976	1,892,513	6.00	8.25
1977	2,006,869	7.00	8.25
1978	2,162,609	7.00	8.25
1979	2,526,000	8.00	5.50
1980	2,815,066	9.00	6.75
1981	2,908,145	11.00	12.50
1982 & 1983	None issued	—	—
1984	1,832,857	7.00	5.00
1985	1,710,571	7.00	5.75
1986	1,153,536	7.00	9.50
1987	2,890,758	7.00	5.25
1988	1,646,204	7.00	4.90
1989	1,987,915	7.00	5.60
1990	1,809,184	7.00	3.50
1991	1,352,101	7.00	6.30
1992	1,500,143	7.00	7.45
1993	1,297,094	8.00	5.00
1994	1,234,813	8.00	10.00
1995	1,038,787	8.00	22.00
1996	—	8.00	9.00
1997	—	8.00	12.00
1998	—	8.00	8.50

UNCIRCULATED ROLLS

Notes: Listings are for rolls containing uncirculated coins. Large-date and small-date varieties for 1960 and 1970 apply to the one-cent coins.

Date	Cents	Nickels	Dimes	Quarters	Halves
1934	225.	1765.	950.	900.	1600.
1934D	850.	3150.	2250.	5550.	—
1934S	—	—	—	—	—
1935	120.	950.	800.	785.	1200.
1935D	265.	2000.	2250.	5650.	4050.
1935S	800.	1450.	1250.	2650.	6300.
1936	66.00	750.	550.	750.	1150.
1936D	145.	900.	1500.	—	2250.
1936S	140.	950.	1050.	2500.	3300.
1937	35.00	500.	550.	700.	1050.
1937D	70.00	700.	1250.	1750.	3900.
1937S	75.00	700.	1325.	3950.	3150.
1938	83.00	100.	880.	2050.	1750.
1938D	110.	120.	900.	—	—
1938D Buffalo	—	550.	—	—	—
1938S	65.00	120.	1200.	2015.	—
1939	35.00	50.00	600.	485.	1150.
1939D	90.00	1750.	500.	1000.	1150.
1939S	71.00	660.	1200.	2015.	2250.
1940	39.00	25.00	350.	565.	950.
1940D	50.00	57.00	600.	2500.	—
1940S	36.00	100.	450.	550.	1150.
1941	44.00	27.50	350.	300.	750.
1941D	110.	95.00	600.	1150.	1150.
1941S	90.00	100.	350.	800.	3000.
1942	19.50	215.	250.	120.	750.
1942P	—	210.	—	—	—
1942D	11.00	785.	550.	350.	1250.
1942S	170.	170.	650.	1850.	1400.
1943	34.00	125.	250.	180.	750.
1943D	44.00	100.	450.	665.	1650.
1943S	100.	100.	550.	950.	1300.
1944	7.00	210.	250.	170.	750.
1944D	12.00	225.	350.	360.	1150.
1944S	11.50	100.	350.	380.	1200.
1945	24.00	135.	230.	100.	700.
1945D	10.00	120.	250.	250.	950.
1945S	7.50	65.00	250.	190.	900.
1946	9.50	9.00	44.00	140.	950.
1946D	10.00	11.50	50.00	105.	800.
1946S	9.50	8.00	50.00	140.	850.
1947	33.00	27.00	65.00	210.	900.
1947D	11.00	20.00	120.	190.	750.
1947S	14.00	16.00	65.00	140.	—
1948	15.00	9.00	145.	100.	265.
1948D	11.50	29.00	125.	140.	240.
1948S	15.50	16.00	120.	140.	—
1949	19.00	25.00	600.	550.	700.
1949D	19.00	19.00	230.	320.	800.
1949S	48.00	30.00	1070.	—	870.
1950	19.50	40.00	120.	90.00	550.
1950D	19.00	225.	110.	90.00	560.
1950S	25.00	—	485.	245.	—
1951	21.00	30.00	45.00	125.	250.
1951D	6.00	24.00	45.00	75.00	550.
1951S	20.00	44.00	315.	600.	500.
1952	16.00	19.00	55.00	105.	225.
1952D	6.30	41.00	40.00	70.00	190.
1952S	50.00	17.50	180.	390.	820.
1953	3.80	5.50	45.00	75.00	275.
1953D	3.20	4.85	46.00	65.00	100.
1953S	8.00	10.00	32.00	100.	265.
1954	5.00	4.85	38.00	65.00	120.
1954D	3.15	4.70	32.00	70.00	100.
1954S	2.25	5.00	38.00	70.00	140.
1955	4.25	6.50	41.00	65.00	130.
1955D	1.90	4.40	32.00	75.00	—
1955S	10.50	—	32.00	—	—
1956	1.90	3.50	41.00	65.00	100.
1956D	1.75	4.00	32.00	75.00	—
1957	2.40	4.35	43.00	76.00	110.
1957D	1.75	3.00	38.00	80.00	84.00
1958	1.60	3.15	35.00	65.00	84.00
1958D	1.60	3.00	32.00	75.00	77.00
1959	1.00	3.30	32.00	65.00	84.00
1959D	.85	3.15	32.00	65.00	100.
1960 lg. dt.	.90	2.85	32.00	64.00	84.00
1960 sm. dt.	90.00	—	—	—	—

Date	Cents	Nickels	Dimes	Quarters	Halves
1960D lg. dt.	1.20	3.30	32.00	64.00	77.00
1960D sm. dt.	1.00	—	—	—	—
1961	.85	3.00	32.00	64.00	77.00
1961D	.85	3.15	32.00	68.00	77.00
1962	1.25	3.50	32.00	68.00	84.00
1962D	1.20	2.85	32.00	64.00	70.00
1963	.85	2.85	32.00	64.00	77.00
1963D	.85	3.30	32.00	64.00	77.00
1964	.90	3.00	32.00	69.00	63.00
1964D	1.00	3.50	32.00	64.00	64.00
1965	1.55	2.85	9.00	16.00	21.00
1966	1.40	2.65	8.00	19.50	22.50
1967	1.75	3.15	8.00	19.00	22.50
1968	1.55	—	10.00	24.00	—
1968D	1.00	3.80	8.80	27.00	—
1968S	1.00	3.50	—	—	21.00
1969	4.00	—	36.00	44.00	—
1969D	1.25	4.25	12.50	38.00	—
1969S	1.55	3.80	—	—	25.00
1970	1.50	—	9.50	17.50	—
1970D	1.25	3.00	8.00	16.00	—
1970S	1.10	2.85	—	—	195.
1970S sm. dt.	1260.	—	—	—	—
1971	5.00	16.50	12.50	23.00	21.00
1971D	2.00	4.75	9.00	23.00	19.50
1971S	2.25	—	—	—	—
1972	1.40	4.75	8.00	14.00	22.00
1972D	1.90	3.15	8.00	17.00	17.50
1972S	1.25	—	—	—	—
1973	1.05	4.10	7.00	15.50	25.00
1973D	1.05	3.50	9.00	15.50	23.00
1973S	1.60	—	—	—	—
1974	.75	3.00	9.00	14.00	27.00
1974D	.75	5.65	8.00	21.00	25.00
1974S	2.10	—	—	—	—
1975	1.10	10.00	10.00	—	—
1975D	.75	4.50	9.50	—	—
1976	1.00	11.50	17.50	15.50	21.00
1976D	1.90	7.50	15.00	17.50	21.00
1977	1.25	3.15	7.50	15.50	20.00
1977D	1.00	5.65	7.90	15.50	25.00
1978	1.90	3.15	7.50	15.50	25.00
1978D	1.25	4.15	9.00	15.50	29.00
1979	1.25	3.50	7.50	16.00	24.00
1979D	.90	4.90	7.50	19.00	21.00
1980	1.10	3.90	7.75	16.00	25.00
1980D	1.20	3.30	7.00	15.50	24.00
1981	1.00	3.30	7.50	15.50	27.00
1981D	1.00	3.30	7.00	15.50	27.00
1982	.85	40.00	65.00	120.	25.00
1982D	.90	36.50	21.00	35.00	34.00
1983	1.25	47.00	41.00	235.	44.00
1983D	1.35	26.50	28.00	80.00	28.00
1984	2.75	38.00	9.50	20.00	25.00
1984D	11.00	5.40	14.00	45.00	25.00
1985	2.50	6.00	10.00	40.00	25.00
1985D	2.25	5.00	10.00	25.00	23.00
1986	8.80	7.00	36.00	100.	57.00
1986D	3.15	27.00	30.00	80.00	52.00
1987	1.60	4.00	7.00	16.00	65.00
1987D	1.60	3.50	7.00	14.00	70.00
1988	3.10	3.15	8.00	25.00	28.00
1988D	3.40	5.00	7.50	19.00	28.00
1989	1.25	3.15	7.50	16.00	23.00
1990	1.20	3.00	7.50	21.00	20.00
1990D	1.20	4.00	7.00	17.50	30.00
1991	1.25	5.00	9.75	17.50	23.00
1991D	1.20	5.65	11.50	22.50	32.00
1992	2.00	8.50	7.00	19.00	16.00
1992D	1.30	3.90	8.25	19.00	29.00
1993	2.00	4.50	8.00	17.50	17.00
1993D	1.15	4.75	7.55	17.50	21.00
1994	1.25	3.50	7.50	14.50	16.00
1994D	1.25	3.50	7.00	15.50	20.00
1995	.75	3.50	7.25	19.50	16.00
1995D	1.40	7.50	7.25	16.00	14.00
1996	1.00	3.15	7.50	15.00	14.00
1996D	1.00	3.15	7.50	15.00	14.00
1997	1.00	3.15	7.00	14.00	21.00
1997D	1.20	3.30	7.00	14.00	15.50
1998	1.00	3.15	7.25	14.00	15.50
1998D	1.00	3.15	7.25	14.00	15.50
1999	1.00	3.15	7.25	14.00	15.50
1999D	1.00	3.15	7.25	14.00	15.50

Commemoratives, 1892-1954

Quarter

Designer: Charles E. Barber. **Size:** 24.3 millimeters. **Weight:** 6.25 grams. **Composition:** 90% silver (0.1809 ounces), 10% copper.

Date	Event	Mintage	AU-50	MS-60	MS-63	MS-64	MS-65
1893	Isabella (25¢)	24,214	230.	270.	475.	975.	2850.

Half dollars

Designers: Alabama: Laura G. Fraser. Albany: Gertrude K. Lathrop. Arkansas: Edward E. Burr. Bay Bridge: Jacques Schnier. Boone: Augustus Lukeman. Bridgeport: Henry Kreis. California Jubilee: Jo Mora. Cincinnati: Constance Ortmayer. Cleveland-Great Lakes: Brenda Putnam. Columbia: A. Wolfe Davidson. Columbian Expo: Olin L. Warner. Connecticut: Henry Kreis. Delaware: Carl L. Schmitz. Elgin: Trygve Rovelstad. Gettysburg: Frank Vittor. Grant: Laura G. Fraser. Hawaiian: Juliette M. Fraser. Hudson: Chester Beach. Huguenot-Walloon: George T. Morgan. Lincoln-Illinois: George T. Morgan. Iowa: Adam Pietz. Lexington-Concord: Chester Beach. Long Island: Howard K. Weinman. Lynchburg: Charles Keck. Maine: Anthony de Francisci. Maryland: Hans Schuler. Missouri: Robert Aitken. Monroe: Chester Beach. New Rochelle: Gertrude K. Lathrop. Norfolk: William M. and Marjorie E. Simpson. Oregon: James E. and Laura G. Fraser. Panama-Pacific: Charles E. Barber (obverse) and George T. Morgan (reverse). Pilgrim: Cyrus E. Dallin. Rhode Island: Arthur G. Carey and John H. Benson. Roanoke: William M. Simpson. Robinson-Arkansas: Henry Kreis (obverse) and Edward E. Burr. San Diego: Robert Aitken. Sesquicentennial: John F. Lewis. Spanish Trail: L.W. Hoffecker. Stone Mountain: Gutzon Borglum. Texas: Pompeo Coppini. Fort Vancouver: Laura G. Fraser. Vermont: Charles Keck. Booker T. Washington: Isaac S. Hathaway. Washington-Carver: Isaac S. Hathaway. Wisconsin: David Parsons. York County: Walter H. Rich. **Size:** 30.6 millimeters. **Weight:** 12.5 grams. **Composition:** 90% silver (0.3618 ounces), 10% copper. **Notes:** Values for "PDS sets" contain one example each from the Philadelphia, Denver and San Francisco mints. "Type coin" values are for the most inexpensive single coin available from the date and mintmark combinations listed. The Alabama half-dollar varieties are distinguished by whether "2x2" appears on the obverse behind the head. The Grant half-dollar varieties are distinguished by whether a star appears above the word "Grant" on the obverse. The Missouri half-dollar varieties are distinguished by whether "2 ★ 2" appears on the obverse to the left of the head.

2x2

Date	Event	Mintage	AU-50	MS-60	MS-63	MS-64	MS-65
1921	Alabama 2X2	6,006	170.	275.	515.	825.	2400.
1921	Alabama	59,038	105.	195.	425.	670.	2550.

Date	Event	Mintage	AU-50	MS-60	MS-63	MS-64	MS-65
1936	Albany	17,671	190.	205.	210.	250.	360.

Date	Event	Mintage	AU-50	MS-60	MS-63	MS-64	MS-65
1937	Antietam	18,028	400.	425.	440.	495.	700.

Date	Event	Mintage	AU-50	MS-60	MS-63	MS-64	MS-65
1935	Arkansas PDS set	5,505	—	200.	215.	300.	700.
1936	Arkansas PDS set	9,660	—	200.	215.	275.	900.
1937	Arkansas PDS set	5,505	—	215.	275.	300.	950.
1938	Arkansas PDS set	3,155	—	315.	400.	460.	1800.
1939	Arkansas PDS set	2,104	—	580.	825.	1000.	2700.
	Arkansas type coin	—	54.00	57.00	68.00	75.00	195.

See also Robinson-Arkansas

Date	Event	Mintage	AU-50	MS-60	MS-63	MS-64	MS-65
1936	Bay Bridge	71,424	95.00	100.	110.	135.	275.

**"1934" added to
1935-1938 issues**

Date	Event	Mintage	AU-50	MS-60	MS-63	MS-64	MS-65
1934	Boone	10,007	61.00	68.00	80.00	100.	170.
1935	Boone PDS set w/1934	5,005	—	580.	730.	1050.	1650.
1935	Boone PDS set	2,003	—	215.	275.	300.	500.
1936	Boone PDS set	5,005	—	215.	275.	300.	485.
1937	Boone PDS set	2,506	—	580.	650.	735.	1100.
1938	Boone PDS set	2,100	—	750.	945.	1100.	1350.
	Boone type coin	—	57.00	65.00	80.00	90.00	140.

Date	Event	Mintage	AU-50	MS-60	MS-63	MS-64	MS-65
1936	Bridgeport	25,015	95.00	110.	115.	120.	270.

Date	Event	Mintage	AU-50	MS-60	MS-63	MS-64	MS-65
1925S	California Jubilee	86,594	95.00	110.	155.	230.	980.

Date	Event	Mintage	AU-50	MS-60	MS-63	MS-64	MS-65
1936	Cincinnati PDS set	5,005	—	670.	730.	800.	1900.
1936	Cincinnati type coin	—	195.	210.	225.	230.	580.

Date	Event	Mintage	AU-50	MS-60	MS-63	MS-64	MS-65
1936	Cleveland - Great Lakes	50,030	54.00	61.00	65.00	90.00	235.

Date	Event	Mintage	AU-50	MS-60	MS-63	MS-64	MS-65
1936	Columbia PDS set	9,007	—	475.	520.	535.	650.
1936	Columbia type coin	—	140.	150.	155.	190.	225.

1892 Columbian Expo Half
Grade MS-60

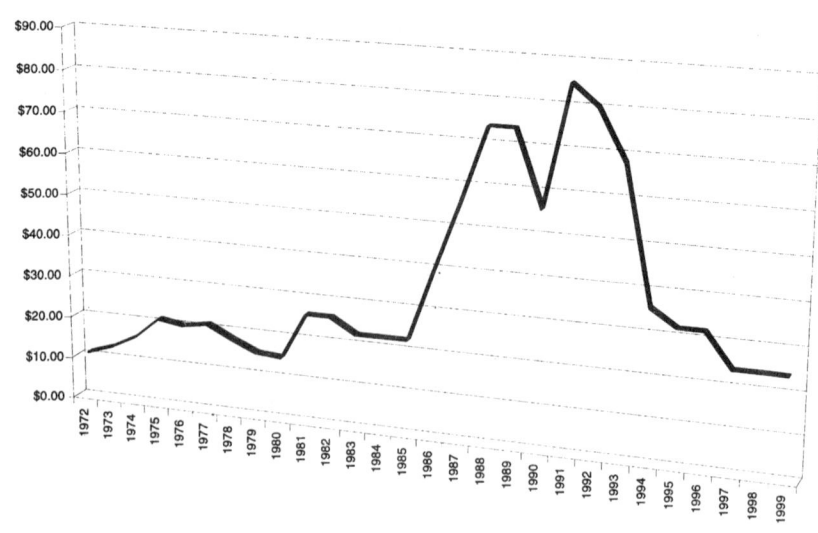

Retail Price

Source: COIN PRICES

Date	Event	Mintage	AU-50	MS-60	MS-63	MS-64	MS-65
1892	Columbian Expo	950,000	12.00	24.00	80.00	150.	650.
1893	Columbian Expo	1,550,405	12.00	24.00	75.00	150.	765.

Date	Event	Mintage	AU-50	MS-60	MS-63	MS-64	MS-65
1935	Connecticut	25,018	155.	175.	190.	235.	600.

Date	Event	Mintage	AU-50	MS-60	MS-63	MS-64	MS-65
1936	Delaware	20,993	175.	195.	210.	230.	350.

Date	Event	Mintage	AU-50	MS-60	MS-63	MS-64	MS-65
1936	Elgin	20,015	155.	160.	170.	195.	250.

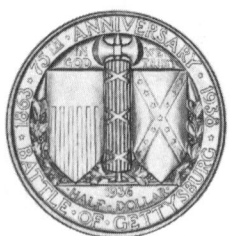

Date	Event	Mintage	AU-50	MS-60	MS-63	MS-64	MS-65
1936	Gettysburg	26,928	250.	275.	285.	330.	610.

  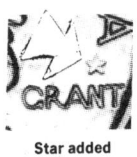

Star added

Date	Event	Mintage	AU-50	MS-60	MS-63	MS-64	MS-65
1922	Grant with star	4,256	620.	910.	1450.	2350.	7000.
1922	Grant	67,405	63.00	80.00	160.	265.	850.

Date	Event	Mintage	AU-50	MS-60	MS-63	MS-64	MS-65
1928	Hawaiian	10,008	1000.	1200.	1750.	2350.	5100.

Date	Event	Mintage	AU-50	MS-60	MS-63	MS-64	MS-65
1935	Hudson	10,008	410.	450.	500.	670.	1250.

Date	Event	Mintage	AU-50	MS-60	MS-63	MS-64	MS-65
1924	Huguenot-Walloon	142,080	85.00	100.	120.	170.	535.

Date	Event	Mintage	AU-50	MS-60	MS-63	MS-64	MS-65
1918	Lincoln-Illinois	100,058	73.00	92.00	110.	170.	610.

Date	Event	Mintage	AU-50	MS-60	MS-63	MS-64	MS-65
1946	Iowa	100,057	58.00	63.00	70.00	75.00	100.

Date	Event	Mintage	AU-50	MS-60	MS-63	MS-64	MS-65
1925	Lexington-Concord	162,013	58.00	68.00	95.00	155.	615.

Date	Event	Mintage	AU-50	MS-60	MS-63	MS-64	MS-65
1936	Long Island	81,826	55.00	61.00	73.00	115.	420.

Date	Event	Mintage	AU-50	MS-60	MS-63	MS-64	MS-65
1936	Lynchburg	20,013	135.	150.	160.	200.	290.

Date	Event	Mintage	AU-50	MS-60	MS-63	MS-64	MS-65
1920	Maine	50,028	85.00	100.	140.	215.	615.

Date	Event	Mintage	AU-50	MS-60	MS-63	MS-64	MS-65
1934	Maryland	25,015	100.	115.	150.	190.	350.

2 ☆ 4

Date	Event	Mintage	AU-50	MS-60	MS-63	MS-64	MS-65
1921	Missouri 2 star 4	5,000	380.	465.	850.	1500.	5850.
1921	Missouri	15,428	210.	400.	610.	1000.	5500.

Date	Event	Mintage	AU-50	MS-60	MS-63	MS-64	MS-65
1923S	Monroe	274,077	27.00	36.00	115.	340.	2150.

Date	Event	Mintage	AU-50	MS-60	MS-63	MS-64	MS-65
1938	New Rochelle	15,266	245.	260.	275.	295.	385.

Date	Event	Mintage	AU-50	MS-60	MS-63	MS-64	MS-65
1936	Norfolk	16,936	340.	350.	360.	380.	500.

1926 Oregon Trail Half
Grade MS-60

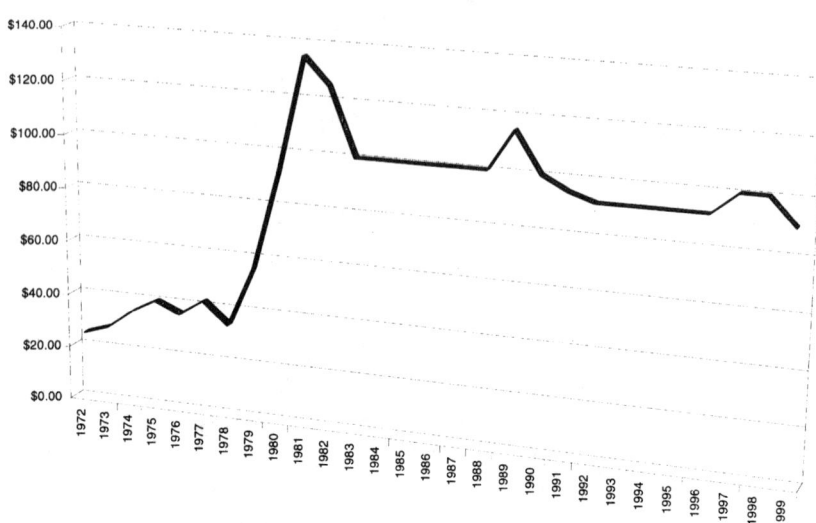

■ Retail Price

Source: COIN PRICES

Date	Event	Mintage	AU-50	MS-60	MS-63	MS-64	MS-65
1926	Oregon	47,955	80.00	90.00	100.	135.	180.
1926S	Oregon	83,055	80.00	95.00	110.	135.	180.
1928	Oregon	6,028	140.	155.	170.	180.	245.
1933D	Oregon	5,008	215.	230.	245.	275.	425.
1934D	Oregon	7,006	120.	140.	155.	180.	275.
1936	Oregon	10,006	95.00	110.	115.	125.	210.
1936S	Oregon	5,006	110.	120.	155.	180.	245.
1937D	Oregon	12,008	115.	130.	140.	170.	195.
1938	Oregon PDS set	6,005	—	515.	580.	620.	650.
1939	Oregon PDS set	3,004	—	1050.	1250.	1350.	1650.
	Oregon type coin	—	80.00	90.00	100.	135.	180.

Date	Event	Mintage	AU-50	MS-60	MS-63	MS-64	MS-65
1915S	Panama - Pacific	27,134	195.	300.	610.	950.	2350.

Date	Event	Mintage	AU-50	MS-60	MS-63	MS-64	MS-65
1920	Pilgrim	152,112	54.00	63.00	80.00	120.	550.
1921	Pilgrim	20,053	100.	110.	145.	225.	750.

Date	Event	Mintage	AU-50	MS-60	MS-63	MS-64	MS-65
1936	Rhode Island PDS set	15,010	—	200.	245.	340.	700.
1936	Rhode Island type coin	—	60.00	70.00	80.00	115.	225.

Date	Event	Mintage	AU-50	MS-60	MS-63	MS-64	MS-65
1937	Roanoke	29,030	140.	155.	170.	200.	245.

Date	Event	Mintage	AU-50	MS-60	MS-63	MS-64	MS-65
1936	Robinson-Arkansas	25,265	80.00	95.00	105.	115.	315.
		(See also Arkansas)					

Date	Event	Mintage	AU-50	MS-60	MS-63	MS-64	MS-65
1935S	San Diego	70,132	49.00	55.00	58.00	75.00	80.00
1936D	San Diego	30,092	54.00	58.00	66.00	75.00	90.00

Date	Event	Mintage	AU-50	MS-60	MS-63	MS-64	MS-65
1926	Sesquicentennial	141,120	49.00	61.00	160.	485.	5000.

Date	Event	Mintage	AU-50	MS-60	MS-63	MS-64	MS-65
1935	Spanish Trail	10,008	765.	790.	800.	910.	1050.

Date	Event	Mintage	AU-50	MS-60	MS-63	MS-64	MS-65
1925	Stone Mountain	1,314,709	30.00	36.00	61.00	90.00	225.

Date	Event	Mintage	AU-50	MS-60	MS-63	MS-64	MS-65
1934	Texas	61,463	80.00	85.00	90.00	100.	160.
1935	Texas PDS set	9,994	—	275.	290.	315.	475.
1936	Texas PDS set	8,911	—	275.	290.	315.	475.
1937	Texas PDS set	6,571	—	285.	300.	315.	475.
1938	Texas PDS set	3,775	—	545.	730.	790.	1075.
	Texas type coins	—	80.00	85.00	90.00	100.	160.

Date	Event	Mintage	AU-50	MS-60	MS-63	MS-64	MS-65
1925	Fort Vancouver	14,994	225.	275.	345.	500.	1200.

Date	Event	Mintage	AU-50	MS-60	MS-63	MS-64	MS-65
1927	Vermont	28,142	130.	150.	155.	250.	900.

Date	Event	Mintage	AU-50	MS-60	MS-63	MS-64	MS-65
1946	B.T. Washington PDS set	200,113	—	35.00	49.00	68.00	110.
1947	B.T. Washington PDS set	100,017	—	46.00	73.00	100.	245.
1948	B.T. Washington PDS set	8,005	—	97.00	105.	140.	170.
1949	B.T. Washington PDS set	6,004	—	170.	195.	215.	270.
1950	B.T. Washington PDS set	6,004	—	85.00	105.	110.	155.
1951	B.T. Washington PDS set	7,004	—	105.	120.	140.	160.
	B.T. Washington type coin	—	9.00	11.00	12.00	15.00	30.00

Date	Event	Mintage	AU-50	MS-60	MS-63	MS-64	MS-65
1951	Washington-Carver PDS set	10,004	—	73.00	85.00	115.	485.
1952	Washington-Carver PDS set	8,006	—	73.00	95.00	120.	340.
1953	Washington-Carver PDS set	8,003	—	73.00	95.00	120.	485.
1954	Washington-Carver PDS set	12,006	—	68.00	85.00	95.00	365.
	Washington-Carver type coin	—	9.00	11.00	12.00	15.00	40.00

Date	Event	Mintage	AU-50	MS-60	MS-63	MS-64	MS-65
1936	Wisconsin	25,015	150.	160.	170.	210.	245.

Date	Event	Mintage	AU-50	MS-60	MS-63	MS-64	MS-65
1936	York County	25,015	140.	145.	155.	175.	190.

Silver dollar

Designer: Charles E. Barber. **Size:** 38.1 millimeters. **Weight:** 26.73 grams. **Composition:** 90% silver (0.7736 ounces), 10% copper.

Date	Event	Mintage	AU-50	MS-60	MS-63	MS-64	MS-65
1900	Lafayette ($1)	36,026	290.	515.	1150.	2300.	9000.

Gold dollars

Designers: Louisiana: Charles E. Barber. Lewis and Clark Expo: Charles E. Barber. Panama-Pacific Expo: Charles Keck. McKinley Memorial: Charles E. Barber (obverse) and George T. Morgan (reverse). Grant: Laura G. Fraser. **Size:** 15 millimeters. **Weight:** 1.672 grams. **Composition:** 90% gold (0.0484 ounces), 10% copper. **Notes:** The Grant gold-dollar varieties are distinguished by whether a star appears on the obverse above the word "Grant."

Jefferson   McKinley

Date	Event	Mintage	AU-50	MS-60	MS-63	MS-64	MS-65
1903	Louisiana, Jefferson	17,500	300.	395.	700.	950.	1750.
1903	Louisiana, McKinley	17,500	280.	350.	600.	900.	1800.

Date	Event	Mintage	AU-50	MS-60	MS-63	MS-64	MS-65
1904	Lewis and Clark Expo	10,025	470.	700.	1750.	2550.	4500.
1905	Lewis and Clark Expo	10,041	470.	800.	2350.	4200.	11,000.

Date	Event	Mintage	AU-50	MS-60	MS-63	MS-64	MS-65
1915S	Panama-Pacific Expo	15,000	295.	330.	450.	750.	1600.

Date	Event	Mintage	AU-50	MS-60	MS-63	MS-64	MS-65
1916	McKinley Memorial	9,977	245.	325.	450.	700.	1600.
1917	McKinley Memorial	10,000	325.	470.	850.	1200.	2050.

With star

Date	Event	Mintage	AU-50	MS-60	MS-63	MS-64	MS-65
1922	Grant Memorial w/o star	5,016	1000.	1050.	1300.	1600.	2250.
1922	Grant Memorial w/star	5,000	1100.	1250.	1600.	1800.	2050.

Gold $2.50

Designers: Panama-Pacific Expo: Charles E. Barber (obverse) and George T. Morgan (reverse). Sesquicentennial: John R. Sinnock. **Size:** 18 millimeters. **Weight:** 4.18 grams. **Composition:** 90% gold (0.121 ounces), 10% copper.

Date	Event	Mintage	AU-50	MS-60	MS-63	MS-64	MS-65
1915S	Panama Pacific Expo.	6,749	1110.	1250.	2550.	2850.	3650.

Date	Event	Mintage	AU-50	MS-60	MS-63	MS-64	MS-65
1926	Philadelphia Sesquicentennial	46,019	240.	265.	500.	950.	3000.

Gold $50

Designer: Robert Aitken. **Size:** 44 millimeters. **Weight:** 83.59 grams. **Composition:** 90% gold (2.42 ounces), 10% copper.

Date	Event	Mintage	AU-50	MS-60	MS-63	MS-64	MS-65
1915S	Panama-Pacific Expo, round	483	22,000.	24,000.	37,500.	47,000.	110,000.
1915S	Panama-Pacific Expo, octagon	645	20,000.	22,000.	32,500.	42,000.	96,500.

Commemoratives 1982-present

Half Dollars

Designer: Elizabeth Jones. **Size:** 30.6 millimeters. **Weight:** 12.5 grams. **Composition:** 90% silver (0.3618 ounces), 10% copper.

Date	Mintage	(Proof)	MS-65	Prf-65
1982D Geo. Washington	2,210,458	—	4.50	—
1982S Geo. Washington	—	(4,894,044)	—	4.50

Date	Mintage	(Proof)	MS-65	Prf-65
1986D Statue of Liberty	928,008	—	4.50	—
1986S Statue of Liberty	—	(6,925,627)	—	4.65

Date	Mintage	(Proof)	MS-65	Prf-65
1989D Congress	163,753	—	8.50	—
1989S Congress	—	767,897	—	5.00

Date	Mintage	(Proof)	MS-65	Prf-65
1991D Mt. Rushmore	172,754	—	9.00	—
1991S Mt. Rushmore	—	753,257	9.00	8.50

Date	Mintage	(Proof)	MS-65	Prf-65
1992P Olympic	161,607	—	5.00	—
1992S Olympic	—	(519,645)	7.50	8.00

Date	Mintage	(Proof)	MS-65	Prf-65
1992D Columbus	135,702	—	12.50	—
1992S Columbus	—	(390,154)	—	12.50

Date	Mintage	(Proof)	MS-65	Prf-65
1993W Madison/Bill of Rights	173,224	—	12.50	—
1993S Madison/Bill of Rights	—	(559,758)	—	12.50

Date	Mintage	(Proof)	MS-65	Prf-65
1993P World War II	192,968	(290,343)	10.00	11.00

Date	Mintage	(Proof)	MS-65	Prf-65
1994W World Cup Soccer	52,836	—	9.00	—
1994P World Cup Soccer	122,412	—	—	10.00

Date	Mintage	(Proof)	MS-65	Prf-65
1995S Civil War	—	—	9.00	10.00

Date	Mintage	(Proof)	MS-65	Prf-65
1995S Olympic Basketball	171,001	(169,655)	12.00	12.00

Date	Mintage	(Proof)	MS-65	Prf-65
1995S Olympic Baseball	164,605	(118,087)	12.00	12.00

Date	Mintage	(Proof)	MS-65	Prf-65
1996S Soccer	52,836	(122,412)	11.50	10.00

Date	Mintage	(Proof)	MS-65	Prf-65
1996S Swimmer	—	—	11.50	7.50

Silver dollars

Designers: 1983 Olympics: Elizabeth Jones. 1984 Olympics: Robert Graham. Statue of Liberty: John Mercanti. Constitution: Patricia Lewis Verani. 1988 Olympics: Patricia Lewis Verani (obverse) and Sherl Joseph Winter (reverse). Congress: William Woodward. Eisenhower: John Mercanti (obverse) and Marcel Jovine (reverse). Mount Rushmore: Marika Somogyi (obverse) and Frank Gasparro (reverse). Korean War: John Mercanti (obverse) and James Ferrell (reverse). United Service Organizations: Robert Lamb (obverse) and John Mercanti (reverse). 1992 Olympics: John R. Deecken (obverse) and Marcel Jovine (reverse). **Size:** 38.1 millimeters. **Weight:** 26.73 grams. **Composition:** 90% silver (0.76 ounces), 10% copper.

Date	Mintage	(Proof)	MS-65	Prf-65
1983P Olympic	294,543	—	9.50	—
1983D Olympic	174,014	—	9.50	—
1983S Olympic	174,014	(1,577,025)	9.50	10.00

Date	Mintage	(Proof)	MS-65	Prf-65
1984P Olympic	217,954	—	14.00	—
1984D Olympic	116,675	—	21.00	—
1984S Olympic	116,675	(1,801,210)	23.00	10.00

Date	Mintage	(Proof)	MS-65	Prf-65
1986P Statue of Liberty	723,635	—	10.00	—
1986S Statue of Liberty	—	(6,414,638)	—	10.00

Date	Mintage	(Proof)	MS-65	Prf-65
1987P Constitution	451,629	—	9.50	—
1987S Constitution	—	(2,747,116)	—	9.50

Date	Mintage	(Proof)	MS-65	Prf-65
1988D Olympic	191,368	—	9.50	—
1988S Olympic	—	(1,359,366)	—	9.50

Date	Mintage	(Proof)	MS-65	Prf-65
1989D Congress	135,203	—	12.50	—
1989S Congress	—	(762,198)	—	11.25

Date	Mintage	(Proof)	MS-65	Prf-65
1990W Eisenhower	241,669	—	11.00	—
1990P Eisenhower	—	(638,335)	—	11.00

Date	Mintage	(Proof)	MS-65	Prf-65
1991P Mt. Rushmore	133,139	—	28.00	—
1991S Mt. Rushmore	—	(738,419)	—	28.00

Date	Mintage	(Proof)	MS-65	Prf-65
1991D Korean War	213,049	—	15.00	—
1991P Korean War	—	(618,488)	—	11.00

Date	Mintage	(Proof)	MS-65	Prf-65
1991D USO	124,958	—	15.00	—
1991S USO	—	(321,275)	—	12.00

Date	Mintage	(Proof)	MS-65	Prf-65
1992D Olympic	187,552	—	21.00	—
1992S Olympic	—	(504,505)	—	28.00

Date	Mintage	(Proof)	MS-65	Prf-65
1992D White House	123,803	—	19.00	—
1992W White House	—	(375,851)	16.50	19.00

Date	Mintage	(Proof)	MS-65	Prf-65
1992D Columbus	106,949	—	29.00	—
1992P Columbus	—	(385,241)	—	29.00

Date	Mintage	(Proof)	MS-65	Prf-65
1993D Madison/Bill of Rights	98,383	—	16.50	—
1993S Madison/Bill of Rights	—	(534,001)	16.00	16.50

Date	Mintage	(Proof)	MS-65	Prf-65
1993D World War II	94,708	—	21.00	—
1993W World War II	—	(322,422)	—	23.00

Date	Mintage	(Proof)	MS-65	Prf-65
1993P Jefferson	266,927	—	23.00	—
1993S Jefferson	—	(332,891)	—	14.00

Date	Mintage	(Proof)	MS-65	Prf-65
1994D World Cup Soccer	81,698	—	26.50	—
1994S World Cup Soccer	—	(576,978)	—	29.00

Date	Mintage	(Proof)	MS-65	Prf-65
1994W Prisoner of War	54,790	—	25.00	—
1994P Prisoner of War	—	(220,100)	—	25.00

Date	Mintage	(Proof)	MS-65	Prf-65
1994W Vietnam Veterans	57,317	—	28.00	—
1994P Vietnam Veterans	—	(226,262)	—	29.00

Date	Mintage	(Proof)	MS-65	Prf-65
1994W Women in Military	53,054	—	23.00	—
1994W Women in Military	—	(213,201)	—	22.00

Date	Mintage	(Proof)	MS-65	Prf-65
1994D U.S. Capitol	68,352	—	18.00	—
1994S U.S. Capitol	—	(279,416)	—	12.50

Date	Mintage	(Proof)	MS-65	Prf-65
1995P Civil War	—	—	23.00	—
1995S Civil War	—	—	—	18.50

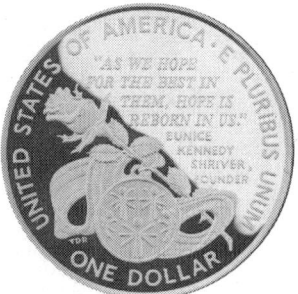

Date	Mintage	(Proof)	MS-65	Prf-65
1995W Shriver	—		24.00	
1995P Shriver	—	—	—	15.00

Date	Mintage	(Proof)	MS-65	Prf-65
1995D Olympic Gymnastics	42,497	—	43.00	—
1995P Olympic Gymnastics	—	(182,676)	—	33.00

Date	Mintage	(Proof)	MS-65	Prf-65
1995D Olympic Blind Runner	28,649	—	43.00	—
1995P Olympic Blind Runner	—	(138,337)	—	33.00

Date	Mintage	(Proof)	MS-65	Prf-65
1995D Olympic Field and Track	24,796	—	32.00	
1995P Olympic Field and Track	—	(136,935)	—	34.00

Date	Mintage	(Proof)	MS-65	Prf-65
1995D Olympic Cycling	19,662	—	32.00	—
1995P Olympic Cycling	—	(118,795)	—	35.00

Date	Mintage	(Proof)	MS-65	Prf-65
1996D Tennis	15,983	—	39.00	—
1996P Tennis	—	(92,016)	—	33.00

Date	Mintage	(Proof)	MS-65	Prf-65
1996D Paralympics	14,497	—	40.00	—
1996P Paralympics	—	(84,280)	—	35.00

Date	Mintage	(Proof)	MS-65	Prf-65
1996D Rowing	16,258	—	37.00	—
1996P Rowing	—	(151,890)	—	35.00

Date	Mintage	(Proof)	MS-65	Prf-65
1996D High Jumper	15,697	—	38.00	—
1996P High Jumper	—	(124,502)	—	35.00

Date	Mintage	(Proof)	MS-65	Prf-65
1996D Community Service	23,468	—	75.00	—
1996S Community Service	—	(100,787)	—	30.00

Date	Mintage	(Proof)	MS-65	Prf-65
1996D Smithsonian	126,616	—	34.00	—
1996P Smithsonian	—	(30,593)	—	29.00

Date	Mintage	(Proof)	MS-65	Prf-65
1997P Botanic Garden	57,272	(264,528)	32.00	30.00

Date	Mintage	(Proof)	MS-65	Prf-65
1997S Jackie Robinson	30,007	(110,495)	29.00	29.00

Date	Mintage	(Proof)	MS-65	Prf-65
1997P Law Enforcement	—	—	38.00	40.00

Date	Mintage	(Proof)	MS-65	Prf-65
1998S Robert E. Kennedy	—	—	37.00	38.00

Date	Mintage	(Proof)	MS-65	Prf-65
1998S Black Patriots	—	—	38.00	40.00

Date	Mintage	(Proof)	MS-65	Prf-65
1999P Dolley Madison	—	—	38.00	40.00

Gold $5

Designers: Statue of Liberty: Elizabeth Jones. Constitution: Marcel Jovine. 1988 Olympics: Elizabeth Jones (obverse) and Marcel Jovine (reverse). Congress: John Mercanti. Mount Rushmore: John Mercanti (obverse) and Robert Lamb (reverse). 1992 Olympics: James C. Sharpe (obverse) and James M. Peed (reverse). **Size:** 21.5 millimeters. **Weight:** 90% gold (0.24 ounces), 10% alloy.

Date	Mintage	(Proof)	MS-65	Prf-65
1986W Statue of Liberty	95,248	(404,013)	145.	145.

Date	Mintage	(Proof)	MS-65	Prf-65
1987W Constitution	214,225	(651,659)	145.	145.

Date	Mintage	(Proof)	MS-65	Prf-65
1988W Olympic	62,913	(281,456)	145.	145.

Date	Mintage	(Proof)	MS-65	Prf-65
1989W Congress	46,899	(164,690)	145.	145.

Date	Mintage	(Proof)	MS-65	Prf-65
1991W Mt. Rushmore	31,959	(111,991)	145.	145.
1992W Olympic	27,732	(77,313)	145.	145.
1992W Columbus	24,329	(79,730)	145.	145.
1993W Madison/Bill of Rights	22,266	(78,651)	135.	110.
1993W World War II	23,089	(65,461)	145.	145.
1994W World Cup Soccer	22,464	(89,619)	145.	145.
1995W Civil War	—	—	280.	150.

Date	Mintage	(Proof)	MS-65	Prf-65
1995W Olympic Torch Runner	14,675	(57,442)	190.	145.

Date	Mintage	(Proof)	MS-65	Prf-65
1995W Olympic Stadium	10,579	(43,124)	200.	175.

Date	Mintage	(Proof)	MS-65	Prf-65
1996W Flag Bearer	9,174	(32,886)	255.	220.

Date	Mintage	(Proof)	MS-65	Prf-65
1996W Cauldron	9,210	(38,555)	255.	220.

Date	Mintage	(Proof)	MS-65	Prf-65
1996W Smithsonian	—	—	260.	190.

Date	Mintage	(Proof)	MS-65	Prf-65
1997W Jackie Robinson	5,202	(24,546)	265.	170.

Date	Mintage	(Proof)	MS-65	Prf-65
1997W Roosevelt	—	—	195.	155.

Gold $10

Date	Mintage	(Proof)	MS-65	Prf-65
1984W Olympic	75,886	(381,085)	250.	250.
1984P Olympic	33,309	—	—	270.
1984D Olympic	34,533	—	—	265.
1984S Olympic	48,551	—	—	250.

Sets

Date	Price
1983 & 1984 proof dollars.	16.00
1983 collectors set1983 PDS uncirculated dollars.	23.00
1984 collectors set1984 PDS uncirculated dollars.	40.00
1983 & 1984 gold and silver uncirculated set. One 1983 and one 1984 uncirculated dollar and one 1984 uncirculated gold $10.	275.
1983 & 1984 gold and silver proof set. One 1983 and one 1984 proof dollar and one 1984 proof gold $10.	275.
1983 & 1984 6 coin set. One 1983 and one 1984 uncirculated and proof dollar. One uncirculated and one proof gold $10.	550.
1988 2 coin set: uncirculated silver dollar and gold $5.	145.
1988 2 coin set: proof silver dollar and gold $5.	135.
1988 4 coin set: 1 each of proof and uncirculated issues.	285.
1992 2 coin set: uncirculated half dollar and silver dollar.	25.00
1992 2 coin set: proof half dollar and silver dollar.	35.00
1992 3 coin set: uncirculated half dollar, silver dollar and gold $5.	150.
1992 3 coin set: proof half dollar, silver dollar and gold $5.	150.
1992 6 coin set: 1 each of proof and uncirculated issues.	295.
1995 4 coin set: uncirculated basketball half $1 gymnast & blind runner, $5 torch runner.	195.
1995 4 coin set: proof basketball half $1 gymnast & blind runner, $5 torch runner.	245.
1995 2 coin set: proof $1 gymnast & blind runner.	69.00
1995 2 coin set: proof $1 track & field, cycling.	69.00
1995-96 4 coin set: proof halves, basketball, baseball swimming, soccer.	50.00

Statue of Liberty

Date	Price
1986 2 coin set: uncirculated silver dollar and clad half dollar.	15.00
1986 2 coin set: proof silver dollar and clad half dollar.	13.00
1986 3 coin set: uncirculated silver dollar, clad half dollar and gold $5.	150.
1986 3 coin set: proof silver dollar, clad half dollar and gold $5.	150.
1986 6 coin set: 1 each of the proof and uncirculated issues.	300.

Constitution

Date	Price
1987 2 coin set: uncirculated silver dollar and gold $5.	150.
1987 2 coin set: proof silver dollar and gold $5.	145.
1987 4 coin set: 1 each of the proof and uncirculated issues.	285.

Congress

Date	Price
1989 2 coin set: uncirculated silver dollar and clad half dollar.	20.00
1989 2 coin set: proof silver dollar and clad half dollar.	18.00
1989 3 coin set: uncirculated silver dollar, clad half and gold $5.	150.
1989 3 coin set: proof silver dollar, clad half and gold $5.	150.
1989 6 coin set: 1 each of the proof and uncirculated issues.	300.

Mt. Rushmore

Date	Price
1991 2 coin set: uncirculated half dollar and silver dollar.	35.00
1991 2 coin set: proof half dollar and silver dollar.	30.00
1991 3 coin set: uncirculated half dollar, silver dollar and gold $5.	150.
1991 3 coin set: proof half dollar, silver dollar and gold $5.	150.
1991 6 coin set: 1 each of proof and uncirculated issues.	300.

Columbus Quincentenary

Date	Price
1992 2 coin set: uncirculated half dollar and silver dollar.	30.00
1992 2 coin set: proof half dollar and silver dollar.	35.00
1992 3 coin set: uncirculated half dollar, silver dollar and gold $5.	160.
1992 3 coin set: proof half dollar, silver dollar and gold $5.	160.
1992 6 coin set: 1 each of proof and uncirculated issues.	350.

Madison/Bill of Rights

Date	Price
1993 2 coin set: uncirculated half dollar and silver dollar.	25.00
1993 2 coin set: proof half dollar and silver dollar.	20.00
1993 3 coin set: uncirculated half dollar, silver dollar and gold $5.	150.
1993 3 coin set: proof half dollar, silver dollar and gold $5.	150.
1993 6 coin set: 1 each of proof and uncirculated issues.	400.

World War II

Date | **Price**
1993 2 coin set: uncirculated half dollar and silver dollar. — 20.00
1993 2 coin set: proof half dollar and silver dollar. — 25.00
1993 3 coin set: uncirculated half dollar, silver dollar and gold $5. — 160.
1993 3 coin set: proof half dollar, silver dollar and gold $5. — 160.
1993 6 coin set: 1 each of proof and uncirculated issues. — 320.

Jefferson

Date | **Price**
1993 Jefferson: dollar, nickel and $2 note. — 90.00

World Cup

Date | **Price**
1994 2 coin set: uncirculated half dollar and silver dollar. — 30.00
1994 2 coin set: proof half dollar and silver dollar. — 30.00
1994 3 coin set: uncirculated half dollar, silver dollar and gold $5. — 145.
1994 3 coin set: proof half dollar, silver dollar and gold $5. — 145.
1994 6 coin set: 1 each of proof and uncirculated issues. — 310.

U.S. Veterans

Date | **Price**
1994 3 coin set: uncirculated POW, Vietnam, Women dollars. — 65.00
1994 3 coin set: proof POW, Vietnam, Women dollars. — 45.00

Civil War

Date | **Price**
1995 2 coin set: uncirculated half and dollar. — 30.00
1995 2 coin set: proof half and dollar. — 25.00
1995 3 coin set: uncirculated half, dollar and gold $5. — 315.
1995 3 coin set: proof half, dollar and gold $5. — 170.
1995 6 coin set: 1 each of proof and uncirculated issues. — 490.

Smithsonian

Date | **Price**
1996 2 coin set: Smithsonian proof dollar and $5 gold. — 205.
1996 4 coin set: proof and B.U. — 480.

Botanic Garden

Date | **Price**
1997 dollar, Jefferson nickel and $1 note. — 150.

Jackie Robinson

Date | **Price**
1997 2 coin set: proof dollar & $5 gold. — 220.
1997 4 coin set: proof & BU. — 440.
1997 legacy set. — 380.

Kennedy

Date | **Price**
1998 2 coin set: proof. — 75.00
1998 2 coin collectors set: matte finished Robert Kennedy dollar and John Kennedy half dollar. — 125.

American Eagle bullion coins

Notes: American Eagle bullion coins are traded for their precious-metal content and compete with similar coins from other countries. Values for the non-proof issues will fluctuate with gold and silver prices.

Silver

One-ounce

Designers: Adolph A. Weinman (obverse) and John Mercanti (reverse). **Size:** 40.6 millimeters. **Weight:** 31.103 grams. **Composition:** 99.93% silver (0.999 ounces), 0.07% copper.

Prices based on $5.16 spot silver.

Date	Mintage	Unc	Prf.
1986	5,393,005	10.00	—
1986S	1,446,778	—	25.00
1987	11,442,335	9.00	—
1987S	904,732	—	25.00
1988	5,004,646	9.00	—
1988S	557,370	—	32.00
1989	5,203,327	9.00	—
1989S	617,694	—	25.00
1990	5,840,210	9.00	—
1990S	695,510	—	25.00
1991	7,191,066	9.00	—
1991S	511,924	—	25.00
1992	5,540,068	10.00	—
1992S	498,552	—	25.00
1993	6,763,762	9.00	—
1993P	403,625	—	44.00
1994	4,227,319	9.00	—
1994P	—	—	44.00
1995	4,672,051	9.00	—
1995P	—	—	43.00
1995W 10th Anniv.	30,125	—	700.
1996	3,603,386	10.00	—
1996P	—	—	27.00
1997	4,295,004	10.00	—
1997P	—	—	27.00
1998	4,847,549	9.00	—
1998P	—	—	25.00
1999	—	9.50	—
1999P	—	—	—

Gold American Eagles

Arabic numeral date   Roman numeral date

Five Dollars - 1/10 oz

Designers: Augustus Saint-Gaudens (obverse) and Miley Busiek (reverse). **Size:** 16.5 millimeters. **Weight:** 3.393 grams. **Composition:** 91.67% gold (0.1 ounces), 5.33% copper, 3% silver.

Prices based on $285.00 spot gold.

Date	Mintage	Unc	Prf.
MCMLXXXVI (1986)	912,609	45.00	—
MCMLXXXVII (1987)	580,266	45.00	—
MCMLXXXVIII (1988)	159,500	48.00	—
MCMLXXXVIII (1988)P	143,881	—	58.00
MCMLXXXIX (1989)	264,790	48.00	—
MCMLXXXIX (1989)P	82,924	—	60.00
MCMXC (1990)	210,210	48.00	—
MCMXC (1990)P	99,349	—	58.00
MCMXCI (1991)	165,200	48.00	—
MCMXCI (1991)P	70,344	—	60.00
1992	209,300	48.00	—
1992P	64,902	—	71.00
1993	210,709	48.00	—
1993P	58,649	—	66.00
1994	206,380	47.00	—
1994W	—	—	60.00
1995	223,025	38.00	—
1995W	—	—	68.00
1996	—	38.00	—
1996W	—	—	74.00
1997	528,515	38.00	—
1997W	—	—	95.00
1998	1,344,520	38.00	—
1998W	—	—	60.00
1999	—	38.00	—
1999W	—	—	—

Ten Dollars - 1/4 oz

Arabic numeral date   Roman numeral date

Size: 22 millimeters. **Weight:** 8.483 grams. **Composition:** 91.67% gold (0.25 ounces), 5.33% copper, 3% silver.

Date	Mintage	Unc	Prf.
MCMLXXXVI (1986)	726,031	100.	—
MCMLXXXVII (1987)	269,255	105.	—
MCMLXXXVIII (1988)	49,000	110.	—
MCMLXXXVIII (1988)P	98,028	—	150.
MCMLXXXIX (1989)	81,789	110.	—
MCMLXXXIX (1989P)	53,593	—	150.
MCMXC (1990)	41,000	110.	—
MCMXC (1990)P	62,674	—	150.
MCMXCI (1991)	36,100	135.	—
MCMXCI (1991)P	50,839	—	150.
1992	59,546	110.	—
1992P	46,290	—	150.
1993	71,864	110.	—
1993P	46,271	—	150.
1994	72,650	105.	—
1994W	—	—	150.
1995	83,752	100.	—
1995W	—	—	150.
1996	60,318	100.	—
1996W	—	—	150.
1997	108,805	100.	—
1997W	—	—	150.
1998	309,829	85.00	—
1998W	—	—	150.
1999	—	85.00	—
1999W	—	—	—

Arabic numeral date   Roman numeral date

Twenty Five Dollars - 1/2 oz

Size: 27 millimeters. **Weight:** 16.966 grams. **Composition:** 91.67% gold (0.5 ounces), 5.33% copper, 3% silver.

Date	Mintage	Unc	Prf.
MCMLXXXVI (1986)	599,566	190.	—
MCMLXXXVII (1987)	131,255	210.	—
MCMLXXXVII (1987)P	143,398	—	285.
MCMLXXXVIII (1988)	45,000	295.	—
MCMLXXXVIII (1988)P	76,528	—	285.
MCMLXXXIX (1989)	44,829	395.	—
MCMLXXXIX (1989)P	44,264	—	285.
MCMXC (1990)	31,000	385.	—
MCMXC (1990)P	51,636	—	285.
MCMXCI (1991)	24,100	415.	—
MCMXCI (1991)P	53,125	—	285.
1992	54,404	225.	—
1992P	40,982	—	285.
1993	73,324	195.	—
1993P	43,319	—	285.
1994	62,400	180.	—
1994W	—	—	285.
1995	53,474	180.	—
1995W	—	—	285.
1996	39,287	315.	—
1996W	—	—	285.
1997	79,605	180.	—
1997W	—	—	285.
1998	169,029	180.	—
1998W	—	—	285.
1999	—	180.	—
1999W	—	—	—

Arabic numeral date

Roman numeral date

Fifty Dollars - 1 oz

Size: 32.7 millimeters. **Weight:** 33.931 grams. **Composition:** 91.67% gold (1 ounce), 5.33% copper, 3% silver.

Date	Mintage	Unc	Prf.
MCMLXXXVI (1986)	1,362,650	325.	—
MCMLXXXVI (1986)W	446,290	—	590.
MCMLXXXVII (1987)	1,045,500	325.	—
MCMLXXXVII (1987)W	147,498	—	590.
MCMLXXXVIII (1988)	465,000	325.	—
MCMLXXXVIII (1988)W	87,133	—	590.
MCMLXXXIX (1989)	415,790	325.	—
MCMLXXXIX (1989)W	53,960	—	590.
MCMXC (1990)	373,210	330.	—
MCMXC (1990)W	62,401	—	590.
MCMXCI (1991)	243,100	330.	—
MCMXCI (1991)W	50,411	—	590.
1992	275,000	330.	—
1992W	44,835	—	590.
1993	480,192	325.	—
1993W	34,389	—	590.
1994	221,633	330.	—
1994W	—	—	590.
1995	200,636	330.	—
1995W	—	—	590.
1996	189,148	335.	—
1996W	—	—	590.
1997	664,508	325.	—
1997W	—	—	590.
1998	1,468,530	325.	—
1998W	—	—	595.
1999	—	325.	—
1999W	—	—	—

The American Eagle gold coin series was minted to compete with other bullion coins of the world. The weight of 1, 1/2, 1/4 and 1/10th ounce indicates the total gold weight of the coin. The composition of all four gold bullion coins is an alloy containing 91.67 percent gold, 3.0 percent silver, and 5.33 percent copper.

PLATINUM EAGLES
Platinum American Eagles

Prices based on $369.00 spot platinum.

The reverse of the American Eagle platinum proof coins changes each year. The reverse for 1998, second in the series, is pictured here.

One Hundred Dollars - 1 oz

Date	Mintage	Unc	Prf.
1997	56,000	420.	—
1997W	—	—	725.
1998	133,002	410.	—
1998W	—	—	715.
1999	—	395.	—
1999W	—	—	—

Fifty Dollars - 1/2 oz

Date	Mintage	Unc	Prf.
1997	20,500	450.	—
1997W	—	—	370.
1998	32,415	250.	—
1998W	—	—	410.
1999	—	210.	—
1999W	—	—	—

Twenty Five Dollars - 1/4 oz

Date	Mintage		Unc	Prf.
1997	27,100		200.	—
1997W	—		—	210.
1998	38,887		160.	—
1998W	—		—	225.
1999	—		120.	—
1999W	—		—	—

Ten Dollars - 1/10 oz

Date	Mintage		Unc	Prf.
1997	70,250		47.00	—
1997W	—		—	125.
1998	39,525		49.00	—
1998W	—		—	125.
1999	—		47.00	—
1999W	—		—	—

U.S. minting varieties and errors

Introduction
By Alan Herbert

The P.D.S. cataloging system used here to list minting varieties was originally compiled by the author in 1971. PDS stands for the three main divisions of the minting process, "planchet," "die" and "striking." Two more divisions cover collectible modifications after the strike, as well as non-collectible alterations, counterfeits and damaged coins.

This listing includes 445 classes, each a distinct part of the minting process or from a specific non-mint change in the coin. Classes from like causes are grouped together. The PDS system applies to coins of the world, but is based on U.S. coinage with added classes for certain foreign minting practices.

Price ranges are based on a U.S. coin in MS-60 grade (uncirculated.) The ranges may be applied in general to foreign coins of similar size or value although collector values are not usually as high as for U.S. coins. Prices are only a guide as the ultimate price is determined by a willing buyer and seller.

To define minting varieties, "A coin which exhibits a variation of any kind from the normal, as a result of any portion of the minting process, whether at the planchet stage, as a result of a change or modification of the die, or during the striking process. It includes those classes considered to be intentional changes, as well as those caused by normal wear and tear on the dies or other minting equipment and classes deemed to be "errors."

The three causes are represented as follows:
1. (I) = Intentional Changes
2. (W) = Wear and Tear
3. (E) = Errors
Note: A class may show more than one cause and could be listed as (IWE).

Rarity level

The rarity ratings are based on the following scale:
1 - Very Common. Ranges from every coin struck down to 1,000,000.
2 - Common. From 1,000,000 down to 100,000.
3 - Scarce. From 100,000 down to 10,000.
4 - Very Scarce. From 10,000 down to 1,000.
5 - Rare. From 1,000 down to 100.
6 - Very Rare. From 100 down to 10.
7 - Extremely Rare. From 10 down to 1.
Unknown: If I don't have a confirmed report of a piece fitting a particular class, it is listed as Unknown and I would appreciate reports from readers in order to update future presentations.

An Unknown does not mean that your piece automatically is very valuable. Even a Rarity 7 piece, extremely rare, even unique, may have a very low collector value because of a lack of demand or interest in that particular class.

Classes, definitions and price ranges are based on material previously offered in my book, *The Official Price Guide to Minting Varieties and Errors*, 5th edition, and in *Coin Prices* Magazine.

Pricing information has also been provided by John A. Wexler and Ken Potter, with special pricing and technical advice from Del Romines.

Also recommended is the *Cherrypicker's Guide to Rare Die Varieties* 3rd edition, by Bill Fivaz and J.T. Stanton, available from Stanton at P.O. Box 932, Savannah, GA 31402.

For help with your coin questions, to report significant new finds and for authentication of your minting varieties, include a loose first class stamp and write to Alan Herbert, Dept.

NA-8, NAC&P, 700 E. State St., Iola, WI 54990-0001. Don't include any numismatic material until you have received specific mailing instructions from me.

Quick check index

If you have a coin and are not sure where to look for the possible variety:

If your coin shows doubling, first check V-B-I.

Then try II-A, II-B, II-C, II-I (4 & 5), III-J, III-L, or IV-C.

If part of the coin is missing, check III-B, III-C, or III-D.

If there is a raised line of coin metal, check II-D, II-G.

If there is a raised area of coin metal, check II-E, II-F, or III-F.

If the coin is out of round, and too thin, check III-G.

If coin appears to be the wrong metal, check III-A, III-E, III-F-3 and III-G.

If the die appears to have been damaged, check II-E, II-G. (Damage to the coin itself usually is not a minting variety.)

If the coin shows incomplete or missing design, check II-A, II-E, III-B-3, III-B-5 or III-D.

If only part of the planchet was struck, check III-M.

If something was struck into the coin, check III-J and III-K.

If something has happened to the edge of the coin, check II-D-6, II-E-10, III-I, III-M and III-O.

If your coin shows other than the normal design, check II-A or II-C.

If a layer of the coin metal is missing, or a clad layer is missing, check III-B and III-D.

If you have an unstruck blank, or planchet, check I-G.

If your coin may be a restrike, check IV-C.

If your coin has a counterstamp, countermark, additional engraving or apparent official modifications, check IV-B and V-A-8.

Do not depend on the naked eye to examine your coins. Use a magnifying lens whenever possible, as circulation damage, wear and alterations frequently can be mistaken for legitimate minting varieties.

Division I: planchet varieties

The first division of the PDS System includes those minting varieties that occur in the manufacture of the planchet upon which the coins will ultimately be struck and includes classes resulting from faulty metallurgy, mechanical damage, faulty processing, or equipment or human malfunction prior to the actual coin striking.

Planchet alloy mix (I-A)

This section includes those classes pertaining to mixing and processing the various metals which will be used to make a coin alloy.

I-A-1 Improper Alloy Mix (WE), Rarity Level: 3-4, Values: $5 to $10.

I-A-2 Slag Inclusion Planchet (WE), Rarity Level: 5-6, Values: $25 up.

Damaged and defective planchets (I-B)

To be a class in this section the blank, or planchet, must for some reason not meet the normal standards or must have been damaged in processing. The classes cover the areas of defects in the melting, rolling, punching and processing of the planchets up to the point where they are sent to the coin presses to be struck.

I-B-1 Defective Planchet (WE), Rarity Level: 6, Values: $25 up.

I-B-2 Mechanically Damaged Planchet (WE), Rarity Level: –, Values: No Value. (See values for the coin struck on a mechanically damaged planchet.)

I-B-3 Rolled Thin Planchet (WE), Rarity Level: 6 - (Less rare on half cents of 1795, 1797 and restrikes of 1831-52.) Values: $10 up.

I-B-4 Rolled Thick Planchet (WE), Rarity Level: 7 - (Less rare in Colonial copper coins. Notable examples occur on the restrike half cents of 1840-52.) Values: $125 up.

I-B-5 Tapered Planchet (WE), Rarity Level: 7, Values: $25 up.

I-B-6 Partially Unplated Planchet (WE), Rarity Level: 6, Values: $15 up.

I-B-7 Unplated Planchet (WE), Rarity Level: 6-7, Values: $50 up.

I-B-8 Bubbled Plating Planchet (WE), Rarity Level: 1, Values: No Value.

I-B-9 Included Gas Bubble Planchet (WE), Rarity Level: 6-7, Values: $50 up.

I-B-10 Partially Unclad Planchet (WE), Rarity Level: 6, Values: $20 up.

I-B-11 Unclad Planchet (WE), Rarity Level: 6-7, Values: $50 up.

I-B-12 Undersize Planchet (WE), Rarity Level: 7, Values: $250 up.

I-B-13 Oversize Planchet (WE), Rarity Level: 7, Values: $250 up.

I-B-14 Improperly Prepared Proof Planchet (WE), Rarity Level: 7, Values: $100 up.

I-B-15 Improperly Annealed Planchet (WE), Rarity Level: - , Values: No Value.

I-B-16 Faulty Upset Edge Planchet (WE), Rarity Level: 5-6, Values: $10 up.

I-B-17 Rolled-In Metal Planchet (WE), Rarity Level: 6-7, Values: $50 up.

I-B-18 Weld Area Planchet (WE), Rarity Level: Unknown, Values: No Value Established. (See values for the coins struck on weld area planchets.)

I-B-19 Strike Clip Planchet (WE), Rarity Level: 7, Values: $150 up.

I-B-20 Unpunched Center-Hole Planchet (WE), Rarity Level: 5-7, Values: $5 and up.

I-B-21 Incompletely Punched Center-Hole Planchet (WE), Rarity Level: 6-7, Values: $15 up.

I-B-22 Uncentered Center-Hole Planchet (WE), Rarity Level: 6-7, Values: $10 up.

I-B-23 Multiple Punched Center-Hole Planchet (WE), Rarity Level: 7, Values: $35 up.

I-B-24 Unintended Center-Hole Planchet (WE), Rarity Level: Unknown, Values: -.

I-B-25 Wrong Size or Shape Center-Hole Planchet (IWE), Rarity Level: 5-7, Values: $10 up.

Clipped planchets (I-C)

Clipped blanks, or planchets, occur when the strip of coin metal fails to move forward between successive strokes of the gang punch to clear the previously punched holes, in the same manner as a cookie cutter overlapping a previously cut hole in the dough. The size of the clip is a function of the amount of overlap of the next punch.

The overlapping round punches produce a missing arc with curve matching the outside circumference of the blanking punch. Straight clips occur when the punch overlaps the beginning or end of a strip which has had the end sheared or sawed off. Ragged clips occur in the same manner when the ends of the strip have been left as they were rolled out.

The term "clip" as used here should not be confused with the practice of clipping or shaving small pieces of metal from a bullion coin after it is in circulation.

I-C-1 Disc Clip Planchet (WE), Rarity Level: 3-5, Values: $5 up.

I-C-2 Curved Clip Planchet - (To 5%) (WE), Rarity Level: 5-6, Values: $5 up.

I-C-3 Curved Clip Planchet - (6 to 10%) (WE), Rarity Level: 6, Values: $10 up.

I-C-4 Curved Clip Planchet - (11 to 25%) (WE), Rarity Level: 5-6, Values: $15 up.

I-C-5 Curved Clip Planchet - (26 to 60%) (WE), Rarity Level: 6-7, Values: $25 up.

I-C-6 Double Curved Clip Planchet (WE), Rarity Level: 6, Values: $10 up.

I-C-7 Triple Curved Clip Planchet (WE), Rarity Level: 5-6, Values: $25 up.

I-C-8 Multiple Curved Clip Planchet (WE), Rarity Level: 6-7, Values: $35 up.

I-C-9 Overlapping Curved Clipped Planchet (WE), Rarity Level: 6-7, Values: $50 up.

I-C-10 Incompletely Punched Curved Clip Planchet (WE), Rarity Level: 6, Values: $35 up.

I-C-11 Oval Curved Clip Planchet (WE), Rarity Level: 6-7, Values: $50 up.

I-C-12 Crescent Clip Planchet - (61% or more) (WE), Rarity Level: 7, Values: $200 up.

I-C-13 Straight Clip Planchet (WE), Rarity Level: 6, Values: $30 up.

I-C-14 Incompletely Sheared Straight Clip Planchet (WE), Rarity Level: 6, Values: $50 up.

I-C-15 Ragged Clip Planchet (WE), Rarity Level: 6-7, Values: $35 up.

I-C-16 Outside Corner Clip Planchet (E), Rarity Level: -, Values: No Value.

I-C-17 Inside Corner Clip Planchet (E), Rarity Level: -, Values: No Value.

I-C-18 Irregularly Clipped Planchet (E) Rarity Level: -, Values: Value not established.

I-C-19 Incompletely Punched Scalloped or Multi-Sided Planchet (E), Rarity Level: 7, Values: $25 up.

Laminated, split, or broken planchet (I-D)

For a variety of reasons the coin metal may split into thin layers (delaminate) and either split completely off the coin, or be retained. Common causes are included gas or alloy mix problems. Lamination cracks usually enter the surface of the planchet at a very shallow angle or are at right angles to the edge. The resulting layers differ from slag in that they appear as normal metal.

Lamination cracks and missing metal of any size below a split planchet are too common in the 35 percent silver 1942-1945 nickels to be collectible or have any significant value.

I-D-1 Small Lamination Crack Planchet (W), Rarity Level: 4-5, Values: $1 up.

I-D-2 Large Lamination Crack Planchet (W), Rarity Level: 3-4, Values: $5 up.

I-D-3 Split Planchet (W), Rarity Level: 5-6, Values: $15 up.

I-D-4 Hinged Split Planchet (W), Rarity Level: 6-7, Values: $75 up.

I-D-5 Clad Planchet With a Clad Layer Missing (W), Rarity Level: 5-6, Values: $35 up.

I-D-6 Clad Planchet With Both Clad Layers Missing (W), Rarity Level: 6-7, Values: $75 up.

I-D-7 Separated Clad Layer (W), Rarity Level: 5, Values: $25 up.

I-D-8 Broken Planchet (WE), Rarity Level: 3-4, Values: $5 up.

Wrong stock planchet (I-E)

The following classes cover those cases where the wrong coin metal stock was run through the blanking press, making blanks of the correct diameter, but of the wrong thickness, alloy or metal or a combination of the wrong thickness and the wrong metal.

I-E-1 Half Cent Stock Planchet (IE), Rarity Level: Unknown, Values: No Value Established.

I-E-2 Cent Stock Planchet (IE), Rarity Level: Unknown, Values: No Value Established.

I-E-3 Two Cent Stock Planchet (E), Rarity Level: Unknown, Values: No Value Established.

I-E-4 Three Cent Silver Stock Planchet (E), Rarity Level: Unknown, Values: No Value Established.

I-E-5 Three Cent Nickel Stock Planchet (E), Rarity Level: Unknown, Values: No Value Established.

I-E-6 Half Dime Stock Planchet (E), Rarity Level: Unknown, Values: No Value Established.

I-E-7 Dime Stock Planchet (E), Rarity Level: 7, Values: $200 up.

I-E-8 Twenty Cent Stock Planchet (E), Rarity Level: Unknown, Values: No Value Established.

I-E-9 Quarter Stock Planchet (E), Rarity Level: Unknown, Values: No Value Established.

I-E-10 Half Dollar Stock Planchet (E), Rarity Level: Unknown, Values: No Value Established.

I-E-11 Dollar Stock Planchet (E), Rarity Level: 7, Values: $300 up.

I-E-12 Token or Medal Stock Planchet (E), Rarity Level: Unknown, Values: No Value Established.

I-E-13 Wrong Thickness Spoiled Planchet (IWE), Rarity Level: Unknown, Values: No Value Established.

I-E-14 Correct Thickness Spoiled Planchet (IWE), Rarity Level: Unknown, Values: No Value Established.

I-E-15 Cut Down Struck Token Planchet (IWE), Rarity Level: Unknown, Values: No Value Established.

I-E-16 Experimental or Pattern Stock Planchet (IE), Rarity Level: Unknown, Values: No Value Established.

I-E-17 Proof Stock Planchet (IE), Rarity Level: Unknown, Values: No Value Established.

I-E-18 Adjusted Specification Stock Planchet (IE), Rarity Level: 7, Values: $25 up.

I-E-19 Trial Strike Stock Planchet (IE), Rarity Level: Unknown, Values: No Value Established.

I-E-20 U.S. Punched Foreign Stock Planchet (E), Rarity Level: 7, Values: $75 up.

I-E-21 Foreign Punched Foreign Stock Planchet (E), Rarity Level: 7, Values: $75 up.

I-E-22 Non-Standard Coin Alloy Planchet (IE), Rarity Level: 7, Values: Unknown.

Extra metal on a blank, or planchet (I-F)

True extra metal is only added to the blank during the blanking operation. This occurs as metal is scraped off the sides of the blanks as they are driven down through the thimble, or lower die in the blanking press. The metal is eventually picked up by a blank passing through, welded to it by the heat of friction.

A second form of extra metal has been moved to this section, the sintered coating planchet, the metal deposited on the planchet in the form of dust during the annealing operation.

I-F-1 Extra Metal on a Type 1 Blank (W), Rarity Level: 7, Values: $50 up.
I-F-2 Extra Metal on a Type 2 Planchet (W), Rarity Level: 6-7, Values: $75 up.
I-F-3 Sintered Coating Planchet (W), Rarity Level: 7, Values: $75 up.

Normal or abnormal planchets (I-G)

This section consists of the two principal forms – the blank as it comes from the blanking press – and in the form of a planchet after it has passed through the upsetting mill. It also includes a class for purchased planchets and one for planchets produced by the mint.
I-G-1 Type I Blank (IWE), Rarity Level: 3-5, Values: $2 up.
I-G-2 Type II Planchet (IWE), Rarity Level: 3-4, Values: 50 up.
I-G-3 Purchased Planchet (I), Rarity Level: 1, Values: No Value.
I-G-4 Mint Made Planchet (I), Rarity Level: 1, Values: No Value.
I-G-5 Adjustment-Marked Planchet (I), Rarity Level: Unknown, Values: No Value.
I-G-6 Hardness Test-Marked Planchet (I), Rarity Level: -, Values: No Value Established.
Note: There are no classes between I-G-6 and I-G-23
I-G-23 Proof Planchet (IE), Rarity Level: 6-7, Values: $1 up.

Coin metal strip (I-H)

When the coin metal strip passes through the blanking press it goes directly to a chopper. This cuts the remaining web into small pieces to be sent back to the melting furnace. Pieces of the web or the chopped up web may escape into the hands of collectors.
I-H-1 Punched Coin Metal Strip (IWE), Rarity Level: 4-6, Values: $5 up, depending on size, denomination and number of holes showing.
I-H-2 Chopped Coin Metal Strip (IE), Rarity Level: 3-5, Values: $5 up.

The die varieties
Division II

Die varieties may be unique to a given die, but will repeat for the full life of the die unless a further change occurs. Anything that happens to the die will affect the appearance of the struck coin. This includes all the steps of the die making:

● Cutting a die blank from a tool steel bar.
● Making the design.
● Transferring it to a model.
● Transferring it to the master die or hub.
● The hubbing process of making the die.
● Punching in the mintmark.
● Heat treating of the die.

The completed dies are also subject to damage in numerous forms, plus wear and tear during the striking process and repair work done with abrasives. All of these factors can affect how the struck coin looks.

Engraving varieties (II-A)

In all cases in this section where a master die, or master hub is affected by the class, the class will affect all the working hubs and all working dies descending from it.
Identification as being on a master die or hub depends on it being traced to two or more of the working hubs descended from the same master tools.
II-A-1 Overdate (IE), Rarity Level: 1-7, Values: $1 up.
II-A-2 Doubled Date (IE), Rarity Level: 1-7, Values: $1 up.
II-A-3 Small Date (IE), Rarity Level: 2-5, Values: $1 up.
II-A-4 Large Date (IE), Rarity Level: 2-5, Values: $1 up.
II-A-5 Small Over Large Date (IE), Rarity Level: 4-6, Values: $15 up.
II-A-6 Large Over Small Date (IE), Rarity Level: 3-5, Values: $10 up.
II-A-7 Blundered Date (E), Rarity Level: 6-7, Values: $50 up.
II-A-8 Corrected Blundered Date (IE), Rarity Level: 3-5, Values: $5 up.

II-A-9 Wrong Font Date Digit (IE), Rarity Level: 5-6, Values: Minimal.

II-A-10 Worn, Broken or Damaged Punch (IWE), Rarity Level: 5-6, Values: $5 up.

II-A-11 Expedient Punch (IWE), Rarity Level: 5-6, Values: $10 up.

II-A-12 Blundered Digit (E), Rarity Level: 4-5, Values: $50 up.

II-A-13 Corrected Blundered Digit (IE), Rarity Level: 3-6, Values: $10 up.

II-A-14 Doubled Digit (IWE), Rarity Level: 2-6, Values: $2 up.

II-A-15 Wrong Style or Font Letter or Digit (IE), Rarity Level: 3-5, Values: Minimal.

II-A-16 One Style or Font Over Another (IE), Rarity Level: 4-6, Values: $10 up.

II-A-17 Letter Over Digit (E), Rarity Level: 6-7, Values: $25 up.

II-A-18 Digit Over Letter (E), Rarity Level: 6-7, Values: $25 up.

II-A-19 Omitted Letter or Digit (IWE), Rarity Level: 4-6, Values: $5 up.

II-A-20 Blundered Letter (E), Rarity Level: 6-7, Values: $50 up.

II-A-21 Corrected Blundered Letter (IE), Rarity Level: 1-3, Values: $10 up.

II-A-22 Doubled Letter (IWE), Rarity Level: 2-6, Values: $2 up.

II-A-23 Blundered Design Element (IE), Rarity Level: 6-7, Values: $50 up.

II-A-24 Corrected Blundered Design Element (IE), Rarity Level: 3-5, Values: $10 up.

II-A-25 Large Over Small Design Element (IE), Rarity Level: 4-6, Values: $2 up.

II-A-26 Omitted Design Element (IWE), Rarity Level: 5-7, Values: $10 up.

II-A-27 Doubled Design Element (IWE), Rarity Level: 2-6, Values: $2 up.

II-A-28 One Design Element Over Another (IE), Rarity Level: 3-6, Values: $5 up.

II-A-29 Reducing Lathe Doubling (WE), Rarity Level: 6-7, Values: $50 up.

II-A-30 Extra Design Element (IE), Rarity Level: 3-5, Values: $10 up.

II-A-31 Modified Design (IWE), Rarity Level: 1-5, Values: No Value up.

II-A-32 Normal Design (I), Rarity Level: 1, Values: No Extra Value.

II-A-33 Design Mistake (IE), Rarity Level: 2-6, Values: $1 up.

II-A-34 Defective Die Design (IWE), Rarity Level: 1, Values: No Value.

II-A-35 Pattern (I), Rarity Level: 6-7, Values: $100 up.

II-A-36 Trial Design (I), Rarity Level: 5-7, Values: $100 up.

II-A-37 Omitted Designer's Initial (IWE), Rarity Level: 3-7, Values: $1 up.

II-A-38 Layout Mark (IE), Rarity Level: 5-7, Values: Minimal.

II-A-39 Abnormal Reeding (IWE), Rarity Level: 2-5, Values: $1 up.

II-A-40 Modified Die or Hub (IWE), Rarity Level: 1-5, Values: No Value up.

II-A-41 Numbered Die (I), Rarity Level: 3-5, Values: $5 up.

II-A-42 Plugged Die (IW), Rarity Level: 5-6, Values: Minimal.

II-A-43 Cancelled Die (IE), Rarity Level: 3-6, Values: No Value up.

II-A-44 Hardness Test Marked Die (IE), Rarity Level: 7, Values: $100 up.

II-A-45 Coin Simulation (IE), Rarity Level: 6-7, Values: $100 up, but may be illegal to own.

II-A-46 Punching Mistake (IE), Rarity Level: 2-6, Values: $1 up.

II-A-47 Small Over Large Design (IE), Rarity Level: 4-6, Values: $5 up.

II-A-48 Doubled Punch (IE), Rarity Level: 5-7, Values: $5 up.

II-A-49 Mint Display Sample (I) Rarity Level: 7, Values not established.

II-A-50 Center Dot, Stud or Circle (IE) Rarity Level: 7, much more common on early cents, Values not established

Hub doubling varieties (II-B)

This section includes eight classes of hub doubling. Each class is from a different cause, described by the title of the class. At the latest count over 2,500 doubled dies have been reported in the U.S. coinage, the most famous being examples of the 1955, 1969-S and 1972 cent dies.

Rotated hub doubling

Hub break

II-B-I Rotated Hub Doubling (WE), Rarity Level: 3-6, Values: $1 up

II-B-II Distorted Hub Doubling (WE), Rarity Level: 3-6, Values: $1 up.

II-B-III Design Hub Doubling (IWE), Rarity Level: 3-6, Values: $1 up to five figure amounts.

II-B-IV Offset Hub Doubling (WE), Rarity Level: 4-6, Values: $15 up.

II-B-V Pivoted Hub Doubling (WE), Rarity Level: 3-6, Values: $10 up.

II-B-VI Distended Hub Doubling (WE), Rarity Level: 2-5, Values: $1 up.

II-B-VII Modified Hub Doubling (IWE), Rarity Level: 2-5, Values: $1 up.

II-B-VIII Tilted Hub Doubling (WE), Rarity Level: 4-6, Values: $5 up.

Mintmark varieties (II-C)

Double   Triple

Mintmarks are punched into U.S. coin dies by hand (Up to 1985 for proof coins, to 1990 for cents and nickels and 1991 for other denominations). Variations resulting from mistakes in the punching are listed in this section. Unless exceptionally mispunched, values are usually estimated at 150 percent of numismatic value. Slightly tilted or displaced mintmarks have no value.

II-C-1 Doubled Mintmark (IE), Rarity Level: 2-6, Values: 50 cents up.

II-C-2 Separated Doubled Mintmark (IE), Rarity Level: 5-6, Values: $15 up.

II-C-3 Over Mintmark (IE), Rarity Level: 3-6, Values: $2 up.

II-C-4 Tripled Mintmark (IE), Rarity Level: 3-5, Values: 50 up.

II-C-5 Quadrupled Mintmark (IE), Rarity Level: 4-6, Values: $1 up.

II-C-6 Small Mintmark (IE), Rarity Level: 2-5, Values: No Extra Value up.

II-C-7 Large Mintmark (IE), Rarity Level: 2-5, Values: No Extra Value up.

II-C-8 Large Over Small Mintmark (IE), Rarity Level: 2-5, Values: $2 up.

II-C-9 Small Over Large Mintmark (IE), Rarity Level: 3-6, Values: $5 up.

II-C-10 Broken Mintmark Punch (W), Rarity Level: 5-6, Values: $5 up.

II-C-11 Omitted Mintmark (IWE), Rarity Level: 4-7, Values: $125 up.

II-C-12 Tilted Mintmark (IE), Rarity Level: 5-7, Values: $5 up.

II-C-13 Blundered Mintmark (E), Rarity Level: 4-6, Values: $5 up.

II-C-14 Corrected Horizontal Mintmark (IE), Rarity Level: 4-6, Values: $5 up.

II-C-15 Corrected Upside Down Mintmark (IE), Rarity Level: 4-6, Values: $5 up.

II-C-16 Displaced Mintmark (IE), Rarity Level: 4-6, Values: $5 to $10.

II-C-17 Modified Mintmark (IWE), Rarity Level: 1-4, Values: No Extra Value up.

II-C-18 Normal Mintmark (I), Rarity Level: 1, Values: No Extra Value.

II-C-19 Doubled Mintmark Punch (I), Rarity Level: 6-7, Values: No Extra Value up.

II-C-20 Upside Down Mintmark (E) Rarity Level 6-7, Values: $5 up.

II-C-21 Horizontal Mintmark (E) Rarity Level 6-7, Values: $5 up.

II-C-22 Wrong Mintmark (E) Rarity Level 6-7, Values $15 up. (Example has a D mintmark in the date, but was used at Philadelphia.)

Die, collar and hub cracks (II-D)

Die cracks

Cracks in the surface of the die allow coin metal to be forced into the crack during the strike, resulting in raised irregular lines of coin metal above the normal surface of the coin. These are one of the commonest forms of die damage and wear, making them easily collectible.

Collar cracks and hub cracks are added to this section because the causes and effects are similar or closely associated.

Die cracks, collar cracks and hub cracks are the result of wear and tear on the tools, with intentional use assumed for all classes.

II-D-1 Die Crack (W), Rarity Level: 1-3, Values: 10 to $1, $25 up on a proof coin with a rarity level of 6-7.

II-D-2 Multiple Die Cracks (W), Rarity Level: 1-3, Values: 25 cents to $2.

II-D-3 Head-To-Rim Die Crack (Lincoln Cent) (W), Rarity Level: 2-6, Values: 25 to $10 for multiple die cracks.

II-D-4 Split Die (W), Rarity Level: 5-6, Values: $10 up.

II-D-5 Rim-To-Rim Die Crack (W), Rarity Level: 2-5, Values: $1 up.

II-D-6 Collar Crack (W), Rarity Level: 4-6, Values: $10 up.

II-D-7 Hub Crack (W), Rarity Level: 3-5, Values: $1-$2.

Die breaks (II-E)

Small die break II-E-2

Clogged letter II-E-1

Major die break II-E-5

Rim die break II-E-4

Breaks in the surface of the die allow coin metal to squeeze into the resulting holes, causing raised irregular areas above the normal surface of the coin. Die chips and small die breaks are nearly as common as the die cracks, but major die breaks, which extend in from the edge of the coin, are quite rare on the larger coins.

If the broken piece of the die is retained, the resulting design will be above or below the level of the rest of the surface.

II-E-1 Die Chip (W), Rarity Level: 1-2, Values: 10 to $1.

II-E-2 Small Die Break (W), Rarity Level: 1-3, Values: 10 to $2.

II-E-3 Large Die Break (W), Rarity Level: 3-5, Values: $1 to $50 and up.

II-E-4 Rim Die Break (W), Rarity Level: 2-3, Values: 25 cents to $5.

II-E-5 Major Die Break (WE), Rarity Level: 3-6, Values: $5 to $100 and up.

II-E-6 Retained Broken Die (W), Rarity Level: 3-5, Values: $1 to $10 and up.

II-E-7 Retained Broken Center of the Die (W), Rarity Level: 6-7, Values: $100 up.

II-E-8 Laminated Die (W), Rarity Level: 3-5, Values: 10 cents to $5.

II-E-9 Chipped Chrome Plating (W), Rarity Level: 4-5, Values: $10 to $25 on proofs.

II-E-10 Collar Break (W), Rarity Level: 4-6, Values: $5 to $25 and up.

II-E-11 Broken Letter or Digit on an Edge Die (W), Rarity Level: 4-6, Values: Minimal.

II-E-12 "Bar" Die Break (W), Rarity Level: 3-5, Values: 25 to $20.

II-E-13 Hub Break (W), Rarity Level: 4-6, Values: 50 to $10 and up.

"BIE" varieties (II-F)

A series of small die breaks or die chips in the letters of "LIBERTY" mostly on the wheat-reverse Lincoln cent are actively collected. The name results from the resemblance to an "I" between the "B" and "E" on many of the dies, but they are found between all of the letters in different cases. Well over 1,500 dies are known and cataloged. Numerous more recent examples are known.

BIE variety II-F-4

II-F-1 ILI Die Variety (W), Rarity Level: 4-5, Values: 25 cents to $10.
II-F-2 LII Die Variety (W), Rarity Level: 3-5, Values: 50 cents to $15.
II-F-3 IIB Die Variety (W), Rarity Level: 3-5, Values: 50 cents to $15.
II-F-4 BIE Die Variety (W), Rarity Level: 3-5, Values: $1 to $20.
II-F-5 EIR Die Variety (W), Rarity Level: 3-5, Values: 50 to $15.
II-F-6 RIT Die Variety (W), Rarity Level: 4-5, Values: $2 to $25.
II-F-7 TIY Die Variety (W), Rarity Level: 4-5, Values: $5 to $30.
II-F-8 TYI Die Variety (W), Rarity Level: 4-5, Values: $2 to $25.

Worn and damaged dies, collars and hubs (II-G)

Die clashes and design transfer

Many dies are continued deliberately in service after they have been damaged, dented, clashed or show design transfer, since none of these classes actually affect anything but the appearance ofthe coin. The root cause is wear, but intent or mistakes may enter the picture.

II-G-1 Dented Die, Collar or Hub (IWE), Rarity Level: 3-5, Values: 25 to $5.

II-G-2 Damaged Die, Collar or Hub (IWE), Rarity Level: 3-5, Values: 25 to $5.

II-G-3 Worn Die, Collar or Hub (IWE), Rarity Level: 2-3, Values: No Extra Value to Minimal Value.

II-G-4 Pitted or Rusted Die, Collar or Hub (IWE), Rarity Level: 3-4, Values:No Extra Value, marker only.

II-G-5 Heavy Die Clash (IWE), Rarity Level: 4-5, Values: $1 to $10 and up.

II-G-6 Heavy Collar Clash (IWE), Rarity Level: 3-4, Values: $1 to $5 and up.

II-G-7 Heavy Design Transfer (IWE), Rarity Level: 3-4, Values: 10 cents to $1.

Die progressions (II-H)

The progression section consists of three classes. These are useful as cataloging tools for many different die varieties, but especially the die cracks and die breaks which may enlarge, lengthen or increase in number.

II-H-1 Progression (W), Rarity Level: 3-5, Values: $1 up.

II-H-2 Die Substitution (IW), Rarity Level: 2-4, Values: No Extra Value to Minimal Value.

II-H-3 Die Repeat (I), Rarity Level: 2-4, Values: No Extra Value to Minimal Value.

Die scratches, polished and abraded dies (II-I)

Die scratches II-I-1

This section consists of those classes having to do with the use of an abrasive in some form to intentionally polish proof dies, or repair the circulating die surface. Several classes which previously were referred to as "polished" now are listed as "abraded."

II-I-1 Die Scratch (IW), Rarity Level: 1-2, Values: No Extra Value to 10 cents to 25 cents, as a marker.

II-I-2 Polished (proof) Die (IW), Rarity Level: 1, Values: No Extra Value.

II-I-3 Abraded (Circulation) Die (IW), Rarity Level: 1-2, Values: No Extra Value up to $10.

II-I-4 Inside Abraded Die Doubling (IW), Rarity Level: 1-3, Values: No Extra Value to $1.

II-I-5 Outside Abraded Die Doubling (IW), Rarity Level: 1-3, Values: No Extra Value to $1.

II-I-6 Lathe Marks (IW), Rarity Level: 5-7, Values: No Extra Value, marker only.

Striking varieties
Division III

Once the dies are made and the planchets have been prepared, they are struck by a pair of dies and become a coin. In this division, we list the misstrikes resulting from human or mechanical malfunction in the striking process. These are one-of-a-kind varieties, but there may be many similar coins that fall in a given class.

Multiples and combinations of classes must be considered on a case by case basis. The first several sections match the planchet sections indicated in the title.

Struck on defective alloy mix planchets (III-A)

This section includes those classes of coins struck on planchets that were made from a defective alloy.

III-A-1 Struck on an Improper Alloy Mix Planchet (IE), Rarity Level: 2-3, Values: 10 cents to $2.

III-A-2 Struck on a Planchet With Slag Inclusions(IE), Rarity Level: 5-6, Values: $10 up.

Struck on damaged, defective or abnormal planchet (III-B)

Coins get struck on many strange objects. The more common of course are planchets which have been damaged in some way in the production process. In most of the classes in this section intent is at least presumed, if not specifically listed as a cause.

III-B-1 Struck on a Defective Planchet (IWE), Rarity Level: 4-6, Values: $5 to $10 and up.

III-B-2 Struck on a Mechanically Damaged Planchet (IWE), Rarity Level: 5-6, Values: $10 to $20 and up.

III-B-3 Struck on a Rolled Thin Planchet (IWE), Rarity Level: 5-6, Values: $2 to $5 and up.

III-B-4 Struck on a Rolled Thick Planchet (IWE), Rarity Level: 5-6, Values: $35 to $50 and up.

III-B-5 Struck on a Tapered Planchet (WE), Rarity Level: 4-6, Values: $2 to $5 and up.

III-B-6 Struck on a Partially Unplated Planchet (WE), Rarity Level: 5, Values: $10 up.

III-B-7 Struck on an Unplated Planchet (WE), Rarity Level: 6-7, Values: $100 up.

III-B-8 Struck on a Bubbled Plating Planchet (IWE), Rarity Level: 1, Values: No Value.

III-B-9 Struck on an Included Gas Bubble Planchet (WE), Rarity Level: 5-6, Values: $5 up.

III-B-10 Struck on a Partially Unclad Planchet (WE), Rarity Level: 5-6, Values: $5 up.

III-B-11 Struck on an Unclad Planchet (WE), Rarity Level: 4-5, Values: $5 and up.

III-B-12 Struck on an Undersize Planchet (WE), Rarity Level: 4-6, Values: Minimal.

III-B-13 Struck on an Oversize Planchet (WE), Rarity Level: 6-7, Values: Minimal.

III-B-14 Struck on an Improperly Prepared Proof Planchet (IWE), Rarity Level: 3-5, Values: $5 up.

III-B-15 Struck on an Improperly Annealed Planchet (IWE), Rarity Level: 4-5, Values: $5 up.

III-B-16 Struck on a Faulty Upset Edge Planchet (IWE), Rarity Level: 4-5, Values: $1 to $2.

III-B-17 Struck on a Rolled In Metal Planchet (WE), Rarity Level: 4-6, Values: $2 up.

III-B-18 Struck on a Weld Area Planchet (WE), Rarity Level: 6, Values: $25 to $50.

III-B-19 Struck on a Strike Clip Planchet (W), Rarity Level: 6-7, Values: $25 up.

III-B-20 Struck on an Unpunched Center Hole Planchet (WE), Rarity Level: 4-6, Values: $1 and up.

III-B-21 Struck on an Incompletely Punched Center Hole Planchet (WE), Rarity Level: 6-7, Values: $5 up.

III-B-22 Struck on an Uncentered Center Hole Planchet (WE), Rarity Level: 6-7, Values: $10 up.

III-B-23 Struck on a Multiple Punched Center Hole Planchet (WE), Rarity Level: 7, Values: $25 up.

III-B-24 Struck on an Unintended Center Hole Planchet (WE), Rarity Level: 6-7, Values: $25 and up.

III-B-25 Struck on a Wrong Size or Shape Center Hole Planchet (WE), Rarity Level: 5-7, Values: $5 up.

III-B-26 Struck on Scrap Coin Metal (E), Rarity Level: 4-6, Values: $10 up.

III-B-27 Struck on Junk Non Coin Metal (E), Rarity Level: 4-6, Values: $15 up.

III-B-28 Struck on a False Planchet (E), Rarity Level: 3-5, Values: $35 up.

III-B-29 Struck on Bonded Planchets (E), Rarity Level: 6-7, Values: $50 up.

Struck on a defective planchet III-B-1   Struck on a tapered planchet III-B-5

Struck on a clipped planchet (III-C)

Coins struck on clipped blanks, or planchets, exhibit the same missing areas as they did before striking, modified by the metal flow from the strike which rounds the edges and tends to move metal into the missing areas. Values for blanks will run higher than planchets with similar clips.

III-C-1 Struck on a Disc Clip Planchet (WE), Rarity Level: 4-5, Values: $1 on regular coins, $20 and up for clad coins.

III-C-2 Struck on a Curved Clip Planchet - to 5% (WE), Rarity Level: 3-5, Values: 50 cents up.

III-C-3 Struck on a Curved Clip Planchet - (6 to 10%) (WE), Rarity Level: 4-5, Values: $1 up.

III-C-4 Struck on a Curved Clip Planchet - (11 to 25%) (WE), Rarity Level: 4-5, Values: $2 up.

III-C-5 Struck on a Curved Clip Planchet - (26 to 60%) (WE), Rarity Level: 4-6, Values: $10 up.

III-C-6 Struck on a Double Curved Clip Planchet (WE), Rarity Level: 3-4, Values: $2 up.

III-C-7 Struck on a Triple Curved Clip Planchet (WE), Rarity Level: 4-5, Values: $5 up.

III-C-8 Struck on a Multiple Curved Clip Planchet (WE), Rarity Level: 4-6, Values: $5 up.

III-C-9 Struck on an Overlapping Curved Clipped Planchet (WE), Rarity Level: 5-6, Values: $15 up.

III-C-10 Struck on an Incomplete Curved Clip Planchet (WE), Rarity Level: 4-5, Values: $10 up.

III-C-11 Struck on an Oval Clip Planchet (WE), Rarity Level: 5-6, Values: $20 up.

III-C-12 Struck on a Crescent Clip Planchet - (61% or more) (WE), Rarity Level: 6-7, Values: $100 up.

III-C-13 Struck on a Straight Clip Planchet (E), Rarity Level: 4-6, Values: $10 up.

III-C-14 Struck on an Incomplete Straight Clip Planchet (WE), Rarity Level: 5-6, Values: $20 up.

III-C-15 Struck on a Ragged Clip Planchet (E), Rarity Level: 4-6, Values: $15 up.

III-C-16 Struck on an Outside Corner Clip Planchet (E), Rarity Level: 7, Values: $100 up.

III-C-17 Struck on an Inside Corner Clip Planchet (E), Rarity Level: Unknown outside mint., Values: -.

III-C-18 Struck on an Irregularly Clipped Planchet (E), Rarity Level: 6-7, Values: $20 up.

III-C-19 Struck on an Incompletely Punched Scalloped or Multi-Sided Planchet (E), Rarity Level: 7, Values: $20 up.

Ragged edge clip III-C-15

Multiple clip III-C-8   **Incomplete curved clip III-C-10**

Struck on a laminated, split or broken planchet (III-D)

This section has to do with the splitting, cracking or breaking of a coin parallel to the faces of the coin, or at least very nearly parallel, or breaks at right angles to the faces of the coin.

Lamination cracks and missing metal of any size below a split planchet are too common in the 35-percent silver 1942-1945 nickels to be collectible or have any significant value.

III-D-1 Struck on a Small Lamination Crack Planchet (W), Rarity Level: 3-4, Values: 10 up.

III-D-2 Struck on a Large Lamination Crack Planchet (W), Rarity Level: 3-6, Values: $1 up.

III-D-3 Struck on a Split Planchet (W), Rarity Level: 4-6, Values: $5 up.

III-D-4 Struck on a Hinged Split Planchet (W), Rarity Level: 5-6, Values: $35 up.

III-D-5 Struck on a Planchet With a Clad Layer Missing (W), Rarity Level: 4-5, Values: $15 up.

III-D-6 Struck on a Planchet With Both Clad Layers Missing (W), Rarity Level: 4-5, Values: $25 up.

III-D-7 Struck on a Separated Clad Layer or Lamination (W), Rarity Level: 6-7, Values: $75 up.

III-D-8 Struck on a Broken Planchet Before the Strike (W), Rarity Level: 3-5, Values: $10 up.

III-D-9 Broken Coin During or After the Strike (W), Rarity Level: 4-6, Values: $20 up.

III-D-10 Struck Coin Fragment Split or Broken During or After the Strike (W), Rarity Level: 3-5, Values: $5 up.

III-D-11 Reedless Coin Broken During or After the Strike (W), Rarity Level: Unknown, Values: -.

Lamination crack III-D-1   **Split planchet III-D-3**   **Layer peeled off III-D-2**

Struck on wrong stock planchets (III-E)

These classes cover those cases where the wrong stock was run through the blanking press, making planchets of the correct diameter, but of the wrong thickness, alloy or metal or a combination of incorrect thickness and metal.

III-E-1 Struck on a Half Cent-Stock Planchet (IE), Rarity Level: Unknown, Values: No Value Established.

III-E-2 Struck on a Cent-Stock Planchet (IE), Rarity Level: Unknown, Values: No Value Established.

III-E-3 Struck on a Two-Cent-Stock Planchet (E), Rarity Level: Unknown, Values: -.

III-E-4 Struck on a Three-Cent-Silver Stock Planchet (E), Rarity Level: Unknown, Values: -.

III-E-5 Struck on a Three-Cent-Nickel Stock Planchet (E), Rarity Level: Unknown, Values: -.

III-E-6 Struck on a Half Dime-Stock Planchet (E), Rarity Level: Unknown, Values: -.

III-E-7 Struck on a Dime-Stock Planchet (E), Rarity Level: 5-6, Values: $20 up.

III-E-8 Struck on a Twenty-Cent-Stock Planchet (E), Rarity Level: Unknown, Values: -.

III-E-9 Struck on a Quarter-Stock Planchet (E), Rarity Level: 6, Values: $50 up.

III-E-10 Struck on a Half Dollar-Stock Planchet (E), Rarity Level: 6-7, Values: $100 up.

III-E-11 Struck on a Dollar-Stock Planchet (E), Rarity Level: 6-7, Values: $300 up.

III-E-12 Struck on a Token/Medal-Stock Planchet (E), Rarity Level: 7, Values: No Value Established.

III-E-13 Struck on a Wrong Thickness Spoiled Planchet (IWE), Rarity Level: 7, Values: $50 up.

III-E-14 Struck on a Correct Thickness Spoiled Planchet (IWE), Rarity Level: Unknown, Values: No Value Established.

III-E-15 Struck on a Cut Down Struck Token (IWE), Rarity Level: 6-7, Values: $50 up.

III-E-16 Struck on an Experimental or Pattern-Stock Planchet (IE), Rarity Level: 7, Values: $50 up.

III-E-17 Struck on a Proof-Stock Planchet (IE), Rarity Level: 7, Values: $100 up.

III-E-18 Struck on an Adjusted Specification-Stock Planchet (IE), Rarity Level: 3-7, Values: No Value to $5 and up.

III-E-19 Struck on a Trial Strike-Stock Planchet (IE), Rarity Level: Unknown, Values: No Value Established.

III-E-20 U.S. Coin Struck on a Foreign-Stock Planchet. (E), Rarity Level: 5, Values: $35 up.

III-E-21 Foreign Coin Struck on a Foreign-Stock Planchet (E), Rarity Level: 5-6, Values: $25 up.

III-E-22 Struck on a Non-Standard Coin Alloy (IE), Rarity Level: 4-7, Values: $20 up.

Quarter on dime stock III-E-7 (lower coin edge)

Extra metal on a struck coin (III-F)

The term "extra metal" for the purpose of this section includes both extra metal added to the blank during the blanking operation and metal powder added to the planchet during the annealing operation.

III-F-1 Struck on a Type 1 Blank With Extra Metal (W), Rarity Level: Unknown, Values:

III-F-2 Struck on a Type 2 Planchet With Extra Metal (W), Rarity Level: 4-5, Values: $10 up.

III-F-3 Struck on a Sintered Coating Planchet (W), Rarity Level: 6-7, Values: $35 up.

Sintered coating III-F-3

Struck on normal or abnormal blanks, or planchets (III-G)

This section includes coins struck on either a blank, as it comes from the blanking press, or as a planchet that has passed through the upsetting mill. Added to this section are those planchets which are normal until they are struck by the wrong dies. These differ from the wrong stock planchets because the wrong stock planchets are already a variety before they are struck.

III-G-1 Struck on a Type 1 Blank (IWE), Rarity Level: 4-6, Values: $10 up.

III-G-2 Struck on a Type 2 Planchet (I), Rarity Level: 1, Values: No Extra Value.

III-G-3 Struck on a Purchased Planchet (I), Rarity Level: 1, Values: No Extra Value.

III-G-4 Struck on a Mint-Made Planchet (I), Rarity Level: 1, Values: No Extra Value.

III-G-5 Struck on an Adjustment-Marked Planchet (I), Rarity Level: 4-7, Values: Minimal, and may reduce value of coin in some cases.

III-G-6 Struck on a Hardness Test-Marked Planchet (I), Rarity Level: 6-7, Values: $10 up.

III-G-7 Wrong Planchet or Metal on a Half Cent Planchet (IE), Rarity Level: 5-7, Values: $100 up.

III-G-8 Wrong Planchet or Metal on a Cent Planchet (IE), Rarity Level: 3-6, Values: $25 up.

III-G-9 Wrong Planchet or Metal on a Nickel Planchet (E), Rarity Level: 4-6, Values: $35 up

III-G-10 Wrong Planchet or Metal on a Dime Planchet (E), Rarity Level: 4-6, Values: $50 up.

III-G-11 Wrong Planchet or Metal on a Quarter Planchet (E), Rarity Level: 4-6. Values: $100 up.

III-G-12 Wrong Planchet or Metal on a Half Dollar Planchet (E), Rarity Level: 6-7, Values: $500 up.

III-G-13 Wrong Planchet or Metal on a Dollar Planchet (E), Rarity Level: 7, Values: $500 up.

III-G-14 Wrong Planchet or Metal on a Gold Planchet (E), Rarity Level: 7, Values: $1000 up.

III-G-15 Struck on a Wrong Series Planchet (IE), Rarity Level: 6-7, Values: $1500 up.

III-G-16 U.S. Coin Struck on a Foreign Planchet (E), Rarity Level: 5-7, Values: $35 up.

III-G-17 Foreign Coin Struck on a U.S. Planchet (E), Rarity Level: 6-7, Values: $50 up.

III-G-18 Foreign Coin Struck on a Wrong Foreign Planchet (E), Rarity Level: 6-7, Values: $50 up.

III-G-19 Struck on a Medal Planchet (E), Rarity Level: 6-7, Values: $100 up.

III-G-20 Medal Struck on a Coin Planchet (IE), Rarity Level: 3-5, Values: $10 up.

III-G-21 Struck on an Official Sample Planchet (IE), Rarity Level: Unknown, Values: No Value Established.

III-G-22 Struck Intentionally on a Wrong Planchet (I), Rarity Level: 6-7, Values: Mainly struck as Presentation Pieces, full numismatic value.

III-G-23 Non-Proof Struck on a Proof Planchet (IE), Rarity Level: 6-7, Values: $500 up.

Cent on dime planchet III-G-10

Half on dime planchet III-G-12

Half on quarter planchet III-G-11

Struck on coin metal strip (III-H)

Pieces of the coin metal strip do manage at times to escape into the coin press.

III-H-1 (See I-H-1 Punched Coin Metal Strip), Rarity Level: Impossible, Values: -.

III-H-2 Struck on Chopped Coin Metal Strip (E), Rarity Level: 6-7, Values: $25 up.

Die adjustment strikes (III-I)

As the dies are set up and adjusted in the coin press, variations in the strike occur until the dies are properly set. Test strikes are normally scrapped, but on occasion reach circulation.

III-I-1 Die Adjustment Strike (IE), Rarity Level: 5-6, Values: $35 up.

III-I-2 Edge Strike (E), Rarity Level: 5-6, Values: $10 to $20 and up.

III-I-3 Weak Strike (W), Rarity Level: 1, Values: No Extra Value.

III-I-4 Strong Strike (IWE), Rarity Level: 1, Values: No value except for the premium that might be paid for a well struck coin.

III-I-5 Jam Strike (IE), Rarity Level: 7, Values: $50 up.

III-I-6 Trial Piece Strike (I), Rarity Level: 6-7, Values: $100 up.

III-I-7 Edge-Die Adjustment Strike (I), Rarity Level: 5-7, Values: $5 up.

III-I-8 Uniface Strike (I), Rarity Level 7, Values: $50 up.

Indented, brockage and counter-brockage strikes (III-J)

Indented and uniface strikes involve an extra unstruck planchet between one of the dies and the planchet being struck. Brockage strikes involve a struck coin between one of the dies and the planchet and a counter-brockage requires a brockage coin between one of the dies and the planchet.

A cap, or capped die strike results when a coin sticks to the die and is squeezed around it in the shape of a bottle cap.

III-J-1 Indented Strike (W), Rarity Level: 3-6, Values: $5 up.

III-J-2 Uniface Strike (W), Rarity Level: 3-5, Values: $15 up.

III-J-3 Indented Strike By a Smaller Planchet (WE), Rarity Level: 5-7, Values: $100 up.

III-J-4 Indented Second Strike (W), Rarity Level: 3-5, Values: $10 up, about the same as a regular double strike of comparable size.

III-J-5 Partial Brockage Strike (W), Rarity Level: 3-6, Values: $15 up.

III-J-6 Full Brockage Strike (W), Rarity Level: 3-6, Values: $5 up.

III-J-7 Brockage Strike of a Smaller Coin (WE), Rarity Level: 6-7, Values: $200 up.

III-J-8 Brockage Strike of a Struck Coin Fragment (WE), Rarity Level: 4-6, Values: $5 up.

III-J-9 Brockage Second Strike (WE), Rarity Level: 3-5, Values: $5 up.

III-J-10 Partial Counter-Brockage Strike (WE), Rarity Level: 3-5, Values: $10 up.

III-J-11 Full Counter-Brockage Strike (WE), Rarity Level: 5-7, Values: $100 up.

III-J-12 Counter-Brockage Second Strike (WE), Rarity Level: 4-6, Values: $10 up.

III-J-13 Full Brockage-Counter-Brockage Strike (WE), Rarity Level: 6-7, Values: $150 up.

III-J-14 Multiple Brockage or Counter-Brockage Strike (WE), Rarity Level: 5-7, Values: $100 up.

III-J-15 Capped Die Strike (WE), Rarity Level: 6-7, Values: $500 up.

III-J-16 Reversed Capped Die Strike (WE), Rarity Level: 7, Values: $1,000 up.

Indented strike III-J-1   Counter-brockage strike III-J-11   Capped die strike III-J-15

Struck through abnormal objects (III-K)

This section covers most of the objects or materials which might come between the planchet and the die and be struck into the surface of the coin. Unless noted, the materials - even the soft ones - are driven into the surface of the coin.

III-K-1 Struck Through Cloth (IWE), Rarity Level: 3-6, Values: $35 up.

III-K-2 Struck Through Wire (IWE), Rarity Level: 3-6, Values: $5 up.

III-K-3 Struck Through Thread (IWE), Rarity Level: 3-6, Values: $5 up.

III-K-4 Struck Through Dirt-and-Grease-Filled Die (IWE), Rarity Level: 1-4, Values: 10 cents to 25 cents up, but no value on a worn or circulated coin.

III-K-5 Struck Through a Dropped Filling (IWE), Rarity Level: 5-6, Values: $10 up.

III-K-6 Struck Through Wrong Metal Fragments (IWE), Rarity Level: 4-6, Values: $1 up.

III-K-7 Struck Through an Unstruck Planchet Fragment (IWE), Rarity Level: 3-5, Values: $1 up.

III-K-8 Struck Through a Rim Burr (IWE), Rarity Level: 3-5, Values: $1 to $2 and up.

III-K-9 Struck Through plit-Off Reeding (IWE), Rarity Level: 5-6, Values: $25 up.

III-K-10 Struck Through a Feed Finger (IWE), Rarity Level: 5-7, Values: $25 to $50 and up.

III-K-11 Struck Through Miscellaneous Objects (IWE), Rarity Level: 4-6, Values: $1 up.

III-K-12 Struck Through Progression (IWE), Rarity Level: 4-6, Values: $1 up.

| Struck through cloth III-K-1 | Struck through a filled die III-K-4 | Struck through dropped filling III-K-5 |

Note: Some 1987 through 1994 quarters are found without mintmarks, classed as III-K-4, a Filled Die. Values depend on market conditions. Filled dies have value ONLY on current, uncirculated grade coins.

Double strikes (III-L)

Only coins which receive two or more strikes by the die pair fall in this section and are identified by the fact that both sides of the coin are affected. Unless some object interferes, an equal area of both sides of the coin will be equally doubled.

The exception is the second strike with a loose die, which will double only one side of a coin, but is a rare form usually occurring only on proofs. A similar effect is flat field doubling from die chatter.

III-L-1 Close Centered Double Strike (WE), Rarity Level: 4-6, Values: $15 up.

III-L-2 Rotated Second Strike Over a Centered First Strike (WE), Rarity Level: 4-6, Values: $15 up.

III-L-3 Off-Center Second Strike Over a Centered First Strike (WE), Rarity Level: 4-6, Values: $15 up.

III-L-4 Off-Center Second Strike Over an Off-Center First Strike (WE), Rarity Level: 4-6, Values: $10 up.

III-L-5 Off-Center Second Strike Over a Broadstrike (WE), Rarity Level: 5-6, Values: $20 up.

III-L-6 Centered Second Strike Over an Off-Center First Strike (WE), Rarity Level: 5-6, Values: $50 up.

III-L-7 Obverse Struck Over Reverse (WE), Rarity Level: 5-6, Values: $25 up.

III-L-8 Nonoverlapping Double Strike (WE), Rarity Level: 5-6 Values: $20 up.

III-L-9 Struck Over a Different Denomination or Series (WE), Rarity Level: 6, Values: $300 and up.

III-L-10 Chain Strike (WE), Rarity Level: 6, Values: $300 up for the pair of coins that were struck together.

III-L-11 Second-Strike Doubling From a Loose Die (W), Rarity Level: 6-7, Values: $200 up.

III-L-12 Second-Strike Doubling From a Loose Screw Press Die (W), Rarity Level: 5-6, Values: $100 up.

III-L-13 Second Strike on an Edge Strike (WE), Rarity Level: 5-6, Values: $20 up.

III-L-14 Folded Planchet Strike (WE), Rarity Level: 5-7, Values: $100 up.

III-L-15 Triple Strike (WE), Rarity Level: 6-7, Values: $100 up.

III-L-16 Multiple Strike (WE), Rarity Level: 6-7, Values: $200 up.

III-L-17 U.S. Coin Struck Over a Struck Foreign Coin (WE), Rarity Level: 6-7, Values: $300 up.

III-L-18 Foreign Coin Struck Over a Struck U.S. Coin (WE), Rarity Level: 6-7, Values: $400 up.

III-L-19 Foreign Coin Struck Over a Struck Foreign Coin (WE), Rarity Level: 7, Values: $500 up.

III-L-20 Double Strike on Scrap or Junk (E), Rarity Level: 6, Values: $50 up.
III-L-21 Struck on a Struck Token or Medal (E), Rarity Level: 5-6, Values: $100 up.
III-L-22 Double-Struck Edge Motto or Design (E), Rarity Level: 6-7, Values: $200 up.
III-L-23 One Edge Motto or Design Struck Over Another (E), Rarity Level: 7, Values: $300 up.
III-L-24 Flat Field Doubling (W), Rarity Level: 2-3, Values: $1 to $5.
III-L-25 Territorial Struck over Struck U.S. Coin: (I) Rarity Level: 6-7, Values: $200 up.
III-L-26 Pattern Struck over Struck U.S. Coin: (I) Rarity Level: 6-7, Values: $200 up.
III-L-27 Pattern Struck over Struck Pattern:(I) Rarity Level 6-7, Values: $200 up.
III-L-28 Pattern Struck Over Foreign Coin:(I) Rarity Level 6-7, Values - $200 up.

Off-center second strike over centered 1st strike III-L-3

Non-overlapping double strike III-L-8

Multiple strike III-L-16

Chain strike III-L-10

Collar striking varieties (III-M)

The collar is often referred to as the "Third Die," and is involved in a number of forms of misstrikes. The collar normally rises around the planchet, preventing it from squeezing sideways between the dies and at the same time forming the reeding on reeded coins.

If the collar is out of position or tilted, a partial collar strike results; if completely missing, it causes a broadstrike; if the planchet is not entirely between the dies, an off-center strike.

III-M-1 Flanged Partial Collar Strike (WE), Rarity Level: 5-6, Values: $20 up.
III-M-2 Reversed Flanged Partial Collar Strike (WE), Rarity Level: 6-7, Values: $35 up.
III-M-3 Tilted Partial Collar Strike (WE), Rarity Level: 5-6, Values: $20 up.
III-M-4 Centered Broadstrike (WE), Rarity Level: 5-6, Values: $5 up.
III-M-5 Uncentered Broadstrike (WE), Rarity Level: 5, Values: $3 up.
III-M-6 Reversed Broadstrike (WE), Rarity Level: 6, Values: $10 up.
III-M-7 Struck Off-Center 10-30% (W), Rarity Level: 3-6, Values: $3 up.
III-M-8 Struck Off-Center 31-70% (W), Rarity Level: 4-6, Values: $5 up.
III-M-9 Struck Off-Center 71% or More (W), Rarity Level: 3-5, Values: $2 up.
III-M-10 Rotated Multi-sided Planchet Strike (W), Rarity Level: 5-6, Values: $10 up.
III-M-11 Wire Edge Strike (IWE), Rarity Level: 1-2, Values: No Extra Value.
III-M-12 Struck With the Collar Too High (WE), Rarity Level: 6-7, Values: $20 up.
III-M-13 Off-Center Slide Strike (W), Rarity Level:3-6 $4 up.

Flanged partial collar III-M-1

Struck off center 10 to 30 percent III-M-7

Struck off center 31 to 70 percent III-M-8

Struck off center 71 percent or more III-M-9

Misaligned and rotated (die) strike varieties (III-N)

Misaligned die III-N-1

Normal rotation   **90 degrees**   **135 degrees**

One (rarely both) of the dies may be Offset Misaligned, off to one side, or may be tilted (Vertically Misaligned). One die may either have been installed so that it is turned in relation to the other die, or may turn in the holder, or the shank may break allowing the die face to rotate in relation to the opposing die.

Vertical misaligned dies are rarely found, and like rotated dies, find only limited collector interest. Ninety and 180 degree rotations are the most popular. Rotations of 14 degrees or less have no value. The 1989-D Congress dollar is found with a nearly 180 degree rotated reverse, currently retailing for around $2,000. Only about 30 have been reported to date.

III-N-1 Offset Die Misalignment Strike (WE), Rarity Level: 3-5, Values: $2 up.

III-N-2 Vertical Die Misalignment Strike (WE), Rarity Level: 4-6, Values: $1 up.

III-N-3 Rotated Die Strike - 15 to 45 Degrees (IWE), Rarity Level: 4-6, Values: $2 up.

III-N-4 Rotated Die Strike - 46 to 135 Degrees (IWE), Rarity Level: 5-6, Values: $10 up.

III-N-5 Rotated Die Strike - 136 to 180 Degrees (IWE), Rarity Level: 5-6, Values: $25 up.

Lettered and design edge strike varieties (III-O)

Early U.S. coins and a number of foreign coins have either lettered edges, or designs on the edge of the coin. Malfunctions of the application of the motto or design to the edge fall in this section.

III-O-1 Overlapping Edge Motto or Design (WE), Rarity Level: 3-4, Values: $5 to $10 and up.

III-O-2 Wrong Edge Motto or Design (WE), Rarity Level: 5-6-7, Values: $50 up.

III-O-3 Missing Edge Motto, Design or Security Edge (IWE), Rarity Level: 5-6-7, Values: $50 up.

III-O-4 Jammed Edge Die Strike (W), Rarity Level: 6, Values: $10 up.

III-O-5 Misplaced Segment of an Edge Die (E), Rarity Level: 4-7, Values: $25 up.

III-O-6 Reeded Edge Struck Over a Lettered Edge (IE), Rarity Level: 3-6, Values: No Extra Value up.

PRICING SECTION

Overlapping edge
letters III-O-1

Defective strikes and mismatched dies (III-P)

The final section of the Striking Division covers coins which are not properly struck for reasons other than those in previous classes, such as coins struck with mismatched (muled) dies. The mismatched die varieties must be taken on a case by case basis, while the other-classes presently have little collector demand or premium.

III-P-1 Defective Strike (WE), Rarity Level: 1, Values: No Extra Value.

III-P-2 Mismatched Die Strike (E), Rarity Level: 4-7, Values: $25 up.

III-P-3 Single-Strike Proof (WE), Rarity Level: 4-5, Values: Minimal.

III-P-4 Single Die-Proof Strike (IE), Rarity Level: 5-6, Values: $100 up.

III-P-5 Reversed Die Strike (I), Rarity Level: 4-5, Values: No Extra Value to Minimal.

Official Mint modifications
Division IV

Several mint produced varieties occur after the coin has been struck, resulting in the addition of the fourth division to my PDS System. Since most of these coins are either unique or are special varieties, each one must be taken on a case by case basis. All classes listed here are by definition intentional.

I have not listed values as the coins falling in these classes which are sold through regular numismatic channels, are cataloged with the regular issues or are covered in specialized catalogs in their particular area.

Matte proofs (IV-A)

Matte proof IV-A-1

Matte proofs as a section include several of the forms of proof coins which have the striking characteristics of a mirror proof but have been treated AFTER striking to give them a grainy, non-reflective surface.

IV-A-1 Matte Proof (I), Rarity Level: 3-5, Values: Normal Numismatic Value.

IV-A-2 Matte Proof on One Side (I), Rarity Level: 7, Values: Normal Numismatic Value.

IV-A-3 Sandblast Proof (I), Rarity Level: 4-6, Values: Normal Numismatic Value.

Additional engraving (IV-B)

Counterstamp IV-B-III

This section includes any added markings which are placed on the struck coin and struck coins which later were cut into pieces for various purposes. The warning is repeated: Anything done to a coin after the strike is extremely difficult to authenticate and is much easier to fake than a die struck coin.

IV-B-1 Counterstamp and Countermark (I), Rarity Level: 3-6, Values: Normal Numismatic Value.

IV-B-2 Perforated and Cut Coins (I), Rarity Level: 4-6, Values: Normal Numismatic Value.

Restrikes (IV-C)

Restrike with new dies IV-C-7

Restrikes cover a complicated mixture of official use of dies from a variety of sources. Whether or not some were officially sanctioned is always a problem for the collector.

IV-C-1) Restrike on the Same Denomination Planchet (I), Rarity Level: 4-6, Values: Normal Numismatic Value.

IV-C-2 Restrike on a Different Denomination or Series Planchet (I), Rarity Level: 4-6, Values: Normal Numismatic Value.

IV-C-3 Restrike on a Foreign Coin (I), Rarity Level: 6-7, Values: Normal Numismatic Value.

IV-C-4 Restrike on a Token or Medal (I), Rarity Level: 5-6, Values: Normal Numismatic Value.

IV-C-5 Restruck With the Original Dies (I), Rarity Level: 4-6, Values: Normal Numismatic Value.

IV-C-6 Restruck With Mismatched Dies (I), Rarity Level: 4-6, Values: Normal Numismatic Value.

IV-C-7 Copy Strike With New Dies (I), Rarity Level: 3-5, Values: Normal Numismatic Value.

IV-C-8 Fantasy Strike (I), Rarity Level: 4-6, Values: Normal Numismatic Value.

After strike modifications
Division V

This division includes both modifications that have value to collectors – and those that don't. I needed a couple of divisions to cover other things that happen to coins to aid in cataloging them. This avoids the false conclusion that an unlisted coin is quite rare, when the exact opposite is more likely to be the case.

Collectible modifications after strike (V-A)

This section includes those classes having to do with deliberate modifications of the coin done with a specific purpose or intent which makes them of some value to collectors. Quite often these pieces were made specifically to sell to collectors, or at least to the public under the guise of being collectible.

V-A-1 Screw Thaler, Rarity Level: 5-6, Values: Normal Numismatic Value.

V-A-2 Love Token, Rarity Level: 3-6, Values: $10 up.

V-A-3 Satirical or Primitive Engraving, Rarity Level: 6-7, Values: $5 up.

V-A-4 Elongated Coin, Rarity Level: 2-7, Values: 50 cents to $1 and up.

V-A-5 Coin Jewelry, Rarity Level: 2-5, Values: $1 up.

V-A-6 Novelty Coin, Rarity Level: 1-3, Values: No Value up to $5 to $10.

V-A-7 Toning, Rarity Level: 3-6, Values: No value up, depending on coloration. Easily faked.

V-A-8 Mint Modification, Rarity Level: 4-7, Values: $5 up. Easily faked.

V-A-9 Mint Packaging Mistake, Rarity Level: 5-7, Values: Nominal $1. Very easily faked.

Mint modification V-A-8

Alterations and damage after the strike(V-B)

This section includes those changes in a coin which have no collector value. In most cases their effect on the coin is to reduce or entirely eliminate any collector value - and in the case of counterfeits they are actually illegal to even own.

V-B-1 Machine Doubling Damage: NOTE: Machine doubling damage is defined as: "Damage to a coin after the strike, due to die bounce or chatter or die displacement, showing on the struck coin as scrapes on the sides of the design elements, with portions of the coin metal in the relief elements either displaced sideways or downward, depending on the direction of movement of the loose die." Machine doubling damage, or MDD, is by far the most common form of doubling found on almost any coin in the world. Rarity Level: 0, Values: Reduces the coin's value.

V-B-2 Accidental or Deliberate Damage, Rarity Level: 0, Values: Reduces the coin's value.

V-B-3 Test Cut or Mark, Rarity Level: 0, Values: Reduces value of coin to face or bullion value.

V-B-4 Alteration, Rarity Level: 0, Values: Reduces value to face or bullion value.

V-B-5 Whizzing, Rarity Level: 0, Values: Reduces value sharply and may reduce it to face or bullion value.

V-B-6 Counterfeit, Copy, Facsimile, Forgery or Fake, Rarity Level: 0, Values: No Value and may be illegal to own.

V-B-7 Planchet Deterioration. Very common on copper-plated zinc cents. Rarity level: 0, Values: No Value

Machine doubling damage V-B-1

Canada

Large cents

1858-1859

1876-1901

1902-1910

1911

1912-1920

KM#	Date	Mintage	VG-8	F-12	VF-20	XF-40	MS-60	MS-63
				BRONZE, 3.24 g				
1	1858	421,000	35.00	45.00	60.00	90.00	215.00	600.00
	1859/8 wide 9	I.A.	22.00	29.00	40.00	60.00	145.00	275.00
	1859 narrow 9	9,579,000	2.25	3.00	4.00	5.00	22.00	140.00
	1859 double punched narrow 9 Type I							
		I.A.	175.00	250.00	350.00	540.00	1150.	2000.
	1859 double punched narrow 9 Type II							
		I.A.	32.00	42.00	60.00	85.00	220.00	400.00
7	1876H	4,000,000	1.50	2.50	4.00	7.00	40.00	180.00
	1881H	2,000,000	2.50	3.50	5.00	10.00	50.00	200.00
	1882H	4,000,000	1.50	2.50	3.00	6.00	30.00	140.00
	1884	2,500,000	2.00	3.00	4.00	7.50	40.00	160.00
	1886	1,500,000	3.25	4.50	7.00	11.50	60.00	220.00
	1887	1,500,000	2.50	3.25	5.00	8.00	40.00	170.00
	1888	4,000,000	1.50	3.00	4.00	5.00	30.00	100.00
	1890H	1,000,000	4.00	6.50	11.50	20.00	100.00	300.00
	1891 lg. date	1,452,000	4.50	7.00	11.00	18.50	90.00	300.00
	1891 S.D.L.L.	I.A.	40.00	60.00	85.00	115.00	300.00	750.00
	1891 S.D.S.L.	I.A.	30.00	45.00	60.00	90.00	200.00	550.00
	1892	1,200,000	3.00	4.50	6.00	10.00	40.00	130.00
	1893	2,000,000	2.00	2.50	4.00	8.00	30.00	100.00
	1894	1,000,000	5.50	8.00	13.00	20.00	85.00	215.00
	1895	1,200,000	3.00	5.00	7.00	10.00	50.00	160.00
	1896	2,000,000	1.75	2.75	3.50	5.50	30.00	100.00
	1897	1,500,000	2.00	3.50	5.00	6.00	30.00	110.00
	1898H	1,000,000	4.00	6.00	8.00	11.00	55.00	200.00

BRONZE

KM#	Date	Mintage	VG-8	F-12	VF-20	XF-40	MS-60	MS-63
	1899	2,400,000	1.50	2.25	3.00	5.00	30.00	100.00
	1900	1,000,000	5.00	8.00	12.00	20.00	65.00	190.00
	1900H	2,600,000	2.50	3.50	4.25	5.00	22.00	70.00
7	1901	4,100,000	1.50	2.50	3.00	5.00	22.00	65.00
8	1902	3,000,000	1.25	1.50	2.00	5.00	16.00	45.00
	1903	4,000,000	1.25	1.50	2.00	4.00	20.00	50.00
	1904	2,500,000	1.50	2.00	3.25	5.00	25.00	75.00
	1905	2,000,000	2.50	4.00	6.00	8.50	35.00	95.00
	1906	4,100,000	1.25	1.50	2.00	4.00	22.00	75.00
	1907	2,400,000	2.50	3.50	4.25	5.00	30.00	85.00
	1907H	800,000	7.00	10.00	16.00	30.00	80.00	275.00
	1908	2,401,506	2.25	3.75	4.50	6.00	26.00	80.00
	1909	3,973,339	1.25	1.50	2.00	4.00	20.00	55.00
	1910	5,146,487	1.25	2.25	2.50	3.00	18.00	55.00
15	1911	4,663,486	1.00	1.25	1.75	3.50	18.50	60.00
21	1912	5,107,642	.75	1.00	1.50	2.50	15.00	50.00
	1913	5,735,405	.75	1.00	1.50	2.50	15.00	50.00
	1914	3,405,958	1.25	1.40	2.00	3.50	28.00	90.00
	1915	4,932,134	.80	1.10	1.75	2.75	18.00	65.00
	1916	11,022,367	.50	.65	.90	2.00	12.00	45.00
	1917	11,899,254	.50	.65	.90	1.50	9.00	45.00
	1918	12,970,798	.50	.65	.90	1.50	9.00	45.00
	1919	11,279,634	.50	.65	.90	1.50	9.00	45.00
	1920	6,762,247	.50	.75	1.00	2.00	12.00	50.00

Small cents

Dot

BRONZE, 3.24 g

KM#	Date	Mintage	VG-8	F-12	VF-20	XF-40	MS-60	MS-63
28	1920	15,483,923	.25	.50	1.00	2.00	9.00	40.00
	1921	7,601,627	.50	.75	1.75	4.00	18.00	70.00
	1922	1,243,635	8.75	10.00	14.50	22.00	120.00	300.00
	1923	1,019,002	14.25	16.25	23.00	34.00	200.00	600.00
	1924	1,593,195	4.00	5.00	6.50	11.50	85.00	200.00
	1925	1,000,622	12.00	15.00	18.75	28.00	130.00	400.00
	1926	2,143,372	2.25	3.00	4.50	8.75	65.00	200.00
	1927	3,553,928	.90	1.25	2.25	4.00	30.00	95.00
	1928	9,144,860	.15	.20	.65	1.50	10.00	40.00
	1929	12,159,840	.15	.20	.65	1.50	10.00	40.00
	1930	2,538,613	1.35	1.80	2.50	5.00	30.00	90.00
	1931	3,842,776	.65	1.00	1.75	3.50	25.00	80.00
	1932	21,316,190	.15	.20	.50	1.50	9.00	35.00
	1933	12,079,310	.15	.20	.50	1.50	9.00	35.00
	1934	7,042,358	.20	.30	.75	1.50	9.00	35.00
	1935	7,526,400	.20	.30	.75	1.50	9.00	35.00
	1936	8,768,769	.15	.20	.75	1.50	9.00	35.00
	1936 dot below dt	678,823	—	—	—	—	Rare	—
	1936 dot below dt	3 known	—	—	—	—	*Specimen	—

*NOTE: David Akers, John Jay Pittman sale 10-97 Gem Specimen realized $110,000.

Maple Leaf

KM#	Date	Mintage	VG-8	F-12	VF-20	XF-40	MS-60	MS-63
32	1937	10,040,231	.50	.70	1.25	1.60	2.50	6.00
	1938	18,365,608	.20	.35	.65	1.00	2.00	6.50
	1939	21,600,319	.20	.35	.60	1.00	2.00	5.00
	1940	85,740,532	.15	.20	.40	.75	2.00	6.00
	1941	56,336,011	.15	.20	.40	1.00	5.00	35.00
	1942	76,113,708	.15	.20	.25	.75	4.50	25.00

KM#	Date	Mintage	VG-8	F-12	VF-20	XF-40	MS-60	MS-63
32	1943	89,111,969	.15	.20	.25	.75	3.00	12.00
	1944	44,131,216	.20	.30	.40	1.00	5.00	32.00
	1945	77,268,591	.15	.20	.25	.50	2.00	5.00
	1946	56,662,071	.15	.20	.30	.60	2.00	5.00
	1947	31,093,901	.15	.20	.25	.50	2.00	6.00
	1947ML	47,855,448	—	.10	.25	.50	2.00	5.00

Modified Obverse Legend

KM#	Date	Mintage	VG-8	F-12	VF-20	XF-40	MS-60	MS-63
41	1948	25,767,779	.10	.20	.40	.80	2.50	8.00
	1949	33,128,933	—	.10	.25	.50	2.00	4.00
	1950	60,444,992	—	.10	.20	.40	1.75	4.00
	1951	80,430,379	—	.10	.20	.40	1.25	4.00
	1952	67,631,736	—	.10	.20	.40	1.00	4.00

Elizabeth II Effigy by Gillick

KM#	Date	Mintage	VG-8	F-12	VF-20	XF-40	MS-60	MS-63
49	1953 w/o strap	67,806,016	.15	.20	.25	.30	.65	2.00
	1953 w/strap	Inc. Ab.	.75	1.50	2.00	3.00	10.00	35.00
	1954 w/strap	22,181,760	.10	.15	.30	.50	2.00	4.00
	1954 w/o strap	Inc. Ab.		Proof-Like Only		—	150.00	250.00
	1955 w/strap	56,403,193	—	.15	.20	.25	.45	1.50
	1955 w/o strap	Inc. Ab.	75.00	100.00	150.00	250.00	500.00	950.00
	1956	78,658,535	—	—	—	.10	.50	.90
	1957	100,601,792	—	—	—	.10	.30	.70
	1958	59,385,679	—	—	—	.10	.30	.70
	1959	83,615,343	—	—	—	.10	.25	.50
	1960	75,772,775	—	—	—	.10	.25	.50
	1961	139,598,404	—	—	—	—	.15	.40
	1962	227,244,069	—	—	—	—	.10	.25
	1963	279,076,334	—	—	—	—	.10	.25
	1964	484,655,322	—	—	—	—	.10	.25

Elizabeth II Effigy by Machin

KM#	Date	Mintage	VG-8	F-12	VF-20	XF-40	MS-60	MS-63
59.1	1965 sm. beads, pointed 5	304,441,082	—	—	—	.45	1.00	1.50
	1965 sm. beads, blunt 5	I.A.	—	—	—	—	.20	.40
	1965 lg. beads, pointed 5	I.A.	—	—	5.25	8.25	20.00	30.00
	1965 lg. beads, blunt 5	I.A.	—	—	—	.10	.35	.70
	1966	184,151,087	—	—	—	—	.10	.20
	1968	329,695,772	—	—	—	—	.10	.20
	1969	335,240,929	—	—	—	—	.10	.20
	1970	311,145,010	—	—	—	—	.10	.20
	1971	298,228,936	—	—	—	—	.10	.20
	1972	451,304,591	—	—	—	—	.10	.20
	1973	457,059,852	—	—	—	—	.10	.20
	1974	692,058,489	—	—	—	—	.10	.20
	1975	642,318,000	—	—	—	—	.10	.20
	1976	701,122,890	—	—	—	—	.10	.20
	1977	453,762,670	—	—	—	—	.10	.20
	1978	911,170,647	—	—	—	—	.10	.20

Smaller Bust

KM#	Date	Mintage	VG-8	F-12	VF-20	XF-40	MS-60	MS-63
59.2	1979	754,394,064	—	—	—	—	.10	.20

Reduced Weight, 2.80 g

KM#	Date	Mintage	VG-8	F-12	VF-20	XF-40	MS-60	MS-63
127	1980	912,052,318	—	—	—	—	.10	.15
	1981	1,209,468,500	—	—	—	—	.10	.15
	1981	199,000	—	—	—	—	Proof	1.50

Reduced Weight, 2.50 g

Edge: Multi-sided.

KM#	Date	Mintage	VG-8	F-12	VF-20	XF-40	MS-60	MS-63
132	1982	911,001,000	—	—	—	—	.10	.15
	1982	180,908	—	—	—	—	Proof	1.50
	1983	975,510,000	—	—	—	—	.10	.15
	1983	168,000	—	—	—	—	Proof	1.50
	1984	838,225,000	—	—	—	—	.10	.15
	1984	161,602	—	—	—	—	Proof	1.50
	1985 pointed 5	771,772,500	—	—	—	4.50	12.50	18.50
	1985 blunt 5	I.A.	—	—	—	—	.10	.15
	1985	157,037	—	—	—	—	Proof	1.50
	1986	740,335,000	—	—	—	—	.10	.15

KM#	Date	Mintage	VG-8	F-12	VF-20	XF-40	MS-60	MS-63
	1986	175,745	—	—	—	—	Proof	2.25
	1987	774,549,000	—	—	—	—	.10	.15
132	1987	179,004	—	—	—	—	Proof	2.25
	1988	482,676,752	—	—	—	—	.10	.15
	1988	175,259	—	—	—	—	Proof	2.25
	1989	1,077,347,200	—	—	—	—	.10	.15
	1989	170,928	—	—	—	—	Proof	2.25

Elizabeth II Effigy by dePedery-Hunt

KM#	Date	Mintage	VG-8	F-12	VF-20	XF-40	MS-60	MS-63
181	1990	218,035,000	—	—	—	—	.10	.15
	1990	140,649	—	—	—	—	Proof	2.50
	1991	831,001,000	—	—	—	—	.10	.15
	1991	131,888	—	—	—	—	Proof	3.50
	1993	752,034,000	—	—	—	—	.10	.15
	1993	145,065	—	—	—	—	Proof	2.00
	1994	639,516,000	—	—	—	—	.10	.15
	1994	146,424	—	—	—	—	Proof	2.50
	1995	624,983,000	—	—	—	—	.10	.15
	1995	—	—	—	—	—	Proof	2.50

COPPER PLATED STEEL

KM#	Date	Mintage	VG-8	F-12	VF-20	XF-40	MS-60	MS-63
181a	1996	445,746,000	—	—	—	—	.10	.15
	1996	—	—	—	—	—	Proof	2.50

BRONZE PLATED STEEL
Edge: Round and plain.

KM#	Date	Mintage	VG-8	F-12	VF-20	XF-40	MS-60	MS-63
289	1997	506,928,000	—	—	—	—	.10	.15
	1997	—	—	—	—	—	Proof	1.50
	1998	—	—	—	—	—	.10	.15
	1998O	—	—	—	—	In Proof sets only		1.50
	1998W	—	—	—	—	In Mint sets only		.20

COMMEMORATIVE CENTS

KM#	Date	Mintage	VG-8	BRONZE F-12	VF-20	XF-40	MS-60	MS-63
65	1967 Confederation Centennial							
		345,140,645	—	—	—	—	.10	.20
204	1992 Confederation 125							
		673,512,000	—	—	—	—	.10	.15
		147,061	—	—	—	—	Proof	2.50

KM#	Date	Mintage	VG-8	5.6700 g, COPPER-PLATED .925 SILVER, .1677 oz ASW F-12	VF-20	XF-40	MS-60	MS-63
309	ND(1998) 90th Anniversary Royal Canadian Mint							
		.025	—	—	—	In Unc sets only		16.50

KM#	Date	Mintage	VG-8	F-12	VF-20	XF-40	MS-60	MS-63
322	ND(1998) 90th Anniversary Royal Canadian Mint							
		.025	—	—	—	—	Proof	16.50

FIVE CENTS

Victoria
1858-1901

Edward VII
1902-1910

George V
1911-1936

Round O's

Oval O's

KM#	Date	Mintage	1.1620 g, .925 SILVER, .0346 oz ASW					
			VG-8	F-12	VF-20	XF-40	MS-60	MS-63
2	1858 sm. date	1,500,000	10.00	15.00	25.00	40.00	225.00	425.00
	1858 lg. date over sm. date							
		Inc. Ab.	100.00	150.00	250.00	375.00	1000.	2250.
	1870 flat rim	2,800,000	9.00	15.00	25.00	45.00	200.00	450.00
	1870 wire rim	Inc. Ab.	9.00	15.00	25.00	45.00	200.00	450.00
	1871	1,400,000	9.00	15.00	25.00	45.00	200.00	500.00
2	1872H	2,000,000	6.00	12.00	25.00	40.00	225.00	600.00
	1874H plain 4	800,000	12.50	27.00	55.00	100.00	325.00	875.00
	1874H crosslet 4	Inc. Ab.	10.00	20.00	40.00	65.00	350.00	750.00
	1875H lg. date	1,000,000	125.00	175.00	325.00	575.00	2200.	4250.
	1875H sm. date	Inc. Ab.	80.00	150.00	250.00	450.00	1400.	3250.
	1880H	3,000,000	4.00	7.50	16.00	35.00	200.00	500.00
	1881H	1,500,000	4.25	9.00	17.50	35.00	200.00	600.00
	1882H	1,000,000	5.00	10.00	18.00	40.00	225.00	650.00
	1883H	600,000	11.50	25.00	60.00	125.00	650.00	1750.
	1884	200,000	75.00	125.00	225.00	475.00	2200.	6000.
	1885 sm. 5	1,000,000	7.50	14.00	35.00	70.00	400.00	1100.
	1885 lg. 5	Inc. Ab.	8.25	15.50	35.00	80.00	425.00	1200.
	1885 lg. 5 over sm. 5							
		Inc. Ab.	35.00	70.00	150.00	400.00	1950.	2750.
	1886 sm. 6	1,700,000	4.50	9.00	17.50	35.00	250.00	700.00
	1886 lg. 6	Inc. Ab.	7.00	10.00	20.00	45.00	300.00	750.00
	1887	500,000	13.00	25.00	45.00	85.00	300.00	675.00
	1888	1,000,000	3.50	6.00	14.00	25.00	140.00	350.00
	1889	1,200,000	14.00	28.00	60.00	100.00	350.00	1000.
	1890H	1,000,000	4.50	8.00	18.00	35.00	165.00	400.00
	1891	1,800,000	3.00	5.00	10.00	16.00	125.00	285.00
	1892	860,000	4.50	8.00	16.00	35.00	200.00	550.00
	1893	1,700,000	3.00	5.00	10.00	18.00	150.00	350.00
	1894	500,000	9.50	20.00	40.00	80.00	285.00	850.00
	1896	1,500,000	3.50	7.00	12.00	25.00	150.00	325.00
	1897	1,319,283	3.75	6.50	12.00	25.00	125.00	265.00
	1898	580,717	8.00	15.00	30.00	50.00	180.00	500.00
	1899	3,000,000	2.75	4.00	7.50	18.00	85.00	250.00
	1900 oval O's	1,800,000	3.00	4.50	8.00	18.00	90.00	265.00
	1900 round O's	Inc. Ab.	13.00	25.00	45.00	90.00	250.00	750.00
	1901	2,000,000	2.75	4.00	8.00	18.00	90.00	265.00
9	1902	2,120,000	1.50	2.00	3.25	7.00	30.00	50.00
	1902 lg. broad H	2,200,000	2.00	2.75	4.50	8.00	40.00	70.00
	1902 sm. narrow H	Inc. Ab.	5.00	10.00	20.00	35.00	130.00	225.00
13	1903	1,000,000	4.00	7.00	14.00	30.00	120.00	280.00
	1903H	2,640,000	1.75	3.00	7.00	13.00	90.00	200.00
	1904	2,400,000	1.75	3.00	7.00	18.00	140.00	400.00
	1905	2,600,000	1.75	3.00	6.00	12.00	85.00	200.00
	1906	3,100,000	1.50	2.00	4.00	8.00	70.00	175.00
	1907	5,200,000	1.50	2.00	4.00	7.00	60.00	125.00
	1908	1,220,524	4.00	6.50	12.00	25.00	95.00	175.00
	1909 round leaves	1,983,725	2.00	2.50	7.00	15.00	125.00	350.00
	1909 pointed leaves	Inc. Ab.	7.75	11.00	27.50	55.00	275.00	800.00
	1910 pointed leaves	3,850,325	1.50	1.75	3.25	7.00	45.00	85.00
	1910 round leaves	Inc. Ab.	9.50	15.00	30.00	75.00	325.00	900.00
16	1911	3,692,350	1.75	2.50	5.00	11.00	65.00	120.00
22	1912	5,863,170	1.50	2.00	3.00	6.00	45.00	125.00
	1913	5,488,048	1.25	2.00	3.00	5.00	24.00	45.00
	1914	4,202,179	1.50	2.20	3.50	7.00	55.00	125.00
	1915	1,172,258	6.50	12.00	20.00	40.00	200.00	475.00
	1916	2,481,675	2.75	4.00	5.50	12.50	90.00	200.00
	1917	5,521,373	1.25	1.75	2.00	4.00	30.00	70.00
	1918	6,052,298	1.25	1.75	2.00	4.00	24.00	60.00
	1919	7,835,400	1.25	1.75	2.00	4.00	27.50	60.00

PRICING SECTION

1.1664 g, .800 SILVER, .0300 oz ASW

22a	1920	10,649,851	1.25	1.75	2.00	4.00	24.00	45.00
	1921	2,582,495	1500.	2000.	2500.	5000.	11,500.	20,000.

NOTE: Approximately 460 known, balance remelted.
NOTE: Stack's A.G. Carter Jr. Sale 12-89 Choice BU finest known realized $57,200.

Near 6   Far 6

Near 6   Far 6

NICKEL

KM#	Date	Mintage	VG-8	F-12	VF-20	XF-40	MS-60	MS-63
29	1922	4,794,119	.25	.75	1.75	7.00	40.00	80.00
	1923	2,502,279	.40	1.25	3.50	12.00	90.00	225.00
	1924	3,105,839	.30	.70	2.50	7.00	75.00	165.00
	1925	201,921	25.00	36.00	60.00	150.00	900.00	2000.
	1926 near 6	938,162	2.25	6.00	14.00	45.00	275.00	900.00
	1926 far 6	Inc. Ab.	65.00	95.00	160.00	300.00	1200.	2200.
	1927	5,285,627	.25	.65	1.75	6.50	45.00	120.00
	1928	4,577,712	.25	.65	1.75	6.50	40.00	80.00
	1929	5,611,911	.25	.65	1.75	6.50	45.00	120.00

KM#	Date	Mintage	VG-8	F-12	VF-20	XF-40	MS-60	MS-63
29	1930	3,704,673	.25	.65	1.75	6.50	70.00	150.00
	1931	5,100,830	.25	.65	2.00	10.25	75.00	200.00
	1932	3,198,566	.25	.65	2.25	10.50	75.00	150.00
	1933	2,597,867	.40	2.75	4.00	11.50	150.00	400.00
	1934	3,827,304	.25	.65	1.75	10.75	80.00	200.00
	1935	3,900,000	.25	.65	1.75	6.50	70.00	160.00
	1936	4,400,450	.25	.65	1.75	6.50	40.00	85.00

KM#	Date	Mintage	VG-8	F-12	VF-20	XF-40	MS-60	MS-63
33	1937 dot	4,593,263	.20	.35	1.25	2.50	9.00	22.00
	1938	3,898,974	.20	1.00	2.00	7.00	65.00	135.00
	1939	5,661,123	.20	.50	1.75	4.50	40.00	70.00
	1940	13,920,197	.15	.30	.75	2.25	14.00	40.00
	1941	8,681,785	.10	.30	.75	2.25	17.00	42.00
	1942 round	6,847,544	.20	.35	.75	1.75	14.00	40.00

Tombac (BRASS)

39	1942 - 12 sided	3,396,234	.40	.65	1.25	1.75	3.00	9.00

Dot   Maple leaf

PRICING SECTION

NICKEL

KM#	Date	Mintage	VG-8	F-12	VF-20	XF-40	MS-60	MS-63
39a	1946	6,952,684	.15	.25	.50	2.00	10.00	25.00
	1947	7,603,724	.15	.25	.50	1.25	10.00	20.00
	1947 dot	Inc. Ab.	12.00	15.00	22.00	50.00	220.00	425.00
	1947 maple leaf	9,595,124	.15	.25	.50	1.25	8.00	16.00

Modified Obverse Legend

KM#	Date	Mintage	VG-8	F-12	VF-20	XF-40	MS-60	MS-63
42	1948	1,810,789	.50	.80	1.00	2.00	15.00	25.00
	1949	13,037,090	.15	.20	.40	.75	4.00	7.00
	1950	11,970,521	.15	.20	.40	.75	4.00	7.00

CHROMIUM and NICKEL-PLATED STEEL

KM#	Date	Mintage	VG-8	F-12	VF-20	XF-40	MS-60	MS-63
42a	1951 low relief*	4,313,410	.15	.25	.50	1.00	2.50	4.50
	1951 high relief* *	Inc. Ab.	325.00	450.00	600.00	1100.	1900.	3800.
	1952	10,891,148	.15	.25	.50	1.00	3.00	5.00

*NOTE: A in GRATIA points between denticles.
* *NOTE: A in GRATIA points to a denticle.

Elizabeth II Effigy by Gillick - 12 Sided Coinage

KM#	Date	Mintage	VG-8	F-12	VF-20	XF-40	MS-60	MS-63
50	1953 w/o strap	16,635,552	.15	.25	.40	1.00	3.00	4.50
	1953 w/strap	Inc.Ab.	.15	.25	.45	1.00	3.50	7.00
	1954	6,998,662	.15	.25	.50	1.00	4.50	8.00

NICKEL

KM#	Date	Mintage	VG-8	F-12	VF-20	XF-40	MS-60	MS-63
50a	1955	5,355,028	.15	.25	.40	.75	3.00	4.50
	1956	9,399,854	—	.20	.30	.45	1.75	3.25
	1957	7,387,703	—	—	.25	.30	1.50	3.00
	1958	7,607,521	—	—	.25	.30	1.50	3.00
	1959	11,552,523	—	—	—	.20	.65	1.25
	1960	37,157,433	—	—	—	.15	.40	.75
	1961	47,889,051	—	—	—	—	.20	.40
	1962	46,307,305	—	—	—	—	.20	.40

Round Coinage

KM#	Date	Mintage	VG-8	F-12	VF-20	XF-40	MS-60	MS-63
57	1963	43,970,320	—	—	—	—	.20	.40
	1964	78,075,068	—	—	—	—	.20	.40
	1964 XWL	—	8.75	11.00	14.00	16.00	23.00	35.00

Elizabeth II Effigy by Machin

KM#	Date	Mintage	VG-8	F-12	VF-20	XF-40	MS-60	MS-63
60.1	1965	84,876,018	—	—	—	—	.20	.30
	1966	27,976,648	—	—	—	—	.20	.30
	1968	101,930,379	—	—	—	—	.20	.30
	1969	27,830,229	—	—	—	—	.20	.30
	1970	5,726,010	—	—	—	.25	.35	.75
	1971	27,312,609	—	—	—	—	.20	.30
	1972	62,417,387	—	—	—	—	.20	.30
	1973	53,507,435	—	—	—	—	.20	.30
	1974	94,704,645	—	—	—	—	.20	.30
	1975	138,882,000	—	—	—	—	.20	.30
	1976	55,140,213	—	—	—	—	.20	.30
	1977	89,120,791	—	—	—	—	.20	.30
	1978	137,079,273	—	—	—	—	.20	.30

Smaller bust

KM#	Date	Mintage	VG-8	F-12	VF-20	XF-40	MS-60	MS-63
60.2	1979	186,295,825	—	—	—	—	.20	.30
	1980	134,878,000	—	—	—	—	.20	.30
	1981	99,107,900	—	—	—	—	.20	.30
	1981	199,000	—	—	—	—	Proof	1.00

COPPER-NICKEL

KM#	Date	Mintage	VG-8	F-12	VF-20	XF-40	MS-60	MS-63
60.2a	1982	64,924,400	—	—	—	—	.20	.30
	1982	180,908	—	—	—	—	Proof	1.00
	1983	72,596,000	—	—	—	—	.20	.30
	1983	168,000	—	—	—	—	Proof	1.00
	1984	84,088,000	—	—	—	—	.20	.30
	1984	161,602	—	—	—	—	Proof	2.00
	1985	126,618,000	—	—	—	—	.20	.30
	1985	157,037	—	—	—	—	Proof	2.00
	1986	156,104,000	—	—	—	—	.20	.30
	1986	175,745	—	—	—	—	Proof	2.00
	1987	106,299,000	—	—	—	—	.10	.15
	1987	179,004	—	—	—	—	Proof	2.00

1988	75,025,000	—	—	—	—	.10	.15
1988	175,259	—	—	—	—	Proof	2.00
1989	141,570,538	—	—	—	—	.10	.15
1989	170,928	—	—	—	—	Proof	2.00

Elizabeth II Effigy by dePedery-Hunt

KM#	Date	Mintage					MS-60	MS-63
182	1990	42,537,000	—	—	—	—	.10	.15
	1990	140,649	—	—	—	—	Proof	2.50
	1991	10,931,000	—	—	—	—	.20	.70
	1991	131,888	—	—	—	—	Proof	6.50
	1993	86,877,000	—	—	—	—	.10	.15
	1993	143,065	—	—	—	—	Proof	2.50
	1994	99,352,000	—	—	—	—	.10	.15
	1994	146,424	—	—	—	—	Proof	3.00
	1995	78,528,000	—	—	—	—	.10	.15
	1995	50,000	—	—	—	—	Proof	2.50

NICKEL PLATED STEEL

KM#	Date	Mintage	VG-8	F-12	VF-20	XF-40	MS-60	MS-63
182a	1996	36,686,000	—	—	—	—	.10	.15
	1997	26,573,000	—	—	—	—	.10	.15
	1998	—	—	—	—	—	.10	.15
	1998W	—	—	—	—	In Unc sets only		.20

5.3500 g, .925 SILVER, .1591 oz ASW

KM#	Date	Mintage	VG-8	F-12	VF-20	XF-40	MS-60	MS-63
182b	1996	—	—	—	—	—	Proof	5.50
	1997	—	—	—	—	—	Proof	5.50
	1998O	—	—	—	—	In Proof sets only		4.00

COMMEMORATIVE FIVE CENTS

KM#	Date	Mintage	VG-8	F-12	VF-20	XF-40	MS-60	MS-63
40	1943 Victory, Tombac (Brass)							
		24,760,256	.20	.30	.40	1.00	2.00	7.00
	1944	8,000	—	—	—	—	Rare	—

CHROMIUM-PLATED STEEL

40a	1944	11,532,784	.15	.25	.50	1.00	2.25	4.50
	1945	18,893,216,	.15	.25	.50	1.00	2.25	4.50

48	1951 Nickel Bicentennial, Nickel							
		9,028,507	.15	.20	.25	.75	2.00	4.00
66	1967 Confederation Centennial, Copper-Nickel							
		36,876,574	—	—	—	—	.20	.30

205	1992 Confederation 125							
		53,732,000	—	—	—	—	.10	.15
		147,061	—	—	—	—	Proof	5.25

KM#	Date	Mintage	1.1670 g, .925 SILVER, .0347 oz ASW VG-8	F-12	VF-20	XF-40	MS-60	MS-63
310	ND(1998) 90th Anniversary Royal Canadian Mint							
		.025	—	—	—		In Unc sets only	2.75
		.025	—	—	—		In Proof sets only	2.75

TEN CENTS

1858-1901   1902-1910

KM#	Date	Mintage	2.3240 g, .925 SILVER, .0691 oz ASW VG-8	F-12	VF-20	XF-40	MS-60	MS-63
3	1858/5	Inc. Below	325.00	500.00	875.00	1350.	3100.	—
	1858	1,250,000	13.50	24.00	45.00	80.00	275.00	700.00
	1870 narrow 0	1,600,000	12.00	25.00	50.00	90.00	285.00	725.00
	1870 wide 0	Inc. Ab.	17.00	30.00	60.00	110.00	350.00	800.00
	1871	800,000	15.00	30.00	70.00	125.00	325.00	1200.
	1871H	1,870,000	18.00	32.50	70.00	125.00	450.00	1000.
	1872H	1,000,000	70.00	125.00	225.00	425.00	1300.	2750.
	1874H	600,000	8.00	15.00	30.00	70.00	275.00	750.00
	1875H	1,000,000	175.00	325.00	575.00	1150.	4050.	7500.
	1880H	1,500,000	7.00	12.00	25.00	55.00	250.00	700.00
	1881H	950,000	8.50	18.00	40.00	90.00	275.00	700.00

KM#	Date	Mintage	VG-8	F-12	VF-20	XF-40	MS-60	MS-63
3	1882H	1,000,000	8.50	18.00	35.00	75.00	300.00	800.00
	1883H	300,000	25.00	60.00	125.00	250.00	800.00	1800.
	1884	150,000	140.00	300.00	575.00	1300.	5150.	10,000.
	1885	400,000	22.00	50.00	125.00	275.00	1500.	3250.
	1886 sm. 6	800,000	12.00	22.00	50.00	110.00	550.00	1500.
	1886 lg. 6	Inc. Ab.	15.00	27.50	60.00	140.00	500.00	1200.
	1887	350,000	23.00	55.00	125.00	275.00	1150.	2750.
	1888	500,000	6.75	13.00	30.00	60.00	250.00	600.00
	1889	600,000	400.00	725.00	1450.	2900.	8750.	14,000.
	1890H	450,000	11.50	20.00	45.00	90.00	325.00	750.00
	1891 21 leaves	800,000	12.00	22.00	50.00	110.00	375.00	825.00
	1891 22 leaves	Inc. Ab.	12.00	22.00	50.00	110.00	375.00	825.00
	1892/1	520,000	115.00	185.00	325.00	525.00	1750.	2550.
	1892	Inc. Ab.	9.50	20.00	37.50	75.00	350.00	800.00
	1893 flat top 3	500,000	14.00	32.00	70.00	130.00	475.00	1300.
	1893 rd. top 3	Inc. Ab.	450.00	900.00	1700.	2900.	6950.	13,000.
	1894	500,000	13.00	25.00	55.00	110.00	350.00	1000.
	1896	650,000	7.00	12.00	25.00	55.00	250.00	550.00
	1898	720,000	7.00	14.00	30.00	60.00	275.00	600.00
	1899 sm. 9's	1,200,000	6.75	10.50	25.00	55.00	210.00	575.00
	1899 lg. 9's	Inc. Ab.	10.00	18.00	35.00	90.00	325.00	850.00
	1900	1,100,000	6.75	10.50	25.00	50.00	150.00	390.00
	1901	1,200,000	6.75	10.50	25.00	50.00	150.00	390.00
10	1902	720,000	3.50	8.00	18.00	45.00	235.00	475.00
	1902H	1,100,000	2.75	5.00	12.50	28.00	100.00	235.00
	1903	500,000	8.00	20.00	60.00	125.00	800.00	1900.
	1903H	1,320,000	3.00	7.00	15.00	42.00	200.00	450.00
	1904	1,000,000	4.50	9.00	30.00	65.00	250.00	500.00
	1905	1,000,000	4.00	8.00	25.00	70.00	350.00	800.00
	1906	1,700,000	2.75	7.50	14.00	40.00	200.00	400.00
	1907	2,620,000	2.75	6.00	12.50	30.00	160.00	350.00
	1908	776,666	5.00	10.00	27.00	65.00	220.00	425.00
	1909 Victorian leaves, similar to 1902-1908 coinage							
		1,697,200	3.50	9.00	20.00	50.00	285.00	700.00
	1909 broad leaves similar to 1910-1912 coinage							
		Inc. Ab.	5.50	12.00	25.00	70.00	375.00	800.00
	1910	4,468,331	2.75	5.00	12.50	28.00	125.00	275.00
17	1911	2,737,584	4.00	9.00	15.00	40.00	110.00	250.00

Small leaves							

KM#	Date	Mintage	VG-8	F-12	VF-20	XF-40	MS-60	MS-63
23	1912	3,235,557	1.75	2.50	6.00	22.00	160.00	400.00
	1913 sm. leaves	3,613,937	1.50	2.25	5.00	17.50	125.00	350.00
	1913 lg. leaves	Inc. Ab.	75.00	140.00	275.00	650.00	3850.	6700.
	1914	2,549,811	1.50	2.50	5.50	18.50	135.00	400.00
	1915	688,057	4.00	10.00	22.00	80.00	340.00	700.00
	1916	4,218,114	1.25	1.50	4.00	11.00	80.00	225.00
	1917	5,011,988	1.25	1.50	3.00	8.75	50.00	110.00
	1918	5,133,602	1.25	1.50	3.00	8.75	45.00	90.00
	1919	7,877,722	1.25	1.50	3.00	8.75	45.00	90.00

2.3328 g, .800 SILVER, .0600 oz ASW

KM#	Date	Mintage	VG-8	F-12	VF-20	XF-40	MS-60	MS-63
23a	1920	6,305,345	1.25	1.50	3.00	9.00	50.00	110.00
	1921	2,469,562	1.25	2.00	4.00	12.50	65.00	200.00
	1928	2,458,602	1.00	1.75	4.00	10.00	55.00	130.00
	1929	3,253,888	1.00	2.25	3.50	9.50	55.00	130.00
	1930	1,831,043	1.25	2.00	4.50	14.00	55.00	150.00
	1931	2,067,421	1.50	1.75	4.00	10.00	55.00	125.00
	1932	1,154,317	1.50	2.50	6.00	20.00	75.00	160.00
	1933	672,368	2.00	3.00	9.00	25.00	175.00	400.00
	1934	409,067	3.00	6.00	18.00	55.00	250.00	500.00
	1935	384,056	3.00	6.00	18.00	55.00	250.00	500.00
	1936	2,460,871	.60	1.25	3.00	8.75	40.00	85.00
	1936 dot on rev.	4 known	—	—	—		*Specimen	—

*NOTE: David Akers, John Jay Pittman sale 10-97 Gem Specimen realized $120,000.

							Maple Leaf	

KM#	Date	Mintage	VG-8	F-12	VF-20	XF-40	MS-60	MS-63
34	1937	2,500,095	1.00	1.75	3.00	4.50	10.00	16.00
	1938	4,197,323	1.25	2.00	3.50	7.00	40.00	70.00
	1939	5,501,748	BV	1.50	2.50	6.00	35.00	60.00
	1940	16,526,470	BV	.75	2.25	3.00	14.00	25.00
	1941	8,716,386	BV	1.50	2.50	6.00	35.00	70.00
	1942	10,214,011	BV	.75	1.25	4.00	25.00	40.00
	1943	21,143,229	BV	.75	1.25	4.00	12.00	25.00
	1944	9,383,582	BV	.75	1.50	4.50	20.00	40.00
	1945	10,979,570	BV	.75	1.25	4.00	12.00	22.00
	1946	6,300,066	BV	1.75	2.00	4.50	20.00	40.00
	1947	4,431,926	BV	2.00	2.50	6.00	32.00	45.00
	1947 maple leaf	9,638,793	BV	.75	1.50	3.00	10.00	16.00

Modified Obverse Legend

KM#	Date	Mintage	VG-8	F-12	VF-20	XF-40	MS-60	MS-63
43	1948	422,741	2.00	3.50	8.00	17.00	40.00	60.00
	1949	11,336,172	—	BV	1.25	2.00	7.00	12.00
	1950	17,823,075	—	BV	1.00	1.50	6.00	10.00
	1951	15,079,265	—	BV	.75	1.50	5.00	9.00
	1952	10,474,455	—	BV	.75	1.50	5.00	9.00

Elizabeth II Effigy by Gillick

51	1953 w/o straps	17,706,395	—	—	BV	1.25	3.00	6.00
	1953 w/straps	Inc. Ab.	—	—	BV	1.25	3.50	6.50
	1954	4,493,150	—	BV	1.00	2.25	6.00	11.00
	1955	12,237,294	—	—	BV	.75	3.00	5.00
	1956	16,732,844	—	—	BV	.75	2.50	4.00
	1956 dot below date	Inc. Ab.	1.00	2.00	3.00	5.00	12.50	22.50
	1957	16,110,229	—	—	—	BV	1.50	2.25
	1958	10,621,236	—	—	—	BV	1.50	2.25
	1959	19,691,433	—	—	—	BV	1.50	2.25
	1960	45,446,835	—	—	—	BV	.75	1.50
	1961	26,850,859	—	—	—	BV	.75	1.50
	1962	41,864,335	—	—	—	BV	.75	1.50
	1963	41,916,208	—	—	—	BV	.75	1.50
	1964	49,518,549	—	—	—	BV	.75	1.50

Elizabeth II Effigy by Machin

61	1965	56,965,392	—	—	—	BV	.75	1.50
	1966	34,567,898	—	—	—	BV	.75	1.50

OTTAWA	Reeding	PHILADELPHIA

2.3240 g, .500 SILVER, .0372 oz ASW

KM#	Date	Mintage	VG-8	F-12	VF-20	XF-40	MS-60	MS-63
72	1968 Ottawa							
		70,460,000	—	—	—	BV	.60	1.25

KM#	Date	Mintage	VG-8	F-12	VF-20	XF-40	MS-60	MS-63
72a	1968 Ottawa							
		87,412,930	—	—	—	.15	.25	.40
73	1968 Philadelphia							
		85,170,000	—	—	—	.15	.25	.40
	1969 lg.date, lg.ship	4 known	—	4750.	6600.	10,000.	14,150.	—

Redesigned Smaller Ship

KM#	Date	Mintage	VG-8	F-12	VF-20	XF-40	MS-60	MS-63
77.1	1969	55,833,929	—	—	—	.15	.25	.40
	1970	5,249,296	—	—	—	.25	.65	.95
	1971	41,016,968	—	—	—	.15	.25	.40
	1972	60,169,387	—	—	—	.15	.25	.40
	1973	167,715,435	—	—	—	.15	.25	.40
	1974	201,566,565	—	—	—	.15	.25	.40
	1975	207,680,000	—	—	—	.15	.25	.40
	1976	95,018,533	—	—	—	.15	.25	.40
	1977	128,452,206	—	—	—	.15	.25	.40
	1978	170,366,431	—	—	—	.15	.25	.40

Smaller bust

KM#	Date	Mintage	VG-8	F-12	VF-20	XF-40	MS-60	MS-63
77.2	1979	237,321,321	—	—	—	.15	.25	.40
	1980	170,111,533	—	—	—	.15	.25	.40
	1981	123,912,900	—	—	—	.15	.25	.40
	1981	199,000	—	—	—	—	Proof	1.50
	1982	93,475,000	—	—	—	.15	.25	.40
	1982	180,908	—	—	—	—	Proof	1.50
	1983	111,065,000	—	—	—	.15	.25	.40
	1983	168,000	—	—	—	—	Proof	2.00
	1984	121,690,000	—	—	—	.15	.25	.40
	1984	161,602	—	—	—	—	Proof	2.00
	1985	143,025,000	—	—	—	.15	.25	.40
	1985	157,037	—	—	—	—	Proof	2.00
	1986	168,620,000	—	—	—	.15	.25	.40
	1986	175,745	—	—	—	—	Proof	2.00
	1987	147,309,000	—	—	—	.15	.25	.40
	1987	179,004	—	—	—	—	Proof	2.00
	1988	162,998,558	—	—	—	.15	.25	.40
	1988	175,259	—	—	—	—	Proof	2.00
	1989	199,104,414	—	—	—	.15	.25	.40
	1989	170,528	—	—	—	—	Proof	3.00

Elizabeth II Effigy by dePedery-Hunt

KM#	Date	Mintage	VG-8	F-12	VF-20	XF-40	MS-60	MS-63
183	1990	65,023,000	—	—	—	.15	.25	.40
	1990	140,649	—	—	—	—	Proof	3.00
	1991	50,397,000	—	—	—	.15	.25	.40
	1991	131,888	—	—	—	—	Proof	6.50
	1993	135,569,000	—	—	—	.15	.25	.40
	1993	143,065	—	—	—	—	Proof	3.00
	1994	145,800,000	—	—	—	.15	.25	.40
	1994	146,424	—	—	—	—	Proof	3.00
	1995	145,800,000	—	—	—	.15	.25	.40
	1995	50,000	—	—	—	—	Proof	3.00

NICKEL PLATED STEEL

KM#	Date	Mintage	VG-8	F-12	VF-20	XF-40	MS-60	MS-63
183a	1996	51,814,000	—	—	—	.15	.25	.40
	1997	42,882,000	—	—	—	.15	.25	.40
	1998	—	—	—	—	.15	.25	.40
	1998W	—	—	—	—	In Mint sets only		.50

2.4000 g, .925 SILVER, .0713 oz ASW

KM#	Date	Mintage	VG-8	F-12	VF-20	XF-40	MS-60	MS-63
183b	1996	—	—	—	—	—	Proof	5.50
	1997	—	—	—	—	—	Proof	5.50
	1998O	—	—	—	—	In Proof sets only		4.00

COMMEMORATIVE TEN CENTS

2.3328 g, .800 SILVER, .0600 oz ASW

KM#	Date	Mintage	VG-8	F-12	VF-20	XF-40	MS-60	MS-63
67	1967 Confederation Centennial							
		62,998,215	—	—	—	BV	.75	1.50

2.3328 g, .500 SILVER, .0372 oz ASW

KM#	Date	Mintage	VG-8	F-12	VF-20	XF-40	MS-60	MS-63
67a	1967 Confederation Centennial							
		Inc. Ab.	—	—	—	BV	.75	1.50

NICKEL

KM#	Date	Mintage	VG-8	F-12	VF-20	XF-40	MS-60	MS-63
206	1992 Confederation 125							
		174,476,000	—	—	—	.15	.25	.40
		147,061	—	—	—	—	Proof	3.00

KM#	Date	Mintage	2.4000 g, .925 SILVER, .0714 oz ASW VG-8	F-12	VF-20	XF-40	MS-60	MS-63
299	ND(1997) John Cabot	*.050	—	—	—	—	Proof	16.25

KM#	Date	Mintage	2.3200 g, .925 SILVER, .0690 oz ASW VG-8	F-12	VF-20	XF-40	MS-60	MS-63
311	ND(1998) 90th Anniversary Royal Canadian Mint	.025	—	—			In Matte sets only	5.50
		.025	—	—			In Proof sets only	5.50

TWENTY CENTS

KM#	Date	Mintage	4.6480 g, .925 SILVER, .1382 oz ASW VG-8	F-12	VF-20	XF-40	MS-60	MS-63
4	1858	750,000	40.00	60.00	90.00	170.00	725.00	1850.

TWENTY-FIVE CENTS

1870-1901   1902-1936

KM#	Date	Mintage	5.8100 g, .925 SILVER, .1728 oz ASW VG-8	F-12	VF-20	XF-40	MS-60	MS-63
5	1870	900,000	11.00	20.00	45.00	100.00	600.00	1350.
	1871	400,000	14.00	25.00	65.00	170.00	700.00	1850.
	1871H	748,000	16.00	27.50	80.00	200.00	700.00	1500.
	1872H	2,240,000	6.00	9.00	25.00	75.00	350.00	975.00
	1874H	1,600,000	7.00	10.00	27.00	80.00	375.00	975.00
	1875H	1,000,000	225.00	450.00	1200.	2200.	8500.	14,150.
	1880H narrow 0	400,000	30.00	60.00	165.00	360.00	900.00	2250.
	1880H wide 0	Inc. Ab.	95.00	175.00	350.00	775.00	2075.	4000.

KM#	Date	Mintage	VG-8	F-12	VF-20	XF-40	MS-60	MS-63
5	1880H wide/narrow 0	Inc. Ab.	90.00	165.00	350.00	650.00	—	—
	1881H	820,000	12.00	25.00	55.00	140.00	800.00	1400.
	1882H	600,000	13.00	27.00	65.00	170.00	800.00	1600.
	1883H	960,000	10.00	18.00	45.00	120.00	600.00	1450.
	1885	192,000	75.00	150.00	325.00	825.00	3000.	6000.
	1886/3	540,000	12.00	25.00	65.00	190.00	950.00	2200.
	1886	Inc. Ab.	10.00	20.00	60.00	175.00	800.00	1950.
	1887	100,000	75.00	160.00	350.00	825.00	3075.	6000.
	1888	400,000	10.00	20.00	50.00	130.00	550.00	1400.
	1889	66,324	95.00	175.00	350.00	825.00	3600.	6750.
	1890H	200,000	15.00	27.00	70.00	175.00	950.00	2250.
	1891	120,000	45.00	90.00	190.00	410.00	1200.	2500.
	1892	510,000	9.00	16.00	45.00	130.00	550.00	1600.
	1893	100,000	75.00	145.00	275.00	540.00	1500.	3000.
	1894	220,000	15.00	28.00	70.00	180.00	700.00	1600.
	1899	415,580	6.00	9.75	27.00	80.00	450.00	1000.
	1900	1,320,000	6.00	9.75	27.00	80.00	350.00	975.00
5	1901	640,000	6.00	9.75	27.00	80.00	375.00	975.00
11	1902	464,000	7.00	15.00	40.00	110.00	500.00	1450.
	1902H	800,000	4.00	7.25	32.00	60.00	225.00	475.00
	1903	846,150	5.00	9.00	30.00	110.00	475.00	1100.
	1904	400,000	10.00	28.00	100.00	250.00	1150.	3000.
	1905	800,000	5.50	15.00	65.00	200.00	1250.	3250.
	1906 lg. crown	1,237,843	5.00	7.25	27.00	70.00	325.00	1100.
	1906 sm. crown	Inc. Ab.	—	—	—	—	Rare	—
	1907	2,088,000	4.00	7.25	27.00	70.00	325.00	1000.
	1908	495,016	6.00	12.00	45.00	125.00	350.00	825.00
	1909	1,335,929	5.00	9.00	40.00	150.00	485.00	1350.

KM#	Date	Mintage	5.8319 g, .925 SILVER, .1734 oz ASW					
			VG-8	F-12	VF-20	XF-40	MS-60	MS-63
11a	1910	3,577,569	4.50	7.25	26.00	65.00	210.00	475.00
18	1911	1,721,341	6.00	14.00	30.00	75.00	250.00	500.00
24	1912	2,544,199	2.25	3.50	10.00	40.00	285.00	1000.
	1913	2,213,595	2.25	3.50	10.00	40.00	265.00	850.00
	1914	1,215,397	2.50	4.00	15.00	50.00	500.00	1500.
	1915	242,382	8.00	25.00	100.00	350.00	2000.	4000.
	1916	1,462,566	2.25	3.00	10.00	30.00	200.00	550.00
	1917	3,365,644	2.25	3.00	9.00	20.00	110.00	200.00
	1918	4,175,649	2.25	3.00	9.00	18.00	75.00	185.00
	1919	5,852,262	2.25	3.00	9.00	18.00	75.00	185.00

KM#	Date	Mintage	5.8319 g, .800 SILVER, .1500 oz ASW					
			VG-8	F-12	VF-20	XF-40	MS-60	MS-63
24a	1920	1,975,278	2.25	3.00	10.00	22.00	140.00	425.00
	1921	597,337	7.00	16.00	65.00	180.00	800.00	1800.
	1927	468,096	16.00	30.00	75.00	200.00	800.00	1500.
	1928	2,114,178	2.25	3.00	9.00	22.00	110.00	320.00
	1929	2,690,562	2.25	2.75	8.00	22.00	110.00	320.00
	1930	968,748	2.25	3.50	10.00	25.00	185.00	500.00
	1931	537,815	2.25	3.50	12.00	27.50	235.00	550.00
	1932	537,994	2.50	4.00	12.00	30.00	200.00	475.00
	1933	421,282	3.00	4.50	16.50	40.00	190.00	400.00
	1934	384,350	3.50	6.00	22.00	55.00	250.00	450.00
	1935	537,772	3.50	5.00	17.50	42.00	200.00	400.00
	1936	972,094	2.25	3.50	9.00	20.00	80.00	200.00

KM#	Date	Mintage	VG-8	F-12	VF-20	XF-40	MS-60	MS-63
	1936 dot	153,322	27.50	60.00	130.00	275.00	700.00	1700.

Maple Leaf Variety

KM#	Date	Mintage	VG-8	F-12	VF-20	XF-40	MS-60	MS-63
35	1937	2,690,176	1.75	3.00	4.00	5.00	10.00	25.00
	1938	3,149,245	1.75	3.00	4.50	6.50	55.00	100.00
	1939	3,532,495	1.50	2.50	3.00	6.50	50.00	85.00
	1940	9,583,650	BV	1.50	2.50	4.50	10.00	25.00
	1941	6,654,672	BV	1.50	2.50	4.50	12.00	26.00
	1942	6,935,871	BV	1.50	2.50	4.50	12.00	26.00
	1943	13,559,575	BV	1.50	2.50	4.00	15.50	30.00
	1944	7,216,237	BV	1.50	2.50	4.50	17.00	36.00
	1945	5,296,495	BV	1.50	2.50	4.00	10.00	26.00
	1946	2,210,810	BV	1.50	3.00	5.00	35.00	60.00
	1947	1,524,554	BV	1.50	3.00	6.00	40.00	75.00
	1947 dot after 7	Inc. Ab.	24.00	40.00	65.00	115.00	200.00	450.00
	1947 maple leaf	4,393,938	BV	1.50	2.75	4 00	12.00	25.00

Modified Obverse Legend

KM#	Date	Mintage	VG-8	F-12	VF-20	XF-40	MS-60	MS-63
44	1948	2,564,424	BV	1.50	3.00	5.00	40.00	90.00
	1949	7,988,830	—	BV	2.25	2.50	9.00	18.00
	1950	9,673,335	—	BV	2.25	2.50	9.00	15.00
	1951	8,290,719	—	BV	2.25	2.50	6.00	12.00
	1952	8,859,642	—	BV	2.25	2.50	6.00	12.00

Elizabeth II Effigy by Gillick

KM#	Date	Mintage	VG-8	F-12	VF-20	XF-40	MS-60	MS-63
52	1953 NSS	10,546,769	—	BV	2.25	2.50	4.00	7.00
	1953 SS	Inc. Ab.	—	BV	2.25	3.00	6.00	12.00
	1954	2,318,891	BV	2.25	3.00	6.00	20.00	30.00
	1955	9,552,505	—	—	BV	2.25	3.50	6.00
	1956	11,269,353	—	—	BV	2.25	3.00	5.00
	1957	12,770,190	—	—	BV	1.50	2.00	4.00
	1958	9,336,910	—	—	BV	1.50	2.00	4.00
	1959	13,503,461	—	—	—	BV	2.25	2.50
	1960	22,835,327	—	—	—	BV	1.50	2.50
	1961	18,164,368	—	—	—	BV	1.50	2.50
	1962	29,559,266	—	—	—	BV	1.50	2.25
	1963	21,180,652	—	—	—	BV	1.25	1.75
	1964	36,479,343	—	—	—	BV	1.25	1.75

Elizabeth II Effigy by Machin

KM#	Date	Mintage	VG-8	F-12	VF-20	XF-40	MS-60	MS-63
62	1965	44,708,869	—	—	—	BV	1.25	1.75
	1966	25,626,315	—	—	—	BV	1.25	1.75

KM#	Date	Mintage	VG-8	F-12	VF-20	XF-40	MS-60	MS-63
			5.8319 g, .500 SILVER, .0937 oz ASW					
62a	1968	71,464,000	—	—	—	BV	1.00	1.75
			NICKEL					
62b	1968	88,686,931	—	—	—	.30	.50	.75
(74.1)	1969	133,037,929	—	—	—	.30	.50	.75
	1970	10,302,010	—	—	—	.30	1.50	2.25
	1971	48,170,428	—	—	—	.30	.50	.75
	1972	43,743,387	—	—	—	.30	.50	.75
	1974	192,360,598	—	—	—	.30	.50	.75
	1975	141,148,000	—	—	—	.30	.50	.75
	1976	86,898,261	—	—	—	.30	.50	.75
	1977	99,634,555	—	—	—	.30	.50	.75
	1978	176,475,408	—	—	—	.30	.50	.75
			Smaller bust					
KM#	Date	Mintage	VG-8	F-12	VF-20	XF-40	MS-60	MS-63
74	1979	131,042,905	—	—	—	.30	.50	.75
	1980	76,178,000	—	—	—	.30	.50	.75
	1981	131,580,272	—	—	—	.30	.50	.75
	1981	199,000	—	—	—	—	Proof	2.00
	1982	171,926,000	—	—	—	.30	.50	.75
	1982	180,908	—	—	—	—	Proof	2.00
	1983	13,162,000	—	—	—	.30	.75	1.50
	1983	168,000	—	—	—	—	Proof	3.00
	1984	121,668,000	—	—	—	.30	.50	.75
	1984	161,602	—	—	—	—	Proof	2.00
	1985	158,734,000	—	—	—	.30	.50	.75
	1985	157,037	—	—	—	—	Proof	2.00
	1986	132,220,000	—	—	—	.30	.50	.75
	1986	175,745	—	—	—	—	Proof	3.00
	1987	53,408,000	—	—	—	.30	.75	1.50
	1987	179,004	—	—	—	—	Proof	3.00
	1988	80,368,473	—	—	—	.30	.75	1.50
	1988	175,259	—	—	—	—	Proof	3.50
	1989	119,796,307	—	—	—	.30	.50	.75
	1989	170,928	—	—	—	—	Proof	3.50

Elizabeth II Effigy by dePedery-Hunt

KM#	Date	Mintage	VG-8	F-12	VF-20	XF-40	MS-60	MS-63
184	1990	31,258,000	—	—	—	.30	.75	1.50
	1990	140,649	—	—	—	—	Proof	3.50
	1991	459,000	—	—	2.00	4.00	8.00	12.00
	1991	131,888	—	—	—	—	Proof	25.00
	1993	73,758,000	—	—	—	.30	.75	1.50
	1993	143,065	—	—	—	—	Proof	3.00
	1994	77,670,000	—	—	—	.30	.75	1.50
	1994	146,424	—	—	—	—	Proof	5.00
	1995	89,210,000	—	—	—	.30	.75	1.50
	1995	50,000	—	—	—	—	Proof	5.00
			NICKEL PLATED STEEL					
KM#	Date	Mintage	VG-8	F-12	VF-20	XF-40	MS-60	MS-63
184a	1996	28,106,000	—	—	—	.30	.75	1.50
	1997	—	—	—	—	.30	.75	1.50
	1998	—	—	—	—	—	—	1.75
	1998W	—	—	—	—	In Mint sets only		2.00
			5.9000 g, .925 SILVER, .1754 oz ASW					
KM#	Date	Mintage	VG-8	F-12	VF-20	XF-40	MS-60	MS-63
184b	1996	—	—	—	—	—	Proof	6.50
	1997	—	—	—	—	—	Proof	6.50
	1998O	—	—	—	—	In Proof sets only		5.00

COMMEMORATIVE TWENTY-FIVE CENTS

KM#	Date	Mintage	VG-8	F-12	VF-20	XF-40	MS-60	MS-63
68	1967 Confederation Centennial, .800 Silver							
		48,855,500	—	—	—	BV	1.25	1.75
68a	1967 Confederation Centennial, .500 Silver							
		Inc. Ab.	—	—	—	BV	1.25	1.75

KM#	Date	Mintage	VG-8	F-12	VF-20	XF-40	MS-60	MS-63
81.1	1973 RCMP Centennial, 120 beads, Nickel							
		134,958,587	—	—	—	.30	.50	.80
81.2	1973 RCMP Centennial, 132 beads, Nickel							
		Inc. Ab.	35.00	55.00	65.00	75.00	100.00	130.00
207	1992 Confederation 125, Nickel							
		442,986	—	—	—	—	—	12.50
		147,061	—	—	—	—	Proof	20.00

125th Anniversary of Confederation

KM#	Date	Mintage	VG-8	F-12	VF-20	XF-40	MS-60	MS-63
203	1992 New Brunswick, Nickel							
		12,174,000	—	—	—	—	—	.80
203a	1992 New Brunswick, .925 Silver							
		149,579	—	—	—	—	Proof	7.50

KM#	Date	Mintage	VG-8	F-12	VF-20	XF-40	MS-60	MS-63
212	1992 North West Territories, Nickel							
		12,582,000	—	—	—	—	—	.80
212a	1992 North West Territories, .925 Silver							
		149,579	—	—	—	—	Proof	7.50
213	1992 Newfoundland, Nickel							
		11,405,000	—	—	—	—	—	.80
213a	1992 Newfoundland, .925 Silver							
		149,579	—	—	—	—	Proof	7.50

KM#	Date	Mintage	VG-8	F-12	VF-20	XF-40	MS-60	MS-63
214	1992 Manitoba, Nickel							
		11,349,000	—	—	—	—	—	.80
214a	1992 Manitoba,.925 Silver	—	—	—	—	—	Proof	7.50
220	1992 Yukon, Nickel	10,388,000	—	—	—	—	—	.80
220a	1992 Yukon, .925 Silver	—	—	—	—	—	Proof	7.50

KM#	Date	Mintage	VG-8	F-12	VF-20	XF-40	MS-60	MS-63
221	1992 Alberta, Nickel	12,133,000	—	—	—	—	—	.80
221a	1992 Alberta, .925 Silver	—	—	—	—	—	Proof	7.50
222	1992 Prince Edward Island, Nickel	13,001,000	—	—	—	—	—	.80
222a	1992 Prince Edward Island, .925 Silver	149,579	—	—	—	—	Proof	7.50

223	1992 Ontario, Nickel	14,263,000	—	—	—	—	—	.80
223a	1992 Ontario, .925 Silver	—	—	—	—	—	Proof	7.50
231	1992 Nova Scotia, Nickel	13,600,000	—	—	—	—	—	.80
231a	1992 Nova Scotia, .925 Silver	149,579	—	—	—	—	Proof	7.50

KM#	Date	Mintage	VG-8	F-12	VF-20	XF-40	MS-60	MS-63
232	1992 British Columbia, Nickel	14,001,000	—	—	—	—	—	.80
232a	1992 British Columbia, .925 Silver	149,579	—	—	—	—	Proof	7.50
233	1992 Saskatchewan, Nickel	14,165,000	—	—	—	—	—	.80
233a	1992 Saskatchewan, .925 Silver	149,579	—	—	—	—	Proof	7.50

KM#	Date	Mintage	VG-8	F-12	VF-20	XF-40	MS-60	MS-63
234	1992 Quebec, Nickel	13,607,000	—	—	—	—	—	.80
234a	1992 Quebec, .925 Silver	149,579	—	—	—	—	Proof	7.50

KM#	Date	Mintage	VG-8	F-12	VF-20	XF-40	MS-60	MS-63
312	ND(1998) 90th Anniversary Royal Canadian Mint	.025	—	—			In Matte sets only	16.50
		—	—	—			In Proof sets only	16.50

FIFTY CENTS

1870-1901
11.6200 g, .925 SILVER, .3456 oz ASW

KM#	Date	Mintage	VG-8	F-12	VF-20	XF-40	MS-60	MS-63
6	1870	450,000	550.00	975.00	1800.	3250.	13,000.	23,600.
	1870 LCW	Inc. Ab.	40.00	70.00	160.00	355.00	3250.	10,000.
	1871	200,000	45.00	100.00	220.00	500.00	4000.	10,500.
	1871H	45,000	90.00	180.00	425.00	925.00	6500.	11,000.
	1872H	80,000	40.00	70.00	170.00	350.00	3600.	10,250.
	1872H inverted A for V in VICTORIA							
		Inc. Ab.	95.00	200.00	495.00	1000.	6600.	11,000.
	1881H	150,000	40.00	80.00	175.00	375.00	4000.	10,500.
	1888	60,000	110.00	220.00	490.00	975.00	5400.	11,000.
	1890H	20,000	700.00	1200.	2000.	3500.	11,000.	20,000.
	1892	151,000	45.00	90.00	225.00	450.00	6000.	10,500.
	1894	29,036	250.00	450.00	920.00	1900.	8100.	15,000.
	1898	100,000	45.00	100.00	225.00	450.00	4500.	10,500.
	1899	50,000	95.00	200.00	435.00	1100.	7100.	12,000.
	1900	118,000	40.00	65.00	160.00	350.00	4000.	10,500.
	1901	80,000	42.00	70.00	165.00	365.00	4200.	10,500.

1902-1910

Victorian Leaves   Edwardian Leaves

KM#	Date	Mintage	VG-8	F-12	VF-20	XF-40	MS-60	MS-63
12	1902	120,000	11.00	22.50	75.00	200.00	1100.	3000.
	1903H	140,000	18.00	35.00	110.00	225.00	1250.	3500.
	1904	60,000	80.00	165.00	300.00	650.00	2800.	7000.
	1905	40,000	100.00	225.00	435.00	1000.	5000.	10,000.
	1906	350,000	10.00	25.00	70.00	190.00	1150.	3250.
	1907	300,000	10.00	25.00	70.00	200.00	1250.	3850.
	1908	128,119	14.75	45.00	120.00	275.00	1150.	2250.
	1909	302,118	13.00	40.00	120.00	325.00	2175.	6000.
	1910 Victorian lvs.	649,521	9.00	22.00	65.00	180.00	950.00	3150.

11.6638 g, .925 SILVER, .3461 oz ASW

KM#	Date	Mintage	VG-8	F-12	VF-20	XF-40	MS-60	MS-63
	1910 Edwardian lvs.	Inc. Ab.	9.00	22.00	65.00	180.00	1000.	3150.

KM#	Date	Mintage	VG-8	F-12	VF-20	XF-40	MS-60	MS-63
19	1911	209,972	9.00	70.00	225.00	475.00	1300.	2900.

Modified Obverse Legend

KM#	Date	Mintage	VG-8	F-12	VF-20	XF-40	MS-60	MS-63
25	1912	285,867	4.50	16.00	75.00	200.00	1100.	2500.
	1913	265,889	4.50	16.00	85.00	210.00	1400.	4000.
	1914	160,128	10.00	45.00	135.00	400.00	2250.	5000.
	1916	459,070	3.00	14.00	50.00	125.00	700.00	2000.
	1917	752,213	3.00	12.00	35.00	90.00	500.00	1200.
	1918	754,989	3.00	8.00	22.00	70.00	425.00	1000.
	1919	1,113,429	3.00	8.00	22.00	70.00	425.00	1000.

1902-1936

| | | 11.6638 g, .800 SILVER, .3000 oz ASW | | | | | | |
KM#	Date	Mintage	VG-8	F-12	VF-20	XF-40	MS-60	MS-63
25a	1920	584,691	3.00	8.50	30.00	110.00	500.00	1250.
	1921	75 to 100 pcs.known	12,300.	17,000.	20,750.	25,000.	35,850.	45,300.

NOTE: Bowers and Merena Victoria Sale 9-89 MS-65 realized $110,000.

	1929	228,328	3.00	8.00	30.00	100.00	550.00	1100.
	1931	57,581	7.00	22.00	65.00	200.00	900.00	2000.
	1932	19,213	32.00	100.00	200.00	500.00	2400.	5500.
	1934	39,539	10.00	25.00	75.00	200.00	650.00	1200.
	1936	38,550	8.50	20.00	65.00	150.00	500.00	1000.

KM#	Date	Mintage	VG-8	F-12	VF-20	XF-40	MS-60	MS-63
36	1937	192,016	2.50	3.00	6.00	10.00	25.00	60.00
	1938	192,018	3.00	5.00	10.00	28.00	100.00	300.00
	1939	287,976	3.00	4.50	8.00	16.50	70.00	220.00
	1940	1,996,566	BV	2.00	3.00	5.00	22.00	60.00
	1941	1,714,874	BV	2.00	3.00	5.00	22.00	60.00
	1942	1,974,164	BV	2.00	3.00	5.00	22.00	60.00
	1943	3,109,583	BV	2.00	3.00	5.00	22.00	60.00
	1944	2,460,205	BV	2.00	3.00	5.00	22.00	60.00
	1945	1,959,528	BV	2.00	3.00	5.00	22.00	60.00
	1946	950,235	BV	4.00	6.00	9.00	60.00	110.00
	1946 hoof in 6	Inc. Ab.	12.00	22.50	45.00	110.00	975.00	1800.
	1947 straight 7	424,885	2.00	4.50	6.00	12.00	80.00	175.00
	1947 curved 7	Inc. Ab.	2.00	4.50	6.00	12.00	80.00	190.00
	1947ML straight 7	38,433	14.00	18.00	30.00	60.00	160.00	225.00
	1947ML curved 7	Inc. Ab.	875.00	1200.	1650.	2000.	3000.	5000.

Modified Obverse Legend

45	1948	37,784	35.00	50.00	65.00	90.00	145.00	225.00
	1949	858,991	2.00	3.00	6.00	10.00	35.00	90.00
	1949 hoof over 9	Inc. Ab.	5.00	12.00	22.00	60.00	350.00	700.00
	1950	2,384,179	3.00	4.50	9.00	20.00	175.00	275.00
	1950 lines in 0	Inc. Ab.	BV	2.50	3.00	4.00	11.00	20.00
	1951	2,421,730	BV	1.75	2.50	3.50	8.00	17.00
	1952	2,596,465	BV	1.75	2.50	3.50	8.00	16.00

Elizabeth II Effigy by Gillick

53	1953 sm. date	1,630,429	—	BV	2.00	2.50	5.50	12.00
	1953 lg.dt,straps	Inc. Ab.	—	BV	3.50	5.00	20.00	30.00
	1953 lg.dt,w/o straps	I.A.	BV	3.00	5.00	12.00	70.00	110.00
	1954	506,305	BV	2.50	4.75	7.00	20.00	30.00
	1955	753,511	BV	2.00	3.00	5.00	12.00	22.00
	1956	1,379,499	—	BV	2.00	3.00	4.50	9.00
	1957	2,171,689	—	—	BV	2.00	3.50	6.00
	1958	2,957,266	—	—	BV	2.00	3.00	5.50

New Reverse Shield

56	1959	3,095,535	—	—	BV	2.00	2.50	4.50
	1960	3,488,897	—	—	—	BV	2.25	3.25
	1961	3,584,417	—	—	—	BV	2.00	3.00
	1962	5,208,030	—	—	—	BV	2.00	3.00
	1963	8,348,871	—	—	—	BV	2.00	3.00
	1964	9,377,676	—	—	—	BV	2.00	3.00

KM#	Date	Mintage	VG-8	F-12	VF-20	XF-40	MS-60	MS-63
				Elizabeth II Effigy by Machin				
63	1965	12,629,974	—	—	—	BV	2.00	3.00
	1966	7,920,496	—	—	—	BV	2.00	3.00

| | 1968-76 | | | 1977 | | 1978- | | |

NICKEL

KM#	Date	Mintage	VG-8	F-12	VF-20	XF-40	MS-60	MS-63
75.1	1968	3,966,932	—	—	—	.50	.65	1.00
	1969	7,113,929	—	—	—	.50	.65	1.00
	1970	2,429,526	—	—	—	.50	.65	1.00
	1971	2,166,444	—	—	—	.50	.65	1.00
	1972	2,515,632	—	—	—	.50	.65	1.00
	1973	2,546,096	—	—	—	.50	.65	1.00
	1974	3,436,650	—	—	—	.50	.65	1.00
	1975	3,710,000	—	—	—	.50	.65	1.00
	1976	2,940,719	—	—	—	.50	.65	1.00
				Smaller bust				
75.2	1977	709,839	—	—	.50	.75	1.50	2.00
75.3	1978 square jewels	3,341,892	—	—	—	.50	.75	1.00
	1978 round jewels	Inc. Ab.	—	—	.50	2.50	3.00	4.00
	1979	3,425,000	—	—	—	.50	.65	1.00
	1980	1,574,000	—	—	—	.50	.65	1.00
	1981	2,690,272	—	—	—	.50	.65	1.00
	1981	199,000	—	—	—	—	Proof	3.00
	1982 small beads	2,236,674	—	—	—	.50	.65	1.00
	1982 small beads	180,908	—	—	—	—	Proof	3.00
	1982 large beads	Inc. Ab.	—	—	—	.50	.65	1.00
	1983	1,177,000	—	—	—	.50	.65	1.00
	1983	168,000	—	—	—	—	Proof	3.00
	1984	1,502,989	—	—	—	.50	.65	1.00
	1984	161,602	—	—	—	—	Proof	3.00
	1985	2,188,374	—	—	—	.50	.65	1.00
	1985	157,037	—	—	—	—	Proof	3.50
	1986	781,400	—	—	—	.50	1.50	2.00
	1986	175,745	—	—	—	—	Proof	3.50
	1987	373,000	—	—	—	.50	2.00	2.50
	1987	179,004	—	—	—	—	Proof	4.00
	1988	220,000	—	—	—	.50	1.50	2.20
	1988	175,259	—	—	—	—	Proof	4.00
	1989	266,419	—	—	—	.50	2.00	2.75
	1989	170,928	—	—	—	—	Proof	4.50

Elizabeth II Effigy by dePedery-Hunt

185	1990	207,000	—	—	—	.50	2.00	3.00
	1990	140,649	—	—	—	—	Proof	7.50
	1991	490,000	—	—	—	.50	.85	1.60
	1991	131,888	—	—	—	—	Proof	10.00
	1993	393,000	—	—	—	.50	.85	1.25
	1993	143,065	—	—	—	—	Proof	5.00
	1994	987,000	—	—	—	.50	.75	1.00
	1994	146,424	—	—	—	—	Proof	6.00
	1995	626,000	—	—	—	.50	.75	1.00
	1995	50,000	—	—	—	—	Proof	6.00

NICKEL PLATED STEEL

185a	1996	458,000	—	—	—	.50	.65	1.00

.925 SILVER

185b	1996	—	—	—	—	—	Proof	7.50
	1997	—	—	—	—	—	Proof	7.50
290	1997 Redesigned Arms, Nickel plated Steel							
		387,000	—	—	—	.50	.65	1.00
	1998	—	—	—	—	.50	.65	1.00
	1998W	—	—	—	—	In Mint sets only		1.75
290a	1997 Redesigned Arms, .925 Silver							
		—	—	—	—	—	Proof	7.00
	1998O	—	—	—	—	In Proof sets only		6.00

COMMEMORATIVE FIFTY CENTS

KM#	Date / Mintage	VG-8	F-12	VF-20	XF-40	MS-60	MS-63
69	1967 Confederation Centennial, .800 Silver						
	4,211,392	—	—	—	3.00	4.00	4.50
208	1992 Confederation 125, Nickel						
	445,000	—	—	—	.50	1.25	1.50
	147,061	—	—	—	—	Proof	8.50

KM#	Date / Mintage	VG-8	F-12	VF-20	XF-40	MS-60	MS-63
261	1995 Atlantic Puffin, .925 Silver	—	—	—	—	Proof	11.50
262	1995 Whooping Crane, .925 Silver	—	—	—	—	Proof	11.50
263	1995 Gray Jays, .925 Silver	—	—	—	—	Proof	11.50

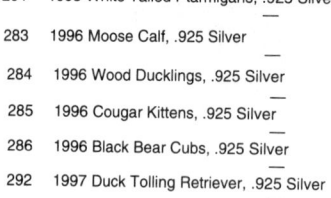

KM#	Date / Mintage	VG-8	F-12	VF-20	XF-40	MS-60	MS-63
264	1995 White Tailed Ptarmigans, .925 Silver	—	—	—	—	Proof	11.50
283	1996 Moose Calf, .925 Silver	—	—	—	—	Proof	12.00
284	1996 Wood Ducklings, .925 Silver	—	—	—	—	Proof	12.00
285	1996 Cougar Kittens, .925 Silver	—	—	—	—	Proof	12.00
286	1996 Black Bear Cubs, .925 Silver	—	—	—	—	Proof	12.00
292	1997 Duck Tolling Retriever, .925 Silver	—	—	—	—	Proof	12.50

KM#	Date	VG-8	F-12	VF-20	XF-40	MS-60	MS-63
293	1997 Labrador Retriever, .925 Silver	—	—	—	—	Proof	13.50
294	1997 Newfoundland, .925 Silver	—	—	—	—	Proof	13.50
295	1997 Eskimo Dog, .925 Silver	—	—	—	—	Proof	12.50

KM#	Date	Mintage	VG-8	F-12	VF-20	XF-40	MS-60	MS-63
313	ND(1998) 90th Anniversary Royal Canadian Mint, .925 Silver							
		.025	—	—			In Matte sets only	32.25
		.025	—	—			In Proof sets only	32.25

KM#	Date	Mintage	VG-8	F-12	VF-20	XF-40	MS-60	MS-63
314	ND(1998) 110 Years Canadian Speed and Figure Skating, .925 Silver							
		—	—	—	—	—	Proof	12.00
315	ND(1998) 100 Years Canadian Ski Racing and Jumping, .925 Silver							
		—	—	—	—	—	Proof	12.00
318	1998 Killer Whales, .925 Silver							
		—	—	—	—	—	Proof	12.00
319	1998 Humpback whale, .925 Silver							
		—	—	—	—	—	Proof	12.00
320	1998 Beluga Whale, .925 Silver							
		—	—	—	—	—	Proof	12.00
321	1998 Blue Whale, .925 Silver							
		—	—	—	—	—	Proof	12.00

327	ND(1998) 110 Years Canadian Soccer, .925 Silver							
		—	—	—	—	—	Proof	12.00
328	ND(1998) 20 Years Canadian Auto Racing, .925 Silver							
		—	—	—	—	—	Proof	12.00

VOYAGEUR DOLLARS

23.3276 g, .800 SILVER, .6000 oz ASW

KM#	Date	Mintage	F-12	VF-20	XF-40	AU-50	MS-60	MS-63
31	1936	339,600	10.00	13.50	18.00	21.50	36.00	75.00

		Pointed 7		Blunt 7	Maple Leaf (blunt 7 only)			
KM#	Date	Mintage	F-12	VF-20	XF-40	AU-50	MS-60	MS-63
37	1937	207,406	9.00	10.50	12.50	15.00	25.00	60.00
	1937	1,295	—	—	—	Proof	—	450.00
	1937	I.A.	—	—	—	Matte Proof	—	250.00
	1938	90,304	25.00	40.00	55.00	60.00	75.00	215.00
	1945	38,391	65.00	115.00	135.00	155.00	200.00	420.00
	1945	—	—	—	—	—	Specimen	1800.
	1946	93,055	13.50	25.00	35.00	40.00	70.00	200.00
	1947 pointed 7	Inc. Bl.	55.00	85.00	110.00	145.00	255.00	950.00
	1947 blunt 7	65,595	35.00	60.00	85.00	100.00	115.00	210.00
	1947 maple leaf	21,135	100.00	140.00	155.00	190.00	225.00	475.00

Modified Left Legend

KM#	Date	Mintage	F-12	VF-20	XF-40	AU-50	MS-60	MS-63
46	1948	18,780	450.00	525.00	615.00	685.00	785.00	1150.
	1950 w/4 water lines	261,002	5.00	8.00	11.00	12.00	18.00	32.00
	1950 w/4 water lines, (1 known)						Matte Proof	—
	1950 Arnprior w/1-1/2 w.l.	I.A.	7.00	10.00	13.50	20.00	36.00	100.00
	1951 w/4 water lines	416,395	4.00	5.00	7.00	8.50	11.50	26.00
	1951 w/4 water lines	—	—	—	—	—	Proof	400.00
	1951 Arnprior w/1-1/2 w.l.	I.A.	25.00	34.00	47.00	65.00	105.00	275.00
	1952 w/4 water lines	406,148	4.00	5.00	7.00	8.00	11.50	26.00
	1952 Arnprior	I.A.	35.00	55.00	70.00	120.00	175.00	375.00
	1952 Arnprior	—	—	—	—	—	Proof	Rare
	1952 w/o water lines	I.A.	5.00	6.50	9.00	10.00	16.50	40.00

Elizabeth II Effigy by Gillick

KM#	Date	Mintage	Mintage	VF-20	XF-40	AU-50	MS-60	MS-63
54	1953 w/o strap, wire rim		1,074,578	3.85	4.50	5.00	8.00	16.00
	1953 w/strap, flat rim		Inc. Ab.	3.85	4.50	5.00	8.00	16.00
54	1954		246,606	7.00	10.00	12.00	16.50	32.50
	1955 w/4 water lines		268,105	7.00	10.00	12.00	16.50	29.00
	1955 Arnprior w/1-1/2 w.l.*		I.A.	60.00	75.00	95.00	110.00	165.00
	1956		209,092	9.00	13.50	15.50	19.00	40.00
	1957 w/4 water lines		496,389	BV	4.75	6.00	8.00	13.50
	1957 w/1 water line		I.A.	5.50	7.50	8.50	12.00	26.50
	1959		1,443,502	—	—	BV	5.00	7.50
	1960		1,420,486	—	—	BV	5.00	7.50
	1961		1,262,231	—	—	BV	5.00	7.50
	1962		1,884,789	—	—	BV	5.00	7.50
	1963		4,179,981	—	—	BV	5.00	7.50

*NOTE: All genuine circulation strike 1955 Arnprior dollars have a die break running along the top of TI in the word GRATIA on the obverse.

Small Beads	Medium Beads	Large Beads

Elizabeth II Effigy by Machin

KM#	Date	Mintage	VF-20	XF-40	AU-50	MS-60	MS-63
64.1	1965 sm. beads, pointed 5	10,768,569	—	—	BV	4.75	6.50
	1965 sm. beads, blunt 5	Inc. Ab.	—	—	BV	4.75	6.50
	1965 lg. beads, blunt 5	Inc. Ab.	—	—	BV	7.50	10.00
	1965 lg. beads, pointed 5	Inc. Ab.	—	—	BV	4.75	6.50
	1965 med. beads, pointed 5	Inc. Ab.	6.75	8.75	10.75	14.00	27.50
	1966 lg. beads	9,912,178	—	—	BV	4.50	6.50
	1966 sm. beads	*485 pcs.	—	750.00	1250.	1400.	1700.

23.3276 g, .500 SILVER, .3750 oz ASW, 36mm

KM#	Date	Mintage	Smaller bust MS-63	Mintage	P/L	Spec.
64.2a	1972	—	—	341,598	—	8.00

NICKEL, 32mm

KM#	Date		Mintage	Large bust MS-63		Mintage	P/L	Spec.
76.1	1968		5,579,714	1.65		1,408,143	3.00	—
	1969		4,809,313	1.65		594,258	3.50	—
	1972		2,676,041	2.00		405,865	3.75	—

KM#	Date	Mintage	Smaller bust MS-63	Mintage	P/L	Spec.
76.2	1975	3,256,000	2.00	322,325	3.75	—
	1976	2,498,204	2.50	274,106	4.00	—

| 76.3 | 1975 mule w/1976 obv. | Inc. Ab. | — | — | * | — |

*NOTE: Only known in proof-like sets w/1976 obv. slightly modified.

KM#	Date	Mintage	Modified Reverse MS-63	Mintage	P/L	Spec.
117	1977	1,393,745	2.50	—	3.50	—
120.1	1978	2,948,488	2.00	—	3.50	—
	1979	2,954,842	2.00	—	3.50	—
	1980	3,291,221	2.00	—	4.50	—

Modified Design

KM#	Date	Mintage	MS-63	Mintage	P/L	Proof
120.1	1981	2,778,900	2.00	—	5.00	6.50
	1982	1,098,500	2.00	—	5.00	6.50
	1983	2,267,525	2.00	—	5.00	8.00
120.1	1984	1,223,486	2.00	—	5.00	—
	1984	161,602	—	—	—	8.00
	1985	3,104,092	2.00	—	5.00	—
	1985	157,037	—	—	—	7.50
	1986	3,089,225	2.00	—	6.00	—
	1986	175,259	—	—	—	10.00
	1987	287,330	2.00	—	7.00	—
	1987	179,004	—	—	—	10.00
120.2	1985 mule w/New Zealand 50 cent, KM-37 obverse	—	—	—	—	—

LOON DOLLARS

AUREATE-BRONZE PLATED NICKEL

KM#	Date	Elizabeth II Effigy by Machin Mintage	MS-63	P/L	Proof
157	1987	205,405,000	2.75	—	—
	1987	178,120	—	—	8.00
	1988	138,893,539	2.75	4.75	—
	1988	175,259	—	—	7.50
	1989	184,773,902	2.75	4.75	—
	1989	170,928	—	—	7.50

KM#	Date	Elizabeth II Effigy by dePedery-Hunt Mintage	MS-63	P/L	Proof
186.1	1990	68,402,000	2.25	4.75	—
	1990	140,649	—	—	9.00
	1991	23,156,000	2.50	6.50	—
	1991	—	—	—	18.00
	1993	33,662,000	2.50	5.50	—
	1993	—	—	—	9.00

KM#	Date	Mintage	MS-63	P/L	Proof
186.1	1994	36,237,000	2.00	5.50	—
	1994	—	—	—	9.00
	1995	41,813,000	2.00	6.50	—
	1995	—	—	—	9.00
	1996	17,101,000	2.00	4.75	—
	1996	—	—	—	7.50
	1997	—	2.50	—	—
	1998	—	2.50	—	—
		—	—	—	10.50
	1998O	—		In Proof sets only	10.00
	1998W	—		In Mint sets only	3.50

COMMEMORATIVE DOLLARS

			23.3276 g, .800 SILVER, .6000 oz ASW					
KM#	Date	Mintage	F-12	VF-20	XF-40	AU-50	MS-60	MS-63
30	1935 Jubilee	428,707	13.50	20.00	30.00	32.50	38.00	65.00

38	1939 Royal Visit	1,363,816	5.00	6.00	7.00	8.50	11.50	25.00
	1939 Royal Visit	—	—	—	—	—	Specimen	475.00
	1939 Royal Visit	—	—	—	—	—	Proof	2500.
47	1949 Newfoundland	672,218	9.00	12.00	18.50	22.00	25.00	31.50
	1949 Newfoundland	—	—	—	—	—	Specimen	725.00

KM#	Date	Mintage	F-12	VF-20	XF-40	AU-50	MS-60	MS-63
55	1958 Br. Columbia	3,039,630	BV	4.50	5.00	5.50	6.50	10.50

KM#	Date	Mintage	F-12	VF-20	XF-40	AU-50	MS-60	MS-63
58	1964 Charlottetown	7,296,832	—	—	—	BV	4.50	7.50

KM#	Date	Mintage	MS-63	P/L	Spec.
70	1967 Goose, Confederation Centennial	6,767,496	7.50	9.00	450.00

KM#	Date	Mintage	MS-63	P/L	Spec.
78	1970 Manitoba (Nickel, 32mm)	4,140,058	2.00	—	—
		645,869	—	2.50	—

KM#	Date	Mintage	MS-63	P/L	Spec.
79	1971 Br. Columbia (Nickel, 32mm)	4,260,781	2.00	2.50	—
		468,729	—	(c) 2.50	—

KM#	Date	Mintage	MS-63	P/L	Spec.
		23.3276 g, .500 SILVER, .3750 oz ASW*			
80	1971 Br. Columbia (.500 Silver, 36mm)	585,674	—	—	7.50

*NOTE: All silver dollars dated 1971 to date are minted to this standard.

82	1973 Pr. Edward Island (Nickel, 32mm)	3,196,452	2.00	—	—
		466,881	—	(c) 2.50	

KM#	Date	Mintage	MS-63	P/L	Spec.
83	1973 Mountie (.500 Silver, 36mm)	1,031,271	—	—	5.00
83v	1973 Mountie, with metal crest on case	Inc. Ab.	—	—	12.00

88	1974 Winnipeg (Nickel, 32mm)	2,799,363	2.00	—	—
		363,786	—	(c) 3.00	—
88a	1974 Winnipeg (.500 Silver, 36mm)	728,947	—	—	5.00

KM#	Date	Mintage	MS-63	P/L	Spec.
97	1975 Calgary (.500 Silver, 36mm)	930,956	—	—	4.25

KM#	Date	Mintage	MS-63	P/L	Spec.
106	1976 Parliament Library (.500 Silver, 36mm)	578,708	—	—	6.00

KM#	Date	Mintage	MS-63	P/L	Spec.
118	1977 Silver Jubilee	744,848	—	—	5.00

KM#	Date	Mintage	MS-63	P/L	Spec.
121	1978 XI Games (.500 Silver, 36mm)	709,602	—	—	5.00

KM#	Date	Mintage	MS-63	P/L	Spec.
124	1979 Griffon (.500 Silver, 36mm)	826,695	—	—	10.00

KM#	Date	Mintage	MS-63	P/L	Spec.
128	1980 Arctic Territories (.500 Silver, 36mm)	539,617	—	—	20.00

KM#	Date	Mintage	MS-63	P/L	Proof
130	1981 Railroad (.500 Silver, 36mm)	699,494	16.00	—	15.50

KM#	Date	Mintage	MS-63	P/L	Proof
133	1982 Regina (.500 Silver, 36mm)	144,930	14.25	—	—
		758,958	—	—	5.00

KM#	Date	Mintage	MS-63	P/L	Proof
134	1982 Constitution (Nickel, 32mm)	9,709,422	3.00	—	6.00

KM#	Date	Mintage	MS-63	P/L	Proof
138	1983 Edmonton University Games	159,450	8.50	—	—
	(.500 Silver, 36mm)	506,847	—	—	6.50

KM#	Date	Mintage	MS-63	P/L	Proof
140	1984 Toronto Sesquicentennial	133,610	22.50	—	—
	(.500 Silver, 36mm)	732,542	—	—	5.50

KM#	Date	Mintage	MS-63	P/L	Proof
141	1984 Cartier (Nickel, 32mm)	7,009,323	2.25	—	—
		87,760	—	—	6.50

KM#	Date	Mintage	MS-63	P/L	Proof
143	1985 National Parks - Moose	163,314	14.50	—	—
	(.500 Silver, 36mm)	733.354	—	—	6.00

KM#	Date	Mintage	MS-63	P/L	Proof
149	1986 Vancouver	125,949	21.50	—	—
	(.500 Silver, 36mm)	680,004	—	—	7.00

KM#	Date	Mintage	MS-63	P/L	Proof
154	1987 John Davis	118,722	16.50	—	—
	(.500 Silver, 36mm)	602,374	—	—	9.50

KM#	Date	Mintage	MS-63	P/L	Proof
161	1988 Ironworks	106,872	25.00	—	—
	(.500 Silver, 36mm)	255,013	—	—	20.00

KM#	Date	Mintage	MS-63	P/L	Proof
168	1989 MacKenzie River	99,774	18.50	—	—
	(.500 Silver, 36mm)	244,062	—	—	30.00

KM#	Date	Mintage	MS-63	P/L	Proof
170	1990 Henry Kelsey	99,455	14.50	—	—
	(.500 Silver, 36mm)	254,959	—	—	15.00

KM#	Date	Mintage	MS-63	P/L	Proof
179	1991 S.S. Frontenac	73,843	15.00	—	—
	(.500 Silver, 36mm)	195,424	—	—	20.00

KM#	Date	Mintage	MS-63	P/L	Proof
210	1992 Stagecoach Service	78,160	14.50	—	—
	(.925 Silver, 36mm)	187,612	—	—	15.00

125th Anniversary of the Confederation

KM#	Date	Mintage	MS-63	P/L	Proof
186.2	ND(1992) Loon, Aureate	4,242,085	2.50	—	—
(209)		—	—	—	10.50

218	ND(1992) Parliament, Aureate	23,915,000	2.50	—	—
		24,227	—	—	11.50

NOTE: (c) Individually cased Proof-likes (P/L), Proofs or Specimens are from broken up Proof-like or specimen sets.

KM#	Date	Mintage	MS-63	P/L	Proof
235	1993 Stanley Cup Hockey	88,150	11.50	—	—
	(.925 Silver, 36mm)	294,314	—	—	14.50

KM#	Date	Mintage	MS-63	P/L	Proof
248	1994 War Memorial	15,000,000	2.50	—	—
	Aureate, 26mm	54,524	—	—	12.50

KM#	Date	Mintage	MS-63	P/L	Proof
251	1994 Last RCMP Sled Dog Patrol	61,561	22.00	—	—
	(.925 Silver, 36mm)	170,374	—	—	25.00

KM#	Date	Mintage	MS-63	P/L	Proof
258	1995 Peacekeeping Monument in Ottawa,	—	2.50	—	—
	Aureate, 26mm	50,000	—	—	12.50

KM#	Date	Mintage	MS-63	P/L	Proof
259	1995 Hudson Bay Company,	—	14.50	—	—
	(.925 Silver, 36mm)	—	—	—	15.00
274	1996 McIntosh Apple	—	17.50	—	—
	(.925 Silver, 36mm)	—	—	—	18.50

KM#	Date	Mintage	MS-63	P/L	Proof
282	ND(1997) 25th Anniversary Hockey Victory	—	14.50	—	—
	(.925 Silver, 36mm)	—	—	—	19.50
291	1997 10th Anniversary - Loon Dollar				
	Aureate. 26mm	—	9.50	—	—

296	1997 10th Anniversary - Loon Dollar (.925 Silver, 36mm)	*.025	—	—	60.00

KM#	Date	Mintage	MS-63	P/L	Proof
306	120th Anniversary Royal Canadian Mounted Police			15.00	
	(.925 Silver, 36mm)	—	—	—	22.50

*NOTE: (c) Individually cased Proof-likes (P/L), Proofs or Specimens are from broken up Proof-like or specimen sets.

2 DOLLARS

ALUMINUM-BRONZE center in NICKEL ring

KM#	Date	Mintage	MS-63	P/L	Proof
270	1996 Polar Bear	375,483,000	3.50	9.00	15.75
	1997	16,942,000	3.50	—	—
	1998	—	3.50	—	—
	1998W	—	—	In Mint sets only	4.00

5.7456 g, GOLD, .1847 oz AGW center within 5.0958 g, SILVER, .1638 oz ASW ring

KM#	Date	Mintage	MS-63	P/L	Proof
270a	1996	5,000	—	—	365.00

25.0000 g, GOLD plated .925 SILVER center in .925 SILVER ring, .7434 oz ASW

KM#	Date	Mintage	MS-63	P/L	Proof
270b	1996	*.015	—	—	80.00

8.8300 g, GOLD plated center, .925 SILVER in .925 SILVER ring, .2626 oz ASW

KM#	Date	Mintage	MS-63	P/L	Proof
270c	1997	—	—	—	23.50
	1998O	—		In Proof sets only	20.00

5 DOLLARS

		8.3592 g, .900 GOLD, .2419 oz AGW					
KM#	Date	Mintage	F-12	VF-20	XF-40	AU-50	MS-60	MS-63
26	1912	165,680	135.00	160.00	190.00	200.00	325.00	725.00
	1913	98,832	135.00	160.00	190.00	200.00	325.00	825.00
	1914	31,122	200.00	300.00	375.00	500.00	800.00	2300.

Olympic Commemoratives

24.3000 g, .925 SILVER, .7227 oz ASW

Series I

KM#	Date	Mintage	MS-63	Proof
84	1973 Sailboats (Kingston)	—	5.25	—
		165,203	—	6.50

KM#	Date	Mintage	MS-63	Proof
85	1973 North America Map	—	5.25	—
		165,203	—	6.50

Series II

KM#	Date	Mintage	MS-63	Proof
89	1974 Olympic Rings	—	5.25	—
		97,431	—	6.50

KM#	Date	Mintage	MS-63	Proof
90	1974 Athlete with torch	—	5.25	—
		97,431	—	6.50

Series III

KM#	Date	Mintage	MS-63	Proof
91	1974 Rowing	—	5.25	—
		104.684	—	6.50

KM#	Date	Mintage	MS-63	Proof
92	1974 Canoeing	—	5.25	—
		104,684	—	6.50

Series IV

KM#	Date	Mintage	MS-63	Proof
98	1975 Marathon	—	5.25	—
		89,155	—	6.50

KM#	Date	Mintage	MS-63	Proof
99	1975 Ladies' Javelin	—	5.25	—
		89,155	—	6.50

Series V

KM#	Date	Mintage	MS-63	Proof
100	1975 Swimmer	—	5.25	—
		89,155	—	6.50

KM#	Date	Mintage	MS-63	Proof
101	1975 Diver	—	5.25	—
		89,155	—	6.50

Series VI

KM#	Date	Mintage	MS-63	Proof
107	1976 Fencing	—	5.25	—
		82,302	—	7.00

KM#	Date	Mintage	MS-63	Proof
108	1976 Boxing	—	5.25	—
		82,302	—	7.00

Series VII

KM#	Date	Mintage	MS-63	Proof
109	1976 Olympic Village	—	5.25	—
		76,908	—	7.00

KM#	Date	Mintage	MS-63	Proof
110	1976 Olympic Flame	—	5.25	—
		79,102	—	7.00

31.3900 g, .9999 SILVER, 1.0091 oz ASW   *.080

316	1998 Dr. Norman Bethune		In Proof sets only	36.50

10 DOLLARS

16.7185 g, .900 GOLD, .4838 oz AGW

KM#	Date	Mintage	F-12	VF-20	XF-40	AU-50	MS-60	MS-63
27	1912	74,759	250.00	350.00	400.00	500.00	750.00	2500.
	1913	149,232	250.00	350.00	400.00	500.00	775.00	3300.
	1914	140,068	275.00	375.00	425.00	600.00	925.00	3100.

PRICING SECTION

Olympic Commemoratives

48.6000 g, .925 SILVER, 1.4454 oz ASW

Series I

KM#	Date	Mintage	MS-63	Proof
86.1	1973 World Map	103,426	10.25	—
		165,203	—	13.00
86.2	1974 World Map (Error-Mule)	320 pcs.	235.00	—

KM#	Date	Mintage	MS-63	Proof
87	1973 Montreal Skyline	—	10.25	—
		165,203	—	13.00

Series II

KM#	Date	Mintage	MS-63	Proof
93	1974 Head of Zeus	—	10.25	—
		104,684	—	13.00

KM#	Date			Mintage	MS-63	Proof
94	1974 Temple of Zeus			—	10.25	—
				104,684	—	13.00

Series III

KM#	Date			Mintage	MS-63	Proof
95	1974 Cycling			—	10.25	—
				97,431	—	13.00

KM#	Date			Mintage	MS-63	Proof
96	1974 Lacrosse			—	10.25	—
				97,431	—	13.00

Series IV

KM#	Date	Mintage	MS-63	Proof
102	1975 Men's Hurdles	—	10.25	—
		82,302	—	13.00

KM#	Date	Mintage	MS-63	Proof
103	1975 Ladies' Shot Put	—	10.25	—
		82,302	—	13.00

Series V

KM#	Date	Mintage	MS-63	Proof
104	1975 Sailing	—	10.25	—
		89,155	—	13.50

KM#	Date	Mintage	MS-63	Proof
105	1975 Canoeing	— 89,155	10.25 —	— 13.50

Series VI

KM#	Date	Mintage	MS-63	Proof
111	1976 Football	— 76,908	10.25 —	— 14.00

KM#	Date	Mintage	MS-63	Proof
112	1976 Field Hockey	— 76,908	10.25 —	— 14.00

Series VII

KM#	Date	Mintage	MS-63	Proof
113	1976 Olympic Stadium	—	10.25	—
		79,102	—	14.00

KM#	Date	Mintage	MS-63	Proof
114	1976 Olympic Velodrome	—	10.25	—
		79,102	—	14.00

15 dollars

Olympic Commemoratives

33.6300 g, .925 SILVER, 1.0000 oz ASW

KM#	Date	Mintage	MS-63	Proof
215	1992 Coaching Track	*275,000	—	28.00

KM#	Date	Mintage	MS-63	Proof
216	1992 High Jump, Rings, Speed Skating	*275,000	—	28.00

33.6300 g, .925 SILVER, 1.0000 oz ASW and
0.3700 g, .9999 GOLD insert, .0118 oz AGW

KM#	Date	Mintage	MS-63	Proof
304	1998 Year of the Tiger	.069	—	55.00
331	1999 Year of the Rabbit	—	—	70.00

20 dollars

18.2733 g, .900 GOLD, .5288 oz AGW

KM#	Date	Mintage	MS-63	Proof
71	1967 Centennial	337,688	—	210.00

Olympic Commemoratives

33.6300 g, .925 SILVER, 1.0000 oz ASW

KM#	Date	Mintage	MS-63	Proof
145	1985 Winter Olympics, Downhill Skier, lettered edge			
		406,360	—	22.50
	1985 Plain edge	Inc. Ab.	—	180.00

KM#	Date	Mintage	MS-63	Proof
146	1985 Winter Olympics, Speed Skater, lettered edge	354,222	—	22.50
	1985 Plain edge	Inc. Ab.	—	180.00

KM#	Date	Mintage	MS-63	Proof
147	1986 Winter Olympics, Biathlon, lettered edge	308,086	—	22.50
	1986 Plain edge	Inc. Ab.	—	180.00

KM#	Date	Mintage	MS-63	Proof
148	1986 Winter Olympics, Hockey, lettered edge	396,602	—	22.50
	1986 Plain edge	Inc. Ab.	—	180.00

KM#	Date	Mintage	MS-63	Proof
150	1986 Winter Olympics, Cross Country Skier	303,199	—	22.50

KM#	Date	Mintage	MS-63	Proof
151	1986 Winter Olympics, Free Style Skier, lettered edge			
		294,322	—	22.50
	1986 Plain edge	Inc. Ab.	—	180.00

34.1070 g, .925 SILVER, 1.0000 oz ASW

KM#	Date	Mintage	MS-63	Proof
155	1987 Winter Olympics, Figure Skater	334,875	—	22.50

KM#	Date	Mintage	MS-63	Proof
156	1987 Winter Olympics, Curling	286.457	—	22.50

KM#	Date	Mintage	MS-63	Proof
159	1987 Winter Olympics, Ski Jumper	290,954	—	22.50

KM#	Date	Mintage	MS-63	Proof
160	1987 Winter Olympics, Bobsled	274,326	—	22.50

Aviation Commemoratives

31.1030 g, .925 SILVER, .9743 oz ASW, w/.0257 oz AGW GOLD Cameo, 1.0000 oz ASW

KM#	Date	Mintage	MS-63	Proof
172	1990 Lancaster/Fauquier	43,596	—	190.00

KM#	Date	Mintage	MS-63	Proof
173	1990 Anson and Harvard	41,844	—	60.00

KM#	Date	Mintage	MS-63	Proof
196	1991 Silver Dart	28,791	—	45.00

PRICING SECTION

KM#	Date	Mintage	MS-63	Proof
197	1991 de Haviland "Beaver"	29,399	—	45.00

KM#	Date	Mintage	MS-63	Proof
224	1992 Curtiss JN-4 Canuck ("Jenny")	33,105	—	45.00

KM#	Date	Mintage	MS-63	Proof
225	1992 de Haviland Gypsy Moth	32,537	—	45.00

KM#	Date	Mintage	MS-63	Proof
236	1993 Fairchild 71C Float plane	32,199	—	45.00

KM#	Date	Mintage	MS-63	Proof
237	1993 Lockheed 14	32,550	—	45.00

KM#	Date	Mintage	MS-63	Proof
246	1994 Curtiss HS-2L Seaplane	31,242	—	45.00
247	1994 Vickers Vedette	30,880	—	45.00

KM#	Date	Mintage	MS-63	Proof
271	1995 C-FEA1 Fleet Cannuck	17,438	—	50.00
272	1995 DHC-1 Chipmunk	17,722	—	50.00

KM#	Date	Mintage	MS-63	Proof
276	1996 CF-100 Cannuck	18,508	—	50.00
277	1996 CF-105 Arrow	27,163	—	50.00
297	1997 Canadair F-86 Sabre	14,389	—	50.00

KM#	Date	Mintage	MS-63	Proof
298	1997 Canadair CT-114 Tutor	15,669	—	50.00
329	1998 CP-107 Argus	*.050	—	45.00
330	1998 CP-215 Waterbomber	*.050	—	45.00

100 DOLLARS

13.3375 g, .583 GOLD, .2500 oz AGW

KM#	Date	Mintage	MS-63	Proof
115	1976 Olympics, beaded borders, 27mm	650,000	90.00	—

16.9655 g, .917 GOLD, .5000 oz AGW

KM#	Date	Mintage	MS-63	Proof
116	1976 Olympics, reduced size, 25mm, plain borders	337,342	—	190.00

KM#	Date	Mintage	MS-63	Proof
119	1977 Queen's Silver Jubilee	180,396	—	190.00
122	1978 Canadian Unification	200,000	—	190.00
126	1979 Year of the Child	250,000	—	190.00
129	1980 Arctic Territories	300,000	—	190.00

KM#	Date	Mintage	MS-63	Proof
131	1981 National Anthem	102,000	—	190.00
137	1982 New Constitution	121,708	—	190.00

KM#	Date	Mintage	MS-63	Proof
139	1983 St. John's, Newfoundland	83,128	—	190.00
142	1984 Jacques Cartier	67,662	—	195.00

KM#	Date	Mintage	MS-63	Proof
144	1985 National Parks - Big horn sheep	61,332	—	195.00
152	1986 Peace	76,409	—	190.00

13.3375 g, .583 GOLD, .2500 oz AGW

KM#	Date	Mintage	MS-63	Proof
158	1987 1988 Olympics - Torch and logo, lettered edge	142,750	—	105.00
	1987 Plain edge	Inc. Ab.	—	350.00
162	1988 Whales	52,594	—	122.50

KM#	Date	Mintage	MS-63	Proof
169	1989 Sainte-Marie	59,657	—	115.00
171	1990 Intl. Literacy Year	49,940	—	115.00

KM#	Date	Mintage	MS-63	Proof
180	1991 S.S. Empress of India	*33,966	—	135.00
211	1992 Montreal	28,162	—	145.00
245	1993 Antique Automobiles	25,971	—	160.00

KM#	Date	Mintage	MS-63	Proof
249	1994 WWII Home Front	16,201	—	175.00
260	1995 Louisbourg	16,916	—	175.00

13.3380 g, .5833 GOLD, and .4167 SILVER alloy
.2500 oz AGW and 1787 oz ASW

KM#	Date	Mintage	MS-63	Proof
273	1996 Klondike Gold Rush	17,973	—	170.00
287	1997 Alexander Graham Bell	*25,000	—	190.00
307	1998 Discovery of Insulin	.025	—	195.00

175 DOLLARS

16.9700 g, .917 GOLD, .5000 oz AGW

KM#	Date	Mintage	MS-63	Proof
217	1992 Olympics - Passing the Torch	22,092	—	325.00

200 DOLLARS

17.1060 g, .917 GOLD, .5042 oz AGW

KM#	Date	Mintage	MS-63	Proof
178	1990 Canada Flag Silver Jubilee	20,980	—	200.00
202	1991 Hockey	10,215	—	245.00
230	1992 Niagara Falls	9,465	—	265.00

17.1350 g, .917 GOLD, .5500 oz AGW

KM#	Date	Mintage	MS-63	Proof
244	1993 Mounted Police	10,807	—	235.00
250	1994 Novel: Anne of Green Gables	8,017	—	235.00
265	1995 Maple Syrup Production	7,621	—	260.00
275	1996 Transcontinental Canadian Railway	7,508	—	265.00

KM#	Date	Mintage	MS-63	Proof
288	1997 Haida Mask	*.025	—	295.00
317	1998 Legendary White Buffalo	*.025	—	305.00

350 DOLLARS

KM#	Date	**38.0500 g, .9999 GOLD, 1.2233 oz AGW** Mintage	MS-63	Proof
308	1998	1,998		745.00

SOVEREIGN

1908-1910   **7.9881 g, .917 GOLD, .2354 oz AGW**   1911-1919

C mint mark below horse's rear hooves

KM#	Date	Mintage	F-12	VF-20	XF-40	AU-50	MS-60	MS-63
14	1908C	636 pcs.	1000.	1750.	2350.	2850.	3450.	4250.
	1909C	16,273	155.00	220.00	285.00	400.00	650.00	1900.
	1910C	28,012	125.00	175.00	250.00	300.00	600.00	1900.
20	1911C	256,946	105.00	115.00	125.00	145.00	200.00	245.00
	1911C	—	—	—	—		Specimen	6500.
	1913C	3,715	400.00	550.00	750.00	1000.	1650.	2800.
	1914C	14,871	175.00	250.00	325.00	550.00	675.00	1400.
	1916C	*About 20 known	7920.	12,500.	14,000.	16,750.	20,000.	31,000.

NOTE: Stacks's A.G. Carter Jr. Sale 12-89 Gem BU realized $82,500.

	1917C	58,845	110.00	120.00	130.00	160.00	200.00	465.00
	1918C	106,516	110.00	120.00	130.00	160.00	200.00	945.00
	1919C	135,889	110.00	120.00	130.00	160.00	200.00	660.00

SILVER BULLION ISSUES
5 DOLLARS

31.1000 g, .9999 SILVER, 1.0000 oz ASW

KM#	Date	Mintage	MS-63	Proof
163	1988 Maple leaf	1,155,931	8.00	—
	1989 Maple leaf	3,288,235	7.25	—
	1989 Maple leaf	43,965	—	28.50

New Elizabeth II Effigy

187	1990 Maple leaf	1,708,800	8.00	—
	1991 Maple leaf	644,300	10.00	—
	1992 Maple leaf	343,800	10.00	—
	1993 Maple leaf	889,946	7.50	—
	1994 Maple leaf	1,133,900	7.75	—
	1995 Maple leaf	326,244	7.75	—
	1996 Maple leaf	250,445	9.50	—
	1997 Maple leaf	100,970	9.50	—
	1998 Maple leaf	—	7.50	—
	1999 Maple leaf	—	7.50	—

50 DOLLARS

311.0350 g, .9999 SILVER, 10.0000 oz ASW

KM#	Date	Mintage	MS-63	Proof
326	1998 10th Anniversary Silver Maple Leaf	*.025	—	150.00

GOLD BULLION ISSUES
1 DOLLAR

1.5551 g, .9999 GOLD, .0500 oz AGW

KM#	Date	Mintage	MS-63	Proof
238	1993 Maple leaf	37,080	BV + 37%	—
	1994 Maple leaf	78,860	BV + 37%	—
	1995 Maple leaf	85,920	BV + 37%	—
	1996 Maple leaf	56,520	BV + 37%	—
	1997 Maple leaf	59,720	BV + 37%	—

2 DOLLARS

2.0735 g, .9999 GOLD, .0666 oz AGW

KM#	Date	Mintage	MS-63	Proof
256	1994 Maple leaf	3,540	BV + 80%	—
	1995 Maple leaf	4,275	BV + 80%	—
	1996 Maple leaf	—	BV + 80%	—
	1997 Maple leaf	—	BV + 80%	—

5 DOLLARS

3.1200 g, .9999 GOLD, .1000 oz AGW

Elizabeth II Effigy by Machin

KM#	Date	Mintage	MS-63	Proof
135	1982 Maple leaf	246,000	BV + 14%	—
	1983 Maple leaf	304,000	BV + 14%	—
	1984 Maple leaf	262,000	BV + 14%	—
	1985 Maple leaf	398,000	BV + 14%	—
	1986 Maple leaf	529,516	BV + 14%	—
	1987 Maple leaf	459,000	BV + 14%	—
	1988 Maple leaf	506,500	BV + 14%	—
	1989 Maple leaf	539,000	BV + 14%	—
	1989 Maple leaf	16,992	—	75.00

Elizabeth II Effigy by dePedery-Hunt

KM#	Date	Mintage	MS-63	Proof
188	1990 Maple leaf	476,000	BV + 14%	—
	1991 Maple leaf	322,000	BV + 14%	—
	1992 Maple leaf	384,000	BV + 14%	—
	1993 Maple leaf	248,630	BV + 14%	—
	1994 Maple leaf	313,150	BV + 14%	—
	1995 Maple leaf	294,890	BV + 14%	—
	1996 Maple leaf	179,220	BV + 14%	—
	1997 Maple leaf	188,540	BV + 14%	—

10 DOLLARS

7.7850 g, .9999 GOLD, .2500 oz AGW

Elizabeth II Effigy by Machin

KM#	Date	Mintage	MS-63	Proof
136	1982 Maple leaf	184,000	BV + 10%	—
	1983 Maple leaf	308,800	BV + 10%	—
	1984 Maple leaf	242,400	BV + 10%	—
	1985 Maple leaf	620,000	BV + 10%	—
	1986 Maple leaf	915,200	BV + 10%	—
	1987 Maple leaf	376,000	BV + 10%	—
	1988 Maple leaf	436,000	BV + 10%	—
	1989 Maple leaf	328,800	BV + 10%	—
	1989 Maple leaf	6,998	—	175.00

Elizabeth II Effigy by dePedery-Hunt

KM#	Date	Mintage	MS-63	Proof
189	1990 Maple leaf	253,600	BV + 10%	—
	1991 Maple leaf	166,400	BV + 10%	—
	1992 Maple leaf	179,600	BV + 10%	—
	1993 Maple leaf	158,452	BV + 10%	—
	1994 Maple leaf	148,792	BV + 10%	—
	1995 Maple leaf	127,596	BV + 10%	—
	1996 Maple leaf	89,148	BV + 10%	—
	1997 Maple leaf	98,104	BV + 10%	—

20 DOLLARS

15.5515 g, .9999 GOLD, .5000 oz AGW
Elizabeth II Effigy by Machin

KM#	Date	Mintage	MS-63	Proof
153	1986 Maple leaf	529,200	*BV + 7%*	—
	1987 Maple leaf	332,800	*BV + 7%*	—
	1988 Maple leaf	538,400	*BV + 7%*	—
	1989 Maple leaf	259,200	*BV + 7%*	—
	1989 Maple leaf	6,998	—	275.00

Elizabeth II Effigy by dePedery-Hunt

190	1990 Maple leaf	174,400	*BV + 7%*	—
	1991 Maple leaf	96,200	*BV + 7%*	—
	1992 Maple leaf	108,000	*BV + 7%*	—
	1993 Maple leaf	99,492	*BV + 7%*	—
	1994 Maple leaf	104,766	*BV + 7%*	—
	1995 Maple leaf	103,162	*BV + 7%*	—
	1996 Maple leaf	66,246	*BV + 7%*	—
	1997 Maple leaf	63,354	*BV + 7%*	—

50 DOLLARS

31.1030 g, .999 GOLD, 1.0000 oz AGW
Rev: 999. Maple Leaf. 999.

KM#	Date	Mintage	MS-63	Proof
125.1	1979 Maple leaf	1,000,000	*BV + 4%*	—
	1980 Maple leaf	1,251,500	*BV + 4%*	—
	1981 Maple leaf	863,000	*BV + 4%*	—
	1982 Maple leaf	883,000	*BV + 4%*	—

31.1030 g, .9999 GOLD, 1.0000 oz AGW
Rev: 9999 Maple Leaf 9999

KM#	Date	Mintage	MS-63	Proof
125.2	1983 Maple leaf	843,000	*BV + 4%*	—
	1984 Maple leaf	1,067,500	*BV + 4%*	—
	1985 Maple leaf	1,908,000	*BV + 4%*	—
	1986 Maple leaf	779,115	*BV + 4%*	—
	1987 Maple leaf	978,000	*BV + 4%*	—
	1988 Maple leaf	826,500	*BV + 4%*	—
	1989 Maple leaf	856,000	*BV + 4%*	—
	1989 Maple leaf	17,781	—	450.00

Elizabeth II Effigy by dePedery-Hunt

191	1990 Maple leaf	815,000	*BV + 4%*	—
	1991 Maple leaf	290,000	*BV + 4%*	—
	1992 Maple leaf	368,900	*BV + 4%*	—
	1993 Maple leaf	321,413	*BV + 4%*	—
	1994 Maple leaf	180,357	*BV + 4%*	—
	1995 Maple leaf	208,729	*BV + 4%*	—
	1996 Maple leaf	143,682	*BV + 4%*	—
	1997 Maple leaf	465,298	*BV + 4%*	—

KM#	Date	Mintage	MS-63	Proof
305	1997 Guaranteed Gold Mountie	12,913	335.00	—

PLATINUM BULLION ISSUES
1 DOLLAR

1.5552 g, .9995 PLATINUM, .0500 oz APW

KM#	Date	Mintage	MS-63	Proof
239	1993 Maple Leaf	2,120	BV + 35%	—
	1994 Maple Leaf	4,260	BV + 35%	—
	1995 Maple Leaf	460 pcs.	BV + 35%	—
	1996 Maple Leaf	1,640	BV + 35%	—
	1997 Maple Leaf	1,340	BV + 35%	—

2 DOLLARS

2.0735 g, .9995 PLATINUM, .0666 oz APW

KM#	Date	Mintage	MS-63	Proof
257	1994 Maple leaf	1,470	395.00	—
	1995 Maple leaf	1,335	BV + 80%	—
	1996 Maple leaf	—	BV + 80%	—
	1997 Maple leaf	—	BV + 80%	—

5 DOLLARS

3.1203 g, .9995 PLATINUM, .1000 oz APW
Elizabeth II Effigy by Machin

KM#	Date	Mintage	MS-63	Proof
164	1988 Maple leaf	74,000	BV + 18%	—
	1989 Maple leaf	18,000	BV + 18%	—
	1989 Maple leaf	11,999	—	90.00

Elizabeth II Effigy by dePedery-Hunt

KM#	Date	Mintage	MS-63	Proof
192	1990 Maple leaf	9,000	BV + 18%	—
	1991 Maple leaf	13,000	BV + 18%	—
	1992 Maple leaf	16,000	BV + 18%	—
	1993 Maple leaf	14,020	BV + 18%	—
	1994 Maple leaf	19,190	BV + 18%	—
	1995 Maple leaf	8,940	BV + 18%	—
	1996 Maple leaf	8,820	BV + 18%	—
	1997 Maple leaf	7,050	BV + 18%	—

10 DOLLARS

7.7857 g, .9995 PLATINUM, .2500 oz APW
Elizabeth II Effigy by Machin

KM#	Date	Mintage	MS-63	Proof
165	1988 Maple leaf	93,600	BV + 13%	—
	1989 Maple leaf	3,200	BV + 13%	—
	1989 Maple leaf	1,999	—	175.00

Elizabeth II Effigy by dePedery-Hunt

KM#	Date	Mintage	MS-63	Proof
193	1990 Maple leaf	1,600	BV + 13%	—
	1991 Maple leaf	7,200	BV + 13%	—
	1992 Maple leaf	11,600	BV + 13%	—
	1993 Maple leaf	8,048	BV + 13%	—
	1994 Maple leaf	9,456	BV + 13%	—
	1995 Maple leaf	6,524	BV + 13%	—
	1996 Maple leaf	6,160	BV + 13%	—
	1997 Maple leaf	4,552	BV + 13%	—

20 DOLLARS

Elizabeth II Effigy by Machin

15.5519 g, .9995 PLATINUM, .5000 oz APW

KM#	Date	Mintage	MS-63	Proof
166	1988 Maple leaf	23,600	BV + 9%	—
	1989 Maple leaf	4,800	BV + 9%	—
	1989 Maple leaf	1,999	—	350.00

KM#	Date	Mintage	MS-63	Proof
	Elizabeth II Effigy by dePedery-Hunt			
194	1990 Maple leaf	2,600	BV + 9%	—
	1991 Maple leaf	5,600	BV + 9%	—
	1992 Maple leaf	12,800	BV + 9%	—
	1993 Maple leaf	6,022	BV + 9%	—
	1994 Maple leaf	6,710	BV + 9%	—
	1995 Maple leaf	6,308	BV + 9%	—
	1996 Maple leaf	5,490	BV + 9%	—
	1997 Maple leaf	3,990	BV + 9%	—

30 DOLLARS

3.1100 g, .999 PLATINUM, .1000 oz APW

KM#	Date	Mintage	MS-63	Proof
174	1990 Polar bear swimming	2,629	Proof	90.00
198	1991 Snowy Owl	*3,500	Proof	90.00
226	1992 Cougar head and shoulders	*3,500	Proof	100.00
240	1993 Arctic fox	*3,500	Proof	90.00

KM#	Date	Mintage	MS-63	Proof
252	1994 Sea otter	1,500 sets only	Proof	95.00
266	1995 Canadian lynx	620 pcs.	Proof	100.00
278	1996 Falcon portrait	489 pcs.	Proof	130.00
300	1997 Bison head	5,000	Proof	115.00
322	1998 Gray wolf	*2,000	Proof	120.00

50 DOLLARS

31.1030 g, .9995 PLATINUM, 1.0000 oz APW

Elizabeth II Effigy by Machin

KM#	Date	Mintage	MS-63	Proof
167	1988 Maple leaf	37,500	BV + 4%	—
	1989 Maple leaf	10,000	BV + 4%	—
	1989 Maple leaf	5,965	—	700.00

Elizabeth II Effigy by dePedery-Hunt

195	1990 Maple leaf	15,100	BV + 4%	—
	1991 Maple leaf	31,900	BV + 4%	—
	1992 Maple leaf	40,500	BV + 4%	—
	1993 Maple leaf	17,666	BV + 4%	—
	1994 Maple leaf	36,245	BV + 4%	—
	1995 Maple leaf	25,829	BV + 4%	—
	1996 Maple leaf	62,273	BV + 4%	—
	1997 Maple leaf	25,480	BV + 4%	—

75 DOLLARS

7.7760 g, .999 PLATINUM, .2500 oz APW

175	1990 Polar bear resting	2,629	Proof	200.00
199	1991 Snowy Owls perched on branch	*3,500	Proof	220.00
227	1992 Cougar prowling	*3,500	Proof	220.00
241	1993 2 Arctic foxes	*3,500	Proof	230.00

253	1994 Sea otter eating urchin	1,500 sets only	Proof	235.00
267	1995 2 lynx kittens	*1,500	Proof	250.00
279	1996 Peregrine falcon - diving falcon	*1,500	Proof	210.00
301	1997 Two bison calves	1,500	Proof	215.00
323	1998 Gray wolf	1,000 sets only	Proof	210.00

150 DOLLARS

15.5520 g, .999 PLATINUM, .5000 oz APW

KM#	Date	Mintage	MS-63	Proof
176	1990 Polar bear walking	2,629	Proof	360.00
200	1991 Snowy Owl flying	*3,500	Proof	375.00
228	1992 Cougar mother and cub	*3,500	Proof	375.00

KM#	Date	Mintage	MS-63	Proof
242	1993 Arctic fox by lake	*3,500	Proof	400.00
254	1994 Sea otter mother carrying pup	1,500 sets only	Proof	435.00
268	1995 Prowling lynx	226 pcs.	Proof	450.00
280	1996 Peregrine falcon - falcon on branch	100 pcs.	Proof	445.00
302	1997 Bison bull	4,000	Proof	420.00
324	1998 2 gray wolf cubs	*2,000	Proof	420.00

300 DOLLARS

31.1035 g, .999 PLATINUM, 1.0000 oz APW

KM#	Date	Mintage	MS-63	Proof
177	1990 Polar bear mother and cub	2,629	Proof	700.00
201	1991 Snowy Owl w/chicks	*3,500	Proof	650.00

KM#	Date	Mintage	MS-63	Proof
229	1992 Cougar resting in tree	*3,500	Proof	650.00
243	1993 Mother fox and 3 kits	*3,500	Proof	800.00
255	1994 2 otters swimming	—	Proof	850.00

KM#	Date	Mintage	MS-63	Proof
269	1995 Female lynx and 3 kittens	*1,500	Proof	875.00
281	1996 Peregrine falcon feeding nestlings	*1,500	Proof	825.00

31.1600 g, .9995 PLATINUM, 1.0013 oz APW

KM#	Date	Mintage	MS-63	Proof
303	1997 Bison family	1,500	Proof	820.00
325	1998 Gray wolf and 2 cubs	1,000 sets only	Proof	820.00

PROOF-LIKE DOLLARS

23.3276 g, .800 SILVER, .6000 oz ASW

KM#	Date	Mintage	Identification	Issue Price	Mkt Value
D3	1953	1,200	KM54, Canoe w/shoulder fold	—	275.00
D4	1954	5,300	KM54, Canoe	1.25	150.00
D5	1955	7,950	KM54, Canoe	1.25	125.00

KM#	Date	Mintage	Identification	Issue Price	Mkt Value
D5a	1955	Inc. Ab.	KM54, Arnprior	1.25	185.00
D6	1956	10,212	KM54, Canoe	1.25	65.00
D7	1957	16,241	KM54, Canoe	1.25	35.00
D8	1958	33,237	KM55, British Columbia	1.25	32.00
D9	1959	45,160	KM54, Canoe	1.25	14.50
D10	1960	82,728	KM54, Canoe	1.25	9.50
D11	1961	120,928	KM54, Canoe	1.25	9.00
D12	1962	248,901	KM54, Canoe	1.25	7.50
D13	1963	963,525	KM54, Canoe	1.25	6.50
D14	1964	2,862,441	KM58, Charlottetown	1.25	6.50
D15	1965	2,904,352	KM64, Canoe	—	6.50
D16	1966	672,514	KM64, Canoe	—	6.50
D17	1967	1,036,176	KM70, Confederation	—	8.50

MINT SETS (MS)
Olympic Commemoratives

KM#	Date	Mintage	Identification	Issue Price	Mkt Value
MS1	1973(4)	—	KM84-87, Series I	45.00	31.00
MS2	1974(4)	—	KM89-90,93-94, Series II	48.00	31.00
MS3	1974(4)	—	KM91-92,95-96, Series III	48.00	31.00
MS4	1975(4)	—	KM98-99,102-103, Series IV	48.00	31.00
MS5	1975(4)	—	KM100-101,104-105, Series V	60.00	31.00
MS6	1976(4)	—	KM107-108,111-112, Series VI	60.00	31.00
MS7	1976(4)	—	KM109-110,113-114, Series VII	60.00	31.00

SPECIMEN SETS (SS)

NOTE: Some authorities list these as proof sets. However, the Canadian Mint does not. The coins are double struck with higher than usual pressure, but are considered to have the same quality as proof issue from the Royal Mint, London.

KM#	Date	Mintage	Identification	Issue Price	Mkt Value
SS1	1858(4)	—	KM1-4 Reeded Edge	—	6000.
SS2	1858(4)	—	KM1-4 Plain Edge	—	6000.
SS3	1858(8)	—	KM1-4 Double Set	—	12,500.
SS4	1858(8)	—	KM1(overdate),2-4 Double Set	—	14,000.
SS5	1870(4)	100*	KM2,3,5,6 (reeded edges)	—	12,500.
SS6	1870(8)	—	KM2,3,5,6 Double Set (plain edges)	—	25,000.
SS7	1872H(4)	—	KM2,3,5,6	—	12,500.
SS8	1875H(2)	—	KM2(Large Date),3,5	—	20,000.
SS9	1880H(3)	—	KM2,3,5(Narrow 0)	—	7000.
SS10	1881H(5)	—	KM7,2,3,5,6	—	12,000.
SS11	1892(2)	—	KM3,5	—	10,000.
SS12	1902(5)	100*	KM8-12	—	10,000.
SS13	1902H(3)	—	KM9(Large H),10,11	—	6500.
SS14	1903H(3)	—	KM10,12,13	—	7000.

NOTE: A 1903H double set has been reported on display in Bombay, India.

KM#	Date	Mintage	Identification	Issue Price	Mkt Value
SS15	1908(5)	1,000*	KM8,10-13	—	2200.
SS16	1911(5)	1,000*	KM15-19	—	5500.
SS17	1911/12(8)	5	KM15-20,26-27	—	52,250.
SS18	1921(5)	—	KM22-25,28	—	80,000.
SS19	1922(2)	—	KM28,29	—	800.00
SS20	1923(2)	—	KM28,29	—	800.00
SS21	1924(2)	—	KM28,29	—	800.00
SS22	1925(2)	—	KM28,29	—	1800.
SS23	1926(2)	—	KM28,29 (Near 6)	—	1800.
SS24	1927(3)	—	KM24a,28,29	—	3200.
SS25	1928(4)	—	KM23a,24a,28,29	—	2800.
SS26	1929(5)	—	KM23a-25a,28,29	—	10,000.
SS27	1930(4)	—	KM23a,24a,28,29	—	6500.
SS28	1931(5)	—	KM23a-25a,28,29	—	8500.
SS29	1932(5)	—	KM23a-25a,28,29	—	10,000.
SS30	1934(5)	—	KM23-25,28,29	—	8500.
SS31	1936(5)	—	KM23-25,28,29	—	8500.
SS32	1936(6)	—	KM23a(dot),24a(dot),25a,28(dot),29,30	—	Rare
SS33	1937(6)	1025*	KM32-37 Matte Finish	—	750.00
SS34	1937(4)	—	KM32-35 Mirror Fields	—	500.00
SS35	1937(6)	75*	KM32-37 Mirror Fields	—	1550.
SS36	1938(6)	—	KM32-37	—	25,000.
SS-A36	1939(6)	—	KM32-35,38 Matte Finish	—	—
SS-B36	1939(6)	—	KM32-35,38 Mirror Fields	—	—
SS-C36	1942(2)	—	KM32,33	—	300.00
SS-D36	1943(2)	—	KM32,40	—	300.00
SS37	1944(5)	3	KM32,34-37,40a	—	11,300.
SS-A37	1944(2)	—	KM32,40a	—	300.00
SS38	1945(6)	6	KM32,34-37,40a	—	6500.
SS-A38	1945(2)	—	KM32,40a	—	300.00
SS39	1946(6)	15	KM32,34-37,39a	—	4000.
SS40	1947(6)	—	KM32,34-36(7 curved),37(pointed 7),39a	—	8500.
SS41	1947(6)	—	KM32,34-36(7 curved),37(blunt 7),39a	—	6200.
SS42	1947ML(6)	—	KM32,34-36(7 curved right),37,39a	—	4250.

PRICING SECTION

KM#	Date	Mintage	Identification	Issue Price	Mkt Value
SS43	1948(6)	30	KM41-46	—	7500.
SS44	1949(6)	20	KM41-45,47	—	3200.
SS44A	1949(2)	—	KM47	—	1550.
SS45	1950(6)	12	KM41-46	—	2300.
SS46	1950(6)	—	KM41-45,46(Arnprior)	—	4500.
SS47	1951(7)	12	KM41,48,42a,43-46 (w/water lines)	—	2725.
SS48	1952(6)	2,317	KM41,42a,43-46 (water lines)	—	3175.
SS48A	1952(6)	—	KM41,42a,43-46 (w/o water lines)	—	—
SS49	1953(6)	28	KM49 w/o straps,50-54	—	1850.
SS50	1953(6)	—	KM49 w/straps,50-54	—	1250.
SS51	1964(6)	—	KM49,51,52,56-58	—	450.00
SS52	1965(6)	—	KM59.1-60.1,61-63,64.1	—	450.00

Double Dollar Prestige Sets

KM#	Date	Mintage	Identification	Issue Price	Mkt Value
SS56	1971(7)	66,860	KM59.1-60.1,62b-75.1,77.1,79(2 pcs.)	12.00	10.00
SS57	1972(7)	36,349	KM59.1-60.1,62b-75.1,76.1,(2 pcs.), 77.1	12.00	15.00
SS58	1973(7)	119,819	KM59.1-60.1,75.1,77.1,81.1,82,83	12.00	10.00
SS59	1973(7)	Inc. Ab.	KM59.1-60.1,75.1,77.1,81.2,82,83	—	135.00
SS60	1974(7)	85,230	KM59.1-60.1,62b-75.1,77.1,88,88a	15.00	10.00
SS61	1975(7)	97,263	KM59.1-60.1,62b-75.1,76.2,77.1,97	15.00	10.00
SS62	1976(7)	87,744	KM59.1-60.1,62b-75.1,76.2,77.1,106	16.00	10.00
SS63	1977(7)	142,577	KM59.1-60.1,62b,75.2,77.1,117.1,118	16.50	10.00
SS64	1978(7)	147,000	KM59.1-60.1,62b,75.3,77.1,120,121	16.50	10.00
SS65	1979(7)	155,698	KM59.2-60.2,74,75.3,77.2,120,124	18.50	12.50
SS66	1980(7)	162,875	KM60.2,74-75.3,77.2,120,127,128	30.50	25.00

Regular Specimen Sets Resumed

KM#	Date	Mintage	Identification	Issue Price	Mkt Value
SS67	1981(6)	71,300	KM60.2,74,75.3,77.2,120,123	10.00	6.00
SS68	1982(6)	62,298	KM60.2a,74,75.3,77.2,120,123	11.50	6.00
SS69	1983(6)	60,329	KM60.2a,74,75.3,77.2,120,132	12.75	6.00
SS70	1984(6)	60,400	KM60.2a,74,75.3,77.2,120,132	10.00	6.00
SS71	1985(6)	61,553	KM60.2a,74,75.3,77.2,120,132	10.00	6.50
SS73	1986(6)	67,152	KM60.2a,74,75.3,77.2,120,132	10.00	6.50
SS72	1987(6)	75,194	KM60.2a,74,75.3,77.2,120,132	11.00	7.00
SS73	1988(6)	70,205	KM60.2a,74,75.3,77.2,132,157	12.30	8.00
SS74	1989(6)	75,306	KM60.2a,74,75.3,77.2,132,157	14.50	14.50
SS75	1990(6)	76,611	KM181-186	15.50	14.50
SS76	1991(6)	68,552	KM181-186	15.50	32.50
SS77	1992(6)	78,328	KM204-209	16.25	21.50
SS78	1993(6)	77,351	KM181-186	16.25	16.50
SS79	1994(6)	77,349	KM181-186	*16.50	19.50
SS80	1995(6)	—	KM181-186	13.95	19.50
SS81	1996(6)	—	KM181-186	—	20.00
SS82	1996(6)	—	KM181a-185a,186	18.95	20.00
SS83	1997(7)	—	KM182a-184a,270,289-291	19.95	22.50
SS84	1998(7)	—	KM182-184,186,270, 289,290	19.95	20.00

NOTE: *Estimated.

V.I.P. SPECIMEN SETS (VS)

NOTE: A very limited number of cased Specimen sets were produced by the Mint beginning in 1969 for presentation to dignitaries visiting the Royal Canadian Mint or other parts of Canada. (A small quantity of 1970 cased Specimen sets were sold to the public for $13.00 each.) The coins, 1¢ to $1.00 were cased in long narrow leather cases (black and other colors).

KM#	Date	Mintage	Identification	Issue Price	Mkt Value
VS1	1969	4 known	—	—	1700.
VS2	1970	100	KM59.1-60.1,74.1-75.1,77.1,78	—	350.00
VS3	1971	69	KM59.1-60.1,74.1-75.1,77.1,79(2 pcs.)	—	375.00
VS4	1972	25	KM59.1-60.1,74.1-75.1,76.1,(2 pcs.),77.1	—	435.00
VS5	1973	26	KM59.1-60.1,75.1,77.1,81.1,82,83	—	435.00
VS6	1974	72	KM59.1-60.1,74.1-75.1,77.1,88,88a	—	375.00
VS7	1975	94	KM59.1-60.1,74.1-75.1,76.2,77.1,97	—	375.00
VS8	1976	—	KM59.1-60.1,74.1-75.1,76.2,77.1,106	—	375.00

PROOF-LIKE SETS (PL)

NOTE: These sets do not have the quality of the Proof or Specimen Set, but are specially produced and packaged.

KM#	Date	Mintage	Identification	Issue Price	Mkt Value
PL1	1953(6)	1,200	KM49 w/o straps, 50-54	2.20	1250.
PL2	1953(6)	Inc. Ab.	KM49-54	2.20	760.00
PL3	1954(6)	3,000	KM49-54	2.50	205.00
PL4	1954(6)	Inc. Ab.	KM49 w/o straps, 50-54	2.50	475.00
PL5	1955(6)	6,300	KM49,50a,51-54	2.50	145.00
PL6	1955(6)	Inc. Ab.	KM49,50a,51-54,Arnprior	2.50	225.00
PL7	1956(6)	6,500	KM49,50a,51-54	2.50	80.00
PL8	1957(6)	11,862	KM49,50a,51-54	2.50	50.00
PL9	1958(6)	18,259	KM49,50a,51-53,55	2.50	40.00
PL10	1959(6)	31,577	KM49,50a,51,52,54,56	2.50	18.00
PL11	1960(6)	64,097	KM49,50a,51,52,54,56	3.00	13.50
PL12	1961(6)	98,373	KM49,50a,51,52,54,56	3.00	12.00
PL13	1962(6)	200,950	KM49,50a,51,52,54,56	3.00	9.00
PL14	1963(6)	673,006	KM49,51,52,54,56,57	3.00	7.50
PL15	1964(6)	1,653,162	KM49,51,52,56-58	3.00	7.50
PL16	1965(6)	2,904,352	KM59.1-60.1,61-63,64.1	4.00	7.50
PL17	1966(6)	672,514	KM59.1-60.1,61-63,64.1	4.00	7.50
PL18	1967(6)	961,887	KM65-70 (pliofilm flat pack)	4.00	12.00
PL18A	1967(6)	70,583	KM65-70 and Silver Medal (red box)	12.00	16.50

PL18B	1967(7)	337,688	KM65-71 (black box)	40.00	250.00
PL19	1968(6)	521,641	KM59.1-60.1,62b,72a,75.1-76.1	4.00	2.50
PL20	1969(6)	326,203	KM59.1-60.1,62b,75.1-77.1	4.00	2.50
PL21	1970(6)	349,120	KM59.1-60.1,62b-75.1,77.1,78	4.00	3.25
PL22	1971(6)	253,311	KM59.1-60.1,62b-75.1,77.1,79	4.00	2.50
PL23	1972(6)	224,275	KM59.1-60.1,62b-77.1	4.00	2.50
PL24	1973(6)	243,695	KM59.1-60.1,62b-75.1 obv. 120 beads, 77.1,81.1,82	4.00	2.50
PL25	1973(6)	Inc. Ab.	KM59.1-60.1,62b-75.1 obv. 132 beads, 77.1,81.2,82	4.00	125.00
PL26	1974(6)	213,589	KM59.1-60.1,62b-75.1,77.1,88	5.00	2.75
PL27.1	1975(6)	197,372	KM59.1,60.1,62b-75.1,76.2,77.1	5.00	2.75
PL27.2	1975(6)	Inc. Ab.	KM59.1,60.1,62b-75.1,76.3,77.1	5.00	—
PL28	1976(6)	171,737	KM59.1,60.1,62b-75.1,76.2,77.1	5.15	3.00
PL29	1977(6)	225,307	KM59.1,60.1,62b,75.2,77.1,117.1	5.15	2.50
PL30	1978(6)	260,000	KM59.1-60.1,62b,75.3,77.1,120	5.25	2.50
PL31	1979(6)	187,624	KM59.2-60.2,74,75.3,77.2,120	6.25	3.00
PL32	1980(6)	410,842	KM60.2,74,75.3,77.2,120,127	6.50	4.50
PL33	1981(6)	186,250	KM60.2,74,75.3,77.2,120,123	5.00	3.75
PL34	1982(6)	203,287	KM60.2,74,75.3,77.2,120,123	6.00	2.75
PL36	1983(6)	190,838	KM60.2a,74,75.3,77.2,120,132	5.00	6.00
PL37	1984(6)	181,249	KM60.2a,74,75.3,77.2,120,132	5.25	5.50
PL38	1985(6)	173,924	KM60.2a,74,75.3,77.2,120,132	5.25	6.50
PL39	1986(6)	167,338	KM60.2a,74,75.3,77.2,120,132	5.25	7.50
PL40	1987(6)	212,136	KM60.2a,74,75.3,77.2,120,132	5.25	5.50
PL41	1988(6)	182,048	KM60.2a,74,75.3,77.2,132,157	6.05	6.75
PL42	1989(6)	173,622	KM60.2a,74,75.3,77.2,132,157	6.60	9.00
PL43	1990(6)	170,791	KM181-186	7.40	9.00
PL44	1991(6)	147,814	KM181-186	7.40	25.00

KM#	Date	Mintage	Identification	Issue Price	Mkt Value
PL45	1992(6)	217,597	KM204-209	8.25	12.50
PL46	1993(6)	171,680	KM181-186	8.25	6.00
PL47	1994(6)	141,676	KM181-185,258	*8.50	7.00
PL48	1994(6)	18,794	KM181-185,258 (Oh Canada holder)	—	12.00
PL49	1995(6)	143,892	KM181-186	6.95	7.00
PL50	1995(6)	50,927	KM181-186 (Oh Canada holder)	14.65	15.00
PL51	1995(6)	36,443	KM181-186 (Baby Gift holder)	—	13.50
PL52	1996(6)	116,736	KM181-186	—	12.50
PL53	1996(6)	29,747	KM181-186 (Oh Canada holder)	—	15.00
PL54	1996(6)	—	KM181a-185a,186	8.95	10.00
PL55	1996(6)	—	KM181a-185a,186 (Oh Canada holder)	14.65	15.00
PL56	1996(6)	—	KM181a-185a,186 (Baby Gift holder)	—	15.00
PL57	1997(7)	—	KM182a-184a,209, 270,289-290	10.45	11.50
PL58	1997(7)	—	KM182a-184a,270, 289-291 (Oh Canada holder)	16.45	16.50
PL59	1997(7)	—	KM182a-184a,209,270 289-290 (Baby Gift holder)	18.50	17.50
PL60	1998W(7)	—	KM182-184,186,270,289-290	10.45	10.50
PL61	1998W(7)	—	KM182-184,186,270,289-290, (Oh Canada holder)	16.45	16.50
PL62	1998W(7)	—	KM182-184,186,270,289-290, (Tiny Treasures holder)	16.45	16.50

CUSTOM PROOF-LIKE SETS (CPL)

KM#	Date	Mintage	Identification	Issue Price	Mkt Value
Each set contains two 1 cent pieces.					
CPL1	1971(7)	33,517	KM59.1(2 pcs.),60.1,62b-75.1,77.1,79	6.50	5.25
CPL2	1972(7)	38,198	KM59.1(2 pcs.),60.1,62b,75.1-77.1	6.50	5.25
CPL3	1973(7)	35,676	KM59.1(2 pcs.),60.1,75.1, 77.1,81.1 obv. 120 beads, 82	6.50	5.25
CPL4	1973(7)	Inc. Ab.	KM59.1(2 pcs.),60.1,75.1, 77.1,81.1 obv. 132 beads,82	6.50	140.00
CPL5	1974(7)	44,296	KM59.1(2 pcs.),60.1,62b-75.1,77.1,88	8.00	5.25
CPL6	1975(7)	36,851	KM59.1(2 pcs.),60.1,62b-75.1,76.2,77.1	8.00	5.25
CPL7	1976(7)	28,162	KM59.1(2 pcs.),60.1,62b-75.1,76.2,77.1	8.00	6.00
CPL8	1977(7)	44,198	KM59.1(2 pcs.),60.1,62b,75.2,77.1,117	8.15	6.00
CPL9	1978(7)	41,000	KM59.1(2 pcs.),60.1,62b,75.3,77.1,120	—	6.00
CPL10	1979(7)	31,174	KM59.2(2 pcs.),60.2,74,75.3,77.2,120	10.75	6.00
CPL11	1980(7)	41,447	KM60.2,74,75.3,77.2,120,127(2 pcs.)	10.75	6.75

PROOF SETS (PS)

KM#	Date	Mintage	Identification	Issue Price	Mkt Value
PS1	1981(7)	199,000	KM60.2,74,75.3,77.2,120,123,130	36.00	20.00
PS2	1982(7)	180,908	KM60.2a,74,75.3,77.2,120,123,133	36.00	10.00
PS3	1983(7)	166,779	KM60.2a,74,75.3,77.2,120,132,138	36.00	15.00
PS4	1984(7)	161,602	KM60.2a,74,75.3,77.2,120,132,140	30.00	15.00
PS5	1985(7)	157,037	KM60.2a,74,75.3,77.2,120,132,143	30.00	15.50
PS6	1986(7)	175,745	KM60.2a,74,75.3,77.2,120,132,149	30.00	15.00
PS7	1987(7)	179,004	KM60.2a,74,75.3,77.2,120,132,154	34.00	17.50
PS8	1988(7)	175,259	KM60.2a,74,75.3,77.2,132,157,161	37.50	26.50
PS9	1989(7)	170,928	KM60.2a,74,75.3,77.2,132,157,168	40.00	26.50
PS10	1989(4)	6,823	KM125.2,135-136,153	1190.	1000.
PS11	1989(4)	1,995	KM164-167	1700.	1325.
PS12	1989(3)	2,550	KM125.2,163,167	1530.	1225.
PS13	1989(3)	9,979	KM135,163-164	165.00	155.00
PS14	1990(7)	158,068	KM170,181-186	41.00	26.50
PS15	1990(4)	2,629	KM174-177	1720.	1175.
PS16	1991(7)	14,629	KM179,181-186	—	80.00
PS17	1991(4)	873	KM198-201	1760.	1275.
PS18	1992(13)	84,397	KM203a,212a-214a,218,220a-223a, 231a-234a	—	95.00
PS19	1992(7)	147,061	KM204-210	42.75	32.50
PS20	1992 (4)	*3,500	KM226-229	1680.	1275.
PS21	1993(7)	143,065	KM181-186,235	42.75	25.00
PS22	1994(7)	47,303	KM181-186,248	47.50	45.00
PS23	1994(7)	99,121	KM181-186,251	*43.00	38.50
PS24	1994(4)	1,500	KM252-255	915.00	1295.
PS25	1995(7)	—	KM181-186,259	37.45	32.50
PS26	1995(7)	50,000	KM181-185,258,259	49.45	55.00
PS27	1995(4)	—	KM261-264	42.00	42.00
PS28	1995(4)	682	KM266-269	1555.	1550.
PS29	1995(2)	—	KM261-262	22.00	21.00
PS30	1995(2)	—	KM263-264	22.00	21.00
PS31	1996(4)	423	KM278-281	1555.	1625.
PS32	1996(7)	—	KM181a,182b-185b,186,274	49.00	50.00
PS33	1996(4)	—	KM283-286	44.45	50.00
PS34	1997(8)	—	KM182b-184b,209,270c,282,289,290a	60.00	65.00
PS35	1997(4)	—	KM292-295	44.45	50.00
PS36	1997(4)	—	KM300-303	1530.	1605.
PS37	1998(8)	—	KM182b-184b,186,270b,289,290a, 306	59.45	60.00
PS38	ND(1998)(5)	.025	KM309-313	73.50	73.50
PS39	ND(1998)(2)	*.080	KM316 w/China Y-727	72.50	72.50
PS40	1998(4)	—	KM318-321	44.45	45.00
PS41	1998(4)	1,000	KM322-325	1552.	1555.
PS42	ND(1998)(5)	.025	KM310-313,332	73.50	73.50

Olympic Commemoratives (OCP)

KM#	Date	Mintage	Identification	Issue Price	Mkt Value
OCP1	1973(4)	—	KM84-87,Series I	78.50	40.00
OCP2	1974(4)	—	KM89,90,93,94,Series II	88.50	40.00
OCP3	1974(4)	—	KM91,92,95,96,Series III	88.50	40.00
OCP4	1975(4)	—	KM98,99,102,103,Series IV	88.50	40.00
OCP5	1975(4)	—	KM100,101,104,105,Series V	88.50	40.00
OCP6	1976(4)	—	KM107,108,111,112, Series VI	88.50	42.00
OCP7	1976(4)	—	KM109,110,113,114,Series VII	88.50	42.00

NEWFOUNDLAND
LARGE

KM#	Date	1865-1896 Mintage	VG-8	BRONZE F-12	VF-20	1904-1936 XF-40	MS-60	MS-63
1	1865	240,000	2.00	3.00	6.00	14.50	120.00	325.00
	1872H	200,000	2.00	3.00	6.00	14.50	65.00	180.00
	1872H	—	—	—	—	—	Proof	800.00
	1873	200,025	2.50	4.50	10.00	25.00	225.00	750.00
	1873	—	—	—	—	—	Proof	800.00
	1876H	200,000	2.00	3.00	6.00	16.00	160.00	450.00
	1876H	—	—	—	—	—	Proof	600.00
	1880 round O, even date							
		400,000	2.00	3.00	6.00	14.50	100.00	300.00
	1880 round O, low O	Inc. Ab.	2.25	4.00	9.00	25.00	150.00	1380.
	1880 oval 0	Inc. Ab.	85.00	130.00	180.00	325.00	850.00	1400.
	1885	40,000	16.50	27.00	55.00	115.00	500.00	1250.
	1888	50,000	15.00	25.00	45.00	100.00	500.00	1970.
	1890	200,000	2.00	3.00	5.50	14.50	140.00	450.00
	1894	200,000	2.00	3.00	5.50	14.50	120.00	350.00
	1896	200,000	2.00	3.00	5.50	14.50	120.00	350.00

KM#	Date	Mintage	VG-8	BRONZE F-12	VF-20	XF-40	MS-60	MS-63
9	1904H	100,000	5.00	10.00	20.00	35.00	275.00	650.00
	1907	200,000	1.50	2.50	4.00	12.00	110.00	375.00
	1909	200,000	1.50	2.50	4.00	10.50	100.00	200.00
	1909	—	—	—	—	—	Proof	400.00
16	1913	400,000	.75	1.50	2.00	4.00	40.00	100.00
	1917C	702,350	.75	1.50	2.00	4.00	65.00	185.00
	1919C	300,000	.75	1.50	2.25	5.00	90.00	275.00
	1919C	—	—	—	—	—	Proof	220.00
	1920C	302,184	.75	1.50	3.50	12.00	145.00	650.00
	1929	300,000	.75	1.50	2.00	4.00	55.00	150.00
	1929	—	—	—	—	—	Proof	185.00
	1936	300,000	.75	1.25	1.75	3.00	28.00	75.00
	1936	—	—	—	—	—	Proof	250.00

SMALL CENTS

KM#	Date	Mintage	VG-8	BRONZE F-12	VF-20	XF-40	MS-60	MS-63
18	1938	500,000	.50	.75	1.50	2.50	16.00	40.00
	1938	—	—	—	—	—	Proof	125.00
	1940	300,000	1.25	2.00	3.00	7.00	35.00	175.00
	1940 re-engraved date	—	16.00	27.50	40.00	70.00	230.00	400.00
	1941C	827,662	.40	.50	.70	1.50	13.50	120.00
	1941C re-engraved date	13.00	22.00	32.50	50.00	165.00	400.00
	1942	1,996,889	.40	.50	.70	1.50	13.50	70.00
	1943C	1,239,732	.40	.50	.70	1.50	13.50	70.00
	1944C	1,328,776	.75	2.00	3.00	4.50	60.00	335.00
	1947C	313,772	.75	1.50	2.25	4.50	40.00	200.00

FIVE CENTS

KM#	Date	Mintage	1.1782 g, .925 SILVER, .0350 oz ASW VG-8	F-12	VF-20	XF-40	MS-60	MS-63
2	1865	80,000	20.00	32.50	60.00	125.00	775.00	1500.
	1870	40,000	35.00	50.00	90.00	175.00	1100.	2000.
	1870	—	—	—	—	—	Proof	3900.
	1872H	40,000	22.00	32.00	60.00	140.00	600.00	1400.
	1873	44,260	45.00	75.00	145.00	355.00	1975.	2850.
	1873H	Inc. Ab.	650.00	1000.	1875.	3300.	8200.	12,500.
	1876H	20,000	75.00	110.00	200.00	350.00	1450.	2750.
	1880	40,000	22.00	40.00	80.00	150.00	1000.	1850.
	1881	40,000	15.00	30.00	45.00	120.00	900.00	1850.
	1882H	60,000	15.00	27.00	40.00	100.00	800.00	1500.
	1882H	—	—	—	—	—	Proof	2800.
	1885	16,000	90.00	150.00	250.00	525.00	2000.	4500.

KM#	Date	Mintage	VG-8	F-12	VF-20	XF-40	MS-60	MS-63
	1888	40,000	20.00	30.00	85.00	140.00	800.00	2450.
	1890	160,000	6.00	12.00	30.00	70.00	600.00	1500.
	1890	—	—	—	—	—	Proof	2100.
	1894	160,000	6.50	12.50	30.00	75.00	600.00	1500.
	1896	400,000	4.00	8.00	20.00	45.00	575.00	1350.
7	1903	100,000	3.00	6.00	18.00	50.00	465.00	1200.
	1904H	100,000	2.00	5.00	14.00	35.00	220.00	475.00
	1908	400,000	1.75	3.50	11.50	25.00	200.00	335.00
13	1912	300,000	1.00	2.00	5.00	20.00	125.00	275.00
	1917C	300,319	1.00	2.00	4.00	14.00	200.00	450.00
	1919C	100,844	2.00	3.00	10.00	30.00	750.00	1250.
	1929	300,000	1.00	1.75	3.25	12.00	165.00	350.00
	1929	—	—	—	—	—	Proof	750.00
19	1938	100,000	.85	.90	1.50	4.00	75.00	200.00
	1938	—	—	—	—	—	Proof	350.00
	1940C	200,000	.85	.90	1.50	4.00	60.00	200.00
	1941C	621,641	.60	.90	1.50	3.00	15.00	30.00
	1942C	298,348	.85	.90	2.50	3.00	25.00	45.00
	1943C	351,666	.60	.90	1.50	3.00	15.00	27.50

		1.1664 g, .800 SILVER, .0300 oz ASW						
19a	1944C	286,504	.85	1.25	2.50	3.00	30.00	65.00
	1945C	203,828	.60	.90	1.50	3.00	18.00	26.00
	1945C	—	—	—	—	—	Proof	250.00
	1946C	2,041	200.00	275.00	355.00	435.00	1100.	1750.
	1946C	—	—	—	—	—	Proof	4000.
	1947C	38,400	3.25	4.50	6.75	15.00	60.00	125.00
	1947C	—	—	—	—	—	Proof	400.00

TEN CENTS

1865-1896

KM#	Date	1865-1896 Mintage	2.3564 g, .925 SILVER, .0701 oz ASW VG-8	F-12	VF-20	XF-40	1903-1947 MS-60	MS-63
3	1865	80,000	13.50	22.00	55.00	160.00	1100.	2250.
	1865 plain edge	—	—	—	—	—	Proof	5500.
	1870	30,000	120.00	190.00	335.00	750.00	2500.	5000.
	1872H	40,000	13.50	20.00	50.00	135.00	800.00	1700.
	1873 flat 3	23,614	15.00	35.00	90.00	345.00	1675.	2900.
	1873 round 3	Inc. Ab.	15.00	35.00	90.00	345.00	1675.	2900.
	1876H	10,000	20.00	35.00	75.00	250.00	1800.	2950.
	1880/70	10,000	22.00	45.00	100.00	275.00	2000.	2950.
	1882H	20,000	12.50	30.00	70.00	310.00	2185.	3410.
	1882H	—	—	—	—	—	Proof	3400.
	1885	8,000	60.00	115.00	210.00	485.00	2100.	4250.
	1888	30,000	11.50	27.50	70.00	345.00	2185.	2500.
	1890	100,000	5.50	11.50	20.00	75.00	700.00	1550.
	1890	—	—	—	—	—	Proof	3200.
	1894	100,000	5.50	11.50	20.00	75.00	700.00	1550.
	1894	—	—	—	—	—	Proof	1750.
	1896	230,000	5.00	10.00	20.00	75.00	600.00	1500.

1901-1910   1910-1936

KM#	Date	1901-1910 Mintage	VG-8	F-12	1910-1936 VF-20	XF-40	MS-60	MS-63
8	1903	100,000	5.00	10.00	35.00	110.00	850.00	2000.
	1904H	100,000	2.50	6.50	20.00	65.00	275.00	400.00
14	1912	150,000	1.50	3.00	9.00	30.00	275.00	400.00
	1917C	250,805	1.00	3.00	6.50	24.00	350.00	1250.
	1919C	54,342	1.50	3.00	9.00	25.00	170.00	325.00

KM#	Date	Mintage	VG-8	F-12	VF-20	XF-40	MS-60	MS-63
20	1938	100,000	1.00	1.50	2.50	7.00	90.00	225.00
	1938	—	—	—	—	—	Proof	500.00
	1940	100,000	.60	1.20	2.50	5.00	80.00	225.00
	1941C	483,630	.55	1.50	2.00	3.25	27.00	85.00
	1942C	293,736	.55	1.50	2.00	3.25	27.00	90.00
	1943C	104,706	.60	1.20	2.50	5.00	50.00	165.00
	2.3328 g, .800 SILVER, .0600 oz ASW							
20a	1944C	151,471	1.00	1.25	3.00	5.00	70.00	225.00
	1945C	175,833	.60	1.00	2.00	3.25	27.00	90.00
	1946C	38,400	3.00	5.00	10.00	20.00	65.00	200.00
	1947C	61,988	1.75	3.00	7.00	12.00	60.00	175.00

TWENTY CENTS

			4.7127 g, .925 SILVER, .1401 oz ASW					
KM#	Date	Mintage	VG-8	F-12	VF-20	XF-40	MS-60	MS-63
4	1865	100,000	11.00	16.00	45.00	125.00	950.00	2000.
	1865 plain edge	—	—	—	—	—	Proof	4500.
	1870	50,000	12.00	20.00	60.00	140.00	1250.	2500.
	1872H	90,000	7.00	14.00	30.00	90.00	750.00	1800.
	1873	45,797	9.00	18.00	60.00	160.00	1500.	3000.
	1876H	50,000	10.00	16.00	50.00	175.00	1350.	2700.
	1880/70	30,000	15.00	25.00	65.00	160.00	1350.	3000.
	1881	60,000	5.00	12.00	35.00	90.00	900.00	1900.
	1882H	100,000	5.00	12.00	27.50	80.00	900.00	1900.
	1882H	—	—	—	—	—	Proof	3700.
	1885	40,000	8.00	12.50	40.00	120.00	1300.	2600.
	1888	75,000	5.00	10.00	32.00	100.00	900.00	2200.
	1890	100,000	4.00	7.00	22.00	70.00	625.00	1600.
	1890	—	—	—	—	—	Proof	2750.
	1894	100,000	4.00	7.00	22.00	60.00	650.00	1700.
	1896 small 96	125,000	3.00	6.00	20.00	70.00	700.00	1800.
	1896 large 96	Inc. Ab.	4.00	10.00	22.00	90.00	725.00	1900.
	1899 small 99	125,000	10.00	25.00	45.00	125.00	850.00	2200.
	1899 large 99	Inc. Ab.	3.25	6.50	18.00	65.00	700.00	1900.
	1900	125,000	3.00	5.00	15.00	55.00	700.00	1900.

KM#	Date	Mintage	VG-8	F-12	VF-20	XF-40	MS-60	MS-63
10	1904H	75,000	9.00	16.00	50.00	175.00	2000.	4250.
	1904H	—	—	—	—	—	Proof	4550.
15	1912	350,000	2.00	3.00	10.00	40.00	350.00	900.00

TWENTY-FIVE CENTS

			5.8319 g, .925 SILVER, .1734 oz ASW					
KM#	Date	Mintage	VG-8	F-12	VF-20	XF-40	MS-60	MS-63
17	1917C	464,779	1.50	2.00	4.00	9.00	120.00	250.00
	1919C	163,939	1.50	2.25	4.25	12.00	220.00	700.00

FIFTY CENTS

1870-1900   **11.7818 g, .925 SILVER, .3504 oz ASW**   **1904-1919**

KM#	Date	Mintage	VG-8	F-12	VF-20	XF-40	MS-60	MS-63
6	1870	50,000	12.00	15.00	45.00	200.00	1400.	3600.
	1870 plain edge	—	—	—	—	—	Proof	6500.
	1872H	48,000	10.00	15.00	40.00	150.00	1250.	3600.
	1873	37,675	28.00	60.00	165.00	615.00	4350.	6000.
	1874	80,000	20.00	30.00	80.00	350.00	2500.	5000.
	1876H	28,000	18.00	30.00	80.00	275.00	2250.	5250.
	1880	24,000	18.00	30.00	80.00	300.00	2250.	5250.
	1881	50,000	10.00	20.00	70.00	225.00	2250.	5250.
	1882H	100,000	8.00	12.50	40.00	150.00	1600.	3600.
	1882H	—	—	—	—	—	Proof	5500.
	1885	40,000	12.00	20.00	70.00	250.00	2250.	5500.
	1888	20,000	13.50	25.00	80.00	300.00	2200.	5200.
	1894	40,000	5.00	12.00	50.00	175.00	2000.	3800.
	1896	60,000	4.00	7.00	26.00	130.00	1400.	3600.
	1898	76,607	5.00	8.00	35.00	140.00	1700.	3600.
	1899 wide 9's	150,000	5.00	8.00	28.00	125.00	1500.	3600.
	1899 narrow 9's	Inc. Ab.	5.00	8.00	28.00	125.00	1500.	3600.
	1900	150,000	5.00	8.00	28.00	125.00	1500.	3600.
11	1904H	140,000	3.25	5.00	16.00	40.00	300.00	850.00
	1907	100,000	4.00	7.00	20.00	45.00	325.00	1000.
	1908	160,000	3.25	4.50	12.50	32.50	175.00	625.00
	1909	200,000	3.25	4.50	12.50	35.00	200.00	700.00
12	1911	200,000	2.75	3.25	8.00	20.00	210.00	500.00
	1917C	375,560	2.75	3.25	6.00	16.50	125.00	285.00
	1918C	294,824	2.75	3.25	6.00	16.50	125.00	285.00
	1919C	306,267	2.75	3.25	6.00	16.50	125.00	380.00

TWO DOLLARS

KM#	Date	Mintage	3.3284 g, .917 GOLD, .0981 oz AGW			AU-50	MS-60	MS-63
			F-12	VF-20	XF-40			
5	1865	10,000	150.00	200.00	275.00	445.00	1450.	5700.
	1865 plain edge	about 10 known	—	—	—	—	Proof	10,000.
	1870	10,000	175.00	225.00	325.00	650.00	1450.	6700.
	1870 plain edge	—	—	—	—	—	Proof	10,000.
	1872	6,050	200.00	285.00	385.00	750.00	2500.	10,300.
	1880	2,500	1000.	1300.	1600.	2300.	4650.	16,500.
	1880	—	—	—	—	—	Proof	18,500.
	1881	10,000	120.00	165.00	225.00	350.00	1550.	5350.
	1882H	25,000	110.00	155.00	210.00	250.00	475.00	1550.
	1882H	—	—	—	—	—	Proof	6000.
	1885	10,000	120.00	165.00	235.00	350.00	580.00	2850.
	1888	25,000	110.00	155.00	210.00	250.00	475.00	1550.

NEW BRUNSWICK
HALF PENNY TOKEN

KM#	Date	Mintage	VG-8	COPPER F-12	VF-20	XF-40	MS-60	MS-63
1	1843	480,000	3.00	6.00	11.50	30.00	100.00	265.00
	1843	—	—	—	—	—	Proof	750.00

KM#	Date	Mintage	VG-8	F-12	VF-20	XF-40	MS-60	MS-63
3	1854	864,000	3.00	6.00	11.50	30.00	100.00	265.00

KM#	Date	Mintage	VG-8	BRONZE F-12	VF-20	XF-40	MS-60	MS-63
3a	1854	—	—	—	—	—	Proof	400.00

ONE PENNY TOKEN

KM#	Date	Mintage	VG-8	COPPER F-12	VF-20	XF-40	MS-60	MS-63
2	1843	480,000	3.75	7.50	15.00	37.50	165.00	325.00
	1843	—	—	—	—	—	Proof	800.00

KM#	Date	Mintage	VG-8	F-12	VF-20	XF-40	MS-60	MS-63
4	1854	432,000	3.75	7.50	15.00	40.00	175.00	350.00

DECIMAL COINAGE
HALF CENT

KM#	Date	Mintage	VG-8	BRONZE F-12	VF-20	XF-40	MS-60	MS-63
5	1861	222,800	65.00	100.00	150.00	200.00	490.00	1510.
	1861	—	—	—	—	—	Proof	2200.

ONE CENT

KM#	Date	Mintage	VG-8	BRONZE F-12	VF-20	XF-40	MS-60	MS-63
6	1861	1,000,000	2.00	4.00	6.00	11.00	90.00	245.00
	1861	—	—	—	—	—	Proof	450.00
	1864 short 6	1,000,000	2.00	4.00	6.00	11.00	90.00	245.00
	1864 long 6	Inc. Ab.	2.00	4.00	6.00	11.00	90.00	245.00

FIVE CENTS

KM#	Date	Mintage	1.1620 g, .925 SILVER, .0346 oz ASW VG-8	F-12	VF-20	XF-40	MS-60	MS-63
7	1862	100,000	35.00	65.00	125.00	250.00	1225.	3200.
	1862	—	—	—	—	—	Proof	3500.
	1864 small 6	100,000	35.00	65.00	125.00	250.00	1225.	3200.
	1864 large 6	Inc. Ab.	35.00	65.00	125.00	250.00	1225.	3200.

TEN CENTS

KM#	Date	Mintage	2.3240 g, .925 SILVER, .0691 oz ASW VG-8	F-12	VF-20	XF-40	MS-60	MS-63
8	1862	150,000	35.00	65.00	125.00	250.00	975.00	2550.
	1862 recut 2	Inc. Ab.	35.00	65.00	140.00	250.00	1100.	4270.
	1862	—	—	—	—	—	Proof	2850.
	1864	100,000	35.00	65.00	125.00	250.00	1650.	2550.

TWENTY CENTS

4.6480 g, .925 SILVER, .1382 oz ASW

KM#	Date	Mintage	VG-8	F-12	VF-20	XF-40	MS-60	MS-63
9	1862	150,000	16.00	29.00	65.00	160.00	825.00	2550.
	1862	—	—	—	—	—	Proof	2850.
	1864	150,000	16.00	29.00	65.00	160.00	825.00	2550.

NOVA SCOTIA
STERLING COINAGE
HALF PENNY TOKEN

COPPER

KM#	Date	Mintage	VG-8	F-12	VF-20	XF-40	MS-60	MS-63
1	1823	400,000	3.00	5.00	8.00	20.00	75.00	150.00
	1823 w/o hyphen	Inc. Ab.	5.00	10.00	20.00	35.00	170.00	350.00
	1824	118,636	3.00	5.00	12.50	25.00	150.00	225.00
	1832	800,000	3.00	5.00	7.50	15.00	60.00	150.00

KM#	Date	Mintage	VG-8	F-12	VF-20	XF-40	MS-60	MS-63
1a	1382(error)	—	150.00	300.00	1650.	—	—	—
	1832/1382	—	500.00	700.00	—	—	—	—
	1832 (imitation)	—	3.00	6.00	9.50	34.00	50.00	100.00

KM#	Date	Mintage	VG-8	F-12	VF-20	XF-40	MS-60	MS-63
3	1840 small 0	300,000	3.50	5.00	10.00	22.00	115.00	165.00
	1840 medium 0	Inc. Ab.	2.50	4.00	7.50	15.00	95.00	125.00
	1840 large 0	Inc. Ab.	4.00	6.00	12.50	27.50	125.00	185.00
	1843	300,000	3.00	5.00	9.00	20.00	85.00	160.00

KM#	Date	Mintage	VG-8	F-12	VF-20	XF-40	MS-60	MS-63
5	1856 w/o LCW	720,000	2.00	4.00	7.50	15.00	70.00	175.00
	1856 w/o LCW	—	—	—	—	—	Proof	600.00
	1856 w/o LCW, inverted A for V in PROVINCE			—	—	Proof	600.00

BRONZE

KM#	Date	Mintage	VG-8	F-12	VF-20	XF-40	MS-60	MS-63
5a	1856 w/LCW	—	—	—	—	—	Proof	600.00

ONE PENNY TOKEN

COPPER

KM#	Date	Mintage	VG-8	F-12	VF-20	XF-40	MS-60	MS-63
2	1824	217,776	3.00	6.00	10.00	25.00	100.00	250.00
	1832	200,000	3.00	6.00	10.00	22.50	80.00	230.00
2a	1832 (imitation)	—	3.75	7.50	22.50	42.50	—	—

KM#	Date	Mintage	VG-8	F-12	VF-20	XF-40	MS-60	MS-63
4	1840	150,000	2.50	5.00	7.50	20.00	100.00	175.00
	1843/0	150,000	12.00	20.00	40.00	80.00	150.00	—
	1843	Inc. Ab.	3.00	6.00	10.00	22.50	110.00	200.00

KM#	Date	Mintage	VG-8	F-12	VF-20	XF-40	MS-60	MS-63
6	1856 w/o LCW	360,000	2.50	5.00	8.50	19.00	110.00	135.00
	1856 w/LCW	Inc. Ab.	2.50	5.00	7.00	15.00	85.00	115.00

BRONZE

KM#	Date	Mintage	VG-8	F-12	VF-20	XF-40	MS-60	MS-63
6a	1856	—	—	—	—	—	Proof	400.00

DECIMAL COINAGE
HALF CENT

KM#	Date	Mintage	VG-8	BRONZE F-12	VF-20	XF-40	MS-60	MS-63
7	1861	400,000	3.00	5.00	8.00	12.00	60.00	165.00
	1864	400,000	3.00	5.00	8.00	12.00	55.00	165.00
	1864	—	—	—	—	—	Proof	300.00

ONE CENT

KM#	Date	Mintage	VG-8	BRONZE F-12	VF-20	XF-40	MS-60	MS-63
8	1861	800,000	2.00	3.00	5.00	10.00	70.00	215.00
	1862	(Est.) 100,000	15.00	22.50	40.00	90.00	360.00	1300.
	1864	800,000	2.00	3.00	5.00	10.00	70.00	215.00

NOTE: The Royal Mint Report records mintage of 1,000,000 for 1862 which is considered incorrect.

PRINCE EDWARD ISLAND
ONE CENT

KM#	Date	Mintage	VG-8	BRONZE F-12	VF-20	XF-40	MS-60	MS-63
4	1871	2,000,000	1.75	2.50	4.50	10.50	75.00	185.00
	1871	—	—	—	—	—	Proof	2000.

Mexico

COLONIAL COB COINAGE

RULERS
Philip V, 1700-1724, 1724-1746
Luis I, 1724

MINT MARKS
Mo, MXo - Mexico City Mint

ASSAYERS INITIALS

Letter	Date	Name
L	1678-1703	Martin Lopez
J	1708-1723	Jose E. de Leon
D	1724-1727	?
R	1729-1730	Nicolas de Roxas
G	1730	—
F	1730-1733	Felipe Rivas de Angulo
F	1733-1784	Francisco de la Pena
M	1733-1763	Manuel de la Pena

.931 SILVER, 1.69 g
Luis I
Obv: Legend around crowned LVDOVICVS
monogram. Rev: Legend around cross,
lions and castles.

KM#	Date	Good	VG	Fine	VF
25	1724 D	225.00	350.00	500.00	600.00
	1725 D	225.00	350.00	500.00	600.00
	1726 D	250.00	370.00	550.00	650.00
	Date off flan	100.00	200.00	250.00	300.00

REAL

ROYAL STRIKES

Philip V

Full struck sample specimens referred to as "Royal"
strikes are seldom encountered and are considered rare.

CIRCULATION STRIKES

.931 SILVER, 3.38 g
Obv. leg: PHILIPVS V DEI G and date
around crowned arms.

1/2 REAL

.931 SILVER, 1.69 g
Philip V
Obv: Legend around crowned PHILIPVS monogram.
Rev: Legend around cross, lions and castles.

KM#	Date	Good	VG	Fine	VF
24	1701 L	30.00	40.00	55.00	90.00
	1702 L	25.00	35.00	50.00	65.00
	1703 L	25.00	35.00	50.00	65.00
	1704 L	30.00	42.50	65.00	85.00
	1705 L	30.00	42.50	65.00	85.00
	1706 L	30.00	42.50	65.00	85.00
	1707 L	30.00	42.50	65.00	85.00
	1708 J	35.00	50.00	70.00	110.00
	1709 J	30.00	42.50	65.00	85.00
	1710 J	30.00	42.50	65.00	85.00
	1711 J	30.00	42.50	65.00	85.00
	1712 J	30.00	42.50	65.00	85.00
	1714 J	30.00	42.50	65.00	85.00
	1715 J	30.00	42.50	65.00	85.00
	1716 J	30.00	42.50	65.00	85.00
	1717 J	30.00	42.50	65.00	85.00
	1718 J	30.00	42.50	65.00	85.00
	1719 J	30.00	42.50	65.00	85.00
	1720 J	30.00	42.50	65.00	85.00
	1721 J	30.00	42.50	65.00	85.00
	1722 J	42.50	55.00	80.00	125.00
	1723 J	42.50	55.00	80.00	125.00
	1724 J	50.00	65.00	85.00	140.00
	1724 D	50.00	65.00	85.00	140.00
	1725 D	50.00	65.00	85.00	140.00
	1726 D	35.00	50.00	70.00	110.00
	1727 D	35.00	50.00	70.00	110.00
	1728 D	35.00	50.00	70.00	110.00

.916 SILVER, 1.69 g

KM#	Date	Good	VG	Fine	VF
24a	1729 D	35.00	50.00	70.00	110.00
	1730 G	35.00	50.00	70.00	110.00
	1730 D	35.00	50.00	70.00	110.00
	1731 F	35.00	50.00	70.00	110.00
	1732 F	35.00	50.00	70.00	110.00
	1733 F	35.00	50.00	70.00	110.00
	Date off flan	15.00	20.00	25.00	30.00

KM#	Date	Good	VG	Fine	VF
30	1701 L	45.00	60.00	70.00	115.00
	1702 L	45.00	60.00	70.00	115.00
	1703 L	45.00	60.00	70.00	115.00
	1703 L	45.00	60.00	70.00	115.00
	1704 L	45.00	60.00	70.00	115.00
	1705 L	45.00	60.00	70.00	115.00
	1706 L	45.00	60.00	70.00	115.00
	1707 L	45.00	60.00	70.00	115.00
	1708 J	45.00	60.00	70.00	115.00
	1709 J	45.00	60.00	70.00	115.00
	1710 J	45.00	60.00	70.00	115.00
	1711 J	45.00	60.00	70.00	115.00
	1712 J	45.00	60.00	70.00	115.00
	1713 J	35.00	45.00	57.50	85.00
	1714 J	35.00	45.00	57.50	85.00
	1715 J	45.00	60.00	70.00	100.00
	1716 J	45.00	60.00	70.00	100.00
	1717 J	45.00	60.00	70.00	100.00
	1718 J	45.00	60.00	70.00	100.00
	1719 J	45.00	60.00	70.00	100.00
	1720 J	45.00	60.00	70.00	100.00
	1721 J	45.00	60.00	70.00	100.00
	1722 J	45.00	60.00	70.00	100.00
	1723 J	45.00	60.00	70.00	100.00
	1724 J	45.00	60.00	70.00	100.00
	1726 D	45.00	60.00	70.00	100.00
	1727 D	45.00	60.00	70.00	100.00
	1728 D	45.00	60.00	70.00	100.00
	1729 F	45.00	60.00	70.00	100.00

.916 SILVER

KM#	Date	Good	VG	Fine	VF
30a	1729 R	45.00	60.00	70.00	100.00
	1730 R	45.00	60.00	70.00	100.00
	1730 F	45.00	60.00	70.00	100.00
	1730 G	45.00	60.00	70.00	100.00
	1731 F	45.00	60.00	70.00	100.00
	Date off flan	10.00	15.00	20.00	30.00

2 REALES

ROYAL STRIKES

Philip V

Fully struck sample specimens referred to as "Royal" strikes are seldom encountered and are considered rare.

CIRCULATION STRIKES

.931 SILVER, 6.77 g
Obv. leg: PHILIPVS V DEI G and date
around crowned arms.

KM#	Date	Good	VG	Fine	VF
35	1701 L	25.00	40.00	50.00	75.00
	1702 L	25.00	40.00	50.00	75.00
	1703 L	25.00	40.00	50.00	75.00
	1704 L	35.00	75.00	150.00	250.00
	1705 L	25.00	40.00	50.00	75.00
	1706 L	25.00	40.00	50.00	75.00
	1707 L	35.00	75.00	150.00	250.00
	1708 J	25.00	40.00	50.00	75.00
	1710 J	25.00	40.00	50.00	75.00
	1711 J	25.00	40.00	50.00	75.00
	1712 J	25.00	40.00	50.00	75.00
	1713 J	25.00	40.00	50.00	75.00
	1714 J	25.00	40.00	50.00	80.00
	1715 J	25.00	40.00	50.00	80.00
	1716 J	25.00	40.00	50.00	75.00
	1717 J	25.00	40.00	50.00	75.00
	1718 J	25.00	40.00	50.00	75.00
	1719 J	25.00	40.00	50.00	75.00
	1720 J	25.00	40.00	50.00	75.00
	1721 J	25.00	40.00	60.00	100.00
	1722 J	25.00	40.00	50.00	75.00
	1723 J	25.00	40.00	50.00	75.00
	1724 J	36.00	50.00	60.00	100.00
	1725 D	36.00	57.50	75.00	125.00
	1725 R	36.00	40.00	50.00	100.00
	1726 D	36.00	57.50	75.00	125.00
	1727 D	36.00	57.50	75.00	125.00
	1728 D	28.00	37.50	75.00	125.00
	.916 SILVER				
35a	1729 R	28.00	37.50	75.00	125.00
	1730 R	28.00	37.50	75.00	125.00
	1731 MF	25.00	30.00	60.00	100.00
	1731/0 J	25.00	30.00	60.00	100.00
	1733 F	25.00	40.00	80.00	150.00
	Date off flan	10.00	20.00	35.00	50.00

4 REALES

ROYAL STRIKES

Philip V

Fully struck sample specimens referred to as "Royal" strikes are seldom encountered and are considered rare.

CIRCULATION STRIKES

.931 SILVER, 13.54 g
Obv. leg: PHILIPVS V DEI G and date
around crowned arms.

KM#	Date	Good	VG	Fine	VF
40	1701 L	80.00	125.00	225.00	375.00
	1702 L	80.00	125.00	225.00	375.00
	1703 L	45.00	90.00	150.00	250.00
	1704 L	80.00	125.00	225.00	375.00
	1705 L	65.00	100.00	200.00	300.00
	1706 L	65.00	100.00	200.00	300.00
	1707 L	65.00	100.00	200.00	300.00
	1708 J	30.00	70.00	120.00	200.00
	1709 J	65.00	100.00	200.00	300.00
	1710 J	50.00	90.00	175.00	250.00
	1711 J	50.00	90.00	175.00	250.00
	1712 J	80.00	125.00	225.00	375.00
	1713 J	80.00	125.00	225.00	375.00
	1714 J	65.00	100.00	200.00	300.00
	1715 J	80.00	125.00	225.00	375.00
	1716 J	65.00	100.00	200.00	300.00
	1717 J	80.00	125.00	225.00	375.00
	1718 J	80.00	125.00	225.00	375.00
	1719 J	65.00	100.00	200.00	300.00
	1720 J	65.00	100.00	200.00	300.00
	1721 J	65.00	100.00	200.00	300.00
	1722 J	90.00	150.00	300.00	500.00
	1723 J	90.00	150.00	300.00	500.00
	1725 D	90.00	150.00	300.00	500.00
	1726 D	90.00	150.00	300.00	500.00
	1727 D	90.00	150.00	300.00	500.00
	1728 D	80.00	125.00	225.00	375.00
	.916 SILVER, 13.54 g				
40a	1729 D	80.00	125.00	250.00	400.00
	1730 R	80.00	125.00	250.00	400.00
	1730 G	80.00	125.00	250.00	400.00
	1731 F	80.00	125.00	250.00	400.00
	1731 F	80.00	125.00	250.00	400.00
	1732/1 F	75.00	100.00	220.00	350.00
	1732 F	65.00	90.00	185.00	300.00
	1733 F	65.00	90.00	185.00	300.00
	1734 F	65.00	90.00	185.00	300.00
	Date off flan	40.00	50.00	70.00	100.00
	(Klippe)				

Similar to KM#40a.

KM#	Date	Good	VG	Fine	VF
41	1733 MF	200.00	250.00	300.00	400.00
	1734 MF	250.00	300.00	400.00	500.00
	1734/3 MF	225.00	250.00	300.00	400.00
	1740/30 MF	250.00	275.00	350.00	450.00
	1742/32 MF	—	—	—	—
	1743/33 MF	—	—	—	—

.931 SILVER, 13.54 g
Luis I
Obv. leg: LVDOVICUS I DEI G
around crowned arms.

KM#	Date	Good	VG	Fine	VF
42	1724 D	650.00	1000.	1500.	2500.
	1725 D	750.00	1200.	2000.	3000.
	Date off flan	225.00	350.00	500.00	850.00

8 REALES
ROYAL STRIKES

Philip V

Fully struck sample specimens referred to as "Royal" strikes are seldom encountered and are considered rare.

CIRCULATION STRIKES

.931 SILVER, 27.07 g
Obv. leg: PHILIPVS V DEI G and date around crowned arms.

KM#	Date	Good	VG	Fine	VF
47	1701 L	100.00	175.00	275.00	400.00
	1702 L	125.00	200.00	300.00	450.00
	1703 L	125.00	200.00	300.00	450.00
	1704 L	150.00	250.00	400.00	600.00
	1706 L	150.00	250.00	400.00	600.00
	1707 L	150.00	250.00	400.00	600.00
	1707 J	150.00	250.00	400.00	600.00
	1708 J	125.00	200.00	300.00	450.00
	1709 J	100.00	175.00	275.00	400.00
	1710 J	150.00	250.00	400.00	600.00
	1711 J	100.00	175.00	275.00	400.00

KM#	Date	Good	VG	Fine	VF
47	1712 J	125.00	200.00	300.00	450.00
	1713 J	60.00	100.00	165.00	250.00
	1714 J	60.00	100.00	165.00	250.00
	1715 J	100.00	175.00	275.00	400.00
	1716 J	100.00	175.00	275.00	400.00
	1717 J	100.00	175.00	275.00	400.00
	1718 J	100.00	175.00	275.00	400.00
	1719 J	100.00	175.00	275.00	400.00
	1720 J	100.00	175.00	275.00	400.00
	1721 J	125.00	200.00	300.00	450.00
	1722 J	100.00	175.00	275.00	400.00
	1723 J	125.00	200.00	300.00	450.00
	1724 D	125.00	200.00	300.00	450.00
	1725 D	180.00	350.00	500.00	900.00
	1726 D	180.00	350.00	500.00	900.00
	1727 D	180.00	350.00	500.00	900.00
	1728 D	200.00	400.00	600.00	1000.
	Date off flan	25.00	50.00	85.00	125.00

.916 SILVER

KM#	Date	Good	VG	Fine	VF
47a	1729 R	75.00	150.00	250.00	375.00
	1730 R	75.00	150.00	250.00	375.00
	1730 G	100.00	175.00	275.00	400.00
	1730 F	75.00	150.00	250.00	375.00
	1731/0 F	250.00	450.00	650.00	1200.
	1731 F	75.00	150.00	250.00	375.00
	1732 F	75.00	150.00	250.00	375.00
	1733 F	75.00	150.00	250.00	400.00
	Date off flan	25.00	50.00	85.00	125.00

(Klippe)

Similar to KM#47a.

KM#	Date	Good	VG	Fine	VF
48	1733 F	150.00	250.00	375.00	600.00
	1733 MF	100.00	150.00	250.00	375.00
	1734/3 MF	100.00	175.00	275.00	400.00
	1734 MF	100.00	175.00	275.00	400.00
	Date off flan	25.00	50.00	85.00	125.00

.931 SILVER, 27.07 g
Luis I
Obv. leg: LVDOVICVS I DEI G.

KM#	Date	Good	VG	Fine	VF
49	1724 D	1500.	2000.	2500.	3000.
	1725 D	1500.	2000.	2500.	3000.
	Date off flan	400.00	600.00	1000.	1500.

ESCUDO
ROYAL STRIKES

Philip V

Fully struck sample specimens referred to as "Royal" strikes are seldom encountered and are considered rare.

CIRCULATION STRIKES

3.3800 g, .917 GOLD, .0997 oz AGW
Mint mark: MXo
Obv. leg: PHILIPVS V DEI G and date around crowned arms.

KM#	Date	Good	VG	Fine	VF
51.1	1702 L	350.00	400.00	450.00	700.00
	1703 L	350.00	400.00	450.00	700.00
	1704 L	350.00	400.00	450.00	700.00
	1706 M	350.00	400.00	450.00	700.00
	1707 L	350.00	400.00	450.00	700.00
	1708 L	350.00	400.00	450.00	700.00
	1709 J	350.00	400.00	450.00	700.00
	1710 J	350.00	400.00	450.00	700.00
	1711 J	350.00	400.00	450.00	700.00
	1712 J	350.00	400.00	450.00	700.00
	Date off flan	250.00	300.00	350.00	450.00

Mint mark: Mo

KM#	Date	Good	VG	Fine	VF
51.2	1713 J	300.00	400.00	450.00	700.00
	1714 J	300.00	375.00	400.00	550.00
	Date off flan	250.00	300.00	350.00	450.00

2 ESCUDOS

6.7700 g, .917 GOLD, .1996 oz AGW
Mint mark: MXo
Obv. leg: CAROLVS II DEI G and date around crowned arms.
Rev: Legend around cross.

KM#	Date	Good	VG	Fine	VF
52	1701 L	600.00	750.00	900.00	1200.
	Date off flan	375.00	400.00	450.00	750.00

ROYAL STRIKES
Philip V

Fully struck sample specimens referred to as "Royal" strikes are seldom encountered and are considered rare.

CIRCULATION STRIKES

Obv. leg: PHILIPVS V DEI G and date around crowned arms.

KM#	Date	Good	VG	Fine	VF
53.1	1704 L	400.00	500.00	650.00	.950.00
	1705 L	400.00	500.00	650.00	950.00
	1707 L	400.00	500.00	650.00	950.00
	1708 J	400.00	500.00	650.00	950.00
	1709 J	400.00	500.00	650.00	950.00
	1710 J	400.00	500.00	650.00	950.00
	1711 J	400.00	500.00	600.00	950.00
	1712 J	400.00	500.00	600.00	950.00
	1713 J	400.00	500.00	600.00	950.00
	Date off flan	300.00	350.00	400.00	600.00

Mint mark: Mo

KM#	Date	Good	VG	Fine	VF
53.2	1714 J	350.00	400.00	600.00	850.00
	1717 J	350.00	400.00	600.00	850.00
	1722 J	350.00	400.00	600.00	900.00
	1723 J	350.00	400.00	600.00	900.00
	1729 R	350.00	400.00	600.00	900.00
	1731 F	350.00	400.00	600.00	800.00
	Date off flan	300.00	350.00	400.00	500.00
	Luis I				
A54	ND D	500.00	1000.	2000.	3000.

4 ESCUDOS
ROYAL STRIKES

Philip V

Fully struck sample specimens referred to as "Royal" strikes are seldom encountered and are considered rare.

CIRCULATION STRIKES

13.5400 g, .917 GOLD, .3992 oz AGW
Mint mark: MXo
Obv. leg: PHILIPVS V DEI G and date
around crowned arms.
Rev: Legend around cross.

KM#	Date	Good	VG	Fine	VF
57.1	1701 L	1150.	1750.	2250.	3000.
	1702 L	1150.	1750.	2250.	3000.
	1703 L	1150.	1750.	2250.	3000.
	1704 L	1150.	1750.	2250.	3000.
	1705 L	1150.	1750.	2250.	3000.
	1706 L	1150.	1750.	2250.	3000.
	1707 L	1150.	1750.	2250.	3000.
	1708 J	1150.	1750.	2250.	3000.
	1709 J	1150.	1750.	2250.	3000.
57.1	1710 J	1150.	1750.	2250.	3000.
	1711 J	1150.	1350.	2000.	3000.
	1712 J	1150.	1350.	2000.	3000.
	1713 J	700.00	1000.	1300.	2000.
	Date off flan	600.00	900.00	1100.	1800.

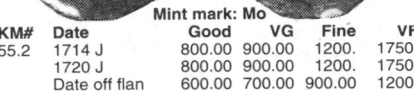

Mint mark: Mo

KM#	Date	Good	VG	Fine	VF
55.2	1714 J	800.00	900.00	1200.	1750.
	1720 J	800.00	900.00	1200.	1750.
	Date off flan	600.00	700.00	900.00	1200.

8 ESCUDOS
ROYAL STRIKES

Philip V

Fully struck sample specimens referred to as "Royal" strikes are seldom encountered and are considered rare.

CIRCULATION STRIKES

27.0700 g, .917 GOLD, .7980 oz AGW
Mint mark: MXo
Obv. leg: PHILIPVS V DEI G and date
around crowned arms.
Rev: Legend around cross.

KM#	Date	Good	VG	Fine	VF
57.1	1701 L	1150.	1750.	2250.	3000.
	1702 L	1150.	1750.	2250.	3000.
	1703 L	1150.	1750.	2250.	3000.
	1704 L	1150.	1750.	2250.	3000.
	1705 L	1150.	1750.	2250.	3000.
	1706 L	1150.	1750.	2250.	3000.
	1707 L	1150.	1750.	2250.	3000.
	1708 J	1150.	1750.	2250.	3000.
	1709 J	1150.	1750.	2250.	3000.
57.1	1710 J	1150.	1750.	2250.	3000.
	1711 J	1150.	1350.	2000.	3000.
	1712 J	1150.	1350.	2000.	3000.
	1713 J	700.00	1000.	1300.	2000.
	Date off flan	600.00	900.00	1100.	1800.

ROYAL STRIKES

Fully struck sample specimens referred to as "Royal" strikes are seldom encountered and are considered rare.

CIRCULATION STRIKES

Mint mark: Mo

KM#	Date	Good	VG	Fine	VF
57.2	1714 J	800.00	1150.	1750.	2500.
	1714 J date on rev.				
		800.00	1150.	1750.	2500.
	1715 J	800.00	1150.	1750.	2500.
	1717 J	900.00	1300.	2250.	3250.
	1718 J	900.00	1300.	2250.	3250.
	1720 J	900.00	1300.	2250.	3250.
	1723 J	900.00	1300.	2250.	3250.
	1728 D	900.00	1300.	2250.	3250.
	1729 R	900.00	1300.	2250.	3250.
	1730 R	900.00	1300.	2250.	3250.
	1730 F	900.00	1300.	2250.	3250.
	1731 F	900.00	1300.	2250.	3250.
	1732 F	900.00	1300.	2250.	3250.
	Date off flan	700.00	950.00	1250.	1850.

Obv. leg: LVDOVICVS I DEI G and date around crowned arms.
Rev: Legend around cross.

KM#	Date	Good	VG	Fine	VF
58	1725 D	3250.	5500.	8500.	13,500.
	Date off flan	1600.	2600.	3700.	5500.

COLONIAL MILLED COINAGE

RULERS

Philip V, 1700-1746
Ferdinand VI, 1746-1759
Charles III, 1760-1788
Charles IV, 1788-1808
Ferdinand VII, 1808-1821

MINT MARKS

Mo - Mexico City Mint

ASSAYERS INITIALS

Letter	Date	Name
F	1733-1784	Francisco de la Pena
M	1733-1763	Manuel de la Pena
M	1754-1770	Manuel Assorin
F	1762-1770	Francisco de Rivera
M	1770-1777	Manuel de Rivera
F	1777-1803	Francisco Arance Cobos
M	1784-1801	Mariano Rodriguez
T	1801-1810	Tomas Butron Miranda
H	1803-1814	Henrique Buenaventura Azorin
J	1809-1833	Joaquin Davila Madrid
J	1812-1833	Jose Garcia Ansaldo

MONETARY SYSTEM

16 Pilones = 1 Real
8 Tlaco = 1 Real
16 Reales = 1 Escudo

1/8 (PILON)
(1/16 Real)

COPPER
Obv: Crowned F VII monogram.
Rev: Castles and lions in wreath.

KM#	Date	VG	Fine	VF	XF
59	1814	10.00	20.00	40.00	120.00
	1815	10.00	20.00	40.00	120.00

1/4 (TLACO)
(1/8 Real)

COPPER
Obv. leg: FERDIN. VII. . around crowned F.VII.

KM#	Date	VG	Fine	VF	XF
63	1814	12.00	25.00	50.00	140.00
	1815	12.00	25.00	50.00	140.00
	1816	12.00	25.00	50.00	140.00

2/4 (2 TLACO)
(1/4 Real)

COPPER
Obv. leg: FERDIN. VII. . around crowned F.VII.

KM#	Date	VG	Fine	VF	XF
64	1814	10.00	20.00	35.00	115.00
	1815/4	12.00	25.00	45.00	135.00
	1815	10.00	20.00	35.00	115.00
	1816	10.00	20.00	35.00	115.00
	1821	20.00	40.00	60.00	185.00

1/4 REAL

.8450 g, .903 SILVER, .0245 oz ASW
Obv: Castle. Rev: Lion.

KM#	Date	VG	Fine	VF	XF
62	1796	10.00	20.00	40.00	80.00
	1797	10.00	25.00	40.00	80.00
	1798	12.50	20.00	35.00	60.00
	1799/8	12.50	17.50	35.00	65.00
	1799	10.00	15.00	27.50	60.00
	1800	10.00	25.00	35.00	80.00
	1801	10.00	15.00	27.50	60.00
	1802	12.50	20.00	27.50	60.00
	1803	12.50	20.00	27.50	60.00
	1804	10.00	20.00	27.50	70.00
	1805/4	12.50	22.50	40.00	65.00
	1805	10.00	20.00	35.00	60.00
	1806	10.00	20.00	35.00	70.00
	1807/797	15.00	30.00	40.00	75.00
	1807	12.50	25.00	35.00	70.00
	1808	12.50	25.00	35.00	70.00
	1809/8	12.50	25.00	35.00	70.00
	1809	12.50	25.00	35.00	70.00
	1810	12.50	25.00	35.00	60.00
	1811	12.50	25.00	35.00	60.00
	1812	12.50	25.00	35.00	60.00
	1813	10.00	20.00	27.50	60.00
	1815	10.00	20.00	35.00	60.00
	1816	10.00	20.00	30.00	50.00

NOTE: Earlier dates (1796-1800) exist for this type.

1/2 REAL

1.6900 g, .917 SILVER, .0498 oz ASW
Obv. leg: PHILIP.V.D.G. HISPAN.ET IND. REX.

KM#	Date	VG	Fine	VF	XF
65	1732	—	—	Rare	—
	1732 F	500.00	800.00	1200.	2000.
	1733 F(MX)	375.00	600.00	1000.	1500.
	1733 MF(MX)				
		400.00	600.00	1000.	1500.
	1733 F	200.00	325.00	550.00	800.00
	1733 MF	300.00	400.00	600.00	800.00
	1734/3 MF	10.00	25.00	35.00	60.00
	1734 MF	10.00	25.00	35.00	60.00
	1735/4 MF	8.00	20.00	35.00	60.00
	1735 MF	8.00	20.00	35.00	60.00
	1736/5 MF	8.00	20.00	35.00	60.00
	1736 MF	8.00	20.00	35.00	60.00
	1737/6 MF	8.00	20.00	35.00	60.00
	1737 MF	8.00	20.00	35.00	60.00
	1738/7 MF	8.00	20.00	35.00	60.00
	1738 MF	8.00	20.00	35.00	60.00
	1739 MF	8.00	20.00	35.00	60.00
	1740/30MF	6.00	14.00	28.00	50.00
	1740/39MF	6.00	14.00	28.00	50.00
	1740 MF	6.00	14.00	28.00	50.00
	1741/39MF	6.00	14.00	28.00	50.00
	1741/0MF	6.00	14.00	28.00	50.00
	1741 MF	6.00	14.00	28.00	50.00

Obv. leg:.PHS.V.D.G. HISP.ET IND.R.

KM#	Date	VG	Fine	VF	XF
66	1742 M	6.00	14.00	28.00	50.00
	1743 M	6.00	14.00	28.00	50.00
	1744/3 M	6.00	14.00	28.00	50.00
	1744 M	6.00	14.00	28.00	50.00
	1745 M	6.00	14.00	28.00	50.00
	1746 M	6.00	14.00	28.00	50.00
	1747 M	6.00	14.00	28.00	50.00

Obv. leg: FRD.VI.D.G.HISP.ET IND.R.

KM#	Date	VG	Fine	VF	XF
67	1747 M	6.50	15.00	30.00	55.00
	1748/7 M	6.50	15.00	30.00	55.00
	1748 M	6.50	15.00	30.00	55.00
	1749 M	6.50	15.00	30.00	55.00
	1750 M	6.50	15.00	30.00	55.00
	1751 M	8.00	20.00	35.00	60.00
	1752 M	6.50	15.00	30.00	55.00
	1753 M	6.50	15.00	30.00	55.00
	1754 M	10.00	25.00	45.00	100.00
	1755/6 M	10.00	25.00	45.00	100.00
	1755 M	6.50	15.00	30.00	55.00
	1756/5 M	6.50	15.00	30.00	55.00
	1756 M	6.50	15.00	30.00	55.00
	1757/6 M	6.50	15.00	30.00	55.00
	1757 M	6.50	15.00	30.00	55.00
	1758/7 M	6.50	15.00	30.00	55.00
	1758 M	6.50	15.00	30.00	55.00
	1759 M	6.50	15.00	30.00	55.00
	1760 M	8.00	20.00	35.00	60.00

Obv. leg: CAR.III.D.G.HISP.ET IND.R.

KM#	Date	VG	Fine	VF	XF
68	1760 M	5.00	10.00	22.00	55.00
	1761 M	5.00	10.00	22.00	55.00
	1762 M	5.00	10.00	22.00	55.00
	1763/2 M	5.00	10.00	22.00	55.00
	1763 M	5.00	10.00	22.00	55.00
	1764 M	5.00	10.00	22.00	55.00
	1765 M	5.00	10.00	22.00	55.00
	1766 M	5.00	10.00	22.00	55.00
	1767 M	7.50	15.00	30.00	65.00
	1768/6 M	6.00	12.00	25.00	60.00
	1768 M	5.00	10.00	22.00	55.00
	1769 M	6.00	12.00	25.00	60.00
	1770 M	6.00	12.00	25.00	60.00
	1770 F	10.00	18.00	35.00	75.00
	1771 F	6.00	12.00	25.00	60.00

1.6900 g, .903 SILVER, .0490 oz ASW
Obv. leg: CAROLUS.III.DEI.GRATIA.
Rev: Inverted FM and mint mark.

KM#	Date	VG	Fine	VF	XF
69.1	1772 FM	4.50	8.00	20.00	65.00
	1773 FM	4.50	7.00	15.00	55.00

Rev: Normal initials and mint mark.

KM#	Date	VG	Fine	VF	XF
69.2	1772 FF	7.00	15.00	30.00	75.00
	1773 FM	4.50	10.00	22.00	60.00
	1773 FM CAROLS (error)				
		300.00	—	—	—
	1774 FM	4.50	10.00	22.00	55.00
	1775 FM	4.50	10.00	22.00	55.00
	1776 FM	4.50	10.00	22.00	55.00
	1777/6 FM	10.00	18.00	35.00	75.00
	1777 FM	7.00	15.00	30.00	65.00
	1778 FF	4.50	10.00	22.00	55.00
	1779 FF	4.50	10.00	22.00	55.00
	1780/g FF	4.50	10.00	22.00	55.00
	1780 FF	4.50	10.00	22.00	55.00
	1781 FF	4.50	10.00	22.00	55.00
	1782/1 FF	6.00	12.50	25.00	75.00
	1782 FF	4.50	10.00	22.00	55.00
	1783 FF	4.50	10.00	22.00	55.00
	1783 FM	125.00	300.00	450.00	—
	1784 FF	4.50	10.00	22.00	55.00
	1784 FM	7.00	15.00	30.00	80.00
	1785 FM	5.00	12.00	25.00	60.00
	1786 FM	4.50	10.00	22.00	55.00
	1787 FM	4.50	10.00	22.00	55.00
	1788 FM	4.50	10.00	22.00	55.00
	1789 FM	7.00	15.00	35.00	100.00

Obv: Armored bust of Charles III, leg: .CAROLUS.IV.

KM#	Date	VG	Fine	VF	XF
70	1789 FM	7.00	15.00	30.00	90.00
	1790 FM	7.00	15.00	30.00	90.00

Obv: Armored bust of Charles III, leg: .CAROLUS.IIII.

KM#	Date	VG	Fine	VF	XF
71	1790 FM	7.00	15.00	30.00	90.00

1/2 REAL

1.6900 g, .903 SILVER, .0490 oz ASW
Obv: Armored bust of Charles IIII.
Rev: Pillars and arms.

KM#	Date	VG	Fine	VF	XF
72	1792 FM	6.00	12.00	22.00	50.00
	1793 FM	6.00	12.00	22.00	50.00
	1794/3 FM	7.50	15.00	30.00	75.00
	1794 FM	5.00	10.00	20.00	45.00
	1795 FM	4.00	10.00	20.00	45.00
	1796 FM	4.00	10.00	20.00	45.00
	1797 FM	4.00	10.00	20.00	45.00
	1798/7 FM	5.00	11.50	22.00	50.00
	1798 FM	4.00	10.00	20.00	45.00
	1799 FM	4.00	10.00	20.00	45.00
	1800/799 FM	5.00	11.50	22.00	50.00
	1800 FM	4.00	10.00	20.00	45.00
	1800 FT	—	—	—	—

Obv: Armored bust of Charles IIII.
Rev: Pillars and arms.

	Date	VG	Fine	VF	XF
	1801 FM	6.50	14.00	28.00	80.00
	1801 FT	4.00	10.00	20.00	45.00
	1802 FT	4.00	10.00	20.00	45.00
	1803 FT	5.00	11.50	22.00	50.00
	1804 TH	4.00	10.00	20.00	45.00
	1805 TH	4.00	10.00	20.00	45.00
	1806 TH	4.00	10.00	20.00	45.00
	1807/6 TH	5.00	11.50	22.00	50.00
	1807 TH	4.00	10.00	20.00	45.00
	1808/7 TH	5.00	11.50	22.00	50.00
	1808 TH	4.00	10.00	20.00	45.00

Obv: Armored bust of Ferdinand VII.

KM#	Date	VG	Fine	VF	XF
73	1808 TH	3.00	7.00	15.00	30.00
	1809 TH	3.00	7.00	15.00	30.00
	1810 TH	5.00	10.00	20.00	40.00
	1810 HJ	3.00	7.00	15.00	30.00
	1811 HJ	3.00	7.00	15.00	30.00
	1812 HJ	3.00	7.00	15.00	30.00
	1812 JJ	10.00	20.00	40.00	100.00
	1813 TH	3.50	7.50	15.00	30.00
	1813 JJ	10.00	20.00	40.00	100.00
	1813 HJ	7.50	15.00	30.00	90.00
	1814 JJ	5.00	10.00	20.00	40.00

Obv: Draped bust of Ferdinand VII.

KM#	Date	VG	Fine	VF	XF
74	1814 JJ	3.00	7.00	16.50	45.00
	1815 JJ	3.00	7.00	15.00	40.00
	1816 JJ	3.00	7.00	15.00	40.00
	1817/6 JJ	—	—	—	—
	1817 JJ	3.00	7.00	16.50	45.00
	1818/7 JJ	3.00	7.00	17.50	50.00
	1818 JJ	3.00	7.00	17.50	50.00
	1819 JJ	3.00	7.00	15.00	40.00
	1820 JJ	3.00	7.00	17.50	50.00
	1821 JJ	3.00	7.00	15.00	40.00

REAL

3.3800 g, .917 SILVER, .0996 oz ASW
Obv. leg: PHILIP.V.D.G.HISPAN.ET IND.REX.

KM#	Date	VG	Fine	VF	XF
75.1	1732	—	—	Rare	—
	1732 F	125.00	225.00	350.00	550.00
	1733 F(MX)	150.00	350.00	425.00	750.00
	1733/2 MF(MX)				
		150.00	350.00	425.00	750.00
	1733 MF(MX)				
		150.00	350.00	425.00	750.00
	1733 F	—	—	Rare	—
	1733 MF	85.00	150.00	225.00	375.00
	1734/3 MF	15.00	30.00	60.00	160.00
	1734 MF	12.00	25.00	50.00	150.00
	1735 MF	12.00	25.00	50.00	150.00
	1736 MF	12.00	20.00	50.00	150.00
	1737 MF	12.00	20.00	50.00	150.00
	1738 MF	12.00	20.00	50.00	150.00
	1739 MF	12.00	20.00	50.00	150.00
	1740 MF	12.00	20.00	50.00	150.00
	1741 MF	12.00	20.00	50.00	150.00

Obv. leg: PHS.V.D.G.HISP.ET.IND.R.

KM#	Date	VG	Fine	VF	XF
75.2	1742 M	8.00	15.00	30.00	90.00
	1743 M	8.00	15.00	30.00	90.00
	1744/3 M	8.00	15.00	30.00	90.00
	1744 M	8.00	15.00	30.00	90.00
	1745 M	7.00	14.00	28.00	80.00
	1746/5 M	10.00	20.00	60.00	200.00
	1746 M	8.00	15.00	35.00	100.00
	1747 M	8.00	15.00	35.00	100.00

Obv. leg: .FRD.VI.D.G.HISP.ET IND.R.

KM#	Date	VG	Fine	VF	XF
76	1747 M	8.00	15.00	30.00	60.00
	1748/7 M	8.00	15.00	30.00	60.00
	1748 M	8.00	15.00	30.00	60.00
	1749/8 M	8.00	15.00	30.00	60.00
	1749 M	8.00	15.00	30.00	60.00
	1750/49 M	8.00	15.00	30.00	60.00
	1750 M	8.00	15.00	30.00	60.00
	1751 M	10.00	20.00	40.00	80.00
	1752 M	8.00	15.00	30.00	60.00
76	1753 M	8.00	15.00	30.00	60.00
	1754 M	10.00	20.00	40.00	80.00
	1755/4 M	8.00	15.00	30.00	60.00
	1755 M	8.00	15.00	30.00	60.00
	1756 M	10.00	20.00	40.00	80.00
	1757 M	10.00	20.00	40.00	80.00
	1758/5 M	8.00	15.00	30.00	60.00
	1758 M	8.00	15.00	30.00	60.00
	1759 M	10.00	20.00	40.00	80.00
	1760 M	10.00	20.00	40.00	80.00

Obv. leg: CAR.III.D.G.HISP.ET IND.R.

Obv. leg: CAR.III.D.G.HISP.ET IND.R.

KM#	Date	VG	Fine	VF	XF
77	1760 M	8.00	12.00	25.00	60.00
	1761/O M	10.00	20.00	50.00	100.00
	1761 M	6.00	10.00	22.00	50.00
	1761/2 M	6.00	10.00	22.00	50.00
	1762 M	6.00	10.00	22.00	50.00
	1763/2 M	12.00	25.00	60.00	120.00
	1763 M	6.00	10.00	22.00	50.00
	1764 M	10.00	20.00	50.00	100.00
	1765 M	10.00	20.00	50.00	100.00
	1766 M	6.00	10.00	22.00	50.00
	1767 M	10.00	20.00	50.00	100.00
	1768 M	6.00	10.00	22.00	50.00
	1769 M	6.00	10.00	22.00	50.00
	1770/69M	6.00	10.00	25.00	65.00
	1770 M	6.00	10.00	25.00	65.00
	1770 F	20.00	40.00	90.00	250.00
	1771 F	20.00	40.00	90.00	250.00

3.3800 g, .903 SILVER, .0981 oz ASW
Obv. leg: CAROLUS.III.DEI.GRATIA.
Rev: Inverted FM and mint mark.

KM#	Date	VG	Fine	VF	XF
78.1	1772 FM	3.00	7.50	15.00	60.00
	1773 FM	3.00	7.50	15.00	60.00

Rev: Normal initials and mint mark.

78.2	1773 FM	6.50	12.50	30.00	90.00
	1774 FM	3.00	7.50	15.00	60.00
	1775 FM	3.00	7.50	15.00	60.00
	1776 FM	3.00	7.50	15.00	60.00
	1777 FM	3.00	7.50	15.00	60.00
	1778 FF	3.00	7.50	15.00	60.00
	1779 FF	3.00	8.50	16.50	60.00
	1780 FF	3.00	7.50	15.00	60.00
	1781 FF	3.00	7.50	15.00	60.00
	1782 FF	3.00	7.50	15.00	60.00
	1783 FF	3.00	8.50	16.50	60.00
	1784 FF	3.00	8.50	16.50	60.00
	1785 FM	3.00	7.50	15.00	60.00
	1785 FF	3.00	8.50	16.50	60.00
	1786 FM	3.00	7.50	15.00	60.00
	1787 FM	12.00	25.00	50.00	125.00
	1787 FF	10.00	20.00	40.00	100.00
	1788 FM	3.00	8.50	16.50	60.00
	1788 FF	3.00	7.50	15.00	60.00
	1789 FM	5.00	10.00	20.00	75.00

Obv: Armored bust of Charles III, leg: CAROLUS.IV. .

79	1789 FM	8.00	15.00	25.00	100.00
	1790 FM	8.00	15.00	25.00	100.00

Obv: Armored bust of Charles III; leg: CAROLUS.IIII.

80	1790 FM	10.00	20.00	35.00	125.00

3.3800 g, .903 SILVER, .0981 oz ASW
Obv: Armored bust of Charles IIII.

KM#	Date	VG	Fine	VF	XF
81	1792 FM	10.00	20.00	30.00	90.00
	1793 FM	15.00	30.00	50.00	150.00
	1794 FM	25.00	50.00	90.00	250.00
	1795 FM	15.00	30.00	50.00	150.00
	1796 FM	3.50	8.50	16.50	65.00
	1797/6 FM	5.00	10.00	20.00	80.00
	1797 FM	3.00	7.50	15.00	60.00
	1798/7 FM	3.50	8.50	16.50	65.00
	1798 FM	3.00	7.50	15.00	60.00
	1799 FM	3.00	7.50	15.00	60.00
	1800 FM	3.00	7.50	15.00	60.00
	1801 FM	8.00	15.00	25.00	80.00
	1801 FT	3.00	8.50	16.50	60.00
	1802 FM	3.00	8.50	16.50	60.00
	1802 FT	3.00	7.50	15.00	60.00
	1803 FT	3.00	8.50	16.50	60.00
	1804 TH	3.00	7.50	15.00	60.00
	1805 TH	3.00	8.50	16.50	60.00
	1806 TH	3.00	7.50	15.00	60.00
	1807/6 TH	3.50	8.50	16.50	65.00
	1807 TH	3.00	7.50	15.00	60.00
	1808/7 TH	3.50	8.50	16.50	65.00
	1808 TH	3.00	7.50	15.00	60.00

Obv: Armored bust of Ferdinand VII.

82	1809 TH	4.00	9.00	18.00	100.00
	1810/09 TH	4.00	9.00	18.00	100.00
	1810 TH	4.00	9.00	18.00	100.00
	1810 HJ	6.00	10.00	20.00	125.00
	1811 HJ	4.00	9.00	12.00	100.00
	1811 TH	25.00	35.00	60.00	250.00
	1812 HJ	4.00	9.00	12.00	80.00
	1812 JJ	6.00	10.00	20.00	125.00
	1813 HJ	6.00	10.00	20.00	125.00
	1813 JJ	50.00	100.00	150.00	250.00
	1814 HJ	50.00	100.00	175.00	300.00
	1814 JJ	50.00	100.00	175.00	300.00

Obv: Draped bust of Ferdinand VII.

83	1814 JJ	25.00	50.00	100.00	350.00
	1815 JJ	5.50	8.50	17.50	125.00
	1815 HJ	15.00	30.00	60.00	150.00
	1816 JJ	4.00	7.50	15.00	75.00
	1817 JJ	4.00	7.50	15.00	75.00
	1818 JJ	30.00	60.00	125.00	500.00
	1819 JJ	5.50	8.50	17.50	75.00
	1820 JJ	5.00	8.50	17.50	75.00
	1821/0 JJ	7.50	12.50	27.50	110.00
	1821 JJ	5.00	8.50	15.00	50.00

2 REALES

6.7700 g, .917 SILVER, .1996 oz ASW
Obv. leg: PHILIP.V.D.G.HISPAN.ET IND. REX.

KM#	Date	VG	Fine	VF	XF
84	1732	—	—	Rare	—
	1732 F	800.00	1300.	1750.	2750.
	1733 F(MX)	600.00	900.00	1500.	2500.
	1733 F	600.00	800.00	1350.	2250.
	1733 MF(MX)	350.00	600.00	1000.	1650.
	1733 MF	600.00	900.00	1500.	2500.
	1734/3 MF	20.00	40.00	80.00	165.00
	1734 MF	20.00	40.00	80.00	165.00
	1735/3 MF	10.00	20.00	40.00	100.00
	1735/4 MF	10.00	20.00	40.00	100.00
	1735 MF	10.00	20.00	40.00	100.00
	1736/3 MF	15.00	30.00	60.00	140.00
	1736/4 MF	15.00	30.00	60.00	140.00
	1736/5 MF	15.00	30.00	60.00	140.00
	1736 MF	15.00	30.00	60.00	140.00
	1737/3 MF	15.00	30.00	60.00	140.00
	1737 MF	15.00	30.00	60.00	140.00
	1738/7 MF	15.00	30.00	60.00	140.00
	1738 MF	15.00	30.00	60.00	140.00
	1739 MF	15.00	30.00	60.00	140.00
	1740/30 MF	15.00	30.00	60.00	140.00
	1740 MF	15.00	30.00	60.00	140.00
	1741 MF	15.00	30.00	60.00	140.00

Obv. leg: PHS.V.D.G.HISP.ET IND.R.

KM#	Date	VG	Fine	VF	XF
85	1742 M	10.00	20.00	40.00	110.00
	1743/2 M	10.00	20.00	40.00	110.00
	1743 M	10.00	20.00	40.00	110.00
	1744/2 M	10.00	20.00	40.00	110.00
	1744/3 M	10.00	20.00	40.00	110.00
	1744 M	10.00	20.00	40.00	110.00
	1745/4 M	10.00	20.00	40.00	110.00
	1745 M	10.00	20.00	40.00	110.00
	1746 M	10.00	20.00	40.00	110.00
	1747 M	10.00	20.00	40.00	110.00
	1749 M	200.00	300.00	500.00	900.00
	1750 M	200.00	300.00	500.00	900.00

Obv. leg: FRD.VI.D.G.HISP.ET IND.R.

KM#	Date	VG	Fine	VF	XF
86	1747 M	12.00	25.00	45.00	125.00

KM#	Date	VG	Fine	VF	XF
86	1748/7 M	12.00	25.00	45.00	125.00
	1748 M	10.00	20.00	40.00	110.00
	1749 M	10.00	20.00	40.00	110.00
	1750 M	10.00	20.00	40.00	110.00
	1751/41 M	12.00	25.00	60.00	140.00
	1751 M	10.00	20.00	40.00	110.00
	1752 M	10.00	20.00	40.00	110.00
	1753/2 M	12.00	25.00	60.00	140.00
	1753 M	12.00	25.00	60.00	140.00
	1754 M	12.00	25.00	60.00	140.00
	1755 M	12.00	25.00	60.00	140.00
	1756 M	12.00	25.00	60.00	140.00
	1757/6 M	10.00	20.00	40.00	110.00
	1757 M	10.00	20.00	40.00	110.00
	1758 M	10.00	20.00	40.00	110.00
	1759/8 M	10.00	20.00	40.00	110.00
	1759 M	15.00	30.00	65.00	175.00
	1760 M	15.00	30.00	65.00	175.00

Obv. leg: CAR.III.D.G.HISP.ET IND.R.

KM#	Date	VG	Fine	VF	XF
87	1760 M	10.00	20.00	40.00	110.00
	1761 M	10.00	20.00	40.00	110.00
	1762 M	10.00	20.00	40.00	110.00
	1763/2 M	10.00	20.00	40.00	110.00
	1763 M	10.00	20.00	40.00	110.00
	1764 M	10.00	20.00	40.00	110.00
	1765 M	10.00	20.00	40.00	110.00
	1766 M	12.00	25.00	70.00	150.00
	1767 M	8.00	16.50	35.00	100.00
	1768/6 M	8.00	16.50	35.00	100.00
	1768 M	8.00	16.50	35.00	100.00
	1769 M	8.00	16.50	35.00	100.00
	1770 M	—	—	Rare	—
	1770 F	—	—	Rare	—
	1771 F	8.00	16.50	35.00	90.00

6.7700 g, .903 SILVER, .1965 oz ASW
Obv. leg: CAROLUS.III.DEI.GRATIA.
Rev: Inverted FM and mint mark.

KM#	Date	VG	Fine	VF	XF
88.1	1772 FM	5.00	10.00	20.00	100.00
	1773 FM	5.00	10.00	20.00	100.00

Rev: Normal initials and mint mark.

KM#	Date	VG	Fine	VF	XF
88.2	1773 FM	5.00	10.00	20.00	100.00
	1774 FM	5.00	10.00	20.00	100.00
	1775 FM	5.00	10.00	20.00	100.00
	1776 FM	5.00	10.00	20.00	100.00
	1777 FM	5.00	10.00	20.00	100.00
	1778 FF	5.00	10.00	20.00	100.00
	1779 FF	5.00	10.00	20.00	100.00
	1780 FF	5.00	10.00	20.00	100.00
	1781 FF	5.00	10.00	20.00	100.00
	1782 FF	5.00	10.00	20.00	100.00
	1783 FF	5.00	10.00	20.00	100.00
	1784 FF	5.00	10.00	20.00	100.00
	1784 FF DEI GRTIA (error)	100.00	150.00	250.00	600.00
	1784 FM	100.00	150.00	250.00	600.00

KM#	Date	VG	Fine	VF	XF
88.2	1785 FM	5.00	10.00	20.00	100.00
	1786 FM	5.00	10.00	20.00	100.00
	1786 FF	100.00	150.00	250.00	600.00
	1787 FM	5.00	10.00	20.00	100.00
	1788 FM	5.00	10.00	20.00	100.00
	1789 FM	11.50	25.00	40.00	150.00

Obv: Armored bust of Charles III; leg: CAROLUS.IV. .

89	1789 FM	11.50	25.00	40.00	150.00
	1790 FM	11.50	25.00	40.00	150.00

Obv: Armored bust of Charles III, leg: CAROLUS.IIII.

90	1790 FM	12.50	27.50	60.00	200.00

6.7700 g, .903 SILVER, .1965 oz ASW
Obv: Armored bust of Carolus IIII.

91	1792 FM	15.00	30.00	60.00	200.00
	1793 FM	15.00	30.00	60.00	200.00
	1794/3 FM	50.00	100.00	200.00	450.00
	1794 FM	40.00	75.00	150.00	400.00
	1795 FM	5.00	10.00	20.00	100.00
	1796 FM	5.00	10.00	20.00	100.00
	1797 FM	5.00	10.00	20.00	100.00
	1798 FM	5.00	10.00	20.00	100.00
	1799/8 FM	5.50	11.50	22.50	110.00
	1799 FM	5.00	10.00	20.00	100.00
	1800 FM	5.00	10.00	20.00	100.00
	1801 FT	5.00	10.00	20.00	100.00
	1801 FM	20.00	40.00	75.00	250.00
	1802 FT	5.00	10.00	20.00	100.00
	1803 FT	5.00	10.00	20.00	100.00
	1804 TH	5.00	10.00	20.00	100.00
	1805 TH	5.00	10.00	20.00	100.00
	1806/5 TH	5.50	11.50	22.50	110.00
	1806 TH	5.00	10.00	20.00	100.00
	1807/5 TH	5.50	11.50	22.50	110.00
	1807/6 TH	15.00	30.00	60.00	200.00
	1807 TH	5.00	10.00	20.00	100.00
	1808/7 TH	5.50	11.50	22.50	110.00
	1808 TH	5.00	10.00	20.00	100.00

Obv: Armored bust of Ferdinand VII.

KM#	Date	VG	Fine	VF	XF
92	1809 TH	6.50	12.50	45.00	150.00
	1810 TH	6.50	12.50	45.00	150.00
	1810 HJ	6.50	12.50	45.00	150.00
	1811 HJ	6.50	12.50	45.00	150.00
	1811 HJ/TH	40.00	80.00	150.00	300.00
	1811 TH	100.00	200.00	300.00	750.00

Obv: Draped bust of Ferdinand VII.

93	1812 HJ	15.00	30.00	100.00	300.00
	1812 TH	60.00	125.00	250.00	500.00
	1812 JJ	10.00	20.00	60.00	200.00
	1813 HJ	40.00	100.00	200.00	500.00
	1813 JJ	20.00	60.00	125.00	350.00
	1813 TH	15.00	30.00	100.00	400.00
	1814/13 JJ	15.00	30.00	100.00	400.00
	1814 JJ	15.00	30.00	100.00	400.00
	1815 JJ	5.50	11.50	32.00	100.00
	1816 JJ	5.50	11.50	32.00	100.00
	1817 JJ	5.50	11.50	32.00	100.00
	1818 JJ	5.50	11.50	32.00	100.00
	1819 JJ	5.50	11.50	32.00	100.00
	1820 JJ	125.00	—	—	—
	1821/0 JJ	5.00	10.00	30.00	110.00
	1821 JJ	5.50	11.50	32.00	100.00

4 REALES

13.5400 g, .917 SILVER, .3992 oz ASW
Obv. leg: PHILLIP.V.D.G.HISPAN.ET IND.REX

KM#	Date	VG	Fine	VF	XF
94	1732	—	—	Rare Specimen	
	1732 F	2000.	3000.	5000.	10,000.
	1733 F	1500.	2000.	4000.	6500.
	1733 MF	1200.	1800.	2500.	4500.
	1733 MF(MX)	1500.	2200.	3250.	5500.
	1733 F(MX)	1500.	2500.	3500.	6000.
	1734/3 MF	150.00	300.00	600.00	1200.
	1734 MF	150.00	300.00	600.00	1200.
	1735 MF	100.00	175.00	300.00	500.00
	1736 MF	100.00	175.00	300.00	500.00
	1737 MF	100.00	175.00	300.00	500.00
	1738/7 MF	100.00	175.00	300.00	500.00
	1738 MF	100.00	175.00	300.00	500.00
	1739 MF	100.00	175.00	300.00	500.00

KM#	Date	VG	Fine	VF	XF
94	1740/30 MF	100.00	200.00	325.00	600.00
	1740 MF	100.00	175.00	300.00	500.00
	1741 MF	100.00	175.00	300.00	500.00
	1742/1 MF	100.00	175.00	300.00	500.00
	1742 MF	100.00	175.00	300.00	500.00
	1743 MF	100.00	175.00	300.00	500.00
	1744/3 MF	100.00	200.00	325.00	600.00
	1744 MF	100.00	175.00	300.00	500.00
	1745 MF	100.00	175.00	300.00	500.00
	1746 MP	100.00	175.00	300.00	500.00
	1747 MF	150.00	275.00	400.00	650.00

13.5400 g, .903 SILVER, .3931 oz ASW
Obv. leg: CAROLUS.III.DEI.GRATIA.
Rev: Inverted FM and mint mark.

KM#	Date	VG	Fine	VF	XF
97.1	1772 FM	90.00	125.00	200.00	450.00
	1773 FM	100.00	175.00	300.00	650.00

Obv. leg: FERDND.VI.D.G.HISPAN.ET IND.REX

KM#	Date	VG	Fine	VF	XF
95	1747 MF	100.00	150.00	300.00	500.00
	1748/7 MF	100.00	150.00	300.00	500.00
	1748 MF	100.00	125.00	250.00	450.00
	1749 MF	150.00	225.00	350.00	650.00
	1750/40 MF	100.00	125.00	250.00	450.00
	1750 MF	100.00	125.00	250.00	450.00
	1751 MF	100.00	125.00	250.00	450.00
	1752 MF	100.00	125.00	250.00	450.00
	1753 MF	100.00	125.00	300.00	500.00
	1754 MM	250.00	375.00	500.00	850.00
	1754 MF	250.00	375.00	500.00	850.00
	1755 MM	100.00	125.00	225.00	425.00
	1756 MM	100.00	150.00	300.00	500.00
	1757 MM	100.00	150.00	300.00	500.00
	1758 MM	100.00	125.00	225.00	425.00
	1759 MM	100.00	125.00	225.00	425.00
	1760/59 MM	100.00	175.00	350.00	550.00
	1760 MM	100.00	175.00	350.00	550.00

Rev: Normal initials and mint mark.

KM#	Date	VG	Fine	VF	XF
97.2	1773 MF	200.00	300.00	400.00	800.00
	1774 FM	25.00	40.00	75.00	350.00
	1775 FM	25.00	40.00	75.00	350.00
	1776 FM	25.00	40.00	75.00	350.00
	1777 FM	25.00	40.00	75.00	350.00
	1778 FF	25.00	40.00	75.00	350.00
	1779 FF	25.00	40.00	75.00	350.00
	1780 FF	25.00	40.00	75.00	350.00
	1781 FF	250.00	350.00	500.00	1000.
	1782 FF	35.00	65.00	150.00	450.00
	1783 FF	25.00	40.00	75.00	350.00
	1784 FF	25.00	40.00	75.00	350.00
	1784 FM	100.00	200.00	350.00	600.00
	1785 FM	100.00	200.00	350.00	600.00
	1786 FM	25.00	40.00	75.00	350.00
	1787 FM	25.00	40.00	75.00	350.00
	1788 FM	25.00	40.00	75.00	350.00
	1789 FM	50.00	100.00	150.00	400.00

Obv. leg: CAROLVS.III.D.G.HISPAN.ET IND.REX

KM#	Date	VG	Fine	VF	XF
96	1760 MM	100.00	150.00	250.00	900.00
	1761 MM	100.00	150.00	250.00	900.00
	1761 MM cross between H and I				
		100.00	150.00	250.00	900.00
	1762 MM	75.00	100.00	150.00	450.00
	1762 MF	100.00	150.00	300.00	600.00
	1763/1 MM	100.00	150.00	300.00	600.00
	1763/2 MF	100.00	150.00	300.00	600.00
	1763 MM	100.00	150.00	300.00	600.00
	1763 MF	100.00	200.00	350.00	800.00
	1764 MM	400.00	600.00	1000.	2000.
	1764 MF	350.00	500.00	1000.	2000.
	1765 MF	350.00	500.00	1000.	2000.
	1766 MF	250.00	350.00	500.00	1250.
	1767 MF	100.00	150.00	300.00	600.00
	1768 MF	75.00	100.00	150.00	450.00
	1769 MF	75.00	100.00	150.00	450.00
	1770 MF	75.00	100.00	150.00	450.00
	1771 MF	125.00	200.00	300.00	700.00
	1771 FM	150.00	275.00	400.00	900.00

Obv: Armored bust of Charles III, leg: CAROLUS.IV. .

KM#	Date	VG	Fine	VF	XF
98	1789 FM	60.00	100.00	150.00	400.00
	1790 FM	25.00	50.00	100.00	350.00

Obv: Armored bust of Charles III, leg: CAROLUS.IIII.

KM#	Date	VG	Fine	VF	XF
99	1790 FM	30.00	60.00	175.00	500.00

Obv: Armored bust of Ferdinand VII.

KM#	Date	VG	Fine	VF	XF
101	1809 HJ	75.00	125.00	175.00	450.00
	1810 TH	75.00	125.00	175.00	450.00
	1810 HJ	75.00	125.00	175.00	450.00
	1811 HJ	75.00	125.00	175.00	450.00
	1812 HJ	500.00	750.00	1000.	2000.

Obv: Draped bust of Ferdinand VII.

		VG	Fine	VF	XF
102	1816 JJ	150.00	200.00	350.00	600.00
	1817 JJ	250.00	400.00	500.00	1000.
	1818/7 JJ	250.00	400.00	500.00	1000.
	1818 JJ	250.00	400.00	500.00	1000.
	1819 JJ	175.00	250.00	350.00	700.00
	1820 JJ	175.00	250.00	350.00	700.00
	1821 JJ	75.00	125.00	200.00	425.00

13.5400 g, .903 SILVER, .3931 oz ASW
Obv: Armored bust of Charles IIII.
Rev: Pillars, arms.

	Date	VG	Fine	VF	XF
100	1792 FM	25.00	40.00	75.00	350.00
	1793 FM	75.00	125.00	200.00	500.00
	1794/3 FM	25.00	40.00	80.00	375.00
	1794 FM	25.00	40.00	80.00	350.00
	1795 FM	25.00	40.00	80.00	350.00
	1796 FM	150.00	250.00	400.00	800.00
	1797 FM	40.00	75.00	150.00	500.00
	1798/7 FM	25.00	40.00	80.00	375.00
	1798 FM	25.00	40.00	80.00	350.00
	1799 FM	25.00	40.00	80.00	350.00
	1800 FM	25.00	40.00	80.00	350.00
	1801 FM	25.00	40.00	80.00	350.00
	1801 FT	60.00	100.00	150.00	500.00
	1802 FT	200.00	300.00	500.00	1000.
	1803 FT	60.00	125.00	200.00	550.00
	1803 FM	350.00	450.00	650.00	1250.
	1804 TH	25.00	50.00	150.00	450.00
	1805 TH	25.00	40.00	80.00	350.00
	1806 TH	25.00	40.00	80.00	350.00
	1807 TH	25.00	40.00	80.00	350.00
	1808/7 TH	25.00	50.00	150.00	450.00
	1808 TH	25.00	50.00	150.00	450.00

8 REALES

27.0700 g, .917 SILVER, .7982 oz ASW
Obv. leg: PHILIP.V.D.G.HISPAN.ET IND.REX.

Obv. leg: FERDND.VI.D.G.HISPAN.ET IND.REX
Rev: W/Royal crown on left pillar.

KM#	Date	VG	Fine	VF	XF
103	1732 F	2750.	4750.	8000.	*Rare
	1733/2 F(MX)	3000.	5250.	9000.	*Rare
	1733 F	2000.	3500.	5850.	*Rare
	1733 F(MX)	—	—	*Rare	—
	1733 MF(MX)	—	—	*Rare	—
	1733 MF	700.00	1500.	2500.	4000.
	1734/3 MF	100.00	150.00	275.00	550.00
	1734 MF	100.00	150.00	250.00	450.00
	1735 MF	100.00	150.00	250.00	450.00
	1736 MF	100.00	150.00	250.00	450.00
	1737 MF	65.00	100.00	150.00	350.00
	1738/6 MF	65.00	100.00	150.00	350.00
	1738/7 MF	65.00	100.00	150.00	350.00
	1738 MF	65.00	100.00	150.00	350.00
	1739/6 MF	65.00	100.00	150.00	350.00
	1739/8 MF	65.00	100.00	150.00	350.00
	1739 MF	65.00	100.00	150.00	350.00
	1740/30 MF	65.00	100.00	150.00	350.00
	1740/39 MF	65.00	100.00	150.00	350.00
	1740 MF	65.00	100.00	150.00	350.00
	1741/31 MF	65.00	100.00	150.00	350.00
	1741 MF	65.00	100.00	150.00	350.00
	1742/32 MF	75.00	125.00	200.00	450.00
	1742/1 MF	75.00	125.00	200.00	450.00
	1742 MF	65.00	100.00	150.00	350.00
	1743/2 MF	65.00	100.00	150.00	350.00
	1743 MF	65.00	100.00	150.00	350.00
	1744/34 MF	65.00	100.00	150.00	350.00
	1744/3 MF	65.00	100.00	135.00	350.00
	1744 MF	65.00	100.00	150.00	350.00
	1745 MF	65.00	100.00	150.00	350.00
	1746/5 MF	65.00	100.00	150.00	350.00
	1746 MF	65.00	100.00	150.00	350.00
	1747 MF	65.00	100.00	150.00	350.00

KM#	Date	VG	Fine	VF	XF
104.1	1747 MF	50.00	100.00	175.00	300.00
	1748/7 MF	60.00	120.00	250.00	450.00
	1748 MF	50.00	75.00	125.00	200.00
	1749 MF	50.00	75.00	125.00	200.00
	1750 MF	50.00	75.00	125.00	200.00
	1751/0 MF	50.00	75.00	125.00	200.00
	1751 MF	50.00	75.00	125.00	200.00
	1752/1 MF	50.00	75.00	125.00	200.00
	1752 MF	50.00	75.00	125.00	200.00
	1753/2 MF	50.00	75.00	125.00	200.00
	1753 MF	50.00	75.00	125.00	200.00
	1754/3 MF	60.00	120.00	200.00	350.00
	1754 MF	50.00	75.00	125.00	200.00
	1754 MM/MF	250.00	600.00	1250.	2500.
	1754 MM	250.00	600.00	1250.	2500.

Rev: Imperial crown.

KM#	Date	VG	Fine	VF	XF
104.2	1754 MM	75.00	125.00	200.00	400.00
	1754 MM	150.00	275.00	425.00	750.00
	1755/4 MM	50.00	80.00	150.00	250.00
	1755 MM	50.00	75.00	125.00	200.00
	1756/5 MM	50.00	75.00	125.00	200.00
	1756 MM	50.00	75.00	125.00	200.00
	1757/6 MM	50.00	75.00	125.00	200.00
	1757 MM	50.00	75.00	125.00	200.00
	1758 MM	50.00	75.00	125.00	200.00
	1759 MM	50.00	75.00	125.00	200.00
	1760/59 MM	60.00	100.00	150.00	250.00
	1760 MM	60.00	100.00	150.00	250.00

*NOTE: Ponterio AMAT sale 3-91 AU 1732 F realized $28,000., XF 1733/2 F (MX) realized $27,000., XF 1733 F realized $11,500., XF 1733 MF (MX) realized $35,000.

*NOTE: Bonhams Patterson sale 7-96 XF 1732 F realized $13,825., gVF 1733 F (MX) $11,710., gVF 1733 MF (MX) realized $21,145.

Obv. leg: CAROLUS.III.D.G.HISPAN.ET IND.REX

KM#	Date	VG	Fine	VF	XF
105	1760/59 MM CAROLUS.III/Ferdin.Vi	—	—	—	—
	1760 MM CAROLUS.III/FERDIN. VI. recut die	60.00	100.00	150.00	325.00

KM#	Date	VG	Fine	VF	XF
105	1760 MM	60.00	100.00	150.00	300.00
	1761/50 MM*				
		65.00	110.00	165.00	325.00
	1761/51 MM*				
		65.00	110.00	165.00	325.00
	1761/0 MM**				
		65.00	110.00	165.00	325.00
	1761 MM**				
		60.00	100.00	150.00	275.00
	1761 MM*				
		65.00	110.00	165.00	325.00
	1762/1 MM**				
		70.00	120.00	175.00	450.00
	1762/1 MM	70.00	120.00	175.00	450.00
	1762 MM**				
		60.00	100.00	150.00	275.00
	1762 MM*				
		50.00	75.00	120.00	200.00
	1762 MF	500.00	750.00	1000.	1500.
	1763/53 MF	50.00	75.00	125.00	250.00
	1763/1 MF	50.00	75.00	125.00	250.00
	1763/2 MM	300.00	450.00	750.00	1500.
	1763/2 MF	50.00	75.00	125.00	250.00
	1763/72 MF	50.00	75.00	125.00	250.00
	1763 MM	450.00	650.00	1150.	2500.
	1763 MF	50.00	75.00	125.00	225.00
	1764/54 MF	50.00	75.00	125.00	250.00
	1764/54 MF CAR/CRA				
		50.00	75.00	125.00	250.00
	1764/1 MF	50.00	75.00	125.00	250.00
	1764/3 MF	50.00	75.00	125.00	250.00
	1764 MF	50.00	75.00	125.00	225.00
	1765 MF	50.00	75.00	125.00	225.00
	1766/5 MF	50.00	75.00	125.00	250.00
	1766 MF	50.00	75.00	125.00	225.00
	1767/17 MF	50.00	75.00	125.00	250.00
	1767/6 MF	50.00	75.00	125.00	250.00
	1767 MF	50.00	75.00	125.00	225.00
	1768/6 MF	50.00	75.00	125.00	250.00
	1768/7 MF	50.00	75.00	125.00	250.00
	1768 MF	50.00	75.00	125.00	225.00
	1769 MF	50.00	75.00	125.00	225.00
	1770/60 MF	50.00	75.00	125.00	250.00
	1770/60 FM	50.00	75.00	125.00	250.00
	1770/69 FM	50.00	75.00	125.00	250.00
	1770 MF	50.00	75.00	125.00	225.00
	1770 FM/F	50.00	75.00	125.00	250.00
	1770 FM	50.00	75.00	125.00	225.00
	1771/0 FM	50.00	75.00	125.00	250.00
	1771 FM	50.00	75.00	125.00	225.00
	1772 FM	—	—	Rare	—

*NOTE: Tip of cross between I and S in legend.
**NOTE: Tip of cross between H and I in legend.

27.0700 g, .903 SILVER, .7859 oz ASW
MF (error) inverted

FM (normal)

Obv. leg: CAROLUS.III.DEI.GRATIA.
Rev: Inverted initials and mint mark.

KM#	Date	VG	Fine	VF	XF
106.1	1772 FM	25.00	50.00	90.00	250.00
	1772 MF	150.00	350.00	750.00	1250.
	1773 FM	25.00	50.00	80.00	175.00

Rev: Normal initials and mint mark.

KM#	Date	VG	Fine	VF	XF
106.2	1773 FM	25.00	50.00	75.00	150.00
	1774 FM	25.00	45.00	60.00	140.00
	1775 FM	25.00	45.00	60.00	140.00
	1776 FM	25.00	45.00	60.00	140.00
	1777/6 FM	35.00	55.00	90.00	300.00
	1777 FM	25.00	45.00	60.00	140.00
	1777 FF	35.00	50.00	80.00	250.00
	1778 FM	—	—	*Rare	—
	1778/7FF	25.00	45.00	60.00	140.00
	1778 FF	25.00	45.00	60.00	140.00
	1779 FF	25.00	45.00	60.00	140.00
	1780 FF	25.00	45.00	60.00	140.00
	1781 FF	25.00	45.00	60.00	140.00
	1782 FF	25.00	45.00	60.00	140.00
	1783 FF	25.00	45.00	60.00	140.00
	1783 FM	4000.	6000.	9000.	—
	1784 FF	150.00	300.00	500.00	1250.
	1784 FM	25.00	45.00	60.00	140.00
	1785 FM	25.00	45.00	60.00	140.00
	1786/5 FM	25.00	45.00	60.00	140.00
	1786 FM	25.00	45.00	60.00	140.00
	1787/6 FM	100.00	250.00	450.00	1200.
	1787 FM	25.00	45.00	60.00	140.00
	1788 FM	25.00	45.00	60.00	140.00
	1789 FM	50.00	100.00	150.00	225.00

*NOTE: Superior Casterline sale 5-89 VF realized
$17,600.

Obv: Armored bust of Charles III, leg: CAROLUS.IV. .

KM#	Date	VG	Fine	VF	XF
107	1789 FM	40.00	65.00	100.00	200.00
	1790 FM	30.00	50.00	80.00	190.00

Obv: Armored bust of Charles III.

KM#	Date	VG	Fine	VF	XF
109	1791 FM	20.00	35.00	50.00	100.00
	1792 FM	20.00	35.00	50.00	100.00
	1793 FM	20.00	35.00	50.00	100.00
	1794 FM	20.00	35.00	50.00	100.00
	1795/4 FM	20.00	35.00	50.00	100.00
	1795 FM	20.00	35.00	50.00	100.00
	1796 FM	20.00	35.00	50.00	100.00
	1797 FM	20.00	35.00	50.00	100.00
	1798 FM	20.00	35.00	50.00	100.00
	1799 FM	20.00	35.00	50.00	100.00
	1800/700 FM	20.00	35.00	50.00	100.00
	1800 FM	20.00	35.00	50.00	100.00
	1801/791 FM	35.00	60.00	100.00	250.00
	1801/0 FM	35.00	60.00	100.00	250.00
	1801/0 FT/FM	20.00	35.00	50.00	100.00
	1801 FM	20.00	40.00	100.00	250.00
	1801 FT/M	35.00	60.00	100.00	250.00
	1801 FT	20.00	35.00	50.00	100.00
	1802/1 FT	35.00	60.00	100.00	250.00
	1802 FT	20.00	35.00	50.00	100.00
	1802 FT/FM	20.00	35.00	50.00	100.00
	1803 FT	20.00	35.00	50.00	110.00
	1803 FM	600.00	900.00	—	—
	1803 FT/FM	20.00	35.00	50.00	100.00
	1803 TH	75.00	150.00	250.00	500.00
	1804/3 TH	35.00	60.00	100.00	250.00
	1804 TH	20.00	35.00	50.00	100.00
	1805/4 TH	40.00	80.00	125.00	275.00
	1805 TH	20.00	35.00	50.00	100.00
	1806 TH	20.00	35.00	50.00	100.00
	1807/6 TH	150.00	250.00	350.00	700.00
	1807 TH	20.00	35.00	50.00	100.00
	1870 TH(error 1807)	150.00	250.00	350.00	700.00
	1808/7 TH	20.00	35.00	50.00	100.00
	1808 TH	20.00	35.00	50.00	100.00

Obv: Armored bust of Charles III, leg: CAROLUS.IIII.

108	1790 FM	30.00	50.00	75.00	175.00

Obv: Armored bust of Ferdinand VII.

KM#	Date	VG	Fine	VF	XF
110	1808 TH	25.00	40.00	75.00	145.00
	1809/8 TH	25.00	40.00	75.00	145.00
	1809 HJ	25.00	40.00	75.00	145.00
	1809 HJ/TH	20.00	35.00	55.00	120.00
	1809 TH/JH	20.00	35.00	55.00	120.00
	1809 TH	20.00	35.00	55.00	120.00
	1810/09 HJ	25.00	40.00	75.00	145.00
	1810 HJ	25.00	40.00	75.00	145.00
	1810 HJ/TH	25.00	40.00	75.00	145.00
	1810 TH	75.00	150.00	300.00	600.00
	1811/0 HJ	20.00	35.00	55.00	120.00
	1811 HJ	20.00	35.00	55.00	120.00
	1811 HJ/TH	20.00	35.00	50.00	100.00

Obv: Draped bust of Ferdinand VII.

KM#	Date	VG	Fine	VF	XF
111	1811 HJ	20.00	40.00	60.00	125.00
	1812 HJ	50.00	75.00	125.00	250.00
	1812 JJ/HJ	20.00	35.00	50.00	90.00
	1812 JJ	20.00	35.00	50.00	90.00
	1813 HJ	50.00	75.00	125.00	250.00
	1813 JJ	20.00	35.00	50.00	90.00
	1814/3 HJ	1200.	2500.	5000.	—
	1814/3 JJ/HJ	20.00	35.00	50.00	90.00
	1814/3 JJ	20.00	35.00	50.00	90.00
	1814 JJ	20.00	35.00	50.00	90.00
	1814 HJ	500.00	800.00	1500.	3000.
	1815/4 JJ	20.00	35.00	50.00	90.00
	1815 JJ	20.00	35.00	50.00	90.00
	1816/5 JJ	20.00	35.00	50.00	85.00
	1816 JJ	20.00	35.00	50.00	85.00
	1817 JJ	20.00	35.00	50.00	85.00
	1818 JJ	20.00	35.00	50.00	85.00
	1819 JJ	20.00	35.00	50.00	85.00
	1820 JJ	20.00	35.00	50.00	85.00
	1821 JJ	20.00	35.00	50.00	85.00

1/2 ESCUDO

1.6900 g, .875 GOLD, .0475 oz AGW
Obv. leg: FERD.VII.D.G.HISP.ET IND.

KM#	Date	VG	Fine	VF	XF
112	1814 JJ	200.00	300.00	400.00	550.00
	1815/4 JJ	150.00	200.00	250.00	350.00
	1815 JJ	150.00	200.00	250.00	350.00
	1816 JJ	100.00	150.00	200.00	300.00
	1817 JJ	150.00	200.00	250.00	350.00
	1818 JJ	150.00	200.00	250.00	350.00
	1819 JJ	150.00	200.00	250.00	350.00
	1820 JJ	200.00	300.00	400.00	550.00

ESCUDO

3.3800 g, .917 GOLD, .0996 oz AGW
Obv. leg: PHILIP.V.D.G.HISPAN.ET IND.REX

KM#	Date	VG	Fine	VF	XF
113	1732 F	1000.	2000.	3000.	4000.
	1733/2 F	1000.	2000.	3000.	4000.
	1733 F	1000.	2000.	3000.	4000.
	1734/3 MF	150.00	250.00	400.00	950.00
	1734 MF	150.00	250.00	400.00	950.00
	1735/4 MF	150.00	250.00	400.00	950.00
	1735 MF	150.00	250.00	400.00	950.00
	1736/5 MF	150.00	250.00	400.00	950.00
	1736 MF	150.00	250.00	400.00	950.00
	1737 MF	200.00	300.00	600.00	1200.
	1738/7 MF	200.00	300.00	600.00	1200.
	1738 MF	200.00	300.00	600.00	1200.
	1739 MF	200.00	300.00	600.00	1200.
	1740 MF	200.00	300.00	600.00	1200.
	1741 MF	200.00	300.00	600.00	1200.
	1742 MF	200.00	300.00	600.00	1200.
	1743/2 MF	150.00	275.00	450.00	900.00
	1743 MF	150.00	250.00	400.00	800.00
	1744 MF	150.00	250.00	400.00	800.00
	1745 MF	150.00	250.00	400.00	800.00
	1746 MF	150.00	250.00	400.00	800.00
	1747 MF	—	—	Rare	—

Obv: Long bust; leg: FERD.VI.D.G.
HISPAN.ET IND.REX.

KM#	Date	VG	Fine	VF	XF
114	1747 MF	600.00	900.00	1500.	2250.

Obv: Short bust.

KM#	Date	VG	Fine	VF	XF
115.1	1748 MF	250.00	350.00	550.00	950.00
	1749 MF	300.00	450.00	700.00	1150.
	1750 MF	200.00	300.00	450.00	800.00
	1751 MF	200.00	300.00	450.00	800.00

Rev: W/o 1 S by arms.

KM#	Date	VG	Fine	VF	XF
115.2	1752 MF	150.00	250.00	400.00	750.00
	1753/2 MF	200.00	300.00	450.00	800.00
	1753 MF	200.00	300.00	450.00	800.00
	1754 MF	200.00	300.00	450.00	800.00
	1755 MM	200.00	300.00	450.00	800.00
	1756 MF	200.00	300.00	450.00	800.00
	1756 MM	200.00	300.00	450.00	800.00

Obv: Armored bust.

KM#	Date	VG	Fine	VF	XF
A116	1757 MM	200.00	300.00	450.00	800.00
	1758 MM	200.00	300.00	450.00	800.00
	1759 MM	200.00	300.00	450.00	800.00

Obv. leg: CAROLVS.III.D.G.HISPAN.ET IND.REX
Rev. leg: NOMINA MAGNA SEQUOR

116	1760 MM	500.00	1000.	1750.	2500.
	1761/0 MM	500.00	1000.	1750.	2500.
	1761 MM	500.00	1000.	1750.	2500.

Obv. leg: CAR.III.D.G.HISP.ET IND.R., large bust.
Rev. leg: IN.UTROQ. FELIX.

117	1762 MF	250.00	375.00	600.00	1100.
	1762 MM	250.00	375.00	600.00	1100.
	1763 MF	250.00	375.00	600.00	1100.
	1763 MM	275.00	425.00	700.00	1200.
	1764 MM	250.00	375.00	600.00	1100.
	1765 MF	250.00	375.00	600.00	1100.
	1766 MF	250.00	375.00	600.00	1100.
	1767 MF	250.00	375.00	600.00	1100.
	1768 MF	250.00	375.00	600.00	1100.
	1769 MF	250.00	375.00	600.00	1100.
	1770 MF	250.00	375.00	600.00	1100.
	1771 MF	250.00	375.00	600.00	1100.

3.3800 g, .901 GOLD, .0979 oz AGW
Obv. leg: CAROL.III.D.G. HISPAN.ET IND.R.
Rev. leg: . . .FELIX.A.D.; initials and mint mark upright.

118.1	1772 FM	125.00	175.00	285.00	550.00
	1773 FM	125.00	175.00	285.00	550.00

Rev: Initials and mint mark inverted.

118.2	1773 FM	125.00	175.00	285.00	550.00
	1774 FM	125.00	175.00	285.00	550.00
	1775 FM	125.00	175.00	285.00	550.00
	1776 FM	125.00	175.00	285.00	550.00

3.3800 g, .875 GOLD, .0950 oz AGW

118.2a	1777 FM	125.00	175.00	285.00	550.00
	1778 FF	125.00	175.00	285.00	550.00
	1779 FF	125.00	175.00	285.00	550.00
	1780 FF	125.00	175.00	285.00	550.00
	1781 FF	125.00	175.00	285.00	550.00
	1782 FF	125.00	175.00	285.00	550.00
	1783/2 FF	125.00	175.00	285.00	550.00
	1783 FF	125.00	175.00	285.00	550.00
	1784 FF	125.00	175.00	285.00	550.00
	1784 FM	125.00	175.00	285.00	550.00
	1785 FM	125.00	175.00	285.00	550.00

KM#	Date	VG	Fine	VF	XF
	1786 FM	125.00	175.00	285.00	550.00
	1787 FM	125.00	175.00	285.00	550.00
	1788 FM	125.00	175.00	285.00	550.00

Rev: Initial letters and mint mark upright.

118.1a	1787 FM	125.00	175.00	285.00	550.00
	1788 FM	125.00	175.00	285.00	550.00

Obv: Bust of Charles III, leg: CAROLUS.IV.D.G. . .

119	1789 FM	125.00	175.00	285.00	550.00
	1790 FM	125.00	175.00	285.00	550.00

3.3800 g, .875 GOLD, .0950 oz AGW
Obv: Armored bust of Charles IV.

120	1792 MF	125.00	165.00	235.00	375.00
	1793 FM	125.00	165.00	235.00	375.00
	1794 FM	125.00	165.00	235.00	375.00
	1795 FM	125.00	165.00	235.00	375.00
	1796 FM	125.00	165.00	235.00	375.00
	1797 FM	125.00	165.00	235.00	375.00
	1798 FM	125.00	165.00	235.00	375.00
	1799 FM	125.00	165.00	235.00	375.00
	1800 FM	125.00	165.00	235.00	375.00
	1801 FT	125.00	165.00	235.00	375.00
	1801 FM	125.00	165.00	235.00	375.00
	1802 FT	125.00	165.00	235.00	375.00
	1803 FT	125.00	165.00	235.00	375.00
	1804/3 TH	125.00	165.00	235.00	375.00
	1804 TH	125.00	165.00	235.00	375.00
	1805 TH	125.00	165.00	235.00	375.00
	1806 TH	125.00	165.00	235.00	375.00
	1807 TH	125.00	165.00	235.00	375.00
	1808 TH	125.00	165.00	235.00	375.00

Obv: Armored bust of Ferdinand VII.

121	1809 HJ	125.00	165.00	235.00	400.00
	1810 HJ	125.00	165.00	235.00	400.00
	1811 HJ	125.00	165.00	235.00	400.00
	1812 HJ	150.00	250.00	300.00	500.00

Obv: Undraped bust of Ferdinand VII.

KM#	Date	VG	Fine	VF	XF
122	1814 HJ	100.00	145.00	225.00	400.00
	1815 JJ	100.00	145.00	225.00	400.00
	1815 HJ	100.00	145.00	225.00	400.00
	1816 JJ	125.00	165.00	275.00	500.00
	1817 JJ	100.00	145.00	225.00	400.00
	1818 JJ	100.00	145.00	225.00	400.00
	1819 JJ	100.00	145.00	225.00	400.00
	1820 JJ	100.00	145.00	225.00	400.00

2 ESCUDOS

6.7700 g, .917 GOLD, .1996 oz AGW
Obv. leg: PHILIP.V.D.G.HISPAN.ET IND.REX.
Rev. leg: INITIUM SAPIENTIAE TIMOR DOMINI.

KM#	Date	VG	Fine	VF	XF
124	1732 F	1000.	1500.	2000.	3000.
	1733 F	750.00	1000.	1500.	2500.
	1734 MF	400.00	500.00	700.00	1300.
	1735 MF	400.00	500.00	700.00	1300.
	1736/5 MF	400.00	500.00	700.00	1300.
	1736 MF	400.00	500.00	700.00	1300.
	1737 MF	400.00	500.00	700.00	1300.
	1738/7 MF	400.00	500.00	700.00	1300.
	1738 MF	400.00	500.00	700.00	1300.
	1739 MF	400.00	500.00	700.00	1300.
	1740 MF	400.00	500.00	700.00	1300.
	1741 MF	400.00	500.00	700.00	1300.
	1742 MF	400.00	500.00	700.00	1300.
	1743 MF	400.00	500.00	700.00	1300.
	1744/3 MF	350.00	450.00	600.00	1200.
	1744 MF	400.00	500.00	700.00	1300.
	1745 MF	400.00	500.00	700.00	1300.
	1746 MF	400.00	500.00	700.00	1300.
	1747 MF	400.00	500.00	700.00	1300.

Obv: Large bust; leg: FERD.VI.D.G. . .
Rev. leg: INITIUM. .

KM#	Date	VG	Fine	VF	XF
125	1747 MF	1500.	2000.	3000.	4500.

Obv. leg: FERD.VI.D.G. . ., small young bust.
Rev. leg: NOMINA MAGNA SEQUOR.

KM#	Date	VG	Fine	VF	XF
126.1	1748 MF	450.00	550.00	700.00	1250.
	1749/8 MF	450.00	550.00	700.00	1250.
	1749 MF	600.00	800.00	1000.	1800.
	1750 MF	400.00	500.00	600.00	1100.
	1751 MF	400.00	500.00	600.00	1100.

Rev: W/o 2 S by arms.

KM#	Date	VG	Fine	VF	XF
126.2	1752 MF	400.00	500.00	600.00	1100.
	1753 MF	400.00	500.00	600.00	1100.
	1754 MF	600.00	800.00	1000.	1800.
	1755 MM	400.00	500.00	600.00	1100.
	1756 MM	600.00	800.00	1000.	1800.
	1756 MF	450.00	550.00	700.00	1250.

Obv: Armored bust; leg: FERDND.VI.D.G. .

KM#	Date	VG	Fine	VF	XF
127	1757 MM	500.00	800.00	1300.	2200.
	1758 MM	500.00	800.00	1300.	2200.
	1759 MM	500.00	800.00	1300.	2200.

Obv. leg: CAROLVS.III.D.G. . ., young bust.

KM#	Date	VG	Fine	VF	XF
128	1760 MM	550.00	900.00	1500.	2500.
	1761 MM	550.00	900.00	1500.	2500.

Obv. leg: CAROLUS.III.D.G. . ., large young bust.
Rev. leg: IN.UTROQ.FELIX.AUSPICE.DEO

KM#	Date	VG	Fine	VF	XF
129	1762 MF	500.00	600.00	800.00	1500.
	1763 MF	500.00	600.00	800.00	1500.
	1764 MF	500.00	600.00	800.00	1500.
	1764 MM	500.00	600.00	800.00	1500.
	1765 MF	500.00	600.00	800.00	1500.
	1766 MF	500.00	600.00	800.00	1500.
	1767 MF	500.00	600.00	800.00	1500.
	1768 MF	500.00	600.00	800.00	1500.
	1769 MF	500.00	600.00	800.00	1500.
	1770 MF	500.00	600.00	1000.	1800.
	1771 MF	500.00	600.00	800.00	1500.

6.7700 g, .901 GOLD, .1961 oz AGW
Obv. leg: CAROLUS.III.D.G. . ., older bust.
Rev: Initials and mint mark upright.

KM#	Date	VG	Fine	VF	XF
130.1	1772 FM	300.00	450.00	600.00	1000.
	1773 FM	300.00	450.00	600.00	1000.

Rev: Initials and mint mark inverted.

KM#	Date	VG	Fine	VF	XF
130.2	1773 FM	300.00	450.00	600.00	1000.
	1774 FM	300.00	450.00	600.00	1000.
	1775 FM	300.00	450.00	600.00	1000.
	1776 FM	300.00	450.00	600.00	1000.

6.7700 g, .875 GOLD, .1904 oz AGW

KM#	Date	VG	Fine	VF	XF
130.2a	1777 FM	300.00	400.00	500.00	800.00
	1778 FF	300.00	400.00	500.00	800.00
	1779 FF	300.00	400.00	500.00	800.00
	1780 FF	300.00	400.00	500.00	800.00
	1781 FF/FM	300.00	400.00	500.00	800.00
	1781 FF	300.00	400.00	500.00	800.00
	1782 FF	300.00	400.00	500.00	800.00
	1783 FF	300.00	400.00	500.00	800.00
	1784 FF	300.00	400.00	500.00	800.00
	1784 FM	500.00	750.00	1000.	1500.
	1785 FM	300.00	400.00	500.00	800.00
	1786 FM	300.00	400.00	500.00	800.00
	1787 FM	300.00	400.00	500.00	800.00
	1788 FM	300.00	400.00	500.00	800.00

Rev: Initial letters and mint mark upright.

KM#	Date	VG	Fine	VF	XF
130.1a	1788 FM	300.00	400.00	500.00	800.00

Obv: Bust of Charles III, leg: CAROL.IV.D.G. . .

KM#	Date	VG	Fine	VF	XF
131	1789 FM	300.00	400.00	650.00	1000.
	1790 FM	300.00	400.00	650.00	1000.

6.7700 g, .875 GOLD, .1904 oz AGW
Obv: Armored bust of Charles IV.

KM#	Date	VG	Fine	VF	XF
132	1791 FM	300.00	400.00	650.00	1000.
	1792 FM	125.00	250.00	375.00	600.00
	1793 FM	125.00	250.00	375.00	600.00
	1794 FM	125.00	250.00	375.00	600.00
	1795 FM	125.00	250.00	375.00	600.00
	1796 FM	125.00	250.00	375.00	600.00
	1797 FM	125.00	250.00	425.00	750.00
	1798 FM	125.00	250.00	375.00	600.00
	1799 FM	125.00	250.00	375.00	600.00
	1800 FM	125.00	250.00	375.00	600.00
	1801 FM	125.00	250.00	375.00	600.00
	1802 FT	125.00	250.00	375.00	600.00
	1803 FT	125.00	250.00	375.00	600.00
	1804 TH	125.00	250.00	375.00	600.00
	1805 TH	125.00	250.00	375.00	600.00
	1806 TH	125.00	250.00	375.00	600.00
	1807 TH	125.00	250.00	375.00	600.00
	1808 TH	125.00	250.00	375.00	600.00

Obv: Undraped bust of Ferdinand VII.

KM#	Date	VG	Fine	VF	XF
134	1814 HJ	250.00	400.00	650.00	1200.
	1814 JJ	250.00	400.00	650.00	1200.
	1815 JJ	250.00	400.00	650.00	1200.
	1816 JJ	250.00	400.00	650.00	1200.
	1817 JJ	250.00	400.00	650.00	1200.
	1818 JJ	250.00	400.00	650.00	1200.
	1819 JJ	250.00	400.00	650.00	1200.
	1820 JJ	250.00	400.00	650.00	1200.

4 ESCUDOS

13.5400 g, .917 GOLD, .3992 oz AGW
Obv: leg: PHILIP.V.D.G.HISPAN.ET IND.REX.
Rev: leg: INITIUM SAPIENTIAE TIMOR DOMINI.

KM#	Date	VG	Fine	VF	XF
135	1732	—	—	Rare	—
	1732 F	—	—	Rare	—
	1733 F	—	—	Rare	—
	1734/3 F	1000.	1500.	2000.	3500.
	1734 MF	800.00	1200.	1750.	3000.
	1735 MF	800.00	1200.	1750.	3000.

KM#	Date	VG	Fine	VF	XF
135	1736 MF	800.00	1200.	1750.	3000.
	1737 MF	600.00	1000.	1500.	2750.
	1738/7 MF	600.00	1000.	1500.	2750.
	1738 MF	600.00	1000.	1500.	2750.
	1739 MF	600.00	1000.	1500.	2750.
	1740/30 MF	600.00	1000.	1500.	2750.
	1740 MF	600.00	1000.	1500.	2750.
	1741 MF	600.00	1000.	1500.	2750.
	1742 MF	600.00	1000.	1500.	2750.
	1743 MF	600.00	1000.	1500.	2750.
	1744 MD	600.00	1000.	1500.	2750.
	1745 MF	600.00	1000.	1500.	2750.
	1746 MF	600.00	1000.	1500.	2750.
	1747 MF	600.00	1000.	1500.	2750.

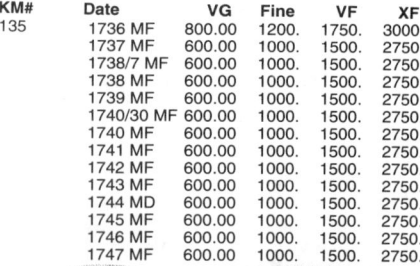

Obv: Large bust; leg: FERDND.VI.D.G. . .

KM#	Date	VG	Fine	VF	XF
136	1747 MF	—	—	Rare	—

Obv: leg: FERDND.VI.D.G. . ., small bust.
Rev: leg: NOMINA MAGNA. . ., 4S divided by arms.

KM#	Date	VG	Fine	VF	XF
137	1748 MF	1500.	3000.	5000.	7000.
	1749 MF	1500.	3000.	5000.	7000.
	1750 MF	1500.	3000.	5000.	7000.
	1751 MF	1500.	3000.	5000.	7000.

Rev: W/o value.

KM#	Date	VG	Fine	VF	XF
138	1752 MF	800.00	1500.	2750.	4000.
	1753 MF	800.00	1500.	2750.	4000.
	1754 MF	800.00	1500.	2750.	4000.
	1755 MM	800.00	1500.	2750.	4000.
	1756 MM	800.00	1500.	2750.	4000.

Obv: Large full bust; leg: FERDND.VI.D.G. .

KM#	Date	VG	Fine	VF	XF
139	1757 MM	1250.	2500.	4500.	6500.
	1758 MM	1250.	2500.	4500.	6500.
	1759 MM	1250.	2500.	4500.	6500.

Obv: Young bust, leg: CAROLVS.III.D.G. . .
Rev. leg: NOMINA MAGNA SEQUOR

140	1760 MM	2500.	5000.	7000.	10,000.
	1761 MM	2500.	5000.	7000.	10,000.

Obv: Large young bust, leg: CAROLUS.III.D.G. . .
Rev. leg: IN.UTROQ.FELIX.AUSPICE.DEO.

141	1762 MF	800.00	1200.	1800.	3000.
	1763 MF	800.00	1200.	1800.	3000.
	1764 MF	—	—	Rare	—
	1765 MF	800.00	1200.	1800.	3000.
	1766 MF	800.00	1200.	1800.	3000.
	1767 MF	800.00	1200.	1800.	3000.
	1768 MF	800.00	1200.	1800.	3000.
	1769 MF	800.00	1200.	1800.	3000.
	1770 MF	800.00	1200.	1800.	3000.
	1771 MF	800.00	1200.	1800.	3000.

13.5400 g, .901 GOLD, .3922 oz AGW
Obv. leg: CAROL.III.D.G. . .
Rev: FM and mint mark upright.

142.1	1772 FM	400.00	650.00	1000.	1850.
	1773 FM	400.00	650.00	1000.	1850.

Rev: Initials and mint mark inverted.

142.2	1773 FM	400.00	600.00	900.00	1600.
	1774 FM	400.00	600.00	900.00	1600.
	1775 FM	400.00	600.00	900.00	1600.
	1776 FM	400.00	600.00	900.00	1600.

13.5400 g, .875 GOLD, .3809 oz AGW

142.2a	1777 FM	400.00	600.00	900.00	1600.
	1778 FF	400.00	600.00	900.00	1600.
	1779 FF	400.00	600.00	900.00	1600.
	1780 FF	400.00	600.00	900.00	1600.
	1781 FF	400.00	600.00	900.00	1600.
	1782 FF	400.00	600.00	900.00	1600.
	1783 FF	400.00	600.00	900.00	1600.
	1784 FF	400.00	600.00	900.00	1600.
	1784 FM	400.00	600.00	900.00	1600.
	1785 FM	400.00	600.00	900.00	1600.

KM#	Date	VG	Fine	VF	XF
	1786 FM	400.00	600.00	900.00	1600.
	1787 FM	400.00	600.00	900.00	1600.
	1788 FM	400.00	600.00	900.00	1600.
	1789 FM	400.00	600.00	900.00	1600.

Rev: Initials and mint mark upright.

142.1a	1788 FM	400.00	650.00	1000.	1850.

Obv. leg: CAROL.IV.D.G. . ., bust of Charles III.

143.1	1789 FM	500.00	700.00	1000.	1750.
	1790 FM	500.00	700.00	1000.	1750.

Obv. leg: CAROL. IIII D.G. . ., bust of Charles III.

143.2	1790 FM	600.00	1000.	1800.	3000.

13.5400 g. .875 GOLD, .3809 oz AGW
Obv: Armored bust of Charles IIII.

144	1792 FM	300.00	500.00	750.00	1400.
	1793 FM	300.00	500.00	750.00	1400.
	1794/3 FM	300.00	500.00	750.00	1400.
	1794 FM	300.00	500.00	750.00	1400.
	1795 FM	300.00	500.00	750.00	1400.
	1796 FM	300.00	500.00	750.00	1400.
	1797 FM	300.00	500.00	750.00	1400.
	1798/7 FM	300.00	500.00	750.00	1400.
	1798 FM	300.00	500.00	750.00	1400.
	1799 FM	300.00	500.00	750.00	1400.
	1800 FM	300.00	500.00	750.00	1400.
	1801 FM	300.00	500.00	750.00	1400.
	1801 FT	300.00	500.00	750.00	1400.
	1802 FT	300.00	500.00	750.00	1400.
	1803 FT	300.00	500.00	750.00	1400.
	1804/3 TH	300.00	500.00	750.00	1400.
	1804 TH	300.00	500.00	750.00	1400.
	1805 TH	300.00	500.00	750.00	1400.
	1806/5 TH	300.00	500.00	750.00	1400.
	1806 TH	300.00	500.00	750.00	1400.
	1807 TH	300.00	500.00	750.00	1400.
	1808/0 TH	300.00	500.00	750.00	1400.
	1808 TH	300.00	500.00	750.00	1400.

Obv: Armored bust of Ferdinand VII.

KM#	Date	VG	Fine	VF	XF
145	1810 HJ	450.00	600.00	950.00	1600.
	1811 HJ	350.00	500.00	850.00	1400.
	1812 HJ	350.00	500.00	850.00	1400.

Obv: Undraped bust of Ferdinand VII.

KM#	Date	VG	Fine	VF	XF
146	1814 HJ	400.00	650.00	900.00	1600.
	1815 HJ	400.00	650.00	900.00	1600.
	1815 JJ	400.00	650.00	900.00	1600.
	1816 JJ	400.00	650.00	900.00	1600.
	1817 JJ	400.00	650.00	900.00	1600.
	1818 JJ	400.00	650.00	900.00	1600.
	1819 JJ	400.00	650.00	900.00	1600.
	1820 JJ	400.00	650.00	900.00	1600.

8 ESCUDOS

27.0700 g, .917 GOLD, .7981 oz AGW
Obv. leg: PHILIP.V.D.G.HISPAN.ET IND.REX.
Rev. leg: INITIUM SAPIENTIAE TIMOR DOMINI.

148	1732	—	—	Rare	—
	1732 F	—	—	Rare	—
	1733 F	—	—	Rare	—
	1734 MF	1000.	1600.	2600.	3750.
	1735 MF	1000.	1500.	2250.	3250.
	1736 MF	1000.	1500.	2250.	3250.
	1737 MF	1000.	1500.	2250.	3250.
	1738/7 MF	1000.	1500.	2250.	3250.
	1738 MF	1000.	1500.	2250.	3250.
	1739 MF	1000.	1500.	2250.	3250.
	1740 MF	1000.	1500.	2250.	3250.
	1741 MF	1000.	1500.	2250.	3250.
	1742 MF	1000.	1500.	2250.	3250.
	1743 MF	1000.	1500.	2250.	3250.
	1744 MF	1000.	1500.	2250.	3250.
	1745 MF	1000.	1500.	2250.	3250.
	1746 MF	1000.	1500.	2250.	3250.
	1747 MF	2000.	3000.	2250.	3250.

Obv: Young bust; leg: FERDND.VI.D.G. .

KM#	Date	VG	Fine	VF	XF
149	1747 MF	3000.	4000.	6500.	12,500.

Obv. leg: FERDND.VI.D.G. . ., small bust.
Rev. leg: NOMINA MAGNA SEQUOR

150	1748 MF	1000.	1500.	2500.	4000.
	1749/8 MF	1000.	1500.	2500.	4000.
	1749 MF	1000.	1500.	2500.	4000.
	1750 MF	1000.	1500.	2500.	4000.
	1751 MF	1000.	1500.	2500.	4000.

Obv. leg: FERDND.VI.D.G. . ., large bust.
Rev: W/o 8 S divided by arms.

KM#	Date	VG	Fine	VF	XF
151	1752 MF	1000.	1500.	2500.	4000.
	1753 MF	1000.	1500.	2500.	4000.
	1754 MF	1000.	1500.	2500.	4000.
	1755 MM	1000.	1500.	2500.	4000.
	1756 MM	1000.	1500.	2500.	4000.

Obv. leg: FERDND.VI.D.G. . ., medium, full bust.

152	1757 MM	1200.	2000.	3000.	4000.
	1758 MM	1200.	2000.	3000.	4000.
	1759 MM	1200.	2000.	3000.	4000.

27.0700 g, .901 GOLD, .7841 oz AGW
Obv: Mature bust, leg: CAROL.III.D.G. . . . .
Rev. leg: . . . . . AUSPICE.DEO.; FM and
mint mark upright.

KM#	Date	VG	Fine	VF	XF
156.1	1772 FM	500.00	750.00	1250.	2000.
	1773 FM	550.00	850.00	1350.	2250.

Rev: Initials and mint mark inverted.

KM#	Date	VG	Fine	VF	XF
156.2	1773 FM	500.00	700.00	1100.	1650.
	1774 FM	500.00	700.00	1100.	1650.
	1775 FM	500.00	700.00	1100.	1650.
	1776 FM	500.00	700.00	1100.	1650.

Obv: Young bust, leg: CAROLVS.III.D.G. .
w/Order of the Golden Fleece at date.

KM#	Date	VG	Fine	VF	XF
153	1760 MM	1500.	2500.	4250.	7000.
	1761 MM	1750.	3000.	5000.	8000.

27.0700 g, .875 GOLD, .7616 oz AGW

KM#	Date	VG	Fine	VF	XF
156.2a	1777/6 FM	500.00	700.00	1100.	1650.
	1777 FM	500.00	700.00	1100.	1650.
	1778 FF	500.00	700.00	1100.	1650.
	1779 FF	500.00	700.00	1100.	1650.
	1780 FF	500.00	700.00	1100.	1650.
	1781 FF	500.00	700.00	1100.	1650.
	1782 FF	500.00	700.00	1100.	1650.
	1783 FF	500.00	700.00	1100.	1650.
	1784 FF	500.00	700.00	1100.	1650.
	1784 FM	500.00	700.00	1100.	1650.
	1785 FM	500.00	700.00	1100.	1650.
	1786 FM	500.00	700.00	1100.	1650.
	1787 FM	500.00	700.00	1100.	1650.
	1788 FM	500.00	700.00	1100.	1650.

Obv: Young bust, leg: CAROLVS.III.D.G. . .
w/Order of the Golden Fleece on chest.

KM#	Date	VG	Fine	VF	XF
154	1761 MM	1500.	2750.	4500.	7500.

Rev: Initials and mint mark upright.

KM#	Date	VG	Fine	VF	XF
156.1a	1788 FM	600.00	900.00	1500.	2500.

Obv. leg: CAROLUS.III.D.G. . ., large bust.
Rev. leg: IN.UTROQ.FELIX.AUSPICE.

KM#	Date	VG	Fine	VF	XF
155	1762 MF	1000.	1500.	2750.	5000.
	1762 MM	1000.	1500.	2750.	5000.
	1763 MF	1000.	1500.	2750.	5000.
	1763 MM	1000.	1500.	2750.	5000.
	1764 MF	1500.	3000.	4000.	6000.
	1764 MM	1500.	3000.	4000.	6000.
	1765/4 MF	1500.	3000.	4000.	6000.
	1765 MF	1500.	3000.	4000.	6000.
	1765 MM	1000.	1500.	2500.	4000.
	1766 MF	1000.	1500.	2500.	4000.
	1767 MF	1000.	1500.	2500.	4000.
	1768 MF	1000.	1500.	2500.	4000.
	1769 MF	1000.	1500.	2500.	4000.
	1770 MF	1000.	1500.	2500.	4000.
	1771 MF	1500.	3000.	4000.	6000.

Obv: Bust of Charles III, leg: CAROL.IV.D.G. . .
Rev: IN UTROQ. . . A.D., arms, order chain.

	Date	VG	Fine	VF	XF
157	1789 FM	500.00	750.00	1500.	3000.
	1790 FM	500.00	750.00	1500.	3000.

Obv: Bust of Charles III, leg: CAROL.IIII.D.G. .

KM#	Date	VG	Fine	VF	XF
158	1790 FM	500.00	750.00	1500.	3000.

27.0700 g, .875 GOLD, .7616 oz AGW
Obv: Armored bust of Charles IIII.
Rev. leg: IN UTROQ. FELIX., arms, Order chain.

159	1791 FM	375.00	475.00	650.00	900.00
	1792 FM	375.00	475.00	650.00	900.00
	1793 FM	375.00	475.00	650.00	900.00
	1794 FM	375.00	475.00	650.00	900.00
	1795 FM	375.00	475.00	650.00	900.00
	1796/5 FM	400.00	500.00	700.00	1000.
	1796 FM	375.00	475.00	650.00	900.00
	1797 FM	375.00	475.00	650.00	900.00
	1798 FM	375.00	475.00	650.00	900.00
	1799 FM	375.00	475.00	650.00	900.00
	1800 FM	375.00	475.00	650.00	900.00
	1801/0 FT	400.00	500.00	700.00	1150.
	1801 FM	375.00	475.00	650.00	900.00
	1801 FT	375.00	475.00	650.00	900.00
	1802 FT	375.00	475.00	650.00	900.00
	1803 FT	375.00	475.00	650.00	900.00
	1804/3 TH	400.00	500.00	700.00	1150.
	1804 TH	375.00	475.00	650.00	900.00
	1805 TH	375.00	475.00	650.00	900.00
	1806 TH	375.00	475.00	650.00	900.00
	1807/6 TH	400.00	500.00	700.00	1150.
	1807 TH	375.00	475.00	675.00	1000.
	1808 TH	450.00	600.00	800.00	1250.

Obv: Armored bust of Ferdinand VII.

KM#	Date	VG	Fine	VF	XF
160	1808 TH	400.00	500.00	750.00	1000.
	1809 HJ	400.00	500.00	750.00	1150.
	1810 HJ	375.00	475.00	650.00	900.00
	1811/0 HJ	400.00	500.00	750.00	1150.
	1811 HJ	400.00	500.00	750.00	1150.
	1811 JJ	375.00	475.00	650.00	900.00
	1812 JJ	375.00	475.00	650.00	900.00

Obv: Undraped bust of Ferdinand VII.

161	1814 JJ	375.00	475.00	650.00	900.00
	1815/4 JJ	400.00	500.00	700.00	1000.
	1815/4 HJ	400.00	500.00	700.00	1000.
	1815 JJ	375.00	475.00	650.00	900.00
	1815 HJ	375.00	475.00	650.00	900.00
161	1816/5 JJ	400.00	500.00	700.00	1000.
	1816 JJ	375.00	475.00	650.00	900.00
	1817 JJ	400.00	500.00	700.00	1000.
	1818/7 JJ	375.00	475.00	650.00	900.00
	1818 JJ	375.00	475.00	650.00	900.00
	1819 JJ	375.00	475.00	650.00	900.00
	1820 JJ	375.00	475.00	650.00	900.00
	1821 JJ	400.00	500.00	700.00	1000.

PROCLAMATION MEDALLIC ISSUES (Q)

The 'Q' used in the following listings refer to *Standard Catalog of Mexican Coins, Paper Money, Stocks, Bonds and Medals*, Krause Publications, Inc., copyright 1981.

Chiapa
REAL

SILVER
Obv. leg: FERNANDO VII REY DE ESPANA Y DE SUS INDIAS, crowned arms between pillars, IR below. INDIAS. Rev: Legend in 5 lines within wreath, PROCLA/MADO/ENCIUD/R.DECHIAPPA/1808.

KM#	Date	Fine	VF	XF	Unc
Q8	1808	22.50	35.00	50.00	—

2 REALES

SILVER
Obv. leg: FERNANDO VII REY DE ESPANA Y DE SUS INDIAS.

Q10	1808	50.00	70.00	100.00	—

Mexico City
1/2 REAL

SILVER, 1.60 g
Obv. leg: A CARLOS IV REY DE ESPANA
Y DE LAS YNDIAS. Rev. leg:
PROCLAMADO EN MEXICO ANO DE 1789.

KM#	Date	Fine	VF	XF	Unc
Q22	1789	20.00	28.50	40.00	—

BRONZE, 18mm

| Q22a | 1789 | 22.50 | 35.00 | 50.00 | — |

SILVER, 17mm
Obv: Crowned arms in double-lined circle.

| Q23 | 1789 | 20.00 | 28.50 | 40.00 | — |

BRONZE

| Q23a | 1789 | 22.50 | 35.00 | 50.00 | — |

REAL

SILVER

| Q24 | 1789 | 20.00 | 28.50 | 40.00 | — |

BRONZE, 21mm
SILVER
Obv: Crowned arms in double-lined circle.

KM#	Date	Fine	VF	XF	Unc
Q-A24	1789	20.00	28.50	40.00	—

COPPER

| Q-A24a | 1789 | 22.50 | 35.00 | 50.00 | — |

2 REALES

SILVER, 6.70 g

| Q25 | 1789 | 35.00 | 50.00 | 75.00 | — |

BRONZE

| Q25a | 1789 | 30.00 | 45.00 | 60.00 | — |

4 REALES

SILVER, 13.60 g

| Q27 | 1789 | 100.00 | 150.00 | 225.00 | — |

BRONZE

KM#	Date	Fine	VF	XF	Unc
Q27a	1789	70.00	100.00	150.00	—

8 REALES

SILVER, 27.00 g

Q28	1789	200.00	275.00	400.00	—

BRONZE

| Q28a | 1789 | 70.00 | 100.00 | 150.00 | — |

Queretaro
2 REALES

SILVER
Obv. leg: FERNANDO VII REY DE ESPANA.

KM#	Date	Fine	VF	XF	Unc
Q64	1808	35.00	50.00	75.00	—

4 REALES

SILVER

Q-A66	1808	140.00	200.00	300.00	—

8 REALES

8 REALES

CAST SILVER
Obv: Imaginary bust of Ferdinand VII;
leg: FERDIN.VII.DEI.GRATIA.
c/m: 'T' at left and pomegranate
pillars at right.

KM#	Date	Good	VG	Fine	VF
123	1810 RP	—	—	Rare	—
	1811 RP	45.00	60.00	100.00	150.00
	1812 RP	30.00	40.00	60.00	90.00
	1813/2 RP	32.50	45.00	70.00	100.00
	1813 RP	30.00	40.00	60.00	90.00

SILVER

KM#	Date	Fine	VF	XF	Unc
Q68	1808	300.00	425.00	600.00	—

WAR OF INDEPENDENCE

ROYALIST ISSUES
(1810-1821)

Provisional Mints
RULER
Ferdinand VII, 1808-1821

MINT MARKS

CA - Chihuahua
D - Durango
GA - Guadalajara
GO - Guanajuato
ZS - Zacatecas

MONETARY SYSTEM
16 Reales = 1 Escudo

CHIHUAHUA

The Chihuahua Mint was established by a decree of October 8, 1810 as a temporary mint. Their first coins were cast 8 reales using Mexico City coins as patterns and obliterating/changing the mint mark and moneyer initials. Two c/m were placed on the obverse - on the left, a T designating its having been received by the Royal Treasurer and on the right crowned pillars of Hercules with pomegranate beneath; the symbol of the comptroller.

In 1814 standard dies were available and from 1814 to 1822 standard 8 reales were struck. Only the one denomination was made at this mint.

MINT MARK: CA

27.0700 g, .903 SILVER, .7860 oz ASW
Obv: Draped bust of Ferdinand VII.
Rev: Similar to KM#123.

KM#	Date	VG	Fine	VF	XF
111.1	1813 RP	—	Reported, not confirmed		
	1814 RP	—	Reported, not confirmed		
	1815 RP	200.00	275.00	350.00	500.00
	1816 RP	80.00	125.00	150.00	275.00
	1817 RP	100.00	150.00	185.00	275.00
	1818 RP	100.00	150.00	185.00	275.00
	1819 RP	125.00	175.00	250.00	350.00
	1820 RP	200.00	275.00	350.00	500.00
	1821 RP	200.00	275.00	350.00	500.00
	1822 RP	400.00	600.00	800.00	1100.

NOTE: KM#111.1 is normally found counterstamped over earlier cast 8 Reales, KM#123.

DURANGO

The Durango mint was authorized as a temporary mint at the same time as the Chihuahua Mint, October 8, 1810. The mint opened sometime in 1811 and made coins of 6 denominations - 5 silver and 1 copper - during the period 1811 to 1822.

MINT MARK: D

1/8 REAL

COPPER
Obv: Crown above double F7 monogram.
Rev: EN DURANGO, value, date.

KM#	Date	VG	Fine	VF	XF
60	1812	35.00	75.00	125.00	225.00
	1813	—	—	Rare	—
	1814	—	—	Rare	—

Rev: Spray added above date.

61	1814	13.50	22.50	45.00	80.00
	1815	15.00	27.50	50.00	85.00
	1816	15.00	27.50	50.00	85.00
	1817	13.50	22.50	45.00	80.00
	1818	13.50	22.50	45.00	80.00
	1818 OCTAVO DD REAL (error)				
		40.00	75.00	—	—

1/2 REAL

1.6900 g, .903 SILVER, .0491 oz ASW
Obv: Draped bust of Ferdinand VII.

74.1	1813 RM	250.00	450.00	750.00	1800.
	1814 MZ	250.00	450.00	750.00	1850.
	1816 MZ	250.00	450.00	750.00	1850.

REAL

3.3800 g, .903 SILVER, .0981 oz ASW
Obv: Draped bust of Ferdinand VII.

83.1	1813 RM	250.00	450.00	650.00	1650.
	1814 MZ	250.00	450.00	650.00	1650.
	1815 MZ	250.00	450.00	650.00	1650.

2 REALES

6.7700 g, .903 SILVER, .1966 oz ASW
Obv: Armored bust of Ferdinand VII.

92.2	1811 RM	250.00	400.00	650.00	1650.
	1812 RM	—	—	Rare	—

Obv: Draped bust of Ferdinand VII.

93.1	1812 MZ	250.00	400.00	650.00	1650.
	1812 RM	—	—	Rare	—
	1813 MZ	300.00	600.00	1000.	2750.
	1813 RM	300.00	600.00	1000.	2750.
	1814 MZ	300.00	600.00	1000.	2750.
	1815 MZ	300.00	600.00	1000.	2750.
	1816 MZ	300.00	600.00	1000.	2750.
	1817 MZ	300.00	600.00	1000.	2750.

4 REALES

13.5400 g, .903 SILVER, .3931 oz ASW
Obv: Draped bust of Ferdinand VII.

KM#	Date	VG	Fine	VF	XF
102.1	1814 MZ	550.00	1000.	1650.	4500.
	1816 MZ	450.00	900.00	1400.	4000.
	1817 MZ	450.00	900.00	1400.	4000.

8 REALES

27.0700 g, .903 SILVER, .7860 oz ASW
Obv: Armored bust of Ferdinand VII.

110.1	1811 RM	600.00	1000.	1750.	5000.
	1812 RM	350.00	650.00	1000.	3500.
	1813 MZ	350.00	650.00	1000.	3500.
	1814 MZ	350.00	650.00	1000.	3500.

Obv: Draped bust of Ferdinand VII.

KM#	Date	VG	Fine	VF	XF
111.2	1812 MZ	350.00	500.00	800.00	1750.
	1812 RM	125.00	175.00	275.00	800.00
	1813 RM	150.00	200.00	325.00	850.00
	1813 MZ	125.00	175.00	275.00	750.00
	1814 MZ	150.00	225.00	275.00	750.00
	1815 MZ	75.00	125.00	225.00	600.00
	1816 MZ	50.00	75.00	125.00	325.00
	1817 MZ	30.00	50.00	90.00	250.00
	1818 MZ	50.00	75.00	125.00	350.00
	1818 RM	50.00	75.00	125.00	325.00
	1818 CG/RM				
		100.00	125.00	150.00	350.00
	1818 CG	50.00	75.00	125.00	325.00
	1819 CG/RM	50.00	100.00	150.00	300.00
	1819 CG	30.00	60.00	100.00	250.00
	1820 CG	30.00	60.00	100.00	250.00
	1821 CG	30.00	40.00	80.00	225.00
	1822 CG	30.00	50.00	90.00	240.00

NOTE: Occasionally these are found struck over Guadalajara 8 reales and are very rare in general, specimens dated prior to 1816 are rather weakly struck.

GUADALAJARA

The Guadalajara Mint made its first coins in 1812 and the mint operated until April 30, 1815. It was to reopen in 1818 and continue operations until 1822. It was the only Royalist mint to strike gold coins, both 4 and 8 escudos. In addition to these it struck the standard 5 denominations in silver.

MINT MARK: GA

1/2 REAL

1.6900 g, .903 SILVER, .0491 oz ASW
Obv: Draped bust of Ferdinand VII.

KM#	Date	VG	Fine	VF	XF
74.2	1812 MR	—	—	Rare	—
	1814 MR	40.00	100.00	200.00	300.00
	1815 MR	200.00	350.00	500.00	1000.

REAL

3.3800 g, .903 SILVER, .0981 oz ASW

KM#	Date	VG	Fine	VF	XF
83.2	1814 MR	125.00	175.00	325.00	600.00
	1815 MR	300.00	500.00	—	—

2 REALES

6.7700 g, .903 SILVER, .1966 oz ASW
Obv: Draped bust of Ferdinand VII.

	Date	VG	Fine	VF	XF
93.2	1812 MR	300.00	500.00	800.00	2500.
	1814 MR	75.00	125.00	250.00	600.00
	1815/4 MR	425.00	725.00	1100.	3600.
	1815 MR	400.00	700.00	1000.	3500.
	1821 FS	200.00	250.00	350.00	900.00

4 REALES

13.5400 g, .903 SILVER, .3931 oz ASW
Obv: Draped bust of Ferdinand VII.

KM#	Date	VG	Fine	VF	XF
102.2	1814 MR	40.00	65.00	150.00	250.00
	1815 MR	80.00	150.00	300.00	500.00

Obv: Large bust.

102.3	1814 MR	50.00	100.00	200.00	400.00

Obv: Large bust w/berries in laurel.

KM#	Date	VG	Fine	VF	XF
102.4	1814 MR	—	—	Rare	—

8 REALES

27.0700 g, .903 SILVER, .7860 oz ASW
Obv: Draped bust of Ferdinand VII.

	Date	VG	Fine	VF	XF
111.3	1812 MR	2000.	3500.	5000.	7000.
	1813/2 MR	60.00	100.00	150.00	400.00
	1813 MR	60.00	100.00	150.00	400.00
	1814 MR	20.00	35.00	60.00	180.00
	1815 MR	150.00	200.00	350.00	750.00
	1818 FS	30.00	50.00	75.00	200.00
	1821/18 FS	30.00	50.00	75.00	200.00
	1821 FS	25.00	35.00	60.00	165.00
	1822/1 FS	30.00	50.00	75.00	200.00
	1822 FS	30.00	50.00	75.00	200.00

NOTE: Die varieties exist. Early dates are also encountered struck over other types.

4 ESCUDOS

13.5400 g, .875 GOLD, .3809 oz ASW
Obv: Uniformed bust of Ferdinand VII.

147	1812 MR	—	—	Rare	—

8 ESCUDOS

27.0700 g, .875 GOLD, .7616 oz AGW
Obv: Large uniformed bust of Ferdinand VII.

KM#	Date	VG	Fine	VF	XF
162	1812 MR	— Reported, not confirmed			
	1813 MR	5000.	8000.	12,000.	20,000.

Obv: Small uniformed bust of Ferdinand VII.

163	1813 MR	10,000.	16,000.	30,000.	50,000.

NOTE: Spink America Gerber sale 6-96 VF or better realized $46,200.

Obv: Undraped bust of Ferdinand VII.

161.1	1821 FS	1500.	2500.	4500.	7500.

Obv: Draped bust of Ferdinand VII.

KM#	Date	VG	Fine	VF	XF
164	1821 FS	6500.	9000.	13,500.	22,500.

GUANAJUATO

The Guanajuato Mint was authorized December 24, 1812 and started production shortly thereafter; closing for unknown reasons on May 15, 1813. The mint was reopened in April, 1821 by the insurgents, who struck coins of the old royal Spanish design to pay their army, even after independence, well into 1822. Only the 2 and 8 reales coins were made.

MINT MARK: Go

2 REALES

6.7700 g, .903 SILVER, .1966 oz ASW
Obv: Draped bust of Ferdinand VII.

KM#	Date	VG	Fine	VF	XF
93.3	1821 JM	35.00	65.00	100.00	185.00
	1822 JM	30.00	50.00	75.00	145.00

8 REALES

27.0700 g, .903 SILVER, .7860 oz ASW
Obv: Draped bust of Ferdinand VII.

111.4	1812 JJ	1250.	2500.	—	—
	1813 JJ	125.00	175.00	275.00	600.00
	1821 JM	25.00	50.00	75.00	200.00
	1822/0 JM	40.00	100.00	150.00	300.00
	1822 JM	20.00	35.00	60.00	185.00

NUEVA VISCAYA

(Later became Durango State)

This 8 reales, intended for the province of Nueva Viscaya, was minted in the newly-opened Durango Mint during February and March of 1811, before the regular coinage of Durango was started.

8 REALES

.903 SILVER
Obv. leg: MON.PROV. DE NUEV.VIZCAYA,
arms of Durango. Rev: Royal arms.

KM#	Date	Good	VG	Fine	VF
181	1811 RM	1250.	2000.	2750.	4500.

NOTE: Several varieties exist.

OAXACA

The city of Oaxaca was in the midst of a coin shortage when it became apparent the city would be taken by insurgent forces. The Royalist forces under Lt. Gen. Saravia had some coins made. They were cast in a blacksmith shop and were made in 3 denominations - 1/2, 1 and 8 reales. They were made only briefly in 1812 before the city fell to the opposing forces.

1/2 REAL

.903 SILVER
Obv: Cross separating castle, lion, F,7O.
Rev. leg: OAXACA around shield.

KM#	Date	Good	VG	Fine	VF
166	1812	1000.	1500.	2500.	3500.

REAL

.903 SILVER

		Good	VG	Fine	VF
167	1812	300.00	600.00	1000.	2000.

8 REALES

.903 SILVER

KM#	Date	Good	VG	Fine	VF
168	1812 c/m:A	1300.	1900.	3300.	4750.
	1812 c/m:B	1300.	1900.	3300.	4750.
	1812 c/m:C	1300.	1900.	3300.	4750.
	1812 c/m:D	1300.	1900.	3300.	4750.
	1812 c/m:K	1300.	1900.	3300.	4750.
	1812 c/m:L	1300.	1900.	3300.	4750.
	1812 c/m:Mo	1300.	1900.	3300.	4750.
	1812 c/m:N	1300.	1900.	3300.	4750.
	1812 c/m:O	1300.	1900.	3300.	4750.
	1812 c/m:R	1300.	1900.	3300.	4750.
	1812 c/m:V	1300.	1900.	3300.	4750.
	1812 c/m:Z	1300.	1900.	3300.	4750.

NOTE: The above issue usually has a second c/m: O between crowned pillars.

REAL DEL CATORCE

(City in San Luis Potosi)

Real del Catorce is an important mining center in the Province of San Luis Potosi. In 1811 an 8 reales coin was issued under very primitive conditions while the city was still in Royalist hands. Few survive.

8 REALES

.903 SILVER
Obv. leg: EL R.D. CATORC. POR FERNA. VII.
Rev. leg: MONEDA. PROVISIONAL.VALE.8R.

KM#	Date	VG	Fine	VF	XF
169	1811	4500.	8500.	15,500.	65,000.

NOTE: Spink America Gerber Sale 6-96 VF or XF realized $63,800.

SAN FERNANDO DE BEXAR

Struck by Jose Antonio de la Garza, the 'jolas' are the only known coins issued under Spanish rule in what has become the continental United States of America.

1/8 REAL

COPPER

KM#	Date	Mintage	Good	VG	Fine	VF
170	1818	8,000	500.00	750.00	1250.	1650.

| 171 | 1818 | Inc. Ab. | 500.00 | 750.00 | 1250. | 1650. |

SAN LUIS POTOSI

Sierra De Pinos
Villa

1/4 REAL

COPPER

KM#	Date	Good	VG	Fine	VF
A172	1814	75.00	125.00	200.00	300.00

SILVER

| A172a | 1814 | — | — | Rare | — |

SOMBRERETE

(Under Royalist Vargas)

The Sombrerete Mint opened on October 8, 1810 in an area that boasted some of the richest mines in Mexico. The mint operated only until July 16, 1811, only to reopen in 1812 and finally close for good at the end

1/2 REAL

.903 SILVER
Obv. leg: FERDIN.VII.SOMBRERETE. . .,
around crowned globes.
Rev. leg: VARGAS above lys in oval, sprays.

KM#	Date	Good	VG	Fine	VF
172	1811	45.00	70.00	150.00	250.00
	1812	50.00	90.00	175.00	275.00

REAL

.903 SILVER
Obv. leg: FERDIN.VII.SOMBRERETE. . .,
around crowned globes.
Rev. leg: VARGAS above lys in oval, sprays.

	Date	Good	VG	Fine	VF
173	1811	45.00	70.00	150.00	250.00
	1812	50.00	90.00	175.00	275.00

2 REALES

.903 SILVER
Obv: R.CAXA.DE.SOMBRERETE, royal arms.
Rev. c/m: VARGAS, 1811, S between crowned pillars.

	Date	Good	VG	Fine	VF
174	1811 SE	100.00	250.00	450.00	700.00

4 REALES

.903 SILVER
Obv. leg: R.CAXA.DE.SOMBRERETE, royal arms.
Rev. leg: Small VARGAS/1811.

	Date				
175.1	1811	75.00	150.00	300.00	650.00

Rev: Large VARGAS/1812.

	Date				
175.2	1812	50.00	100.00	200.00	450.00

PRICING SECTION

8 REALES

.903 SILVER
Obv. leg: R.CAXA. DE SOMBRERETE.
Rev. c/m: VARGAS, date, S between crowned pillars.

KM#	Date	Good	VG	Fine	VF
176	1810	1000.	1750.	2750.	4000.
	1811	225.00	325.00	450.00	600.00

Obv. leg: R.CAXA. DE SOMBRETE, crowned arms.
Rev. leg: VARGAS/date/3

177	1811	125.00	185.00	245.00	500.00
	1812	125.00	175.00	225.00	475.00

VALLADOLID MICHOACAN
(Now Morelia)

Valladolid, capitol of Michoacan province, was a strategically important center for military thrusts into the adjoining provinces. The Royalists made every effort to retain the position. In 1813, with the advance of the insurgent forces, it became apparent that to maintain the position would be very difficult. During 1813 it was necessary to make coins in the city due to lack of traffic with other areas. These were made only briefly before the city fell and were also used by the insurgents with appropriate countermarks.

8 REALES
.903 SILVER
Obv: Royal arms in wreath, value at sides.
Rev: PROVISIONAL/DE VALLADOLID/1813.

KM#	Date	Good	VG	Fine	VF
178	1813	—	—	Rare	—

Obv: Bust, leg: FERDIN. VII.
Rev: Arms, pillars.

179	1813	—	—	*Rare	—

*NOTE: Spink America Gerber sale 6-96 good realized $23,100.

ZACATECAS

The city of Zacatecas, in a rich mining region has provided silver for the world since the mid-1500's. On November 14, 1810 a mint began production for the Royalist cause. Zacatecas was the most prolific during the War of Independence. Four of the 5 "standard" silver denominations were made here, 4 Reales were not. The first, a local type showing mountains of silver on the coins were made only in 1810 and 1811. Some 1811's were made by the Insurgents who took the city on April 15, 1811, later retaken by the Royalists on May 21, 1811. Zacatecas struck the standard Ferdinand VII bust type until 1922.

MINT MARKS: Z, ZS, Zs

1/2 REAL

.903 SILVER
Obv: Local arms w/flowers and castles.

KM#	Date	Good	VG	Fine	VF
180	1810	75.00	125.00	200.00	400.00
1181	(error 1811)	30.00	50.00	90.00	175.00

Obv: Royal arms.
Rev. leg: MONEDA PROVISIONAL DE ZACATECAS., mountain.

KM#	Date	Good	VG	Fine	VF
181	1811	30.00	50.00	90.00	175.00

Obv: Provincial bust FERDIN. VII.
Rev. leg: MONEDA PROVISIONAL DE ZACATECAS.

182	1811	30.00	40.00	65.00	135.00
	1812	25.00	35.00	60.00	120.00

1.6900 g, .903 SILVER, .0491 oz ASW
Obv: Armored bust of Ferdinand VII.

73.1	1813 FP	25.00	45.00	85.00	175.00
	1813 AG	20.00	40.00	60.00	100.00
	1814 AG	15.00	30.00	60.00	100.00
	1815 AG	12.50	25.00	40.00	60.00
	1816 AG	10.00	15.00	25.00	50.00
	1817 AG	10.00	15.00	25.00	50.00
	1818 AG	10.00	15.00	25.00	50.00
	1819 AG	10.00	15.00	25.00	50.00

Obv: Draped bust Ferdinand VII.

KM#	Date	VG	Fine	VF	XF
74.3	1819 AG	8.00	12.00	25.00	50.00
	1820 AG	8.00	12.00	25.00	50.00
	1820 RG	5.00	10.00	20.00	45.00
	1821 AG	150.00	250.00	450.00	850.00
	1821 RG	5.00	10.00	20.00	45.00

REAL

.903 SILVER
Obv: Local arms w/flowers and castles.

KM#	Date	Good	VG	Fine	VF
183	1810	100.00	150.00	300.00	500.00
	1181 (error 1811)	20.00	40.00	75.00	150.00

Obv: Royal arms.
Rev. leg: MONEDA PROVISIONAL DE ZACATECAS., mountain.

184	1811	15.00	30.00	55.00	125.00

Obv: Provincial bust, leg: FERDIN. VII.
Rev. leg: MONEDA PROVISIONAL DE ZACATECAS, arms, pillars.

185	1811	50.00	85.00	120.00	175.00
	1812	40.00	70.00	100.00	175.00

3.3800 g, .903 SILVER, .0981 oz ASW
Obv: Armored bust of Ferdinand VII.

KM#	Date	Good	VG	Fine	VF
82.1	1813 FP	50.00	100.00	150.00	250.00
	1814 FP	20.00	35.00	50.00	85.00
	1814 AG	20.00	35.00	50.00	85.00
	1815 AG	20.00	35.00	50.00	85.00
	1816 AG	10.00	20.00	30.00	65.00
	1817 AG	6.50	12.50	20.00	45.00
	1818 AG	6.50	12.50	20.00	45.00
	1819 AG	5.00	9.00	15.00	35.00
	1820 AG	4.00	7.50	12.50	30.00

Obv: Draped bust of Ferdinand VII.

KM#	Date	VG	Fine	VF	XF
83.3	1820 AG	5.00	10.00	17.50	42.00
	1820 RG	5.00	10.00	17.50	42.00
	1821 AG	15.00	30.00	45.00	80.00
	1821 AZ	10.00	20.00	30.00	65.00
	1821 RG	6.00	12.00	17.50	45.00
	1822 AZ	6.00	12.00	17.50	45.00
	1822 RG	15.00	30.00	45.00	80.00

2 REALES

.903 SILVER
Obv: Local arms w/flowers and castles.

KM#	Date	Good	VG	Fine	VF
186	1810	—	—	Rare	—
	1181 (error 1811)	25.00	40.00	60.00	100.00

Obv: Royal arms.
Rev. leg: MONEDA PROVISIONAL DE ZACATECAS., mountain above L.V.O.

187	1811	15.00	30.00	50.00	90.00

Obv: Armored bust, leg: FERDIN. VII.
Rev. leg: MONEDA PROVISIONAL DE ZACATECAS, crowned arms, pillars.

KM#	Date	Good	VG	Fine	VF
188	1811	35.00	65.00	135.00	225.00
	1812	30.00	60.00	125.00	200.00

6.7700 g, .903 SILVER, .1966 oz ASW
Obv: Large armored bust of Ferdinand VII.

92.1	1813 FP	35.00	50.00	75.00	125.00
	1814 FP	35.00	50.00	75.00	125.00
	1814 AG	35.00	50.00	75.00	125.00
	1815 AG	6.50	12.50	25.00	55.00
	1816 AG	6.50	12.50	25.00	55.00
	1817 AG	6.50	12.50	25.00	55.00
	1818 AG	6.50	12.50	25.00	55.00

Obv: Small armored bust of Ferdinand VII.

KM#	Date	Good	VG	Fine	VF
A92	1819 AG	45.00	100.00	200.00	400.00

Obv: Draped bust of Ferdinand VII.

KM#	Date	VG	Fine	VF	XF
93.4	1818 AG	6.50	12.50	25.00	50.00
	1819 AG	10.00	20.00	40.00	85.00
	1820 AG	10.00	20.00	40.00	85.00
	1820 RG	10.00	20.00	40.00	85.00
	1821 AG	10.00	20.00	40.00	85.00
	1821 AZ/RG	10.00	20.00	40.00	85.00
	1821 AZ	10.00	20.00	40.00	85.00
	1821 RG	10.00	20.00	40.00	85.00
	1822 AG	10.00	20.00	40.00	85.00
	1822 AZ	15.00	30.00	60.00	125.00
	1822 RG	10.00	20.00	40.00	85.00

8 REALES

.903 SILVER
Obv: Local arm w/flowers and castles.
Rev: Similar to KM#190.

KM#	Date	Good	VG	Fine	VF
189	1810	300.00	500.00	750.00	1250.
	1181 (error 1811)				
		100.00	150.00	225.00	350.00

NOTE: Also exists with incomplete date.

Obv. leg: FERDIN.VII.DEI. ., royal arms.
Rev. leg: MONEDA PROVISIONAL DE
ZACATECAS, mountain above L.V.O.

KM#	Date	Good	VG	Fine	VF
190	1811	65.00	100.00	135.00	220.00

Obv: Armored bust of Ferdinand VII.
Rev. leg: MONEDA PROVISIONAL DE
ZACATECAS, crowned arms, pillars.

KM#	Date	Good	VG	Fine	VF
191	1811	45.00	75.00	145.00	275.00
	1812	50.00	85.00	160.00	300.00

Obv: Draped bust of Ferdinand VII.
Rev. leg: MONEDA PROVISIONAL DE
ZACATECAS, crowned arms, pillars.

KM#	Date	Good	VG	Fine	VF
192	1812	75.00	150.00	275.00	450.00

KM#	Date	Year	Good	VG	Fine	VF
193.1	ND	1809 TH	75.00	150.00	200.00	300.00

c/m: LCM on Zacatecas KM#187.

KM#	Date	Year	Good	VG	Fine	VF
193.2	ND	1811	75.00	150.00	200.00	300.00

8 REALES

27.0700 g, .903 SILVER, .7860 oz ASW
Obv: Draped bust of Ferdinand VII.

KM#	Date	VG	Fine	VF	XF
111.5	1813 AG	125.00	200.00	250.00	350.00
	1813 FP	75.00	125.00	175.00	275.00
	1814 AG	100.00	150.00	200.00	300.00
	1814 AG D over horizontal D in IND				
		125.00	175.00	225.00	325.00
	1814 AG/FP	100.00	150.00	200.00	300.00
	1814 FP	150.00	250.00	350.00	450.00
	1815 AG	50.00	100.00	150.00	250.00
	1816 AG	35.00	50.00	65.00	125.00
	1817 AG	35.00	50.00	65.00	125.00
	1818 AG	30.00	40.00	50.00	100.00
	1819 AG	30.00	40.00	50.00	100.00
	1820 AG 18/11 error				
		100.00	200.00	300.00	400.00
	1820 AG	30.00	40.00	50.00	100.00
	1820 RG	30.00	40.00	50.00	100.00
	1821/81 RG	75.00	150.00	225.00	300.00
	1821 RG	15.00	25.00	35.00	65.00
	1821 AZ	50.00	100.00	150.00	200.00
	1822 RG	40.00	60.00	100.00	175.00

CAST SILVER
c/m: LCM on Chihuahua KM#123.

KM#	Date	Year	Good	VG	Fine	VF
194.1	ND	1811 RP	100.00	200.00	300.00	450.00
	ND	1812 RP	100.00	200.00	300.00	450.00

Rev: Crown with lower rear arc.

KM#	Date	VG	Fine	VF	XF
111.6	1821 RG	160.00	320.00	550.00	750.00

COUNTERMARKED COINAGE
Crown and Flag
(Refer to Multiple Countermarks)

LCM - La Comandancia Militar
NOTE: This countermark exists in 15 various sizes.

2 REALES

.903 SILVER
c/m: LCM on Mexico KM#92.

.903 SILVER
c/m: LCM on Chihuahua KM#111.1 struck
over KM#123.

KM#	Date	Year	Good	VG	Fine	VF
194.2	ND	1815 RP	200.00	275.00	400.00	550.00
	ND	1817 RP	125.00	175.00	225.00	300.00
	ND	1820 RP	125.00	175.00	225.00	300.00
	ND	1821 RP	125.00	175.00	225.00	300.00

c/m: LCM on Durango KM#111.2.

KM#	Date		Good	VG	Fine	VF
194.3	ND	1812 RM	70.00	125.00	190.00	250.00
	ND	1821 CG	70.00	125.00	190.00	250.00

c/m: LCM on Guadalajara KM#111.3.

194.4	ND	1813 MR	150.00	225.00	300.00	475.00
	ND	1820 FS	—	—	Rare	—

c/m: LCM on Guanajuato KM#111.4.

194.5	ND	1813 JM	225.00	350.00	475.00	650.00

c/m: LCM on Nueva Vizcaya KM#165.

KM#	Date	Year	Good	VG	Fine	VF
194.6	ND	1811 RM	—	—	Rare	—

c/m: LCM on Mexico KM#111.

194.7	ND	1811 HJ	125.00	225.00	350.00	600.00
	ND	1812 JJ	110.00	135.00	190.00	325.00
	ND	1817 JJ	50.00	65.00	85.00	125.00
	ND	1818 JJ	50.00	65.00	85.00	125.00
	ND	1820 JJ	—	—	—	—

c/m: LCM on Sombrerete KM#176.

KM#	Date	Year	Good	VG	Fine	VF
194.8	ND	1811	—	—	Rare	—
	ND	1812	—	—	Rare	—

c/m: LCM on Zacatecas KM#190.

194.9	ND	1811	225.00	350.00	450.00	—

c/m: LCM on Zacatecas KM#111.5.

194.10	ND	1813 FP	—	—	—	—
	ND	1814 AG	—	—	—	—
	ND	1822 RG	—	—	—	—

LCV - Las Cajas de Veracruz
(The Royal Treasury
of the City of Veracruz)

7 REALES
SILVER
c/m: LCV and 7 on underweight 8 Reales.

KM#	Date	Year	Good	VG	Fine	VF
195	ND	(-)	—	—	Rare	—

7-1/4 REALES
SILVER
c/m: LCV and 7-1/4 on underweight 8 Reales.

196	ND	(-)	—	—	Rare	—

7-1/2 REALES
SILVER
c/m: LCV and 7-1/2 on underweight 8 Reales.

197	ND	(-)	—	—	Rare	—

7-3/4 REALES

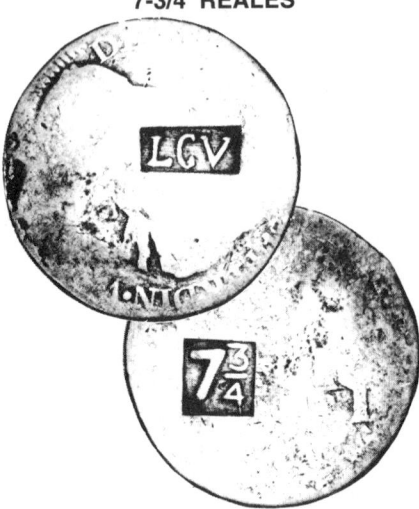

SILVER
c/m: LCV and 7-3/4 on underweight 8 Reales.

KM#	Date	Year	Good	VG	Fine	VF
198	ND	(-)	300.00	375.00	450.00	600.00

8 REALES
CAST SILVER
c/m: LCV on Chihuahua KM#123.

A198	ND	1811 RP	150.00	250.00	400.00	500.00

SILVER
c/m: LCV on Zacatecas KM#191.

KM#	Date	Year	Good	VG	Fine	VF
199	ND	1811	175.00	225.00	275.00	350.00
	ND	1812	175.00	225.00	275.00	350.00

MS (Monogram) - Manuel Salcedo

8 REALES

SILVER
c/m: MS monogram on Mexico KM#110.

KM#	Date	Year	Good	VG	Fine	VF
200	ND	1809 TH	150.00	250.00	400.00	500.00
	ND	1810 HJ	150.00	250.00	400.00	500.00
	ND	1811 HJ	150.00	250.00	400.00	500.00

MVA - Monclova

8 REALES
SILVER
c/m: MVA/1811 on Chihuahua KM#111.1; struck
over cast Mexico KM#110.

201	ND	1809	250.00	450.00	700.00	1000.
	ND	1816 RP	250.00	450.00	700.00	1000.
	ND	1821 RP	250.00	450.00	700.00	1000.

c/m: MVA/1812 on Chihuahua KM#111.1; struck
over cast Mexico KM#109.

KM#	Date	Year	Good	VG	Fine	VF
202.1	1812	1810	125.00	175.00	250.00	350.00

c/m: MVA/1812 on cast Mexico KM#109.

KM#	Date		Good	VG	Fine	VF
202.2	1812 1798 FM		100.00	150.00	250.00	350.00
	1812 1802 FT		100.00	150.00	250.00	350.00

c/m: MVA/1812 on cast Mexico KM#110.

202.3	1812 1809 HJ	100.00	150.00	250.00	350.00
	1812 1809 TH	100.00	150.00	250.00	350.00
	1812 1810 HJ	100.00	150.00	250.00	350.00

c/m: MVA/1812 on Zacatecas KM#189.

202.5	1812	1813	300.00	350.00	450.00	550.00

PDV - Provisional de Valladolid
VTIL - (Util = useful)
(Refer to Multiple countermarks)

INSURGENT COINAGE
Supreme National Congress
of America
1/2 REAL
COPPER
Obv. leg: FERDIN. VII DEI GRATIA, eagle on bridge.
Rev. leg: S.P.CONG.NAT.IND.
GUV.T., value, bow, quiver, etc.

KM#	Date	Good	VG	Fine	VF
203	1811	27.50	45.00	60.00	100.00

REAL
STRUCK SILVER
Similar to 1/2 Real, KM#203.

204	1811	45.00	75.00	125.00	200.00

2 REALES

STRUCK SILVER

KM#	Date	Good	VG	Fine	VF
205	1812	225.00	325.00	475.00	700.00

8 REALES

CAST SILVER

KM#	Date	Good	VG	Fine	VF
206	1811	150.00	250.00	350.00	500.00
	1812	150.00	250.00	350.00	500.00

STRUCK SILVER

KM#	Date	Good	VG	Fine	VF
207	1811	—	—	—	—
	1812	300.00	600.00	1000.	1500.

COPPER
Obv. leg: FERDIN.VII. . ., eagle on bridge.
Rev. leg: PROVICIONAL POR LA SUPREMA JUNTA DE AMERICA, bow, sword and quiver.

KM#	Date	Good	VG	Fine	VF
208	1811	100.00	150.00	225.00	450.00
	1812	100.00	150.00	225.00	450.00

National Congress
1/2 REAL

STRUCK COPPER
Obv. leg: VICE FERD. VII DEI GRATIA ET, eagle on bridge.
Rev. leg: S. P. CONG. NAT. IND.
GUV. T., value, bow, quiver, etc.

KM#	Date	Good	VG	Fine	VF
209	1811	45.00	85.00	150.00	200.00
	1812	27.50	60.00	100.00	150.00
	1813	27.50	60.00	100.00	150.00
	1814	45.00	85.00	150.00	200.00

.903 SILVER

KM#	Date	Good	VG	Fine	VF
210	1812	27.50	60.00	100.00	150.00
	1813	45.00	90.00	175.00	275.00

NOTE: 1812 exists with the date reading inwards and outwards.

REAL

.903 SILVER

211	1812	22.50	45.00	65.00	100.00
	1813	22.50	45.00	65.00	100.00

NOTE: 1812 exists with the date reading either inward or outward.

2 REALES

STRUCK COPPER

212	1812	100.00	150.00	200.00	275.00
	1813	23.50	50.00	75.00	120.00
	1814	32.50	75.00	110.00	165.00

.903 SILVER

213	1813	75.00	155.00	265.00	375.00

NOTE: These dies were believed to be intended for the striking of 2 Escudos.

4 REALES

.903 SILVER
Mint: Mexico City

KM#	Date	Good	VG	Fine	VF
214	1813	600.00	1200.	2250.	3500.

8 REALES

.903 SILVER
Mint: Mexico City
Obv: Small crowned eagle.

KM#	Date	Good	VG	Fine	VF
215.1	1812	500.00	1000.	2000.	3750.

Obv: Large crowned eagle.

KM#	Date	Good	VG	Fine	VF
215.2	1813	500.00	1000.	2000.	3750.

American Congress
REAL

.903 SILVER
Obv: Eagle on cactus,
leg: CONGRESO AMERICANO.
Rev: F.7 on spread mantle,
leg: DEPOSIT D.L.AUCTORI J.

KM#	Date	Good	VG	Fine	VF
216	ND(1813)	35.00	65.00	100.00	175.00

Obv: Eagle on cactus, leg: CONGR.AMER.
Rev: F.7 on spread mantle,
leg: DEPOS.D.L.AUT.D.

KM#	Date	Good	VG	Fine	VF
217	ND(1813)	35.00	65.00	100.00	175.00

NUEVA GALICIA

(Later became Jalisco State)

In early colonial times, Nueva Galicia was an extensive province which substantially combined later provinces of Zacatecas and Jalisco. These are states of Mexico today although the name was revived during the War of Independence. The only issue was 2 reales of rather enigmatic origin. No decrees or other authorization to strike this coin has yet been located or reported.

2 REALES

Obv. leg: PROVYCIONAL. . ., N.G. in center, date.
Rev:. . .a.juniana82R. . . in center.

KM#	Date	Good	VG	Fine	VF
218	1813	1000.	2500.	4500.	—

OAXACA

Oaxaca was the hub of Insurgent activity in the south where coinage started in July 1811 and continued until October 1814. The Oaxaca issues represent episodic strikings, usually under dire circumstances by various individuals. Coins were commonly made of copper due to urgency and were intended to be redeemed at face value in gold or silver once silver was available to the Insurgents. Some were later made in silver, but most appear to be of more recent origin, to statisfy collectors.

SUD

(Under General Morelos)

1/2 REAL

STRUCK COPPER
Obv: Bow, arrow, SUD.
Rev: Morelos monogram Mo, date.

KM#	Date	Good	VG	Fine	VF
219	1811	6.75	11.50	20.00	35.00
	1812	6.75	11.50	20.00	35.00
	1813	5.50	9.00	17.50	30.00
	1814	9.00	16.50	25.00	40.00

NOTE: Uniface strikes exist of #219.

STRUCK SILVER

KM#	Date	Good	VG	Fine	VF
220.1	1811	—	—	—	—
	1812	—	—	—	—
	1813	—	—	—	—

CAST SILVER

KM#	Date	Good	VG	Fine	VF
220.2	1811	—	—	—	—
	1812	—	—	—	—
	1813	25.00	50.00	100.00	150.00

NOTE: Use caution as most silver specimens examined appear questionable and may be considered spurious.

STRUCK SILVER
Obv. leg: PROVICIONAL DE OAXACA, bow, arrow.
Rev. leg: AMERICA MORELOS, lion.

221	1812	35.00	60.00	100.00	150.00
	1813	35.00	60.00	100.00	150.00

STRUCK COPPER

221a	1812	27.50	42.50	70.00	100.00
	1813	20.00	35.00	60.00	85.00

Obv: Similar to KM#220.
Rev: Similar to KM#221 but w/1/2 at left of lion.

A222	1813	27.50	42.50	70.00	100.00

REAL

STRUCK COPPER

KM#	Date	Good	VG	Fine	VF
222	1811	4.75	9.00	18.00	38.00
	1812	3.75	7.00	14.00	30.00
	1813	3.75	7.00	14.00	30.00

STRUCK SILVER

222a	1812	—	—	—	—
	1813	—	—	—	—

CAST SILVER

223	1812	—	—	—	—
	1813	27.50	60.00	115.00	160.00

NOTE: See note below 1/2 Real, KM#220.2

STRUCK COPPER
Obv: Bow, arrow/SUD.
Rev. leg: AMERICA MORELOS, lion.

224	1813	27.50	42.50	75.00	110.00

SILVER

225	1813	—	—	Rare	—

2 REALES

STRUCK COPPER

KM#	Date	Good	VG	Fine	VF
226.1	1811	11.00	22.50	45.00	90.00
	1812	2.50	3.75	5.00	9.00
	1813	2.50	3.75	5.00	9.00
	1814	12.50	25.00	50.00	100.00
226.1a	1812	175.00	300.00	500.00	750.00

Obv: 3 large stars added.

226.2	1814	10.00	20.00	40.00	60.00

Obv. leg: SUD-OXA, bow, arrow.
Rev: Morelos monogram, value, date.

227	1813	60.00	100.00	200.00	300.00
	1814	60.00	100.00	200.00	300.00

Obv. leg: SUD. OAXACA

228	1814	60.00	100.00	200.00	325.00

CAST SILVER

229	1812	60.00	100.00	150.00	225.00
	1812 filled D in SUD				
		60.00	100.00	150.00	225.00

NOTE: See note below 1/2 Real, KM#220.2.

4 REALES

NOTE: All known examples are modern fabrications.

CAST SILVER

230	1811	—	—	—	—
	1812	—	—	—	—

Obv. leg: SUD-OXA, bow, arrow.
Rev: Morelos monogram.

231	1813	125.00	250.00	400.00	800.00

COPPER
Obv. leg: SUD-OXA, bow, arrow.
Rev: Morelos monogram.

KM#	Date	Good	VG	Fine	VF
232	1814	100.00	150.00	200.00	400.00

8 REALES

STRUCK COPPER
Plain fields.

KM#	Date	Good	VG	Fine	VF
233.1	1812	15.00	30.00	60.00	90.00

STRUCK SILVER

KM#	Date	Good	VG	Fine	VF
233.1a	1812	100.00	150.00	250.00	450.00

Ornate flowery fields.

KM#	Date	Good	VG	Fine	VF
234	1811	75.00	125.00	150.00	225.00
	1812	4.00	5.00	7.50	15.00
	1813	4.00	5.00	7.50	15.00
	1814	10.00	15.00	25.00	50.00

KM#	Date	Good	VG	Fine	VF
233.2	1812	6.00	8.00	12.00	15.00
	1813	6.00	8.00	12.00	15.00
	1814	10.00	12.00	15.00	20.00

Similar to KM#233.4 but lines below bow slant left.

KM#	Date	Good	VG	Fine	VF
233.3	1813	10.00	17.50	30.00	50.00

CAST SILVER

KM#	Date	Good	VG	Fine	VF
235	1811	—	—	—	—
	1812	75.00	125.00	200.00	350.00
	1813	60.00	100.00	175.00	300.00
	1814	—	—	—	—

NOTE: Most silver specimens available in today's market are considered spurious.

.903 SILVER, struck
Obv: PROV. D. OAXACA, M monogram.
Rev: Lion shield w/or w/o bow above.

KM#	Date	Good	VG	Fine	VF
236	1812	—	—	Rare	—

Obv: W/o leg.

KM#	Date	Good	VG	Fine	VF
237	1813	—	—	Rare	—

Obv: Bow/M/SUD. .
Rev: PROV. DE, . . ., arms.

KM#	Date	Good	VG	Fine	VF
238	1813	—	—	Rare	—

Obv: Lines below bow slant right.

KM#	Date	Good	VG	Fine	VF
233.4	1813	10.00	17.50	30.00	50.00

CAST SILVER
Similar to 4 Reales, KM#231.

KM#	Date	Good	VG	Fine	VF
239	1814	—	—	Rare	—

COPPER
Obv: Bow, T.C., SUD.
Rev: Morelos monogram, value, date.

KM#	Date	Good	VG	Fine	VF
243	1813	37.50	70.00	125.00	200.00

REAL

STRUCK COPPER
Similar to 1/2 Real, KM#243.

KM#	Date	Good	VG	Fine	VF
244	1813	13.50	25.00	50.00	80.00

2 REALES

STRUCK COPPER
Similar to 1/2 Real, KM#243.

KM#	Date	Good	VG	Fine	VF
245	1813	9.00	22.50	35.00	50.00

COPPER

KM#	Date	Good	VG	Fine	VF
240	1814	35.00	70.00	150.00	250.00

OAXACA spelled out.

KM#	Date	Good	VG	Fine	VF
241	1814	100.00	200.00	350.00	550.00

KM#	Date	Good	VG	Fine	VF
246	1814	22.50	50.00	100.00	175.00

CAST SILVER

KM#	Date	Good	VG	Fine	VF
247	1814	—	—	Rare	—

NOTE: See note below 1/2 Real, KM#220.2.

Huautla
8 REALES

8 REALES

COPPER
Obv. leg: MONEDA PROVI.CIONAL PS.ES.
around bow, arrow/SUD.
Rev. leg: FABRICADO EN HUAUTLA.

KM#	Date	Good	VG	Fine	VF
242	1812	1000.	1500.	2000.	—

Tierra Caliente
(Hot Country)
Under General Morelos
1/2 REAL

STRUCK COPPER

KM#	Date	Good	VG	Fine	VF
248	1813	10.00	20.00	40.00	75.00

CAST SILVER

KM#	Date	Good	VG	Fine	VF
249	1813	—	—	—	—

NOTE: See note below 1/2 Real, KM#220.2.

PUEBLA

The coins of Puebla emanated from Zacatlan, the headquarters of the hit-and-run Insurgent leader Osorno. The mint opened in April 1812 and operated through 1813.

Zacatlan

(Struck by General Osorno)

1/2 REAL

COPPER
Obv: Osorno monogram, ZACATLAN, date.
Rev: Crossed arrows, wreath, value.

KM#	Date	Good	VG	Fine	VF
250	1813	—	—	Rare	—

REAL

COPPER

KM#	Date	Good	VG	Fine	VF
251	1813	100.00	150.00	225.00	450.00

COPPER

KM#	Date	Good	VG	Fine	VF
252	1813	125.00	175.00	275.00	500.00

VERACRUZ

In Zongolica, in the province of Veracruz, 2 priests and a lawyer decided to raise an army to fight for independence. Due to isolation from other Insurgent forces, they decided to make their own coins. Records show that they intended to mint coins of 1/2, 1, 2, 4, and 8 reales, but specimens are extant of only the three higher denominations.

Zongolica

2 REALES

.903 SILVER
Obv. leg: VIVA FERNANDO VII Y AMERICA,
bow and arrow.
Rev. leg: ZONGOLICA, value, crossed
palm branch, sword, date.

KM#	Date	Good	VG	Fine	VF
253	1812	85.00	175.00	300.00	500.00

4 REALES

.903 SILVER
Similar to 2 Reales, KM#253.

		Good	VG	Fine	VF
254	1812	600.00	800.00	1200.	2000.

8 REALES

.903 SILVER

KM#	Date	Good	VG	Fine	VF
255	1812	—	—	*Rare	—

*NOTE: Spink America Gerber sale 6-96 VF to XF realized $57,200.

COUNTERMARKED COINAGE
Congress of Chilpanzingo

Type A: Hand holding bow and arrow between quiver w/arrows, sword and bow.

Type B: Crowned eagle on bridge.

1/2 REAL

SILVER
c/m: Type A on cast Mexico City KM#72.

KM#	Date	Year	Good	VG	Fine	VF
256.1	ND	1812	42.50	70.00	90.00	120.00

c/m: Type A on Zacatecas KM#181.

			Good	VG	Fine	VF
256.2	ND	1811	50.00	75.00	100.00	125.00

REAL

CAST SILVER
c/m: Type A on cast Mexico City KM#81.

KM#	Date	Year	Good	VG	Fine	VF
A257	ND	1803	18.50	30.00	50.00	80.00

2 REALES

SILVER
c/m: Type B on 1/4 cut of 8 Reales.

KM#	Date	Year	Good	VG	Fine	VF
257.1	ND	—	—	—	Unique	—

c/m: Type B on Zacatecas KM#186.

257.2	ND	1811	—	—	Unique	—

8 REALES

SILVER
c/m: Type A on cast Mexico City KM#109.

258.1	ND	1805 TH	45.00	65.00	85.00	125.00

c/m: Type A on cast Mexico City KM#110.

258.2	ND	1810 HJ	50.00	75.00	100.00	150.00

c/m: Type A on cast Mexico City KM#111.

258.3	ND	1811 HJ	45.00	65.00	85.00	125.00
	ND	1812 HJ	100.00	125.00	175.00	275.00

c/m: Type B on Chihuahua KM#111.1.

259.1	ND	1816 RP	200.00	250.00	300.00	350.00

c/m: Type B on cast Mexico City KM#111.

259.2	ND	1811 HJ	130.00	140.00	150.00	175.00

c/m: Type B on Valladolid KM#178.

KM#	Date	Year	Good	VG	Fine	VF
259.3	ND	1813	1000.	2000.	3000.	5000.

c/m: Type B on Zacatecas KM#190.

259.4	ND	1810	400.00	500.00	600.00	750.00

Ensaie
8 REALES

SILVER
c/m: Eagle over ENSAIE on Mexico City KM#110.

260.1	ND	1811 HJ	150.00	200.00	275.00	350.00

c/m: Eagle over ENSAIE crude sling below on Zacatecas KM#189.

260.2	ND	1811	200.00	400.00	600.00	800.00

c/m: Eagle over ENSAIE, crude sling below on Zacatecas KM#190.

260.3	ND	1810	—	—	—	—
	ND	1811	100.00	150.00	200.00	300.00

c/m: Eagle over ENSAIE, crude sling below on Zacatecas KM#191.

260.4	ND	1810	500.00	700.00	900.00	1200.
	ND	1811	250.00	300.00	375.00	500.00
	ND	1812	200.00	250.00	285.00	400.00

Jose Maria Liceaga

J.M.L. with banner on cross, crossed olive branches.
(J.M.L./V., D.s, S.M.,S.Y.S.L., Ve, A.P.,
s.r.a., Sea, P.G.,S.,S.M.,E.)

1/2 REAL

SILVER
c/m: JML/SM on cast Mexico City 1/2 Real.

KM#	Date	Year	Good	VG	Fine	VF
A260	ND	—	100.00	150.00	200.00	275.00

2 REALES

SILVER
c/m: J.M.L./Ve on 1/4 cut of 8 Reales.

261.1	ND	—	175.00	225.00	300.00	—

c/m: J.M.L./V. on Zacatecas KM#186-187.

261.2	ND	1811	200.00	225.00	250.00	300.00

c/m: J.M.L./DS on Zacatecas KM#186-187.

261.3	ND	1811	200.00	235.00	275.00	325.00

c/m: J.M.L./S.M. on Zacatecas KM#186-187.

261.4	ND	1811	200.00	235.00	275.00	325.00

c/m: J.M.L./S.Y. on Zacatecas KM#186-187.

261.5	ND	1811	200.00	235.00	275.00	325.00

8 REALES

SILVER
c/m: J.M.L./D.S. on Zacatecas KM#189-190.

262.1	ND	1811	250.00	325.00	425.00	550.00

c/m: J.M.L./E on Zacatecas KM#189-190.

KM#	Date	Year	Good	VG	Fine	VF
262.2	ND	1811	225.00	300.00	400.00	550.00

c/m: J.M.L./P.G. on Durango KM#111.2.

262.3	ND	1813 RM	200.00	275.00	375.00	525.00

c/m: J.M.L./S.F. on Zacatecas KM#189-190.

262.4	ND	1811	200.00	275.00	375.00	525.00

c/m: J.M.L./S.M. on Zacatecas KM#189-190.

262.5	ND	1811	200.00	275.00	375.00	525.00

c/m: J.M.L./V.E. on Zacatecas KM#189-190.

KM#	Date	Year	Good	VG	Fine	VF
262.6	ND	1811	200.00	275.00	375.00	525.00

Don Jose Maria De Linares

8 REALES

SILVER
c/m: LINA/RES* on Mexico City KM#110.

KM#	Date		Good	VG	Fine	VF
263.1	ND	1808 TH	250.00	300.00	375.00	500.00

c/m: LINA/RES * on Zacatecas KM#189-190.

263.2	ND	1811	300.00	375.00	450.00	575.00

c/m: LINA/RES* on Zacatecas, KM#191-192.

263.3	ND	1812	250.00	300.00	375.00	500.00

L.V.S. - Labor Vincit Semper

NOTE: Some authorities believe L.V.S. is for 'La Villa de Sombrerete'.

8 REALES

CAST SILVER
c/m: L.V.S. on Chihuahua KM#123.

264.1	ND	1811 RP	275.00	350.00	450.00	550.00
	ND	1812 RP	200.00	250.00	300.00	375.00

c/m: L.V.S. on Chihuahua KM#111.1 overstruck on KM#123.

KM#	Date	Year	Good	VG	Fine	VF
264.2	ND	1816 RP	250.00	300.00	325.00	375.00
	ND	1817 RP	250.00	300.00	325.00	375.00
	ND	1818 RP	250.00	300.00	325.00	375.00
	ND	1819 RP	400.00	450.00	500.00	600.00
	ND	1820 RP	450.00	500.00	550.00	650.00

c/m: L.V.S. on Guadalajara KM#111.3.

264.3	ND	1817	185.00	220.00	250.00	310.00

c/m: L.V.S. on Nueva Vizcaya KM#165.

264.4	ND	1811 RM	1150.	3150.	5250.	8250.

c/m: L.V.S. on Sombrerete KM#177.

264.5	ND	1811	300.00	350.00	450.00	550.00
	ND	1812	300.00	350.00	450.00	550.00

c/m: L.V.S. on Zacatecas KM#189-190.

264.6	ND	1811	350.00	400.00	450.00	550.00

c/m: L.V.S. on Zacatecas KM#192.

264.7	ND	1813	350.00	400.00	450.00	550.00

Morelos
Morelos monogram

Type A: Stars above and below monogram in circle.

Type B: Dots above and below monogram in oval.

Type C: Monogram in rectangle.
NOTE: Many specimens of Type C available in today's market are considered spurious.

2 REALES

COPPER
c/m: Type A on Oaxaca Sud, KM#226.1.

A265	1812	—	—	—	—

8 REALES

SILVER
c/m: Type A on cast Mexico City KM#109.

KM#	Date	Year	Good	VG	Fine	VF
265.1	ND	1797 FM	45.00	50.00	60.00	85.00
	ND	1798 FM	45.00	50.00	60.00	85.00
	ND	1800 FM	45.00	50.00	60.00	85.00
	ND	1807 TH	45.00	50.00	60.00	85.00

c/m: Type A on Mexico City KM#110.

265.2	ND	1809 TH	55.00	65.00	85.00	120.00
	ND	1811 HJ	55.00	65.00	85.00	120.00

c/m: Type A on Mexico City KM#111.

265.3	ND	1812 JJ	50.00	60.00	75.00	110.00

COPPER
c/m: Type A on Oaxaca Sud KM#233.

265.4	ND	1811	12.50	17.50	25.00	40.00
	ND	1812	12.50	17.50	25.00	40.00
	ND	1813	12.50	17.50	25.00	40.00
	ND	1814	12.50	17.50	25.00	40.00

CAST SILVER
c/m: Type A on Supreme National Congress KM#206.

KM#	Date	Year	Good	VG	Fine	VF
265.5	ND	1811	200.00	250.00	375.00	600.00

SILVER
c/m: Type A on Zacatecas KM#189-190.

265.6	ND	1811	200.00	250.00	375.00	600.00

c/m: Type A on Zacatecas KM#191.

265.7	ND	1811	200.00	250.00	375.00	600.00

c/m: Type B on Guatemala 8 Reales, C#67.

266.1	ND	1810 M	—	—	Rare	—

c/m: Type B on Mexico City KM#110.

266.2	ND	1809 TH	45.00	55.00	65.00	90.00

c/m: Type C on Zacatecas KM#189-190.

267	ND	1811	300.00	350.00	425.00	650.00

Norte

Issued by the Supreme National Congress and the Army of the North.

c/m: Eagle on cactus; star to left; NORTE below.

1/2 REAL

SILVER
c/m: On Zacatecas KM#180.

268	ND	1811	250.00	300.00	375.00	450.00

2 REALES

SILVER
c/m: On Zacatecas KM#187.

KM#	Date	Year	Good	VG	Fine	VF
269	ND	1811	225.00	275.00	325.00	400.00

c/m: On Zacatecas KM#188.

A269	ND	1812	—	—	—	—

4 REALES

SILVER
c/m: On Sombrerete KM#175.

KM#	Date		Good	VG	Fine	VF
B269	ND	1812	100.00	150.00	200.00	275.00

8 REALES

SILVER
c/m: On Chihuahua KM#111.1.

270.1	ND	1813 RP	250.00	350.00	450.00	550.00

c/m: On Guanajuato KM#111.4.

270.2	ND	1813 JM	400.00	550.00	700.00	800.00

c/m: On Zacatecas KM#189-190.

270.3	ND	1811	300.00	400.00	500.00	650.00

c/m: On Zacatecas KM#191.

KM#	Date	Year	Good	VG	Fine	VF
270.4	ND	1811	200.00	300.00	400.00	550.00
	ND	1812	200.00	300.00	400.00	550.00

Osorno

c/m: Osorno monogram.
(Jose Francisco Osorno)

1/2 REAL

SILVER
c/m: On Mexico City KM#72.

271.1	ND	1798 FM	65.00	100.00	150.00	200.00
	ND	1802 FT	65.00	100.00	150.00	200.00
	ND	1806	65.00	100.00	150.00	200.00

c/m: On Mexico City KM#73.

271.2	ND	1809	65.00	100.00	150.00	200.00

REAL

SILVER
c/m: On Mexico City KM#81.

272.1	ND	1803 FT	65.00	100.00	150.00	200.00
	ND	1803 FT	65.00	100.00	150.00	200.00

c/m: On Potosi Real.

272.2	ND	—	75.00	115.00	175.00	250.00
272.3	ND	1804	75.00	115.00	175.00	250.00

2 REALES

SILVER
c/m: On Mexico City KM#88.2.

KM#	Date	Year	Good	VG	Fine	VF
A272.1		1788 FM	75.00	125.00	175.00	250.00

c/m: On Mexico City KM#91.

KM#	Date	Good	VG	Fine	VF
A272.2	1808 TH	75.00	125.00	175.00	250.00

c/m: On cast Mexico City KM#92.

A272.3 ND	1809 TH	75.00	125.00	175.00	250.00
(A272.1)					

c/m: On Zacatlan KM#252.

A272.4 ND	1813	150.00	200.00	300.00	400.00
(A272.2)					

4 REALES

SILVER
c/m: On Mexico City KM#97.2.

273.1	ND	1782 FF	85.00	150.00	200.00 275.00

c/m: On Mexico City KM#100.

KM#	Date	Year	Good	VG	Fine	VF
273.2	ND	1799 FM	85.00	150.00	200.00	275.00

8 REALES

SILVER
c/m: On Lima 8 Reales, C#101.

274.1	ND	1811 JP	200.00	225.00	250.00 300.00

c/m: On Mexico City KM#110.

KM#	Date	Year	Good	VG	Fine	VF
274.2	ND	1809 TH	125.00	150.00	225.00	300.00
	ND	1810 HJ	125.00	150.00	225.00	300.00
	ND	1811 HJ	125.00	150.00	225.00	300.00

S.J.N.G. - Suprema Junta National Gubernativa

(Refer to Multiple countermarks)

VILLA/GRAN

(Julian Villagran)

2 REALES

CAST SILVER
c/m: On cast Mexico City KM#91.

KM#	Date	Year	Good	VG	Fine	VF
298	ND	1799 FM	150.00	200.00	250.00	350.00
	ND	1802 FT	150.00	200.00	250.00	350.00

8 REALES

CAST SILVER
c/m: VILLA/GRAN on cast Mexico City KM#109.

275	ND	1796 FM	200.00	250.00	300.00 400.00
	ND	1806 TH	200.00	250.00	300.00 400.00

UNCLASSIFIED COUNTERMARKS
General Vicente Guerrero

The countermark of an eagle facing left within a pearled oval has been attributed by some authors as that of General Vicente Guerrero, a leader of the insurgents in the

1/2 REAL

SILVER
c/m: Eagle on Mexico City 1/2 Real.

KM#	Date	Year	Good	VG	Fine	VF
276	ND	—	40.00	60.00	80.00	175.00

REAL

SILVER
c/m: Eagle on Mexico City KM#78.

KM#	Date		Good	VG	Fine	VF
277	ND	1772 FM	35.00	50.00	75.00	165.00

2 REALES

SILVER
c/m: Eagle on Mexico City KM#88.

278.1	ND	1784 FM	40.00	60.00	100.00	225.00
		1798	40.00	60.00	100.00	220.00

c/m: Eagle on Mexico City KM#91.

KM#	Date	Year	Good	VG	Fine	VF
278.2	ND	1807 PJ	30.00	50.00	80.00	200.00

8 REALES

SILVER
c/m: Eagle on Zacatecas KM#191.

279	ND	1811	100.00	150.00	200.00	350.00

ZMY

8 REALES

SILVER
c/m: ZMY on Zacatecas KM#191.

286	ND	1812	100.00	150.00	210.00	275.00

MULTIPLE COUNTERMARKS

Many combinations of Royalist and Insurgent counter-marks are usually found on the cast copies produced by Chihuahua and Mexico City and on the other crude provisional issues of this period. Struck Mexico City coins were used to make molds for casting necessity issues and countermarked afterwards to show issuing authority. Some were marked again by either both or separate opposing friendly forces to authorize circulation in their areas of occupation. Some countermarks are only obtainable with companion markings.

Chilpanzingo Crown and Flag
8 REALES

SILVER
c/m: Chilpanzingo Type B and crown and flag on Zacatecas KM#189-190.

KM#	Date	Year	Good	VG	Fine	VF
280	ND	1811	—	—	—	—

Chilpanzingo/ENSAIE
8 REALES

SILVER
c/m: Chilpanzingo Type B and ENSAIE on Zacatecas KM#189.

A297	ND		—	175.00	250.00	350.00	—

Chilpanzingo/LVA
8 REALES

SILVER
c/m: Chilpanzingo Type A and LVA on Mexico City KM#109.

KM#	Date	Year	Good	VG	Fine	VF
297	ND	1805 TH	45.00	75.00	145.00	250.00

Chilpanzingo/LVS
8 REALES

SILVER
c/m: Chilpanzingo Type A and
script LVS on cast Mexico City KM#110.

KM#	Date	Year	Good	VG	Fine	VF
281	ND	1809 HJ	45.00	65.00	135.00	250.00

Chilpanzingo/Morelos
8 REALES

SILVER
c/m: Chilpanzingo Type A and Morelos
monogram Type A on cast Mexico City KM#109.

KM#	Date		Good	VG	Fine	VF
284	ND	1806 TH	35.00	50.00	100.00	200.00
	ND	1807 TH	35.00	50.00	100.00	200.00

c/m: Chilpanzingo Type A and Morelos monogram
Type A on struck Mexico City KM#110.

285.1	ND	1809 TH	45.00	65.00	135.00	250.00

c/m: Chilpanzingo Type A and Morelos monogram
Type A on cast Mexico City KM#110.

KM#	Date	Year	Good	VG	Fine	VF
285.2	ND	1810 HJ	35.00	45.00	60.00	140.00
	ND	1811 HJ	35.00	45.00	60.00	140.00

c/m: Chilpanzingo Type A and Morelos monogram
Type A on cast Mexico City KM#111.

285.3	ND	1811 HJ	75.00	120.00	175.00	275.00

Chilpanzingo/Morelos/LVS
8 REALES

SILVER
c/m: Chilpanzingo Type A, Morelos Type A and
LVS monogram on cast Mexico City KM#110.

KM#	Date	Year	Good	VG	Fine	VF
286	ND	1809 HJ	50.00	75.00	125.00	275.00

Chilpanzingo/P.D.V.
8 REALES

SILVER
c/m: Chilpanzingo Type B and P.D.V. (Provisional
De Valladolid) on Valladolid KM#178.

KM#	Date	Year	Good	VG	Fine	VF
287	ND	1813	—	—	—	—

Chilpanzingo/S.J.N.G.
8 REALES

SILVER
c/m: Chilpanzingo Type B and S.J.N.G.
(Suprema Junta Nacional Gubernativa)
on Zacatecas KM#189-190.

KM#	Date	Year	Good	VG	Fine	VF
288	ND	1811	—	—	—	—

C.M.S./S.C.M.
2 REALES

SILVER
c/m: C.M.S. (Comandancia Militar Suriana) and
eagle w/S.C.M. (Soberano Congreso Mexicano)
on Mexico City 2 Reales.

289	ND		—	—	—	—	—

ENSAIE/J.M.L.
8 REALES

SILVER
c/m: ENSAIE and J.M.L. on Zacatecas, KM#190.

KM#	Date	Year	Good	VG	Fine	VF
A290	ND	1811	100.00	175.00	275.00	350.00

ENSAIE/VTIL
8 REALES

SILVER
c/m: ENSAIE and VTIL on Zacatecas KM#189-190.

KM#	Date	Year	Good	VG	Fine	VF
290	ND	1811	100.00	175.00	275.00	350.00

J.M.L./VTIL
2 REALES

SILVER
c/m: J.M.L./D.S. and VTIL on Zacatecas, KM#186.

A286	ND	1811	75.00	125.00	175.00	250.00

c/m: J.M.L./V.E. and VTIL on Zacatecas KM#186.

B286	ND	1810	75.00	125.00	175.00	250.00
	ND	1811	75.00	125.00	175.00	250.00

8 REALES

SILVER
c/m: J.M.L./D.S. and VTIL on Mexico City KM#110.

KM#	Date	Year	Good	VG	Fine	VF
291	ND	1810 HJ	85.00	150.00	250.00	400.00

L.C.M./Morelos
8 REALES

SILVER
c/m: LCM and Morelos monogram
Type A on cast Mexico City KM#109.

KM#	Date	Year	Good	VG	Fine	VF
282	ND	1792 FM	—	—	—	—

Morelos/Morelos
8 REALES

SILVER
c/m: Morelos Type A and C on cast
Mexico City KM#109.

283	ND	1806 TH	—	—	—	—

LCM/MVA-1812
8 REALES

SILVER
c/m: LCM and MVA/1812 on Chihuahua KM#123.

KM#	Date		Good	VG	Fine	VF
292	1812 1810 RP		—	—	—	—

c/m: LCM and MVA 1812 on Chihuahua KM#110.

KM#	Date	Year	Good	VG	Fine	VF
A293	1812	1810 HJ	—	—	—	—

c/m: LCM and MVA 1812 on Chihuahua KM#111.1.

KM#	Date	Year	Good	VG	Fine	VF
293	1812	(1817)	200.00	300.00	550.00	850.00
	1812	(1818)	200.00	300.00	550.00	850.00

NOTE: KM293 represents questionable issues - as the
host date is later than the c/m date. However, there is no
documentation existing to indicate for how long or even
when these c/m's were applied.

L.V.A./Morelos
8 REALES

SILVER
c/m: Script LVA and Morelos monogram Type A
on cast Mexico City KM#110.

KM#	Date	Year	Good	VG	Fine	VF
294	ND		HJ	45.00	75.00	135.00 250.00

SILVER
c/m: L.V.S. and MVA/1812 on Chihuahua KM#111.1.

KM#	Date	Year	Good	VG	Fine	VF
A295	1812	(1817)	400.00	650.00	1000.	1500.

NOTE: KM#295 represents a questionable issue - as the
host date is later than the c/m date. However, there is no
documentation existing to indicate for how long or even
when these c/m's were applied.

M.d.S./S.C.M.
2 REALES

SILVER
c/m: M.d.S. (Militar del Sur) and eagle
w/S.C.M. (Soberano Congreso Mexicano)
on Mexico City 2 Reales.

295	ND		—	250.00	450.00	650.00	—

OSORNO/VILLAGRAN
8 REALES

SILVER
c/m: Osorno monogram and VILLA/GRAN on cast
Mexico City KM#110.

KM#	Date	Year	Good	VG	Fine	VF
296	ND	1809 TH	—	—	—	—

S.J.N.G./VTIL
8 REALES

SILVER
c/m: S.J.N.G. and VTIL on Zacatecas KM#191.

298	ND		—	35.00	50.00	75.00	200.00

EMPIRE OF ITURBIDE
RULERS
Augustin I Iturbide, 1822-1823

MINT MARKS
Mo - Mexico City

ASSAYERS INITIALS
JA - Jose Garcia Ansaldo, 1812-1833
JM - Joaquin Davila Madrid,
 1809-1833

1/8 REAL

COPPER
Mint: Nueva Viscaya

KM#	Date	Mintage	Good	VG	Fine	VF
299	1821	—	22.50	50.00	85.00	150.00
	1822	—	6.00	12.50	25.00	45.00
	1823	—	6.00	12.50	25.00	45.00

1/4 REAL

COPPER
Mint: Nueva Viscaya

KM#	Date	Mintage	Good	VG	Fine	VF
300	1822	—	150.00	275.00	400.00	500.00

1/2 REAL

.903 SILVER
Mint mark: Mo

KM#	Date	Mintage	Fine	VF	XF	Unc
301	1822 JM	—	17.50	30.00	60.00	300.00
	1823 JM	—	12.50	25.00	50.00	250.00

REAL

.903 SILVER
Mint mark: Mo

302	1822 JM	—	50.00	110.00	225.00	800.00

2 REALES

.903 SILVER
Mint mark: Mo

303	1822 JM	—	25.00	55.00	225.00	900.00
	1823 JM	—	20.00	45.00	175.00	800.00

8 REALES

.903 SILVER
Mint mark: Mo

KM#	Date	Mintage	Fine	VF	XF	Unc
304	1822 JM	—	45.00	95.00	250.00	900.00

Obv: Bust similar to 8 Escudos, KM#313.
Rev: Similar to KM#304.

| 305 | 1822 JM | — | — | — | Rare | — |

Type IV. Obv: Similar to KM#308.
Rev: Similar to KM#310.

KM#	Date	Mintage	Fine	VF	XF	Unc
309	1822 JM	—	50.00	125.00	225.00	850.00

Type I. Obv: Leg. divided. Rev: 8 R.J.M. at upper
left of eagle.

| 306.1 | 1822 JM | — | 60.00 | 145.00 | 350.00 | 1300. |

Rev: Cross on crown.

| 306.2 | 1822 JM | — | — | — | Rare | — |

Type II. Obv: Similar to KM#306.
Rev: Similar to KM#310.

| 307 | 1822 JM | — | 135.00 | 325.00 | 550.00 | 2250. |

Type V. Obv. continuous leg. w/short
irregular truncation. Rev: 8 R.J.M. below eagle.

| 310 | 1822 JM | — | 50.00 | 125.00 | 200.00 | 900.00 |
| | 1823 JM | — | 50.00 | 125.00 | 200.00 | 900.00 |

Type VI. Obv: Bust w/long truncation.
Rev: Similar to KM#310.

| 311 | 1822 JM | — | — | — | Rare | — |

4 SCUDOS

Type III. Obv: Continuous leg. w/long smooth
truncation. Rev: Similar to KM#306.

| 308 | 1822 JM | — | 175.00 | 500.00 | 950.00 | 2000. |

NOTE: Variety with long, straight truncation is valued at
$5,000. in uncirculated condition.

.875 GOLD
Mint mark: Mo

KM#	Date	Mintage	Fine	VF	XF	Unc
312	1823 JM	—	1000.	1750.	2750.	4500.

8 SCUDOS

.875 GOLD
Mint mark: Mo
Obv. leg: AUGUSTINUS.

KM#	Date	Mintage	Fine	VF	XF	Unc
313.1	1822 JM	—	1200.	2000.	3250.	

NOTE: Superior Casterline sale 5-89 choice AU realized $11,000.

Obv. leg: AUGSTINUS (error).

313.2	1822 JM	—	1250.	2250.	3750.	—

314	1823 JM	—	1000.	1800.	3000.	4500.

REPUBLIC

MINT MARKS

A, AS - Alamos
CE - Real de Catorce
CA,CH - Chihuahua
C, Cn, Gn(error) - Culiacan
D, Do - Durango
EoMo - Estado de Mexico
Ga - Guadalajara
GC - Guadalupe y Calvo
G, Go - Guanajuato
H, Ho - Hermosillo
M, Mo - Mexico City
O, OA - Oaxaca
SLP, PI, P, I/P - San Luis Potosi
Z, Zs - Zacatecas

ASSAYERS INITIALS

ALAMOS MINT

Initials	Years	Mintmaster
PG	1862-1868	Pascual Gaxiola
DL, L	1866-1879	Domingo Larraguibel
AM	1872-1874	Antonio Moreno
ML, L	1878-1895	Manuel Larraguibel

REAL DE CATORCE MINT

ML	1863	Mariano Leon

CHIHUAHUA MINT

MR	1831-1834	Mariano Cristobal Ramirez
AM	1833-1839	Jose Antonio Mucharraz
MJ	1832	Jose Mariano Jimenez
RG	1839-1856	Rodrigo Garcia
JC	1856-1865	Joaquin Campa
BA	1858	Bruno Arriada
FP	1866	Francisco Potts
JG	1866-1868	Jose Maria Gomez del Campo
MM, M	1868-1895	Manuel Merino
AV	1873-1880	Antonio Valero
EA	1877	Eduardo Avila
JM	1877	Jacobo Mucharraz
GR	1877	Guadalupe Rocha
MG	1880-1882	Manuel Gameros

CULIACAN MINT

CE	1846-1870	Clemente Espinosa de los Monteros
C	1870	???
PV	1860-1861	Pablo Viruega
MP, P	1871-1876	Manuel Onofre Parodi
GP	1876	Celso Gaxiola & Manuel Onofre Parodi
CG, G	1876-1878	Celso Gaxiola
JD, D	1878-1882	Juan Dominguez
AM, M	1882-1899	Antonio Moreno
F	1870	Fernando Ferrari
JQ, Q	1899-1903	Jesus S. Quiroz
FV, V	1903	Francisco Valdez
MH, H	1904	Merced Hernandez
RP, P	1904-1905	Ramon Ponce de Leon

DURANGO MINT

RL	1825-1832	???
RM	1830-1848	Ramon Mascarenas
OMC	1840	Octavio Martinez de Castro
CM	1848-1876	Clemente Moron
JMR	1849-1852,	Jose Maria Ramirez
CP, P	1853-1864, 1867-1873	Carlos Leon de la Pena
LT	1864-1865	???
JMP, P	1877	Carlos Miguel de la Palma
PE, E	1878	Pedro Espejo
TB, B	1878-1880	Trinidad Barrera
JP	1880-1894	J. Miguel Palma
MC, C	1882-1890	Manuel M. Canseco or Melchor Calderon

Initials	Years	Mintmaster
ML	1863	Mariano Leon
JB	1885	Jacobo Blanco
ND, D	1892-1895	Norberto Dominguez

ESTADO DE MEXICO MINT

Initials	Years	Mintmaster
L	1828-1830	Luis Valazquez de la Cadena
F	1828-1830	Francisco Parodi

GUADALAJARA MINT

Initials	Years	Mintmaster
FS	1818-1835	Francisco Suarez
JM	1830-1832	???
JG	1836-1839	Juan de Dios Guzman
	1842-1867	
MC	1839-1846	Manuel Cueras
JM	1867-1869	Jesus P. Manzano
IC, C	1869-1877	Ignacio Canizo y Soto
MC	1874-1875	Manuel Contreras
JA, A	1877-1881	Julio Arancivia
FS, S	1880-1882	Fernando Sayago
TB, B	1883-1884	Trinidad Barrera
AH, H	1884-1885	Antonio Hernandez y Prado
JS, S	1885-1895	Jose S. Schiafino

GUADALUPE Y CALVO MINT

Initials	Years	Mintmaster
MP	1844-1852	Manuel Onofre Parodi

GUANAJUATO MINT

Initials	Years	Mintmaster
JJ	1825-1826	Jose Mariano Jimenez
MJ, MR, JM, PG, PJ, PF		???
PM	1841-1848, 1853-1861	Patrick Murphy
YF	1862-1868	Yldefonso Flores
YE	1862-1863	Ynocencio Espinoza
FR	1870-1878	Faustino Ramirez
SB, RR	???	
RS	1891-1900	Rosendo Sandoval

HERMOSILLO MINT

Initials	Years	Mintmaster
PP	1835-1836	Pedro Peimbert
FM	1871-1876	Florencio Monteverde
MP	1866	Manuel Onofre Parodi
PR	1866-1875	Pablo Rubio
R	1874-1875	Pablo Rubio
GR	1877	Guadalupe Rocha
AF, F	1876-1877	Alejandro Fourcade
JA, A	1877-1883	Jesus Acosta
FM, M	1883-1886	Fernando Mendez
FG, G	1886-1895	Fausto Gaxiola

MEXICO CITY MINT

Because of the great number of assayers for this mint (Mexico City is a much larger mint than any of the others) there is much confusion as to which initial stands for which assayer at any one time. Therefore we feel that it would be of no value to list the assayers.

OAXACA MINT

Initials	Years	Mintmaster
AE	1859-1891	Agustin Endner
E	1889-1890	Agustin Endner
FR	1861-1864	Francisco de la Rosa
EN	1890	Eduardo Navarro Luna
N	1890	Eduardo Navarro Luna

POTOSI MINT

Initials	Years	Mintmaster
JS	1827-1842	Juan Sanabria
AM	1838,1843-1849	Jose Antonio Mucharraz
PS	1842-1843,1848-1849, 1857-1861,1867-1870	Pompaso Sanabria
S	1869-1870	Pomposo Sanabria
MC	1849-1859	Mariano Catano
RO	1859-1865	Romualdo Obregon
MH, H	1870-1885	Manuel Herrera Razo
O	1870-1873	Juan R. Ochoa
CA, G	1867-1870	Carlos Aguirre Gomez
BE, E	1879-1881	Blas Escontria
LC, C	1885-1886	Luis Cuevas
MR, R	1886-1893	Mariano Reyes

ZACATECAS MINT

Initials	Years	Mintmaster
A	1825-1829	Adalco
Z	1825-1826	Mariano Zaldivar
V	1824-1831	Jose Mariano Vela
O	1829-1867	Manuel Ochoa
M	1831-1867	Manuel Miner
VL	1860-1866	Vicente Larranaga
JS	1867-1868, 1876-1886	J.S. de Santa Ana
YH	1868-1874	Ygnacio Hierro
JA	1874-1876	Juan H. Acuna
FZ	1886-1905	Francisco de P. Zarate
FM	1904-1905	Francisco Mateos

State and Federal Issues

1/16 REAL

(Medio Octavo)

COPPER
Mint: Jalisco
Obv. leg: DEPARTAMENTO DE JALISCO

KM#	Date	Mintage	Good	VG	Fine	VF
316	1860	—	3.00	5.00	10.00	50.00

Obv. leg: ESTADO LIBRE DE JALISCO

KM#	Date	Mintage	Good	VG	Fine	VF
317	1861	—	2.50	4.00	8.50	42.50

Mint: Mexico City
Obv. leg: REPUBLICA MEXICANA

KM#	Date	Mintage	VG	Fine	VF	XF
315	1831	—	10.00	15.00	35.00	100.00
	1832/1	—	12.00	17.50	35.00	125.00
	1832	—	10.00	15.00	35.00	100.00
	1833	—	8.50	15.00	35.00	100.00

BRASS

KM#	Date	Mintage	VG	Fine	VF	XF
315a	1832	—	13.50	22.50	60.00	150.00
	1833	—	10.00	17.50	50.00	100.00
	1835	—	400.00	800.00	1250.	2500.

1/8 REAL

(Octavo Real)

COPPER
Mint: Chihuahua
Obv. leg: ESTADO SOBERANO DE CHIHUAHUA

KM#	Date	Mintage	Good	VG	Fine	VF
318	1833	—	—	—	Rare	—
	1834	—	—	—	Rare	—
	1835/3	—	—	—	Rare	—

Obv. leg: ESTADO DE CHIHUAHUA

KM#	Date	Mintage	Good	VG	Fine	VF
319	1855	—	3.50	5.00	18.00	60.00

Mint: Durango
Rev. leg: LIBERTAD

KM#	Date	Mintage	Good	VG	Fine	VF
320	1824	—	5.00	10.00	35.00	100.00
	1828	—	150.00	250.00	400.00	1000.

NOTE: These pieces were frequently struck over 1/8 Real, dated 1821-23 of Nueva Vizcaya. All known examples with these host dates are collectable contemporary counterfeits.

Rev. leg: OCTo.DE.R.DE DO., date.

KM#	Date	Mintage	Good	VG	Fine	VF
321	1828	—	6.00	15.00	35.00	100.00

Obv. leg: ESTADO DE DURANGO

KM#	Date	Mintage	Good	VG	Fine	VF
322	1833	—	—	—	Rare	—

Obv. leg: REPUBLICA MEXICANA

KM#	Date	Mintage	Good	VG	Fine	VF
323	1842/33	—	13.50	20.00	40.00	115.00
	1842	—	8.50	15.00	32.50	100.00

Obv. leg: REPUBLICA MEXICANA
Rev. leg: DEPARTAMENTO DE DURANGO

KM#	Date	Mintage	Good	VG	Fine	VF
324	1845	—	22.50	50.00	100.00	250.00
	1846	—	—	—	Rare	—
	1847	—	3.50	5.00	9.00	32.50

Obv. leg: REPUBLICA MEXICANA
Rev. leg: ESTADO DE DURANGO

KM#	Date	Mintage	Good	VG	Fine	VF
325	1851	—	3.50	6.50	10.00	30.00
	1852/1	—	3.50	6.50	10.00	30.00
	1852	—	3.00	5.00	8.00	30.00
	1854	—	6.00	10.00	17.50	65.00

Mint: Guanajuato
Obv. leg: ESTADO LIBRE DE GUANAJUATO

KM#	Date	Mintage	Good	VG	Fine	VF
326	1829	—	3.00	5.00	10.00	25.00
	1829 error w/GUANJUATO					
		—	4.00	6.50	12.50	27.50
	1830	—	7.50	12.00	20.00	75.00

BRASS, 29mm

KM#	Date	Mintage	Good	VG	Fine	VF
327	1856	—	7.50	12.00	20.00	75.00

25mm

	Date	Mintage	Good	VG	Fine	VF
328	1856	—	3.50	6.00	10.00	30.00
	1857	—	3.50	6.00	10.00	30.00

COPPER

328a	1857	—	8.50	20.00	35.00	60.00

Mint: Jalisco
Obv. leg: ESTADO LIBRE DE JALISCO

	Date	Mintage	Good	VG	Fine	VF
329	1828	—	3.00	5.00	8.00	22.50
	1831	—	100.00	200.00	300.00	400.00
	1832/28	—	3.50	5.50	9.00	25.00
	1832	—	3.50	5.50	9.00	25.00
	1833	—	3.50	5.50	9.00	25.00
	1834	—	50.00	100.00	175.00	300.00

	Date	Mintage	Good	VG	Fine	VF
330	1856	—	4.00	7.00	10.00	25.00
	1857	—	4.00	7.00	10.00	25.00

KM#	Date	Mintage	Good	VG	Fine	VF
330	1858	—	4.00	7.00	10.00	25.00
	1861	—	100.00	200.00	300.00	400.00
	1862/1	—	4.00	7.00	10.00	25.00
	1862	—	4.00	7.00	10.00	25.00

Obv. leg: DEPARTAMENTO DE JALISCO

KM#	Date	Mintage	Good	VG	Fine	VF
331	1858	—	3.25	6.00	9.00	22.50
	1859	—	2.75	5.50	8.00	20.00
	1860/59	—	3.25	6.00	9.00	22.50
	1860	—	3.25	6.00	9.00	22.50
	1862	—	4.50	9.00	22.50	50.00

Mint: Mexico City
27mm
Obv. leg: REPUBLICA MEXICANA

KM#	Date	Mintage	VG	Fine	VF	XF
332	1829	—	450.00	900.00	1500.	2500.

21mm
Obv. leg: REPUBLICA MEXICANA

KM#	Date	Mintage	Good	VG	Fine	VF
333	1829	—	7.50	12.00	25.00	55.00
	1830	—	1.00	2.00	5.00	15.00
	1831	—	1.50	3.50	6.00	20.00
	1832	—	1.50	3.50	6.00	20.00
	1833/2	—	1.50	3.50	6.00	20.00
	1833	—	1.50	2.75	5.00	15.00
	1834	—	1.50	2.75	5.00	15.00
	1835/4	—	1.75	3.50	6.00	20.00
	1835	—	1.50	2.75	5.00	15.00

Obv. leg: LIBERTAD

334	1841	—	6.00	15.00	30.00	75.00
	1842	—	2.50	5.00	10.00	30.00
	1850	—	12.50	20.00	30.00	80.00
	1861	—	5.00	12.00	25.00	70.00

Mint: Occidente
Obv. leg: ESTADO DE OCCIDENTE

KM#	Date	Mintage	Good	VG	Fine	VF
335	1828 reverse S					
		—	13.50	28.50	45.00	100.00
	1829	—	13.50	28.50	45.00	100.00

Mint: Potosi
Obv. leg: ESTADO LIBRE DE SAN LUIS POTOSI

336	1829	—	6.00	9.00	15.00	50.00
	1830	—	8.00	12.00	20.00	60.00
	1831	—	5.00	8.00	12.00	40.00
	1859	—	5.00	8.00	12.00	40.00
	1865/1	—	— Reported, not confirmed			

Mint: Sonora
Obv. leg: ESTO LIBE Y SOBO DE SONORA, 28mm.

KM#	Date	Mintage	Good	VG	Fine	VF
337	1859	—	—	Rare	—	—

Mint: Zacatecas
Obv. leg: ESTo LIBe FEDo DE ZACATECAS

338	1825	—	3.00	5.50	12.00	25.00
	1827	—	3.00	5.50	12.00	25.00
	1827 inverted A for V in OCTAVO					
		—	12.00	20.00	40.00	100.00
	1829	—	—	—	Rare	—
	1830	—	2.75	5.00	8.00	20.00
	1831	—	4.50	6.75	13.50	27.50
	1832	—	2.75	5.00	8.00	20.00
	1833	—	2.75	5.00	8.00	20.00
	1835	—	3.50	6.00	10.00	25.00
	1846	—	3.50	6.00	10.00	25.00
	1851	—	125.00	175.00	250.00	350.00
	1852	—	3.50	6.00	10.00	25.00
	1858	—	2.75	5.00	8.00	20.00
	1859	—	2.75	5.00	8.00	20.00
	1862	—	2.75	5.00	8.00	20.00
	1863 reversed 6 in date					
		—	2.75	5.00	8.00	20.00

Obv. leg: DEPARTAMENTO DE ZACATECAS

339	1836	—	4.00	8.00	15.00	40.00
	1845	—	6.00	10.00	20.00	50.00
	1846	—	5.00	9.00	18.50	45.00

1/4 REAL
(Un Quarto/Una Quartilla)
(Copper/Brass Series)

COPPER
Mint: Chihuahua
Obv. leg: ESTADO SOBERANO DE CHIHUAHUA

KM#	Date	Mintage	Good	VG	Fine	VF
340	1833	—	8.00	12.00	35.00	75.00
	1834	—	6.00	10.00	25.00	55.00
	1835	—	5.00	8.00	12.00	50.00

Obv. leg: ESTADO LIBRE DE CHIHUAHUA

KM#	Date	Mintage	Good	VG	Fine	VF
341	1846	—	3.50	6.00	12.00	50.00

NOTE: Varieties with or without fraction bar.

Obv. leg: ESTADO DE CHIHUAHUA

342	1855	—	2.50	5.00	11.50	50.00
	1856	—	2.50	5.00	11.50	50.00

Obv. leg: DEPARTAMENTO DE CHIHUAHUA

343	1855	—	3.00	5.00	10.00	50.00
	1855 DE (reversed D)	—	3.00	5.00	10.00	50.00

Obv. leg: E. CHIHA LIBERTAD

344	1860	—	2.00	4.00	8.00	25.00
	1861	—	2.00	4.00	8.00	25.00
	1865/1	—	2.50	5.50	10.00	30.00
	1865	—	10.00	20.00	35.00	95.00
	1866/5	—	10.00	20.00	35.00	95.00
	1866	—	2.00	4.00	8.00	25.00

Mint: Durango
Obv. leg: REPUBLICA MEXICANA

KM#	Date	Mintage	Good	VG	Fine	VF
345	1845	—	—	—	Rare	—

Rev: DURANGO, date, value.

KM#	Date	Mintage	Good	VG	Fine	VF
346	1858	—	—	—	Rare	—

Obv. leg: ESTADO DE DURANGO
Rev. leg: CONSTITUCION

347	1858	—	3.00	6.50	13.50	50.00

NOTE: Variety exists in brass.

Obv. leg: DEPARTAMENTO DE DURANGO
Rev. leg: LIBERTAD EN EL ORDEN.

348	1860	—	2.00	5.00	13.50	38.50
	1866	—	2.00	5.00	13.50	38.50

Obv. leg: ESTADO DE DURANGO
Rev. leg: INDEPENDENCIA Y LIBERTAD

349	1866	—	2.75	6.00	15.00	45.00

Rev. leg: SUFRAGIO LIBRE

350	1872	—	2.00	4.00	10.00	22.50

NOTE: Variety exists in brass.

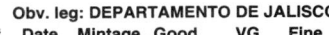

Obv. leg: DEPARTAMENTO DE JALISCO

KM#	Date	Mintage	Good	VG	Fine	VF
354	1836	—	—	—	Rare	—

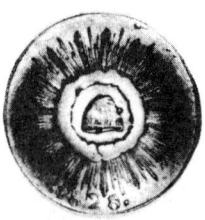

Mint: Guanajuato
Obv. leg: ESTADO LIBRE DE GUANAJUATO

KM#	Date	Mintage	Good	VG	Fine	VF
351	1828	—	3.75	7.00	11.00	40.00
	1828 error w/GUANJUATO					
		—	3.75	7.00	11.00	40.00
	1829	—	4.50	9.00	13.50	40.00

Obv. leg: EST. LIB. DE GUANAXUATO
Rev. leg: OMNIA VINCIT LABOR

352	1856	—	12.00	25.00	50.00	100.00
	1857	—	6.00	9.00	15.00	45.00

BRASS

352a	1856	—	3.25	6.75	11.00	27.50
	1857	—	3.25	6.75	11.00	27.50

COPPER
Mint: Jalisco
Obv. leg: ESTADO LIBRE DE JALISCO

353	1828	—	3.25	6.00	12.00	35.00
	1829/8	—	2.50	5.00	8.00	35.00
	1829	—	2.50	5.00	8.00	35.00
	1830/20	—	2.50	5.00	8.00	30.00
	1830/29	—	2.50	5.00	8.00	30.00
	1830	—	2.50	5.00	8.00	30.00
	1831	—	—	—	Rare	—
	1832/20	—	2.50	5.00	8.00	30.00
	1832/28	—	2.50	5.00	8.00	30.00
	1832	—	2.50	5.00	8.00	30.00
	1833/2	—	2.50	5.00	8.00	30.00
	1834	—	2.50	5.00	8.00	30.00
	1835/3	—	2.50	5.00	8.00	30.00
	1835	—	2.50	5.00	8.00	30.00
	1836	—	—	—	Rare	—

Obv. leg: ESTADO LIBRE DE JALISCO

KM#	Date	Mintage	Good	VG	Fine	VF
355	1858	—	3.00	5.00	8.00	20.00
	1861	—	3.00	5.00	10.00	25.00
	1862	—	3.00	5.00	8.00	20.00

Obv. leg: DEPARTAMENTO DE JALISCO

356	1858	—	3.00	5.00	8.00	20.00
	1859/8	—	3.00	5.00	8.00	20.00
	1859	—	3.00	5.00	8.00	20.00
	1860	—	3.00	5.00	8.00	20.00

Mint: Mexico City
Obv. leg: REPUBLICA MEXICANA.

KM#	Date	Mintage	VG	Fine	VF	XF
357	1829	—	7.00	22.50	50.00	135.00

Reduced size.

358	1829	—	12.00	25.00	50.00	150.00
	1830	—	1.50	2.75	4.50	10.00
	1831	—	1.50	2.75	4.50	10.00
	1832	—	5.50	10.00	20.00	35.00
	1833	—	1.50	2.75	4.50	10.00
	1834/3	—	1.50	2.75	4.50	10.00
	1834	—	1.50	2.75	4.50	10.00
	1835	—	1.50	2.75	4.50	10.00
	1836	—	1.50	2.75	4.50	10.00
	1837	—	6.50	13.50	22.50	45.00

BRASS
c/m: JM

KM#	Date	Mintage	VG	Fine	VF	XF
358a.1	1831	—	8.00	15.00	35.00	75.00

W/o countermark

358a.2	1831	—	—	—	—	—

COPPER
Mint: Potosi
Obv. leg: ESTADO LIBRE DE SAN LUIS POTOSI
Rev. leg: MEXICO LIBRE

KM#	Date	Mintage	Good	VG	Fine	VF
359	1828	—	2.50	4.00	6.75	15.00
	1829	—	2.50	4.00	6.75	15.00
	1830		2.50	4.00	6.75	15.00
	1832	—	2.50	4.00	6.75	15.00
	1859 large LIBRE					
		—	2.50	4.00	6.75	15.00
	1859 small LIBRE					
		—	2.50	4.00	6.75	15.00
	1860	—	2.50	4.00	6.75	15.00

Rev. leg: REPUBLICA MEXICANA

360	1862	1,367	2.50	4.00	6.75	13.50
	1862 LIBR					
	Inc. Ab.		2.50	4.00	6.75	13.50

Milled edge
Obv. leg: ESTADO LIBRE Y SOBERANO DE
S.L. POTOSI
Rev. leg: LIBERTAD Y REFORMA

361	1867	3.177	2.50	3.75	7.00	18.50
	1867 AFG I.A.		2.50	3.75	7.00	18.50

Plain edge

362	1867	Inc. Ab.	2.50	3.75	7.00	18.50
	1867 AFG I.A.		2.50	3.75	7.00	18.50

Mint: Sinaloa
Obv. leg: ESTADO LIBRE Y SOBERANO
DE SINALOA

KM#	Date	Mintage	Good	VG	Fine	VF
363	1847	—	3.50	5.50	9.00	20.00
	1848	—	3.50	5.50	9.00	20.00
	1859	—	3.00	4.50	6.00	13.50
	1861	—	1.50	3.00	4.00	9.00
	1862	—	1.50	3.00	4.00	9.00
	1863	—	2.50	4.00	5.00	10.00
	1864/3	—	2.50	4.00	5.00	10.00
	1864	—	1.50	3.00	4.00	9.00
	1865	—	3.00	5.50	7.00	15.00
	1866/5	7.401	2.50	3.50	5.00	10.00
	1866	Inc. Ab.	1.50	3.00	4.00	9.00

BRASS

363a	1847	—	5.00	10.00	20.00	50.00

COPPER
Mint: Sonora
Obv. leg: EST.D.SONORA UNA CUART

364	1831	—	—	—	Rare	—
	1832	—	3.00	5.00	13.50	50.00
	1833/2	—	2.00	4.00	11.00	37.50
	1833	—	2.00	4.00	11.00	37.50
	1834	—	2.00	4.00	11.00	37.50
	1835/3	—	2.00	4.00	11.00	37.50
	1835	—	2.00	4.00	11.00	37.50
	1836	—	2.00	4.00	11.00	37.50

Obv. leg: ESTO.LIBE.Y SOBO.DE SONORA

365	1859	—	2.00	5.00	8.00	20.00
	1861/59	—	3.00	6.50	11.00	25.00
	1861	—	2.00	5.00	8.00	20.00
	1862	—	2.00	5.00	8.00	20.00
	1863/2	—	6.00	15.00	30.00	50.00

BRASS
Mint: Zacatecas
Obv. leg: ESTO LIBE FEDO DE ZACATECAS

KM#	Date	Mintage	Good	VG	Fine	VF
366	1824	—	—	—	Rare	—
	1825	—	2.50	5.00	8.00	20.00
	1826	—	100.00	150.00	200.00	300.00
	1827/17	—	2.50	5.00	8.00	20.00
	1829	—	2.50	5.00	8.00	20.00
	1830	—	2.50	5.00	8.00	20.00
	1831	—	50.00	100.00	125.00	250.00
	1832	—	2.50	5.00	8.00	20.00
	1833	—	2.50	5.00	8.00	20.00
	1834	—	—	—	Rare	—
	1835	—	2.50	5.00	8.00	20.00
	1846	—	2.50	5.00	8.00	20.00

KM#	Date	Mintage	Good	VG	Fine	VF
366	1847	—	2.50	5.00	8.00	20.00
	1852	—	2.50	5.00	8.00	20.00
	1853	—	2.50	5.00	8.00	20.00
	1855	—	4.50	10.00	20.00	65.00
	1858	—	2.50	5.00	8.00	20.00
	1859	—	2.50	5.00	8.00	20.00
	1860	—	100.00	150.00	200.00	300.00
	1862/57	—	2.50	5.00	8.00	20.00
	1862/59/7	—	10.00	20.00	40.00	80.00
	1862	—	2.50	5.00	8.00	20.00
	1863/2	—	2.50	5.00	8.00	20.00
	1863	—	2.50	5.00	8.00	20.00
	1864/58	—	4.00	10.00	25.00	60.00

COPPER
Obv. leg: DEPARTAMENTO DE ZACATECAS

			Good	VG	Fine	VF
367	1836	—	4.00	8.50	13.50	25.00
	1845	—	—	—	Rare	—
	1846	—	3.50	6.75	9.00	20.00

SILVER SERIES

0.8450 g, .903 SILVER, .0245 oz ASW
Mint mark: CA

KM#	Date	Mintage	VG	Fine	VF	XF
368	1843 RG	—	75.00	125.00	300.00	500.00

Mint mark: C

368.1	1855 LR	—	50.00	100.00	200.00	400.00

Mint mark: Do

368.2	1842 LR	—	12.00	20.00	40.00	125.00
	1843 LR	—	20.00	25.00	60.00	150.00

Mint mark: Ga

368.3	1842 JG	—	2.50	5.50	8.00	20.00
	1843/2 JG	—	—	—	—	—
	1843 JG	—	6.00	9.00	12.50	30.00
	1843 MC	—	4.00	6.50	9.00	25.00
	1844 MC	—	4.00	6.50	9.00	25.00
	1844 LR	—	2.50	5.00	7.50	15.00
	1845 LR	—	2.50	4.50	7.50	15.00
	1846 LR	—	5.00	8.00	10.00	25.00
	1847 LR	—	4.00	6.50	9.00	25.00
	1848 LR	—	—	—	Rare	—
	1850 LR	—	—	—	Rare	—
	1851 LR	—	6.00	10.00	20.00	50.00
	1852 LR	—	50.00	100.00	135.00	200.00
	1854/3 LR	—	50.00	100.00	135.00	200.00
	1854 LR	—	5.00	10.00	12.50	30.00
	1855 LR	—	5.00	8.00	10.00	30.00
	1857 LR	—	6.50	10.00	15.00	27.50
	1862 LR	—	5.50	10.00	15.00	30.00

Mint mark: GC

KM#	Date	Mintage	VG	Fine	VF	XF
368.4	1844 LR	—	50.00	75.00	125.00	200.00

Mint mark: Go

368.5	1842 PM	—	4.00	6.00	10.00	20.00
	1842 LR	—	2.00	4.00	8.00	15.00
	1843/2 LR	—	4.00	6.00	10.00	20.00
	1843 LR	—	2.00	4.00	8.00	15.00
	1844/3 LR	—	—	—	—	—
	1844 LR	—	2.00	4.00	8.00	15.00
	1845 LR	—	8.00	15.00	30.00	60.00
	1846/5 LR	—	—	—	—	—
	1846 LR	—	4.00	6.00	10.00	20.00

KM#	Date	Mintage	VG	Fine	VF	XF
368.5	1847 LR	—	2.00	4.00	8.00	15.00
	1848/7 LR	—	2.00	4.00	8.00	15.00
	1848 LR	—	2.00	4.00	8.00	15.00
	1849/7 LR	—	8.00	15.00	30.00	60.00
	1849 LR	—	2.00	4.00	8.00	15.00
	1850 LR	—	2.00	4.00	8.00	15.00
	1851 LR	—	2.00	4.00	8.00	15.00
	1852 LR	—	2.00	4.00	8.00	15.00
	1853 LR	—	2.00	4.00	8.00	15.00
	1855 LR	—	4.00	8.00	15.00	30.00
	1856/4 LR	—	—	—	—	—
	1856 LR	—	5.00	10.00	20.00	35.00
	1862/1 LR	—	3.00	5.00	10.00	20.00
	1862 LR	—	2.00	4.00	8.00	15.00
	1863 LR	—	2.00	4.00	8.00	15.00

Mint mark: Mo

368.6	1842 LR	—	2.00	4.00	8.00	15.00
	1843 LR	—	2.00	4.00	8.00	15.00
	1844/3 LR	—	8.00	12.00	20.00	40.00
	1844 LR	—	4.00	6.00	10.00	20.00
	1845 LR	—	4.00	6.00	10.00	20.00
	1846 LR	—	2.00	4.00	8.00	15.00
	1850 LR	—	5.00	10.00	20.00	35.00
	1858 LR	—	4.00	8.00	15.00	30.00
	1859 LR	—	4.00	6.00	10.00	20.00
	1860 LR	—	4.00	6.00	10.00	20.00
	1861 LR	—	4.00	6.00	10.00	20.00
	1862 LR	—	4.00	6.00	10.00	20.00
	1863/53 LR	—	—	—	—	—
	1863 LR	—	4.00	6.00	10.00	20.00

Mint mark: S.L.Pi

368.7	1842	—	2.00	4.00	8.00	15.00
	1843/2	—	4.00	6.00	10.00	20.00
	1843	—	2.00	4.00	8.00	15.00
	1844	—	2.00	4.00	8.00	15.00
	1845/3	—	4.00	6.00	10.00	25.00
	1845/4	—	4.00	6.00	10.00	25.00
	1845	—	2.00	4.00	8.00	15.00
	1847/5	—	4.00	6.00	10.00	20.00
	1847	—	2.00	4.00	8.00	15.00
	1851/47	—	4.00	8.00	15.00	30.00
	1854	—	125.00	200.00	275.00	400.00
	1856	—	4.00	8.00	15.00	30.00
	1857	—	5.00	10.00	20.00	35.00
	1862/57	—	10.00	20.00	40.00	85.00

Mint mark: Zs

368.8	1842/1 LR	—	4.00	8.00	15.00	30.00
	1842 LR	—	4.00	6.00	10.00	20.00

1/2 REAL

1.6900 g, .903 SILVER, .0490 oz ASW
Mint mark: Mo
Obv: Hooked-neck eagle.

KM#	Date	Mintage	Fine	VF	XF	Unc
369	1824 JM	—	40.00	60.00	125.00	500.00

Mint mark: A

KM#	Date	Mintage	Fine	VF	XF	Unc
370	1862 PG	—	—	—	Rare	—

Mint mark: Ca
Obv: Facing eagle.

370.1	1844 RG	—	75.00	125.00	175.00	275.00
	1845 RG	—	75.00	125.00	150.00	250.00

KM#	Date	Mintage	Fine	VF	XF	Unc
		Mint mark: C, Co				
370.2	1846 CE	—	30.00	50.00	75.00	150.00
	1848/7 CE	—	15.00	25.00	45.00	90.00
	1849/8 CE	—	15.00	25.00	45.00	90.00
	1849 CE	—	—	—	—	—
	1852 CE	—	12.50	20.00	40.00	80.00
	1853/1 CE	—	12.50	20.00	40.00	80.00
	1854 CE	—	20.00	35.00	50.00	100.00
	1856 CE	—	12.50	20.00	40.00	80.00
	1857/6 CE	—	20.00	35.00	50.00	100.00
	1857 CE	—	15.00	25.00	45.00	90.00
	1858 CE (error 1 for 1/2)					
		—	12.50	20.00	40.00	80.00
	1860/59 PV	—	20.00	35.00	50.00	100.00
	1860 PV	—	12.50	20.00	40.00	80.00
	1861 PV	—	12.50	20.00	40.00	80.00
	1863 CE (error 1 for 1/2)					
		—	15.00	25.00	45.00	90.00
	1867 CE	—	12.50	20.00	40.00	80.00
	1869 CE (error 1 for 1/2)					
		—	12.50	20.00	40.00	80.00
		Mint mark: D, Do				
370.3	1832 RM	—	125.00	225.00	350.00	600.00
	1832 RM/L	—	—	—	—	—
	1833/2 RM/L					
		—	75.00	100.00	150.00	225.00
	1833/1 RM/L					
		—	12.50	20.00	40.00	80.00
	1833 RM	—	25.00	40.00	75.00	150.00
	1834/1 RM	—	25.00	40.00	75.00	150.00
	1834 RM	—	12.50	20.00	40.00	80.00
	1837/1 RM	—	12.50	20.00	40.00	80.00
	1837/4 RM	—	12.50	20.00	40.00	80.00
	1837/6 RM	—	12.50	20.00	40.00	80.00
	1841/33 RM	—	15.00	25.00	50.00	100.00
	1842/32 RM	—	12.50	20.00	40.00	80.00
	1842 RM	—	12.50	20.00	40.00	80.00
	1842 RM 8R (error)					
		—	12.50	20.00	40.00	80.00
	1842 RM 1/2/8R					
		—	12.50	20.00	40.00	80.00
	1843/33 RM	—	15.00	25.00	50.00	100.00
	1843 RM	—	—	—	—	—
	1845/31 RM	—	12.50	20.00	40.00	80.00
	1845/34 RM	—	12.50	20.00	40.00	80.00
	1845/35 RM	—	12.50	20.00	40.00	80.00
	1845 RM	—	15.00	25.00	50.00	100.00
	1846 RM	—	30.00	50.00	80.00	200.00
	1848/5 RM	—	35.00	55.00	110.00	250.00
	1848/36 RM	—	25.00	40.00	75.00	200.00
	1849 JMR	—	25.00	40.00	75.00	200.00
	1850 RM	—	—	Rare	—
	1850 JMR	—	25.00	40.00	75.00	200.00
	1851 JMR	—	20.00	35.00	50.00	100.00
	1852/1 JMR	—	65.00	125.00	250.00	600.00
	1852 JMR	—	30.00	50.00	80.00	200.00
	1853 CP	—	12.50	20.00	40.00	80.00
	1854 CP	—	25.00	40.00	75.00	200.00
	1855 CP	—	25.00	40.00	60.00	150.00
	1856/5 CP	—	20.00	35.00	50.00	100.00
	1857 CP	—	20.00	35.00	50.00	100.00
	1858/7 CP	—	20.00	35.00	50.00	100.00
	1859 CP	—	20.00	35.00	50.00	100.00
	1860/59 CP	—	40.00	65.00	135.00	300.00
	1861 CP	—	125.00	200.00	300.00	600.00
	1862 CP	—	25.00	40.00	60.00	125.00
	1864 LT	—	50.00	100.00	200.00	450.00
	1869 CP	—	40.00	65.00	125.00	275.00

KM#	Date	Mintage	Fine	VF	XF	Unc
		Mint mark: EoMo				
370.4	1829 LF	—	175.00	300.00	500.00	1400
		Mint mark: Ga				
370.5	1825 FS	—	25.00	40.00	75.00	150.00
	1826 FS	—	10.00	15.00	35.00	80.00
	1828/7 FS	—	12.50	20.00	40.00	90.00
	1829 FS	—	7.50	15.00	30.00	70.00
	1830/29 FS	—	40.00	60.00	100.00	200.00
	1831 LP	—	—	Rare	—
	1832 FS	—	10.00	20.00	35.00	80.00
	1834/3 FS	—	65.00	100.00	175.00	250.00
	1834 FS	—	10.00	20.00	35.00	80.00
	1835/4/3 FS/LP					

KM#	Date	Mintage	Fine	VF	XF	Unc
370.5		—	15.00	25.00	40.00	90.00
	1837/6 JG	—	50.00	100.00	150.00	250.00
	1838/7 JG	—	15.00	25.00	40.00	90.00
	1839/8 JG/FS					
		—	35.00	75.00	150.00	250.00
	1839 MC	—	10.00	20.00	35.00	80.00
	1840/39 MC/JG					
		—	—	—	—	—
	1840 MC	—	15.00	25.00	40.00	90.00
	1841 MC	—	20.00	35.00	50.00	100.00
	1842/1 JG	—	15.00	25.00	40.00	90.00
	1842 JG	—	10.00	20.00	35.00	80.00
	1843/2 JG	—	15.00	30.00	50.00	100.00
	1843 JG	—	10.00	20.00	35.00	80.00
	1843 MC/JG	—	10.00	20.00	35.00	80.00
	1843 MC	—	10.00	20.00	35.00	80.00
	1844 MC	—	10.00	20.00	35.00	80.00
	1845 MC	—	10.00	20.00	35.00	80.00
	1845 JG	—	10.00	20.00	35.00	80.00
	1846 MC	—	10.00	20.00	35.00	80.00
	1846 JG	—	10.00	20.00	35.00	80.00
	1847 JG	—	10.00	20.00	35.00	80.00
	1848/7 JG	—	10.00	20.00	35.00	80.00
	1849 JG	—	10.00	20.00	35.00	80.00
	1850/49 JG	—	—	—	—	—
	1850 JG	—	10.00	20.00	35.00	80.00
	1851/0 JG	—	10.00	20.00	35.00	80.00
	1852 JG	—	10.00	20.00	35.00	80.00
	1853 JG	—	10.00	20.00	35.00	80.00
	1854 JG	—	10.00	20.00	35.00	80.00
	1855/4 JG	—	10.00	20.00	35.00	80.00
	1855 JG	—	10.00	20.00	35.00	80.00
	1856 JG	—	10.00	20.00	35.00	80.00
	1857 JG	—	10.00	20.00	35.00	80.00
	1858/7 JG	—	10.00	20.00	35.00	80.00
	1858 JG	—	10.00	20.00	35.00	80.00
	1859/7 JG	—	10.00	20.00	35.00	80.00
	1860/59 JG	—	10.00	20.00	35.00	80.00
	1861 JG	—	5.00	12.50	25.00	60.00
	1862/1 JG	—	15.00	25.00	40.00	90.00
		Mint mark: GC				
370.6	1844 MP	—	50.00	100.00	150.00	350.00
	1845 MP	—	25.00	50.00	100.00	200.00
	1846 MP	—	25.00	50.00	100.00	200.00
	1847 MP	—	25.00	50.00	100.00	300.00
	1848 MP	—	20.00	40.00	75.00	150.00
	1849 MP	—	25.00	50.00	100.00	200.00
	1850 MP	—	30.00	60.00	125.00	250.00
	1851 MP	—	25.00	50.00	100.00	200.00
		Mint mark: Go				
370.7	1826 MJ	—	125.00	250.00	400.00	1000.
	1827/6 MJ	—	7.50	15.00	30.00	75.00
	1828/7 MJ	—	7.50	15.00	30.00	75.00
	1828 MJ denomination 2/1					
		—	—	—	—	—
	1828 JG	—	—	—	—	—
	1828 MR	—	50.00	100.00	150.00	250.00
	1829/8 MJ	—	5.00	10.00	25.00	50.00
	1829 MJ	—	5.00	10.00	25.00	50.00
	1829 MJ reversed N in MEXICANA					
		—	5.00	10.00	25.00	50.00
	1830 MJ	—	5.00	10.00	25.00	50.00
	1831/29 MJ	—	15.00	30.00	60.00	150.00
	1831 MJ	—	10.00	20.00	40.00	80.00
	1832/1 MJ	—	7.50	15.00	30.00	75.00
	1832 MJ	—	7.50	15.00	30.00	75.00
	1833 MJ round top 3					
		—	10.00	20.00	40.00	80.00
	1833 MJ flat top 3					
		—	10.00	20.00	40.00	80.00
	1834 PJ	—	5.00	10.00	25.00	50.00
	1835 PJ	—	5.00	10.00	25.00	50.00
	1836/5 PJ	—	7.50	15.00	30.00	75.00
	1836 PJ	—	5.00	10.00	25.00	50.00
	1837 PJ	—	5.00	10.00	25.00	50.00
	1838/7 PJ	—	5.00	10.00	25.00	50.00
	1839 PJ	—	5.00	10.00	25.00	50.00
	1839 PJ (error: REPUBLIGA)					
		—	5.00	10.00	25.00	50.00
	1840/39 PJ	—	7.50	10.00	25.00	75.00
	1840 PJ straight J					
		—	5.00	10.00	25.00	50.00

KM#	Date	Mintage	Fine	VF	XF	Unc
370.7	1840 PJ curved J					
		—	5.00	10.00	25.00	50.00
	1841/31 PJ	—	5.00	10.00	25.00	50.00
	1841 PJ	—	5.00	10.00	25.00	50.00
	1842/1 PJ	—	5.00	10.00	25.00	50.00
	1842/1 PM	—	5.00	10.00	25.00	50.00
	1842 PM/J	—	5.00	10.00	25.00	50.00
	1842 PJ	—	5.00	10.00	25.00	50.00
	1842 PM	—	5.00	10.00	25.00	50.00
	1843/33 PM 1/2 over 8					
		—	5.00	10.00	25.00	50.00
	1843 PM convex wings					
		—	5.00	10.00	25.00	50.00
	1843 PM concave wings					
		—	5.00	10.00	25.00	50.00
	1844/3 PM	—	5.00	10.00	25.00	50.00
	1844 PM	—	10.00	20.00	40.00	90.00
	1845/4 PM	—	5.00	10.00	25.00	50.00
	1845 PM	—	5.00	10.00	25.00	50.00
	1846/4 PM	—	5.00	10.00	25.00	50.00
	1846/5 PM	—	5.00	10.00	25.00	50.00
	1846 PM	—	5.00	10.00	25.00	50.00
	1847/6 PM	—	7.50	15.00	30.00	60.00
	1847 PM	—	7.50	15.00	30.00	60.00
	1848/35 PM	—	5.00	10.00	25.00	50.00
	1848 PM	—	5.00	10.00	25.00	50.00
	1848 PF/M	—	5.00	10.00	25.00	50.00
	1849/39 PF	—	5.00	10.00	25.00	50.00
	1849 PF	—	5.00	10.00	25.00	50.00
	1849 PF (error: MEXCANA)					
		—	5.00	10.00	25.00	50.00
	1850 PF	—	5.00	10.00	25.00	50.00
	1851 PF	—	5.00	10.00	25.00	50.00
	1852/1 PF	—	5.00	10.00	25.00	50.00
	1852 PF	—	2.50	7.50	17.50	40.00
	1853 PF/R	—	5.00	10.00	25.00	50.00
	1853 PF	—	5.00	10.00	25.00	50.00
	1854 PF	—	5.00	10.00	25.00	50.00
	1855 PF	—	5.00	10.00	25.00	50.00
	1856/4 PF	—	5.00	10.00	25.00	50.00
	1856/5 PF	—	5.00	10.00	25.00	50.00
	1856 PF	—	5.00	10.00	25.00	50.00
	1857/6 PF	—	5.00	10.00	25.00	50.00
	1857 PF	—	5.00	10.00	25.00	50.00
	1858/7 PF	—	7.50	15.00	30.00	60.00
	1858 PF	—	5.00	10.00	25.00	50.00
	1859 PF	—	5.00	10.00	25.00	50.00
	1860 PF small 1/2					
		—	5.00	10.00	25.00	50.00
	1860 PF large 1/2					
		—	5.00	10.00	25.00	50.00
	1860/59 PF	—	5.00	10.00	25.00	50.00
	1861 PF small 1/2					
		—	5.00	10.00	25.00	50.00
	1861 PF large 1/2					
		—	5.00	10.00	25.00	50.00
	1862/1 YE	—	5.00	10.00	25.00	50.00
	1862 YE	—	2.50	7.50	17.50	40.00
	1862 YF	—	5.00	10.00	25.00	50.00
	1867 YF	—	2.50	7.50	17.50	40.00
	1868 YF	—	2.50	7.50	17.50	40.00

NOTE: Varieties exist.

Mint mark: Ho

KM#	Date	Mintage	Fine	VF	XF	Unc
370.8	1839 PP	—	—	—	Unique	—
	1862 FM	—	500.00	650.00	1000.	—
	1867 PR/FM 6/inverted 6, & 7/1					
		—	100.00	175.00	250.00	500.00

Mint mark: Mo

KM#	Date	Mintage	Fine	VF	XF	Unc
370.9	1825 JM	—	10.00	20.00	40.00	80.00
	1826/5 JM	—	10.00	20.00	40.00	80.00
370.9	1826 JM	—	5.00	10.00	20.00	60.00
	1827/6 JM	—	5.00	10.00	20.00	60.00
	1827 JM	—	5.00	10.00	20.00	60.00
	1828/7 JM	—	7.50	15.00	25.00	85.00
	1828 JM	—	10.00	20.00	40.00	90.00
	1829 JM	—	7.50	15.00	25.00	75.00
	1830 JM	—	5.00	10.00	20.00	60.00
	1831 JM	—	5.00	10.00	20.00	60.00
	1832 JM	—	7.50	12.50	27.50	60.00
	1833 MJ	—	7.50	12.50	27.50	60.00
	1834 ML	—	5.00	10.00	20.00	60.00
	1835 ML	—	5.00	10.00	20.00	60.00
	1836/5 ML/MF					

KM#	Date	Mintage	Fine	VF	XF	Unc
370.9		—	7.50	15.00	25.00	65.00
	1836 ML	—	7.50	15.00	25.00	65.00
	1838 ML	—	5.00	10.00	20.00	60.00
	1839/8 ML	—	5.00	10.00	25.00	65.00
	1839 ML	—	5.00	10.00	20.00	50.00
	1840 ML	—	5.00	10.00	20.00	50.00
	1841 ML	—	5.00	10.00	20.00	50.00
	1842 ML	—	5.00	10.00	20.00	50.00
	1842 MM	—	5.00	10.00	20.00	50.00
	1843 MM	—	10.00	20.00	40.00	80.00
	1844 MF	—	5.00	10.00	20.00	50.00
	1845/4 MF	—	5.00	10.00	25.00	60.00
	1845 MF	—	5.00	10.00	20.00	50.00
	1846 MF	—	5.00	10.00	20.00	50.00
	1847 RC	—	10.00	20.00	40.00	80.00
	1848/7 GC/RC					
		—	5.00	10.00	20.00	50.00
	1849 GC	—	5.00	10.00	20.00	50.00
	1850 GC	—	5.00	10.00	20.00	50.00
	1851 GC	—	5.00	10.00	20.00	50.00
	1852 GC	—	5.00	10.00	20.00	50.00
	1853 GC	—	5.00	10.00	20.00	50.00
	1854 GC	—	5.00	10.00	20.00	50.00
	1855 GC	—	5.00	10.00	20.00	50.00
	1855 GF/GC	—	7.50	12.50	25.00	65.00
	1856/5 GF	—	7.50	12.50	25.00	65.00
	1857 GF	—	5.00	10.00	20.00	50.00
	1858 FH	—	3.00	5.00	12.50	40.00
	1858/9 FH	—	5.00	10.00	20.00	50.00
	1859 FH	—	3.00	6.00	15.00	50.00
	1860 FH/GC					
		—	5.00	10.00	20.00	50.00
	1860/59 FH	—	7.50	12.50	25.00	65.00
	1860 FH	—	3.00	6.00	15.00	50.00
	1860 TH	—	5.00	10.00	20.00	50.00
	1861 CH	—	3.00	6.00	15.00	45.00
	1862/52 CH	—	5.00	10.00	20.00	50.00
	1862 CH	—	3.00	6.00	15.00	45.00
	1863/55 TH/GC					
		—	5.00	10.00	20.00	50.00
	1863 CH/GC	—	5.00	10.00	20.00	50.00
	1863 CH	—	3.00	6.00	15.00	45.00

Mint mark: Pi

KM#	Date	Mintage	Fine	VF	XF	Unc
370.10	1831 JS	—	7.50	12.50	25.00	65.00
	1841/36 JS	—	20.00	40.00	75.00	125.00
	1842/1 PS	—	20.00	40.00	75.00	125.00
	1842/1 PS P/J					
		—	60.00	80.00	150.00	300.00
	1842 PS/JS	—	50.00	75.00	125.00	250.00
	1842 JS	—	20.00	40.00	75.00	125.00
	1843/2 PS	—	17.50	25.00	40.00	80.00
	1843 PS	—	15.00	25.00	35.00	70.00
	1843 AM	—	10.00	15.00	25.00	60.00
	1844 AM	—	10.00	15.00	30.00	65.00
	1845 AM	—	250.00	375.00	500.00	1500.
	1846/5 AM	—	40.00	75.00	125.00	200.00
	1847/6 AM	—	15.00	25.00	40.00	80.00
	1848 AM	—	15.00	25.00	40.00	80.00
	1849 MC/AM	—	15.00	25.00	40.00	80.00
	1849 MC	—	12.50	20.00	35.00	70.00
	1850/49 MC	—	—	—	—	—
	1850Pi MC	—	10.00	15.00	25.00	60.00
	1850P MC	—	—	—	—	—
	1851 MC	—	10.00	15.00	25.00	60.00
	1852 MC	—	10.00	20.00	30.00	65.00
	1853 MC	—	7.50	12.50	20.00	60.00
	1854 MC	—	7.50	12.50	20.00	60.00
	1855 MC	—	15.00	20.00	35.00	70.00
	1856 MC	—	15.00	25.00	50.00	100.00
	1857 MC	—	7.50	12.50	20.00	60.00
370.10	1857 PS	—	10.00	15.00	30.00	65.00
	1858 MC	—	12.50	20.00	35.00	70.00
	1858 PS	—	12.50	20.00	35.00	70.00
	1859 MC	—	—	—	Rare	—
	1860/59 PS	—	12.50	20.00	35.00	70.00
	1861 RO	—	10.00	15.00	30.00	60.00
	1862/1 RO	—	15.00	25.00	50.00	125.00
	1862 RO	—	15.00	25.00	50.00	125.00
	1863/2 RO	—	15.00	25.00	45.00	100.00

Mint mark: Z, Zs

KM#	Date	Mintage	Fine	VF	XF	Unc
370.11	1826 AZ	—	5.00	10.00	20.00	60.00
	1826 AO	—	5.00	10.00	20.00	60.00
	1827 AO	—	5.00	10.00	20.00	60.00

KM#	Date	Mintage	Fine	VF	XF	Unc
370.11	1828/7 AO	—	5.00	10.00	20.00	60.00
	1829 AO	—	5.00	10.00	20.00	60.00
	1830 OV	—	5.00	10.00	20.00	60.00
	1831 OV	—	25.00	50.00	75.00	150.00
	1831 OM	—	5.00	10.00	20.00	60.00
	1832 OM	—	5.00	10.00	20.00	60.00
	1833 OM	—	5.00	10.00	20.00	60.00
	1834 OM	—	5.00	10.00	20.00	60.00
	1835/4 OM	—	5.00	10.00	20.00	60.00
	1835 OM	—	5.00	10.00	20.00	60.00
	1836 OM	—	5.00	10.00	20.00	60.00
	1837 OM	—	10.00	20.00	40.00	80.00
	1838 OM	—	5.00	10.00	20.00	60.00
	1839 OM	—	7.50	15.00	30.00	65.00
	1840 OM	—	10.00	25.00	45.00	90.00
	1841 OM	—	10.00	25.00	45.00	90.00
	1842/1 OM	—	5.00	10.00	20.00	60.00
	1842 OM	—	5.00	10.00	20.00	60.00
	1843 OM	—	40.00	75.00	115.00	250.00
	1844 OM	—	5.00	10.00	20.00	60.00
	1845 OM	—	5.00	10.00	20.00	60.00
	1846 OM	—	7.50	15.00	30.00	65.00
	1847 OM	—	5.00	10.00	20.00	50.00
	1848 OM	—	5.00	10.00	20.00	50.00
	1849 OM	—	5.00	10.00	20.00	50.00
	1850 OM	—	5.00	10.00	20.00	50.00
	1851 OM	—	5.00	10.00	20.00	50.00
	1852 OM	—	5.00	10.00	20.00	50.00
	1853 OM	—	5.00	10.00	20.00	50.00
	1854/3 OM	—	5.00	10.00	20.00	50.00
	1854 OM	—	5.00	10.00	20.00	50.00
	1855/3 OM	—	7.50	15.00	30.00	65.00
	1855 OM	—	5.00	10.00	20.00	50.00
	1856 OM	—	5.00	10.00	20.00	50.00
	1857 MO	—	5.00	10.00	20.00	50.00
	1858 MO	—	5.00	10.00	20.00	50.00
	1859 MO	—	6.00	8.50	17.50	35.00
	1859 VL	—	6.00	8.50	17.50	40.00
	1860/50 VL inverted A for V					
		—	5.00	10.00	20.00	50.00
	1860/59 VL inverted A for V					
			5.00	10.00	20.00	50.00
	1860 MO	—	5.00	10.00	20.00	50.00
	1860 VL	—	5.00	10.00	20.00	50.00
	1861/0 VL inverted A for V					
		—	7.50	15.00	30.00	65.00
	1861 VL inverted A for V					
		—	5.00	10.00	20.00	50.00
	1862 VL inverted A for V					
		—	5.00	10.00	20.00	50.00
	1863/1 VL inverted A for V					
		—	7.50	15.00	30.00	65.00
	1863 VL inverted A for V					
		—	5.00	10.00	20.00	50.00
	1869 YH	—	5.00	10.00	20.00	50.00

REAL

3.3800 g, .903 SILVER, .0981 oz ASW
Mint mark: Do

KM#	Date	Mintage	Fine	VF	XF	Unc
371	1824 RL	—	3250.	4000.	5250.	7500.

Mint mark: Ca

KM#	Date	Mintage	Fine	VF	XF	Unc
372	1844 RG	—	500.00	1000.	1500.	2750.
	1845 RG	—	500.00	1000.	1500.	2750.
	1855 RG	—	100.00	150.00	225.00	450.00

KM#	Date	Mintage	Fine	VF	XF	Unc
	Mint mark: C					
372.1	1846 CE	—	12.50	25.00	40.00	110.00
	1848 CE	—	12.50	25.00	40.00	110.00
	1850 CE	—	12.50	25.00	40.00	110.00
	1851/0 CE	—	12.50	25.00	40.00	110.00
	1852/1 CE	—	7.50	15.00	30.00	100.00
	1853/2 CE	—	7.50	15.00	30.00	100.00
	1854 CE	—	7.50	15.00	30.00	100.00
	1856 CE	—	40.00	65.00	100.00	225.00
	1857/4 CE	—	10.00	20.00	35.00	100.00
	1857/6 CE	—	10.00	20.00	35.00	100.00
	1858 CE	—	5.00	7.50	15.00	100.00
	1859 CE	—	—	—	—	—
	1860 PV	—	5.00	7.50	15.00	100.00
	1861 PV	—	5.00	7.50	15.00	100.00
	1863 CE					
	3 known	—		1650.	2250.	
	1869 CE	—	5.00	7.50	15.00	100.00
	Mint mark: Do					
372.2	1832/1 RM	—	5.00	10.00	20.00	90.00
	1832 RM/RL	—	10.00	15.00	30.00	100.00
	1832 RM	—	5.00	10.00	20.00	100.00
	1834/24 RM/RL					
		—	15.00	25.00	50.00	150.00
	1834/3 RM/RL					
		—	15.00	25.00	50.00	150.00
	1834 RM	—	10.00	20.00	40.00	110.00
	1836/4 RM	—	5.00	7.50	15.00	100.00
	1836 RM	—	5.00	7.50	15.00	100.00
	1837 RM	—	12.50	20.00	40.00	110.00
	1841 RM	—	7.50	15.00	30.00	100.00
	1842/32 RM	—	10.00	20.00	40.00	110.00
	1842 RM	—	7.50	15.00	30.00	100.00
	1843 RM	—	5.00	7.50	15.00	100.00
	1844/34 RM	—	15.00	25.00	45.00	125.00
	1845 RM	—	5.00	7.50	15.00	100.00
	1846 RM	—	7.50	15.00	30.00	100.00
	1847 RM	—	10.00	15.00	35.00	100.00
	1848/31 RM	—	10.00	15.00	35.00	100.00
	1848/33 RM	—	10.00	15.00	35.00	100.00
	1848/5 RM	—	10.00	15.00	35.00	100.00
	1848 RM	—	7.50	12.50	20.00	100.00
	1849/8 CM	—	10.00	15.00	30.00	100.00
	1850 JMR	—	15.00	25.00	45.00	125.00
	1851 JMR	—	15.00	25.00	45.00	120.00
	1852 JMR	—	15.00	25.00	45.00	120.00
	1853 CP	—	12.50	20.00	35.00	100.00
	1854/1 CP	—	10.00	15.00	25.00	100.00
	1854 CP	—	7.50	12.50	20.00	100.00
	1855 CP	—	10.00	15.00	25.00	100.00
	1856 CP	—	12.50	20.00	35.00	100.00
	1857 CP	—	12.50	20.00	35.00	100.00
	1858 CP	—	12.50	20.00	35.00	100.00
	1859 CP	—	7.50	12.50	20.00	100.00
	1860/59 CP	—	10.00	15.00	25.00	100.00
	1861 CP	—	15.00	25.00	40.00	110.00
	1862/1 CP	—	225.00	300.00	450.00	1250.
	1864 LT	—	15.00	25.00	40.00	110.00
	Mint mark: EoMo					
372.3	1828 LF	—	200.00	300.00	450.00	1500.
	Mint mark: Ga					
372.4	1826 FS	—	15.00	30.00	50.00	125.00
	1828/7 FS	—	15.00	30.00	50.00	125.00
	1829/8/7 FS	—	—	—	—	—
	1829 FS	—	15.00	30.00	50.00	125.00
	1830 FS	—	250.00	350.00	500.00	—
	1831 LP	—	15.00	30.00	50.00	125.00
	1831 LP/FS	—	300.00	450.00	600.00	—
	1832 FS	—	250.00	350.00	500.00	—
	1833/2 G FS	—	100.00	150.00	275.00	550.00
	1833 FS	—	75.00	125.00	225.00	500.00
	1834/3 FS	—	75.00	125.00	225.00	500.00
	1835 FS	—	—	—	—	—
	1837/6 JG/FS					
		—	12.50	20.00	35.00	100.00
	1838/7 JG/FS					
		—	12.50	20.00	35.00	100.00
	1839 JG	—	250.00	350.00	500.00	—
	1840 JG	—	12.50	20.00	35.00	100.00
	1840 MC	—	7.50	12.50	25.00	70.00
	1841 MC	—	50.00	75.00	125.00	250.00
	1842/0 JG/MC					
		—	10.00	15.00	30.00	100.00

PRICING SECTION

KM#	Date	Mintage	Fine	VF	XF	Unc
372.4	1842 JG	—	7.50	12.50	20.00	100.00
	1843 JG	—	150.00	200.00	300.00	750.00
	1843 MC	—	5.00	7.50	15.00	100.00
	1844 MC	—	7.50	12.50	20.00	100.00
	1845 MC	—	10.00	15.00	25.00	100.00
	1845 JG	—	5.00	7.50	20.00	100.00
	1846 JG	—	12.50	20.00	35.00	100.00
	1847/6 JG	—	10.00	15.00	25.00	100.00
	1847 JG	—	10.00	15.00	25.00	100.00
	1848 JG	—	400.00	550.00	700.00	—
	1849 JG	—	7.50	12.50	20.00	100.00
	1850 JG	—	175.00	275.00	400.00	—
	1851 JG	—	10.00	15.00	25.00	100.00
	1852 JG	—	10.00	15.00	25.00	100.00
	1853/2 JG	—	10.00	15.00	25.00	100.00
	1854 JG	—	10.00	15.00	25.00	100.00
	1855 JG	—	15.00	25.00	40.00	100.00
	1856 JG	—	7.50	12.50	20.00	100.00
	1857/6 JG	—	12.50	20.00	35.00	100.00
	1858/7 JG	—	15.00	25.00	40.00	110.00
	1859/8 JG	—	25.00	50.00	75.00	150.00
	1860/59 JG	—	30.00	60.00	90.00	225.00
	1861/0 JG	—	20.00	30.00	50.00	125.00
	1861 JG	—	25.00	50.00	100.00	250.00
	1862 JG	—	7.50	12.50	20.00	100.00

Mint mark: GC

KM#	Date	Mintage	Fine	VF	XF	Unc
372.5	1844 MP	—	40.00	60.00	100.00	250.00
	1845 MP	—	40.00	60.00	100.00	250.00
	1846 MP	—	40.00	60.00	100.00	250.00
	1847 MP	—	40.00	60.00	100.00	250.00
	1848 MP	—	40.00	60.00	100.00	250.00
	1849/7 MP	—	40.00	60.00	100.00	250.00
	1849/8 MP	—	40.00	60.00	100.00	250.00
	1849 MP	—	40.00	60.00	100.00	250.00
	1850 MP	—	40.00	60.00	100.00	250.00
	1851 MP	—	40.00	60.00	100.00	250.00

Mint mark: Go

KM#	Date	Mintage	Fine	VF	XF	Unc
372.6	1826/5 JJ	—	5.00	7.50	15.00	85.00
	1826 MJ	—	4.00	6.00	15.00	85.00
	1827 MJ	—	4.00	6.00	15.00	65.00
	1827 JM	—	10.00	15.00	25.00	75.00
	1828/7 MR	—	4.00	6.00	15.00	85.00
	1828 MJ, straight J, small 8					
		—	4.00	6.00	15.00	85.00
	1828Go MJ, full J, large 8					
		—	4.00	6.00	15.00	85.00
	1828G MJ, full J, large 8					
		—	4.00	6.00	15.00	85.00
	1828 MR	—	4.00	6.00	15.00	85.00
	1829/8 MG small eagle					
		—	4.00	6.00	15.00	85.00
	1829 MJ small eagle					
		—	4.00	6.00	15.00	85.00
	1829 MJ large eagle					
		—	4.00	6.00	15.00	85.00
	1830 MJ small initials					
		—	4.00	6.00	15.00	85.00
	1830 MJ medium initials					
		—	4.00	6.00	15.00	85.00
	1830 MJ large initials					
		—	4.00	6.00	15.00	85.00
	1830 MJ reversed N in MEXICANA					
		—	4.00	6.00	15.00	85.00
	1831/0 MJ reversed N in MEXICANA					
		—	4.00	6.00	15.00	85.00
	1831 MJ	—	4.00	6.00	15.00	85.00
	1832/1 MJ	—	15.00	30.00	50.00	125.00
	1832 MJ	—	15.00	30.00	50.00	125.00
372.6	1833 MJ top of 3 round					
		—	4.00	6.00	15.00	85.00
	1833 MJ top of 3 flat					
		—	4.00	6.00	15.00	85.00
	1834 PJ	—	4.00	6.00	15.00	85.00
	1835 PJ	—	7.50	12.50	20.00	85.00
	1836 PJ	—	4.00	6.00	15.00	85.00
	1837 PJ	—	15.00	30.00	50.00	125.00
	1838/7 PJ	—	10.00	20.00	35.00	85.00
	1839 PJ	—	4.00	6.00	15.00	85.00
	1840/39 PJ	—	4.00	6.00	15.00	85.00
	1840 PJ	—	4.00	6.00	15.00	85.00
	1841/31 PJ	—	10.00	20.00	35.00	85.00
	1841 PJ	—	4.00	6.00	15.00	85.00

KM#	Date	Mintage	Fine	VF	XF	Unc
372.6	1842 PJ	—	4.00	6.00	15.00	85.00
	1842 PM	—	4.00	6.00	15.00	85.00
	1843 PM convex wings					
		—	4.00	6.00	15.00	85.00
	1843 PM concave wings					
		—	4.00	6.00	15.00	85.00
	1844 PM	—	4.00	6.00	15.00	85.00
	1845/4 PM	—	4.00	6.00	15.00	85.00
	1845 PM	—	4.00	6.00	15.00	85.00
	1846/5 PM	—	7.50	12.50	20.00	85.00
	1846 PM	—	4.00	6.00	15.00	85.00
	1847/6 PM	—	4.00	6.00	15.00	85.00
	1847 PM	—	4.00	6.00	15.00	85.00
	1848 PM	—	4.00	6.00	15.00	85.00
	1849 PF	—	10.00	20.00	35.00	85.00
	1850 PF	—	4.00	6.00	15.00	85.00
	1851 PF	—	10.00	20.00	35.00	100.00
	1853/2 PF	—	7.50	12.50	20.00	75.00
	1853 PF	—	4.00	6.00	15.00	75.00
	1854/3 PF	—	4.00	6.00	15.00	75.00
	1854 PF large eagle					
		—	4.00	6.00	15.00	75.00
	1854 PF small eagle					
		—	4.00	6.00	15.00	75.00
	1855/3 PF	—	4.00	6.00	15.00	75.00
	1855/4 PF	—	4.00	6.00	15.00	75.00
	1855 PF	—	4.00	6.00	15.00	75.00
	1856/5 PF	—	4.00	6.00	15.00	75.00
	1856 PF	—	4.00	6.00	15.00	75.00
	1857/6 PF	—	4.00	6.00	15.00	75.00
	1857 PF	—	4.00	6.00	15.00	75.00
	1858 PF	—	4.00	6.00	15.00	75.00
	1859 PF	—	4.00	6.00	15.00	75.00
	1860/50 PF	—	4.00	6.00	15.00	75.00
	1860 PF	—	4.00	6.00	15.00	75.00
	1861 PF	—	4.00	6.00	15.00	75.00
	1862 YE	—	4.00	6.00	15.00	75.00
	1862/1 YF	—	7.50	12.50	20.00	75.00
	1862 YF	—	4.00	6.00	15.00	75.00
	1867 YF	—	4.00	6.00	15.00	75.00
	1868/7 YF	—	4.00	6.00	15.00	75.00

Mint mark: Ho

KM#	Date	Mintage	Fine	VF	XF	Unc
372.7	1867 small 7/1 PR					
		—	50.00	65.00	100.00	250.00
	1867 large 7/small 7 PR					
		—	50.00	65.00	100.00	250.00
	1868 PR	—	50.00	65.00	100.00	250.00

Mint mark: Mo

KM#	Date	Mintage	Fine	VF	XF	Unc
372.8	1825 JM	—	10.00	20.00	40.00	110.00
	1826 JM	—	7.50	15.00	30.00	100.00
	1827/6 JM	—	7.50	15.00	30.00	75.00
	1827 JM	—	5.00	10.00	20.00	70.00
	1828 JM	—	7.50	15.00	30.00	100.00
	1830/29 JM	—	5.00	10.00	20.00	100.00
	1831 JM	—	100.00	200.00	300.00	750.00
	1832 JM	—	5.00	10.00	20.00	100.00
	1833/2 MJ	—	5.00	10.00	20.00	100.00
	1850 GC	—	5.00	10.00	20.00	100.00
	1852 GC	—	275.00	425.00	575.00	—
	1854 GC	—	10.00	20.00	40.00	100.00
	1855 GF	—	5.00	10.00	20.00	80.00
	1856 GF	—	5.00	10.00	20.00	80.00
	1857 GF	—	5.00	10.00	20.00	80.00
	1858 FH	—	5.00	10.00	20.00	80.00
	1859 FH	—	5.00	10.00	20.00	80.00
	1861 CH	—	5.00	10.00	20.00	80.00
	1862 CH	—	5.00	10.00	20.00	80.00
	1863/2 CH	—	7.50	12.50	25.00	80.00
372.9	1831 JS	—	5.00	10.00	20.00	125.00
	1837 JS	—	750.00	850.00	1000.	—
	1838/7 JS	—	250.00	300.00	375.00	—
	1838 JS	—	20.00	35.00	60.00	125.00
	1840/39 JS	—	7.50	15.00	30.00	125.00
	1840 JS	—	7.50	15.00	30.00	125.00
	1841 JS	—	7.50	15.00	30.00	125.00
	1842 JS	—	15.00	30.00	55.00	150.00
	1842 PS	—	5.00	10.00	20.00	125.00
	1843 PS	—	12.50	20.00	35.00	125.00
	1843 AM	—	40.00	60.00	80.00	150.00
	1844 AM	—	40.00	60.00	80.00	150.00
	1845 AM	—	7.50	15.00	30.00	125.00
	1846/5 AM	—	7.50	15.00	30.00	125.00

KM#	Date	Mintage	Fine	VF	XF	Unc
372.9	1847/6 AM	—	7.50	15.00	30.00	125.00
	1847 AM	—	7.50	15.00	30.00	125.00
	1848/7 AM	—	7.50	15.00	30.00	125.00
	1849 PS	—	7.50	15.00	30.00	125.00
	1849/8 SP	—	60.00	100.00	150.00	—
	1849 SP	—	15.00	25.00	40.00	125.00
	1850 MC	—	5.00	10.00	20.00	125.00
	1851/0 MC	—	7.50	15.00	30.00	125.00
	1851 MC	—	7.50	15.00	30.00	125.00
	1852/1/0 MC					
		—	10.00	20.00	35.00	125.00
	1852 MC	—	7.50	15.00	30.00	125.00
	1853/1 MC	—	12.50	20.00	35.00	125.00
	1853 MC	—	10.00	20.00	35.00	125.00
	1854/3 MC	—	20.00	40.00	60.00	150.00
	1855/4 MC	—	20.00	40.00	60.00	150.00
	1855 MC	—	15.00	25.00	45.00	125.00
	1856 MC	—	15.00	25.00	45.00	125.00
	1857 PS	—	20.00	35.00	55.00	135.00
	1857 MC	—	20.00	40.00	60.00	150.00
	1858 MC	—	12.50	20.00	35.00	125.00
	1859 PS	—	10.00	15.00	30.00	125.00
	1860/59 PS	—	10.00	15.00	30.00	125.00
	1861 PS	—	7.50	12.50	20.00	125.00
	1861 RO	—	12.50	20.00	35.00	125.00
	1862/1 RO	—	12.50	20.00	35.00	90.00
	1862 RO	—	7.50	12.50	20.00	125.00

Mint mark: Zs

KM#	Date	Mintage	Fine	VF	XF	Unc
372.10	1826 AZ	—	5.00	12.50	35.00	120.00
	1826 AO	—	5.00	12.50	35.00	120.00
	1827 AO	—	5.00	12.50	35.00	120.00
	1828/7 AO	—	5.00	12.50	35.00	120.00
	1828 AO	—	5.00	12.50	35.00	120.00
	1828 AO inverted V for A					
		—	5.00	12.50	35.00	120.00
	1829 AO	—	5.00	12.50	35.00	120.00
	1830 ZsOV	—	5.00	12.50	35.00	120.00
	1830 ZOV	—	5.00	12.50	35.00	120.00
	1831 OV	—	5.00	12.50	35.00	120.00
	1831 OM	—	5.00	12.50	35.00	120.00
	1832 OM	—	5.00	12.50	30.00	120.00
	1833/2 OM	—	5.00	12.50	30.00	120.00
	1833 OM	—	5.00	12.50	30.00	120.00
	1834/3 OM	—	5.00	12.50	30.00	120.00
	1834 OM	—	5.00	12.50	30.00	120.00
	1835/4 OM	—	20.00	35.00	60.00	150.00
	1835 OM	—	4.00	8.00	20.00	65.00
	1836/5 OM	—	4.00	8.00	20.00	85.00
	1836 OM	—	4.00	8.00	20.00	85.00
	1837 OM	—	4.00	8.00	20.00	85.00
	1838 OM	—	4.00	8.00	20.00	85.00
	1839 OM	—	4.00	8.00	20.00	85.00
	1840 OM	—	4.00	8.00	20.00	85.00
	1841 OM	—	20.00	40.00	60.00	150.00
	1842/1 OM	—	4.00	8.00	20.00	85.00
	1842 OM	—	4.00	8.00	20.00	85.00
	1843 OM	—	4.00	8.00	20.00	85.00
	1844 OM	—	4.00	8.00	20.00	85.00
	1845/4 OM	—	5.00	12.50	30.00	100.00
	1845 OM	—	4.00	8.00	20.00	85.00
	1846 OM old font and obv.					
		—	4.00	8.00	20.00	85.00
	1846 OM new font and obv.					
		—	4.00	8.00	20.00	85.00
	1847 OM	—	4.00	8.00	20.00	85.00
	1848 OM	—	4.00	8.00	20.00	85.00
	1849 OM	—	10.00	25.00	50.00	125.00
	1850 OM	—	4.00	6.00	15.00	85.00
372.10	1851 OM	—	4.00	6.00	15.00	85.00
	1852 OM	—	4.00	6.00	15.00	85.00
	1853 OM	—	4.00	6.00	15.00	85.00
	1854/2 OM	—	4.00	6.00	15.00	85.00
	1854/3 OM	—	4.00	6.00	15.00	85.00
	1854 OM	—	4.00	6.00	15.00	85.00
	1855/4 OM	—	4.00	6.00	15.00	85.00
	1855 OM	—	4.00	6.00	15.00	85.00
	1855 MO	—	4.00	6.00	15.00	85.00
	1856 MO	—	4.00	6.00	15.00	85.00
	1856 MO/OM	—	4.00	6.00	15.00	85.00
	1857 MO	—	4.00	6.00	15.00	85.00
	1858 MO	—	4.00	6.00	15.00	85.00
	1859 MO	—	4.00	6.00	15.00	75.00
	1860 VL	—	4.00	6.00	15.00	75.00
	1861 VL	—	4.00	6.00	15.00	75.00

KM#	Date	Mintage	Fine	VF	XF	Unc
372.10	1862 VL	—	5.00	12.50	30.00	100.00
	1868 JS	—	25.00	45.00	90.00	175.00
	1869 YH	—	4.00	8.00	20.00	75.00

2 REALES

6.7600 g, .903 SILVER, .1962 oz ASW
Mint mark: D, Do
Obv: Hooked-neck eagle.

KM#	Date	Mintage	Fine	VF	XF	Unc
373	1824 Do RL	—	50.00	125.00	300.00	850.00
	1824 D RL	—	100.00	200.00	500.00	1650.

Mint mark: Mo

KM#	Date	Mintage	Fine	VF	XF	Unc
373.1	1824 JM	—	20.00	50.00	100.00	350.00

Mint mark: A
Obv: Facing eagle, reeded edge.

KM#	Date	Mintage	Fine	VF	XF	Unc
374	1872 AM	.015	40.00	100.00	200.00	500.00

Mint mark: Ce

KM#	Date	Mintage	Fine	VF	XF	Unc
374.1	1863 ML	—	125.00	200.00	325.00	675.00

Mint mark: Ca

KM#	Date	Mintage	Fine	VF	XF	Unc
374.2	1832 MR	—	30.00	60.00	100.00	200.00
	1833 MR	—	30.00	60.00	125.00	500.00
	1834 MR	—	35.00	75.00	125.00	500.00
	1834 AM	—	35.00	75.00	125.00	500.00
	1835 AM	—	35.00	75.00	125.00	500.00
	1836 AM	—	20.00	40.00	80.00	200.00
	1844 RG	—	—		Unique	—
	1845 RG	—	20.00	40.00	80.00	200.00
	1855 RG	—	20.00	40.00	80.00	200.00

Mint mark: C

KM#	Date	Mintage	Fine	VF	XF	Unc
374.3	1846/1146 CE					
		—	25.00	50.00	100.00	225.00
	1847 CE	—	12.50	20.00	40.00	200.00
	1848 CE	—	12.50	20.00	40.00	200.00
	1850 CE	—	25.00	50.00	75.00	200.00
	1851 CE	—	12.50	20.00	40.00	200.00
	1852/1 CE	—	12.50	20.00	40.00	200.00
	1853/2 CE	—	12.50	20.00	40.00	200.00
	1854 CE	—	15.00	30.00	50.00	200.00
	1856 CE	—	20.00	35.00	70.00	200.00
	1857 CE	—	12.50	20.00	40.00	200.00
	1860 PV	—	12.50	20.00	40.00	200.00
	1861 PV	—	12.50	20.00	40.00	200.00
	1869 CE	—	12.50	20.00	40.00	200.00

Mint mark: Do

KM#	Date	Mintage	Fine	VF	XF	Unc
374.4	1826 RL	—	20.00	40.00	60.00	200.00
	1832 RM style of pre-1832					
		—	20.00	40.00	60.00	200.00
	1832 RM style of post-1832					
		—	20.00	40.00	60.00	200.00
	1834/2 RM	—	20.00	40.00	60.00	200.00
	1834/3 RM	—	20.00	40.00	60.00	200.00
	1835/4 RM/RL					
		—	200.00	300.00	500.00	—
	1841/31 RM	—	50.00	75.00	125.00	250.00
	1841 RM	—	50.00	75.00	125.00	250.00
	1842/32 RM	—	12.50	20.00	40.00	200.00
	1843 RM/RL	—	12.50	20.00	40.00	200.00
	1844 RM	—	35.00	50.00	80.00	200.00

KM#	Date	Mintage	Fine	VF	XF	Unc
374.4	1845/34 RM/RL					
		—	12.50	20.00	40.00	200.00
	1846/36 RM	—	100.00	150.00	200.00	350.00
	1848/36 RM	—	12.50	20.00	40.00	200.00
	1848/37 RM	—	12.50	20.00	40.00	200.00
	1848/7 RM	—	12.50	20.00	40.00	200.00
	1848 RM	—	12.50	20.00	40.00	200.00
	1849 CM/RM	—	12.50	20.00	40.00	200.00
	1849 CM	—	12.50	20.00	40.00	200.00
	1851 JMR/RL					
		—	12.50	20.00	40.00	200.00
	1852 JMR	—	12.50	20.00	40.00	200.00
	1854 CP/CR	—	30.00	50.00	80.00	200.00
	1855 CP	—	250.00	350.00	500.00	—
	1856 CP	—	100.00	150.00	250.00	500.00
	1858 CP	—	12.50	20.00	40.00	200.00
	1859/8 CP	—	12.50	20.00	40.00	200.00
	1861 CP	—	12.50	20.00	40.00	200.00

Mint mark: EoMo

374.5	1828 LF	—	325.00	525.00	900.00	2500.

Mint mark: Ga

374.6	1825 FS	—	20.00	40.00	80.00	200.00
	1826 FS	—	20.00	40.00	80.00	200.00
	1828/7 FS	—	100.00	150.00	225.00	400.00
	1829 FS	—	—	—	Rare	—
	1832/0 FS/LP					
		—	100.00	150.00	225.00	350.00
	1832 FS	—	12.50	20.00	40.00	200.00
	1833/2 FS/LP					
		—	12.50	20.00	40.00	200.00
	1834/27 FS	—	—	—	Rare	—
	1834 FS	—	12.50	20.00	40.00	200.00
	1835 FS	—	2100.	—	—	—
	1837 JG	—	12.50	20.00	40.00	200.00
	1838 JG	—	12.50	20.00	40.00	200.00
	1840/30 MC	—	12.50	20.00	40.00	200.00
	1841 MC	—	12.50	20.00	40.00	200.00
	1842/32 JG/MC					
		—	35.00	50.00	100.00	200.00
	1842 JG	—	20.00	40.00	80.00	200.00
	1843 JG	—	12.50	20.00	40.00	200.00
	1843 MC/JG	—	12.50	20.00	40.00	200.00
	1844 MC	—	12.50	20.00	40.00	200.00
	1845/3 MC/JG					
		—	12.50	20.00	40.00	200.00
	1845/4 MC/JG					
		—	12.50	20.00	40.00	200.00
	1845 JG	—	12.50	20.00	40.00	200.00
	1846 JG	—	12.50	20.00	40.00	200.00
	1847/6 JG	—	25.00	40.00	80.00	200.00
	1848/7 JG	—	12.50	20.00	40.00	200.00
	1849 JG	—	12.50	20.00	40.00	200.00
	1850/40 JG	—	12.50	20.00	40.00	200.00
	1851 JG	—	250.00	350.00	500.00	—
	1852 JG	—	12.50	20.00	40.00	200.00
	1853/1 JG	—	12.50	20.00	40.00	200.00
	1854/3 JG	—	250.00	350.00	500.00	—
	1855 JG	—	35.00	50.00	80.00	200.00
	1856 JG	—	12.50	20.00	40.00	200.00
	1857 JG	—	250.00	350.00	500.00	—
	1859/8 JG	—	12.50	20.00	40.00	200.00
	1859 JG	—	12.50	20.00	40.00	200.00
	1862/1 JG	—	12.50	20.00	40.00	200.00

Mint mark: GC

374.7	1844 MP	—	40.00	60.00	125.00	275.00
	1845 MP	—	40.00	60.00	125.00	275.00
	1846 MP	—	50.00	100.00	150.00	300.00
	1847 MP	—	35.00	50.00	100.00	250.00
	1848 MP	—	50.00	100.00	150.00	300.00
	1849 MP	—	50.00	100.00	150.00	300.00
	1850 MP	—	125.00	250.00	—	—
	1851/0 MP	—	50.00	100.00	150.00	300.00
	1851 MP	—	50.00	100.00	150.00	300.00

Mint mark: Go

374.8	1825 JJ	—	7.50	15.00	30.00	150.00
	1826/5 JJ	—	7.50	15.00	30.00	150.00
	1826 JJ	—	7.50	10.00	25.00	150.00
	1826 MJ	—	7.50	10.00	25.00	150.00
	1827/6 MJ	—	7.50	10.00	25.00	150.00
	1827 MJ	—	7.50	10.00	25.00	150.00
	1828/7 MR	—	7.50	15.00	30.00	150.00

KM#	Date	Mintage	Fine	VF	XF	Unc
374.8	1828 MJ	—	7.50	10.00	20.00	150.00
	1828 JM	—	7.50	10.00	20.00	150.00
	1829 MJ	—	7.50	10.00	20.00	150.00
	1831 MJ	—	7.50	10.00	20.00	150.00
	1832 MJ	—	7.50	10.00	20.00	150.00
	1833 MJ	—	7.50	10.00	20.00	150.00
	1834 PJ	—	7.50	10.00	20.00	150.00
	1835/4 PJ	—	7.50	15.00	30.00	150.00
	1835 PJ	—	7.50	10.00	20.00	150.00
	1836 PJ	—	7.50	10.00	20.00	150.00
	1837/6 PJ	—	7.50	10.00	20.00	150.00
	1837 PJ	—	7.50	10.00	20.00	150.00
	1838/7 PJ	—	7.50	10.00	20.00	150.00
	1838 PJ	—	7.50	10.00	20.00	150.00
	1839/8 PJ	—	7.50	15.00	30.00	150.00
	1839 PJ	—	7.50	10.00	20.00	150.00
	1840 PJ	—	7.50	10.00	20.00	150.00
	1841 PJ	—	7.50	10.00	20.00	150.00
	1842 PJ	—	7.50	10.00	20.00	150.00
	1842 PM/PJ	—	7.50	10.00	20.00	150.00
	1842 PM	—	7.50	10.00	20.00	150.00
	1843/2 PM concave wings, thin rays, sm. letters					
		—	7.50	10.00	20.00	150.00
	1843 PM convex wings, thick rays, lg. letters					
		—	7.50	10.00	20.00	150.00
	1844 PM	—	7.50	10.00	20.00	150.00
	1845/4 PM	—	7.50	10.00	20.00	150.00
	1845 PM	—	7.50	10.00	20.00	150.00
	1846/5 PM	—	10.00	15.00	35.00	150.00
	1846 PM	—	7.50	10.00	20.00	150.00
	1847 PM	—	7.50	10.00	20.00	150.00
	1848/7 PM	—	7.50	15.00	30.00	150.00
	1848 PM	—	7.50	15.00	30.00	150.00
	1848 PF	—	100.00	150.00	250.00	500.00
	1849/8 PF/PM					
		—	7.50	10.00	20.00	150.00
	1849 PF	—	7.50	10.00	20.00	150.00
	1850/40 PF	—	7.50	10.00	20.00	150.00
	1850 PF	—	7.50	10.00	20.00	150.00
	1851 PF	—	7.50	10.00	20.00	150.00
	1852/1 PF	—	7.50	10.00	20.00	150.00
	1852 PF	—	7.50	10.00	20.00	150.00
	1853 PF	—	7.50	10.00	20.00	150.00
	1854/3 PF	—	7.50	10.00	20.00	150.00
	1854 PF old font and obv.					
		—	7.50	10.00	20.00	150.00
	1854 PF new font and obv.					
		—	7.50	10.00	20.00	150.00
	1855 PF	—	7.50	10.00	20.00	150.00
	1855 PF star in G of mint mark					
		—	7.50	10.00	20.00	150.00
	1856/5 PF	—	10.00	15.00	35.00	150.00
	1856 PF	—	10.00	15.00	25.00	150.00
	1857/6 PF	—	7.50	10.00	20.00	150.00
	1857 PF	—	7.50	10.00	20.00	150.00
	1858/7 PF	—	7.50	10.00	20.00	150.00
	1858 PF	—	7.50	10.00	20.00	150.00
	1859/7 PF	—	7.50	10.00	20.00	150.00
	1859 PF	—	7.50	10.00	20.00	150.00
	1860/50 PF	—	7.50	10.00	20.00	150.00
	1860/59 PF	—	7.50	10.00	20.00	150.00
	1860 PF	—	7.50	10.00	20.00	150.00
	1861/51 PF	—	7.50	10.00	20.00	150.00
	1861/57 PF	—	7.50	10.00	20.00	150.00
	1861/0 PF	—	7.50	10.00	20.00	150.00
	1861 PF	—	7.50	10.00	20.00	150.00
	1862/1 YE	—	7.50	10.00	20.00	125.00
	1862 YE	—	7.50	10.00	20.00	125.00
	1862/57 YE	—	7.50	10.00	20.00	125.00
374.8	1862 YE/PF	—	7.50	10.00	20.00	125.00
	1862 YF	—	7.50	10.00	20.00	125.00
	1863/52 YF	—	7.50	10.00	20.00	125.00
	1863 YF	—	7.50	10.00	20.00	125.00
	1867/57 YF	—	7.50	10.00	20.00	125.00
	1868/57 YF	—	10.00	15.00	25.00	125.00

NOTE: Varieties exist.

Mint mark: Ho

374.9	1861 FM	—	200.00	300.00	400.00	650.00
	1862/52 Ho FM/C. CE					
		—	250.00	350.00	500.00	—
	1867/1 PR/FM					
		—	75.00	150.00	250.00	500.00

PRICING SECTION

KM#	Date	Mintage	Fine	VF	XF	Unc
		Mint mark: Mo				
374.10	1825 JM	—	10.00	15.00	30.00	175.00
	1826 JM	—	10.00	15.00	30.00	175.00
	1827 JM	—	10.00	15.00	30.00	175.00
	1828 JM	—	10.00	15.00	30.00	175.00
	1829/8 JM	—	10.00	15.00	30.00	175.00
	1829 JM	—	10.00	15.00	30.00	175.00
	1830 JM	—	40.00	60.00	125.00	250.00
	1831 JM	—	10.00	15.00	30.00	175.00
	1832 JM.	—	100.00	200.00	400.00	—
	1833/2 MJ/JM					
		—	10.00	15.00	30.00	175.00
	1834 ML	—	50.00	100.00	200.00	400.00
	1836 ML	—	—	Reported, not confirmed		
	1836 MF	—	10.00	15.00	30.00	175.00
	1837 ML	—	10.00	15.00	30.00	175.00
	1840 ML	—	150.00	225.00	350.00	—
	1841 ML	—	10.00	15.00	30.00	175.00
	1842 ML	—	—	—	Rare	—
	1847 RC	—	10.00	15.00	30.00	175.00
	1848 GC	—	10.00	15.00	30.00	175.00
	1849 GC	—	10.00	15.00	30.00	175.00
	1850 GC	—	10.00	15.00	30.00	175.00
	1851 GC	—	40.00	60.00	125.00	250.00
	1852 GC	—	10.00	15.00	30.00	175.00
	1853 GC	—	10.00	15.00	30.00	175.00
	1854/44 GC	—	10.00	15.00	30.00	175.00
	1855 GC	—	10.00	15.00	30.00	175.00
	1855 GF/GC	—	10.00	15.00	30.00	175.00
	1855 GF	—	10.00	15.00	30.00	175.00
	1856/5 GF/GC					
		—	10.00	15.00	30.00	175.00
	1857 GF	—	10.00	15.00	30.00	175.00
	1858 FH	—	7.50	12.50	25.00	150.00
	1858 FH/GF	—	7.50	12.50	25.00	150.00
	1859 FH	—	7.50	12.50	25.00	150.00
	1860 FH	—	7.50	12.50	25.00	150.00
	1860 TH	—	7.50	12.50	25.00	150.00
	1861 TH	—	—	Reported, not confirmed		
	1861 CH	—	7.50	12.50	25.00	150.00
	1862 CH	—	7.50	12.50	25.00	150.00
	1863 CH	—	7.50	12.50	25.00	150.00
	1863 TH	—	7.50	12.50	25.00	150.00
	1867 CH	—	7.50	12.50	25.00	150.00
	1868 CH	—	10.00	15.00	30.00	150.00
	1868 PH	—	7.50	12.50	25.00	150.00

NOTE: Varieties exist.

KM#	Date	Mintage	Fine	VF	XF	Unc
		Mint mark: Pi				
374.11	1829 JS	—	10.00	15.00	30.00	200.00
	1830/20 JS	—	20.00	30.00	60.00	200.00
	1837 JS	—	10.00	15.00	30.00	200.00
	1841 JS	—	10.00	15.00	30.00	200.00
	1842/1 JS	—	10.00	15.00	30.00	200.00
	1842 JS	—	10.00	15.00	30.00	200.00
	1842 PS	—	20.00	35.00	60.00	200.00
	1843 PS	—	12.50	20.00	40.00	200.00
	1843 AM	—	10.00	15.00	30.00	200.00
	1844 AM	—	10.00	15.00	30.00	200.00
	1845 AM	—	10.00	15.00	30.00	200.00
	1846 AM	—	10.00	15.00	30.00	200.00
	1849 MC	—	10.00	15.00	30.00	200.00
	1850 MC	—	10.00	15.00	30.00	200.00
	1856 MC	—	40.00	60.00	125.00	250.00
	1857 MC	—	—	—	—	—
	1858 MC	—	12.50	20.00	40.00	200.00
	1859 MC	—	50.00	70.00	100.00	200.00
	1861 PS	—	10.00	15.00	30.00	200.00
	1862 RO	—	12.50	20.00	40.00	200.00
	1863 RO	—	100.00	250.00	350.00	500.00
	1868 PS	—	10.00	15.00	30.00	200.00
	1869/8 PS	—	10.00	15.00	30.00	200.00
	1869 PS	—	10.00	15.00	30.00	200.00
		Mint mark: Zs				
374.12	1825 AZ	—	10.00	15.00	30.00	150.00
	1826 AV (A is inverted V)					
		—	7.50	10.00	25.00	150.00
	1826 AZ (A is inverted V)					
		—	7.50	10.00	25.00	150.00
	1826 AO	—	10.00	15.00	30.00	150.00
	1827 AO (A is inverted V)					
		—	6.00	8.00	12.00	150.00
	1828/7 AO	—	15.00	30.00	60.00	175.00
	1828 AO	—	7.50	10.00	25.00	100.00

KM#	Date	Mintage	Fine	VF	XF	Unc
374.12	1828 AO (A is inverted V)					
		—	7.50	10.00	25.00	150.00
	1829 AO	—	7.50	10.00	25.00	150.00
	1829 OV	—	7.50	10.00	25.00	150.00
	1830 OV	—	7.50	10.00	25.00	150.00
	1831 OV	—	7.50	10.00	25.00	150.00
	1831 OM/OV	—	7.50	10.00	25.00	150.00
	1831 OM	—	7.50	10.00	25.00	150.00
	1832/1 OM	—	15.00	30.00	60.00	150.00
	1832 OM	—	7.50	10.00	25.00	150.00
	1833/27 OM	—	7.50	10.00	25.00	150.00
	1833/2 OM	—	7.50	10.00	25.00	150.00
	1833 OM	—	7.50	10.00	25.00	150.00
	1834 OM	—	40.00	60.00	125.00	200.00
	1835 OM	—	7.50	10.00	25.00	150.00
	1836 OM	—	7.50	10.00	25.00	150.00
	1837 OM	—	7.50	10.00	25.00	150.00
	1838 OM	—	15.00	30.00	60.00	150.00
	1839 OM	—	7.50	10.00	20.00	150.00
	1840 OM	—	7.50	10.00	20.00	150.00
	1841/0 OM	—	7.50	10.00	20.00	150.00
	1841 OM	—	7.50	10.00	20.00	150.00
	1842 OM	—	7.50	10.00	20.00	150.00
	1843 OM	—	7.50	10.00	20.00	150.00
	1844 OM	—	7.50	10.00	20.00	150.00
	1845 OM small letters and leaves					
		—	7.50	10.00	20.00	150.00
	1845 OM large letters and leaves					
		—	7.50	10.00	20.00	150.00
	1846 OM	—	7.50	10.00	20.00	150.00
	1847 OM	—	7.50	10.00	20.00	150.00
	1848 OM	—	7.50	10.00	20.00	150.00
	1849 OM	—	7.50	10.00	20.00	150.00
	1850 OM	—	7.50	10.00	20.00	150.00
	1851 OM	—	7.50	10.00	20.00	150.00
	1852 OM	—	7.50	10.00	20.00	150.00
	1853 OM	—	7.50	10.00	20.00	150.00
	1854/3 OM	—	7.50	10.00	20.00	150.00
	1854 OM	—	7.50	10.00	20.00	150.00
	1855/4 OM	—	7.50	10.00	20.00	150.00
	1855 OM	—	7.50	10.00	20.00	150.00
	1855 MO	—	7.50	10.00	20.00	150.00
	1856/5 MO	—	7.50	10.00	20.00	150.00
	1856 MO	—	7.50	10.00	20.00	150.00
	1857 MO	—	7.50	10.00	20.00	150.00
	1858 MO	—	7.50	10.00	20.00	150.00
	1859 MO	—	7.50	10.00	20.00	150.00
	1860/59 MO	—	7.50	10.00	20.00	150.00
	1860 MO	—	7.50	10.00	20.00	100.00
	1860 VL	—	7.50	10.00	20.00	150.00
	1861 VL	—	7.50	10.00	20.00	150.00
	1862 VL	—	7.50	10.00	20.00	100.00
	1863 MO	—	12.50	20.00	40.00	150.00
	1863 VL	—	7.50	10.00	20.00	150.00
	1864 MO	—	7.50	10.00	20.00	150.00
	1864 VL	—	7.50	10.00	20.00	150.00
	1865 MO	—	7.50	10.00	20.00	150.00
	1867 JS	—	7.50	.10.00	20.00	150.00
	1868 JS	—	10.00	15.00	35.00	150.00
	1868 YH	—	7.50	10.00	20.00	150.00
	1869 YH	—	7.50	10.00	20.00	150.00
	1870 YH	—	7.50	10.00	20.00	150.00

4 REALES

13.5400 g, .903 SILVER, .3925 oz ASW
Mint mark: Ce   Obv: Facing eagle.

Mint mark: C

KM#	Date	Mintage	Fine	VF	XF	Unc
375	1863 ML large C					
		—	200.00	500.00	850.00	4000.
	1863 ML small C					
		—	350.00	650.00	1250.	4750.

Mint mark: C

KM#	Date	Mintage	Fine	VF	XF	Unc
375.1	1846 CE	—	400.00	550.00	900.00	—
	1850 CE	—	75.00	125.00	250.00	600.00
	1852 CE	—	200.00	300.00	500.00	1250.
	1857 CE	—	—	—	Rare	—
	1858 CE	—	100.00	200.00	350.00	1000.
	1860 PV	—	25.00	50.00	125.00	600.00

Mint mark: Ga

KM#	Date	Mintage	Fine	VF	XF	Unc
375.2	1842/1 JG	—	—	Reported, not confirmed		
	1842 JG	—	—	Reported, not confirmed		
	1843 MC	—	20.00	40.00	80.00	400.00
	1844/3 MC	—	30.00	60.00	125.00	400.00
	1844 MC	—	20.00	40.00	80.00	400.00
	1845 MC	—	20.00	40.00	80.00	400.00
	1845 JG	—	20.00	40.00	80.00	400.00
	1846 JG	—	20.00	40.00	80.00	400.00
	1847 JG	—	40.00	80.00	150.00	400.00
	1848/7 JG	—	40.00	80.00	150.00	400.00
	1849 JG	—	40.00	80.00	150.00	400.00
	1850 JG	—	65.00	125.00	250.00	550.00
	1852 JG	—	—	—	Rare	—
	1854 JG	—	—	—	Rare	—
	1855 JG	—	100.00	200.00	400.00	1250.
	1856 JG	—	—	—	Rare	—
	1857/6 JG	—	65.00	125.00	250.00	550.00
	1858 JG	—	125.00	250.00	450.00	1250.
	1859/8 JG	—	125.00	250.00	450.00	1250.
	1860 JG	—	—	—	Rare	—
	1863/2 JG	—	150.00	300.00	1250.	6000.
	1863 JG	—	150.00	300.00	1250.	6000.

Mint mark: GC

KM#	Date	Mintage	Fine	VF	XF	Unc
375.3	1844 MP	—	1000.00	2000.	3000.	—
	1845 MP	—	3000.00	4000.	5000.	9000.
	1846 MP	—	1700.00	2800.	—	—
	1847 MP	—	1500.00	2500.	—	—
	1849 MP	—	2000.00	3000.	—	—
	1850 MP	—	500.00	1000.	—	—

Mint mark: Go

KM#	Date	Mintage	Fine	VF	XF	Unc
375.4	1835 PJ	—	12.50	25.00	60.00	350.00
	1836/5 PJ	—	15.00	30.00	75.00	350.00
	1836 PJ	—	15.00	30.00	75.00	350.00
	1837 PJ	—	12.50	25.00	60.00	350.00
	1838/7 PJ	—	15.00	30.00	75.00	350.00
	1838 PJ	—	12.50	30.00	75.00	350.00
	1839 PJ	—	12.50	25.00	60.00	350.00
	1840/30 PJ	—	20.00	50.00	100.00	350.00
	1841/31 PJ	—	150.00	250.00	450.00	1250.
	1842 PJ	—	—	—	Rare	—
	1842 PM	—	15.00	30.00	75.00	350.00
	1843/2 PM eagle w/convex wings, thick rays					
		—	12.50	25.00	60.00	350.00
	1843 PM eagle w/concave wings, thin rays					
		—	12.50	25.00	60.00	350.00
	1844/3 PM	—	15.00	30.00	75.00	350.00
	1844 PM	—	20.00	50.00	100.00	350.00
	1845/4 PM	—	20.00	50.00	100.00	350.00
	1845 PM	—	20.00	50.00	100.00	350.00
	1846/5 PM	—	15.00	30.00	75.00	350.00
375.4	1846 PM	—	15.00	30.00	75.00	350.00
	1847/6 PM	—	15.00	30.00	75.00	350.00
	1847 PM	—	15.00	30.00	75.00	350.00
	1848/7 PM	—	20.00	50.00	100.00	350.00
	1848 PM	—	20.00	50.00	100.00	350.00
	1849 PF	—	20.00	50.00	100.00	350.00
	1850 PF	—	12.50	25.00	60.00	350.00
	1851 PF	—	12.50	25.00	60.00	350.00
	1852 PF	—	15.00	30.00	75.00	350.00
	1853 PF	—	15.00	30.00	75.00	350.00
	1854 PF large eagle					
		—	15.00	30.00	75.00	350.00
	1854 PF small eagle					
		—	15.00	30.00	75.00	350.00
	1855/4 PF	—	15.00	30.00	75.00	350.00
	1855 PF	—	12.50	25.00	60.00	350.00
	1856 PF	—	12.50	25.00	60.00	350.00
	1857 PF	—	20.00	50.00	100.00	350.00

KM#	Date	Mintage	Fine	VF	XF	Unc
	1858 PF	—	20.00	50.00	100.00	350.00
	1859 PF	—	20.00	50.00	100.00	350.00
	1860/59 PF	—	15.00	30.00	75.00	350.00
	1860 PF	—	15.00	30.00	75.00	350.00
	1861/51 PF	—	15.00	30.00	75.00	350.00
	1861 PF	—	20.00	50.00	100.00	350.00
	1862/1 YE	—	15.00	30.00	75.00	350.00
	1862/1 YF	—	15.00	30.00	75.00	350.00
	1862 YE/PF	—	15.00	30.00	75.00	350.00
	1862 YE	—	15.00	30.00	75.00	350.00
	1862 YF	—	15.00	30.00	75.00	350.00
	1863/53 YF	—	15.00	30.00	75.00	350.00
	1863 YF/PF	—	15.00	30.00	75.00	350.00
	1863 YF	—	15.00	30.00	75.00	350.00
	1867/57 YF/PF					
		—	15.00	30.00	75.00	350.00
	1868/58 YF/PF					
		—	15.00	30.00	75.00	350.00
	1870 FR	—	15.00	30.00	75.00	350.00

NOTE: Varieties exist. Some 1862 dates appear to be 1869 because of weak dies.

Mint mark: Ho

KM#	Date	Mintage	Fine	VF	XF	Unc
375.5	1861 FM	—	200.00	350.00	500.00	1850.
	1867/1 PR/FM	—	150.00	275.00	400.00	1750.

Mint mark: Mo

KM#	Date	Mintage	Fine	VF	XF	Unc
375.6	1827/6 JM	—	200.00	400.00	—	—
	1850 GC	—	—	—	Rare	—
	1852 GC	—	—	—	Rare	—
	1854 GC	—	—	—	Rare	—
	1855 GF/GC	—	50.00	100.00	200.00	500.00
	1855 GF	—	100.00	200.00	350.00	800.00
	1856 GF/GC	—	20.00	50.00	100.00	350.00
	1856 GF	—	—	—	Rare	—
	1859 FH	—	20.00	50.00	100.00	350.00
	1861 CH	—	15.00	30.00	75.00	300.00
	1862 CH	—	20.00	50.00	100.00	350.00
	1863/2 CH	—	20.00	50.00	100.00	350.00
	1863 CH	—	75.00	150.00	300.00	650.00
	1867 CH	—	20.00	50.00	100.00	350.00
	1868 CH/PH	—	30.00	75.00	150.00	400.00
	1868 CH	—	20.00	50.00	100.00	350.00
	1868 PH	—	30.00	75.00	150.00	400.00

Mint mark: O

KM#	Date	Mintage	Fine	VF	XF	Unc
375.7	1861 FR ornamental edge					
		—	225.00	450.00	750.00	2750.
	1861 FR herringbone edge					
		—	300.00	550.00	850.00	2850.
	1861 FR obliquely reeded edge					
		—	200.00	400.00	700.00	—

Mint mark: Pi

KM#	Date	Mintage	Fine	VF	XF	Unc
375.8	1837 JS	—	200.00	350.00	—	—
	1838 JS	—	150.00	250.00	400.00	850.00
	1842 PS	—	50.00	100.00	200.00	450.00
	1843/2 PS	—	50.00	100.00	200.00	450.00
	1843/2 PS 3 cut from 8 punch					
		—	50.00	100.00	200.00	450.00
	1843 AM	—	30.00	75.00	150.00	450.00
	1843 PS	—	50.00	100.00	200.00	450.00
	1844 AM	—	30.00	75.00	150.00	450.00
	1845/4 AM	—	20.00	50.00	100.00	450.00
	1845 AM	—	20.00	50.00	100.00	450.00
	1846 AM	—	20.00	50.00	100.00	450.00
	1847 AM	—	75.00	150.00	250.00	550.00
	1848 AM	—	—	—	Rare	—
	1849 MC/AM	—	20.00	50.00	100.00	450.00
	1849 MC	—	20.00	50.00	100.00	450.00
	1849 PS	—	20.00	50.00	100.00	450.00
	1850 MC	—	20.00	50.00	100.00	450.00
	1851 MC	—	20.00	50.00	100.00	450.00
	1852 MC	—	20.00	50.00	100.00	450.00
	1853 MC	—	20.00	50.00	100.00	450.00
	1854 MC	—	100.00	200.00	400.00	1100.
	1855 MC	—	175.00	300.00	500.00	1500.
	1856 MC	—	250.00	400.00	700.00	—

KM#	Date	Mintage	Fine	VF	XF	Unc
	Mint mark: Zs					
375.8	1857 MC	—	—	—	Rare	—
	1857 PS	—	—	—	Rare	—
	1858 MC	—	100.00	200.00	400.00	1000.
	1859 MC	—	2000.	3000.	—	—
	1860 PS	—	300.00	450.00	700.00	—
	1861 PS	—	30.00	75.00	150.00	450.00
	1861 RO/PS	—	30.00	75.00	150.00	450.00
	1861 RO	—	50.00	100.00	200.00	450.00
	1862 RO	—	30.00	75.00	150.00	450.00
	1863 RO	—	30.00	75.00	150.00	450.00
	1864 RO	—	1600.	2600.	—	—
	1868 PS	—	30.00	75.00	150.00	450.00
	1869/8 PS	—	30.00	75.00	150.00	450.00
	1869 PS	—	30.00	75.00	150.00	450.00
	Mint mark: Zs					
375.9	1830 OM	—	20.00	50.00	100.00	350.00
	1831 OM	—	15.00	30.00	75.00	350.00
	1832/1 OM	—	20.00	50.00	100.00	350.00
	1832 OM	—	20.00	50.00	100.00	350.00
	1833/2 OM	—	20.00	50.00	100.00	350.00
	1833/27 OM	—	15.00	30.00	75.00	350.00
	1833 OM	—	15.00	30.00	75.00	350.00
	1834/3 OM	—	20.00	50.00	100.00	350.00
	1834 OM	—	15.00	30.00	75.00	350.00
	1835 OM	—	15.00	30.00	75.00	350.00
	1836 OM	—	15.00	30.00	75.00	350.00
	1837/5 OM	—	20.00	50.00	100.00	350.00
	1837/6 OM	—	20.00	50.00	100.00	350.00
	1837 OM	—	20.00	50.00	100.00	350.00
	1838/7 OM	—	15.00	30.00	75.00	350.00
	1839 OM	—	250.00	375.00	500.00	—
	1840 OM	—	—	—	Rare	—
	1841 OM	—	15.00	30.00	75.00	350.00
	1842 OM large letters					
		—	15.00	30.00	75.00	350.00
	1842 OM small letters					
		—	75.00	150.00	300.00	800.00
	1843 OM	—	15.00	30.00	75.00	350.00
	1844 OM	—	20.00	50.00	100.00	350.00
	1845 OM	—	20.00	50.00	100.00	350.00
	1846/5 OM	—	25.00	60.00	125.00	350.00
	1846 OM	—	20.00	50.00	100.00	350.00
	1847 OM	—	15.00	30.00	75.00	350.00
	1848/6 OM	—	50.00	75.00	125.00	350.00
	1848 OM	—	20.00	50.00	100.00	350.00
	1849 OM	—	20.00	50.00	100.00	350.00
	1850 OM	—	20.00	50.00	100.00	350.00
	1851 OM	—	15.00	30.00	75.00	350.00
	1852 OM	—	15.00	30.00	75.00	350.00
	1853 OM	—	20.00	50.00	100.00	350.00
	1854/3 OM	—	30.00	75.00	150.00	350.00
	1855/4 OM	—	20.00	50.00	100.00	350.00
	1855 OM	—	15.00	30.00	75.00	350.00
	1856 OM	—	15.00	30.00	75.00	350.00
	1856 MO	—	20.00	50.00	100.00	350.00
	1857/5 MO	—	20.00	50.00	100.00	350.00
	1857 O/M	—	20.00	50.00	100.00	350.00
	1857 MO	—	15.00	30.00	75.00	350.00
	1858 MO	—	20.00	50.00	100.00	350.00
	1859 MO	—	15.00	30.00	75.00	350.00
	1860/59 MO	—	20.00	50.00	100.00	350.00
	1860 MO	—	15.00	30.00	75.00	350.00
	1860 VL	—	20.00	50.00	100.00	350.00
	1861/0 VL	—	20.00	50.00	100.00	350.00
	1861 VL	—	15.00	30.00	75.00	350.00
	1862/1 VL	—	20.00	50.00	100.00	350.00
	1862 VL	—	20.00	50.00	100.00	350.00
	1863 VL	—	20.00	50.00	100.00	350.00
	1863 MO	—	20.00	50.00	100.00	350.00
	1864 VL	—	15.00	30.00	75.00	350.00
	1868 JS	—	20.00	50.00	100.00	350.00
	1868 YH	—	15.00	30.00	75.00	350.00
	1869 YH	—	15.00	30.00	75.00	350.00
	1870 YH	—	15.00	30.00	75.00	350.00

8 REALES

27.0700 g, .903 SILVER, .7859 oz ASW

KM#	Date	Mintage	Fine	VF	XF	Unc
	Mint mark: Do					
	Obv: Hooked-neck eagle.					
376	1824 RL	—	200.00	350.00	1250.	2750.
	Mint mark: Go					
376.1	1824 JM	—	200.00	325.00	1000.	3500.
	1825/4 JJ	—	550.00	800.00	1500.	6000.
	1825 JJ	—	500.00	750.00	1400.	5500.

KM#	Date	Mintage	Fine	VF	XF	Unc
	Mint mark: Mo					
376.2	1823 JM edge: circle and rectangle pattern					
		—	—	—	Rare	—
	1823 JM edge: laurel leaves					
		—	150.00	275.00	600.00	2250.
	1824 JM	—	125.00	225.00	450.00	1850.
	1824 JM (error) REPULICA					
		—	7000.	9000.	—	—

NOTE: These are rarely found with detail on the eagles breast and bring a premium if even slight feather detail is present there.

KM#	Date	Mintage	Fine	VF	XF	Unc
	Mint mark: A, As					
377	1864 PG	—	750.00	1250.	2000.	—
	1865/4 PG	—	—	—	Rare	—
	1865 PG	—	500.00	750.00	1000.	—
	1866/5 PG	—	—	—	Rare	—
	1866 PG	—	1250.	2250.	—	—
	1866 DL	—	—	—	Rare	—
	1867 DL	—	1150.	2150.	—	—
	1868 DL	—	50.00	90.00	150.00	300.00
	1869/8 DL	—	50.00	90.00	150.00	—
	1869 DL	—	50.00	80.00	120.00	300.00
	1870 DL	—	30.00	60.00	120.00	300.00
	1871 DL	—	20.00	35.00	75.00	200.00

KM#	Date	Mintage	Fine	VF	XF	Unc
377	1872 AM/DL	—	25.00	50.00	100.00	300.00
	1872 AM	—	25.00	50.00	100.00	250.00
	1873 AM	.509	15.00	25.00	50.00	150.00
	1874 DL	—	15.00	25.00	50.00	150.00
	1875A DL 7/7	—	40.00	80.00	120.00	300.00
	1875A DL	—	15.00	25.00	50.00	150.00
	1875AsDL	—	30.00	60.00	110.00	250.00
	1876 DL	—	15.00	25.00	50.00	150.00
	1877 DL	.515	15.00	25.00	50.00	150.00
	1878 DL	.513	15.00	25.00	50.00	150.00
	1879 DL	—	20.00	35.00	75.00	175.00
	1879 ML	—	30.00	60.00	125.00	350.00
	1880 ML	—	12.00	15.00	30.00	140.00
	1881 ML	.966	12.00	15.00	30.00	140.00
	1882 ML	.480	12.00	15.00	30.00	140.00
	1883 ML	.464	12.00	15.00	30.00	140.00
	1884 ML	—	12.00	15.00	30.00	140.00
	1885 ML	.280	12.00	15.00	30.00	140.00
	1886 ML	.857	12.00	15.00	25.00	110.00
	1886/0 As/Cn ML/JD					
		I.A.	15.00	20.00	35.00	160.00
	1887 ML	.650	12.00	15.00	25.00	110.00
	1888/7 ML	.508	30.00	60.00	100.00	400.00
	1888 ML	I.A.	12.00	15.00	25.00	110.00
	1889 ML	.427	12.00	15.00	25.00	110.00
	1890 ML	.450	12.00	15.00	25.00	110.00
	1891 ML	.533	12.00	15.00	25.00	110.00
	1892 ML	.465	12.00	15.00	25.00	110.00
	1893 ML	.734	10.00	12.00	22.00	85.00
	1894 ML	.725	10.00	12.00	22.00	85.00
	1895 ML	.477	10.00	12.00	22.00	85.00

NOTE: Varieties exist.

Mint mark: Ce

KM#	Date	Mintage	Fine	VF	XF	Unc
377.1	1863 ML	—	425.00	700.00	1350.	3000.
	1863 CeML/PiMC					
		—	425.00	750.00	1500.	3250.

Mint mark: Ca

KM#	Date	Mintage	Fine	VF	XF	Unc
377.2	1831 MR	—	1000.	1750.	2250.	3250.
	1832 MR	—	125.00	200.00	300.00	600.00
	1833 MR	—	350.00	650.00	1250.	—
	1834 MR	—	—	—	Rare	—
	1834 AM	—	350.00	650.00	—	—
	1835 AM	—	150.00	250.00	400.00	800.00
	1836 AM	—	100.00	150.00	225.00	450.00
	1837 AM	—	450.00	850.00	—	—
	1838 AM	—	100.00	200.00	300.00	600.00
	1839 RG	—	1250.	2500.	3500.	—
	1840 RG 1 dot after date					
		—	300.00	500.00	800.00	1500.
	1840 RG 3 dots after date					
		—	300.00	500.00	800.00	1500.
	1841 RG	—	50.00	100.00	150.00	300.00
	1842 RG	—	25.00	40.00	75.00	150.00
	1843 RG	—	40.00	80.00	125.00	250.00
	1844/1 RG	—	35.00	70.00	100.00	200.00
	1844 RG	—	25.00	40.00	75.00	150.00
	1845 RG	—	25.00	40.00	75.00	150.00
	1846 RG	—	30.00	60.00	100.00	250.00
	1847 RG	—	40.00	80.00	125.00	250.00
	1848 RG	—	30.00	60.00	100.00	200.00
	1849 RG	—	30.00	60.00	100.00	200.00
	1850/40 RG	—	40.00	80.00	125.00	250.00
	1850 RG	—	30.00	60.00	100.00	200.00

KM#	Date	Mintage	Fine	VF	XF	Unc
377.2	1851/41 RG	—	100.00	200.00	300.00	500.00
	1851 RG	—	150.00	250.00	400.00	750.00
	1852/42 RG	—	150.00	250.00	400.00	750.00
	1852 RG	—	150.00	250.00	400.00	750.00
	1853/43 RG	—	150.00	250.00	400.00	750.00
	1853 RG	—	150.00	250.00	400.00	750.00
	1854/44 RG	—	100.00	200.00	300.00	500.00
	1854 RG	—	50.00	100.00	150.00	300.00
	1855/45 RG	—	100.00	200.00	350.00	650.00
	1855 RG	—	75.00	125.00	200.00	400.00
	1856/45 RG	—	300.00	550.00	1000.	1750.
	1856/5 JC	—	400.00	650.00	1150.	2000.
	1857 JC/RG	—	40.00	80.00	125.00	250.00
	1857 JC	—	50.00	100.00	150.00	250.00
	1858 JC	—	20.00	35.00	75.00	150.00
	1858 BA	—	2000.	3500.	—	—
	1859 JC	—	40.00	80.00	125.00	250.00
	1860 JC	—	20.00	40.00	90.00	175.00
	1861 JC	—	15.00	25.00	50.00	125.00
	1862 JC	—	15.00	25.00	50.00	125.00
	1863 JC	—	20.00	35.00	75.00	150.00
	1864 JC	—	20.00	35.00	75.00	150.00
	1865 JC	—	100.00	200.00	350.00	600.00
	1865 FP	—	1350.	—	—	—
	1866 JC	—	—	—	Rare	—
	1866 FP	—	1000.	2000.	3250.	5000.
	1866 JG	—	850.00	1650.	2750.	—
	1867 JG	—	100.00	200.00	350.00	600.00
	1868 JG	—	75.00	150.00	200.00	350.00
	1868 MM	—	50.00	100.00	150.00	300.00
	1869 MM	—	20.00	35.00	65.00	125.00
	1870 MM	—	20.00	35.00	65.00	125.00
	1871/0 MM	—	15.00	25.00	50.00	120.00
	1871 MM	—	15.00	25.00	50.00	120.00
	1871 MM first M/inverted M					
		—	20.00	35.00	65.00	125.00
	1873 MM	—	20.00	35.00	65.00	125.00
	1873 MM/T					
		—	15.00	25.00	50.00	120.00
	1874 MM	—	12.00	15.00	30.00	100.00
	1875 MM	—	12.00	15.00	30.00	100.00
	1876 MM	—	12.00	15.00	30.00	100.00
	1877 EA	.472	12.00	15.00	30.00	100.00
	1877 GR	I.A.	25.00	45.00	65.00	150.00
	1877 JM	I.A.	12.00	15.00	30.00	100.00
	1877 AV	I.A.	100.00	200.00	350.00	750.00
	1878 AV	.439	12.00	15.00	25.00	80.00
	1879 AV	—	12.00	15.00	25.00	80.00
	1880 AV	—	250.00	400.00	650.00	1250.
	1880 PM	—	500.00	800.00	1150.	1750.
	1880 MG normal initials					
		—	12.00	15.00	25.00	100.00
	1880 MG tall initials					
		—	12.00	15.00	25.00	100.00
	1880 MM	—	12.00	15.00	25.00	100.00
	1881 MG	1.085	10.00	12.00	20.00	65.00
	1882 MG	.779	10.00	12.00	20.00	65.00
	1882 MM	I.A.	10.00	12.00	20.00	65.00
	1882 MM M sideways					
		Inc. Ab.	20.00	40.00	90.00	150.00
	1883 sideways M MM					
		.818	—	—	—	—
	1883 MM	I.A.	10.00	12.00	20.00	65.00
	1884/3 MM	—	12.00	15.00	30.00	80.00
	1884 MM	—	10.00	12.00	20.00	65.00
	1885/4 MM					
		1.345	15.00	25.00	50.00	120.00
	1885/6 MM	I.A.	15.00	25.00	50.00	120.00
	1885 MM	I.A.	10.00	12.00	20.00	65.00
	1886 MM	2.483	10.00	12.00	20.00	65.00
	1887 MM	2.625	10.00	12.00	20.00	65.00
	1888/7 MM					
		2.434	15.00	25.00	50.00	120.00
	1888 MM	I.A.	10.00	12.00	20.00	65.00
	1889 MM	2.681	10.00	12.00	20.00	65.00
	1890 MM	2.137	10.00	12.00	20.00	65.00
	1891/0 MM					
		2.268	15.00	25.00	50.00	120.00
	1891 MM	I.A.	10.00	12.00	20.00	80.00
	1892 MM	2.527	10.00	12.00	20.00	65.00
	1893 MM	2.632	10.00	12.00	20.00	65.00
	1894 MM	2.642	10.00	12.00	20.00	65.00
377.2	1895 MM	1.112	10.00	12.00	20.00	65.00
	1895 MM	1.112	10.00	12.00	20.00	65.00

NOTE: Varieties exist.

Mint mark: C, Cn

KM#	Date	Mintage	Fine	VF	XF	Unc
377.3	1846 CE	—	150.00	300.00	800.00	1500.
	1847 CE	—	600.00	1000.	1500.	—
	1848 CE	—	150.00	300.00	600.00	1000.
	1849 CE	—	75.00	125.00	200.00	400.00
	1850 CE	—	75.00	125.00	200.00	400.00
	1851 CE	—	125.00	250.00	450.00	1000.
	1852/1 CE	—	100.00	150.00	250.00	500.00
	1852 CE	—	100.00	200.00	350.00	650.00
	1853/0 CE	—	200.00	350.00	700.00	1300.
	1853/2/0 CE	—	200.00	400.00	750.00	1400.
	1853 CE thick rays					
		—	100.00	175.00	300.00	600.00
	1853 CE (error:) MEXIGANA					
		—	200.00	350.00	650.00	—
	1854 CE	—	—	—	Rare	—
	1854 CE large eagle & hat					
		—	175.00	350.00	750.00	1200.
	1855/6 CE	—	40.00	60.00	100.00	200.00
	1855 CE	—	25.00	40.00	75.00	150.00
	1856 CE	—	50.00	100.00	175.00	350.00
	1857 CE	—	20.00	35.00	75.00	150.00
	1858 CE	—	30.00	40.00	75.00	150.00
	1859 CE	—	20.00	35.00	75.00	150.00
	1860/9 PV/CV					
		—	50.00	70.00	100.00	200.00
	1860/9 PV/E	—	50.00	70.00	100.00	200.00
	1860 CE	—	25.00	40.00	75.00	150.00
	1860 PV	—	40.00	60.00	90.00	175.00
	1861/0 CE	—	40.00	60.00	100.00	250.00
	1861 PV/CE	—	75.00	125.00	200.00	350.00
	1861 CE	—	20.00	35.00	60.00	150.00
	1862 CE	—	20.00	35.00	60.00	150.00
	1863/2 CE	—	30.00	50.00	75.00	200.00
	1863 CE	—	20.00	30.00	60.00	150.00
	1864 CE	—	30.00	60.00	100.00	300.00
	1865 CE	—	125.00	200.00	325.00	650.00
	1866 CE	—	—	—	Rare	—
	1867 CE	—	125.00	200.00	375.00	750.00
	1868/7 CE	—	30.00	40.00	75.00	150.00
	1868/8	—	50.00	100.00	150.00	300.00
	1868 CE	—	30.00	40.00	75.00	150.00
	1869 CE	—	30.00	40.00	75.00	175.00
	1870 CE	—	35.00	50.00	90.00	200.00
	1873 MP	—	50.00	100.00	150.00	300.00
	1874C MP	—	20.00	30.00	45.00	100.00
	1874CN MP	—	125.00	200.00	300.00	600.00
	1875 MP	—	12.00	15.00	22.00	80.00
	1876 GP	—	12.00	15.00	30.00	90.00
	1876 CG	—	12.00	15.00	22.00	80.00
	1877 CG	.339	12.00	15.00	22.00	80.00
	1877 Gn CG (error)					
		—	65.00	125.00	200.00	400.00
	1877 JA	I.A.	35.00	75.00	125.00	250.00
	1878/7 CG	.483	35.00	75.00	125.00	250.00
	1878 CG	I.A.	15.00	25.00	35.00	125.00
	1878 JD	I.A.	15.00	20.00	30.00	125.00
	1878 JD D/retrograde D					
		I.A.	20.00	30.00	40.00	150.00
	1879 JD	—	12.00	15.00	30.00	90.00
	1880/70 JD	—	15.00	20.00	30.00	90.00
	1880 JD	—	12.00	15.00	22.00	80.00
	1881/0 JD					
		1.032	15.00	20.00	30.00	90.00
	1881C JD	I.A.	12.00	15.00	22.00	80.00
	1881CnJD	I.A.	40.00	60.00	90.00	150.00
	1882 JD	.397	12.00	15.00	22.00	80.00
	1882 AM	I.A.	12.00	15.00	22.00	80.00
	1883 AM	.333	12.00	15.00	22.00	125.00
	1884 AM	—	12.00	15.00	22.00	80.00
	1885/6 AM	.227	20.00	30.00	45.00	110.00
	1885C AM	I.A.	75.00	125.00	250.00	500.00
	1885CnAM	I.A.	12.00	15.00	22.00	80.00
	1885GnAM (error)					
		Inc. Ab.	60.00	100.00	150.00	300.00
	1886 AM	.571	12.00	15.00	22.00	80.00
	1887 AM	.732	12.00	15.00	22.00	80.00
	1888 AM	.768	12.00	15.00	22.00	80.00
	1889 AM	1.075	12.00	15.00	22.00	80.00
	1890 AM	.874	10.00	12.00	20.00	65.00
	1891 AM	.777	10.00	12.00	20.00	65.00
	1892 AM	.681	10.00	12.00	20.00	65.00
	1893 AM	1.144	10.00	12.00	20.00	65.00
	1894 AM	2.118	10.00	12.00	20.00	65.00

KM#	Date	Mintage	Fine	VF	XF	Unc
377.3	1895 AM	1.834	10.00	12.00	20.00	65.00
	1896 AM	2.134	10.00	12.00	20.00	65.00
	1897 AM	1.580	10.00	12.00	20.00	65.00

NOTE: Varieties exist.

Mint mark: Do

KM#	Date	Mintage	Fine	VF	XF	Unc
377.4	1825 RL	—	30.00	55.00	90.00	200.00
	1826 RL	—	40.00	100.00	250.00	500.00
	1827/6 RL	—	35.00	60.00	85.00	200.00
	1827 RL	—	30.00	50.00	80.00	175.00
	1828/7 RL	—	35.00	60.00	90.00	200.00
	1828 RL	—	25.00	50.00	80.00	175.00
	1829 RL	—	25.00	50.00	80.00	175.00
	1830 RM B on eagles claw					
		—	25.00	50.00	80.00	175.00
	1831 RM B on eagles claw					
		—	20.00	30.00	60.00	150.00
	1832 RM Mexican dies, B on eagles claw					
		—	25.00	50.00	100.00	200.00
	1832/1 RM/RL French dies					
		—	25.00	35.00	75.00	165.00
	1833/2 RM/RL					
		—	20.00	35.00	75.00	165.00
	1833 RM	—	15.00	30.00	60.00	150.00
	1834/3/2 RM/RL					
		—	20.00	35.00	75.00	165.00
	1834 RM	—	15.00	25.00	50.00	150.00
	1835/4 RM/RL					
		—	25.00	40.00	80.00	175.00
	1835 RM	—	20.00	35.00	65.00	150.00
	1836/1 RM	—	20.00	35.00	65.00	150.00
	1836/4 RM	—	20.00	35.00	65.00	150.00
	1836/5/4 RM/RL					
		—	75.00	150.00	250.00	500.00
	1836 RM	—	20.00	30.00	55.00	150.00
	1836 RM M on snake					
		—	20.00	30.00	55.00	150.00
	1837/1 RM	—	20.00	30.00	55.00	150.00
	1837 RM	—	20.00	30.00	55.00	150.00
	1838/1 RM	—	20.00	30.00	55.00	150.00
	1838/7 RM	—	20.00	30.00	55.00	150.00
	1838 RM	—	20.00	30.00	55.00	150.00
	1839/1 RM/RL					
		—	20.00	30.00	55.00	150.00
	1839/1 RM	—	20.00	30.00	55.00	150.00
	1839 RM	—	20.00	30.00	55.00	150.00
	1840/38/31 RM					
		—	20.00	30.00	55.00	150.00
	1840/39 RM	—	20.00	30.00	55.00	150.00
	1840 RM	—	20.00	30.00	55.00	150.00
	1841/31 RM	—	25.00	50.00	85.00	200.00
	1842/31 RM B below cactus					
		—	125.00	250.00	400.00	750.00
	1842/31 RM	—	40.00	80.00	125.00	250.00
	1842/32 RM	—	40.00	80.00	125.00	250.00
	1842 RM eagle of 1832-41					
		—	20.00	30.00	55.00	150.00
	1842 RM pre 1832 eagle resumed					
		—	20.00	30.00	55.00	150.00
	1842 RM	—	40.00	80.00	125.00	250.00
	1843/33 RM	—	50.00	90.00	150.00	250.00
	1844/34 RM	—	100.00	200.00	300.00	500.00
	1844/35 RM	—	100.00	200.00	300.00	500.00
	1845/31 RM	—	35.00	75.00	125.00	250.00

KM#	Date	Mintage	Fine	VF	XF	Unc
377.4	1845/34 RM	—	35.00	75.00	125.00	250.00
	1845/35 RM	—	35.00	75.00	125.00	250.00
	1845 RM	—	20.00	30.00	55.00	150.00
	1846/31 RM	—	20.00	30.00	55.00	150.00
	1846/36 RM	—	20.00	30.00	55.00	150.00
	1846 RM	—	20.00	30.00	55.00	150.00
	1847 RM	—	25.00	50.00	80.00	185.00
	1848/7 RM	—	125.00	250.00	400.00	750.00
	1848/7 CM/RM	—	100.00	200.00	350.00	700.00
	1848 CM/RM	—	100.00	200.00	350.00	700.00
	1848 RM	—	100.00	200.00	300.00	600.00
	1848 CM	—	50.00	100.00	200.00	400.00
	1849/39 CM	—	100.00	200.00	350.00	700.00
	1849 CM	—	100.00	200.00	350.00	700.00
	1849 JMR/CM oval 0	—	200.00	325.00	450.00	800.00
	1849 DoJMR oval O	—	200.00	400.00	600.00	1000.
	1849 DoJMR round O	—	200.00	400.00	600.00	1000.
	1850 JMR	—	100.00	150.00	250.00	500.00
	1851/0 JMR	—	100.00	150.00	250.00	500.00
	1851 JMR	—	100.00	150.00	250.00	500.00
	1852 CP/JMR	—	—	—	Rare	—
	1852 CP	—	—	—	Rare	—
	1852 JMR	—	175.00	250.00	375.00	650.00
	1853 CP/JMR	—	175.00	275.00	400.00	700.00
	1853 CP	—	200.00	350.00	600.00	1200.
	1854 CP	—	25.00	35.00	65.00	300.00
	1855 CP eagle type of 1854	—	50.00	100.00	175.00	350.00
	1855 CP eagle type of 1856	—	50.00	100.00	175.00	350.00
	1856 CP	—	50.00	100.00	175.00	350.00
	1857 CP	—	35.00	75.00	175.00	350.00
	1858/7 CP	—	25.00	35.00	70.00	165.00
	1858 CP	—	20.00	30.00	60.00	165.00
	1859 CP	—	20.00	30.00	60.00	165.00
	1860/59 CP	—	30.00	50.00	100.00	200.00
	1860 CP	—	20.00	30.00	60.00	165.00
	1861/0 CP	—	30.00	50.00	100.00	200.00
	1861 CP	—	20.00	30.00	50.00	125.00
	1862/1 CP	—	25.00	35.00	60.00	125.00
	1862 CP	—	20.00	30.00	55.00	100.00
	1863/2 CP	—	25.00	50.00	75.00	175.00
	1863/53 CP	—	30.00	60.00	90.00	200.00
	1863 CP	—	25.00	50.00	75.00	175.00
	1864 CP	—	100.00	150.00	250.00	500.00
	1864 LT	—	25.00	40.00	80.00	175.00
	1865 LT	—	—	—	Rare	—
	1866 CM	—	1750.	3250.	5500.	8000.
	1867 CM	—	—	—	Rare	—
	1867/6 CP	—	200.00	400.00	600.00	1200.
	1867 CP	—	175.00	300.00	500.00	1000.
	1867 CP/CM	—	175.00	300.00	500.00	1000.
	1867 CP/LT	—	175.00	300.00	500.00	1000.
	1868 CP	—	25.00	40.00	80.00	175.00
	1869 CP	—	20.00	30.00	50.00	125.00
	1870/69 CP	—	20.00	30.00	50.00	125.00
	1870/9 CP	—	20.00	30.00	50.00	125.00
	1870 CP	—	20.00	30.00	50.00	125.00
	1873 CP	—	125.00	225.00	325.00	600.00
	1873 CM	—	30.00	50.00	100.00	200.00
	1874/3 CM	—	12.00	15.00	22.00	100.00
	1874 CM	—	10.00	15.00	22.00	75.00
	1874 JH	—	1500.	2500.	—	—
	1875 CM	—	10.00	15.00	22.00	80.00
	1875 JH	—	100.00	175.00	275.00	500.00
	1876 CM	—	10.00	15.00	22.00	80.00
	1877 CM	.431	1650.	2750.	—	—
	1877 CP	I.A.	10.00	15.00	22.00	80.00
	1877 JMP	I.A.	—	—	Rare	—
	1878 PE	.409	15.00	25.00	40.00	100.00
	1878 TB	I.A.	10.00	15.00	22.00	80.00

KM#	Date	Mintage	Fine	VF	XF	Unc
377.4	1879 TB	—	10.00	15.00	22.00	80.00
	1880/70 TB	—	150.00	250.00	375.00	650.00
	1880/70 TB/JP	—	150.00	250.00	375.00	650.00
	1880/70 JP	—	15.00	25.00	40.00	100.00
	1880 TB	—	150.00	250.00	375.00	650.00
	1880 JP	—	10.00	15.00	22.00	80.00
	1881 JP	.928	10.00	15.00	22.00	80.00
	1882 JP	.414	10.00	15.00	22.00	80.00
	1882 MC/JP	Inc. Ab.	30.00	60.00	100.00	200.00
	1882 MC	I.A.	25.00	50.00	75.00	150.00
	1883/73 MC	.452	15.00	25.00	40.00	90.00
	1883 MC	I.A.	10.00	15.00	22.00	80.00
	1884/3 MC	—	20.00	30.00	60.00	110.00
	1884 MC	—	10.00	15.00	22.00	80.00
	1885 MC	.547	10.00	12.00	20.00	70.00
	1885 JB	I.A.	25.00	35.00	50.00	125.00
	1886/3 MC	.955	15.00	25.00	40.00	100.00
	1886 MC	I.A.	10.00	12.00	20.00	70.00
	1887 MC	1.004	10.00	12.00	20.00	70.00
	1888 MC	.996	10.00	12.00	20.00	70.00
	1889 MC	.874	10.00	12.00	20.00	70.00
	1890 MC	1.119	10.00	12.00	20.00	70.00
	1890 JP	I.A.	10.00	12.00	20.00	70.00
	1891 JP	1.487	10.00	12.00	20.00	70.00
	1892 JP	1.597	10.00	12.00	20.00	70.00
	1892 ND	I.A.	25.00	50.00	100.00	200.00
	1893 ND	1.617	10.00	12.00	20.00	70.00
	1894 ND	1.537	10.00	12.00	20.00	70.00
	1895/3 ND	.761	15.00	25.00	40.00	100.00
	1895 ND	I.A.	10.00	12.00	20.00	70.00

NOTE: Varieties exist.

Mint mark: EoMo

KM#	Date	Mintage	Fine	VF	XF	Unc
377.5	1828 LF/LP	—	350.00	850.00	2000.	—
	1828 LF	—	350.00	850.00	2000.	—
	1829 LF	—	300.00	750.00	1850.	—
	1830/20 LF	—	—	—	Rare	—
	1830 LF	—	1000.	2000.	3250.	—

KM#	Date	Mintage	Fine	VF	XF	Unc
377.6			Mint mark: Ga			
	1825 FS	—	150.00	275.00	425.00	850.00
	1826/5 FS	—	125.00	250.00	400.00	800.00
	1827/87 FS	—	125.00	250.00	400.00	800.00
	1827 FS	—	225.00	350.00	500.00	1000.
	1287 FS (error)	8500.	9500.		—	—
	1828 FS	—	200.00	375.00	550.00	1200.
	1829/8 FS	—	200.00	375.00	550.00	1200.
	1829 FS	—	175.00	325.00	475.00	950.00
	1830/29 FS	—	175.00	300.00	450.00	900.00
	1830 FS	—	100.00	175.00	300.00	600.00
	1830 LP/FS	—	—	—	Rare	—
	1831 LP	—	200.00	400.00	600.00	1200.
	1831 FS/LP	—	300.00	500.00	750.00	1500.
	1831 FS	—	150.00	350.00	—	—
	1832/1 FS	—	50.00	100.00	175.00	300.00
	1832/1 FS/LP					
		—	60.00	125.00	200.00	350.00
	1832 FS	—	25.00	50.00	100.00	225.00
	1833/2/1 FS/LP					
		—	45.00	75.00	125.00	250.00
	1833/2 FS	—	25.00	50.00	100.00	225.00
	1834/2 FS	—	60.00	125.00	200.00	350.00
	1834/3 FS	—	60.00	125.00	200.00	350.00
	1834/0 FS	—	60.00	125.00	200.00	350.00
	1834 FS	—	50.00	100.00	150.00	300.00
	1835 FS	—	25.00	50.00	100.00	225.00
	1836/1 JG/FS					
		—	40.00	80.00	125.00	250.00
	1836 FS	—	400.00	750.00	—	—
	1836 JG/FS	—	25.00	50.00	100.00	225.00
	1836 JG	—	25.00	50.00	100.00	225.00
	1837/6 JG/FS					
		—	50.00	100.00	175.00	300.00
	1837 JG	—	40.00	80.00	125.00	250.00
	1838/7 JG	—	100.00	175.00	300.00	550.00
	1838 JG	—	100.00	150.00	275.00	500.00
	1839 MC	—	100.00	200.00	300.00	550.00
	1839 MC/JG	—	100.00	200.00	300.00	550.00
	1839 JG	—	60.00	125.00	200.00	350.00
	1840/30 MC	—	50.00	75.00	150.00	275.00
	1840 MC	—	30.00	60.00	125.00	250.00
	1841 MC	—	30.00	60.00	125.00	250.00
	1842/1 JG/MG					
		—	100.00	150.00	250.00	450.00
	1842/1 JG/MC					
		—	100.00	150.00	250.00	450.00
	1842 JG	—	25.00	50.00	100.00	225.00
	1842 JG/MG	—	25.00	50.00	100.00	225.00
	1843/2 MC/JG					
		—	25.00	50.00	100.00	225.00
	1843 MC/JG	—	25.00	50.00	100.00	225.00
	1843 JG	—	400.00	600.00	800.00	1500.
	1843 MC	—	50.00	100.00	150.00	300.00
	1844 MC	—	50.00	100.00	150.00	300.00
	1845 MC	—	75.00	150.00	250.00	450.00
	1845 JG	—	650.00	1150.	1750.	—
	1846 JG	—	40.00	80.00	150.00	300.00
	1847 JG	—	100.00	150.00	225.00	400.00
	1848/7 JG	—	55.00	85.00	125.00	250.00
	1848 JG	—	50.00	75.00	100.00	225.00
	1849 JG	—	90.00	125.00	175.00	325.00
	1850 JG	—	50.00	100.00	150.00	300.00
	1851 JG	—	125.00	200.00	350.00	650.00
	1852 JG	—	100.00	150.00	250.00	450.00
	1853/2 JG	—	125.00	175.00	250.00	475.00
	1853 JG	—	90.00	125.00	175.00	300.00
	1854/3 JG	—	65.00	90.00	125.00	250.00
	1854 JG	—	50.00	75.00	125.00	250.00
	1855/4 JG	—	50.00	100.00	150.00	275.00
	1855 JG	—	25.00	50.00	100.00	225.00
	1856/4 JG	—	60.00	125.00	175.00	300.00
	1856/5 56	—	60.00	125.00	175.00	300.00
	1856 JG	—	50.00	100.00	150.00	275.00
	1857 JG	—	50.00	100.00	225.00	400.00
	1858 JG	—	100.00	150.00	300.00	500.00
	1859/7 JG	—	25.00	50.00	100.00	200.00
	1859/8 JG	—	25.00	50.00	100.00	200.00
	1859 JG	—	20.00	40.00	80.00	175.00
	1860 JG w/o dot					
		—	350.00	750.00	1200.	2250.
	1860 JG dot in loop of snakes tail (base alloy)	—	2000.	3250.	—	—
	1861 JG	—	—	—	Rare	—

KM#	Date	Mintage	Fine	VF	XF	Unc
377.6	1862 JG	—	—	—	Rare	—
	1863/52 JG	—	—	—	—	—
	1863/59 JG	—	45.00	50.00	85.00	145.00
	1863/2 JG	—	30.00	50.00	90.00	175.00
	1863/4 JG	—	40.00	60.00	125.00	200.00
	1863 JG	—	25.00	45.00	75.00	150.00
	1863 FV	—	—	—	Rare	—
	1867 JM	—	—	—	Rare	—
	1868/7 JM	—	50.00	75.00	125.00	200.00
	1868 JM	—	50.00	75.00	125.00	200.00
	1869 JM	—	50.00	75.00	125.00	200.00
	1869 IC	—	75.00	125.00	200.00	375.00
	1870/60 IC	—	60.00	90.00	150.00	275.00
	1870 IC	—	60.00	90.00	150.00	275.00
	1873 IC	—	15.00	25.00	50.00	125.00
	1874 IC	—	10.00	15.00	22.00	90.00
	1874 MC	—	25.00	50.00	100.00	200.00
	1875 IC	—	15.00	30.00	60.00	125.00
	1875 MC	—	10.00	15.00	22.00	90.00
	1876 IC	.559	15.00	30.00	50.00	100.00
	1876 MC	I.A.	125.00	175.00	250.00	375.00
	1877 IC	.928	10.00	15.00	22.00	90.00
	1877 JA	I.A.	10.00	15.00	22.00	90.00
	1878 JA	.764	10.00	15.00	22.00	90.00
	1879 JA	—	10.00	15.00	22.00	90.00
	1880/70 FS	—	15.00	25.00	50.00	125.00
	1880 JA	—	10.00	15.00	22.00	90.00
	1880 FS	—	10.00	15.00	22.00	90.00
	1881 FS	1.300	10.00	15.00	22.00	90.00
	1882/1 FS	.537	15.00	25.00	50.00	125.00
	1882 FS	I.A.	10.00	15.00	22.00	90.00
	1882 TB/FS	I.A.	75.00	150.00	250.00	450.00
	1882 TB	I.A.	50.00	100.00	175.00	300.00
	1883 TB	.561	15.00	25.00	40.00	125.00
	1884 TB	—	10.00	12.00	20.00	85.00
	1884 AH	—	10.00	12.00	20.00	85.00
	1885 AH	.443	10.00	12.00	20.00	85.00
	1885 JS	I.A.	30.00	60.00	100.00	200.00
	1886 JS	1.039	10.00	12.00	20.00	85.00
	1887 JS	.878	10.00	12.00	20.00	85.00
	1888 JS	1.159	10.00	12.00	20.00	85.00
	1889 JS	1.583	10.00	12.00	20.00	85.00
	1890 JS	1.658	10.00	12.00	20.00	85.00
	1891 JS	1.507	10.00	12.00	20.00	85.00
	1892/1 JS					
		1.627	15.00	25.00	50.00	125.00
	1892 JS	I.A.	10.00	12.00	20.00	80.00
	1893 JS	1.952	10.00	12.00	20.00	80.00
	1894 JS	2.046	10.00	12.00	20.00	80.00
	1895 JS	1.146	10.00	12.00	20.00	65.00

NOTE: Varieties exist. The 1830 LP/FS is currently only known with a Philippine countermark.

KM#	Date	Mintage	Fine	VF	XF	Unc
		Mint mark: GC				
377.7	1844 MP	—	350.00	500.00	1000.	2000.
	1844 MP (error) reversed S in Ds, Gs					
		—	400.00	600.00	1200.	2250.
	1845 MP eagle's tail square					
		—	125.00	200.00	325.00	700.00
	1845 MP eagle's tail round					
		—	175.00	350.00	650.00	1200.
	1846 MP eagle's tail square					
		—	125.00	200.00	350.00	750.00
	1846 MP eagle's tail round					
		—	125.00	200.00	350.00	750.00
	1847 MP	—	150.00	250.00	400.00	800.00
	1848 MP	—	175.00	300.00	500.00	900.00
	1849 MP	—	175.00	300.00	525.00	1000.
	1850 MP	—	175.00	300.00	575.00	1100.
	1851 MP	—	300.00	500.00	900.00	1600.
	1852 MP	—	350.00	600.00	1150.	2250.

Mint mark: Go

KM#	Date	Mintage	Fine	VF	XF	Unc
377.8	1825 JJ	—	40.00	70.00	150.00	300.00
	1825 JJ error mint mark G	—	1250.	1650.	—	—
	1826 JJ straight J's	—	40.00	80.00	175.00	350.00
	1826 JJ full J's	—	30.00	60.00	125.00	250.00
	1826 MJ	—	250.00	450.00	850.00	—
	1827 MJ	—	40.00	75.00	125.00	250.00
	1827 MJ/JJ	—	40.00	75.00	125.00	250.00
	1827 MR	—	100.00	200.00	350.00	600.00
	1828 MJ	—	30.00	60.00	125.00	250.00
	1828/7 MR	—	200.00	400.00	600.00	1200.
	1828 MR	—	200.00	400.00	600.00	1200.
	1829 MJ	—	20.00	35.00	55.00	165.00
	1830 MJ oblong beading and narrow J	—	20.00	30.00	55.00	165.00
	1830 MJ regular beading and wide J	—	20.00	30.00	55.00	165.00
	1831 MJ colon after date	—	12.00	20.00	40.00	150.00
	1831 MJ 2 stars after date	—	12.00	20.00	40.00	150.00
	1832 MJ	—	12.00	20.00	40.00	150.00
	1832 MJ 1 of date over inverted 1	—	20.00	35.00	65.00	175.00
	1833 MJ	—	12.00	20.00	40.00	150.00
	1833 JM	—	900.00	1400.	2000.	2500.
	1834 PJ	—	12.00	20.00	40.00	150.00
	1835 PJ star on cap	—	12.00	20.00	40.00	150.00
	1835 PJ dot on cap	—	12.00	20.00	40.00	150.00
	1836 PJ	—	12.00	20.00	40.00	150.00
	1837 PJ	—	12.00	20.00	40.00	150.00
	1838 PJ	—	12.00	20.00	40.00	150.00
	1839 PJ/JJ	—	12.00	20.00	40.00	150.00
	1839 PJ	—	12.00	20.00	40.00	150.00
	1840/30 PJ	—	20.00	30.00	50.00	150.00
	1840 PJ	—	12.00	20.00	35.00	125.00
	1841/31 PJ	—	12.00	20.00	35.00	125.00
	1841 PJ	—	12.00	20.00	35.00	125.00
	1842/31 PM/PJ	—	25.00	35.00	60.00	150.00
	1842 PJ	—	20.00	30.00	50.00	125.00
	1842 PM/PJ	—	12.00	20.00	35.00	125.00
	1842 PM	—	12.00	20.00	35.00	125.00
	1843 PM dot after date	—	12.00	20.00	35.00	125.00
	1843 PM triangle of dots after date	—	12.00	20.00	35.00	125.00
	1844 PM	—	12.00	20.00	35.00	125.00
	1845 PM	—	12.00	20.00	35.00	125.00
	1846/5 PM eagle type of 1845	—	20.00	30.00	50.00	150.00
	1846 PM early type of 1847	—	15.00	25.00	40.00	135.00
	1847 PM	—	12.00	20.00	35.00	125.00
	1848/7 PM	—	20.00	35.00	65.00	150.00
	1848 PM	—	20.00	35.00	65.00	150.00
	1848 PF	—	12.00	20.00	35.00	125.00
	1849 PF	—	12.00	20.00	35.00	125.00
	1850 PF	—	12.00	20.00	35.00	125.00
	1851/0 PF	—	20.00	30.00	50.00	150.00
	1851 PF	—	12.00	20.00	35.00	125.00
	1852/1 PF	—	20.00	30.00	50.00	150.00
	1852 PF	—	12.00	20.00	35.00	125.00
	1853/2 PF	—	20.00	30.00	50.00	150.00
	1853 PF	—	12.00	20.00	35.00	125.00
	1854 PF	—	12.00	20.00	35.00	125.00
	1855 PF large letters	—	12.00	20.00	35.00	125.00
	1855 PF small letters	—	12.00	20.00	35.00	125.00
	1856/5 PF	—	20.00	30.00	50.00	150.00
	1856 PF	—	12.00	20.00	35.00	125.00
	1857/5 PF	—	20.00	30.00	50.00	150.00
	1857/6 PF	—	20.00	30.00	50.00	150.00
	1857 PF	—	12.00	20.00	35.00	125.00

KM#	Date	Mintage	Fine	VF	XF	Unc
377.8	1858 PF	—	12.00	20.00	35.00	125.00
	1859/7 PF	—	20.00	30.00	50.00	150.00
	1859/8 PF	—	20.00	30.00	50.00	150.00
	1859 PF	—	12.00	20.00	35.00	125.00
	1860/50 PF	—	20.00	30.00	50.00	150.00
	1860/59 PF	—	12.00	18.00	25.00	85.00
	1860 PF	—	12.00	15.00	20.00	75.00
	1861/51 PF	—	15.00	20.00	30.00	100.00
	1861/0 PF	—	12.00	15.00	20.00	75.00
	1861 PF	—	12.00	15.00	20.00	75.00
	1862 YE/PF	—	12.00	15.00	20.00	75.00
	1862 YE	—	12.00	15.00	20.00	75.00
	1862 YF	—	12.00	15.00	20.00	75.00
	1862 YF/PF	—	12.00	15.00	20.00	75.00
	1863/53 YF	—	12.00	18.00	25.00	75.00
	1863/54 YF	—	15.00	20.00	30.00	100.00
	1863 YE	—	—	—	Rare	—
	1863 YF	—	12.00	15.00	20.00	75.00
	1867/57 YF	—	15.00	20.00	30.00	100.00
	1867 YF	—	12.00	15.00	20.00	75.00
	1868/58 YF	—	15.00	20.00	30.00	100.00
	1868 YF	—	12.00	15.00	20.00	75.00
	1870/60 FR	—	20.00	30.00	50.00	150.00
	1870 YF	—	—	—	Rare	—
	1870 FR/YF	—	12.00	18.00	25.00	85.00
	1870 FR	—	12.00	15.00	20.00	75.00
	1873 FR	—	12.00	15.00	20.00	75.00
	1874/3 FR	—	15.00	20.00	30.00	85.00
	1874 FR	—	15.00	25.00	35.00	100.00
	1875/6 FR	—	15.00	20.00	30.00	85.00
	1875 FR small circle w/dot on eagle	—	12.00	15.00	20.00	75.00
	1876/5 FR	—	15.00	20.00	30.00	85.00
	1876 FR	—	12.00	15.00	20.00	60.00
	1877 FR	2.477	12.00	15.00	20.00	60.00
	1878/7 FR	2.273	15.00	20.00	30.00	75.00
	1878/7 SM	—	15.00	20.00	30.00	75.00
	1878 FR	I.A.	12.00	15.00	20.00	65.00
	1878 SM,S/F	—	15.00	20.00	25.00	70.00
	1878 SM	—	12.00	15.00	20.00	65.00
	1879/7 SM	—	15.00	20.00	30.00	75.00
	1879/8 SM	—	15.00	20.00	30.00	75.00
	1879/8 SM/FR	—	15.00	20.00	30.00	75.00
	1879 SM	—	12.00	15.00	20.00	65.00
	1879 SM/FR	—	15.00	20.00	30.00	75.00
	1880/70 SB	—	15.00	20.00	30.00	75.00
	1880 SB/SM	—	12.00	15.00	20.00	65.00
	1881/71 SB	— 3.974	15.00	20.00	30.00	75.00
	1881/0 SB	I.A.	15.00	20.00	30.00	75.00
	1881 SB	I.A.	12.00	15.00	20.00	65.00
	1882 SB	2.015	12.00	15.00	20.00	75.00
	1883 SB	2.100	35.00	75.00	125.00	250.00
	1883 BR	I.A.	12.00	15.00	20.00	65.00
	1883 BR/SR	—	12.00	15.00	20.00	65.00
	1883 BR/SB	Inc. Ab.	12.00	15.00	20.00	65.00
	1884/73 BR	—	20.00	30.00	40.00	100.00
	1884/74 BR	—	20.00	30.00	40.00	100.00
	1884/3 BR	—	20.00	30.00	40.00	100.00
	1884 BR	—	12.00	15.00	20.00	65.00
	1884/74 RR	—	50.00	100.00	175.00	350.00
	1884 RR	—	50.00	100.00	175.00	350.00
	1885/75 RR	2.363	15.00	20.00	30.00	75.00
	1885 RR	I.A.	12.00	15.00	20.00	65.00
	1886/75 RR	4.127	15.00	20.00	25.00	70.00
	1886/76 RR	Inc. Ab.	12.00	15.00	20.00	65.00
	1886/5 RR/BR	Inc. Ab.	12.00	15.00	20.00	65.00
	1886 RR	I.A.	12.00	15.00	20.00	65.00
	1887 RR	4.205	10.00	15.00	20.00	65.00
	1888 RR	3.985	10.00	15.00	20.00	65.00
	1889 RR	3.646	10.00	15.00	20.00	65.00
	1890 RR	3.615	10.00	15.00	20.00	65.00
	1891 RS	3.197	10.00	15.00	20.00	65.00
	1891 RR	—	Contemporary counterfeit			
	1892 RS	3.672	10.00	15.00	20.00	65.00
	1893 RS	3.854	10.00	15.00	20.00	65.00
	1894 RS	4.127	10.00	15.00	20.00	65.00
	1895/1 RS					

KM#	Date	Mintage	Fine	VF	XF	Unc
		3.768	15.00	20.00	25.00	75.00
	1895/3 RS	I.A.	15.00	20.00	25.00	75.00
	1895 RS	I.A.	10.00	15.00	20.00	65.00
	1896/1 Go/As RS/ML					
		5.229	15.00	20.00	25.00	75.00
	1896/1 RS	I.A.	12.00	15.00	20.00	65.00
	1896 Go/Ga RS					
		Inc. Ab.	—	—	—	—
	1896 RS	I.A.	10.00	12.00	18.00	60.00
	1897 RS	4.344	10.00	12.00	18.00	60.00

NOTE: Varieties exist.

KM#	Date	Mintage	Fine	VF	XF	Unc
	1892 FG	.643	12.00	18.00	25.00	100.00
	1893 FG	.518	12.00	18.00	25.00	100.00
	1894 FG	.504	12.00	18.00	25.00	100.00
	1895 FG	.320	12.00	18.00	25.00	100.00

NOTE: Varieties exist.

Mint mark: Mo

KM#	Date	Mintage	Fine	VF	XF	Unc
377.10	1824 JM round tail					
		—	75.00	125.00	250.00	500.00
	1824 JM square tail					
		—	75.00	125.00	250.00	500.00
	1825 JM	—	25.00	35.00	60.00	175.00
	1826/5 JM	—	25.00	40.00	75.00	190.00
	1826 JM	—	20.00	30.00	55.00	165.00
	1827 JM medal alignment					
		—	25.00	35.00	60.00	175.00
	1827 JM coin alignment					
		—	25.00	35.00	60.00	175.00
	1828 JM	—	30.00	60.00	100.00	240.00
	1829 JM	—	20.00	30.00	60.00	175.00
	1830/20 JM	—	35.00	55.00	100.00	240.00
	1830 JM	—	30.00	50.00	90.00	220.00
	1831 JM	—	30.00	50.00	100.00	240.00
	1832/1 JM	—	25.00	40.00	65.00	180.00
	1832 JM	—	20.00	30.00	55.00	165.00
	1833 MJ	—	25.00	40.00	80.00	200.00
	1833 ML	—	500.00	750.00	950.00	2000.
	1834/3 ML	—	25.00	35.00	60.00	175.00
	1834 ML	—	20.00	30.00	55.00	165.00
	1835 ML	—	20.00	30.00	55.00	165.00

8 REALES

Date	Mintage	Fine	VF	XF	Unc
1836 ML	—	50.00	100.00	150.00	325.00
1836 ML/MF	—	50.00	100.00	150.00	325.00
1836 MF	—	30.00	50.00	90.00	220.00
1836 MF/ML	—	35.00	60.00	100.00	240.00
1837/6 ML	—	30.00	50.00	80.00	200.00
1837/6 MM	—	30.00	50.00	80.00	200.00
1837/6 MM/ML					
	—	30.00	50.00	80.00	200.00
1837/6 MM/MF					
	—	30.00	50.00	80.00	200.00
1837 ML	—	30.00	50.00	80.00	200.00
1837 MM	—	75.00	125.00	175.00	325.00
1838 MM	—	30.00	50.00	80.00	200.00
1838 ML	—	20.00	35.00	60.00	180.00
1838 ML/MM	—	20.00	35.00	60.00	180.00
1839 ML	—	15.00	25.00	50.00	165.00
1840 ML	—	15.00	25.00	50.00	165.00
1841 ML	—	15.00	25.00	45.00	150.00
1842 ML	—	15.00	25.00	45.00	150.00
1842 MM	—	15.00	25.00	45.00	150.00
1843 MM	—	15.00	25.00	45.00	150.00
1844 MF/MM	—	—	—	—	—
1844 MF	—	15.00	25.00	45.00	150.00
1845/4 MF	—	15.00	25.00	45.00	150.00
1845 MF	—	15.00	25.00	45.00	150.00
1846/5 MF	—	15.00	25.00	50.00	165.00
1846 MF	—	15.00	25.00	50.00	165.00
1847/6 MF	—	—	—	Rare	—
1847 MF	—	1650.	3000.	5000.	7500.
1847 RC	—	20.00	30.00	50.00	165.00
1847 RC/MF	—	15.00	25.00	45.00	150.00
1848 GC	—	15.00	25.00	45.00	150.00
1849/8 GC	—	20.00	35.00	60.00	180.00
1849 GC	—	15.00	25.00	45.00	150.00

Mint mark: Ho

KM#	Date	Mintage	Fine	VF	XF	Unc
377.9	1835 PP	—	—	—	Rare	—
	1836 PP	—	—	—	Rare	—
	1839 PR	—	—	—	Unique	—
	1861 FM reeded edge					
		—	4500.	7500.	—	—
	1862 FM plain edge, snakes tail left, long ray over *8R					
		—	—	—	Rare	—
	1862 FM plain edge, snakes tail left					
		—	1550.	2700.	—	—
	1862 FM reeded edge, snakes tail right					
		—	1650.	2750.	—	—
377.9	1863 FM	—	150.00	300.00	800.00	—
	1864 FM	—	—	—	Rare	—
	1864 PR	—	650.00	1250.	2150.	3350.
	1865 FM	—	250.00	500.00	950.00	—
	1866 FM	—	1150.	2150.	3500.	5500.
	1866 MP	—	950.00	1750.	3000.	4650.
	1867 PR	—	100.00	175.00	275.00	500.00
	1868 PR	—	20.00	35.00	65.00	175.00
	1869 PR	—	40.00	60.00	125.00	250.00
	1870 PR	—	50.00	80.00	150.00	300.00
	1871/0 PR	—	50.00	75.00	125.00	250.00
	1871 PR	—	30.00	50.00	90.00	200.00
	1872/1 PR	—	35.00	60.00	90.00	200.00
	1872 PR	—	30.00	50.00	75.00	175.00
	1873 PR	.351	30.00	50.00	85.00	150.00
	1874 PR	—	15.00	20.00	40.00	125.00
	1875 PR	—	15.00	20.00	40.00	125.00
	1876 AF	—	15.00	20.00	40.00	125.00
	1877 AF	.410	20.00	30.00	50.00	150.00
	1877 GR	I.A.	100.00	150.00	225.00	400.00
	1877 JA	I.A.	25.00	50.00	85.00	175.00
	1878 JA	.451	15.00	20.00	40.00	120.00
	1879 JA	—	15.00	20.00	40.00	120.00
	1880 JA	—	15.00	20.00	40.00	120.00
	1881 JA	.586	15.00	20.00	40.00	120.00
	1882 HoJA O above H					
		.240	25.00	40.00	65.00	125.00
	1882 HoJA O after H					
		I.A.	25.00	40.00	65.00	125.00
	1883/2 JA	.204	225.00	375.00	550.00	1000.
	1883/2 FM/JA					
		I.A.	25.00	40.00	75.00	150.00
	1883 FM	I.A.	20.00	30.00	60.00	125.00
	1883 JA	I.A.	275.00	450.00	800.00	1500.
	1884/3 FM	—	20.00	25.00	50.00	125.00
	1884 FM	—	15.00	20.00	40.00	120.00
	1885 FM	.132	15.00	20.00	40.00	120.00
	1886 FM	.225	20.00	30.00	45.00	125.00
	1886 FG	I.A.	20.00	30.00	45.00	125.00
	1887 FG	.150	20.00	35.00	65.00	150.00
	1888 FG	.364	12.00	18.00	25.00	100.00
	1889 FG	.490	12.00	18.00	25.00	100.00
	1890 FG	.565	12.00	18.00	25.00	100.00
	1891 FG	.738	12.00	18.00	25.00	100.00

KM#	Date	Mintage	Fine	VF	XF	Unc
377.10	1850/40 GC	—	25.00	50.00	100.00	240.00
	1850/49 GC	—	25.00	50.00	100.00	240.00
	1850 GC	—	20.00	40.00	75.00	190.00
	1851 GC	—	20.00	40.00	60.00	175.00
	1852 GC	—	15.00	30.00	55.00	160.00
	1853 GC	—	15.00	25.00	50.00	160.00
	1854 GC	—	15.00	25.00	50.00	160.00
	1855 GC	—	20.00	35.00	65.00	180.00
	1855 GF	—	12.00	15.00	30.00	125.00
	1855 GF/GC	—	12.00	15.00	30.00	125.00
	1856/4 GF	—	15.00	25.00	45.00	145.00
	1856/5 GF	—	15.00	25.00	45.00	145.00
	1856 GF	—	12.00	15.00	30.00	125.00
	1857 GF	—	10.00	15.00	30.00	125.00
	1858/7 FH/GF	—	10.00	15.00	30.00	125.00
	1858 FH	—	10.00	15.00	30.00	125.00
	1859 FH	—	10.00	15.00	30.00	125.00
	1860/59 FH	—	15.00	20.00	30.00	125.00
	1860 FH	—	10.00	15.00	30.00	125.00
	1860 TH	—	12.00	18.00	40.00	145.00
	1861 TH	—	10.00	15.00	20.00	75.00
	1861 CH	—	10.00	15.00	20.00	75.00
	1862 CH	—	10.00	15.00	20.00	75.00
	1863 CH	—	10.00	15.00	20.00	75.00
	1863 CH/TH	—	10.00	15.00	20.00	75.00
	1863 TH	—	10.00	15.00	20.00	75.00
	1867 CH	—	10.00	15.00	20.00	65.00
	1868 CH	—	10.00	15.00	20.00	65.00
	1868 CH/PH	—	10.00	15.00	20.00	65.00
	1868 PH	—	10.00	15.00	20.00	65.00
	1869 CH	—	10.00	15.00	20.00	65.00
	1873 MH	—	10.00	15.00	20.00	65.00
	1873 MH/HH	—	12.00	18.00	25.00	75.00
	1874/69 MH	—	15.00	25.00	45.00	100.00
	1874 MH	—	12.00	18.00	25.00	75.00
	1874 BH/MH	—	12.00	15.00	20.00	65.00
	1874 BH	—	10.00	15.00	20.00	65.00
	1875 BH	—	10.00	15.00	20.00	65.00
	1876/4 BH	—	12.00	18.00	25.00	75.00
	1876/5 BH	—	12.00	18.00	25.00	75.00
	1876 BH	—	10.00	15.00	20.00	65.00
	1877 MH	.898	10.00	15.00	20.00	65.00
	1877 MH/BH Inc. Ab.		12.00	18.00	25.00	75.00
	1878 MH	2.154	10.00	15.00	20.00	65.00
	1879/8 MH	—	10.00	15.00	20.00	75.00
	1879 MH	—	10.00	15.00	20.00	65.00
	1880/79 MH	—	15.00	20.00	30.00	75.00
	1880 MH	—	10.00	15.00	20.00	75.00
	1881 MH	5.712	10.00	15.00	20.00	65.00
	1882/1 MH	2.746	12.00	15.00	20.00	75.00
	1882 MH	I.A.	10.00	15.00	20.00	65.00
	1883/2 MH	2.726	12.00	18.00	25.00	85.00
	1883 MH	I.A.	10.00	15.00	20.00	65.00
	1884/3 MH	—	15.00	20.00	30.00	75.00
	1884 MH	—	10.00	15.00	20.00	65.00
	1885 MH	3.649	10.00	15.00	20.00	65.00
	1886 MH	7.558	10.00	12.00	18.00	60.00
	1887 MH	7.681	10.00	12.00	18.00	60.00
	1888 MH	7.179	10.00	12.00	18.00	60.00
	1889 MH	7.332	10.00	15.00	20.00	65.00
	1890 MH	7.412	10.00	12.00	18.00	60.00
	1890 AM	I.A.	10.00	12.00	18.00	60.00
	1891 AM	8.076	10.00	12.00	18.00	60.00
	1892 AM	9.392	10.00	12.00	18.00	60.00
	1893 AM	10.773	10.00	12.00	18.00	55.00
	1894 AM	12.394	10.00	12.00	18.00	45.00
	1895 AM	10.474	10.00	12.00	18.00	45.00
	1895 AB	I.A.	10.00	12.00	18.00	60.00
	1896 AB	9.327	10.00	12.00	18.00	60.00
	1896 AM	I.A.	10.00	12.00	18.00	60.00
	1897 AM	8.621	10.00	12.00	18.00	60.00

NOTE: Varieties exist. 1874 CP is a die struck counterfeit.

Mint mark: O, Oa

KM#	Date	Mintage	Fine	VF	XF	Unc
377.11	1858O AE	—	5500.	—	—	—
	1858OaAE	—	—	—	Unique	—
	1859 AE A in O of mm	—	300.00	650.00	1150.	—
	1860 AE A in O of mm	—	200.00	450.00	750.00	—
	1861 O FR	—	125.00	250.00	500.00	1100.
	1861OaFR	—	150.00	350.00	600.00	—
	1862O FR	—	40.00	80.00	200.00	375.00
	1862OaFR	—	65.00	125.00	250.00	450.00
	1863O FR	—	30.00	60.00	100.00	250.00
	1863O AE	—	30.00	60.00	100.00	250.00
	1863OaAE A in O of mm	—	100.00	150.00	250.00	450.00
	1863OaAE A above O in mm	—	1650.	2750.	—	—
	1864 FR	—	25.00	50.00	75.00	200.00
	1865 AE	—	1850.	3000.	—	—
	1867 AE	—	40.00	80.00	150.00	400.00
	1868 AE	—	25.00	50.00	100.00	250.00
	1869 AE	—	30.00	60.00	100.00	250.00
	1873 AE	—	200.00	300.00	600.00	1350.
	1874 AE	.142	15.00	30.00	50.00	200.00
	1875/4 AE	.131	25.00	50.00	75.00	200.00
	1875 AE	I.A.	15.00	30.00	40.00	135.00
	1876 AE	.140	20.00	35.00	55.00	200.00
	1877 AE	.139	20.00	30.00	50.00	200.00
	1878 AE	.125	15.00	25.00	50.00	200.00
	1879 AE	.153	15.00	30.00	45.00	150.00
	1880 AE	.143	15.00	30.00	45.00	150.00
	1881 AE	.134	20.00	35.00	60.00	150.00
	1882 AE	.100	20.00	35.00	60.00	150.00
	1883 AE	.122	15.00	30.00	45.00	150.00
	1884 AE	.142	15.00	30.00	50.00	150.00
	1885 AE	.158	15.00	25.00	40.00	135.00
	1886 AE	.120	15.00	30.00	45.00	150.00
	1887/6 AE	.115	25.00	50.00	80.00	200.00
	1887 AE	I.A.	15.00	25.00	40.00	135.00
	1888 AE	.145	15.00	25.00	40.00	135.00
	1889 AE	.150	20.00	30.00	60.00	175.00
	1890 AE	.181	20.00	30.00	60.00	175.00
	1891 EN	.160	15.00	25.00	40.00	135.00
	1892 EN	.120	15.00	25.00	40.00	135.00
	1893 EN	.066	45.00	75.00	115.00	225.00

NOTE: Varieties exist.

Mint mark: Pi

KM#	Date	Mintage	Fine	VF	XF	Unc
377.12	1827 JS	—	—	—	Rare	—
	1828/7 JS	—	275.00	425.00	650.00	1250.
	1828 JS	—	225.00	375.00	550.00	1100.
	1829 JS	—	35.00	65.00	125.00	250.00
	1830 JS	—	30.00	50.00	100.00	200.00
	1831/0 JS	—	30.00	60.00	125.00	250.00
	1831 JS	—	25.00	35.00	75.00	200.00
	1832/22 JS	—	25.00	35.00	65.00	165.00
	1832 JS	—	25.00	35.00	65.00	165.00
	1833/2 JS	—	30.00	40.00	70.00	175.00

KM#	Date Mintage	Fine	VF	XF	Unc
	1833 JS —	20.00	30.00	50.00	150.00
	1834/3 JS —	25.00	35.00	60.00	150.00
	1834 JS —	15.00	25.00	50.00	150.00
	1835 JS denomination 8R				
	—	20.00	30.00	65.00	175.00
	1835 JS denomination 8Rs				
	—	15.00	25.00	50.00	150.00
	1836 JS —	20.00	30.00	55.00	150.00
	1837 JS —	30.00	50.00	85.00	200.00
	1838 JS —	20.00	30.00	55.00	150.00
	1839 JS —	20.00	40.00	70.00	150.00
	1840 JS —	20.00	30.00	60.00	150.00
	1841PiJS —	25.00	40.00	85.00	200.00
	1841iPJS (error)				
	—	50.00	100.00	200.00	400.00
	1842/1 JS —	40.00	60.00	100.00	200.00
	1842/1 PS/JS				
	—	35.00	55.00	90.00	200.00
	1842 JS eagle type of 1843				
	—	30.00	50.00	80.00	175.00
	1842 PS —	30.00	50.00	80.00	175.00
	1842 PS/JS eagle type of 1841				
	—	30.00	50.00	80.00	175.00
	1843/2 PS round top 3				
	—	50.00	75.00	150.00	250.00
	1843 PS flat top 3				
	—	30.00	60.00	125.00	225.00
	1843 AM round top 3				
	—	20.00	30.00	55.00	150.00
	1843 AM flat top 3				
	—	20.00	30.00	55.00	150.00
	1844 AM —	20.00	30.00	55.00	150.00
	1845/4 AM —	25.00	50.00	100.00	225.00
	1845 AM —	25.00	50.00	100.00	225.00
	1846/5 AM —	20.00	35.00	55.00	150.00
	1846 AM —	15.00	25.00	50.00	150.00
	1847 AM —	30.00	50.00	85.00	175.00
	1848/7 AM —	30.00	60.00	100.00	200.00
	1848 AM —	30.00	50.00	85.00	175.00
	1849/8 PS/AM				
	—	1750.	3000.	—	—
	1849 PS —	2250.	3750.	—	—
	1849 MC/PS —	60.00	125.00	250.00	500.00
	1849 AM —	1250.	2250.	4000.	—
	1849 MC —	60.00	125.00	250.00	500.00
	1850 MC —	40.00	80.00	150.00	300.00
	1851 MC —	150.00	300.00	450.00	900.00
	1852 MC —	75.00	125.00	200.00	400.00
	1853 MC —	150.00	275.00	400.00	850.00
	1854 MC —	100.00	150.00	250.00	500.00
	1855 MC —	100.00	150.00	250.00	500.00
	1856 MC —	65.00	100.00	200.00	400.00
	1857 MC —	500.00	900.00	1500.	—
	1857 PS/MC —	150.00	225.00	375.00	700.00
	1857 PS —	125.00	200.00	350.00	650.00
	1858 MC/PS —	250.00	400.00	650.00	1200.
	1858 MC —	250.00	400.00	650.00	1200.
	1858 PS —	—	Rare	—	
	1859/8 MC/PS				
	—	3650.	5750.	—	—
	1859 MC —	3500.	5500.	—	—
	1859 PS/MC —	3500.	5500.	—	—
	1860 FC —	2000.	4000.	6500.	—
	1860 FE —	—	—	Rare	—
	1860 MC —	2000.	4000.	6500.	—
	1860 PS —	400.00	600.00	900.00	1750.
	1860 RO —	—	—	*Rare	—
	1861 PS —	30.00	60.00	90.00	175.00
	1861 RO —	25.00	35.00	55.00	125.00
	1862/1 RO —	20.00	25.00	50.00	125.00
	1862 RO —	15.00	20.00	40.00	100.00
	1862 RO oval O in RO				
	—	15.00	20.00	40.00	100.00
	1862 RO round O in RO, 6 is inverted 9				
	—	20.00	30.00	50.00	125.00
	1863/2 RO —	25.00	35.00	65.00	150.00
	1863 RO —	15.00	20.00	40.00	125.00
	1863 6/inverted 6				
	—	25.00	35.00	55.00	125.00
	1863 FC —	—	—	Rare	—
	1864 RO —	—	—	Rare	—
	1867 CA —	650.00	950.00	—	—
	1867 LR —	525.00	850.00	—	—

KM#	Date Mintage	Fine	VF	XF	Unc
377.12	1867 PS/CA —	—	—	Rare	—
	1867 PS —	30.00	60.00	125.00	275.00
	1868/7 PS —	30.00	60.00	125.00	250.00
	1868 PS —	20.00	30.00	50.00	125.00
	1869/8 PS —	20.00	25.00	45.00	125.00
	1869 PS —	15.00	20.00	40.00	125.00
	1870/69 PS —	1150.	2250.	4000.	—
	1870 PS —	1000.	2000.	3500.	—
	1873 MH —	18.00	25.00	45.00	150.00
	1874/3 MH —	15.00	20.00	30.00	135.00
	1874 MH —	10.00	12.00	22.00	120.00
	1875 MH —	10.00	12.00	22.00	100.00
	1876/5 MH —	18.00	25.00	45.00	150.00
	1876 MH —	10.00	12.00	22.00	100.00
	1877 MH 1.018	10.00	12.00	22.00	120.00
	1878 MH 1.046	12.00	15.00	25.00	125.00
	1879/8 MH —	10.00	20.00	30.00	125.00
	1879 MH —	10.00	12.00	22.00	100.00
	1879 BE —	25.00	50.00	75.00	150.00
	1879 MH —	30.00	50.00	100.00	200.00
	1880 MR —	250.00	400.00	800.00	—
	1880 MH —	10.00	12.00	22.00	100.00
	1881 MH 2.100	10.00	12.00	22.00	100.00
	1882/1 MH				
	1.602	15.00	20.00	30.00	125.00
	1882 MH I.A.	10.00	12.00	22.00	100.00
	1883 MH 1.545	10.00	12.00	22.00	100.00
	1884/3 MH —	15.00	20.00	30.00	125.00
	1884 MH/MM				
	—	12.00	15.00	22.00	90.00
	1884 MH —	10.00	12.00	20.00	80.00
	1885/4 MH				
	1.736	15.00	20.00	30.00	125.00
	1885/8 MH I.A.	15.00	20.00	30.00	125.00
	1885 MH I.A.	10.00	12.00	20.00	80.00
	1885 LC I.A.	12.00	15.00	18.00	100.00
	1886 LC 3.347	10.00	12.00	20.00	80.00
	1886 MR I.A.	10.00	12.00	20.00	80.00
	1887 MR 2.922	10.00	12.00	20.00	80.00
	1888 MR 2.438	10.00	12.00	20.00	80.00
	1889 MR 2.103	10.00	12.00	20.00	80.00
	1890 MR 1.562	10.00	12.00	20.00	70.00
	1891 MR 1.184	10.00	12.00	20.00	70.00
	1892 MR 1.336	10.00	12.00	20.00	70.00
	1893 MR .530	10.00	12.00	20.00	80.00

NOTE: Varieties exist.

*NOTE: Spink America Gerber sale 6-96 cleaned VF or better realized $33,000.

Mint mark: Zs

KM#	Date Mintage	Fine	VF	XF	Unc
377.13	1825 AZ —	25.00	35.00	65.00	175.00
	1826/5 AZ —	25.00	45.00	85.00	200.00
	1826 AZ —	20.00	35.00	65.00	175.00
	1826 AV —	200.00	400.00	700.00	1500.
	1826 AO —	300.00	600.00	1000.	2000.
	1827 AO/AZ —	35.00	50.00	125.00	250.00
	1827 AO —	25.00	45.00	85.00	200.00
	1828 AO —	15.00	20.00	45.00	165.00
	1829 AO —	15.00	20.00	45.00	165.00
	1829 OV —	50.00	90.00	150.00	300.00
	1830 OV —	15.00	20.00	45.00	165.00
	1831 OV —	25.00	50.00	90.00	200.00
	1831 OM —	15.00	25.00	55.00	165.00
	1832/1 OM —	20.00	25.00	45.00	165.00
	1832 OM —	15.00	20.00	40.00	150.00
	1833/2 OM —	20.00	30.00	45.00	165.00
	1833 OM/MM				

KM#	Date	Mintage	Fine	VF	XF	Unc
377.13						
		—	15.00	25.00	40.00	150.00
	1833 OM	—	15.00	20.00	35.00	150.00
	1834 OM	—	15.00	20.00	35.00	150.00
	1835 OM	—	15.00	20.00	40.00	150.00
	1836/4 OM	—	20.00	30.00	50.00	165.00
	1836/5 OM	—	20.00	30.00	50.00	165.00
	1836 OM	—	15.00	20.00	35.00	150.00
	1837 OM	—	15.00	20.00	35.00	150.00
	1838/7 OM	—	20.00	30.00	45.00	165.00
	1838 OM	—	15.00	20.00	35.00	150.00
	1839 OM	—	15.00	20.00	35.00	150.00
	1840 OM	—	15.00	20.00	35.00	150.00
	1841 OM	—	15.00	20.00	35.00	150.00
	1842 OM eagle type of 1841					
		—	15.00	20.00	35.00	150.00
	1842 OM eagle type of 1843					
		—	15.00	20.00	35.00	150.00
	1843 OM	—	15.00	20.00	35.00	150.00
	1844 OM	—	15.00	20.00	35.00	150.00
	1845 OM	—	15.00	20.00	35.00	150.00
	1846 OM	—	15.00	20.00	35.00	150.00
	1847 OM	—	15.00	20.00	35.00	150.00
	1848/7 OM	—	20.00	30.00	45.00	165.00
	1848 OM	—	15.00	20.00	35.00	150.00
	1849 OM	—	15.00	20.00	35.00	150.00
	1850 OM	—	15.00	20.00	35.00	150.00
	1851 OM	—	15.00	20.00	35.00	150.00
	1852 OM	—	15.00	20.00	35.00	150.00
	1853 OM	—	30.00	45.00	75.00	200.00
	1854/3 OM	—	20.00	30.00	60.00	175.00
	1854 OM	—	15.00	25.00	45.00	165.00
	1855 OM	—	20.00	30.00	60.00	175.00
	1855 MO	—	30.00	60.00	90.00	200.00
	1856/5 MO	—	20.00	30.00	45.00	165.00
	1856 MO	—	15.00	20.00	35.00	150.00
	1857/5 MO	—	20.00	30.00	45.00	165.00
	1857 MO	—	15.00	20.00	35.00	150.00
	1858/7 MO	—	15.00	20.00	35.00	150.00
	1858 MO	—	15.00	20.00	35.00	150.00
	1859 MO	—	15.00	20.00	30.00	100.00
	1859 VL/MO	—	25.00	50.00	75.00	150.00
	1859 VL	—	20.00	40.00	60.00	125.00
	1860/50 MO	—	10.00	12.00	18.00	75.00
	1860/59 MO	—	10.00	12.00	18.00	75.00
	1860 MO	—	10.00	12.00	18.00	75.00
	1860 VL/MO	—	10.00	12.00	18.00	75.00
	1860 VL	—	10.00	12.00	18.00	75.00
	1859/8 MO	—	15.00	20.00	35.00	150.00
	1859 MO	—	15.00	20.00	35.00	150.00
	1859 VL/MO	—	25.00	50.00	75.00	175.00
	1859 VL	—	20.00	40.00	60.00	165.00
	1860/50 MO	—	10.00	12.00	20.00	80.00
	1860/59 MO	—	10.00	12.00	20.00	80.00
	1860 MO	—	10.00	12.00	20.00	80.00
	1860 VL/MO	—	10.00	12.00	20.00	80.00
	1860 VL	—	10.00	12.00	20.00	80.00
	1861/0 VL/MO					
		—	10.00	12.00	20.00	80.00
	1861/0 VL	—	10.00	12.00	20.00	80.00
	1861 VL	—	10.00	12.00	20.00	80.00
	1862/1 VL	—	15.00	20.00	35.00	100.00
	1862 VL	—	10.00	12.00	20.00	80.00
	1863 VL	—	10.00	12.00	20.00	80.00
	1863 MO	—	10.00	12.00	20.00	80.00
	1864/3 VL	—	15.00	20.00	35.00	100.00
	1864 VL	—	10.00	12.00	20.00	80.00
	1864 MO	—	15.00	20.00	35.00	100.00
	1865/4 MO	—	200.00	450.00	800.00	1550.
	1865 MO	—	150.00	300.00	600.00	1250.
	1866 VL	Contemporary counterfeit				
	1867 JS	—	—	—	Rare	—
	1868 JS	—	10.00	12.00	20.00	80.00
	1868 YH	—	10.00	12.00	20.00	80.00
	1869 YH	—	10.00	12.00	20.00	80.00
	1870 YH	—	—	—	Rare	—
	1873 YH	—	10.00	12.00	20.00	80.00
	1874 YH	—	10.00	12.00	20.00	80.00
	1874 JA/YA	—	10.00	12.00	20.00	80.00
	1874 JA	—	10.00	12.00	20.00	80.00
	1875 JA	—	10.00	12.00	20.00	80.00
	1876 JA	—	10.00	12.00	20.00	80.00
	1876 JS	—	10.00	12.00	20.00	80.00
	1877 JS	2.700	10.00	12.00	20.00	80.00
	1878 JS	2.310	10.00	12.00	20.00	80.00
	1879/8 JS	—	15.00	20.00	35.00	100.00

KM#	Date	Mintage	Fine	VF	XF	Unc
377.13	1879 JS	—	10.00	12.00	20.00	80.00
	1880 JS	—	10.00	12.00	20.00	80.00
	1881 JS	5.592	10.00	12.00	20.00	80.00
	1882/1 JS					
		2.485	15.00	20.00	35.00	100.00
	1882 JS straight J					
		Inc. Ab.	10.00	12.00	20.00	65.00
	1882 JS full J					
		Inc. Ab.	10.00	12.00	20.00	65.00
	1883/2 JS					
		2.563	15.00	20.00	35.00	100.00
	1883 JS	I.A.	10.00	12.00	20.00	80.00
	1884 JS	—	10.00	12.00	20.00	80.00
	1885 JS	2.252	10.00	12.00	20.00	65.00
	1886/5 JS					
		5.303	15.00	20.00	35.00	100.00
	1886/8 JS	I.A.	15.00	20.00	35.00	100.00
	1886 JS	I.A.	10.00	12.00	20.00	65.00
	1886 FZ	I.A.	10.00	12.00	20.00	65.00
	1887ZsFZ					
		4.733	10.00	12.00	20.00	65.00
	1887Z FZ	I.A.	20.00	30.00	50.00	100.00
	1888/7 FZ					
		5.132	12.00	15.00	25.00	80.00
	1888 FZ	I.A.	10.00	12.00	20.00	65.00
	1889 FZ	4.344	10.00	12.00	20.00	65.00
	1890 FZ	3.887	10.00	12.00	20.00	65.00
	1891 FZ	4.114	10.00	12.00	20.00	65.00
	1892/1 FZ					
		4.238	12.00	15.00	25.00	80.00
	1892 FZ	I.A.	10.00	12.00	20.00	65.00
	1893 FZ	3.872	10.00	12.00	20.00	65.00
	1894 FZ	3.081	10.00	12.00	20.00	65.00
	1895 FZ	4.718	10.00	12.00	20.00	65.00
	1896 FZ	4.226	10.00	12.00	20.00	55.00
	1897 FZ	4.877	10.00	12.00	20.00	55.00

NOTE: Varieties exist.

1/2 ESCUDO

1.6900 g, .875 GOLD, .0475 oz AGW
Mint mark: C
Obv: Facing eagle.

KM#	Date	Mintage	Fine	VF	XF	Unc
378	1848 CE	—	35.00	50.00	75.00	150.00
	1853 CE	—	35.00	50.00	75.00	150.00
	1854 CE	—	35.00	50.00	75.00	150.00
	1856 CE	—	50.00	100.00	150.00	250.00
	1857 CE	—	35.00	50.00	75.00	150.00
	1859 CE	—	35.00	50.00	75.00	150.00
	1860 CE	—	35.00	50.00	75.00	150.00
	1862 CE	—	35.00	50.00	75.00	125.00
	1863 CE	—	35.00	50.00	75.00	125.00
	1866 CE	—	35.00	50.00	75.00	125.00
	1867 CE	—	35.00	50.00	75.00	125.00
	1870 CE	—	—	—	—	—

Mint mark: Do

KM#	Date	Mintage	Fine	VF	XF	Unc
378.1	1833 RM/RL	—	35.00	50.00	75.00	150.00
	1834/3 RM	—	35.00	50.00	75.00	150.00
	1835/3 RM	—	35.00	50.00	75.00	150.00
	1836/4 RM	—	35.00	50.00	75.00	150.00
	1837 RM	—	35.00	50.00	75.00	150.00
	1838 RM	—	40.00	60.00	100.00	175.00
	1843 RM	—	40.00	60.00	100.00	175.00
	1844/33 RM	—	40.00	60.00	100.00	175.00
	1844/33 RM/RL					
		—	65.00	125.00	275.00	450.00
	1846 RM	—	40.00	60.00	100.00	175.00
	1848 RM	—	40.00	60.00	100.00	175.00
	1850/33 JMR	—	40.00	60.00	100.00	175.00
	1851 JMR	—	40.00	60.00	100.00	200.00
	1852 JMR	—	40.00	60.00	100.00	175.00
	1853/33 CP	—	75.00	150.00	300.00	500.00
	1853 CP	—	35.00	50.00	75.00	150.00
	1854 CP	—	35.00	50.00	75.00	150.00
	1855 CP	—	35.00	50.00	75.00	150.00
	1859 CP	—	35.00	50.00	75.00	150.00

PRICING SECTION

PRICING SECTION

Mint mark: Ga

KM#	Date Mintage	VG	Fine	VF	XF
	1861 CP —	35.00	50.00	75.00	150.00
	1864 LT —	75.00	125.00	250.00	400.00

Mint mark: Ga

KM#	Date Mintage	VG	Fine	VF	XF
378.2	1825 FS —	40.00	60.00	100.00	175.00
	1829 FS —	40.00	60.00	100.00	175.00
	1831 FS —	40.00	60.00	100.00	175.00
	1834 FS —	40.00	60.00	100.00	175.00
	1835 FS —	40.00	60.00	100.00	175.00
	1837 JG —	40.00	60.00	100.00	175.00
	1838 JG —	40.00	60.00	100.00	175.00
	1839 JG —	40.00	60.00	100.00	175.00
	1842 JG —	40.00	60.00	100.00	175.00
	1847 JG —	40.00	60.00	100.00	175.00
	1850 JG —	35.00	50.00	75.00	150.00
	1852 JG —	35.00	50.00	75.00	150.00
	1859 JG —	40.00	60.00	100.00	175.00
	1861 JG —	35.00	50.00	75.00	150.00

Mint mark: GC

KM#	Date Mintage	VG	Fine	VF	XF
378.3	1846 MP —	50.00	75.00	100.00	175.00
	1847 MP —	50.00	75.00	100.00	175.00
	1848/7 MP —	50.00	75.00	100.00	200.00
	1850 MP —	50.00	75.00	100.00	175.00
	1851 MP —	50.00	75.00	100.00	175.00

Mint mark: Go

KM#	Date Mintage	VG	Fine	VF	XF
378.4	1845 PM —	30.00	40.00	65.00	125.00
	1849 PF —	30.00	40.00	65.00	125.00
	1851/41 PF —	30.00	40.00	65.00	125.00
	1851 PF —	30.00	40.00	65.00	125.00
	1852 PF —	30.00	40.00	65.00	125.00
	1853 PF —	30.00	40.00	65.00	125.00
	1855 PF —	30.00	50.00	80.00	150.00
	1857 PF —	30.00	40.00	65.00	125.00
	1858/7 PF —	30.00	40.00	65.00	125.00
	1859 PF —	30.00	40.00	65.00	125.00
	1860 PF —	30.00	40.00	65.00	125.00
	1861 PF —	30.00	40.00	65.00	125.00
	1862/1 YE —	30.00	40.00	65.00	125.00
	1863 PF —	30.00	50.00	80.00	150.00
	1863 YF —	30.00	40.00	65.00	125.00

Mint mark: Mo

KM#	Date Mintage	VG	Fine	VF	XF
378.5	1825/1 JM —	50.00	75.00	125.00	200.00
	1825/4 JM —	50.00	75.00	125.00	200.00
	1825 JM —	30.00	40.00	80.00	150.00
	1827/6 JM —	30.00	40.00	80.00	150.00
	1827 JM —	30.00	40.00	80.00	150.00
	1829 JM —	30.00	40.00	80.00	150.00
	1831/0 JM —	30.00	40.00	80.00	150.00
	1831 JM —	30.00	40.00	60.00	125.00
	1832 JM —	30.00	40.00	60.00	125.00
	1833 MJ olive & oak branches reversed —	30.00	50.00	60.00	175.00
	1834 ML —	30.00	40.00	60.00	125.00
	1835 ML —	30.00	40.00	80.00	150.00
	1838 ML —	30.00	50.00	90.00	175.00
	1839 ML —	30.00	50.00	90.00	175.00
	1840 ML —	30.00	40.00	60.00	125.00
	1841 ML —	30.00	40.00	60.00	125.00
	1842 ML —	30.00	40.00	80.00	150.00
	1842 MM —	30.00	40.00	80.00	150.00
	1843 MM —	30.00	40.00	60.00	125.00
	1844 MF —	30.00	40.00	60.00	125.00
	1845 MF —	30.00	40.00	60.00	125.00
	1846/5 MF —	30.00	40.00	60.00	125.00
	1846 MF —	30.00	40.00	60.00	125.00
	1848 GC —	30.00	40.00	60.00	125.00
	1850 GC —	30.00	40.00	60.00	125.00
	1851 GC —	30.00	40.00	60.00	125.00
	1852 GC —	30.00	40.00	60.00	125.00
	1853 GC —	30.00	40.00	60.00	125.00
	1854 GC —	30.00	40.00	60.00	125.00
	1855 GF —	30.00	40.00	60.00	125.00
	1856/4 GF —	30.00	40.00	60.00	125.00
	1857 GF —	30.00	40.00	60.00	125.00
	1858/7 FH/GF —	35.00	50.00	75.00	150.00
	1858 FH —	30.00	40.00	60.00	125.00
	1859 FH —	30.00	40.00	60.00	125.00
	1860/59 FH —	30.00	40.00	60.00	125.00
	1861 CH/FH —	30.00	40.00	80.00	150.00
	1862 CH —	30.00	40.00	60.00	125.00
	1863/57 CH/GF				

KM#	Date Mintage	VG	Fine	VF	XF
378.5	—	30.00	40.00	60.00	125.00
	1868/58 PH —	30.00	40.00	80.00	150.00
	1869/59 CH —	30.00	40.00	80.00	150.00

Mint mark: Zs

KM#	Date Mintage	VG	Fine	VF	XF
378.6	1860 VL —	35.00	50.00	75.00	150.00
	1862/1 VL —	35.00	50.00	75.00	150.00
	1862 VL —	30.00	40.00	65.00	125.00

ESCUDO

3.3800 g, .875 GOLD, .0950 oz AGW
Mint mark: C
Obv: Facing eagle.

KM#	Date Mintage	VG	Fine	VF	XF
379	1846 CE —	75.00	100.00	200.00	350.00
	1847 CE —	50.00	75.00	125.00	175.00
	1848 CE —	50.00	75.00	125.00	175.00
	1849/8 CE —	60.00	100.00	150.00	225.00
	1850 CE —	50.00	75.00	125.00	175.00
	1851 CE —	60.00	100.00	150.00	225.00
	1853/1 CE —	60.00	100.00	150.00	225.00
	1854 CE —	50.00	75.00	125.00	175.00
	1856/5/4 CE —	60.00	100.00	150.00	225.00
	1856 CE —	50.00	75.00	125.00	175.00
	1857/1 CE —	60.00	100.00	150.00	225.00
	1857 CE —	50.00	75.00	125.00	175.00
	1861 PV —	50.00	75.00	125.00	175.00
	1862 CE —	50.00	75.00	125.00	175.00
	1863 CE —	50.00	75.00	125.00	175.00
	1866 CE —	50.00	75.00	125.00	175.00
	1870 CE —	50.00	75.00	125.00	175.00

Mint mark: Do

KM#	Date Mintage	VG	Fine	VF	XF
379.1	1833/2 RM/RL —	75.00	125.00	200.00	300.00
	1834 RM —	60.00	100.00	150.00	200.00
	1835 RM —	—	—	—	—
	1836 RM/RL —	60.00	100.00	150.00	200.00
	1838 RM —	60.00	100.00	150.00	200.00
	1846/38 RM —	75.00	125.00	200.00	300.00
	1850 JMR —	75.00	125.00	175.00	225.00
	1851/31 JMR				
379.1	—	75.00	125.00	200.00	300.00
	1851 JMR —	75.00	125.00	175.00	225.00
	1853 CP —	75.00	125.00	175.00	225.00
	1854/34 CP —	75.00	125.00	175.00	225.00
	1854/44 CP/RP —	75.00	125.00	175.00	225.00
	1855 CP —	75.00	125.00	175.00	225.00
	1859 CP —	75.00	125.00	175.00	225.00
	1861 CP —	75.00	125.00	175.00	225.00
	1864 LT/CP —	75.00	125.00	175.00	225.00

Mint mark: Ga

KM#	Date Mintage	VG	Fine	VF	XF
379.2	1825 FS —	60.00	90.00	125.00	200.00
	1826 FS —	60.00	90.00	125.00	200.00
	1829 FS —	—	—	—	—
	1831 FS —	60.00	90.00	125.00	200.00
	1834 FS —	60.00	90.00	125.00	200.00
	1835 JG —	60.00	90.00	125.00	200.00
	1842 JG/MC —	60.00	90.00	125.00	200.00
	1843 MC —	60.00	90.00	125.00	200.00
	1847 JG —	60.00	90.00	125.00	200.00
	1848/7 JG —	60.00	90.00	125.00	200.00
	1849 JG —	60.00	90.00	125.00	200.00
	1850/40 JG —	65.00	125.00	225.00	325.00
	1850 JG —	60.00	90.00	125.00	200.00
	1852/1 JG —	60.00	90.00	125.00	200.00
	1856 JG —	60.00	90.00	125.00	200.00
	1857 JG —	60.00	90.00	125.00	200.00
	1859/7 JG —	60.00	90.00	125.00	200.00
	1860/59 JG —	65.00	100.00	175.00	275.00
	1860 JG —	60.00	90.00	125.00	200.00

Mint mark: GC

KM#	Date	Mintage	VG	Fine	VF	XF
379.3	1844 MP	—	75.00	100.00	175.00	250.00
	1845 MP	—	75.00	100.00	175.00	250.00
	1846 MP	—	75.00	100.00	175.00	250.00
	1847 MP	—	75.00	100.00	175.00	250.00
	1848 MP	—	75.00	100.00	175.00	250.00
	1849 MP	—	75.00	100.00	175.00	250.00
	1850 MP	—	75.00	100.00	175.00	250.00
	1851 MP	—	75.00	100.00	175.00	250.00

Mint mark: Go

KM#	Date	Mintage	VG	Fine	VF	XF
379.4	1845 PM	—	60.00	75.00	125.00	200.00
	1849 PF	—	60.00	75.00	125.00	200.00
	1851 PF	—	60.00	75.00	125.00	200.00
	1853 PF	—	60.00	75.00	125.00	200.00
	1860 PF	—	75.00	125.00	200.00	300.00
	1862 YE	—	60.00	75.00	125.00	200.00

Mint mark: Mo

KM#	Date	Mintage	VG	Fine	VF	XF
379.5	1825 JM	—	50.00	70.00	100.00	150.00
	1827/6 JM	—	50.00	70.00	100.00	150.00
	1827 JM	—	50.00	70.00	100.00	150.00
	1830/29 JM	—	50.00	70.00	100.00	150.00
	1831 JM	—	50.00	70.00	100.00	150.00
	1832 JM	—	50.00	70.00	125.00	175.00
	1833 MJ	—	50.00	70.00	100.00	150.00
	1834 ML	—	50.00	70.00	125.00	175.00
	1841 ML	—	50.00	70.00	125.00	175.00
	1843 MM	—	50.00	70.00	100.00	150.00
	1845 MF	—	50.00	70.00	100.00	150.00
	1846/5 MF	—	50.00	70.00	100.00	150.00
	1848 GC	—	50.00	70.00	125.00	175.00
	1850 GC	—	50.00	70.00	125.00	175.00
	1856/4 GF	—	50.00	70.00	100.00	150.00
	1856/5 GF	—	50.00	70.00	100.00	150.00
	1856 GF	—	50.00	70.00	100.00	150.00
	1858 FH	—	50.00	70.00	125.00	175.00
	1859 FH	—	50.00	70.00	100.00	150.00
	1860 TH	—	50.00	70.00	125.00	175.00
	1861 CH	—	50.00	70.00	100.00	150.00
	1862 CH	—	50.00	70.00	125.00	175.00
	1863 TH	—	50.00	70.00	100.00	150.00
	1869 CH	—	50.00	70.00	100.00	150.00

Mint mark: Zs

KM#	Date	Mintage	VG	Fine	VF	XF
379.6	1853 OM	—	100.00	125.00	200.00	300.00
	1860/59 VL V is inverted A					
		—	75.00	100.00	200.00	350.00
	1860 VL	—	75.00	100.00	150.00	200.00
	1862 VL	—	75.00	100.00	150.00	200.00

2 ESCUDOS

6.7700 g, .875 GOLD, .1904 oz AGW
Mint mark: C
Obv: Facing eagle.

KM#	Date	Mintage	VG	Fine	VF	XF
380	1846 CE	—	100.00	150.00	225.00	325.00
	1847 CE	—	100.00	150.00	225.00	325.00
	1848 CE	—	100.00	150.00	225.00	325.00
	1852 CE	—	100.00	150.00	225.00	325.00
	1854 CE	—	100.00	175.00	250.00	375.00
	1856/4 CE	—	100.00	175.00	250.00	375.00
	1857 CE	—	100.00	150.00	225.00	325.00

Mint mark: Do

KM#	Date	Mintage	VG	Fine	VF	XF
380.1	1833 RM	—	300.00	450.00	700.00	1200.
	1837/4 RM	—	—	—	—	—
	1837 RM	—	—	—	—	—
	1844 RM	—	275.00	400.00	600.00	1000.

Mint mark: EoMo

KM#	Date	Mintage	VG	Fine	VF	XF
380.2	1828 LF	—	700.00	1000.	1750.	2500.

Mint mark: Ga

KM#	Date	Mintage	VG	Fine	VF	XF
380.3	1835 FS	—	100.00	150.00	225.00	325.00
	1836/5 JG	—	100.00	150.00	225.00	300.00
	1839/5 JG	—	—	—	—	—
	1839 JG	—	100.00	150.00	200.00	275.00
	1840 MC	—	100.00	150.00	200.00	275.00
	1841 MC	—	100.00	150.00	250.00	400.00
	1847/6 JG	—	100.00	150.00	225.00	300.00
	1848/7 JG	—	100.00	150.00	225.00	300.00
	1850/40 JG	—	100.00	150.00	200.00	250.00
	1851 JG	—	100.00	150.00	200.00	275.00
	1852 JG	—	100.00	150.00	225.00	325.00
	1853 JG	—	100.00	150.00	200.00	275.00
	1854/2 JG	—	—	—	—	—
	1858 JG	—	100.00	150.00	200.00	275.00
	1859/8 JG	—	100.00	150.00	225.00	300.00
	1859 JG	—	100.00	150.00	200.00	275.00
	1860/50 JG	—	100.00	150.00	225.00	300.00
	1860 JG	—	100.00	150.00	225.00	300.00
	1861/59 JG	—	100.00	150.00	200.00	275.00
	1861/0 JG	—	100.00	150.00	200.00	275.00
	1863/1 JG	—	100.00	150.00	200.00	275.00
	1870 IC	—	100.00	150.00	200.00	275.00

Mint mark: GC

KM#	Date	Mintage	VG	Fine	VF	XF
380.4	1844 MP	—	150.00	200.00	275.00	400.00
	1845 MP	—	750.00	1250.	2000.	3000.
	1846 MP	—	750.00	1250.	2000.	3000.
	1847 MP	—	125.00	175.00	350.00	500.00
	1848 MP	—	150.00	200.00	350.00	450.00
	1849 MP	—	150.00	200.00	300.00	400.00
	1850 MP	—	150.00	200.00	300.00	400.00

Mint mark: Go

KM#	Date	Mintage	VG	Fine	VF	XF
380.5	1845 PM	—	100.00	150.00	250.00	400.00
	1849 PF	—	100.00	150.00	250.00	400.00
	1853 PF	—	100.00	150.00	250.00	400.00
	1856 PF	—	100.00	150.00	250.00	400.00
	1859 PF	—	100.00	150.00	250.00	400.00
	1860/59 PF	—	100.00	150.00	250.00	400.00
	1860 PF	—	100.00	150.00	250.00	400.00
	1862 YE	—	100.00	150.00	250.00	400.00

Mint mark: Ho

KM#	Date	Mintage	VG	Fine	VF	XF
380.6	1861 FM	—	500.00	1000.	1500.	2000.

Mint mark: Mo

KM#	Date	Mintage	VG	Fine	VF	XF
380.7	1825 JM	—	100.00	150.00	200.00	275.00
	1827/6 JM	—	100.00	150.00	200.00	275.00
	1827 JM	—	100.00	150.00	200.00	275.00
	1830/29 JM	—	100.00	150.00	200.00	275.00
	1831 JM	—	100.00	150.00	200.00	275.00
	1833 ML	—	100.00	150.00	200.00	275.00
	1841 ML	—	100.00	150.00	200.00	275.00
	1844 MF	—	100.00	150.00	200.00	275.00
	1845 MF	—	100.00	150.00	200.00	275.00
	1846 MF	—	125.00	200.00	400.00	600.00
	1848 GC	—	100.00	150.00	200.00	275.00
	1850 GC	—	100.00	150.00	200.00	275.00
	1856/5 GF	—	100.00	150.00	200.00	275.00
	1856 GF	—	100.00	150.00	200.00	275.00
	1858 FH	—	100.00	150.00	200.00	275.00
	1859 FH	—	100.00	150.00	200.00	275.00
	1861 TH	—	100.00	150.00	200.00	275.00
	1861 CH	—	100.00	150.00	200.00	300.00
	1862 CH	—	100.00	150.00	200.00	300.00
	1863 TH	—	100.00	150.00	200.00	300.00
	1868 PH	—	100.00	150.00	200.00	300.00
	1869 CH	—	100.00	150.00	200.00	300.00

Mint mark: Zs

KM#	Date	Mintage	VG	Fine	VF	XF
380.8	1860 VL	—	150.00	300.00	600.00	1200.
	1862 VL	—	250.00	500.00	800.00	1200.
	1864 MO	—	150.00	300.00	600.00	1200.

4 ESCUDOS

Mint mark: Do

13.5400 g, .875 GOLD, .3809 oz AGW

Mint mark: C
Facing eagle

KM#	Date	Mintage	VG	Fine	VF	XF
381	1846 CE	—	1200.	1700.	—	—
	1847 CE	—	400.00	650.00	850.00	1250.
	1848 CE	—	600.00	900.00	1250.	1750.

Mint mark: Do

381.1	1832 RM/LR	—	—	—	Rare	—
	1832 RM	—	600.00	900.00	1250.	1750.
	1833 RM/RL	—	—	—	Rare	—
	1852 JMR	—	—	—	Rare	—

Mint mark: Ga

381.2	1844 MC	—	500.00	750.00	1000.	1500.
	1844 JG	—	400.00	650.00	850.00	1250.

Mint mark: GC

381.3	1844 MP	—	400.00	650.00	850.00	1250.
	1845 MP	—	350.00	500.00	700.00	1000.
	1846 MP	—	400.00	650.00	850.00	1250.
	1848 MP	—	400.00	650.00	850.00	1250.
	1850 MP	—	500.00	750.00	1000.	1500.

Mint mark: Go

381.4	1829/8 MJ	—	200.00	300.00	450.00	700.00
	1829 JM	—	200.00	300.00	450.00	700.00
	1829 MJ	—	200.00	300.00	450.00	700.00
	1831 MJ	—	200.00	300.00	450.00	700.00
	1832 MJ	—	200.00	300.00	450.00	700.00
	1833 MJ	—	200.00	300.00	500.00	800.00
	1834 PJ	—	250.00	450.00	650.00	1000.
	1835 PJ	—	250.00	450.00	650.00	1000.
	1836 PJ	—	200.00	300.00	500.00	800.00
	1837 PJ	—	200.00	300.00	500.00	800.00
	1838 PJ	—	200.00	300.00	500.00	800.00
	1839 PJ	—	250.00	450.00	650.00	1000.
	1840 PJ	—	200.00	300.00	500.00	800.00
	1841 PJ	—	250.00	450.00	650.00	1000.
	1845 PM	—	200.00	300.00	500.00	800.00
	1847/5 YE	—	250.00	450.00	650.00	1000.
	1847 PM	—	250.00	450.00	650.00	1000.
	1849 PF	—	250.00	450.00	650.00	1000.
	1851 PF	—	250.00	450.00	650.00	1000.
	1852 PF	—	200.00	300.00	500.00	800.00
	1855 PF	—	200.00	300.00	500.00	800.00
	1857/5 PF	—	200.00	300.00	500.00	800.00
	1858/7 PF	—	200.00	300.00	500.00	800.00
	1858 PF	—	200.00	300.00	500.00	800.00
	1859/7 PF	—	250.00	450.00	650.00	1000.
381.4	1860 PF	—	275.00	475.00	750.00	1200.
	1862 YE	—	200.00	300.00	500.00	800.00
	1863 YF	—	200.00	300.00	500.00	800.00

Mint mark: Ho

381.5	1861 FM	—	1000.	1500.	2500.	3750.

Mint mark: Mo

381.6	1825 JM	—	200.00	300.00	500.00	850.00
	1827/6 JM	—	200.00	300.00	500.00	800.00
	1829 JM	—	200.00	350.00	650.00	1000.
	1831 JM	—	200.00	350.00	650.00	1000.
	1832 JM	—	275.00	475.00	750.00	1200.
	1844 MF	—	200.00	350.00	650.00	1000.
	1850 GC	—	200.00	350.00	650.00	1000.
	1856 GF	—	200.00	300.00	500.00	800.00
	1857/6 GF	—	200.00	300.00	500.00	800.00
	1857 GF	—	200.00	300.00	500.00	800.00
	1858 FH	—	200.00	350.00	650.00	1000.
	1859/8 FH	—	200.00	350.00	650.00	1000.

KM#	Date	Mintage	VG	Fine	VF	XF
	1861 CH	—	400.00	800.00	1200.	1600.
	1863 CH	—	200.00	350.00	650.00	1000.
	1868 PH	—	200.00	300.00	500.00	800.00
	1869 CH	—	200.00	300.00	500.00	800.00

Mint mark: O, Oa

381.7	1861 FR	—	1500.	2500.	4000.	6500.

Mint mark: Zs

381.8	1862 VL	—	750.00	1250.	2250.	3500.

8 ESCUDOS

Tail Curved   **Tail Looped**

27.0700 g, .875 GOLD, .7616 oz AGW
Mint mark: Mo
Obv: Hooked-neck eagle.

KM#	Date	Mintage	Fine	VF	XF	Unc
382.1	1823 JM snake's tail curved					
		—	3750.	7000.	11,000.	—

NOTE: Superior Casterline sale 5-89 choice AU realized $18,700.

KM#	Date	Mintage	Fine	VF	XF	Unc
382.2	1823 JM snake's tail looped					
		—	3750.	7000.	11,000.	—

Mint mark: A
Obv: Facing eagle.

KM#	Date	Mintage	Fine	VF	XF	Unc
383	1864 PG	—	650.00	1250.	2250.	—
	1866 DL	—	—	—	7500.	—
	1868/7 DL	—	1500.	2250.	3250.	—
	1869 DL	—	650.00	1250.	2250.	—
	1870 DL	—	1500.	2250.	3250.	—
	1872 AM	—	—	—	Rare	—

Mint mark: Ca

KM#	Date	Mintage	Fine	VF	XF	Unc
383.1	1841 RG	—	400.00	750.00	1250.	1750.
	1842 RG	—	375.00	500.00	1000.	1500.
	1843 RG	—	375.00	500.00	1000.	1500.
	1844 RG	—	350.00	500.00	1000.	1500.
	1845 RG	—	350.00	500.00	1000.	1500.
	1846 RG	—	500.00	1250.	1500.	2000.
	1847 RG	—	1000.	2500.	—	—
	1848 RG	—	350.00	500.00	1000.	1500.
	1849 RG	—	350.00	500.00	1000.	1500.
	1850/40 RG	—	350.00	500.00	1000.	1500.
	1851/41 RG	—	350.00	500.00	1000.	1500.
	1852/42 RG	—	350.00	500.00	1000.	1500.
	1853/43 RG	—	350.00	500.00	1000.	1500.
	1854/44 RG	—	350.00	500.00	1000.	1500.
	1855/43 RG	—	400.00	650.00	1250.	1750.
	1856/46 RG	—	350.00	500.00	750.00	1250.
	1857 JC/RG	—	350.00	500.00	750.00	1250.
	1858 JC	—	350.00	500.00	750.00	1250.
	1858 BA/RG	—	350.00	500.00	750.00	1250.
	1859 JC/RG	—	350.00	500.00	750.00	1250.
	1860 JC/RG	—	350.00	500.00	1000.	1500.
	1861 JC	—	375.00	500.00	750.00	1250.
	1862 JC	—	375.00	500.00	750.00	1250.
	1863 JC	—	500.00	1000.	1750.	2250.
	1864 JC	—	400.00	750.00	1250.	1750.
	1865 JC	—	750.00	1500.	2500.	3500.
	1866 JC	—	375.00	500.00	1000.	1500.
	1866 FP	—	600.00	1250.	2000.	2500.
	1866 JG	—	375.00	500.00	1000.	1500.
	1867 JG	—	375.00	500.00	750.00	1250.
	1868 JG concave wings					
		—	375.00	500.00	750.00	1250.
	1869 MM regular eagle					
		—	375.00	500.00	750.00	1250.
	1870/60 MM	—	375.00	500.00	750.00	1250.
	1871/61 MM	—	375.00	500.00	750.00	1250.

Mint mark: C

KM#	Date	Mintage	Fine	VF	XF	Unc
383.2	1846 CE	—	375.00	500.00	1000.	1750.
	1847 CE	—	375.00	500.00	800.00	1250.

KM#	Date	Mintage	Fine	VF	XF	Unc
383.2	1848 CE	—	375.00	500.00	1000.	1750.
	1849 CE	—	375.00	450.00	700.00	1250.
	1850 CE	—	375.00	450.00	700.00	1250.
	1851 CE	—	375.00	500.00	800.00	1250.
	1852 CE	—	375.00	500.00	800.00	1250.
	1853/1 CE	—	375.00	450.00	700.00	1250.
	1854 CE	—	375.00	450.00	700.00	1250.
	1855/4 CE	—	375.00	500.00	1000.	1750.
	1855 CE	—	375.00	500.00	800.00	1250.
	1856 CE	—	375.00	450.00	700.00	1250.
	1857 CE	—	375.00	450.00	700.00	1250.
	1857 CE w/o periods after C's					
		—	—	—	—	—
	1858 CE	—	375.00	450.00	700.00	1250.
	1859 CE	—	375.00	450.00	700.00	1250.
	1860/58 CE	—	375.00	500.00	800.00	1250.
	1860 CE	—	375.00	500.00	800.00	1250.
	1860 PV	—	375.00	450.00	700.00	1250.
	1861 PV	—	375.00	500.00	800.00	1250.
	1861 CE	—	375.00	500.00	800.00	1250.
	1862 CE	—	375.00	500.00	800.00	1250.
	1863 CE	—	375.00	500.00	800.00	1250.
	1864 CE	—	375.00	450.00	700.00	1250.
	1865 CE	—	375.00	500.00	800.00	1250.
	1866/5 CE	—	375.00	450.00	700.00	1250.
	1866 CE	—	375.00	450.00	700.00	1250.
	1867 CB (error)					
		—	375.00	450.00	700.00	1250.
	1867 CE/CB	—	375.00	450.00	700.00	1250.
	1868 CB (error)					
		—	375.00	500.00	800.00	1250.
	1869 CE	—	375.00	500.00	800.00	1250.
	1870 CE	—	375.00	500.00	800.00	1250.

Mint mark: Do

KM#	Date	Mintage	Fine	VF	XF	Unc
383.3	1832 RM	—	850.00	1750.	2000.	3000.
	1833 RM/RL	—	375.00	500.00	800.00	1250.
	1834 RM	—	375.00	500.00	800.00	1250.
	1835 RM	—	375.00	500.00	800.00	1250.
	1836 RM/RL	—	375.00	500.00	800.00	1250.
	1836 RM M on snake					
		—	375.00	500.00	800.00	1250.
	1837 RM	—	375.00	500.00	800.00	1250.
	1838/6 RM	—	375.00	500.00	800.00	1250.
	1838 RM	—	375.00	500.00	800.00	1250.
	1839 RM	—	375.00	450.00	700.00	1250.
	1840/30 RM/RL					
		—	400.00	600.00	1000.	1750.
	1841/30 RM	—	550.00	750.00	1250.	2000.
	1841/31 RM	—	375.00	500.00	800.00	1250.
	1841/34 RM	—	375.00	500.00	800.00	1250.
	1841 RM/RL	—	375.00	500.00	800.00	1250.
	1842/32 RM	—	375.00	500.00	800.00	1250.
	1843/33 RM	—	550.00	750.00	1250.	2000.
	1843/1 RM	—	375.00	500.00	800.00	1250.
	1843 RM	—	375.00	500.00	800.00	1250.
	1844/34 RM/RL					
		—	500.00	1000.	1500.	2500.
	1844 RM	—	450.00	800.00	1250.	2000.
	1845/36 RM	—	400.00	600.00	1000.	1750.
	1845 RM	—	400.00	600.00	1000.	1750.
	1846 RM	—	375.00	500.00	800.00	1250.
	1847/37 RM	—	375.00	500.00	800.00	1250.
	1848/37 RM	—	—	—	—	—
	1848/38 CM	—	375.00	500.00	800.00	1250.
	1849/39 CM	—	375.00	500.00	800.00	1250.
	1849 JMR	—	400.00	750.00	1250.	2000.
	1850 JMR	—	400.00	750.00	1250.	2000.

KM#	Date Mintage	Fine	VF	XF	Unc
383.3	1851 JMR	— 400.00	750.00	1250.	2000.
	1852/1 JMR	— 450.00	800.00	1250.	2000.
	1852 CP	— 450.00	800.00	1250.	2000.
	1853 CP	— 450.00	800.00	1250.	2000.
	1854 CP	— 400.00	600.00	1000.	1750.
	1855/4 CP	— 375.00	500.00	800.00	1250.
	1855 CP	— 375.00	500.00	800.00	1250.
	1856 CP	— 400.00	600.00	1000.	1750.
	1857 CP French style eagle, 1832-57				
		— 375.00	500.00	800.00	1250.
	1857 CP Mexican style eagle				
		— 375.00	500.00	800.00	1250.
	1858 CP	— 375.00	500.00	800.00	1250.
	1859 CP	— 375.00	500.00	800.00	1250.
	1860/59 CP	— 450.00	700.00	1250.	2200.
	1861/0 CP	— 400.00	600.00	1000.	1750.
	1862/52 CP	— 375.00	500.00	800.00	1250.
	1862/1 CP	— 375.00	500.00	800.00	1250.
	1862 CP	— 375.00	500.00	800.00	1250.
	1863/53 CP	— 375.00	500.00	800.00	1250.
	1864 LT	— 375.00	500.00	800.00	1250.
	1865/4 LT	— 500.00	1000.	1650.	2750.
	1866/4 CM	— 1250.	2000.	2500.	—
	1866 CM	— 400.00	600.00	1000.	1750.
	1867/56 CP	— 400.00	600.00	1000.	1750.
	1867/4 CP	— 375.00	500.00	800.00	1250.
	1868/4 CP/LT				
		—	—	—	—
	1869 CP	— 500.00	1250.	1750.	2750.
	1870 CP	— 400.00	600.00	1000.	1750.

Mint mark: EoMo

KM#	Date	Fine	VF	XF	Unc
383.4	1828 LF	— 3500.	5500.	8500.	—
	1829 LF	— 3500.	5500.	8500.	—

Mint mark: Ga

KM#	Date	Fine	VF	XF	Unc
383.5	1825 FS	— 500.00	1000.	1250.	1750.
	1826 FS	— 500.00	1000.	1250.	1750.
	1830 FS	— 500.00	1000.	1250.	1750.
	1836 FS	— 750.00	1500.	2000.	3000.
	1836 JG	— 1000.	2500.	3500.	—
	1837 JG	— 1000.	2500.	3500.	—
	1840 MC	— 750.00	1500.	2000.	3000.
	1841/31 MC	— 1000.	2500.	—	—
	1841 MC	— 850.00	1650.	2250.	—
	1842 JG	—	—	—	—
	1843 MC	—	—	—	—
	1845 MC	— 400.00	850.00	1100.	1650.
	1847 JG	— 2250.	—	—	—
	1849 JG	— 500.00	1000.	1250.	1750.
	1850 JG	— 400.00	850.00	1100.	1650.
	1851 JG	— 400.00	850.00	1100.	1650.
	1852/1 JG	— 500.00	1000.	1250.	1750.
	1855 JG	— 1000.	2500.	3500.	—
	1856 JG	— 400.00	850.00	1100.	1650.
	1857 JG	— 400.00	850.00	1100.	1650.
	1861/0 JG	— 500.00	1000.	1250.	1750.
	1861 JG	— 400.00	700.00	1200.	1750.
	1863/1 JG	— 500.00	1000.	1250.	1750.
	1866 JG	— 400.00	850.00	1100.	1650.

Mint mark: GC

KM#	Date	Mintage	Fine	VF	XF	Unc
383.6	1844 MP	—	550.00	750.00	1250.	2000.

KM#	Date	Mintage	Fine	VF	XF	Unc
383.6	1845 MP eagle's tail square					
		—	550.00	750.00	1250.	2000.
	1845 MP eagle's tail round					
		—	550.00	750.00	1250.	2000.
	1846 MP eagle's tail square					
		—	450.00	650.00	1000.	1750.
	1846 MP eagle's tail round					
		—	450.00	650.00	1000.	1750.
	1847 MP	—	450.00	650.00	1000.	1750.
	1848 MP	—	550.00	750.00	1250.	2000.
	1849 MP	—	550.00	750.00	1250.	2000.
	1850 MP	—	450.00	650.00	1000.	1750.
	1851 MP	—	450.00	650.00	1000.	1750.
	1852 MP	—	550.00	750.00	1250.	2000.

Mint mark: Go

KM#	Date	Fine	VF	XF	Unc
383.7	1828 MJ	— 700.00	1750.	2250.	3000.
	1829 MJ	— 600.00	1500.	2000.	2750.
	1830 MJ	— 375.00	500.00	750.00	1000.
	1831 MJ	— 600.00	1500.	2000.	2750.
	1832 MJ	— 500.00	1250.	1750.	2500.
	1833 MJ	— 375.00	500.00	700.00	700.00
	1834 PJ	— 375.00	500.00	700.00	700.00
	1835 PJ	— 375.00	500.00	700.00	700.00
	1836 PJ	— 400.00	650.00	900.00	1250.
	1837 PJ	— 400.00	650.00	900.00	1250.
	1838/7 PJ	— 375.00	500.00	700.00	1000.
	1838 PJ	— 375.00	500.00	800.00	1200.
	1839/8 PJ	— 375.00	500.00	700.00	1000.
	1839 PJ regular eagle				
		— 375.00	500.00	800.00	1200.
	1840 PJ concave wings				
		— 375.00	500.00	700.00	1000.
	1841 PJ	— 375.00	500.00	700.00	1000.
	1842 PJ	— 375.00	475.00	650.00	1000.
	1842 PM	— 375.00	500.00	700.00	1000.
	1843 PM small eagle				
		— 375.00	500.00	700.00	1000.
	1844/3 PM	— 400.00	650.00	900.00	1250.
	1844 PM	— 375.00	500.00	700.00	1000.
	1845 PM	— 375.00	500.00	700.00	1000.
	1846/5 PM	— 375.00	500.00	800.00	1200.
	1846 PM	— 375.00	500.00	700.00	1000.
	1847 PM	— 400.00	650.00	900.00	1250.
	1848/7 PM	— 375.00	500.00	700.00	1000.
	1848 PM	— 375.00	500.00	700.00	1000.
	1848 PF	— 375.00	500.00	700.00	1000.
	1849 PF	— 375.00	425.00	600.00	900.00
	1850 PF	— 375.00	425.00	600.00	900.00
	1851 PF	— 375.00	500.00	700.00	1000.
	1852 PF	— 375.00	500.00	700.00	1000.
	1853 PF	— 375.00	425.00	600.00	900.00
	1854 PF eagle of 1853				
		— 375.00	500.00	700.00	1000.
	1854 PF eagle of 1855				
		— 375.00	500.00	700.00	1000.
	1855/4 PF	— 400.00	650.00	900.00	1250.
	1855 PF	— 375.00	500.00	700.00	1000.
	1856 PF	— 375.00	500.00	700.00	1000.
	1857 PF	— 375.00	500.00	700.00	1000.
	1858 PF	— 375.00	500.00	700.00	1000.
	1859 PF	— 375.00	400.00	550.00	750.00
	1860/50 PF	— 375.00	425.00	600.00	900.00
	1860/59 PF	— 400.00	650.00	900.00	1250.
	1860 PF	— 375.00	500.00	700.00	1100.
	1861/0 PF	— 375.00	400.00	500.00	750.00
	1861 PF	— 375.00	400.00	500.00	750.00
	1862/1 YE	— 375.00	500.00	700.00	1000.
	1862 YE	— 375.00	500.00	700.00	1000.

KM#	Date Mintage	Fine	VF	XF	Unc
383.7	1862 YF	—	—	—	—
	1863/53 YF —	375.00	500.00	700.00	1000.
	1863 PF —	375.00	500.00	700.00	1000.
	1867/57 YF/PF				
	—	375.00	500.00	700.00	1000.
	1867 YF —	375.00	500.00	700.00	1000.
	1868/58 YF —	375.00	500.00	700.00	1000.
	1870 FR —	375.00	425.00	600.00	900.00

Mint mark: Ho

KM#	Date Mintage	Fine	VF	XF	Unc
383.8	1863 FM —	400.00	650.00	1000.	2000.
	1864 FM —	600.00	1250.	1750.	2750.
	1864 PR/FM —	400.00	650.00	1000.	2000.
	1865 FM/PR —	500.00	800.00	1250.	2500.
	1867/57 PR —	400.00	650.00	1000.	2000.
	1868 PR —	500.00	800.00	1250.	2500.
	1868 PR/FM —	500.00	800.00	1250.	2500.
	1869 PR/FM —	400.00	650.00	1000.	2000.
	1869 PR —	400.00	650.00	1000.	2000.
	1870 PR —	400.00	650.00	1000.	2000.
	1871/0 PR —	500.00	800.00	1250.	2500.
	1871 PR —	500.00	800.00	1250.	2500.
	1872/1 PR —	600.00	1250.	1750.	2750.
	1873 PR —	400.00	650.00	1000.	2000.

Large book.

Small book.

Mint mark: Mo

KM#	Date Mintage	Fine	VF	XF	Unc
383.9	1824 JM lg. book reverse				
	—	500.00	1000.	1250.	2000.
	1825 JM sm. book reverse				
	—	375.00	450.00	600.00	1000.
	1826/5 JM —	700.00	1750.	2250.	3000.
	1827 JM —	375.00	600.00	725.00	1000.
	1828 JM —	375.00	600.00	725.00	1000.
	1829 JM —	375.00	600.00	725.00	1000.
	1830 JM —	375.00	600.00	725.00	1000.
	1831 JM —	375.00	600.00	725.00	1000.
	1832/1 JM —	375.00	600.00	725.00	1000.
	1832 JM —	375.00	600.00	725.00	1000.
	1833 MJ —	400.00	750.00	1000.	1500.
	1833 ML —	375.00	450.00	600.00	900.00
	1834 ML —	400.00	750.00	1000.	1500.
	1835/4 ML —	500.00	1000.	1250.	2000.
	1836 ML —	375.00	450.00	600.00	900.00
	1836 MF —	500.00	700.00	1200.	2000.
	1837/6 ML —	375.00	450.00	600.00	900.00
	1838 ML —	375.00	450.00	600.00	900.00
	1839 ML —	375.00	450.00	600.00	900.00
	1840 ML —	375.00	450.00	600.00	900.00
	1841 ML —	375.00	450.00	600.00	900.00

KM#	Date Mintage	Fine	VF	XF	Unc
383.9	1842/1 ML	—	—	—	—
	1842 ML —	375.00	450.00	600.00	900.00
	1842 MM	—	—	—	—
	1843 MM —	375.00	450.00	600.00	900.00
	1844 MF —	375.00	450.00	600.00	900.00
	1845 MF —	375.00	450.00	600.00	900.00
	1846 MF —	500.00	1000.	1250.	2000.
	1847 MF —	950.00	2250.	—	—
	1847 RC —	375.00	500.00	800.00	1250.
	1848 GC —	375.00	450.00	600.00	900.00
	1849 GC —	375.00	450.00	600.00	900.00
	1850 GC —	375.00	450.00	600.00	900.00
	1851 GC —	375.00	450.00	600.00	900.00
	1852 GC —	375.00	450.00	600.00	900.00
	1853 GC —	375.00	450.00	600.00	900.00
	1854/44 GC —	375.00	450.00	600.00	900.00
	1854/3 GC —	375.00	450.00	600.00	900.00
	1855 GF —	375.00	450.00	600.00	900.00
	1856/5 GF —	375.00	450.00	600.00	900.00
	1856 GF —	375.00	450.00	600.00	900.00
	1857 GF —	375.00	450.00	600.00	900.00
	1858 FH —	375.00	450.00	600.00	900.00
	1859 FH —	400.00	750.00	'1000.	1500.
	1860 FH —	375.00	450.00	600.00	900.00
	1860 TH —	375.00	450.00	600.00	900.00
	1861/51 CH —	375.00	450.00	600.00	900.00
	1862 CH —	375.00	450.00	600.00	900.00
	1863/53 CH —	375.00	450.00	600.00	900.00
	1863/53 TH —	375.00	450.00	600.00	900.00
	1867 CH —	375.00	450.00	600.00	900.00
	1868 CH —	375.00	450.00	600.00	900.00
	1868 PH —	375.00	450.00	600.00	900.00
	1869 CH —	375.00	450.00	600.00	900.00

NOTE: Formerly reported 1825/3 JM is merely a reworked 5.

Mint mark: O

KM#	Date Mintage	Fine	VF	XF	Unc
383.10	1858 AE —	2000.	3000.	4000.	6000.
	1859 AE —	1000.	2500.	3750.	5500.
	1860 AE —	1000.	2500.	3750.	5500.
	1861 FR —	450.00	850.00	1250.	2750.
	1862 FR —	450.00	850.00	1250.	2750.
	1863 FR —	450.00	850.00	1250.	2750.
	1864 FR —	450.00	850.00	1250.	2750.
	1867 AE —	450.00	850.00	1250.	2750.
	1868 AE —	450.00	850.00	1250.	2750.
	1869 AE —	450.00	850.00	1250.	2750.

Mint mark: Zs

KM#	Date Mintage	Fine	VF	XF	Unc
383.11	1858 MO —	400.00	750.00	1000.	2000.
	1859 MO —	375.00	475.00	650.00	900.00
	1860/59 VL/MO				
	—	2000.	3000.	4000.	—
	1860/9 MO —	400.00	750.00	1000.	2000.
	1860 MO —	375.00	500.00	700.00	1000.
	1861/0 VL —	375.00	500.00	700.00	1000.
	1861 VL —	375.00	500.00	700.00	1000.
	1862 VL —	375.00	500.00	700.00	1100.
	1863 VL —	375.00	525.00	750.00	1150.
	1863 MO —	375.00	500.00	700.00	1000.
	1864 MO —	750.00	1000.	1500.	3000.
	1865 MO —	375.00	500.00	700.00	1000.
	1865 MP	—	Contemporary counterfeit		
	1868 JS —	400.00	600.00	800.00	1250.
	1868 YH —	400.00	600.00	800.00	1250.
	1869 YH —	400.00	600.00	800.00	1250.
	1870 YH —	400.00	600.00	800.00	1250.
	1871 YH —	400.00	600.00	800.00	1250.

EMPIRE OF MAXIMILIAN
RULER
Maximilian, Emperor, 1864-1867
MINT MARKS
Refer To Republic Coinage
MONETARY SYSTEM
100 Centavos = 1 Peso (8 Reales)
CENTAVO

COPPER
Mint mark: M

KM#	Date	Mintage	Fine	VF	XF	Unc
384	1864	—	35.00	60.00	150.00	1000.

5 CENTAVOS

1.3537 g, .903 SILVER, .0393 oz ASW
Mint mark: G

KM#	Date	Mintage	Fine	VF	XF	Unc
385	1864	.090	17.50	35.00	75.00	300.00
	1865	—	20.00	30.00	55.00	275.00
	1866	—	75.00	150.00	300.00	1800.
		Mint mark: M				
385.1	1864	—	12.50	20.00	55.00	275.00
	1866/4	—	25.00	40.00	75.00	385.00
	1866	—	20.00	35.00	65.00	375.00
		Mint mark: P				
385.2	1864	—	100.00	215.00	950.00	2300.
		Mint mark: Z				
385.3	1865	—	25.00	45.00	150.00	425.00

10 CENTAVOS

2.7073 g, .903 SILVER, .0786 oz ASW
Mint mark: G

KM#	Date	Mintage	Fine	VF	XF	Unc
386	1864	.045	20.00	40.00	80.00	300.00
	1865	—	25.00	45.00	85.00	325.00
		Mint mark: M				
386.1	1864	—	15.00	25.00	55.00	275.00
	1866/4	—	25.00	35.00	60.00	300.00
	1866/5	—	25.00	35.00	75.00	375.00
	1866	—	25.00	35.00	75.00	375.00
		Mint mark: P				
386.2	1864	—	70.00	150.00	300.00	600.00
		Mint mark: Z				
386.3	1865	—	25.00	55.00	145.00	475.00

50 CENTAVOS

13.5365 g, .903 SILVER, .3929 oz ASW
Mint mark: Mo

KM#	Date	Mintage	Fine	VF	XF	Unc
387	1866	.031	40.00	95.00	200.00	600.00

PESO

27.0700 g, .903 SILVER, .7857 oz ASW
Mint mark: Go

KM#	Date	Mintage	Fine	VF	XF	Unc
388	1866	—	300.00	500.00	800.00	2150.
		Mint mark: Mo				
388.1	1866	2.148	30.00	45.00	150.00	375.00
	1867	1.238	40.00	65.00	175.00	400.00
		Mint mark: Pi				
388.2	1866	—	55.00	125.00	275.00	725.00

20 PESOS

33.8400 g, .875 GOLD, .9520 oz AGW
Mint mark: Mo

KM#	Date	Mintage	Fine	VF	XF	Unc
389	1866	8,274	500.00	800.00	1200.	2400.

GOLD PESO FANTASIES

Modern gold 'Peso' fantasies of Maximilian exist. Five varieties exist, some dated 1865. One has an eagle in a plain field above a wreath on the reverse. On the second type a numeral '1' appears to either side of the eagle, and the metallic content is designated below: LEY-ORO-K22.

TRIAL STRIKES (TS)

KM#	Date	Mintage	Identification	Mkt.Val.
TS1	1866 Mo	—	20 Pesos, Copper	—

REPUBLIC
DECIMAL COINAGE

100 Centavos = 1 Peso

UN (1) CENTAVO

COPPER
Mint mark: Mo
Obv: Seated Liberty.

KM#	Date	Mintage	Fine	VF	XF	Unc
390	1863 round top 3, reeded edge					165.00
	—		12.00	20.00	40.00	160.00
	1863 round top 3, plain edge					
	—		12.00	20.00	40.00	165.00
	1863 flat top 3					
	—		10.00	18.00	35.00	160.00

Mint mark: SLP

390.1	1863	1.025	15.00	30.00	60.00	300.00

Mint mark: As
Obv: Standing eagle.

KM#	Date	Mintage	Fine	VF	XF	Unc
391	1875	—	—	—	Rare	—

KM#	Date	Mintage	Fine	VF	XF	Unc
391	1876	.050	100.00	200.00	300.00	650.00
	1880	—	25.00	50.00	100.00	400.00
	1881	—	30.00	60.00	125.00	250.00

		Mint mark: Cn				
391.1	1874	.266	12.50	17.50	35.00	150.00
	1875/4	.153	15.00	20.00	45.00	150.00
	1875	Inc. Ab.	10.00	15.00	25.00	150.00
	1876	.154	5.00	8.00	15.00	150.00
	1877/6	.993	7.50	11.50	17.50	175.00
	1877	Inc. Ab.	6.00	9.00	15.00	150.00
	1880	.142	7.50	10.00	12.50	150.00
	1881	.167	7.50	10.00	25.00	175.00
	1897 large N in mm.					
		.300	2.50	5.00	12.00	50.00
	1897 small N in mm.					
		Inc. Ab.	2.50	5.00	9.00	45.00

		Mint mark: Do				
391.2	1879	.110	10.00	17.50	35.00	150.00
	1880	.069	40.00	90.00	175.00	500.00
	1891	—	8.00	11.00	30.00	150.00
	1891 Do/Mo	—	8.00	11.00	30.00	150.00

		Mint mark: Ga				
391.3	1872	.263	15.00	30.00	60.00	200.00
	1873	.333	6.00	9.00	25.00	150.00
	1874	.076	15.00	25.00	50.00	175.00
	1875	—	10.00	15.00	30.00	150.00
	1876	.303	3.00	6.00	17.50	150.00
	1877	.108	4.00	6.00	20.00	150.00
	1878	.543	4.00	6.00	15.00	150.00
	1881/71	.975	7.00	9.00	20.00	175.00
	1881	Inc. Ab.	7.00	9.00	20.00	175.00
	1889 Ga/Mo	—	3.50	5.00	25.00	125.00
	1890	—	4.00	7.50	20.00	100.00

		Mint mark: Go				
391.4	1874	—	20.00	40.00	80.00	250.00
	1875	.190	11.50	30.00	60.00	200.00
	1876	—	125.00	200.00	350.00	750.00
	1877	—	—	—	Rare	—
	1878	.576	8.00	11.00	30.00	175.00
	1880	.890	6.00	10.00	25.00	175.00

		Mint mark: Ho				
391.5	1875	3,500	450.00	—	—	—
	1876	8,508	50.00	100.00	225.00	500.00
	1880 short H, round O					
		.102	7.50	15.00	35.00	150.00
	1880 tall H, oval O					
		Inc. Ab.	7.50	15.00	35.00	150.00
	1881	.459	5.00	10.00	25.00	150.00

		Mint mark: Mo				
391.6	1869	1.874	7.50	25.00	60.00	200.00
	1870/69	1.200	10.00	25.00	60.00	225.00
	1870	Inc. Ab.	8.00	20.00	50.00	200.00
	1871	.918	8.00	15.00	40.00	200.00
	1872/1	1.625	6.50	10.00	30.00	200.00
	1872	Inc. Ab.	6.00	9.00	25.00	200.00
	1873	1.605	4.00	7.50	20.00	200.00
	1874/3	1.700	5.00	7.00	15.00	100.00
	1874	Inc. Ab.	3.00	5.50	15.00	100.00
	1874.	Inc. Ab.	5.00	10.00	25.00	200.00
	1875	1.495	6.00	8.00	30.00	100.00
	1876	1.600	3.00	5.50	12.50	100.00
	1877	1.270	3.00	5.50	13.50	100.00
	1878/5	1.900	7.50	11.00	22.50	125.00
	1878/6	Inc. Ab.	7.50	11.00	22.50	125.00
	1878/7	Inc. Ab.	7.50	11.00	20.00	125.00
	1878	Inc. Ab.	6.00	9.00	13.50	100.00
	1879/8	1.505	4.50	6.50	13.50	100.00
	1879	Inc. Ab.	3.00	5.50	11.50	75.00
	1880/70	1.130	5.50	7.50	15.00	100.00
	1880/72	I.A.	20.00	50.00	100.00	250.00
	1880/79	I.A.	15.00	35.00	75.00	175.00
	1880	Inc. Ab.	4.25	6.00	12.50	75.00
	1881	1.060	4.50	7.00	15.00	75.00
	1886	12.687	1.50	2.00	8.50	40.00
	1887	7.292	1.50	2.00	5.00	35.00
	1888/78	9.984	2.50	3.00	10.00	30.00
	1888/7	Inc. Ab.	2.50	3.00	10.00	30.00
	1888	Inc. Ab.	1.50	2.00	8.50	30.00
	1889	19.970	2.00	3.00	8.00	30.00
	1890/89					

KM#	Date	Mintage	Fine	VF	XF	Unc
391.6		18.726	2.50	3.00	10.00	40.00
	1890/990	I.A.	2.50	3.00	10.00	40.00
	1890	Inc. Ab.	1.50	2.00	8.50	30.00
	1891	14.544	1.50	2.00	8.50	30.00
	1892	12.908	1.50	2.00	8.50	30.00
	1893/2	5.078	2.50	3.00	10.00	35.00
	1893	Inc. Ab.	1.50	2.00	8.50	30.00
	1894/3	1.896	3.00	6.00	15.00	50.00
	1894	Inc. Ab.	2.00	3.00	10.00	35.00
	1895/3	3.453	3.00	4.50	12.50	35.00
	1895/85	I.A.	3.00	6.00	15.00	50.00
	1895	Inc. Ab.	2.00	3.00	8.50	25.00
	1896	3.075	2.00	3.00	8.50	25.00
	1897	4.150	1.50	2.00	8.50	25.00

NOTE: Varieties exist.

Mint mark: Oa

KM#	Date	Mintage	Fine	VF	XF	Unc
391.7	1872	.016	300.00	500.00	1200.	—
	1873	.011	350.00	600.00	—	—
	1874	4,835	450.00	—	—	—
	1875	2,860	500.00	—	—	—

Mint mark: Pi

KM#	Date	Mintage	Fine	VF	XF	Unc
391.8	1871	—	—	—	Rare	—
	1877	.249	—	—	Rare	—
	1878	.751	12.50	25.00	50.00	200.00
	1891 Pi/Mo	—	10.00	17.50	35.00	150.00
	1891	—	8.00	15.00	30.00	150.00

Mint mark: Zs

KM#	Date	Mintage	Fine	VF	XF	Unc
391.9	1872	.055	22.50	30.00	100.00	300.00
	1873	1.460	4.00	8.00	25.00	150.00
	1874/3	.685	5.50	11.00	30.00	250.00
	1874	Inc. Ab.	4.00	8.00	25.00	200.00
	1875/4	.200	8.50	17.00	45.00	250.00
	1875	Inc. Ab.	7.00	14.00	35.00	200.00
	1876	—	5.00	10.00	25.00	200.00
	1877	—	50.00	125.00	300.00	750.00
	1878	—	4.50	9.00	25.00	200.00
	1880	.100	5.00	10.00	30.00	200.00
	1881	1.200	4.25	8.00	25.00	150.00

COPPER-NICKEL
Mint: Mexico City

KM#	Date	Mintage	Fine	VF	XF	Unc
392	1882	99.955	7.50	12.50	17.50	35.00
	1883	Inc. Ab.	.50	.75	1.00	1.50

COPPER
Obv: Restyled eagle.

KM#	Date	Mintage	Fine	VF	XF	Unc
393	1898	1.529	4.00	6.00	15.00	40.00

NOTE: Varieties exist.

Mint mark: C
Reduced size.

KM#	Date	Mintage	Fine	VF	XF	Unc
394	1901	.220	15.00	22.50	35.00	65.00
	1902	.320	15.00	22.50	45.00	90.00
	1903	.536	7.50	12.50	20.00	45.00
	1904/3	.148	35.00	50.00	75.00	125.00
	1905	.110	100.00	150.00	300.00	550.00

NOTE: Varieties exist.

Mint mark: M,Mo

KM#	Date	Mintage	Fine	VF	XF	Unc
394.1	1899	.051	150.00	175.00	300.00	800.00
	1900 wide date					
		4.010	2.50	4.00	7.50	25.00
	1900 narrow date					
		Inc. Ab.	2.50	4.00	7.50	25.00
	1901	1.494	3.00	8.00	17.50	50.00
	1902/899					
		2.090	30.00	60.00	100.00	175.00
	1902	Inc. Ab.	2.25	4.00	10.00	35.00
	1903	8.400	1.50	2.25	4.00	20.00
	1904	10.250	1.50	2.00	4.00	20.00
	1905	3.643	2.25	4.00	10.00	40.00

NOTE: Varieties exist.

2 CENTAVOS

COPPER-NICKEL
Mint: Mexico City

KM#	Date	Mintage	Fine	VF	XF	Unc
395	1882	50.023	2.00	3.00	7.50	15.00
	1883/2	Inc. Ab.	2.00	3.00	7.50	15.00
	1883	Inc. Ab.	.50	.75	1.00	2.50

5 CENTAVOS

1.3530 g, .903 SILVER, .0392 oz ASW
Mint mark: Ca
Obv: Facing eagle. Rev: Denomination in wreath.

KM#	Date	Mintage	Fine	VF	XF	Unc
396	1868	—	40.00	65.00	125.00	400.00
	1869	*.030	25.00	40.00	100.00	350.00
	1870	.035	30.00	50.00	100.00	350.00

Mint mark: SLP

KM#	Date	Mintage	Fine	VF	XF	Unc
396.1	1863	—	75.00	125.00	350.00	1200.

Mint mark: Mo
Rev: Cap and rays.

KM#	Date	Mintage	Fine	VF	XF	Unc
397	1867/3	—	25.00	50.00	125.00	275.00
	1867	—	20.00	40.00	100.00	250.00
	1868/7	—	25.00	50.00	150.00	325.00
	1868	—	20.00	40.00	100.00	250.00

NOTE: Varieties exist.

Mint mark: P

KM#	Date	Mintage	Fine	VF	XF	Unc
397.1	1868/7	.034	25.00	50.00	125.00	300.00
	1868	Inc. Ab.	20.00	45.00	100.00	250.00
	1869	.014	200.00	300.00	600.00	—

Mint mark: As
Obv: Standing eagle.

KM#	Date	Mintage	Fine	VF	XF	Unc
398	1874 DL	—	10.00	20.00	40.00	150.00
	1875 DL	—	10.00	20.00	40.00	150.00
	1876 L	—	22.00	45.00	70.00	160.00
	1878 L mule, gold peso obverse					
		—	250.00	350.00	650.00	—
	1879 L mule, gold peso obverse					
		—	40.00	65.00	120.00	275.00

KM#	Date	Mintage	Fine	VF	XF	Unc
398	1880 L mule, gold peso obverse					
		.012	55.00	85.00	165.00	325.00
	1886 L	.043	12.00	25.00	50.00	165.00
	1886 L mule, gold peso obverse					
		Inc. Ab.	55.00	85.00	165.00	300.00
	1887 L	.020	25.00	50.00	75.00	165.00
	1888 L	.032	12.00	25.00	50.00	125.00
	1889 L	.016	25.00	50.00	100.00	200.00
	1890 L	.030	25.00	50.00	85.00	175.00
	1891 L	8,000	65.00	125.00	200.00	400.00
	1892 L	.013	20.00	40.00	60.00	125.00
	1893 L	.024	10.00	20.00	45.00	90.00
	1895 L	.020	10.00	20.00	45.00	90.00

Mint mark: CH, Ca

KM#	Date	Mintage	Fine	VF	XF	Unc
398.1	1871 M	.014	20.00	40.00	100.00	250.00
	1873 M crude date					
		—	100.00	150.00	250.00	500.00
	1874 M crude date					
		—	25.00	50.00	75.00	150.00
	1886 M	.025	7.50	15.00	30.00	100.00
	1887 M	.037	7.50	15.00	30.00	100.00
	1887 Ca/MoM					
		Inc. Ab.	10.00	20.00	40.00	125.00
	1888 M	.145	1.50	3.00	6.00	25.00
	1889 M	.044	5.00	10.00	20.00	50.00
	1890 M	.102	1.50	3.00	6.00	25.00
	1891 M	.164	1.50	3.00	6.00	25.00
	1892 M	.085	1.50	3.00	6.00	25.00
	1892 M 9/inverted 9					
		Inc. Ab.	2.00	4.00	7.50	30.00
	1893 M	.133	1.50	3.00	6.00	25.00
	1894 M	.108	1.50	3.00	6.00	25.00
	1895 M	.074	2.00	4.00	7.50	30.00

Mint mark: Cn

KM#	Date	Mintage	Fine	VF	XF	Unc
398.2	1871 P	—	125.00	200.00	350.00	—
	1873 P	4,992	50.00	100.00	200.00	400.00
	1874 P	—	25.00	50.00	100.00	200.00
	1875 P	—	—	—	Rare	—
	1876 P	—	25.00	50.00	100.00	200.00
	1886 M	.010	25.00	50.00	100.00	200.00
	1887 M	.010	25.00	50.00	100.00	200.00
	1888 M	.119	1.50	3.00	6.00	30.00
	1889 M	.066	4.00	7.50	15.00	50.00
	1890 M	.180	1.50	3.00	6.00	25.00
	1890 D (error)					
		Inc. Ab.	125.00	175.00	250.00	—
	1891 M	.087	2.00	4.00	7.50	25.00
	1894 M	.024	4.00	7.50	15.00	40.00
	1896 M	.016	7.50	12.50	25.00	75.00
	1897 M	.223	1.50	2.50	5.00	20.00

Mint mark: Do

KM#	Date	Mintage	Fine	VF	XF	Unc
398.3	1874 M	—	100.00	150.00	225.00	500.00
	1877 P	4,795	75.00	125.00	225.00	450.00
	1878/7 E/P					
		4,300	200.00	300.00	450.00	—
	1879 B	—	125.00	200.00	350.00	—
	1880 B	—	—	—	Rare	—
	1881 P	3,020	300.00	500.00	800.00	—
	1887 C	.042	5.00	8.00	17.50	60.00
	1888/9 C	.091	6.00	10.00	20.00	70.00
	1888 C	Inc. Ab.	4.00	7.50	15.00	55.00
	1889 C	.049	3.50	6.00	12.50	50.00
	1890 C	.136	4.00	7.50	15.00	55.00
	1890 P	Inc. Ab.	5.00	8.00	17.50	60.00
	1891/0 P	.048	3.50	6.00	12.50	50.00
	1891 P	Inc. Ab.	3.00	5.00	10.00	45.00
	1894 D	.038	3.50	6.00	12.50	50.00

Mint mark: Ga

KM#	Date	Mintage	Fine	VF	XF	Unc
398.4	1877 A	—	15.00	30.00	60.00	150.00
	1881 S	.156	4.00	7.50	15.00	60.00
	1886 S	.087	2.00	4.00	7.50	25.00
	1888 S lg.G					
		.262	2.00	4.00	10.00	30.00
	1888 S sm.g					
		Inc. Ab.	2.00	4.00	10.00	30.00
	1889 S	.178	1.50	3.00	7.50	25.00
	1890 S	.068	4.00	7.50	12.50	35.00
	1891 S	.050	4.00	6.50	10.00	35.00
	1892 S	.078	2.00	4.00	7.50	25.00
	1893 S	.044	4.00	7.50	15.00	45.00

Mint mark: Go

KM#	Date	Mintage	Fine	VF	XF	Unc
398.5	1869 S	.080	15.00	30.00	75.00	175.00
	1871 S	.100	5.00	10.00	25.00	75.00
	1872 S	.030	30.00	60.00	125.00	250.00
	1873 S	.040	30.00	60.00	125.00	250.00
	1874 S	—	7.00	12.00	25.00	75.00
	1875 S	—	8.00	15.00	30.00	75.00
	1876 S	—	8.00	15.00	30.00	75.00
	1877 S	—	7.00	12.00	20.00	75.00
	1878/7 S	.020	8.00	15.00	25.00	75.00
	1879 S	—	8.00	15.00	25.00	75.00
	1880 S	.055	15.00	30.00	60.00	200.00
	1881/0 S	.160	5.00	8.00	17.50	60.00
	1881 S	Inc. Ab.	4.00	6.00	12.00	45.00
	1886 R	.230	1.50	3.00	6.00	30.00
	1887 R	.230	1.50	2.50	5.00	30.00
	1888 R	.320	1.50	2.50	5.00	20.00
	1889 R	.060	4.00	6.00	12.00	45.00
	1890 R	.250	1.50	2.50	5.00	20.00
	1891/0 R	.168	1.80	3.00	6.00	30.00
	1891 R	Inc. Ab.	1.50	2.50	5.00	20.00
	1892 R	.138	1.50	3.00	6.00	25.00
	1893 R	.200	1.25	2.50	5.00	20.00
	1894 R	.200	1.25	2.50	5.00	20.00
	1896 R	.525	1.25	2.00	4.00	15.00
	1897 R	.596	1.50	2.00	4.00	15.00

Mint mark: Ho

KM#	Date	Mintage	Fine	VF	XF	Unc
398.6	1874/69 R	—	125.00	225.00	350.00	—
	1874 R	—	100.00	200.00	325.00	—
	1878/7 A	.022	—	—	Rare	—
	1878 A	Inc. Ab.	20.00	40.00	80.00	175.00
	1878 A mule, gold peso obverse					
		Inc. Ab.	40.00	80.00	150.00	300.00
	1880 A	.043	7.50	15.00	30.00	75.00
	1886 G	.044	5.00	10.00	20.00	75.00
	1887 G	.020	5.00	10.00	20.00	75.00
	1888 G	.012	7.50	15.00	30.00	85.00
	1889 G	.067	3.00	6.00	12.50	40.00
	1890 G	.050	3.00	6.00	12.50	40.00
	1891 G	.046	3.00	6.00	12.50	40.00
	1893 G	.084	2.50	5.00	10.00	30.00
	1894 G	.068	2.00	4.00	10.00	30.00

Mint mark: Mo

KM#	Date	Mintage	Fine	VF	XF	Unc
398.7	1869/8 C	.040	8.00	15.00	40.00	120.00
	1870 C	.140	4.00	7.00	20.00	60.00
	1871 C	.103	9.00	20.00	40.00	100.00
	1871 M	Inc. Ab.	7.50	12.50	25.00	60.00
	1872 M	.266	5.00	8.00	20.00	55.00
	1873 M	.020	40.00	60.00	100.00	225.00
	1874/69 M	—	7.50	15.00	30.00	75.00
	1874 M	—	4.00	7.00	17.50	50.00
	1874/3 B	—	5.00	8.00	22.50	55.00
	1874 B	—	5.00	8.00	22.50	55.00
	1875 B	—	4.00	7.00	15.00	50.00
	1875 B/M	—	6.00	9.00	17.50	60.00
	1876/5 B	—	4.00	7.00	15.00	50.00
	1876 B	—	4.00	7.00	12.50	50.00
	1877/6 M	.080	4.00	7.00	15.00	60.00
	1877 M	Inc. Ab.	4.00	7.00	12.50	60.00
	1878/7 M	.100	4.00	7.00	15.00	55.00
	1878 M	Inc. Ab.	2.50	5.00	12.50	45.00
	1879/8 M	—	8.00	12.50	22.50	55.00
	1879 M	—	4.50	7.00	15.00	50.00
	1879 M 9/inverted 9					
		—	10.00	15.00	25.00	75.00
	1880/76 M/B					
		—	5.00	7.50	15.00	50.00
	1880/76 M	—	5.00	7.50	15.00	50.00
	1880 M	—	4.00	6.00	12.00	40.00
	1881/0 M	.180	4.00	6.00	10.00	35.00
	1881 M	Inc. Ab.	3.00	4.50	9.00	35.00
	1886/0 M	.398	2.00	2.75	7.50	25.00
	1886/1 M	I.A.	2.00	2.75	7.50	25.00
	1886 M	Inc. Ab.	1.75	2.25	6.00	20.00
	1887 m	.720	1.75	2.00	5.00	20.00
	1887 M/m	I.A.	1.75	2.00	6.00	20.00
	1888/7 M	1.360	2.25	2.50	6.00	20.00
	1888 M	Inc. Ab.	1.75	2.00	5.00	20.00
	1889/8 M	1.242	2.25	2.50	6.00	20.00
	1889 M	Inc. Ab.	1.75	2.00	5.00	20.00
	1890/00 M					
		1.694	1.75	2.75	6.00	20.00
	1890 M	Inc. Ab.	1.50	2.00	5.00	20.00
	1891 M	1.030	1.75	2.00	5.00	20.00

KM#	Date	Mintage	Fine	VF	XF	Unc
398.7	1892 M	1.400	1.75	2.00	5.00	20.00
	1892 M 9/inverted 9					
	Inc. Ab.		2.00	2.75	7.50	20.00
	1893 M	.220	1.75	2.00	5.00	15.00
	1894 M	.320	1.75	2.00	5.00	15.00
	1895 M	.078	3.00	5.00	8.00	25.00
	1896 B	.080	1.75	2.00	5.00	20.00
	1897 M	.160	1.75	2.00	5.00	15.00

NOTE: Varieties exist.

Mint mark: Oa

KM#	Date	Mintage	Fine	VF	XF	Unc
398.8	1890 E	.048	—	—	Rare	—
	1890 N	Inc. Ab.	65.00	125.00	200.00	350.00

Mint mark: Pi

KM#	Date	Mintage	Fine	VF	XF	Unc
398.9	1869 S	—	300.00	400.00	500.00	—
	1870 G/MoC					
		.020	—	—	Rare	—
	1870 O	Inc. Ab.	200.00	300.00	400.00	—
	1871 O	5,400	—	—	Rare	—
	1872 O	—	75.00	100.00	175.00	400.00
	1873	5,000	—	—	Rare	—
	1874 H	—	30.00	50.00	100.00	225.00
	1875 H	—	7.50	12.50	30.00	75.00
	1876 H	—	10.00	20.00	45.00	100.00
	1877 H	—	7.50	12.50	20.00	60.00
	1878/7 H	—	—	—	Rare	—
	1878 H	—	60.00	90.00	150.00	300.00
	1880 H	6,200	—	—	Rare	—
	1881 H	4,500	—	—	Rare	—
	1886 R	.033	12.50	25.00	50.00	125.00
	1887/0 R	.169	4.00	7.50	15.00	45.00
	1887 R	Inc. Ab.	3.00	5.00	10.00	32.00
	1888 R	.210	2.00	4.00	9.00	30.00
	1889/7 R	.197	2.50	5.00	10.00	32.00
	1889 R	Inc. Ab.	2.00	4.00	9.00	30.00
	1890 R	.221	2.00	3.00	6.00	25.00
	1891/89 R/B					
		.176	2.00	4.00	8.00	25.00
	1891 R	Inc. Ab.	2.00	3.00	6.00	20.00
	1892/89 R	.182	2.00	4.00	8.00	25.00
	1892/0 R	I.A.	2.00	4.00	8.00	25.00
	1892 R	Inc. Ab.	2.00	3.00	6.00	20.00
	1893 R	.041	5.00	10.00	20.00	60.00

NOTE: Varieties exist.

Mint mark: Zs

KM#	Date	Mintage	Fine	VF	XF	Unc
398.10	1870 H	.040	12.50	25.00	50.00	125.00
	1871 H	.040	12.50	25.00	50.00	125.00
	1872 H	.040	12.50	25.00	50.00	125.00
	1873/2 H	.020	35.00	65.00	125.00	275.00
	1873 H	Inc. Ab.	25.00	50.00	100.00	250.00
	1874 H	—	7.50	12.50	25.00	75.00
	1874 A	—	40.00	75.00	150.00	300.00
	1875 A	—	7.50	12.50	25.00	75.00
	1876 A	—	50.00	75.00	100.00	200.00
	1876 S	—	12.50	25.00	50.00	125.00
	1877 S	—	3.00	6.00	12.00	40.00
	1878 S	.060	3.00	6.00	12.00	40.00
	1879/8 S	—	3.00	6.00	15.00	50.00
	1879 S	—	3.00	6.00	12.00	40.00
	1880/79 S	.130	6.00	10.00	20.00	60.00
	1880 S	Inc. Ab.	5.00	8.00	16.00	45.00
	1881 S	.210	2.50	5.00	10.00	35.00
	1886/4 S	.360	6.00	10.00	20.00	60.00
	1886 S	Inc. Ab.	2.00	3.00	6.00	20.00
	1886 Z	Inc. Ab.	5.00	10.00	25.00	65.00
	1887 Z	.400	2.00	3.00	6.00	25.00
	1888/7 Z	.500	2.00	3.00	6.00	25.00
	1888 Z	Inc. Ab.	2.00	3.00	6.00	25.00
	1889 Z	.520	2.00	3.00	6.00	25.00
	1889 Z 9/inverted 9					
		Inc. Ab.	2.00	3.00	6.00	25.00
	1889 ZsZ/MoM					
		Inc. Ab.	2.00	3.00	6.00	25.00
	1890 Z	.580	1.75	2.50	5.00	20.00
	1890 ZsZ/MoM					
		Inc. Ab.	2.00	3.00	6.00	25.00
	1891 Z	.420	1.75	2.50	5.00	20.00
	1892 Z	.346	1.75	2.50	5.00	20.00
	1893 Z	.258	1.75	2.50	5.00	20.00
	1894 Z	.228	1.75	2.50	5.00	20.00
	1894 ZoZ (error)					
		Inc. Ab.	2.00	4.00	8.00	30.00
398.10	1895 Z	.260	1.75	2.50	5.00	20.00

KM#	Date	Mintage	Fine	VF	XF	Unc
398.10	1895 Z	.260	1.75	2.50	5.00	20.00
	1896 Z	.200	1.75	2.50	5.00	20.00
	1896 6/inverted 6					
		Inc. Ab.	2.00	3.00	6.00	25.00
	1897/6 Z	.200	2.00	3.00	6.00	25.00
	1897 Z	Inc. Ab.	1.75	2.50	5.00	20.00

COPPER-NICKEL
Mint: Mexico City

KM#	Date	Mintage	Fine	VF	XF	Unc
399	1882	Inc. Ab.	.50	1.00	2.50	7.50
	1883	Inc. Ab.	25.00	50.00	80.00	250.00

.903 SILVER
Mint mark: Cn
Obv: Restyled eagle.

KM#	Date	Mintage	Fine	VF	XF	Unc
400	1898 M	.044	1.75	4.00	8.00	20.00
	1899 M	.111	5.50	8.50	20.00	50.00
	1899 Q	Inc. Ab.	1.75	2.25	4.50	12.50
	1900/800 Q					
		.239	3.50	5.00	12.50	30.00
	1900 Q round Q, single tail					
		Inc. Ab.	1.75	2.50	6.00	15.00
	1900 Q narrow C, oval Q					
		Inc. Ab.	1.75	2.50	6.00	15.00
	1900 Q wide C, oval Q					
		Inc. Ab.	1.75	2.50	6.00	15.00
	1901 Q	.148	1.75	2.25	4.50	12.50
	1902 Q narrow C, heavy serifs					
		.262	1.75	2.50	6.00	15.00
	1902 Q wide C, light serifs					
		Inc. Ab.	1.75	2.50	6.00	15.00
	1903/1 Q	.331	2.00	2.50	6.00	15.00
	1903 Q	Inc. Ab.	1.75	2.25	4.50	12.50
	1903/1898 V					
		Inc. Ab.	3.50	4.50	9.00	22.50
	1903 V	Inc. Ab.	1.75	2.25	4.50	12.50
	1904 H	.352	1.75	2.25	5.00	15.00

NOTE: Varieties exist.

Mint mark: Go

KM#	Date	Mintage	Fine	VF	XF	Unc
400.1	1898 R mule, gold peso obverse					
		.180	7.50	15.00	30.00	75.00
	1899 R	.260	1.75	2.25	4.50	12.50
	1900 R	.200	1.75	2.25	4.50	12.50

NOTE: Varieties exist.

Mint mark: Mo

KM#	Date	Mintage	Fine	VF	XF	Unc
400.2	1898 M	.080	2.00	4.00	7.00	25.00
	1899 M	.168	1.75	2.25	4.50	12.50
	1900/800 M					
		.300	4.50	6.50	10.00	30.00
	1900 M	Inc. Ab.	1.75	2.25	4.50	12.50
	1901 M	.100	1.75	2.25	4.50	12.50
	1902 M	.144	1.25	2.00	3.75	10.00
	1903 M	.500	1.25	2.00	3.75	10.00
	1904/804 M					
		1.090	1.75	2.50	6.00	15.00
	1904/94 M	I.A.	1.75	2.50	6.00	15.00
	1904 M	Inc. Ab.	1.25	2.00	6.00	12.50
	1905 M	.344	1.75	3.75	7.50	17.50

Mint mark: Zs

KM#	Date	Mintage	Fine	VF	XF	Unc
400.3	1898 Z	.100	1.75	2.25	4.50	12.50
	1899 Z	.050	2.00	3.00	7.00	20.00
	1900 Z	.055	1.75	2.50	5.00	15.00
	1901 Z	.040	1.75	2.50	5.00	15.00
	1902/1 Z	.034	2.00	4.50	9.00	22.50
	1902 Z	Inc. Ab.	1.75	3.75	7.50	17.50

KM#	Date	Mintage	Fine	VF	XF	Unc
400.3	1903 Z	.217	1.25	2.00	5.00	12.50
	1904 Z	.191	1.75	2.50	5.00	12.50
	1904 M Inc. Ab.		1.75	2.50	6.00	15.00
	1905 M	.046	2.00	4.50	9.00	22.50

10 CENTAVOS

2.7070 g, .903 SILVER, .0785 oz ASW
Mint mark: Ca
Obv: Eagle. Rev: Value within wreath.

KM#	Date	Mintage	Fine	VF	XF	Unc
401	1868/7	—	30.00	60.00	150.00	550.00
	1868	—	30.00	60.00	150.00	550.00
	1869	.015	25.00	50.00	125.00	600.00
	1870	.017	22.50	45.00	100.00	550.00

Mint mark: SLP

401.2	1863	—	75.00	150.00	275.00	900.00

Mint mark: Mo

402	1867/3	—	50.00	100.00	150.00	450.00
	1867	—	20.00	40.00	60.00	250.00
	1868/7	—	20.00	40.00	80.00	275.00
	1868	—	20.00	45.00	75.00	250.00

Mint mark: P

402.1	1868/7	.038	45.00	90.00	175.00	650.00
	1868	Inc. Ab.	20.00	40.00	100.00	550.00
	1869/7	4,900	55.00	125.00	250.00	800.00

Mint mark: As

403	1874 DL	—	20.00	40.00	80.00	175.00
	1875 L	—	5.00	10.00	25.00	90.00
	1876 L	—	10.00	18.00	40.00	110.00
	1878/7 L	—	10.00	18.00	45.00	120.00
	1878 L	—	5.00	10.00	30.00	100.00
	1879 L	—	10.00	18.00	40.00	110.00
	1880 L	.013	10.00	18.00	40.00	110.00
	1882 L	.022	10.00	18.00	40.00	110.00
	1883 L	8,520	25.00	50.00	100.00	225.00
	1884 L	—	7.50	12.50	35.00	100.00
	1885 L	.015	7.50	12.50	35.00	100.00
	1886 L	.045	7.50	12.50	35.00	100.00
	1887 L	.015	7.50	12.50	35.00	100.00
	1888 L	.038	7.50	12.50	35.00	100.00
	1889 L	.020	7.50	12.50	35.00	100.00
	1890 L	.040	7.50	12.50	35.00	100.00
	1891 L	.038	7.50	12.50	35.00	100.00
	1892 L	.057	5.00	10.00	25.00	90.00
	1893 L	.070	10.00	18.00	40.00	110.00

NOTE: Varieties exist. An 1891 As L over 1889 HoG exists which was evidently produced at the Alamos Mint using dies sent from the Hermosillo Mint.

2.7070 g, .903 SILVER, .0785 oz ASW
Mint mark: CH, Ca

403.1	1871 M	8,150	15.00	30.00	60.00	150.00
	1873 M crude date					
		—	35.00	75.00	125.00	175.00
	1874 M	—	10.00	17.50	35.00	100.00
	1880/70 G					
		7,620	20.00	40.00	80.00	175.00
	1880 G/g	I.A.	15.00	25.00	50.00	125.00
	1881	340 pcs.	—	—	Rare	—

KM#	Date	Mintage	Fine	VF	XF	Unc
403.1	1883 M	9,000	10.00	20.00	40.00	125.00
	1884 M	—	10.00	20.00	40.00	125.00
	1886 M	.045	7.50	12.50	30.00	100.00
	1887/3 M/G					
		.096	5.00	10.00	20.00	75.00
	1887 M Inc. Ab.		2.00	4.00	8.00	75.00
	1888 M	.299	1.50	2.50	5.00	75.00
	1888 Ca/Mo					
		Inc. Ab.	1.50	2.50	5.00	75.00
	1889/8 M	.115	2.00	4.00	8.00	75.00
	1889 M small 89 (5 Centavo font)					
		Inc. Ab.	2.00	4.00	8.00	75.00
	1890/80 M	.140	2.00	4.00	8.00	75.00
	1890/89 M	I.A.	2.00	4.00	8.00	75.00
	1890 M Inc. Ab.		1.50	3.00	7.00	75.00
	1891 M	.163	1.50	3.00	7.00	75.00
	1892 M	.169	1.50	3.00	7.00	75.00
	1892 M 9/inverted 9					
		Inc. Ab.	2.00	4.00	8.00	75.00
	1893 M	.246	1.50	3.00	7.00	75.00
	1894 M	.163	1.50	3.00	7.00	75.00
	1895 M	.127	1.50	3.00	7.00	75.00

NOTE: Varieties exist.

Mint mark: Cn

403.2	1871 P	—	—	—	Rare	—
	1873 P	8,732	20.00	50.00	100.00	225.00
	1881 D	9,440	75.00	175.00	325.00	500.00
	1882 D	.012	75.00	125.00	200.00	400.00
	1885 M mule gold 2-1/2 Peso obv.					
		.018	25.00	50.00	100.00	200.00
	1886 M mule, gold 2-1/2 Peso obv.					
		.013	50.00	100.00	150.00	300.00
	1887 M	.011	20.00	40.00	75.00	175.00
	1888 M	.056	5.00	10.00	25.00	125.00
	1889 M	.042	5.00	10.00	20.00	75.00
	1890 M	.132	2.00	4.00	7.50	75.00
	1891 M	.084	5.00	10.00	20.00	75.00
	1892/1 M	.037	4.00	8.00	15.00	75.00
	1892 M Inc. Ab.		2.50	5.00	10.00	75.00
	1894 M	.043	2.50	5.00	10.00	75.00
	1895 M	.023	2.50	5.00	10.00	60.00
	1896 M	.121	1.50	2.50	5.00	50.00

Mint mark: Do

403.3	1878 E	2,500	100.00	175.00	300.00	600.00
	1879 B	—	—	—	Rare	—
	1880/70 B	—	—	—	Rare	—
	1880/79 B	—	—	—	Rare	—
	1884 C	—	30.00	60.00	100.00	225.00
	1886 C	.013	75.00	150.00	300.00	500.00
	1887 C	.081	4.00	8.00	15.00	100.00
	1888 C	.031	6.00	12.00	30.00	100.00
	1889 C	.055	4.00	8.00	15.00	100.00
	1890 C	.050	4.00	8.00	15.00	100.00
	1891 P	.139	2.00	4.00	8.00	80.00
	1892 P	.212	2.00	4.00	8.00	80.00
	1892 D Inc. Ab.		2.00	4.00	8.00	80.00
	1893 D	.258	2.00	4.00	8.00	80.00
	1893 D/C	I.A.	2.50	5.00	10.00	80.00
	1894 D	.184	1.50	3.00	6.00	80.00
	1894 D/C	I.A.	2.00	4.00	8.00	80.00
	1895 D	.142	1.50	3.00	6.00	80.00

Mint mark: Ga

403.4	1871 C	4,734	75.00	125.00	200.00	500.00
	1873/1 C	.025	10.00	15.00	35.00	150.00
	1873 C Inc.Ab.		10.00	15.00	35.00	150.00
	1874 C	—	10.00	15.00	35.00	150.00
	1877 A	—	10.00	15.00	30.00	150.00
	1881 S	.115	5.00	10.00	25.00	150.00
	1883 B	.090	4.00	8.00	15.00	90.00
	1884 B	—	5.00	10.00	20.00	90.00
	1884 B/S	—	6.00	12.50	25.00	90.00
	1884 H	—	3.00	5.00	10.00	90.00
	1885 H	.093	3.00	5.00	10.00	90.00
	1886 S	.151	2.50	4.00	9.00	90.00
	1887 S	.162	1.50	3.00	6.00	90.00
	1888 S	.225	1.50	3.00	6.00	90.00
	1888 GaS/HoG					
		Inc. Ab.	1.50	3.00	6.00	90.00
	1889 S	.310	1.50	3.00	6.00	40.00
	1890 S	.303	1.50	3.00	6.00	40.00
	1891 S	.199	5.00	10.00	20.00	45.00

PRICING SECTION

KM#	Date	Mintage	Fine	VF	XF	Unc
403.4	1892 S	.329	1.50	3.00	6.00	40.00
	1893 S	.225	1.50	3.00	6.00	40.00
	1894 S	.243	3.00	6.00	12.00	40.00
	1895 S	.080	1.50	3.00	6.00	40.00

NOTE: Varieties exist.

Mint mark: Go

KM#	Date	Mintage	Fine	VF	XF	Unc
403.5	1869 S	7,000	20.00	40.00	80.00	200.00
	1871/0 S	.060	15.00	25.00	50.00	125.00
	1872 S	.060	15.00	25.00	50.00	125.00
	1873 S	.050	15.00	25.00	50.00	125.00
	1874 S	—	15.00	25.00	50.00	125.00
	1875 S	—	250.00	350.00	500.00	800.00
	1876 S	—	10.00	20.00	40.00	100.00
	1877 S	—	80.00	120.00	200.00	400.00
	1878/7 S	.010	10.00	20.00	45.00	110.00
	1878 S Inc. Ab.		7.50	12.00	20.00	75.00
	1879 S	—	7.50	12.00	20.00	75.00
	1880 S	—	100.00	200.00	300.00	450.00
	1881/71 S	.100	3.00	5.00	10.00	75.00
	1881/0 S	I.A.	3.50	5.00	10.00	75.00
	1881 S Inc. Ab.		3.00	5.00	10.00	75.00
	1882/1 S	.040	3.00	6.00	12.00	75.00
	1883 B	—	3.00	5.00	10.00	75.00
	1884 B	—	1.50	3.00	6.00	75.00
	1884 S	—	6.00	12.50	25.00	90.00
	1885 R	.100	1.50	3.00	6.00	75.00
	1886 R	.095	3.00	5.00	10.00	75.00
	1887 R	.330	2.50	5.00	10.00	75.00
	1888 R	.270	1.50	3.00	6.00	75.00
	1889 R	.205	2.00	4.00	8.00	75.00
	1889 GoR/HoG					
	Inc. Ab.		3.00	5.00	10.00	75.00
	1890 R	.270	1.50	3.00	6.00	35.00
	1890 GoR/Cn M					
	Inc. Ab.		1.50	3.00	6.00	35.00
	1891 R	.523	1.50	3.00	6.00	35.00
	1891 GoR/HoG					
	Inc. Ab.		1.50	3.00	6.00	35.00
	1892 R	.440	1.50	3.00	6.00	35.00
	1893/1 R	.389	3.00	5.00	10.00	35.00
	1893 R Inc. Ab.		1.50	3.00	6.00	35.00
	1894 R	.400	1.50	2.50	5.00	35.00
	1895 R	.355	1.50	2.50	5.00	35.00
	1896 R	.190	1.50	2.50	5.00	35.00
	1897 R	.205	1.50	2.50	5.00	35.00

NOTE: Varieties exist.

Mint mark: Ho

KM#	Date	Mintage	Fine	VF	XF	Unc
403.6	1874 R	—	30.00	60.00	100.00	200.00
	1876 F	3,140	200.00	300.00	450.00	750.00
	1878 A	—	5.00	10.00	15.00	85.00
	1879 A	—	25.00	50.00	90.00	175.00
	1880 A	—	3.00	6.00	12.50	85.00
	1881 A	.028	4.00	7.00	15.00	85.00
	1882/1 A	.025	5.00	10.00	20.00	85.00
	1882/1 a	I.A.	6.00	12.50	25.00	85.00
	1882 A Inc. Ab.		4.00	7.00	15.00	85.00
	1883	7,000	65.00	100.00	200.00	400.00
	1884 A	—	35.00	75.00	150.00	300.00
	1884 M	—	7.50	15.00	30.00	85.00
	1885 M	.021	12.50	25.00	50.00	100.00
	1886 M	.010	—	—	Rare	—
	1886 G Inc. Ab.		7.50	12.50	25.00	85.00
	1887 G	—	25.00	50.00	75.00	150.00
	1888 G	.025	6.00	12.50	25.00	85.00
	1889 G	.042	3.00	6.00	10.00	85.00
	1890 G	.048	3.00	6.00	10.00	85.00
	1891/80 G	.136	3.00	6.00	10.00	85.00
	1891/0 G	I.A.	3.00	6.00	10.00	85.00
	1891 G Inc. Ab.		3.00	6.00	10.00	85.00
	1892 G	.067	3.00	6.00	10.00	85.00
	1893 G	.067	3.00	6.00	10.00	85.00

Mint mark: Mo

KM#	Date	Mintage	Fine	VF	XF	Unc
403.7	1869/8 C	.030	10.00	20.00	40.00	100.00
	1869 C Inc. Ab.		8.00	17.50	35.00	90.00
	1870 C	.110	3.00	7.50	15.00	50.00
	1871 C	.084	50.00	75.00	125.00	250.00
	1871 M Inc. Ab.		12.00	17.50	45.00	125.00
	1872/69 M	.198	10.00	20.00	35.00	100.00
	1872 M Inc. Ab.		3.00	7.50	15.00	65.00
	1873 M	.040	10.00	15.00	30.00	75.00
	1874 M	—	5.00	10.00	20.00	65.00

KM#	Date	Mintage	Fine	VF	XF	Unc
403.7	1874/64 B	—	5.00	10.00	20.00	65.00
	1874 B/M	—	20.00	40.00	60.00	125.00
	1874 B	—	5.00	10.00	15.00	65.00
	1875 B	—	20.00	40.00	60.00	125.00
	1876/5 B	—	3.00	5.00	9.00	65.00
	1876/5 B/M	—	3.00	5.00	9.00	65.00
	1877/6 M	—	3.00	5.00	9.00	65.00
	1877/6 M/B	—	3.00	5.00	9.00	65.00
	1877 M	—	3.00	5.00	9.00	65.00
	1878/7 M	.100	3.00	5.00	9.00	65.00
	1878 M Inc. Ab.		3.00	5.00	9.00	65.00
	1879/69 M	—	3.00	5.00	9.00	65.00
	1879 M/C	—	3.00	5.00	9.00	65.00
	1880/79 M	—	3.00	5.00	9.00	65.00
	1881/0 M	.510	3.00	5.00	9.00	35.00
	1881 M Inc. Ab.		3.00	5.00	9.00	35.00
	1882/1 M	.550	3.00	5.00	9.00	35.00
	1882 M Inc. Ab.		3.00	5.00	9.00	35.00
	1883/2 M	.250	3.00	5.00	9.00	35.00
	1884 M	—	3.00	5.00	9.00	35.00
	1885 M	.470	3.00	5.00	9.00	35.00
	1886 M	.603	3.00	5.00	9.00	35.00
	1887 M	.580	3.00	5.00	9.00	35.00
	1888/7 MoM					
		.710	3.00	5.00	9.00	35.00
	1888 MoM I.A.		3.00	5.00	9.00	35.00
	1888 MOM I.A.		3.00	5.00	9.00	35.00
	1889/8 M	.622	3.00	5.00	9.00	35.00
	1889 M Inc. Ab.		3.00	5.00	9.00	35.00
	1890/89 M	.815	3.00	5.00	9.00	35.00
	1890 M Inc. Ab.		3.00	5.00	9.00	35.00
	1891 M	.859	1.50	2.50	7.00	25.00
	1892 M	1.030	1.50	2.50	7.00	25.00
	1893 M	.310	1.50	2.50	7.00	25.00
	1893 M/C	I.A.	1.50	2.50	7.00	25.00
	1894 M	.350	5.00	10.00	20.00	60.00
	1895 M	.320	1.50	2.50	7.00	25.00
	1896 B/G	.340	1.50	2.50	7.00	25.00
	1896 M Inc. Ab.		35.00	70.00	100.00	150.00
	1897 M	.170	1.50	2.50	5.00	20.00

NOTE: Varieties exist.

Mint mark: Oa

KM#	Date	Mintage	Fine	VF	XF	Unc
403.8	1889 E	.021	200.00	400.00	600.00	—
	1890 E	.031	100.00	150.00	250.00	500.00
	1890 N Inc. Ab.		—	—	Rare	—

Mint mark: Pi

KM#	Date	Mintage	Fine	VF	XF	Unc
403.9	1869/8 S	4,000	—	—	Rare	—
	1870/69 O	.018	—	—	Rare	—
	1870 G Inc. Ab.		125.00	200.00	325.00	600.00
	1871 O	.021	50.00	100.00	150.00	300.00
	1872 O	.016	150.00	225.00	350.00	650.00
	1873 O	4,750	—	—	Rare	—
	1874 H	—	25.00	50.00	100.00	200.00
	1875 H	—	75.00	125.00	200.00	400.00
	1876 H	—	75.00	125.00	200.00	400.00
	1877 H	—	75.00	125.00	200.00	400.00
	1878 H	—	250.00	500.00	750.00	—
	1879 H	—	—	—	—	—
	1880 H	—	150.00	250.00	350.00	—
	1881 H	7,600	250.00	350.00	500.00	—
	1882 H	4,000	—	—	—	—
	1883 H	—	125.00	200.00	300.00	500.00
	1884 H	—	25.00	50.00	100.00	200.00
	1885 H	.051	25.00	50.00	100.00	200.00
	1885 C Inc. Ab.		—	—	Rare	—
	1886 C	.052	15.00	30.00	60.00	150.00
	1886 R Inc. Ab.		5.00	10.00	20.00	65.00
	1887 R	.118	2.50	5.00	10.00	50.00
	1888 R	.136	2.50	5.00	10.00	50.00
	1889/7 R	.131	7.50	12.50	20.00	60.00
	1890 R	.204	1.50	3.00	7.50	40.00
	1891/89 R	.163	2.50	5.00	10.00	40.00
	1891 R Inc. Ab.		1.50	3.50	6.00	30.00
	1892/0 R	.200	2.00	4.00	8.00	40.00
	1892 R Inc. Ab.		1.50	2.50	5.00	40.00
	1893 R	.048	7.50	10.00	17.50	60.00

NOTE: Varieties exist.

Mint mark: Zs

KM#	Date	Mintage	Fine	VF	XF	Unc
403.10	1870 H	.020	100.00	150.00	200.00	400.00
	1871/0 H	.010	—	—	—	—
	1871 H Inc. Ab.		—	—	—	—

KM#	Date	Mintage	Fine	VF	XF	Unc
403.10	1872 H	.010	150.00	200.00	275.00	500.00
	1873 H	.010	250.00	350.00	600.00	—
	1874/3 H	—	50.00	75.00	150.00	300.00
	1874 A	—	200.00	300.00	500.00	—
	1875 A	—	5.00	10.00	25.00	100.00
	1876 A	—	5.00	10.00	25.00	100.00
	1876 S	—	100.00	200.00	300.00	500.00
	1877 S small S					
		—	7.50	12.50	25.00	100.00
	1877 S regular S					
		—	7.50	12.50	25.00	100.00
	1878/7 S	.030	5.00	10.00	20.00	80.00
	1878 S	Inc. Ab.	5.00	10.00	20.00	80.00
	1879 S	—	5.00	10.00	20.00	80.00
	1880 S	—	5.00	10.00	20.00	80.00
	1881/0 S	.120	3.00	6.00	12.50	50.00
	1881 S	Inc. Ab.	3.00	6.00	12.50	50.00
	1882/1 S	.064	12.50	25.00	50.00	125.00
	1882 S	Inc. Ab.	12.50	25.00	50.00	125.00
	1883/73 S	.102	2.00	4.00	8.00	50.00
	1883 S	Inc. Ab.	2.00	4.00	8.00	50.00
	1884/3 S	—	2.00	4.00	8.00	50.00
	1884 S	—	2.00	4.00	8.00	50.00
	1885 S	.297	1.50	2.50	5.00	50.00
	1885 S small S in mint mark					
		Inc. Ab.	2.50	4.00	8.00	50.00
	1885 Z w/o assayers initial (error)					
		Inc. Ab.	3.50	7.50	15.00	65.00
	1886 S	.274	1.50	2.50	5.00	30.00
	1886 Z	I.A.	12.50	25.00	50.00	125.00
	1887 ZsZ	.233	1.50	2.50	5.00	30.00
	1887 Z Z (error)					
		Inc. Ab.	3.50	7.50	15.00	50.00
	1888 ZsZ	.270	1.50	2.50	5.00	30.00
	1888 Z Z (error)					
		Inc. Ab.	3.50	7.50	15.00	40.00
	1889/7 Z/S					
		.240	4.00	8.00	12.50	40.00
	1889 Z/S	I.A.	1.50	4.00	8.00	30.00
	1889 Z	Inc. Ab.	1.50	2.50	5.00	30.00
	1890 ZsZ	.410	1.50	2.50	5.00	30.00
	1890 Z Z (error)					
		Inc. Ab.	3.75	7.50	15.00	40.00
	1891 Z	1.105	1.50	2.50	5.00	30.00
	1891 ZsZ double s					
		Inc. Ab.	2.00	4.00	7.00	30.00
	1892 Z	1.102	1.50	2.50	5.00	30.00
	1893 Z	1.011	1.50	2.50	5.00	25.00
	1894 Z	.892	1.50	2.50	5.00	30.00
	1895 Z	.920	1.50	2.50	5.00	30.00
	1896/5 ZsZ	.700	1.50	2.50	5.00	30.00
	1896 ZsZ	I.A.	1.50	2.50	5.00	30.00
	1896 Z Z (error)					
		Inc. Ab.	3.75	7.50	15.00	40.00
	1897/6 ZsZ	.900	2.00	5.00	10.00	30.00
	1897/6 Z Z (error)					
		Inc. Ab.	3.75	7.50	15.00	40.00
	1897 Z	Inc. Ab.	1.50	2.50	5.00	30.00

NOTE: Varieties exist.

Mint mark: Cn
Obv: Restyled eagle.

KM#	Date	Mintage	Fine	VF	XF	Unc
404	1898 M	9,870	50.00	100.00	150.00	300.00
	1899 Q round Q, single tail					
		.080	5.00	7.50	15.00	40.00
	1899 Q oval Q, double tail					
		Inc. Ab.	5.00	7.50	15.00	40.00
	1900 Q	.160	1.50	2.50	5.00	20.00
	1901 Q	.235	1.50	2.50	5.00	20.00
	1902 Q	.186	1.50	2.50	5.00	20.00
	1903 Q	.256	1.50	2.50	6.00	20.00
	1903 V	Inc. Ab.	1.50	2.50	5.00	15.00
	1904 H	.307	1.50	2.50	5.00	15.00

NOTE: Varieties exist.

Mint mark: Go

KM#	Date	Mintage	Fine	VF	XF	Unc
404.1	1898 R	.435	1.50	2.50	5.00	20.00
	1899 R	.270	1.50	2.50	5.00	25.00

KM#	Date	Mintage	Fine	VF	XF	Unc
	1900 R	.130	7.50	12.50	25.00	60.00

Mint mark: Mo

KM#	Date	Mintage	Fine	VF	XF	Unc
404.2	1898 M	.130	1.50	2.50	5.00	17.50
	1899 M	.190	1.50	2.50	5.00	17.50
	1900 M	.311	1.50	2.50	5.00	17.50
	1901 M	.080	2.50	3.50	7.00	20.00
	1902 M	.181	1.50	2.50	5.00	17.50
	1903 M	.581	1.50	2.50	5.00	17.50
	1904 M	1.266	1.25	2.00	4.50	15.00
	1904 MM (error)					
		Inc. Ab.	2.50	5.00	10.00	25.00
	1905 M	.266	2.00	3.75	7.50	20.00

Mint mark: Zs

KM#	Date	Mintage	Fine	VF	XF	Unc
404.3	1898 Z	.240	1.50	2.50	7.50	20.00
	1899 Z	.105	1.50	3.00	10.00	22.00
	1900 Z	.219	7.50	10.00	20.00	45.00
	1901 Z	.070	2.50	5.00	10.00	25.00
	1902 Z	.120	2.50	5.00	10.00	25.00
	1903 Z	.228	1.50	3.00	10.00	20.00
	1904 Z	.368	1.50	3.00	10.00	20.00
	1904 M	Inc. Ab.	1.50	3.00	10.00	25.00
	1905 M	.066	7.50	15.00	30.00	60.00

20 CENTAVOS

5.4150 g, .903 SILVER, .1572 oz ASW
Mint mark: Cn
Obv: Restyled eagle.

KM#	Date	Mintage	Fine	VF	XF	Unc
405	1898 M	.114	5.00	12.50	35.00	140.00
	1899 M	.044	12.00	20.00	45.00	225.00
	1899 Q	Inc. Ab.	20.00	35.00	100.00	250.00
	1900 Q	.068	6.50	12.50	35.00	140.00
	1901 Q	.185	5.00	10.00	30.00	120.00
	1902/802 Q					
		.098	6.00	10.00	30.00	120.00
	1902 Q	Inc. Ab.	4.00	9.00	30.00	120.00
	1903 Q	.093	4.00	9.00	30.00	120.00
	1904/3 H	.258	—	—	—	—
	1904 H	Inc. Ab.	5.00	10.00	30.00	120.00

Mint mark: Go

KM#	Date	Mintage	Fine	VF	XF	Unc
405.1	1898 R	.135	4.00	8.00	20.00	100.00
	1899 R	.215	4.00	8.00	20.00	100.00
	1900/800 R					
		.038	10.00	20.00	50.00	150.00

Mint mark: Mo

KM#	Date	Mintage	Fine	VF	XF	Unc
405.2	1898 M	.150	4.00	8.00	20.00	85.00
	1899 M	.425	4.00	8.00	20.00	85.00
	1900/800 M					
		.295	4.00	8.00	20.00	85.00
	1901 M	.110	4.00	8.00	20.00	85.00
	1902 M	.120	4.00	8.00	20.00	85.00
	1903 M	.213	4.00	8.00	20.00	85.00
	1904 M	.276	4.00	8.00	20.00	85.00
	1905 M	.117	6.50	20.00	50.00	150.00

NOTE: Varieties exist.

Mint mark: Zs

KM#	Date	Mintage	Fine	VF	XF	Unc
405.3	1898 Z	.195	5.00	10.00	20.00	100.00
	1899 Z	.210	5.00	10.00	20.00	100.00
	1900/800 Z					
		.097	5.00	10.00	20.00	100.00
	1901/O Z	.130	25.00	50.00	100.00	250.00
	1901 Z	Inc. Ab.	5.00	10.00	20.00	100.00
	1902 Z	.105	5.00	10.00	20.00	100.00
	1903 Z	.143	5.00	10.00	20.00	100.00
	1904 Z	.246	5.00	10.00	20.00	100.00
	1904 M	Inc. Ab.	5.00	10.00	20.00	100.00
	1905 M	.059	10.00	20.00	50.00	150.00

PRICING SECTION

25 CENTAVOS

6.7680 g, .903 SILVER, .1965 oz ASW
Mint mark: A, As

KM#	Date	Mintage	Fine	VF	XF	Unc
406	1874 L	—	20.00	40.00	90.00	200.00
	1875 L	—	15.00	30.00	70.00	200.00
	1876 L	—	30.00	50.00	100.00	200.00
	1877 L	.011	200.00	300.00	500.00	—
	1877. Inc. Ab.		10.00	25.00	60.00	200.00
	1878 L	.025	10.00	25.00	60.00	200.00
	1879 L	—	10.00	25.00	60.00	200.00
	1880 L	—	10.00	25.00	60.00	200.00
	1880.L	—	10.00	25.00	60.00	200.00
	1881 L	8,800	500.00	700.00	—	—
	1882 L	7,777	15.00	35.00	80.00	200.00
	1883 L	.028	10.00	25.00	60.00	200.00
	1884 L	—	10.00	25.00	60.00	200.00
	1885 L	—	20.00	40.00	90.00	200.00
	1886 L	.046	15.00	30.00	70.00	200.00
	1887 L	.012	12.50	27.50	65.00	200.00
	1888 L	.020	12.50	27.50	65.00	200.00
	1889 L	.014	12.50	27.50	65.00	200.00
	1890 L	.023	10.00	25.00	60.00	200.00

Mint mark: CA, CH, Ca
KM#	Date	Mintage	Fine	VF	XF	Unc
406.1	1871 M	.018	25.00	50.00	100.00	200.00
	1872 M very crude date					
		.024	50.00	100.00	150.00	300.00
	1883 M	.012	10.00	25.00	50.00	175.00
	1885/3 M	.035	10.00	25.00	50.00	175.00
	1885 M Inc.Ab.		10.00	25.00	50.00	175.00
	1886 M	.022	10.00	25.00	50.00	175.00
	1887/6 M	.026	10.00	15.00	30.00	175.00
	1887 M Inc. Ab.		10.00	15.00	30.00	175.00
	1888 M	.014	10.00	25.00	50.00	175.00
	1889 M	.050	10.00	15.00	30.00	175.00

Mint mark: Cn
KM#	Date	Mintage	Fine	VF	XF	Unc
406.2	1871 P	—	250.00	500.00	750.00	—
	1872 P	2,780	300.00	550.00	800.00	—
	1873 P	.020	100.00	150.00	250.00	500.00
	1874 P	—	20.00	50.00	125.00	250.00
	1875 P	—	250.00	500.00	750.00	—
	1876 P	—	—	—	Rare	—
	1878/7 D/S	—	100.00	150.00	250.00	500.00
	1878 D	—	100.00	150.00	250.00	500.00
	1879 D	—	15.00	35.00	70.00	175.00
	1880 D	—	250.00	500.00	750.00	—
	1881/0 D	.018	15.00	30.00	60.00	175.00
	1882 D	—	200.00	350.00	600.00	—
	1882 M	—	—	—	Rare	—
	1883 M	.015	50.00	100.00	150.00	300.00
	1884 M	—	20.00	40.00	80.00	175.00
	1885/4 M	.019	20.00	40.00	80.00	175.00
	1886 M	.022	12.50	20.00	50.00	175.00
	1887 M	.032	12.50	20.00	50.00	175.00
	1888 M	.086	7.50	15.00	30.00	175.00
	1889 M	.050	10.00	25.00	50.00	175.00
	1890 M	.091	7.50	17.50	40.00	175.00
	1892/0 M	.016	20.00	40.00	80.00	200.00
	1892 M Inc. Ab.		20.00	40.00	80.00	200.00

Mint mark: Do
KM#	Date	Mintage	Fine	VF	XF	Unc
406.3	1873 P 892 pcs.	—	—	Rare	—	
	1877 P	—	25.00	50.00	100.00	200.00
	1878/7 E	—	250.00	500.00	750.00	—
	1878 B	—	—	—	Rare	—
	1879 B	—	50.00	75.00	125.00	250.00
	1880 B	—	—	—	Rare	—
	1882 C	.017	25.00	50.00	100.00	225.00
	1884/3 C	—	25.00	50.00	100.00	200.00
	1885 C	.015	20.00	40.00	80.00	200.00
	1886 C	.033	15.00	30.00	60.00	200.00
	1887 C	.027	10.00	20.00	50.00	200.00

KM#	Date	Mintage	Fine	VF	XF	Unc
406.3	1888 C	.025	10.00	20.00	50.00	200.00
	1889 C	.029	10.00	20.00	50.00	200.00
	1890 C	.068	7.50	15.00	40.00	200.00

Mint mark: Ga
KM#	Date	Mintage	Fine	VF	XF	Unc
406.4	1880 A	.038	25.00	50.00	100.00	200.00
	1881/0 S	.039	25.00	50.00	100.00	200.00
	1881 S Inc. Ab.		25.00	50.00	100.00	200.00
	1882 S	.018	25.00	50.00	100.00	200.00
	1883/2 B/S	—	50.00	100.00	150.00	300.00
	1884 B	—	20.00	40.00	80.00	150.00
	1889 S	.030	20.00	40.00	80.00	150.00

Mint mark: Go
KM#	Date	Mintage	Fine	VF	XF	Unc
406.5	1870 S	.128	10.00	20.00	50.00	125.00
	1871 S	.172	10.00	20.00	50.00	125.00
	1872/1 S	.178	10.00	20.00	50.00	125.00
	1872 S Inc. Ab.		10.00	20.00	50.00	125.00
	1873 S	.120	10.00	20.00	50.00	125.00
	1874 S	—	15.00	30.00	60.00	150.00
	1875/4 S	—	15.00	30.00	60.00	150.00
	1875 S	—	10.00	20.00	50.00	125.00
	1876 S	—	20.00	40.00	80.00	175.00
	1877 S	.124	10.00	20.00	50.00	125.00
	1878 S	.146	10.00	20.00	50.00	125.00
	1879 S	—	10.00	20.00	50.00	125.00
	1880 S	—	20.00	40.00	80.00	175.00
	1881 S	.408	7.50	17.50	45.00	125.00
	1882 S	.204	7.50	17.50	45.00	125.00
	1883 B	.168	7.50	17.50	45.00	125.00
	1884/69 B	—	7.50	17.50	45.00	125.00
	1884/3 B	—	7.50	17.50	45.00	125.00
	1884 B	—	7.50	17.50	45.00	125.00
	1885/65 R	.300	7.50	17.50	45.00	125.00
	1885/69 R I.A.		7.50	17.50	45.00	125.00
	1885 R Inc. Ab.		7.50	17.50	45.00	125.00
	1886/66 R	.322	7.50	17.50	45.00	125.00
	1886/69 R/S					
	Inc. Ab.		7.50	17.50	45.00	125.00
	1886/5/69R					
	Inc. Ab.		7.50	15.00	45.00	125.00
	1886 R Inc. Ab.		7.50	15.00	45.00	125.00
	1887 R	.254	7.50	15.00	45.00	125.00
	1887 Go/Cn R/D					
	Inc. Ab.		7.50	15.00	45.00	125.00
	1888 R	.312	7.50	15.00	45.00	125.00
	1889/8 R	.304	7.50	15.00	45.00	125.00
	1889/8 Go/Cn R/D					
	Inc. Ab.		7.50	15.00	45.00	125.00
	1889 R Inc. Ab.		7.50	15.00	45.00	125.00
	1890 R	.236	7.50	15.00	45.00	125.00

NOTE: Varieties exist.

Mint mark: Ho
KM#	Date	Mintage	Fine	VF	XF	Unc
406.6	1874 R	.023	10.00	20.00	40.00	125.00
	1874/64 R I.A.		10.00	20.00	40.00	125.00
	1875 R	—	—	—	Rare	—
	1876/4 F/R					
		.034	10.00	20.00	50.00	150.00
	1876 F/R I.A.		10.00	25.00	60.00	150.00
	1876 F Inc. Ab.		10.00	25.00	55.00	135.00
	1877 F	—	10.00	20.00	50.00	125.00
	1878 A	.023	10.00	20.00	50.00	125.00
	1879 A	—	10.00	20.00	50.00	125.00
	1880 A	—	15.00	30.00	60.00	125.00
	1881 A	.019	15.00	30.00	60.00	125.00
	1882 A	8,120	20.00	40.00	80.00	150.00
	1883 M	2,000	100.00	200.00	300.00	600.00
	1884 M	—	12.50	25.00	50.00	150.00
	1885 M	—	10.00	20.00	50.00	125.00
	1886 G	6,400	30.00	60.00	125.00	250.00
	1887 G	.012	10.00	20.00	40.00	125.00
	1888 G	.020	10.00	20.00	40.00	125.00
	1889 G	.028	10.00	20.00	40.00	125.00
	1890/80 G	.018	25.00	50.00	100.00	125.00
	1890 G Inc. Ab.		25.00	50.00	100.00	125.00

NOTE: Varieties exist.

Mint mark: Mo
KM#	Date	Mintage	Fine	VF	XF	Unc
406.7	1869 C	.076	10.00	25.00	50.00	125.00
	1870/9 C	.136	6.00	12.00	30.00	125.00
	1870 C Inc. Ab.		6.00	12.00	30.00	125.00
	1871 M	.138	6.00	12.00	30.00	125.00
	1872 M	.220	6.00	12.00	30.00	125.00
	1873/1 M	.048	10.00	25.00	50.00	125.00

KM#	Date	Mintage	Fine	VF	XF	Unc
406.7	1873 M Inc. Ab.		10.00	25.00	50.00	125.00
	1874/69 B/M					
		—	10.00	25.00	50.00	125.00
	1874/3 M	—	10.00	25.00	50.00	125.00
	1874/3 B	—	10.00	25.00	50.00	125.00
	1874 M	—	6.00	12.00	30.00	125.00
	1874 B/M	—	10.00	25.00	50.00	125.00
	1875 B	—	6.00	12.00	30.00	125.00
	1876/5 B	—	7.50	15.00	40.00	125.00
	1876 B	—	6.00	12.00	30.00	125.00
	1877 M	.056	10.00	25.00	50.00	125.00
	1878/1 M	.120	10.00	25.00	50.00	125.00
	1878/7 M	I.A.	10.00	25.00	50.00	125.00
	1878 M Inc. Ab.		6.00	12.00	30.00	125.00
	1879 M	—	10.00	20.00	40.00	125.00
	1880 M	—	7.50	15.00	35.00	125.00
	1881/0 M	.300	10.00	25.00	50.00	125.00
	1881 M Inc. Ab.		10.00	25.00	50.00	125.00
	1882 M	.212	7.50	15.00	35.00	125.00
	1883 M	.108	7.50	15.00	35.00	125.00
	1884 M	—	10.00	20.00	40.00	125.00
	1885 M	.216	10.00	25.00	40.00	125.00
	1886/5 M	.436	7.50	15.00	35.00	125.00
	1886 M Inc. Ab.		7.50	15.00	35.00	125.00
	1887 M	.376	7.50	15.00	35.00	125.00
	1888 M	.192	7.50	15.00	35.00	125.00
	1889 M	.132	7.50	15.00	35.00	125.00
	1890 M	.060	10.00	20.00	40.00	125.00

NOTE: Varieties exist.

Mint mark: Pi

KM#	Date	Mintage	Fine	VF	XF	Unc
406.8	1869 S	—	25.00	75.00	150.00	300.00
	1870 G	.050	10.00	30.00	75.00	150.00
	1870 O Inc. Ab.		15.00	35.00	85.00	175.00
	1871 O	.030	10.00	30.00	75.00	150.00
	1872 O	.046	10.00	30.00	75.00	150.00
	1873 O	.013	15.00	40.00	90.00	175.00
	1874 H	—	15.00	40.00	90.00	200.00
	1875 H	—	10.00	25.00	60.00	150.00
	1876/5 H	—	15.00	30.00	80.00	175.00
	1876 H	—	10.00	25.00	65.00	150.00
	1877 H	.019	10.00	25.00	65.00	150.00
	1878 H	—	15.00	30.00	60.00	150.00
	1879/8 H	—	10.00	25.00	60.00	150.00
	1879 H	—	10.00	25.00	60.00	150.00
	1879 E	—	100.00	200.00	300.00	600.00
	1880 H	—	20.00	40.00	100.00	200.00
	1881 H	.050	20.00	40.00	80.00	175.00
	1881 E Inc. Ab.		—	—	Rare	—
	1882 H	.020	10.00	20.00	60.00	150.00
	1883 H	.017	10.00	25.00	65.00	150.00
	1884 H	—	10.00	25.00	65.00	150.00
	1885 H	.043	10.00	20.00	60.00	150.00
	1886 C	.078	10.00	25.00	65.00	150.00
	1886 R Inc. Ab.		7.50	20.00	50.00	150.00
	1886 R 6/inverted 6					
	Inc. Ab.		7.50	20.00	50.00	150.00
	1887 Pi/ZsR					
		.092	7.50	20.00	50.00	150.00
	1887 Pi/ZsB					
	Inc. Ab.		100.00	150.00	300.00	500.00
	1888 R	.106	7.50	20.00	50.00	150.00
	1888 Pi/ZsR					
	Inc. Ab.		10.00	20.00	50.00	150.00
	1888 R/B	I.A.	10.00	20.00	50.00	150.00
	1889 R	.115	7.50	15.00	40.00	150.00
	1889 Pi/ZsR					
	Inc. Ab.		10.00	20.00	50.00	150.00
	1889 R/B	I.A.	10.00	20.00	50.00	150.00
	1890 R	.064	10.00	20.00	50.00	150.00
	1890 Pi/ZsR/B					
	Inc. Ab.		7.50	15.00	40.00	150.00
	1890 R/B	I.A.	10.00	20.00	50.00	150.00

NOTE: Varieties exist.

Mint mark: Zs

KM#	Date	Mintage	Fine	VF	XF	Unc
406.9	1870 H	.152	6.00	15.00	50.00	125.00
	1871 H	.250	6.00	15.00	50.00	125.00
	1872 H	.260	6.00	15.00	50.00	125.00
	1873 H	.132	6.00	15.00	50.00	125.00
	1874 H	—	10.00	20.00	60.00	125.00
	1874 A	—	10.00	20.00	60.00	125.00
	1875 A	—	7.00	20.00	60.00	125.00
	1876 A	—	6.00	15.00	50.00	125.00
	1876 S	—	6.00	15.00	50.00	125.00

KM#	Date	Mintage	Fine	VF	XF	Unc
406.9	1877 S	.350	6.00	15.00	50.00	125.00
	1878 S	.252	6.00	15.00	50.00	125.00
	1879 S	—	6.00	15.00	50.00	125.00
	1880 S	—	6.00	15.00	50.00	125.00
	1881/0 S	.570	6.00	15.00	50.00	125.00
	1881 S Inc. Ab.		6.00	15.00	50.00	125.00
	1882/1 S	.300	10.00	17.50	55.00	125.00
	1882 S Inc. Ab.		6.00	15.00	50.00	125.00
	1883/2 S	.193	10.00	17.50	55.00	125.00
	1883 S Inc. Ab.		6.00	15.00	50.00	125.00
	1884/3 S	—	10.00	17.50	55.00	125.00
	1884 S	—	6.00	15.00	50.00	125.00
	1885 S	.309	6.00	15.00	50.00	125.00
	1886/5 S	.613	6.00	15.00	50.00	125.00
	1886 S Inc. Ab.		6.00	15.00	50.00	125.00
	1886 Z Inc. Ab.		6.00	15.00	55.00	125.00
	1887 Z	.389	6.00	15.00	50.00	125.00
	1888 Z	.408	6.00	15.00	50.00	125.00
	1889 Z	.400	6.00	15.00	50.00	125.00
	1890 Z	.269	6.00	15.00	50.00	125.00

NOTE: Varieties exist.

50 CENTAVOS

13.5360 g, .903 SILVER, .3930 oz ASW
Mint mark: A, As
Rev: Balance scale.

KM#	Date	Mintage	Fine	VF	XF	Unc
407	1875 L	—	12.00	25.00	70.00	400.00
	1876/5 L	—	25.00	50.00	120.00	450.00
	1876 L	—	12.00	25.00	70.00	400.00
	1876.L	—				
	1877 L	.026	15.00	30.00	85.00	450.00
	1878 L	—	12.00	25.00	70.00	400.00
	1879 L	—	25.00	50.00	120.00	450.00
	1880 L	.057	12.00	25.00	70.00	400.00
	1881 L	.018	15.00	30.00	80.00	450.00
	1884 L	6,286	65.00	120.00	250.00	650.00
	1885 As/HoL					
		.021	15.00	35.00	90.00	450.00
	1888 L	—	Contemporary counterfeits			

Mint mark: Ca, CHa

KM#	Date	Mintage	Fine	VF	XF	Unc
407.1	1883 M	.012	30.00	60.00	125.00	500.00
	1884 M	—	25.00	50.00	125.00	500.00
	1885 M	.013	15.00	35.00	90.00	400.00
	1886 M	.018	20.00	40.00	100.00	450.00
	1887 M	.026	25.00	65.00	150.00	500.00

Mint mark: Cn

KM#	Date	Mintage	Fine	VF	XF	Unc
407.2	1871 P	—	400.00	550.00	750.00	1500.
	1873 P	—	400.00	550.00	750.00	1500.
	1874 P	—	200.00	300.00	500.00	1000.
	1875/4 P	—	20.00	40.00	75.00	450.00
	1875 P	—	12.00	25.00	50.00	450.00
	1876 P	—	15.00	30.00	60.00	450.00
	1877/6 G	—	15.00	30.00	60.00	450.00
	1877 G	—	12.00	25.00	50.00	450.00
	1878 G	.018	20.00	40.00	75.00	450.00
	1878 D Cn/Mo					
	Inc. Ab.		30.00	60.00	100.00	450.00
	1878 D Inc. Ab.		15.00	35.00	75.00	450.00
	1879 D	—	12.00	25.00	50.00	450.00
	1879 D/G	—	12.00	25.00	50.00	450.00
	1880 D	—	15.00	30.00	60.00	450.00
	1881/0 D	.188	15.00	30.00	60.00	450.00
	1881 D Inc. Ab.		15.00	30.00	60.00	450.00
	1881 G Inc. Ab.		125.00	175.00	275.00	550.00
	1882 D	—	175.00	225.00	325.00	1000.
	1882 G	—	100.00	250.00	300.00	1000.
	1883 D	.019	25.00	50.00	100.00	500.00
	1885/3 CN/Pi M/H					
		9,254	30.00	60.00	100.00	500.00
	1886 M/G	7,030	50.00	100.00	150.00	800.00

KM#	Date	Mintage	Fine	VF	XF	Unc
407.2	1886 M Inc. Ab.		40.00	80.00	150.00	800.00
	1887 M	.076	20.00	40.00	100.00	450.00
	1888 M	—	Contemporary counterfeits			
	1892 M	8,200	40.00	80.00	150.00	800.00

Mint mark: Do

KM#	Date	Mintage	Fine	VF	XF	Unc
407.3	1871 P	591 pcs.	—	—	Rare	—
	1873 P	4,010	150.00	250.00	500.00	1250.
	1873 M/P	I.A.	150.00	250.00	500.00	1250.
	1874 M	—	20.00	40.00	175.00	750.00
	1875 M	—	20.00	40.00	80.00	350.00
	1875 H	—	150.00	250.00	450.00	1000.
	1876/5 M	—	35.00	70.00	150.00	500.00
	1876 M	—	35.00	70.00	150.00	500.00
	1877 P	2,000	30.00	45.00	150.00	1250.
	1878 B	—	—	—	Rare	—
	1879 B	—	—	—	Rare	—
	1880 P	—	30.00	60.00	125.00	500.00
	1881 P	.010	40.00	80.00	150.00	500.00
	1882 C	8,957	30.00	75.00	200.00	800.00
	1884/2 C	—	20.00	50.00	125.00	600.00
	1884 C	—	—	—	—	—
	1885 B	—	15.00	40.00	100.00	500.00
	1886 C	.016	15.00	40.00	100.00	500.00
	1887 Do/MoC					
		.028	15.00	40.00	100.00	500.00

Mint mark: Go

KM#	Date	Mintage	Fine	VF	XF	Unc
407.4	1869 S	—	15.00	35.00	75.00	550.00
	1870 S	.166	12.00	25.00	50.00	450.00
	1871 S	.148	12.00	25.00	50.00	450.00
	1872/1 S	.144	15.00	30.00	60.00	500.00
	1872 S Inc. Ab.		12.00	25.00	50.00	450.00
	1873 S	.050	12.00	25.00	50.00	450.00
	1874 S	—	12.00	25.00	50.00	450.00
	1875 S	—	15.00	35.00	75.00	450.00
	1876/5 S	—	12.00	25.00	50.00	450.00
	1877 S	.076	12.00	25.00	60.00	450.00
	1878 S	.037	15.00	30.00	75.00	550.00
	1879 S	—	12.00	25.00	50.00	450.00
	1880 S	—	12.00	25.00	50.00	450.00
	1881/79 S	.032	15.00	30.00	60.00	500.00
	1881 S Inc. Ab.		12.00	25.00	50.00	450.00
	1882 S	.018	12.00	25.00	50.00	450.00
	1883/2 B/S	—	15.00	30.00	60.00	500.00
	1883 B	—	12.00	25.00	50.00	450.00
	1883 S	—	—	—	Rare	—
	1884 B/S	—	15.00	30.00	75.00	500.00
	1885 R	.053	12.00	25.00	50.00	450.00
	1886/5 R/B					
		.059	15.00	30.00	60.00	500.00
	1886/5 R/S					
	Inc. Ab.		20.00	40.00	75.00	500.00
	1886 R Inc. Ab.		20.00	40.00	75.00	450.00
	1887 R	.018	20.00	40.00	75.00	550.00
	1888 R	—	Contemporary counterfeits			

NOTE: Varieties exist.

13.5360 g, .903 SILVER, .3930 oz ASW

Mint mark: Ho

KM#	Date	Mintage	Fine	VF	XF	Unc
407.5	1874 R	—	20.00	40.00	100.00	600.00
	1875/4 R	—	20.00	50.00	125.00	600.00
	1875 R	—	20.00	50.00	125.00	600.00
	1876/5 F/R	—	15.00	35.00	100.00	550.00
	1876 F	—	15.00	35.00	100.00	550.00
	1877 F	—	50.00	75.00	150.00	650.00
	1880/70 A	—	15.00	35.00	100.00	550.00
	1880 A	—	15.00	35.00	100.00	550.00
	1881 A	.013	15.00	35.00	100.00	550.00
	1882 A	—	75.00	150.00	250.00	750.00
	1888 G	—	Contemporary counterfeits			
	1894 G	.059	15.00	30.00	100.00	450.00
	1895 G	8,000	250.00	350.00	500.00	1250.

NOTE: Varieties exist.

Mint mark: Mo

KM#	Date	Mintage	Fine	VF	XF	Unc
407.6	1869 C	.046	15.00	35.00	95.00	600.00
	1870 C	.052	15.00	30.00	90.00	550.00
	1871 C	.014	40.00	75.00	150.00	650.00
	1871 M/C	I.A.	35.00	75.00	150.00	600.00
	1872/1 M	.060	35.00	75.00	150.00	600.00
	1872 M Inc. Ab.		35.00	75.00	150.00	550.00
	1873 M	6,000	35.00	75.00	150.00	600.00
	1874/3 M	—	200.00	400.00	600.00	1250.
	1874/2 B	—	15.00	30.00	75.00	500.00

KM#	Date	Mintage	Fine	VF	XF	Unc
407.6	1874/3 B/M	—	15.00	30.00	75.00	500.00
	1874 B	—	15.00	30.00	75.00	500.00
	1875 B	—	15.00	30.00	75.00	550.00
	1876/5 B	—	15.00	30.00	75.00	500.00
	1876 B	—	12.00	25.00	75.00	500.00
	1877/2 M	—	20.00	40.00	100.00	550.00
	1877 M	—	15.00	30.00	90.00	500.00
	1878/7 M					
		8,000	25.00	50.00	125.00	600.00
	1878 M Inc. Ab.		15.00	35.00	100.00	550.00
	1879 M	—	25.00	50.00	125.00	550.00
	1880 M	—	100.00	150.00	250.00	750.00
	1881 M	.016	25.00	50.00	125.00	600.00
	1882/1 M					
		2,000	30.00	60.00	150.00	750.00
	1883/2 M	4,000	150.00	225.00	350.00	1000.
	1884 M	—	150.00	225.00	350.00	1000.
	1885 M	.012	30.00	60.00	150.00	600.00
	1886/5 M	.066	15.00	35.00	90.00	450.00
	1886 M Inc. Ab.		12.00	25.00	75.00	400.00
	1887/6 M	.088	15.00	35.00	90.00	450.00
	1887 M Inc. Ab.		15.00	35.00	75.00	450.00
	1888 M	—	Contemporary counterfeits			

Mint mark: Pi

KM#	Date	Mintage	Fine	VF	XF	Unc
407.7	1870/780 G					
		.050	25.00	45.00	110.00	500.00
	1870 G Inc. Ab.		20.00	40.00	100.00	450.00
	1870 O Inc. Ab.		20.00	40.00	100.00	450.00
	1871 O/G	.064	15.00	30.00	80.00	400.00
	1872 O	.052	15.00	30.00	80.00	400.00
	1872 O/G	I.A.	15.00	30.00	80.00	400.00
	1873 O	.032	20.00	40.00	100.00	450.00
	1873 H Inc. Ab.		25.00	50.00	125.00	550.00
	1874 H/O	—	15.00	30.00	80.00	400.00
	1875 H	—	15.00	30.00	80.00	400.00
	1876 H	—	30.00	60.00	150.00	700.00
	1877 H	.034	20.00	40.00	100.00	450.00
	1878 H	9,700	20.00	40.00	100.00	450.00
	1879/7 H	—	15.00	35.00	90.00	450.00
	1879 H	—	15.00	35.00	90.00	400.00
	1880 H	—	20.00	40.00	100.00	450.00
	1881 H	.028	20.00	40.00	100.00	450.00
	1882 H	.022	15.00	30.00	80.00	400.00
	1883 H 8/8					
		.029	50.00	100.00	200.00	750.00
	1883 H Inc. Ab.		15.00	30.00	80.00	400.00
	1884 H	—	50.00	100.00	175.00	600.00
	1885/0 H	.045	20.00	40.00	100.00	450.00
	1885/4 H	I.A.	20.00	40.00	100.00	450.00
	1885 H Inc. Ab.		25.00	50.00	125.00	450.00
	1885 C Inc. Ab.		15.00	30.00	80.00	400.00
	1886/1 R	.092	50.00	100.00	175.00	600.00
	1886 C Inc. Ab.		15.00	30.00	80.00	400.00
	1886 R Inc. Ab.		15.00	30.00	80.00	400.00
	1887 R	.032	15.00	30.00	90.00	450.00
	1888 R	—	Contemporary counterfeits			

Mint mark: Zs

KM#	Date	Mintage	Fine	VF	XF	Unc
407.8	1870 H	.086	12.00	25.00	60.00	450.00
	1871 H	.146	12.00	25.00	50.00	400.00
	1872 H	.132	12.00	25.00	50.00	400.00
	1873 H	.056	12.00	25.00	50.00	400.00
	1874 H	—	12.00	25.00	50.00	400.00
	1874 A	—	—	—	Rare	—
	1875 A	—	12.00	25.00	50.00	400.00
	1876/5 A	—	15.00	30.00	60.00	450.00
	1876 A	—	12.00	25.00	50.00	400.00
	1876 S	—	100.00	200.00	350.00	750.00
	1877 S	.100	12.00	25.00	50.00	400.00
	1878/7 S	.254	15.00	30.00	60.00	450.00
	1878 S Inc. Ab.		15.00	30.00	60.00	400.00
	1879 S	—	12.00	25.00	50.00	400.00
	1880 S	—	12.00	25.00	50.00	400.00
	1881 S	.201	12.00	25.00	50.00	400.00
	1882/1 S	2,000	50.00	100.00	250.00	650.00
	1882 S Inc. Ab.		50.00	100.00	250.00	650.00
	1883 Zs/Za S					
		.031	30.00	60.00	100.00	450.00
	1883 S Inc. Ab.		25.00	50.00	100.00	450.00
	1884/3 S	—	15.00	30.00	60.00	450.00
	1884 S	—	12.00	25.00	50.00	400.00
	1885/4 S	2,000	25.00	50.00	125.00	450.00
	1885 S Inc. Ab.		25.00	50.00	125.00	450.00
	1886 Z	2,000	150.00	275.00	400.00	1000.
	1887 Z	.063	30.00	60.00	125.00	450.00

PESO

27.0730 g, .903 SILVER, .7860 oz ASW
Mint mark: CH
Rev: Balance scale.

KM#	Date	Mintage	Fine	VF	XF	Unc
408	1872 P/M	.747	750.00	1500.	3500.	—
	1872 P	Inc. Ab.	350.00	700.00	1500.	—
	1872/1 M	I.A.	25.00	40.00	75.00	400.00
	1872 M	Inc. Ab.	17.50	25.00	50.00	250.00
	1873 M	.320	20.00	30.00	60.00	265.00
	1873 M/P	I.A.	25.00	40.00	75.00	350.00

Mint mark: Cn

KM#	Date	Mintage	Fine	VF	XF	Unc
408.1	1870 E	—	40.00	80.00	150.00	500.00
	1871/11 P	.478	25.00	45.00	90.00	350.00
	1871 P	Inc. Ab.	20.00	40.00	75.00	300.00
	1872 P	.209	20.00	40.00	75.00	300.00
	1873 P	.527	20.00	40.00	75.00	300.00

Mint mark: Do

KM#	Date	Mintage	Fine	VF	XF	Unc
408.2	1870 P	—	50.00	100.00	175.00	450.00
	1871 P	.427	25.00	50.00	75.00	300.00
	1872 P	.296	20.00	40.00	75.00	350.00
	1872 PT	I.A.	100.00	175.00	250.00	675.00
	1873 P	.203	25.00	45.00	85.00	350.00

Mint mark: Ga

KM#	Date	Mintage	Fine	VF	XF	Unc
408.3	1870 C	—	650.00	850.00	—	—
	1871 C	.829	25.00	65.00	135.00	600.00
	1872 C	.485	40.00	90.00	175.00	650.00
	1873/2 C	.277	40.00	90.00	175.00	700.00
	1873 C	Inc. Ab.	25.00	65.00	135.00	600.00

Mint mark: Go

KM#	Date	Mintage	Fine	VF	XF	Unc
408.4	1871/0 S	3.946	30.00	50.00	90.00	350.00
	1871/3 S	I.A.	20.00	35.00	70.00	275.00
	1871 S	Inc. Ab.	12.00	20.00	40.00	220.00
	1872 S	4.067	12.00	20.00	40.00	250.00
	1873/2 S	1.560	15.00	25.00	50.00	250.00
	1873 S	Inc. Ab.	12.00	20.00	45.00	250.00
	1873/Go/Mo/S/M					
		Inc. Ab.	12.00	20.00	45.00	250.00

Mint mark: Mo

KM#	Date	Mintage	Fine	VF	XF	Unc
408.5	1869 C	—	35.00	65.00	135.00	450.00
	1870/69 C					
		5.115	15.00	25.00	55.00	275.00
	1870 C	Inc. Ab.	12.00	20.00	40.00	250.00
	1870 M/C	I.A.	18.00	30.00	60.00	275.00
	1870 M	Inc. Ab.	18.00	30.00	60.00	275.00
	1871/0 M					
		6.974	15.00	25.00	55.00	275.00
	1871 M	Inc. Ab.	12.00	20.00	40.00	250.00
	1872/1 M/C					
		4.801	15.00	25.00	50.00	275.00
	1872 M	Inc. Ab.	12.00	20.00	40.00	250.00
	1873 M	1.765	12.00	20.00	40.00	250.00

NOTE: The 1869 C with large LEY on the scroll is a pattern.

Mint mark: Oa

KM#	Date	Mintage	Fine	VF	XF	Unc
408.6	1869 E	—	275.00	400.00	600.00	2000.
	1870 OAE small A					
		Inc. Ab.	15.00	30.00	75.00	400.00
	1870 OA E large A					
		Inc. Ab.	100.00	150.00	300.00	900.00
	1871/69 E	.140	30.00	50.00	125.00	550.00
	1871 OaE small A					
		Inc. Ab.	15.00	30.00	60.00	300.00
	1871 OA E large A					
		Inc. Ab.	15.00	30.00	75.00	400.00
	1872 OaE small A					
		.180	15.00	30.00	75.00	400.00
	1872 OA E large A					
		Inc. Ab.	50.00	100.00	200.00	450.00
	1873 E	.105	15.00	30.00	75.00	350.00

Mint mark: Pi

KM#	Date	Mintage	Fine	VF	XF	Unc
408.7	1870 S	1.967	200.00	350.00	500.00	1000.
	1870 S/A	I.A.	200.00	350.00	500.00	1000.
	1870 G	Inc. Ab.	25.00	50.00	125.00	450.00
	1870 H	Inc. Ab.	Contemporary counterfeit			
	1870 O/G	I.A.	25.00	35.00	125.00	450.00
	1870 O	Inc. Ab.	20.00	30.00	100.00	350.00
	1871/69 O					
		2.103	75.00	150.00	250.00	500.00
	1871 O/G	I.A.	15.00	30.00	60.00	300.00
	1872 O	1.873	15.00	30.00	60.00	300.00
	1873 O	.893	15.00	30.00	60.00	300.00
	1873 H	Inc. Ab.	15.00	30.00	60.00	300.00

NOTE: Varieties exist.

Mint mark: Zs

KM#	Date	Mintage	Fine	VF	XF	Unc
408.8	1870 H	4.519	12.00	30.00	40.00	220.00
	1871 H	4.459	12.00	20.00	40.00	220.00
	1872 H	4.039	12.00	20.00	40.00	220.00
	1873 H	1.782	12.00	20.00	40.00	220.00

NOTE: Varieties exist.

Mint mark: Cn
Liberty cap

KM#	Date	Mintage	Fine	VF	XF	Unc
409	1898 AM	1.720	10.00	15.00	30.00	65.00
	1898 Cn/MoAM					
		I.A.	15.00	30.00	90.00	150.00
	1899 AM	1.722	25.00	50.00	90.00	175.00
	1899 JQ	I.A.	10.00	15.00	50.00	125.00
	1900 JQ	1.804	10.00	15.00	30.00	80.00
	1901 JQ	1.473	10.00	15.00	30.00	80.00
	1902 JQ	1.194	10.00	15.00	45.00	125.00
	1903 JQ	1.514	10.00	15.00	30.00	80.00
	1903 FV	I.A.	25.00	50.00	100.00	225.00
	1904 MH	1.554	10.00	15.00	30.00	80.00
	1904 RP	I.A.	45.00	85.00	125.00	300.00
	1905 RP	.598	20.00	40.00	75.00	225.00

Mint mark: Go

KM#	Date	Mintage	Fine	VF	XF	Unc
409.1	1898 RS	4.256	10.00	15.00	35.00	75.00
	1898 Go/MoRS					
		Inc. Ab.	20.00	30.00	60.00	125.00
	1899 RS	3.207	10.00	15.00	30.00	75.00
	1900 RS	1.489	25.00	50.00	100.00	250.00

NOTE: Varieties exist.

Mint mark: Mo

KM#	Date	Mintage	Fine	VF	XF	Unc
409.2	1898 AM original strike - rev. w/139 Beads					
		10.156	7.50	10.00	17.50	60.00
	1898 AM restrike (1949) - rev. w/134 Beads					
		10.250	7.50	10.00	15.00	40.00
	1899 AM	7.930	10.00	12.50	20.00	70.00

KM#	Date	Mintage	Fine	VF	XF	Unc
409.2	1900 AM	8.226	10.00	12.50	20.00	70.00
	1901 AM	14.505	7.50	10.00	20.00	70.00
	1902/1 AM	16.224	150.00	300.00	500.00	950.00
	1902 AM	I.A.	7.50	10.00	20.00	70.00
	1903 AM	22.396	7.50	10.00	20.00	70.00
	1903 MA (error) Inc. Ab.		1500.	2500.	3500.	7500.
	1904 AM	14.935	7.50	10.00	20.00	70.00
	1905 AM	3.557	15.00	25.00	55.00	125.00
	1908 AM	7.575	10.00	12.50	20.00	60.00
	1908 GV	I.A.	10.00	12.50	17.50	40.00
	1909 GV	2.924	10.00	12.50	17.50	45.00

NOTE: Varieties exist.

Mint mark: Zs

KM#	Date	Mintage	Fine	VF	XF	Unc
409.3	1898 FZ	5.714	10.00	12.50	20.00	60.00
	1899 FZ	5.618	10.00	12.50	20.00	65.00
	1900 FZ	5.357	10.00	12.50	20.00	65.00
	1901 AZ	5.706	4000.	6500.	10,000.	—
	1901 FZ	I.A.	10.00	12.50	20.00	60.00
	1902 FZ	7.134	10.00	12.50	20.00	60.00
	1903/2 FZ	3.080	12.50	15.00	50.00	125.00
	1903 FZ	I.A.	10.00	12.50	20.00	65.00
	1904 FZ	2.423	10.00	15.00	25.00	70.00
	1904 FM	I.A.	10.00	15.00	25.00	85.00
	1905 FM	.995	20.00	40.00	60.00	150.00

NOTE: Varieties exist.

PESO

1.6920 g, .875 GOLD, .0476 oz AGW
Mint mark: As

KM#	Date	Mintage	Fine	VF	XF	Unc
410	1888 L	—	—	—	Rare	—
	1888 AsL/MoM	—	—	—	Rare	—

Mint mark: Ca

KM#	Date	Mintage	Fine	VF	XF	Unc
410.1	1888 Ca/MoM	104 pcs.	—	—	Rare	—

Mint mark: Cn

KM#	Date	Mintage	Fine	VF	XF	Unc
410.2	1873 P	1,221	75.00	100.00	150.00	250.00
	1875 P	—	85.00	125.00	150.00	250.00
	1878 G	248 pcs.	100.00	175.00	225.00	450.00
	1879 D	—	100.00	150.00	175.00	275.00
	1881/0 D	338 pcs.	100.00	150.00	175.00	275.00
	1882 D	340 pcs.	100.00	150.00	175.00	275.00
	1883 D	—	100.00	150.00	175.00	275.00
	1884 M	—	100.00	150.00	175.00	275.00
	1886/4 M	277 pcs.	100.00	150.00	225.00	450.00
	1888/7 M	2,586	100.00	175.00	225.00	450.00
	1888 M Inc. Ab.		65.00	100.00	150.00	250.00
	1889 M	—	—	—	Rare	—
	1891/89 M	969 pcs.	75.00	100.00	150.00	250.00
	1892 M	780 pcs.	75.00	100.00	150.00	250.00
	1893 M	498 pcs.	85.00	125.00	150.00	250.00
	1894 M	493 pcs.	80.00	125.00	150.00	250.00
	1895 M	1,143	65.00	100.00	150.00	250.00
	1896/5 M	1,028	65.00	100.00	150.00	250.00
	1897 M	785 pcs.	65.00	100.00	150.00	250.00
	1898 M	3,521	65.00	100.00	150.00	225.00
	1898 Cn/MoM Inc. Ab.		65.00	100.00	150.00	250.00
	1899 Q	2,000	65.00	100.00	150.00	225.00
	1901/0 Q	2,350	65.00	100.00	150.00	225.00
	1902 Q	2,480	65.00	100.00	150.00	225.00
	1902 Cn/MoQ/C Inc. Ab.		65.00	100.00	150.00	225.00
	1904 H	3,614	65.00	100.00	150.00	225.00

KM#	Date	Mintage	Fine	VF	XF	Unc
410.2	1904 Cn/Mo/ H Inc. Ab.		65.00	100.00	150.00	250.00
	1905 P	1,000	—	Reported, not confirmed		

Mint mark: Go

KM#	Date	Mintage	Fine	VF	XF	Unc
410.3	1870 S	—	100.00	125.00	150.00	250.00
	1871 S	500 pcs.	100.00	175.00	225.00	450.00
	1888 R	210 pcs.	125.00	200.00	250.00	500.00
	1890 R	1,916	75.00	100.00	150.00	250.00
	1892 R	533 pcs.	100.00	150.00	175.00	325.00
	1894 R	180 pcs.	150.00	200.00	250.00	500.00
	1895 R	676 pcs.	100.00	150.00	175.00	300.00
	1896/5 R	4,671	65.00	100.00	150.00	250.00
	1897/6 R	4,280	65.00	100.00	150.00	250.00
	1897 R Inc. Ab.		65.00	100.00	150.00	250.00
	1898 R regular obv.	5,193	65.00	100.00	150.00	250.00
	1898 R mule, 5 Centavos obv., normal rev. Inc. Ab.		75.00	100.00	150.00	250.00
	1899 R	2,748	65.00	100.00	150.00	250.00
	1900/800 R	864 pcs.	75.00	125.00	150.00	275.00

Mint mark: Ho

KM#	Date	Mintage	Fine	VF	XF	Unc
410.4	1875 R	310 pcs.	—	—	Rare	—
	1876 F	—	—	—	Rare	—
	1888 G/MoM	—	—	—	Rare	—

Mint mark: Mo

KM#	Date	Mintage	Fine	VF	XF	Unc
410.5	1870 C	2,540	40.00	60.00	80.00	175.00
	1871 M/C	1,000	50.00	100.00	150.00	225.00
	1872 M/C	3,000	40.00	60.00	80.00	175.00
	1873/1 M	2,900	40.00	60.00	80.00	175.00
	1873 M Inc. Ab.		40.00	60.00	80.00	175.00
	1874 M	—	40.00	60.00	80.00	175.00
	1875 B/M	—	40.00	60.00	80.00	175.00
	1876/5 B/M	—	40.00	60.00	80.00	175.00
	1877 M	—	40.00	60.00	80.00	175.00
	1878 M	2,000	40.00	60.00	80.00	175.00
	1879 M	—	40.00	60.00	80.00	175.00
	1880/70 M	—	40.00	60.00	80.00	175.00
	1881/71 M	1,000	40.00	60.00	80.00	175.00
	1882/72 M	—	40.00	60.00	80.00	175.00
	1883/72 M	1,000	40.00	60.00	80.00	175.00
	1884 M	—	40.00	60.00	80.00	175.00
	1885/71 M	—	40.00	60.00	80.00	175.00
	1885 M	—	40.00	60.00	80.00	175.00
	1886 M	1,700	40.00	60.00	80.00	175.00
	1887 M	2,200	40.00	60.00	80.00	175.00
	1888 M	1,000	40.00	60.00	80.00	175.00
	1889 M	500 pcs.	100.00	150.00	200.00	275.00
	1890 M	570 pcs.	100.00	150.00	200.00	275.00
	1891 M	746 pcs.	100.00	150.00	200.00	275.00
	1892/0 M	2,895	40.00	60.00	80.00	175.00
	1893 M	5,917	40.00	60.00	80.00	175.00
	1894 M	6,244	40.00	60.00	80.00	175.00
	1895 M	8,994	40.00	60.00	80.00	175.00
	1895 B Inc. Ab.		40.00	60.00	80.00	175.00
	1896 B	7,166	40.00	60.00	80.00	175.00
	1896 M Inc. Ab.		40.00	60.00	80.00	175.00
	1897 M	5,131	40.00	60.00	80.00	175.00
	1898/7 M	5,368	40.00	60.00	80.00	175.00
	1899 M	9,515	40.00	60.00	80.00	175.00
	1900/800 M	9,301	40.00	60.00	80.00	175.00
	1900/880 M Inc. Ab.		40.00	60.00	80.00	175.00
	1900/890 M Inc. Ab.		40.00	60.00	80.00	175.00
	1900 M Inc. Ab.		40.00	60.00	80.00	175.00

KM#	Date	Mintage	Fine	VF	XF	Unc
410.5	1901/801 M large date					
		8,293	40.00	60.00	80.00	175.00
	1901 M small date					
		Inc. Ab.	40.00	60.00	80.00	175.00
	1902 M large date					
		.011	40.00	60.00	80.00	175.00
	1902 M small date					
		Inc. Ab.	40.00	60.00	80.00	175.00
	1903 M large date					
		.010	40.00	60.00	80.00	175.00
	1903 M small date					
		Inc. Ab.	50.00	80.00	120.00	180.00
	1904 M	9,845	40.00	60.00	80.00	175.00
	1905 M	3,429	40.00	60.00	80.00	175.00

Mint mark: Zs

KM#	Date	Mintage	Fine	VF	XF	Unc
410.6	1872 H	2,024	125.00	150.00	175.00	250.00
	1875/3 A	—	125.00	150.00	200.00	300.00
	1878 S	—	125.00	150.00	175.00	250.00
	1888 Z	280 pcs.	175.00	225.00	300.00	650.00
	1889 Z	492 pcs.	150.00	175.00	225.00	425.00
	1890 Z	738 pcs.	150.00	175.00	225.00	425.00

2-1/2 PESOS

4.2300 g, .875 GOLD, .1190 oz AGW
Mint mark: As

KM#	Date	Mintage	Fine	VF	XF	Unc
411	1888 As/MoL	—	—	—	Rare	—

Mint mark: Cn

411.1	1893 M	141 pcs.	1500.	2000.	2500.	3500.

Mint mark: Do

411.2	1888 C	—	—	—	Rare	—

Mint mark: Go

411.3	1871 S	600 pcs.	1250.	2000.	2500.	3250.
	1888 Go/MoR					
		110 pcs.	1750.	2250.	2750.	3500.

Mint mark: Ho

411.4	1874 R	—	—	—	Rare	—
	1888 G	—	—	—	Rare	—

Mint mark: Mo

411.5	1870 C					
		820 pcs.	150.00	250.00	350.00	650.00
	1872 M/C					
		800 pcs.	150.00	250.00	350.00	650.00
	1873/2 M	—	200.00	350.00	750.00	1250.
	1874 M	—	200.00	350.00	750.00	1250.
	1874 B/M	—	200.00	350.00	750.00	1250.
	1875 B	—	200.00	350.00	750.00	1250.
	1876 B	—	250.00	500.00	1000.	1500.
	1877 M	—	200.00	350.00	750.00	1250.
	1878 M					
		400 pcs.	200.00	350.00	750.00	1250.
	1879 M	—	200.00	350.00	750.00	1250.
	1880/79 M	—	200.00	350.00	750.00	1250.
	1881 M					
		400 pcs.	200.00	350.00	750.00	1250.
	1882 M	—	200.00	350.00	750.00	1250.
	1883/73 M					
		400 pcs.	200.00	350.00	750.00	1250.
	1884 M	—	250.00	500.00	1000.	1500.
	1885 M	—	200.00	350.00	750.00	1250.
	1886 M					
		400 pcs.	200.00	350.00	750.00	1250.
	1887 M					
		400 pcs.	200.00	350.00	750.00	1250.
	1888 M					
		540 pcs.	200.00	350.00	750.00	1250.
	1889 M					
		240 pcs.	150.00	300.00	525.00	850.00
	1890 M					
		420 pcs.	200.00	350.00	750.00	1250.
	1891 M					
		188 pcs.	200.00	350.00	750.00	1250

KM#	Date	Mintage	Fine	VF	XF	Unc
	1892 M					
		240 pcs.	200.00	350.00	750.00	1250.

Mint mark: Zs

411.6	1872 H	1,300	200.00	350.00	500.00	1000.
	1873 H	—	175.00	325.00	450.00	700.00
	1875/3 A	—	200.00	350.00	750.00	1250.
	1877 S	—	200.00	350.00	750.00	1250.
	1878 S	300 pcs.	200.00	350.00	750.00	1250.
	1888 Zs/MoS					
		80 pcs.	300.00	500.00	1000.	1750.
	1889 Zs/MoZ					
		184 pcs.	250.00	450.00	950.00	1500.
	1890 Z	326 pcs.	200.00	350.00	750.00	1250.

CINCO (5) PESOS

8.4600 g, .875 GOLD, .2380 oz AGW
Mint mark: As

KM#	Date	Mintage	Fine	VF	XF	Unc
412	1875 L	—	—	—	—	—
	1878 L	383 pcs.	900.00	1700.	3000.	4500.

Mint mark: Ca

412.1	1888 M					
		120 pcs.	—	—	Rare	—

8.4600 g, .875 GOLD, .2380 oz AGW
Mint mark: Cn

412.2	1873 P	—	300.00	600.00	1000.	1500.
	1874 P	—	—	—	—	—
	1875 P	—	300.00	500.00	700.00	1250.
	1876 P	—	300.00	500.00	700.00	1250.
	1877 G	—	300.00	500.00	700.00	1250.
	1882	174 pcs.	—	—	Rare	—
	1888 M	—	500.00	1000.	1350.	2000.
	1890 M					
		435 pcs.	250.00	500.00	750.00	1250.
	1891 M	1,390	250.00	400.00	500.00	1000.
	1894 M					
		484 pcs.	250.00	500.00	750.00	1600.
	1895 M					
		142 pcs.	500.00	750.00	1500.	2500.
	1900 Q	1,536	200.00	300.00	400.00	950.00
	1903 Q	1,000	200.00	300.00	400.00	800.00

Mintmark: Do

412.3	1873/2 P	—	700.00	1250.	1800.	3000.
	1877 P	—	700.00	1250.	1800.	3000.
	1878 E	—	700.00	1250.	1800.	3000.
	1879/7 B	—	700.00	1250.	1800.	3000.
	1879 B	—	700.00	1250.	1800.	3000.

Mint mark: Go

412.4	1871 S	1,600	400.00	800.00	1250.	2500.
	1887 M					
		140 pcs.	600.00	1200.	1500.	2750.
	1888 R	65 pcs.	—	—	Rare	—
	1893 R	16 pcs.	—	—	Rare	—

Mint mark: Ho

412.5	1874 R	—	1750.	2500.	3000.	4500.
	1877 R					
		990 pcs.	750.00	1250.	2000.	3000.
	1877 A	Inc. Ab.	650.00	1100.	1750.	2750.
	1888 G	—	—	—	Rare	—

Mint mark: Mo

412.6	1870 C					
		550 pcs.	200.00	400.00	550.00	900.00
	1871/69 M					
		1,600	175.00	350.00	475.00	750.00
	1871 M	Inc. Ab.	175.00	350.00	475.00	750.00
	1872 M	1,600	175.00	350.00	475.00	750.00
	1873/2 M	—	200.00	400.00	550.00	850.00
	1874 M	—	200.00	400.00	550.00	850.00

KM#	Date	Mintage	Fine	VF	XF	Unc
412.6	1875/3 B/M	—	200.00	400.00	550.00	950.00
	1875 B	—	200.00	400.00	550.00	950.00
	1876/5 B/M	—	200.00	400.00	550.00	1000.
	1877 M	—	250.00	450.00	750.00	1250.
	1878/7 M					
		400 pcs.	200.00	400.00	550.00	1250.
	1878 M Inc. Ab.	200.00	400.00	550.00	1250.	
	1879/8 M	—	200.00	400.00	550.00	1250.
	1880 M	—	200.00	400.00	550.00	1250.
	1881 M	—	200.00	400.00	550.00	1250.
	1882 M					
		200 pcs.	250.00	450.00	750.00	1250.
	1883 M					
		200 pcs.	250.00	450.00	750.00	1250.
	1884 M	—	250.00	450.00	750.00	1250.
	1886 M					
		200 pcs.	250.00	450.00	750.00	1250.
	1887 M					
		200 pcs.	250.00	450.00	750.00	1250.
	1888 M					
		250 pcs.	200.00	400.00	550.00	1250.
	1889 M					
		190 pcs.	250.00	450.00	750.00	1250.
	1890 M					
		149 pcs.	250.00	450.00	750.00	1250.
	1891 M					
		156 pcs.	250.00	450.00	750.00	1250.
	1892 M					
		214 pcs.	250.00	450.00	750.00	1250.
	1893 M	1,058	200.00	400.00	500.00	800.00
	1897 M					
		370 pcs.	200.00	400.00	550.00	1000.
	1898 M					
		376 pcs.	200.00	400.00	550.00	1000.
	1900 M	1,014	175.00	350.00	450.00	750.00
	1901 M	1,071	175.00	350.00	450.00	750.00
	1902 M	1,478	175.00	350.00	450.00	750.00
	1903 M	1,162	175.00	350.00	450.00	750.00
	1904 M	1,415	175.00	350.00	450.00	750.00
	1905 M					
		563 pcs.	200.00	400.00	550.00	1500.

Mint mark: Zs

KM#	Date	Mintage	Fine	VF	XF	Unc
412.7	1874 A	—	250.00	500.00	750.00	1500.
	1875 A	—	200.00	400.00	500.00	1000.
	1877 S/A	—	200.00	400.00	550.00	1000.
	1878/7 S/A	—	200.00	400.00	550.00	1000.
	1883 S	—	175.00	375.00	500.00	750.00
	1888 Z	70 pcs.	1000.	1500.	2000.	3000.
	1889 Z					
		373 pcs.	200.00	300.00	500.00	850.00
	1892 Z	1,229	200.00	300.00	450.00	750.00

DIEZ (10) PESOS

16.9200 g, .875 GOLD, .4760 oz AGW
Mint mark: As
Rev: Balance scale.

KM#	Date	Mintage	Fine	VF	XF	Unc
413	1874 DL	—	—	—	Rare	—
	1875 L	642 pcs.	600.00	1250.	2500.	3500.
	1878 L	977 pcs.	500.00	1000.	2000.	3000.
	1879 L	1,078	500.00	1000.	2000.	3000.
	1880 L	2,629	500.00	1000.	2000.	3000.
	1881 L	2,574	500.00	1000.	2000.	3000.
	1882 L	3,403	500.00	1000.	2000.	3000.
	1883 L	3,597	500.00	1000.	2000.	3000.
	1884 L	—	—	—	Rare	—
	1885 L	4,562	500.00	1000.	2000.	3000.
	1886 L	4,643	500.00	1000.	2000.	3000.
	1887 L	3,667	500.00	1000.	2000.	3000.
	1888 L	4,521	500.00	1000.	2000.	3000.
	1889 L	5,615	500.00	1000.	2000.	3000.
	1890 L	4,920	500.00	1000.	2000.	3000.
	1891 L	568 pcs.	500.00	1000.	2000.	3000.
	1892 L	—	—	—	—	—
	1893 L	817 pcs.	500.00	1000.	2000.	3000.
	1894/3 L	1,658	—	—	—	—
	1894 L Inc. Ab.	500.00	1000.	2000.	3000.	
	1895 L	1,237	500.00	1000.	2000.	3000.

Mint mark: Ca

KM#	Date	Mintage	Fine	VF	XF	Unc
413.1	1888 M	175 pcs.	—	—	7500.	—

16.9200 g, .875 GOLD, .4760 oz AGW
Mint mark: Cn

KM#	Date	Mintage	Fine	VF	XF	Unc
413.2	1881 D	—	400.00	600.00	1000.	1750.

KM#	Date	Mintage	Fine	VF	XF	Unc
	1882 D					
		874 pcs.	400.00	600.00	1000.	1750.
	1882 E Inc. Ab.	400.00	600.00	1000.	1750.	
	1883 D					
		221 pcs.	—	—	—	—
	1883 M Inc. Ab.	400.00	600.00	1000.	1750.	
	1884 D	—	400.00	600.00	1000.	1750.
	1884 M	—	400.00	600.00	1000.	1750.
	1885 M	1,235	400.00	600.00	1000.	1750.
	1886 M					
		981 pcs.	400.00	600.00	1000.	1750.
	1887 M	2,289	400.00	600.00	1000.	1750.
	1888 M					
		767 pcs.	400.00	600.00	1000.	1750.
	1889 M					
		859 pcs.	400.00	600.00	1000.	1750.
	1890 M	1,427	400.00	600.00	1000.	1750.
	1891 M					
		670 pcs.	400.00	600.00	1000.	1750.
	1892 M					
		379 pcs.	400.00	600.00	1000.	1750.
	1893 M	1,806	400.00	600.00	1000.	1750.
	1895 M					
		179 pcs.	500.00	1000.	1500.	2500.
	1903 Q					
		774 pcs.	400.00	600.00	1000.	1750.

Mint mark: Do

KM#	Date	Mintage	Fine	VF	XF	Unc
413.3	1872 P	1,755	350.00	550.00	850.00	1250.
	1873/2 P	1,091	350.00	550.00	900.00	1500.
	1873/2 M/P					
	Inc. Ab.	350.00	550.00	900.00	1500.	
	1874 M	—	350.00	550.00	900.00	1500.
	1875 M	—	350.00	550.00	900.00	1500.
	1876 M	—	450.00	750.00	1250.	2000.
	1877 P	—	350.00	550.00	900.00	1500.
	1878 E					
		582 pcs.	350.00	550.00	900.00	1500.
	1879/8 B	—	350.00	550.00	900.00	1500.
	1879 B	—	350.00	550.00	900.00	1500.
	1880 P	2,030	350.00	550.00	900.00	1500.
	1881/79 P					
		2,617	350.00	550.00	900.00	1500.
	1882 P	1,528	—	—	Rare	—
	1882 C Inc. Ab.	350.00	550.00	900.00	1500.	
	1883 C					
		793 pcs.	450.00	750.00	1250.	2000.
	1884 C					
		108 pcs.	450.00	750.00	1250.	2000.

Mint mark: Ga

KM#	Date	Mintage	Fine	VF	XF	Unc
413.4	1870 C					
		490 pcs.	500.00	800.00	1000.	1500.
	1871 C	1,910	400.00	800.00	1500.	2250.
	1872 C					
		780 pcs.	500.00	1000.	2000.	2500.
	1873 C					
		422 pcs.	500.00	1000.	2000.	3000.
	1874/3 C					
		477 pcs.	500.00	1000.	2000.	3000.
	1875 C					
		710 pcs.	500.00	1000.	2000.	3000.
	1878 A					
		183 pcs.	600.00	1200.	2500.	3500.
	1879 A					
		200 pcs.	600.00	1200.	2500.	3500.
	1880 S					
		404 pcs.	500.00	1000.	2000.	3000.
	1881 S					
		239 pcs.	600.00	1200.	2500.	3500.
	1891 S					
		196 pcs.	600.00	1200.	2500.	3500.

Mint mark: Go

KM#	Date	Mintage	Fine	VF	XF	Unc
413.5	1872 S	1,400	2000.	4000.	6500.	10,000.
	1887 R	80 pcs.	—	—	*Rare	—
	1888 R	68 pcs.	—	—	Rare	—

*NOTE: Stack's Rio Grande Sale 6-93, P/L AU realized, $12,650.

Mint mark: Ho

KM#	Date	Mintage	Fine	VF	XF	Unc
413.6	1874 R	—	—	—	Rare	—
	1876 F					
		357 pcs.	—	—	Rare	—

Mint mark: Mo

KM#	Date	Mintage	Fine	VF	XF	Unc
	1878 A					
		814 pcs.	1750.	3000.	3500.	5500.
	1879 A	—	1000.	2000.	2500.	4000.
	1880 A	—	1000.	2000.	2500.	4000.
	1881 A	—	—	—	Rare	—

Mint mark: Mo

KM#	Date	Mintage	Fine	VF	XF	Unc
413.7	1870 C					
		480 pcs.	500.00	900.00	1200.	2000.
	1872/1 M/C					
		2,100	350.00	550.00	900.00	1400.
	1873 M	—	400.00	600.00	950.00	1500.
	1874/3 M	—	400.00	600.00	950.00	1500.
	1875 B/M	—	400.00	600.00	950.00	1500.
	1876 B	—	—	—	Rare	—
	1878 M					
		300 pcs.	400.00	600.00	950.00	1500.
	1879 M	—	—	—	—	—
	1881 M					
		100 pcs.	500.00	1000.	1600.	2500.
	1882 M	—	400.00	600.00	950.00	1500.
	1883 M					
		100 pcs.	600.00	1000.	1600.	2500.
	1884 M	—	600.00	1000.	1600.	2500.
	1885 M	—	400.00	600.00	950.00	1500.
	1886 M					
		100 pcs.	600.00	1000.	1600.	2500.
	1887 M					
		100 pcs.	600.00	1000.	1625.	2750.
	1888 M					
		144 pcs.	450.00	750.00	1200.	2000.
	1889 M	88 pcs.	600.00	1000.	1600.	2500.
	1890 M					
		137 pcs.	600.00	1000.	1600.	2500.
	1891 M					
		133 pcs.	600.00	1000.	1600.	2500.
	1892 M	45 pcs.	600.00	1000.	1600.	2500.
	1893 M	1,361	350.00	550.00	900.00	1400.
	1897 M					
		239 pcs.	400.00	600.00	950.00	1500.
	1898/7 M					
		244 pcs.	425.00	625.00	1000.	1750.
	1900 M					
		733 pcs.	400.00	600.00	950.00	1500.
	1901 M					
		562 pcs.	350.00	500.00	800.00	1400.
	1902 M					
		719 pcs.	350.00	500.00	800.00	1400.
	1903 M					
		713 pcs.	350.00	500.00	800.00	1400.
	1904 M					
		694 pcs.	350.00	500.00	800.00	1400.
	1905 M					
		401 pcs.	400.00	600.00	950.00	1500.

Mint mark: Oa

KM#	Date	Mintage	Fine	VF	XF	Unc
413.8	1870 E	4,614	400.00	600.00	900.00	1350.
	1871 E	2,705	400.00	600.00	900.00	1350.
	1872 E	5,897	400.00	600.00	900.00	1350.
	1873 E	3,537	400.00	600.00	950.00	1500.
	1874 E	2,205	400.00	600.00	1200.	1800.
	1875 E					
		312 pcs.	450.00	750.00	1400.	2250.
	1876 E					
		766 pcs.	450.00	750.00	1400.	2250.
	1877 E					
		463 pcs.	450.00	750.00	1400.	2250.
	1878 E					
		229 pcs.	450.00	750.00	1400.	2250.
	1879 E					
413.8		210 pcs.	450.00	750.00	1400.	2250.
	1880 E					
		238 pcs.	450.00	750.00	1400.	2250.
	1881 E					
		961 pcs.	400.00	600.00	1200.	2000.
	1882 E					
		170 pcs.	600.00	1000.	1500.	2500.
	1883 E					
		111 pcs.	600.00	1000.	1500.	2500.
	1884 E					
		325 pcs.	450.00	750.00	1400.	2250.
	1885 E					
		370 pcs.	450.00	750.00	1400.	2250.

KM#	Date	Mintage	Fine	VF	XF	Unc
413.8	1886 E					
		400 pcs.	450.00	750.00	1400.	2250.
	1887 E	—	700.00	1250.	2250.	4000.
	1888 E	—	—	—	—	—

Mint mark: Zs

KM#	Date	Mintage	Fine	VF	XF	Unc
413.9	1871 H	2,000	350.00	550.00	850.00	1200.
	1872 H	3,092	300.00	500.00	700.00	1000.
	1873 H					
		936 pcs.	400.00	600.00	950.00	1500.
	1874 H	—	400.00	600.00	950.00	1500.
	1875/3 A	—	400.00	600.00	1000.	1750.
	1876/5 S	—	400.00	600.00	1000.	1750.
	1877 S/H					
		506 pcs.	400.00	600.00	1000.	1750.
	1878 S					
		711 pcs.	400.00	600.00	1000.	1750.
	1879/8 S	—	450.00	750.00	1400.	2250.
	1879 S	—	450.00	750.00	1400.	2250.
	1880 S	2,089	350.00	550.00	950.00	1500.
	1881 S					
		736 pcs.	400.00	600.00	1000.	1750.
	1882 S	1,599	350.00	550.00	950.00	1500.
	1883/2 S					
		256 pcs.	400.00	600.00	1000.	1750.
	1884/3 S	—	350.00	550.00	950.00	1600.
	1884 S	—	350.00	550.00	950.00	1600.
	1885 S	1,588	350.00	550.00	950.00	1500.
	1886 S	5,364	350.00	550.00	950.00	1500.
	1887 Z	2,330	350.00	550.00	950.00	1500.
	1888 Z	4,810	350.00	550.00	950.00	1500.
	1889 Z	6,154	300.00	500.00	750.00	1350.
	1890 Z	1,321	350.00	550.00	950.00	1500.
	1891 Z	1,930	350.00	550.00	950.00	1500.
	1892 Z	1,882	350.00	550.00	950.00	1500.
	1893 Z	2,899	350.00	550.00	950.00	1500.
	1894 Z	2,501	350.00	550.00	950.00	1500.
	1895 Z	1,217	350.00	550.00	950.00	1500.

VEINTE (20) PESOS

33.8400 g, .875 GOLD, .9520 oz AGW
Mint mark: As
Rev: Balance scale.

KM#	Date	Mintage	Fine	VF	XF	Unc
414	1876 L	276 pcs.	—	—	Rare	—
	1877 L	166 pcs.	—	—	Rare	—
	1878 L	—	—	—	—	—
	1888 L	—	—	—	Rare	—

Mint mark: CH, Ca

KM#	Date	Mintage	Fine	VF	XF	Unc
414.1	1872 M					
		995 pcs.	500.00	650.00	950.00	2500.
	1873 M					
		950 pcs.	500.00	650.00	950.00	2500.
	1874 M	1,116	500.00	650.00	950.00	2500.
	1875 M					
		750 pcs.	500.00	650.00	950.00	2500.
	1876 M					
		600 pcs.	500.00	800.00	1250.	2750.
	1877	55 pcs.	—	—	Rare	—
	1882 M	1,758	500.00	650.00	950.00	2500.
	1883 M					
		161 pcs.	600.00	1000.	1500.	3000.
	1884 M					
		496 pcs.	500.00	650.00	950.00	2500.
	1885 M					
		122 pcs.	600.00	1000.	1500.	3000.
	1887 M					
		550 pcs.	500.00	650.00	950.00	2500.
	1888 M					
		351 pcs.	500.00	650.00	950.00	2500.

KM#	Date	Mintage	Fine	VF	XF	Unc
413.1	1889 M	464 pcs.	500.00	650.00	950.00	2500.
	1890 M	1,209	500.00	650.00	950.00	2500.
	1891 M	2,004	500.00	600.00	900.00	2250.
	1893 M	418 pcs.	500.00	650.00	950.00	2500.
	1895 M	133 pcs.	600.00	1000.	1500.	3000.

Mint mark: Cn

KM#	Date	Mintage	Fine	VF	XF	Unc
414.2	1870 E	3,749	500.00	650.00	950.00	2000.
	1871 P	3,046	500.00	650.00	950.00	2000.
	1872 P	972 pcs.	500.00	650.00	950.00	2000.
	1873 P	1,317	500.00	650.00	950.00	2000.
	1874 P	—	500.00	650.00	950.00	2000.
	1875 P	—	600.00	1200.	1800.	2500.
	1876 P	—	500.00	650.00	950.00	2000.
	1876 G	—	500.00	650.00	950.00	2000.
	1877 G	167 pcs.	600.00	1000.	1500.	3000.
	1878	842 pcs.	—	—	Rare	—
	1881/0 D	2,039	—	—	—	—
	1881 D	Inc. Ab.	500.00	650.00	950.00	2000.
	1882/1 D	736 pcs.	500.00	650.00	950.00	2000.
	1883 M	1,836	500.00	650.00	950.00	2000.
	1884 M	—	500.00	650.00	950.00	2000.
	1885 M	544 pcs.	500.00	650.00	950.00	2000.
	1886 M	882 pcs.	500.00	650.00	950.00	2000.
	1887 M	837 pcs.	500.00	650.00	950.00	2000.
	1888 M	473 pcs.	500.00	650.00	950.00	2000.
	1889 M	1,376	500.00	650.00	950.00	2000.
	1890 M	—	500.00	650.00	950.00	2000.
	1891 M	237 pcs.	500.00	900.00	1200.	2250.
	1892 M	526 pcs.	500.00	650.00	950.00	2000.
	1893 M	2,062	500.00	650.00	950.00	2000.
	1894 M	4,516	500.00	650.00	950.00	2000.
	1895 M	3,193	500.00	650.00	950.00	2000.
	1896 M	4,072	500.00	650.00	950.00	2000.
	1897/6 M	959 pcs.	500.00	650.00	950.00	2000.
	1897 M	Inc. Ab.	500.00	650.00	950.00	2000.
	1898 M	1,660	500.00	650.00	950.00	2000.
	1899 M	1,243	500.00	650.00	950.00	2000.
	1899 Q	Inc. Ab.	500.00	900.00	1200.	2250.
	1900 Q	1,558	500.00	650.00	950.00	2000.
	1901/0 Q	1,496	—	—	—	—
	1901 Q	Inc. Ab.	500.00	650.00	950.00	2000.
	1902 Q	1,059	500.00	650.00	950.00	2000.
	1903 Q	1,121	500.00	650.00	950.00	2000.
	1904 H	4,646	500.00	650.00	950.00	2000.
	1905 P	1,738	500.00	900.00	1200.	2250.

Mint mark: Do

KM#	Date	Mintage	Fine	VF	XF	Unc
414.3	1870 P	416 pcs.	1000.	1500.	2000.	2500.
	1871/0 P	1,073	1000.	1750.	2250.	2750.
	1871 P	Inc. Ab.	1000.	1500.	2000.	2500.
	1872/1 PT	—	1500.	3000.	4500.	7000.
	1876 M	—	1000.	1500.	2000.	2500.
	1877 P	94 pcs.	1500.	2250.	2750.	3250.
	1878	258 pcs.	—	—	Rare	—

Mint mark: Go

KM#	Date	Mintage	Fine	VF	XF	Unc
414.4	1870 S	3,250	500.00	650.00	900.00	1250.
	1871 S	.020	500.00	650.00	900.00	1250.
	1872 S	.018	500.00	650.00	900.00	1250.
	1873 S	7,000	500.00	650.00	900.00	1250.
	1874 S	—	500.00	650.00	900.00	1250.
	1875 S	—	500.00	650.00	900.00	1250.
	1876 S	—	500.00	650.00	900.00	1250.
	1876 M/S	—	—	—	—	—
	1877 M/S	.015	—	—	Rare	—
	1877 R	Inc. Ab.	500.00	650.00	900.00	1250.
	1877 S	Inc. Ab.	—	—	Rare	—
	1878/7 M/S	.013	650.00	1250.	2000.	2800.
	1878 M	Inc. Ab.	650.00	1250.	2000.	2800.
414.4	1878 S	Inc. Ab.	500.00	650.00	900.00	1250.
	1879 S	8,202	500.00	800.00	1200.	2300.
	1880 S	7,375	500.00	650.00	900.00	1250.
	1881 S	4,909	500.00	650.00	900.00	1250.
	1882 S	4,020	500.00	650.00	900.00	1250.
	1883/2 B	3,705	550.00	750.00	1150.	2250.
	1883 B	Inc. Ab.	500.00	650.00	900.00	1250.
	1884 B	1,798	500.00	650.00	900.00	1250.
	1885 R	2,660	500.00	650.00	900.00	1250.
	1886 R	1,090	550.00	800.00	1250.	2500.
	1887 R	1,009	550.00	800.00	1250.	2500.
	1888 R	1,011	550.00	800.00	1250.	2500.
	1889 R	956 pcs.	550.00	800.00	1250.	2500.
	1890 R	879 pcs.	550.00	800.00	1250.	2500.
	1891 R	818 pcs.	550.00	800.00	1250.	2500.
	1892 R	730 pcs.	550.00	800.00	1250.	2500.
	1893 R	3,343	500.00	650.00	1000.	2000.
	1894/3 R	6,734	500.00	650.00	900.00	1250.
	1894 R	I.A.	500.00	650.00	900.00	1250.
	1895/3 R	7,118	500.00	650.00	900.00	1250.
	1895 R	I.A.	500.00	650.00	900.00	1250.
	1896 R	9,219	500.00	650.00	900.00	1250.
	1897/6 R	6,781	500.00	650.00	900.00	1250.
	1897 R	I.A.	500.00	650.00	900.00	1250.
	1898 R	7,710	500.00	650.00	900.00	1250.
	1899 R	8,527	500.00	650.00	900.00	1250.
	1900 R	4,512	550.00	800.00	1250.	2350.

Mint mark: Ho

KM#	Date	Mintage	Fine	VF	XF	Unc
414.5	1874 R	—	—	—	Rare	—
	1875 R	—	—	—	Rare	—
	1876 F	—	—	—	Rare	—
	1888 G	—	—	—	Rare	—

33.8400 g, .875 GOLD, .9520 oz AGW
Mint mark: Mo

KM#	Date	Mintage	Fine	VF	XF	Unc
414.6	1870 C	.014	500.00	600.00	800.00	1300.
	1871 M	.021	500.00	600.00	800.00	1300.
	1872/1 M	.011	500.00	600.00	800.00	1600.
	1872 M	I.A.	500.00	600.00	800.00	1300.
	1873 M	5,600	500.00	600.00	800.00	1300.
	1874/2 M	—	500.00	600.00	800.00	1350.
	1874/2 B	—	500.00	700.00	1000.	1600.
	1875 B	—	500.00	650.00	900.00	1500.
	1876 B	—	500.00	650.00	900.00	1500.
	1876 M	—	—	Reported, not confirmed		
	1877 M	2,000	500.00	700.00	1100.	2000.
	1878 M	7,000	500.00	650.00	900.00	1500.
	1879 M	—	500.00	650.00	900.00	1750.
	1880 M	—	500.00	650.00	900.00	1750.
	1881/0 M	.011	500.00	600.00	800.00	1350.
	1881 M	I.A.	500.00	600.00	800.00	1350.
	1882/1 M	5,800	500.00	600.00	800.00	1350.
	1882 M	I.A.	500.00	600.00	800.00	1350.
	1883/1 M	4,000	500.00	600.00	800.00	1350.
	1883 M	I.A.	500.00	600.00	800.00	1250.
	1884/3 M	—	500.00	650.00	900.00	1400.
	1884 M	—	500.00	650.00	900.00	1400.
	1885 M	6,000	500.00	650.00	900.00	1750.
	1886 M	.010	500.00	600.00	800.00	1500.
	1887 M	.012	600.00	800.00	1500.	2500.
	1888 M	7,300	500.00	600.00	800.00	1500.
	1889 M	6,477	500.00	600.00	900.00	1650.
	1890 M	7,852	500.00	600.00	800.00	1500.
	1891/0 M	8,725	500.00	600.00	800.00	1500.
	1891 M	I.A.	500.00	600.00	800.00	1500.
	1892 M	.011	500.00	600.00	800.00	1300.
	1893 M	.015	500.00	600.00	800.00	1300.
	1894 M	.014	500.00	600.00	800.00	1300.
	1895 M	.013	500.00	600.00	800.00	1300.
	1896 B	.014	500.00	600.00	800.00	1300.
	1897/6 M	.012	500.00	600.00	800.00	1300.
	1897 M	I.A.	500.00	600.00	800.00	1300.
	1898 M	.020	500.00	600.00	800.00	1300.
	1899 M	.023	500.00	600.00	800.00	1300.
	1900 M	.021	500.00	600.00	800.00	1300.
	1901 M	.029	500.00	600.00	800.00	1300.
	1902 M	.038	500.00	600.00	800.00	1300.
	1903/2 M	.031	500.00	600.00	800.00	1300.
	1903 M	I.A.	500.00	600.00	800.00	1300.

KM#	Date	Mintage	Fine	VF	XF	Unc
414.6	1904 M	.052	500.00	600.00	800.00	1300.
	1905 M	9,757	500.00	600.00	800.00	1300.
	Mint mark: Oa					
414.7	1870 E	1,131	750.00	1500.	2500.	5000.
	1871 E	1,591	750.00	1500.	2500.	5000.
	1872 E					
		255 pcs.	1000.	1750.	3000.	7000.
	1888 E					
		170 pcs.	2000.	3000.	5000.	—

KM#	Date	Mintage	Fine	VF	XF	Unc
	Mint mark: Zs					
414.8	1871 H	1,000	3500.	6500.	7000.	9000.
	1875 A	—	4000.	6000.	7500.	9500.
	1878 S					
		441 pcs.	4000.	6000.	7500.	9500.
	1888 Z	50 pcs.	—	—	Rare	—
	1889 Z					
		640 pcs.	3500.	5500.	7000.	9000.

United States of Mexico

PRICING SECTION

MINT MARK

o
M - Mexico City

CENTAVO

BRONZE, 20mm

KM#	Date	Mintage	Fine	VF	XF	Unc
415	1905	6.040	3.25	5.75	12.50	95.00
	1906 narrow date					
		*67.505	.50	.75	1.25	14.00
	1906 wide date					
		Inc. Ab.	.65	1.25	2.25	22.00
	1910	8.700	1.50	2.50	6.50	90.00
	1911	16.450	.60	1.00	2.75	22.50
	1912	12.650	.75	1.25	3.00	32.00
	1913	12.850	.65	1.00	2.75	33.00
	1914	17.350	.60	.85	2.50	14.50
	1915	2.277	9.00	21.50	65.00	300.00
	1916	.500	40.00	72.00	160.00	1200.
	1920	1.433	20.00	45.00	100.00	400.00
	1921	3.470	4.25	13.50	42.50	275.00
	1922	1.880	8.00	15.00	45.00	300.00
	1923	4.800	.50	.75	1.75	13.50
	1924/3	2.000	50.00	140.00	250.00	500.00
	1924	Inc. Ab.	4.00	10.00	20.00	275.00
	1925	1.550	3.75	9.25	22.00	225.00
	1926	5.000	.90	1.75	3.50	26.00
	1927/6	6.000	25.00	40.00	60.00	140.00
	1927	Inc. Ab.	.60	1.25	4.50	36.00
	1928	5.000	.60	.80	3.25	16.50
	1929	4.500	.60	.80	1.75	18.00
	1930	7.000	.75	1.00	2.25	19.00
	1933	10.000	.25	.35	1.75	16.50
	1934	7.500	.40	.95	3.25	35.00
	1935	12.400	.15	.25	.40	11.50
	1936	20.100	.15	.20	.30	8.00
	1937	20.000	.15	.25	.35	3.50
	1938	10.000	.10	.15	.30	2.25
	1939	30.000	.10	.20	.30	1.25
	1940	10.000	.20	.30	.60	6.50
	1941	15.800	.15	.25	.35	2.25
	1942	30.400	.15	.20	.30	1.25
	1943	4.310	.30	.50	.75	9.00
	1944	5.645	.15	.25	.50	7.00
	1945	26.375	.10	.15	.25	1.00
	1946	42.135	—	.15	.20	.60
	1947	13.445	—	.10	.15	.80
	1948	20.040	—	.15	.30	1.10
	1949	6.235	.10	.15	.30	1.75

*NOTE: 50,000,000 pcs. were struck at the Birmingham Mint.

NOTE: Varieties exist. Wide and narrow dates exist for 1911 and 1914.

Zapata Issue
Reduced size, 16mm.

416	1915	.179	16.00	27.50	50.00	75.50

BRASS, 16mm

KM#	Date	Mintage	VF	XF	Unc	BU
417	1950	12.815	.15	.30	1.75	2.00
	1951	25.740	.15	.25	.65	1.10
	1952	24.610	.10	.25	.40	.75
	1953	21.160	.10	.25	.40	.85
	1954	25.675	.10	.15	.85	1.20
	1955	9.820	.15	.25	.85	1.50
	1956	11.285	.15	.25	.80	1.45
	1957	9.805	.15	.25	.85	1.35
	1958	12.155	.10	.25	.45	.80
	1959	11.875	.10	.25	.75	1.25
	1960	10.360	.10	.15	.40	.65
	1961	6.385	.10	.15	.45	.85
	1962	4.850	.10	.15	.55	.90
	1963	7.775	.10	.15	.25	.45
	1964	4.280	.10	.15	.20	.35
	1965	2.255	.10	.15	.25	.40
	1966	1.760	.10	.25	.60	.75
	1967	1.290	.10	.15	.40	.70
	1968	1.000	.10	.20	.85	1.25
	1969	1.000	.10	.15	.75	1.25

Reduced size, 13mm.

418	1970	1.000	.20	.40	1.30	1.80
	1972	1.000	.20	.45	2.50	3.25
	1972/2	—	.50	1.25	3.25	5.00
	1973	1.000	1.65	2.75	8.00	9.75

2 CENTAVOS

BRONZE, 25mm

KM#	Date	Mintage	Fine	VF	XF	Unc
419	1905	.050	125.00	275.00	425.00	1200.
	1906/inverted 6					
		9.998	25.00	50.00	110.00	375.00
	1906 wide date					
		I.A.	4.00	10.00	21.50	80.00
	1906 narrow date					
		*I.A.	6.50	12.50	25.00	85.00
	1920	1.325	6.50	21.50	60.00	350.00
	1921	4.275	2.50	4.75	10.00	90.00
	1922	—	275.00	600.00	1500.	4000.
	1924	.750	8.50	20.00	55.00	450.00
	1925	3.650	2.50	3.50	9.00	40.00
	1926	4.750	1.00	2.25	5.50	35.00
	1927	7.250	.60	1.00	4.50	22.75
	1928	3.250	.75	1.50	3.75	25.00
	1929	.250	55.00	150.00	550.00	1000.
	1935	1.250	4.25	9.25	22.50	200.00
	1939	5.000	.60	.90	2.25	20.00
	1941	3.550	.45	.60	1.25	18.00

*NOTE: 5,000,000 pcs. were struck at the Birmingham Mint.

KM#	Date	Mintage	Fine	VF	XF	Unc
422	1931	—	525.00	725.00	1150.	3250.
	1933	8.000	1.25	2.00	3.25	25.00
	1934	10.000	1.00	1.50	2.50	22.50
	1935	21.980	.75	1.20	2.25	22.50

Zapata Issue
Reduced size, 20mm.

420	1915	.487	6.50	9.00	13.50	65.00

COPPER-NICKEL

KM#	Date	Mintage	VF	XF	Unc	BU
423	1936	46.700	.65	1.25	6.50	9.00
	1937	49.060	.50	1.00	6.00	9.00
	1938	3.340	5.00	12.50	65.00	250.00
	1940	22.800	.75	1.50	8.00	12.00
	1942	7.100	1.50	3.20	35.00	45.00

5 CENTAVOS

BRONZE
'Josefa' Ortiz de Dominguez

KM#	Date	Mintage	VF	XF	Unc	BU
424	1942	.900	20.00	60.00	375.00	525.00
	1943	54.660	.40	.65	3.00	4.00
	1944	53.463	.25	.35	.75	1.00
	1945	44.262	.25	.35	.90	1.65
	1946	49.054	.50	.75	2.00	2.75
	1951	50.758	.60	.85	3.00	4.75
	1952	17.674	1.25	2.25	9.25	11.50
	1953	31.568	1.10	1.75	7.00	10.00
	1954	58.680	.40	.75	2.75	4.00
	1955	31.114	1.85	2.50	11.00	15.00

NICKEL

421	1905	1.420	6.00	9.50	22.50	290.00
	1906/5	10.615	12.00	23.50	60.00	375.00
	1906	*Inc. Ab.	.75	1.20	3.25	50.00
	1907	4.000	1.25	3.50	10.00	350.00
	1909	2.052	3.25	9.50	42.50	360.00
	1910	6.181	1.15	3.20	5.50	77.00
	1911 narrow date					
		4.487	.75	3.00	5.00	85.00
	1911 wide date					
		Inc. Ab.	2.50	4.25	9.00	110.00
	1912 small mint mark					
		.420	97.50	120.00	210.00	725.00
	1912 large mint mark					
		Inc. Ab.	60.00	85.00	160.00	575.00
	1913	2.035	1.65	3.75	9.00	100.00
	1914	2.000	.75	1.75	3.50	65.00

NOTE: 5,000,000 pcs. appear to have been struck at the Birmingham Mint in 1914 and all of 1909-1911. The Mexican Mint report does not mention receiving the 1914 dated coins.

NOTE: Varieties exist. Wide and narrow dates exist for 1913.

COPPER-NICKEL
'White Josefa'

425	1950	5.700	.75	1.50	6.25	8.00

NOTE: 5,600,000 pieces struck at Connecticut melted.

BRONZE

422	1914	2.500	10.00	21.50	45.00	250.00
	1915	11.424	2.50	4.50	14.50	145.00
	1916	2.860	13.50	32.00	170.00	690.00
	1917	.800	60.00	150.00	320.00	820.00
	1918	1.332	32.00	80.00	200.00	625.00
	1919	.400	100.00	190.00	335.00	925.00
	1920	5.920	3.00	7.50	40.00	285.00
	1921	2.080	9.00	21.50	70.00	275.00
	1924	.780	35.00	80.00	235.00	625.00
	1925	4.040	4.75	10.00	42.50	225.00
	1926	3.160	5.50	11.00	43.50	300.00
	1927	3.600	3.25	6.75	27.50	220.00
	1928 large date					
		1.740	10.00	17.50	68.00	250.00
	1928 small date					
		Inc. Ab.	25.00	45.00	90.00	385.00
	1929	2.400	4.75	10.00	40.00	180.00
	1930 large oval 0 in date					
		2.600	4.00	7.50	27.50	210.00
	1930 small square 0 in date					
		Inc. Ab.	50.00	115.00	220.00	565.00

BRASS

426	1954 dot	—	9.00	32.00	325.00	375.00
	1954 w/o dot	—	12.00	25.00	250.00	290.00
	1955	12.136	.75	1.50	9.00	12.50
	1956	60.216	.20	.30	.90	1.50
	1957	55.288	.15	.20	.90	1.50
	1958	104.624	.15	.20	.60	1.00
	1959	106.000	.15	.25	.90	1.50
	1960	99.144	.10	.15	.50	.75
	1961	61.136	.10	.15	.40	.70
	1962	47.232	.10	.15	.30	.55
	1963	156.680	—	.15	.20	.35
	1964	71.168	—	.15	.20	.40
	1965	155.720	—	.15	.25	.35
	1966	124.944	—	.15	.40	.65
	1967	118.816	—	.15	.25	.40
	1968	189.588	—	.15	.50	.75
	1969	210.492	—	.15	.55	.80

COPPER-NICKEL

KM#	Date	Mintage	VF	XF	Unc	BU
426a	1960	— 300.00	—	—	—
	1962	19 pcs. 300.00	—	—	—

BRASS
Reduced size, 18mm.

KM#	Date	Mintage	VF	XF	Unc	BU
427	1970	163.368	.10	.15	.35	.45
	1971	198.844	.10	.15	.25	.30
	1972	225.000	.10	.15	.25	.30
	1973 flat top 3					
		595.070	.10	.15	.25	.40
	1973 round top 3					
		Inc. Ab.	.10	.15	.20	.30
	1974	401.584	.10	.15	.30	.40
	1975	342.308	.10	.15	.25	.35
	1976	367.524	.10	.15	.40	.60

NOTE: Due to some minor alloy variations this type is often encountered with a bronze color toning.

10 CENTAVOS

2.5000 g, .800 SILVER, .0643 oz ASW

	Date	Mintage	VF	XF	Unc	BU
428	1905	3.920	5.25	7.00	35.00	50.00
	1906	8.410	4.75	6.25	25.00	35.00
	1907/6	5.950	45.00	115.00	275.00	350.00
	1907	Inc. Ab.	5.50	7.75	35.00	42.50
	1909	2.620	8.00	12.50	70.00	90.00
	1910/00	3.450	12.00	35.00	75.00	100.00
	1910	Inc. Ab.	8.00	12.50	25.00	30.00
	1911 narrow date					
		2.550	10.00	15.00	88.00	125.00
	1911 wide date					
		Inc. Ab.	6.00	8.50	42.50	60.00
	1912	1.350	10.00	16.00	135.00	155.00
	1912 low 2 I.A.	8.00	16.00	125.00	150.00
	1913/2	1.990	7.75	15.00	35.00	65.00
	1913	Inc. Ab.	6.00	8.50	33.50	45.00
	1914	3.110	4.50	5.75	13.50	18.50

NOTE: Wide and narrow dates exist for 1914.

1.8125 g, .800 SILVER, .0466 oz ASW
Reduced size, 15mm.

	Date	Mintage	VF	XF	Unc	BU
429	1919	8.360	10.00	17.50	85.00	115.00

BRONZE

KM#	Date	Mintage	VF	XF	Unc	BU
430	1919	1.232	20.00	47.50	440.00	525.00
	1920	6.612	12.50	38.50	400.00	475.00
	1921	2.255	30.00	65.00	625.00	875.00
	1935	5.970	12.00	23.50	125.00	175.00

1.6600 g, .720 SILVER, .0384 oz ASW

	Date	Mintage	VF	XF	Unc	BU
431	1925/15	5.350	18.00	35.00	110.00	125.00
	1925/3	Inc. Ab.	18.00	35.00	115.00	130.00
	1925	Inc. Ab.	2.00	4.00	35.00	47.50
	1926/16	2.650	25.00	55.00	160.00	175.00
	1926	Inc. Ab.	3.50	6.00	62.50	80.00
	1927	2.810	2.25	3.00	17.50	21.50
	1928	5.270	1.75	2.25	12.00	14.25
	1930	2.000	3.75	5.00	18.75	22.50
	1933	5.000	1.50	3.00	10.00	12.50
	1934	8.000	1.75	2.25	8.00	9.50
	1935	3.500	2.75	4.00	11.50	14.00

COPPER-NICKEL

	Date	Mintage	VF	XF	Unc	BU
432	1936	33.030	.65	2.25	8.25	10.00
	1937	3.000	2.75	42.50	225.00	250.00
	1938	3.650	1.75	5.50	60.00	75.00
	1939	6.920	1.00	3.50	30.00	40.00
	1940	12.300	.40	1.00	5.00	6.50
	1942	14.380	.60	1.50	7.00	8.50
	1945	9.558	.40	.70	3.50	4.00
	1946	46.230	.25	.45	2.25	3.10

BRONZE
Benito Juarez

	Date	Mintage	VF	XF	Unc	BU
433	1955	1.818	.60	3.00	22.00	30.00
	1956	5.255	.50	3.00	22.00	35.00
	1957	11.925	.20	.40	5.50	8.00
	1959	26.140	.20	.35	.65	1.25
	1966	5.873	.15	.25	.65	1.50
	1967	32.318	.10	.15	.30	.40

COPPER-NICKEL
Variety I
Rev: 5 full rows of kernels, sharp stem, wide date.

KM#	Date	Mintage	VF	XF	Unc	BU
434.1	1974	6.000	—	.35	.85	1.00
	1975	5.550	.10	.35	.85	1.75
	1976	7.680	.10	.20	.30	.40
	1977	144.650	1.25	2.25	3.50	4.50
	1978	271.870	—	1.00	1.50	2.25
	1979	375.660	—	.50	1.00	1.75
	1980/79	21.290	2.45	3.75	6.00	7.00
	1980	I.A.	1.50	2.00	4.50	5.00

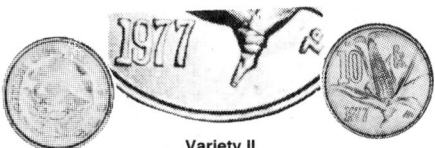

Variety II
Rev: 5 full, plus 1 partial row at left, blunt stem,
narrow date.

KM#	Date	Mintage	VF	XF	Unc	BU
434.2	1974	Inc. Ab.	—	.10	.25	.35
	1977	Inc. Ab.	—	.10	.30	.35
	1978	Inc. Ab.	—	.10	.30	.40
	1979	Inc. Ab.	.15	.50	1.00	2.00
	1980	Inc. Ab.	—	.10	.30	.35

Variety III
Rev: 5 full, plus 1 partial row, blunt
stem and wide date.

434.3	1980/79	—	—	—	—	—

Variety III
Rev: 5 full, plus 1 partial row,
sharp stem and narrow date.

434.4	1979	—	—	—	—	—

20 CENTAVOS

5.0000 g, .800 SILVER, .1286 oz ASW

435	1905	2.565	9.00	15.00	150.00	175.00
	1906	6.860	7.25	14.50	60.00	80.00
	1907 straight 7					
		4.000	8.50	17.50	70.00	100.00
	1907 curved 7					
		5.435	7.50	13.50	75.00	95.00
	1908	.350	85.00	200.00	1500.	—
	1910	1.135	9.50	15.00	80.00	95.00
	1911	1.150	14.00	32.00	125.00	150.00
	1912	.625	35.00	70.00	335.00	375.00
	1913	1.000	14.50	30.00	95.00	115.00
	1914	1.500	10.00	21.50	72.50	85.00

Reduced size, 19mm.

KM#	Date	Mintage	VF	XF	Unc	BU
436	1919	4.155	25.00	50.00	195.00	245.00

BRONZE

437	1920	4.835	40.00	110.00	650.00	725.00
	1935	20.000	5.50	8.50	95.00	135.00

3.3333 g, .720 SILVER, .0772 oz ASW

KM#	Date	Mintage	VF	XF	Unc	BU
438	1920	3.710	4.75	10.00	165.00	215.00
	1921	6.160	4.50	10.00	100.00	145.00
	1925	1.450	8.00	17.00	125.00	150.00
	1926/5	1.465	18.00	45.00	325.00	375.00
	1926	Inc. Ab.	4.50	6.25	80.00	110.00
	1927	1.405	3.75	6.25	80.00	115.00
	1928	3.630	2.50	4.50	14.50	19.50
	1930	1.000	3.50	6.25	25.00	32.00
	1933	2.500	2.25	2.75	10.00	12.50
	1934	2.500	2.25	3.00	12.00	14.00
	1935	2.460	2.25	2.75	10.00	12.50
	1937	10.000	2.25	2.50	4.75	5.50
	1939	8.800	1.75	2.00	4.00	4.50
	1940	3.000	1.75	2.00	3.50	5.00
	1941	5.740	1.50	2.00	3.00	3.50
	1942	12.460	1.50	2.00	3.25	3.80
	1943	3.955	2.00	2.50	3.50	4.25

BRONZE

439	1943	46.350	.75	2.75	18.00	25.00
	1944	83.650	.40	.65	9.00	11.00
	1945	26.801	1.10	3.50	10.50	13.00
	1946	25.695	.90	2.00	6.00	8.25
	1951	11.385	2.50	5.50	80.00	100.00
	1952	6.560	2.50	4.50	25.00	32.50
	1953	26.948	.35	.75	8.25	12.00
	1954	40.108	.35	.80	9.00	12.50
	1955	16.950	2.50	6.00	65.00	80.00

440	1955					
		Inc. KM439	.65	1.50	15.00	20.00
	1956	22.431	.30	.35	3.00	5.00
	1957	13.455	.45	1.25	9.00	12.00
	1959	6.017	4.00	7.50	65.00	95.00
	1960	39.756	.15	.25	.85	1.25
	1963	14.869	.25	.35	.90	1.25
	1964	28.654	.25	.40	.90	1.25
	1965	74.162	.20	.40	.85	1.20
	1966	43.745	.15	.25	.90	1.30
	1967	46.487	.20	.55	1.20	1.50
	1968	15.477	.30	.55	1.35	1.65
	1969	63.647	.20	.40	1.00	1.50
	1970	76.287	.15	.20	.90	1.30
	1971	49.892	.30	.50	1.40	1.75

KM#	Date	Mintage	VF	XF	Unc	BU
441	1971					
		Inc. KM440	.20	.35	1.75	2.35
	1973	78.398	.25	.35	.95	1.50
	1974	34.200	.20	.35	1.25	1.75

COPPER-NICKEL
Francisco Madero

KM#	Date	Mintage	VF	XF	Unc	BU
442	1974	112.000	.10	.15	.25	.30
	1975	611.000	.10	.15	.30	.35
	1976	394.000	.10	.15	.35	.45
	1977	394.350	.10	.15	.40	.45
	1978	527.950	.10	.15	.25	.30
	1979	524.615	.10	.15	.30	.40
	1979 Doubled die obv. large/small letters					
		—	1.25	2.00	4.00	8.00
	1980	326.500	.15	.25	.40	.60
	1981 open 8					
		106.205	.30	.50	1.00	2.00
	1981 closed 8, high date					
		248.500	.30	.50	1.00	2.00
	1981 closed 8, low date					
		—	1.00	1.50	3.50	4.25
	1981/1982	—	30.00	75.00	160.00	190.00
	1982	286.855	.40	.60	.90	1.10
	1983 round top 3					
		100.930	.25	.40	1.75	2.25
	1983 flat top 3					
		Inc. Ab.	.25	.50	1.25	1.75
	1983	998 pcs.	—	—	Proof	15.00

NOTE: The 1981/1982 overdate is often mistaken as 1982/1981.

BRONZE
Olmec Culture

KM#	Date	Mintage	VF	XF	Unc	BU
491	1983	260.000	.20	.25	.90	1.10
	1983	53 pcs.	—	—	Proof	165.00
	1984	180.320	.20	.25	1.50	1.70

25 CENTAVOS

3.3330 g, .300 SILVER, .0321 oz ASW

KM#	Date	Mintage	VF	XF	Unc	BU
443	1950	77.060	.50	.75	1.75	2.25
	1951	41.172	.50	.75	1.60	2.00
	1952	29.264	.75	1.10	1.80	2.50
	1953	38.144	.60	.70	1.50	2.00

COPPER-NICKEL
Francisco Madero

KM#	Date	Mintage	VF	XF	Unc	BU
444	1964	20.686	—	.15	.25	.40
	1966 closed beak					
		.180	.65	1.00	2.50	3.00
	1966 open beak					
		Inc. Ab.	1.75	3.50	10.00	14.00

50 CENTAVOS

12.5000 g, .800 SILVER, .3215 oz ASW

KM#	Date	Mintage	VF	XF	Unc	BU
445	1905	2.446	14.00	21.50	150.00	225.00
	1906	16.966	4.50	8.50	27.50	40.00
	1907 straight 7					
		18.920	4.50	7.25	25.00	28.50
	1907 curved 7					
		14.841	5.25	8.00	25.00	28.50
	1908	.488	65.00	150.00	525.00	625.00
	1912	3.736	10.00	12.50	45.00	60.00
	1913/07	10.510	30.00	70.00	225.00	275.00
	1913/2	Inc. Ab.	18.00	22.50	65.00	85.00
	1913	Inc. Ab.	5.50	8.50	25.00	30.00
	1914	7.710	6.75	13.50	35.00	45.00
	1916	.480	50.00	75.00	200.00	290.00
	1917	37.112	5.50	8.50	20.00	22.50
	1918	1.320	60.00	110.00	250.00	335.00

9.0625 g, .800 SILVER, .2331 oz ASW
Reduced size, 27mm.

KM#	Date	Mintage	VF	XF	Unc	BU
446	1918/7	2.760	525.00	625.00	1250.	—
	1918	Inc. Ab.	16.00	50.00	325.00	400.00
	1919	29.670	8.00	17.50	100.00	125.00

8.3333 g, .720 SILVER, .1929 oz ASW

KM#	Date	Mintage	VF	XF	Unc	BU
447	1919	10.200	8.00	18.50	87.50	110.00
	1920	27.166	6.00	8.50	75.00	85.00
	1921	21.864	6.50	9.00	85.00	100.00
	1925	3.280	14.00	30.00	130.00	160.00
	1937	20.000	3.75	5.00	7.50	8.50
	1938	.100	40.00	75.00	275.00	350.00
	1939	10.440	5.25	7.25	14.00	16.50
	1942	.800	5.50	7.50	15.00	17.00
	1943	41.512	2.75	4.00	5.50	6.50
	1944	55.806	3.00	3.75	5.50	6.50
	1945	56.766	3.00	3.75	6.00	6.50

7.9730 g, .420 SILVER, .1076 oz ASW

KM#	Date	Mintage	VF	XF	Unc	BU
448	1935	70.800	2.20	2.75	5.00	6.00

6.6600 g, .300 SILVER, .0642 oz ASW
Cuauhtemoc

KM#	Date	Mintage	VF	XF	Unc	BU
449	1950	13.570	1.50	1.80	3.00	4.00
	1951	3.650	2.00	2.50	3.75	5.00

BRONZE

KM#	Date	Mintage	VF	XF	Unc	BU
450	1955	3.502	1.20	2.20	27.50	35.00
	1956	34.643	.65	1.00	3.25	4.50
	1957	9.675	1.00	2.00	6.50	7.50
	1959	4.540	.35	.50	1.50	2.00

COPPER-NICKEL

KM#	Date	Mintage	VF	XF	Unc	BU
451	1964	43.806	.15	.20	.45	.65
	1965	14.326	.20	.25	.45	.65
	1966	1.726	.20	.40	1.30	1.75
	1967	55.144	.20	.30	.65	1.00
	1968	80.438	.15	.30	.65	.80
	1969	87.640	.20	.35	.80	1.15

Obv: Stylized eagle.

KM#	Date	Mintage	VF	XF	Unc	BU
452	1970	76.236	.15	.20	.90	1.25
	1971	125.288	.15	.20	.90	1.30
	1972	16.000	1.25	2.00	3.00	4.75
	1975 Dots					
		177.958	.60	1.25	3.50	6.00
	1975 No dots					
		Inc. Ab.	.15	.20	.50	.75
	1976 Dots					
		37,480	.75	1.25	5.00	6.00
	1976 No dots					
		Inc. Ab.	.15	.20	.50	.75
	1977	12.410	6.50	10.00	32.50	42.50
	1978	85.400	.15	.25	.50	.75
	1979 round 2nd 9 in date					
		229.000	.15	.25	.50	.65
	1979 square 9's in date					
		Inc. Ab.	.20	.40	1.60	2.10
	1980 narrow date, square 9					
		89.978	.45	.75	1.00	2.00
	1980 wide date, round 9					
		178.188	.20	.25	1.00	1.15
	1981 rectangular 9, narrow date					
		142.212	.50	.75	1.75	2.50
	1981 round 9, wide date					
		Inc. Ab.	.30	.50	1.25	1.75
	1982	45.474	.20	.40	1.50	2.40
	1983	90.318	.50	.75	2.25	2.85
	1983	998 pcs.	—	—	Proof	15.00

NOTE: Coins dated 1975 and 1976 exist with and without dots in centers of three circles on plumage on reverse. Edge varieties exist.

STAINLESS STEEL
Palenque Culture

KM#	Date	Mintage	VF	XF	Unc	BU
492	1983	99.540	—	.30	1.50	2.50
	1983	53 pcs.	—	—	Proof	165.00

UN (1) PESO

27.0700 g, .903 SILVER, .7859 oz ASW
'Caballito'

KM#	Date	Mintage	VF	XF	Unc	BU
453	1910	3.814	35.00	55.00	160.00	215.00
	1911 long lower left ray on rev.					
		1.227	40.00	65.00	200.00	235.00
	1911 short lower left ray on rev.					
		Inc. Ab.	125.00	200.00	600.00	725.00
	1912	.322	95.00	200.00	350.00	400.00
	1913/2	2.880	35.00	65.00	275.00	350.00
	1913	Inc. Ab.	35.00	60.00	180.00	220.00
	1914	.120	600.00	950.00	2750.	—

NOTE: 1913 coins exist with even and unevenly spaced date.

18.1300 g, .800 SILVER, .4663 oz ASW

454	1918	3.050	32.00	120.00	1400.	2150.
	1919	6.151	18.50	45.00	900.00	1600.

16.6600 g, .720 SILVER, .3856 oz ASW

KM#	Date	Mintage	VF	XF	Unc	BU
455	1920/10	8.830	40.00	80.00	300.00	—
	1920	Inc. Ab.	6.50	21.50	160.00	200.00
	1921	5.480	8.00	21.50	160.00	200.00
	1922	33.620	3.50	5.00	22.00	28.00
	1923	35.280	3.50	5.00	22.00	28.00
	1924	33.060	3.50	5.00	22.00	28.00
	1925	9.160	4.50	9.50	60.00	80.00
	1926	28.840	3.50	5.00	20.00	25.00
	1927	5.060	6.50	9.50	72.50	90.00
	1932	50.770	3.00	4.00	5.00	6.50
	1933/2	43.920	15.00	25.00	80.00	—
	1933	Inc. Ab.	3.00	4.00	5.25	6.75
	1934	22.070	3.75	4.50	9.50	10.50
	1935	8.050	4.50	6.00	11.50	13.50
	1938	30.000	3.00	4.00	6.00	7.25
	1940	20.000	3.00	3.50	5.00	6.00
	1943	47.662	3.00	3.25	4.50	5.00
	1944	39.522	3.00	3.50	4.50	5.00
	1945	37.300	3.00	3.50	4.50	5.00

14.0000 g, .500 SILVER, .2250 oz ASW
Jose Morelos y Pavon

KM#	Date	Mintage	VF	XF	Unc	BU
456	1947	61.460	2.00	2.75	5.00	6.00
	1948	22.915	2.50	4.00	6.00	7.00
	1949	*4.000	—	1200.	1600.	2500.
	1949	—	—	—	Proof	5000.

*NOTE: Not released for circulation.

13.3300 g, .300 SILVER, .1285 oz ASW
Jose Morelos y Pavon

457	1950	3.287	3.00	4.25	8.00	9.50

16.0000 g, .100 SILVER, .0514 oz ASW
100th Anniversary of Constitution

KM#	Date	Mintage	VF	XF	Unc	BU
458	1957	.500	4.00	5.50	14.00	18.00

Jose Morelos y Pavon

KM#	Date	Mintage	VF	XF	Unc	BU
459	1957	28.273	.75	1.00	2.25	3.00
	1958	41.899	.75	.85	1.85	2.60
	1959	27.369	1.60	2.00	5.50	7.00
	1960	26.259	.75	1.10	3.25	3.50
	1961	52.601	.60	.90	2.25	3.00
	1962	61.094	.60	.90	2.25	3.00
	1963	26.394	BV	.80	2.00	2.40
	1964	15.615	BV	.75	2.00	2.40
	1965	5.004	BV	.65	1.85	2.10
	1966	30.998	BV	.65	1.85	2.25
	1967	9.308	BV	.65	2.75	3.50

COPPER-NICKEL

Jose Morelos y Pavon

KM#	Date	Mintage	VF	XF	Unc	BU
460	1970 narrow date					
		102.715	.25	.35	.75	.90
	1970 wide date					
		Inc. Ab.	1.25	2.50	8.00	10.00
	1971	426.222	.20	.25	.50	.65
	1972	120.000	.20	.25	.40	.65
	1974	63.700	.20	.25	.65	.90

1975 tall narrow date					
	205.979	.25	.45	1.00	1.35

1975 short wide date					
	Inc. Ab.	.30	.40	.75	1.00
1976	94.489	.15	.20	.50	.75
1977 thick date					
	94.364	.25	.45	1.00	1.25
1977 thin date					
	Inc. Ab.	1.00	1.75	4.50	12.00
1978 closed 8					
	208.300	.20	.30	1.00	1.15
1978 open 8					
	55.140	.75	1.25	9.00	15.00
1979 thin date					
	117.884	.20	.30	1.25	1.75
1979 thick date					
	Inc. Ab.	.40	.60	1.45	1.90
1980 closed 8					
	318.800	.25	.35	.80	1.00
1980 open 8					
	23.865	.75	1.50	9.00	12.75
1981 closed 8					
	413.349	.20	.30	.85	1.00
1981 open 8					
	58.616	.50	1.25	7.00	8.50
1982	235.000	.25	.75	2.25	2.50
1983 wide date					
	100.000	.50	1.10	3.00	3.50
1983 narrow date					
	Inc. Ab.	.30	.45	3.25	3.75
1983	1,051	—	—	Proof	15.00

STAINLESS STEEL
Jose Morelos y Pavon

KM#	Date	Mintage	VF	XF	Unc	BU
496	1984	722.802	.10	.25	.80	1.00
	1985	985.000	.10	.25	.50	.75
	1986	740.000	.10	.25	.50	.75
	1987	250.000	—	.25	.50	.80
	1987	2 known	—	—	Proof	1250.

DOS (2) PESOS

1.6666 g, .900 GOLD, .0482 oz AGW

KM#	Date	Mintage	Fine	VF	XF	Unc
461	1919	1.670	—	BV	25.00	32.00
	1920	4.282	—	BV	25.00	32.00
	1944	.010	27.50	35.00	50.00	80.00
	1945	*.140	—	—	BV + 20%	
	1946	.168	30.00	45.00	55.00	80.00
	1947	.025	27.50	35.00	50.00	65.00
	1948	.045	—	no specimens known		

*NOTE: During 1951-1972 a total of 4,590,493 pieces were restruck, most likely dated 1945. In 1996 matte restrikes were produced.

26.6667 g, .900 SILVER, .7717 oz ASW
Centennial of Independence

KM#	Date	Mintage	VF	XF	Unc	BU
462	1921	1.278	30.00	55.00	300.00	400.00

DOS Y MEDIO (2-1/2) PESOS

2.0833 g, .900 GOLD, .0602 oz AGW

KM#	Date	Mintage	Fine	VF	XF	Unc
463	1918	1.704	—	BV	28.00	45.00
	1919	.984	—	BV	28.00	45.00
	1920/10	.607	—	BV	55.00	100.00
	1920	Inc. Ab.	—	BV	28.00	45.00
	1944	.020	—	BV	28.00	45.00
	1945	*.180	—	—	BV + 18%	
	1946	.163	—	BV	28.00	45.00
	1947	.024	200.00	265.00	325.00	500.00
	1948	.063	BV	35.00	40.00	65.00

*NOTE: During 1951-1972 a total of 5,025,087 pieces were restruck, most likely dated 1945. In 1996 matte restrikes were produced.

CINCO (5) PESOS

4.1666 g, .900 GOLD, .1205 oz AGW

KM#	Date	Mintage	Fine	VF	XF	Unc
464	1905	.018	100.00	150.00	200.00	500.00
	1906	4.638	—	BV	50.00	70.00
	1907	1.088	—	BV	50.00	70.00
	1910	.100	BV	55.00	70.00	120.00
	1918/7	.609	BV	55.00	70.00	120.00
	1918	Inc. Ab.	—	BV	50.00	70.00
	1919	.506	—	BV	50.00	70.00
	1920	2.385	—	BV	50.00	70.00
	1955	*.048	—	—	BV + 11%	

*NOTE: During 1955-1972 a total of 1,767,645 pieces were restruck, most likely dated 1955. In 1996 matte restrikes were produced.

30.0000 g, .900 SILVER, .8681 oz ASW
Cuauhtemoc

KM#	Date	Mintage	VF	XF	Unc	BU
465	1947	5.110	BV	6.25	8.75	9.75
	1948	26.740	BV	6.00	8.00	8.75

27.7800 g, .720 SILVER, .6431 oz ASW
Opening of Southern Railroad

KM#	Date	Mintage	VF	XF	Unc	BU
466	1950	.200	30.00	35.00	45.00	55.00

NOTE: It is recorded that 100,000 pieces were melted to be used for the 1968 Mexican Olympic 25 Pesos.

Miguel Hidalgo y Costilla

KM#	Date	Mintage	VF	XF	Unc	BU
467	1951	4.958	BV	5.75	7.50	10.00
	1952	9.595	BV	5.50	7.00	9.50
	1953	20.376	BV	5.25	7.00	9.50
	1954	.030	30.00	50.00	75.00	85.00

Bicentennial of Hidalgo's Birth

KM#	Date	Mintage	VF	XF	Unc	BU
468	1953	1.000	BV	5.50	7.50	10.00

18.0500 g, .720 SILVER, .4178 oz ASW
Reduced size, 36mm.

469	1955	4.271	3.75	4.25	4.75	7.00
	1956	4.596	3.75	4.25	4.75	7.00
	1957	3.464	3.75	4.25	4.75	7.00

100th Anniversary of Constitution

KM#	Date	Mintage	VF	XF	Unc	BU
470	1957	.200	6.00	8.00	14.00	16.00

Centennial of Carranza's Birth

KM#	Date	Mintage	VF	XF	Unc	BU
471	1959	1.000	BV	5.00	7.00	9.50

Small date   Large date
COPPER-NICKEL
Vicente Guerrero

KM#	Date	Mintage	VF	XF	Unc	BU
472	1971	28.457	.50	.95	2.50	3.25
	1972	75.000	.60	1.25	2.00	2.50
	1973	19.405	1.25	2.10	5.00	7.50
	1974	34.500	.50	.80	1.75	2.25
	1976 small date					
		26.121	.75	1.45	3.50	4.25
	1976 large date					
		121.550	.35	.50	1.50	1.75
	1977	102.000	.50	.75	1.50	2.00
	1978	25.700	1.00	1.50	5.25	6.75

Quetzalcoatl

KM#	Date	Mintage	VF	XF	Unc	BU
485	1980	266.900	.25	.50	1.75	2.25
	1981	30.500	.45	.65	2.75	3.25
	1982	20.000	1.50	2.35	4.25	5.25
	1982	1,051	—	—	Proof	18.00
	1983	7 known	—	—	Proof	1150.
	1984	16.300	1.25	2.00	4.75	6.00
	1985	76.900	2.25	4.00	4.50	5.25

BRASS
Circulation Coinage

KM#	Date	Mintage	VF	XF	Unc	BU
502	1985	30.000	—	.15	.35	.50
	1987	81.900	8.00	9.50	12.50	15.00
	1988	76.600	—	.10	.25	.35
	1988	2 known	—	—	Proof	600.00

DIEZ (10) PESOS

8.3333 g, .900 GOLD, .2411 oz AGW
Miguel Hidalgo

KM#	Date	Mintage	Fine	VF	XF	Unc
473	1905	.039	110.00	125.00	155.00	200.00
	1906	2.949	—	BV	100.00	150.00
	1907	1.589	—	BV	100.00	150.00
	1908	.890	—	BV	100.00	150.00
	1910	.451	—	BV	100.00	150.00
	1916	.026	110.00	120.00	150.00	275.00
	1917	1.967	—	BV	100.00	150.00
	1919	.266	—	BV	100.00	150.00
	1920	.012	150.00	250.00	400.00	650.00
	1959	*.050	—	—		BV + 7%

NOTE: During 1961-1972 a total of 954,983 pieces were restruck, most likely dated 1959. In 1996 matte restrikes were produced.

28.8800 g, .900 SILVER, .8357 oz ASW
Miguel Hidalgo

KM#	Date	Mintage	VF	XF	Unc	BU
474	1955	.585	BV	6.00	8.75	10.75
	1956	3.535	BV	5.50	8.50	11.00

100th Anniversary of Constitution

KM#	Date	Mintage	VF	XF	Unc	BU
475	1957	100	12.50	25.00	42.00	48.00

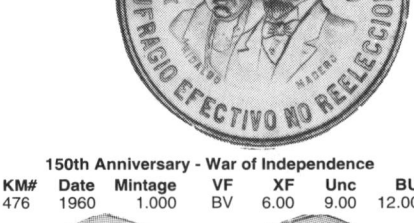

150th Anniversary - War of Independence

KM#	Date	Mintage	VF	XF	Unc	BU
476	1960	1.000	BV	6.00	9.00	12.00

COPPER-NICKEL
Miguel Hidalgo
Thin flan, 1.6mm.

KM#	Date	Mintage	VF	XF	Unc	BU
477.1	1974	3.900	.50	1.00	3.50	4.25
	1974	—	—	—	Proof	625.00
	1975	1.000	2.25	3.25	7.75	15.00
	1976	74.500	.25	.75	1.75	2.25
	1977	79.620	.50	1.00	2.00	3.00
	Thick flan, 2.3mm.					
477.2	1978	124.850	.50	.75	2.50	2.75
	1979	57.200	.50	.75	2.25	2.50
	1980	55.200	.50	.75	2.50	3.75
	1981	222.768	.40	.60	2.25	2.60
	1982	151.770	.50	.80	2.50	3.50
	1982	1.051	—	—	Proof	18.00
	1983	3 known	—	—	Proof	1600.
	1985	58.000	1.25	1.75	5.75	7.50

STAINLESS STEEL
Miguel Hidalgo

KM#	Date	Mintage	VF	XF	Unc	BU
512	1985	257.000	—	.15	.50	.75
	1986	392.000	—	.15	.50	1.50
	1987	305.000	—	.15	.35	.50
	1988	500.300	—	.15	.25	.35
	1989	—	.20	.25	.75	1.50
	1990	—	—	.25	.75	1.25
	1990	2 known	—	—	Proof	500.00

NOTE: Date varieties exist.

VEINTE (20) PESOS

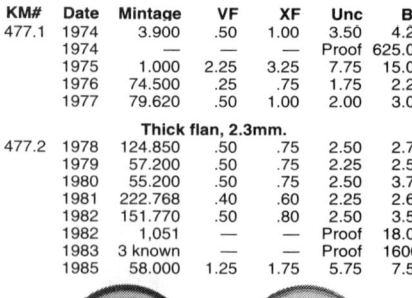

16.6666 g, .900 GOLD, .4823 oz AGW

KM#	Date	Mintage	Fine	VF	XF	Unc
478	1917	.852	—	BV	170.00	200.00
	1918	2.831	—	BV	170.00	200.00
	1919	1.094	—	BV	170.00	200.00
	1920/10	.462	—	BV	175.00	210.00
	1920	Inc. Ab.	—	BV	170.00	200.00
	1921/11	.922	—	BV	175.00	210.00
	1921	Inc. Ab.	—	BV	170.00	200.00
	1959	*.013	—	—	BV + 4%	

*NOTE: During 1960-1971 a total of 1,158,414 pieces were restruck, most likely dated 1959. In 1996 matte restrikes were produced.

COPPER-NICKEL

KM#	Date	Mintage	VF	XF	Unc	BU
486	1980	84.900	.50	.85	2.50	3.40
	1981	250.573	.60	.80	2.50	3.50
	1982	236.892	1.00	1.75	2.75	3.85
	1982	1.051	—	—	Proof	18.00
	1983	3 known	—	—	Proof	—
	1984	55.000	1.00	1.50	3.75	7.50

BRASS
Guadalupe Victoria, First President

508	1985 wide date				
	25.000	.10	.20	1.00	1.25
	1985 narrow date				
	Inc. Ab.	.10	.25	1.50	2.00
1986	10.000	1.00	1.75	5.00	6.00
1988	355.200	.10	.20	.50	1.00
1989	—	.15	.30	1.50	2.00
1990	—	.15	.30	1.50	2.50
1990	3 known	—	—	Proof	475.00

VEINTICINCO (25) PESOS

22.5000 g, .720 SILVER, .5209 oz ASW
Summer Olympics - Mexico City
Type I, rings aligned.

KM#	Date	Mintage	VF	XF	Unc	BU
479.1	1968	27.182	BV	4.00	4.75	6.00

Type II, center ring low.

479.2	1968	Inc. Ab.	4.00	5.00	9.00	10.50

Normal tongue   Long curved tongue
Type III, center rings low.
Snake with long curved tongue.

479.3	1968	Inc. Ab.	4.25	5.25	9.50	11.00

Benito Juarez

KM#	Date	Mintage	VF	XF	Unc	BU
480	1972	2.000	BV	4.00	5.50	6.50

7.7760 g, .720 SILVER, .1800 oz ASW
1986 World Cup Soccer Games

497	1985	.354	—	—	—	7.50

8.4060 g, .925 SILVER, .2450 oz ASW
Rev: W/o fineness statement.

497a	1986	—	—	—	Proof	9.00

1986 World Cup Soccer Games

503	1985	.277	—	—	Proof	9.00

1986 World Cup Soccer Games

514	1985	.234	—	—	Proof	9.00

1986 World Cup Soccer Games

KM#	Date	Mintage	VF	XF	Unc	BU
519	1986	—	—	—	Proof	9.00

50 PESOS

COPPER-NICKEL
Coyolxauhqui

KM#	Date	Mintage	VF	XF	Unc	BU
490	1982	222.890	1.00	2.50	5.00	6.25
	1983	45.000	1.50	3.00	6.00	6.50
	1983	1,051	—	—	Proof	22.00
	1984	73.537	1.00	1.35	3.50	4.00
	1984	4 known	—	—	Proof	750.00

NOTE: Doubled die examples of 1982 and 1983 dates exist.

Benito Juarez

KM#	Date	Mintage	VF	XF	Unc	BU
495	1984	94.216	.65	1.25	2.75	3.50
	1985	296.000	.25	.45	1.50	2.25
	1986	50.000	5.00	7.00	11.00	12.50
	1987	210.000	.25	.45	1.00	1.25
	1988	80.200	6.25	9.00	12.50	14.50

STAINLESS STEEL

KM#	Date	Mintage	VF	XF	Unc	BU
495a	1988	353.300	—	.20	.75	1.50
	1990	—	—	.30	1.00	2.00
	1992	—	—	.25	1.00	2.75

41.6666 g, .900 GOLD, 1.2057 oz AGW
Centennial of Independence

KM#	Date	Mintage	Fine	VF	XF	Unc
481	1921	.180	—	—	BV	650.00
	1922	.463	—	—	BV	510.00
	1923	.432	—	—	BV	510.00
	1924	.439	—	—	BV	510.00
	1925	.716	—	—	BV	510.00
	1926	.600	—	—	BV	510.00
	1927	.606	—	—	BV	510.00
	1928	.538	—	—	BV	510.00
	1929	.458	—	—	BV	510.00
	1930	.372	—	—	BV	510.00
	1931	.137	—	—	BV	565.00
	1944	.593	—	—	BV	510.00
	1945	1.012	—	—	BV	510.00
	1946	1.588	—	—	BV	510.00
	1947	.309	—	—		BV + 3%
	1947	—	—	—		Specimen 6500.

NOTE: During 1949-1972 a total of 3,975,654 pieces were restruck, most likely dated 1947. In 1996 matte restrikes were produced.

15.5520 g, .720 SILVER, .3601 oz ASW
1986 World Cup Soccer Games

KM#	Date	Mintage	VF	XF	Unc	BU
498	1985	.347	—	—	—	8.50

16.8310 g, .925 SILVER, .5000 oz ASW
Rev: W/o fineness statement.

KM#	Date	Mintage	VF	XF	Unc	BU
498a	1986	.010	—	—	Proof	13.50

1986 World Cup Soccer Games

KM#	Date	Mintage	VF	XF	Unc	BU
504	1985	.347	—	—	Proof	13.50

1986 World Cup Soccer Games

KM#	Date	Mintage	VF	XF	Unc	BU
515	1985	.234	—	—	Proof	13.50

1986 World Cup Soccer Games

KM#	Date	Mintage	VF	XF	Unc	BU
523	1986	.190	—	—	Proof	13.50

15.5500 g, .999 SILVER, .5000 oz ASW
50th Anniversary - Nationalization of Oil Industry

532	ND(1988)	.030	—	—	12.00	15.00

CIEN (100) PESOS

Low 7's   High 7's
27.7700 g, .720 SILVER, .6429 oz ASW
Jose Morelos y Pavon

KM#	Date	Mintage	VF	XF	Unc	BU
483.1	1977 low 7's, sloping shoulder					
		5.225	BV	4.25	6.00	10.00
	1977 high 7's, sloping shoulder					
		Inc. Ab.	BV	4.25	6.00	10.50

KM#	Date	Mintage	VF	XF	Unc	BU
483.2	1977 date in line, higher right shoulder					
(484)		Inc. KM483	BV	4.25	5.00	6.50
	1978	9.879	BV	4.25	6.50	8.50
	1979	.784	BV	4.25	6.50	8.50
	1979	—	—	—	Proof	550.00

ALUMINUM-BRONZE
Venustiano Carranza

493	1984	227.809	.45	.60	2.75	4.00
	1985	377.423	.30	.50	2.00	3.00
	1986	43.000	1.00	2.50	4.75	7.50
	1987	165.000	.60	1.25	2.50	3.50
	1988	433.100	.30	.50	2.00	2.75
	1989	—	.35	.65	2.00	2.75
	1990	—	.15	.40	1.50	2.50
	1990	1 known	—	—	Proof	650.00
	1991	—	.15	.25	1.00	2.50
	1992	—	.30	.75	1.75	3.00

31.1030 g, .720 SILVER, .7201 oz ASW
1986 World Cup Soccer Games

KM#	Date	Mintage	VF	XF	Unc	BU
499	1985	.302	—	—	—	12.50

1986 World Cup Soccer Games
Rev: W/o fineness statement.

KM#	Date	Mintage	VF	XF	Unc	BU
521	1986	.208	—	—	Proof	18.50

32.6250 g, .925 SILVER, 1.0000 oz ASW
Rev: W/o fineness statement.

KM#	Date	Mintage	VF	XF	Unc	BU
499a	1985	9,006	—	—	Proof	18.50

1986 World Cup Soccer Games
Rev: W/o fineness statement.

524	1986	.190	—	—	Proof	18.50

1986 World Cup Soccer Games
Rev: W/o fineness statement.

505	1985	9,006	—	—	Proof	18.50

World Wildlife Fund - Monarch Butterflies

KM#	Date	Mintage	VF	XF	Unc	BU
537	1987	*.030	—	—	Proof	47.50

31.1030 g, .999 SILVER, 1.0000 oz ASW
50th Anniversary - Nationalization of Oil Industry

KM#	Date	Mintage	VF	XF	Unc	BU
533	1988	.010	—	—	28.00	35.00

33.6250 g, .925 SILVER, 1.0000 oz ASW
Save the Children

KM#	Date	Mintage	VF	XF	Unc	
539	1991	.030	—	—	Proof	40.00

27.0000 g, .925 SILVER, .8029 oz ASW
Ibero - American Series - Pillars

KM#	Date	Mintage	VF	XF	Unc	BU
540	1991	.050	—	—	Proof	48.00
	1992	.075	—	—	Proof	42.00

31.1035 g, .999 SILVER, 1.0000 oz ASW
Eagle Warrior

KM#	Date	Mintage	VF	XF	Unc
556	1992	.205	—	—	11.50
	1992	4,000	—	Proof	36.00

Xochipilli - The God of Joy, Music and Dance

562	1992	4,000	—	Proof	36.00

Brasero Efigie - The God of Rain

563	1992	4,000	—	Proof	36.00

Huehueteotl - The God of Fire

KM#	Date	Mintage	VF	XF	Unc
564	1992	4,000	—	Proof	36.00

31.1030 g, .999 SILVER, 1.0000 oz ASW
Save the Harbor Porpoise

KM#	Date	Mintage	VF	XF	Unc	BU
566	1992	—	—	—	Proof	45.00

200 PESOS

COPPER-NICKEL
175th Anniversary of Independence

509	1985	75.000	—	.25	3.25	4.75

75th Anniversary of 1910 Revolution

510	1985	98.590	—	.25	3.25	4.25

1986 World Cup Soccer Games

KM#	Date	Mintage	VF	XF	Unc	BU
525	1986	50.000	—	1.00	3.50	4.50

62.2060 g, .999 SILVER, 2.0000 oz ASW
1986 World Cup Soccer Games

526	1986	.050	—	—	40.00	50.00

250 PESOS

8.6400 g, .900 GOLD, .2500 oz AGW
1986 World Cup Soccer Games

500.1	1985	.100	—	—	—	100.00
	1986	—	—	—	—	100.00

Rev: W/o fineness statement.

500.2	1985	4,506	—	—	Proof	110.00
	1986	—	—	—	Proof	135.00

1986 World Cup Soccer Games

506.1	1985	.088	—	—	—	110.00

Rev: W/o fineness statement.

KM#	Date	Mintage	VF	XF	Unc	BU
506.2	1985	*.080	—	—	Proof	115.00

7.7758 g, .999 GOLD, .2500 oz AGW
Native Culture - Sculpture of Jaguar Head

KM#	Date	Mintage	VF	XF	Unc
558	1992	.010	—	—	145.00
	1992	2,000		Proof	275.00

500 PESOS

17.2800 g, .900 GOLD, .5000 oz AGW
1986 World Cup Soccer Games
Obv: Eagle facing left w/snake in beak.

KM#	Date	Mintage	VF	XF	Unc	BU
501.1	1985	.102	—	—	—	210.00
	1986	—	—	—	—	210.00

Rev: W/o fineness statement.

| 501.2 | 1985 | 5,506 | — | — | Proof | 225.00 |
| | 1986 | — | — | — | Proof | 225.00 |

1986 World Cup Soccer Games

| 507.1 | 1985 | — | — | — | — | 225.00 |

Rev: W/o fineness statement.

| 507.2 | 1985 | — | — | — | Proof | 225.00 |

33.4500 g, .925 SILVER, 1.0000 oz ASW
75th Anniversary of 1910 Revolution

| 511 | 1985 | .040 | — | — | Proof | 32.50 |

COPPER-NICKEL
Francisco Madero

KM#	Date	Mintage	VF	XF	Unc	BU
529	1986	20.000	—	1.00	2.50	3.00
	1987	180.000	—	.75	2.00	2.50
	1988	230.000	—	.50	2.00	2.50
	1988	2 known	—	—	Proof	650.00
	1989	—	—	.75	2.00	3.00
	1990	—	—	.75	2.00	3.50
	1992	—	—	1.00	2.25	3.50

17.2800 g, .900 GOLD, .5000 oz AGW
50th Anniversary - Nationalization of Oil Industry
Rev: Monument.
Similar to 5000 Pesos, KM#531.

| 534 | 1988 | — | — | — | — | 225.00 |

15.5517 g, .999 GOLD, .5000 oz AGW
Native Culture - Sculpture of Jaguar Head

KM#	Date	Mintage	VF	XF	Unc
559	1992	.010	—	—	200.00
	1992	2,000		Proof	400.00

1000 PESOS

17.2800 g, .900 GOLD, .5000 oz AGW
175th Anniversary of Independence

KM#	Date	Mintage	VF	XF	Unc	BU
513	1985	—	—	—	Proof	325.00

31.1030 g, .999 GOLD, 1.0000 oz AGW
1986 World Cup Soccer Games

| 527 | 1986 | — | — | — | — | 550.00 |

34.5590 g, .900 GOLD, 1.0000 oz AGW

50th Anniversary - Nationalization of Oil Industry
Similar to 5000 Pesos, KM#531.
Rev: Portrait of Cardenas.

KM#	Date	Mintage	VF	XF	Unc	BU
535	1988	—	—	—	Proof	440.00

ALUMINUM-BRONZE
Juana de Asbaje

536	1988	229.300	.85	1.25	3.75	4.25
	1989	—	.85	1.25	3.45	4.25
	1990	—	.85	1.25	2.25	4.25
	1990	2 known	—	—	Proof	550.00
	1991	—	1.00	1.50	2.50	4.25
	1992	—	1.00	1.50	2.25	3.50

31.1035 g, .999 GOLD, 1.0000 oz AGW
Native Culture - Sculpture of Jaguar Head

560	1992	.018	—	—	400.00
	1992	2,000	—	Proof	600.00

2000 PESOS

62.2000 g, .999 GOLD, 2.0000 oz AGW
1986 World Cup Soccer Games

528	1986	—	—	—	—	900.00

5000 PESOS

COPPER-NICKEL
50th Anniversary - Nationalization of Oil Industry

531	ND(1988)					
		50.000	—	4.75	7.75	10.00

10000 PESOS

155.5175 g, .999 SILVER, 5.0000 oz ASW
Illustration reduced. Actual size: 65mm.
Native Warriors Taking Female Captive

KM#	Date	Mintage	VF	XF	Unc
557	1992	.052	—	—	46.00
	1992	3,005	—	Proof	80.00

MONETARY REFORM

1 New Peso = 1000 Old Pesos

5 CENTAVOS

STAINLESS STEEL

KM#	Date	Mintage	VF	XF	Unc
546	1992	—	—	.15	.25
	1993	—	—	.15	.25
	1994	—	—	.15	.25
	1995	—	—	.15	.25
	1996	—	—	.15	.25
	1997	—	—	.15	.25

10 CENTAVOS

STAINLESS STEEL

547	1992	—	—	.20	.30
	1993	—	—	.20	.30
	1994	—	—	.20	.30
	1995	—	—	.20	.30
	1996	—	—	.20	.30
	1997	—	—	.20	.30

20 CENTAVOS

ALUMINUM-BRONZE

548	1992	—	—	.25	.35
	1993	—	—	.25	.35
	1994	—	—	.25	.35
	1995	—	—	.25	.35
	1996	—	—	.25	.35

Chaac Mool

572	1994	.030	—	Matte	6.50
	1994	2,000	—	Proof	10.50

PESO

50 CENTAVOS

ALUMINUM-BRONZE

549	1992	—	—	.45	.85
	1993	—	—	.45	.75
	1994	—	—	.45	.75
	1995	—	—	.45	.75
	1996	—	—	.45	.75
	1997	—	—	.45	.75

7.775 g, .999 SILVER, .2500 oz ASW
Senor De Las Limas
Similar to 5 Pesos, KM#595.

593	1996	.010	—	—	4.00
	1996	—	—	Proof	25.00
	1998	—	—	Matte	3.25

NEW PESO

STAINLESS STEEL ring,
ALUMINUM-BRONZE center
Similar to KM#550, but denom. w/o N.

603	1996	—	—	—	1.35
	1997	—	—	—	1.35

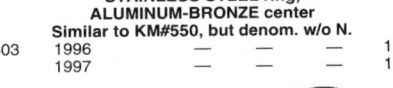

STAINLESS STEEL ring,
ALUMINUM-BRONZE center

KM#	Date	Mintage	VF	XF	Unc
550	1992	—	—	.60	1.25
	1993	—	—	.60	1.25
	1994	—	—	.60	1.25
	1995	—	—	.60	1.25
	1996	—	—	.60	1.25

7.7759 g, .999 SILVER, .2500 oz ASW
Disco De La Muerte
Obv: Mexican eagle.

KM#	Date	Mintage	VF	XF	Unc
617	1997	—	—	—	4.00
	1997	—	—	Proof	10.50
	1998	—	—	Matte	10.50

2 NEW PESOS

7.7601 g, .999 SILVER, .2498 oz ASW
Bajorrelieve Del El Tajin

567	1993	.100	—	—	6.50
	1993	3,000	—	Proof	10.50

STAINLESS STEEL ring,
ALUMINUM-BRONZE center

STAINLESS STEEL ring,
ALUMINUM-BRONZE center

KM#	Date	Mintage	VF	XF	Unc
551	1992	—	—	1.50	2.50
	1993	—	—	1.00	2.25
	1994	—	—	1.00	2.25
	1995	—	—	1.00	2.25

15.5516 g, .999 SILVER, .4995 oz ASW
Bajorrelieve Del El Tajin

KM#	Date	Mintage	VF	XF	Unc
568	1993	.100	—	—	6.50
	1993	3,000	—	Proof	10.50

Chaac Mool

KM#	Date	Mintage	VF	XF	Unc
573	1994	.030	—	Matte	6.50
	1994	2,000	—	Proof	10.50

2 PESOS

15.5517 g, .999 SILVER, .5000 oz ASW
Senor De Las Limas
Similar to 5 Pesos. KM#595.

KM#	Date	Mintage	VF	XF	Unc
594	1996	.010	—	—	6.00
	1996	—	—	Proof	18.50
	1998	—	—	Matte	8.50

STAINLESS STEEL ring,
ALUMINUM-BRONZE center
Similar to KM#551, but denom. w/o N.

KM#	Date	Mintage	VF	XF	Unc
604	1996	—	—	—	2.35
	1997	—	—	—	2.35

15.5517 g, .999 SILVER, .5000 oz ASW
Disco De La Muerte
Obv: Mexican eagle.

KM#	Date	Mintage	VF	XF	Unc
618	1996	—	—	—	6.00
	1996	.010	—	Proof	18.50
	1997	—	—	—	6.00
	1997	—	—	Proof	10.50
	1998	—	—	—	6.50

5 NEW PESOS

STAINLESS STEEL ring,
ALUMINUM-BRONZE center

KM#	Date	Mintage	VF	XF	Unc
552	1992	—	—	2.00	4.00
	1993	—	—	2.00	4.00
	1994	—	—	2.00	4.00
	1995	—	—	Proof	25.00

31.1035 g, .999 SILVER, .9991 oz ASW
Bajorrelieve Del El Tajin

KM#	Date	Mintage	VF	XF	Unc
569	1993	.100	—	—	12.00
	1993	2,200	—	Proof	36.00

Palma Con Cecodrilo
Obv: National emblem.
Rev: Aerial view of crocodile.

582   1993   2,655   —   Proof   36.00

KM#	Date	Mintage	VF	XF	Unc
574	1994	.050	—	Matte	12.00
	1994	2,200	—	Proof	36.00

Anciano Con Brasero
Rev: Kneeling figure sculpture.

583   1993   2,655   —   Proof   36.00

Tomb of Palenque Memorial Stone

575   1994   2,200   —   Proof   36.00

Carita Sonriente
Rev: Sculptured head.

584   1993   3,000   —   Proof   36.00

Mascaron Del Dios Chaac
Rev: Elaborately carved wall segment
w/hook or loop.

577   1994   2,200   —   Proof   36.00

Chaac Mool

Dintel 26
Rev: 2 seated figures wall carving.

KM#	Date	Mintage	VF	XF	Unc
578	1994	2,200	—	Proof	36.00

27.0000 g, .925 SILVER, .8030 oz ASW
Environmental Protection - Pacific Ridley Sea Turtle

588	1994	.020	—	Proof	37.50

5 PESOS

El Luchador

597	1996	.030	—	—	13.50
	1996	—	—	Proof	36.00
	1998	—	—	Matte	10.00

Hacha Ceremonial

598	1996	.030	—	—	13.50
	1996	—	—	Proof	36.00
	1998	—	—	Matte	10.00

31.1035 g, .999 SILVER, 1.0000 oz ASW
Senor De Las Limas

595	1996	.030	—	—	12.00
	1996	.030	—	Proof	36.00
	1998	—	—	Matte	16.25

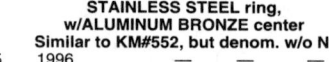

STAINLESS STEEL ring,
w/ALUMINUM BRONZE center
Similar to KM#552, but denom. w/o N.

605	1996	—	—	—	4.00
	1997	—	—	—	4.00

Hombre Jaguar

KM#	Date	Mintage	VF	XF	Unc
596	1996	.030	—	—	13.50
	1996	—	—	Proof	36.00
	1998	—	—	Matte	10.00

31.1035 g, .999 SILVER, 1.0000 oz ASW
Teohituacan - Disco de la Muerte
Obv: Eagle and snake.

617	1997	*.030	—	Proof	36.00
	1998	—	—	—	13.50

Teohituacan - Mascara
Obv: Eagle and snake.

618	1997	*.030	—	Proof	36.00
	1998	—	—		13.50

Teohituacan - Vasija
Obv: Eagle and snake.

619	1997	—	—	—	9.00
	1997	*.030	—	Proof	36.00
	1998	—	—	Matte	13.50

Teohituacan - Jugador of Pelota
Obv: Eagle and snake.

620	1997	—	—	—	9.00
	1997	*.030	—	Proof	36.50
	1998	—	—	Matte	10.00

31.1035 g, .999 SILVER, 1.0000 oz ASW
World Wildlife Fund - 2 Lobo
Obv: Mexican eagle.

625	1997	*.015	—	Proof	50.00

27.0000 g, .925 SILVER, .8030 oz ASW
Jarabe Tapatio - 2 Dancers
Obv: Mexican emblem within circle of arms.

629	1997	.020	—	Proof	30.00

10 NEW PESOS

ALUMINUM-BRONZE ring w/
11.1400 g, .925 SILVER, .1666 oz ASW center

KM#	Date	Mintage	VF	XF	Unc
553	1992	—	—	—	8.50
	1993	—	—	—	8.50
	1994	—	—	—	8.50
	1995	—	—	—	8.50

155.5175 g, .999 SILVER, 4.9956 oz ASW
Illustration reduced. Actual size: 64.9mm.
Piramide Del El Tajin

			VF	XF	Unc
570	1993	.050	—	—	46.00
	1993	3,000	—	Proof	78.00

Illustration reduced. Actual size: 64.9mm.
Pyramid del Castillo

KM#	Date	Mintage	VF	XF	Unc
576	1994	.020	—	Matte	46.50
	1994	1,000	—	Proof	80.00

10 PESOS

1555.5175 g, .999 SILVER, 5.0000 oz ASW
Illustration reduced. Actual size: 65mm.
Cabeza Olmeca

			VF	XF	Unc
599	1996	.010	—	Proof	80.00
	1998	—	—	Matte	46.00

11.1400 g, .925 SILVER, .1666 oz ASW center
Similar to KM#553, but denom. w/o N.

KM#	Date	Mintage	VF	XF	Unc
606	1996	—	—	—	7.50

1555.5175 g, .999 SILVER, 5.0000 oz ASW
Teohituacan - Piramide del Sol
Obv: Eagle and snake.

			VF	XF	Unc
621	1997	*.010	—	Proof	80.00

COPPER-NICKEL ZINC center in BRASS ring
Obv: National emblem. Rev: Aztec design.

					Unc
616	1997	—	—	—	6.00
	1998	—	—	—	6.00

25 PESOS

7.7758 g, .999 SILVER, .2500 oz ASW
Eagle Warrior

554	1992	.050	—	—	6.50
	1992	3,000	—	Proof	10.50

7.7758 g, .999 GOLD, .2500 oz AGW
Sacerdote
Similar to 100 Pesos, KM#602.

600	1995	.010	—	—	225.00
	1996	—	—	Proof	275.00

Teohituacan - Serpiente Emplumada
Obv: Eagle and snake.

622	1997	*.010	—	Proof	100.00

Serpiente Emplumada
Similar to 100 Pesos, KM#626.
Obv: Mexican eagle.

624	1997	—	—	—	200.00
	1997	.010	—	Proof	275.00

1,555.5175 g, .999 SILVER, 5.0000 oz ASW
Piramide Del Sol
Obv: Mexican eagle.

623	1997	—	—	—	50.00
	1997	.010	—	Proof	95.00
	1998	—	—	Matte	46.00

50 NEW PESOS

20 NEW PESOS

ALUMINUM-BRONZE ring w/
16.9000 g, .925 SILVER, .2499 oz ASW center

561	1993	—	—	—	13.50
	1994	—	—	—	13.50
	1995	—	—	—	13.50

34.0000 g, .925 SILVER, .5051 oz ASW center
in BRASS ring
Nino Heroes

571	1993	—	—	—	26.50
	1994	—	—	—	26.50
	1995	—	—	—	26.50

20 PESOS

ALUMINUM-BRONZE ring w/
16.9000 g, .925 SILVER, .2499 oz ASW center
Similar to KM#561, but denom. w/o N.

607	1996	—	—	—	13.50

15.5517 g, .999 GOLD, .5000 oz AGW
Hacha Ceremonial
Similar to 100 New Pesos, KM#587.

KM#	Date	Mintage	VF	XF	Unc
586	1993	.016	—	—	275.00
	1993	500 pcs.	—	Proof	425.00

25 NEW PESOS

7.7758 g, .999 GOLD, .2500 oz AGW
Hacha Ceremonial
Similar to 100 New Pesos, KM#587.

KM#	Date	Mintage	VF	XF	Unc
585	1993	.016	—	—	145.00
	1993	800 pcs.	—	Proof	275.00

Personaje de Jaina
Rev: Seated figure.

579	1994	2,000	—	—	165.00
	1994	500 pcs.	—	Proof	325.00

Personaje de Jaina
Rev: Seated figure.

580	1994	1,000	—	—	300.00
	1994	500 pcs.	—	Proof	525.00

50 PESOS

15.5517 g, .999 SILVER, .5000 oz ASW
Eagle Warrior

| 555 | 1992 | .050 | — | — | 8.50 |
| | 1992 | 3,000 | — | Proof | 18.50 |

15.5517 g, .999 GOLD, .5000 oz AGW
Sacerdote
Similar to 100 Pesos, KM#602.

| 601 | 1995 | .010 | — | — | 425.00 |
| | 1996 | | — | Proof | 475.00 |

15.5517 g, .999 SILVER, .5000 oz ASW
Similar to 50 New Pesos, KM#571 w/o "N"
before denomination.

| 608 | 1996 | — | — | — | 22.00 |

Teohituacan - Serpiente Emplumada
Obv: Eagle and snake.

| 623 | 1997 | *.010 | — | Proof | 100.00 |

15.5517 g, .999 GOLD, .5000 oz AGW
Serpiente Emplumada
Similar to 100 Pesos, KM#626.
Obv: Mexico City.

| 625 | 1997 | — | — | — | 350.00 |
| | 1997 | .010 | — | Proof | 475.00 |

100 NEW PESOS

31.1035 g, .999 GOLD, 1.0000 oz AGW
Hacha Ceremonial

| 587 | 1993 | 7,158 | — | — | 525.00 |
| | 1993 | 500 pcs. | — | Proof | 675.00 |

Personaje de Jaina

KM#	Date	Mintage	VF	XF	Unc
581	1994	1,000	—	—	575.00
	1994	500 pcs.	—	Proof	800.00

100 PESOS

31.1035 g, .999 GOLD, 1.0000 oz AGW
Sacerdote

| 602 | 1995 | .010 | — | — | 600.00 |
| | 1996 | | — | Proof | 600.00 |

Teohituacan - Serpiente Emplumada
Obv: Eagle and snake.

| 624 | 1997 | | — | — | 600.00 |
| | 1997 | *.010 | — | Proof | 670.00 |

SILVER BULLION ISSUES
1/20 ONZA TROY de PLATA
(1/20 Troy Ounce of Silver)

1.5551 g, .999 SILVER, .0500 oz ASW

542	1991	.054	—	—	—	2.45
	1992	.296	—	—	—	2.45
	1992	5,000	—	—	Proof	10.00
	1993	.100	—	—	—	2.45
	1993	—	—	—	Proof	10.00
	1994	.090	—	—	—	2.45
	1994	.050	—	—	Proof	10.00
	1995	.010	—	—	—	2.45
	1995	2,000	—	—	Proof	10.00

Obv: Mexican eagle. Rev: Winged Victory.

609	1996	—	—	—	—	2.45
	1996	—	—	—	Proof	10.00
	1997	—	—	—	—	2.45
	1997	—	—	—	Proof	10.00
	1998	—	—	—	—	2.45
	1998	—	—	—	Proof	10.00

1/10 ONZA TROY de PLATA
(1/10 Troy Ounce of Silver)

3.1103 g, .999 SILVER, .1000 oz ASW

KM#	Date	Mintage	VF	XF	Unc	BU
543	1991	.054	—	—	—	2.55
	1992	.300	—	—	—	2.55
	1992	5,000	—	—	Proof	12.00
	1993	.100	—	—	—	2.55
	1993	—	—	—	Proof	12.00
	1994	.090	—	—	—	2.55
	1994	.050	—	—	Proof	12.00
	1995	.010	—	—	—	2.55
	1995	2,000	—	—	Proof	12.00

Obv: Mexican eagle. Rev: Winged Victory.

KM#	Date	Mintage	VF	XF	Unc	BU
610	1996	—	—	—	—	2.55
	1996	—	—	—	Proof	12.00
	1997	—	—	—	—	2.55
	1997	—	—	—	Proof	12.00
	1998	—	—	—	—	2.55
	1998	—	—	—	Proof	12.00

1/4 ONZA TROY de PLATA
(1/4 Troy Ounce of Silver)

7.7758 g, .999 SILVER, .2500 oz ASW

KM#	Date	Mintage	VF	XF	Unc	BU
544	1991	.050	—	—	—	4.50
	1992	.104	—	—	—	4.50
	1992	5,000	—	—	Proof	15.00
	1993	.087	—	—	—	4.50
	1993	—	—	—	Proof	15.00
	1994	.090	—	—	—	4.50
	1994	.050	—	—	Proof	15.00
	1995	.015	—	—	—	4.50
	1995	2,000	—	—	Proof	15.00

Obv: Mexican eagle. Rev: Winged Victory.

KM#	Date	Mintage	VF	XF	Unc	BU
611	1996	—	—	—	—	4.50
	1996	—	—	—	Proof	15.00
	1997	—	—	—	—	4.50
	1997	—	—	—	Proof	15.00
	1998	—	—	—	—	4.50
	1998	—	—	—	Proof	15.00

1/2 ONZA TROY de PLATA
(1/2 Troy Ounce of Silver)

15.5517 g, .999 SILVER, .5000 oz ASW

KM#	Date	Mintage	VF	XF	Unc	BU
545	1991	.051	—	—	—	6.00
	1992	.119	—	—	—	6.00
	1992	5,000	—	—	Proof	17.50
	1993	.072	—	—	—	6.00
	1993	—	—	—	Proof	17.50
	1994	.090	—	—	—	6.00
	1994	.050	—	—	Proof	17.50
	1995	.015	—	—	—	6.00
	1995	2,000	—	—	Proof	17.50

Obv: Mexican eagle. Rev: Winged Victory.

KM#	Date	Mintage	VF	XF	Unc	BU
612	1996	—	—	—	—	6.00
	1996	—	—	—	Proof	17.50
	1997	—	—	—	—	6.00
	1997	—	—	—	Proof	17.50
	1998	—	—	—	—	6.00
	1998	—	—	—	Proof	17.50

ONZA TROY de PLATA
(Troy Ounce of Silver)

33.6250 g, .925 SILVER, 1.0000 oz ASW
Obv: Mint mark above coin press.

KM#	Date	Mintage	VF	XF	Unc	BU
M49a	1949	1.000	10.00	12.50	17.50	25.00

Type 1. Obv: Wide spacing between DE MONEDA
Rev: Mint mark below balance scale.

M49b.1 1978 .280 — BV 6.75 14.00

Type 2. Obv: Close spacing between DE MONEDA

M49b.2 1978 Inc. Ab. — BV 6.75 12.00

Type 5.

M49b.5	1980	6.104	—	BV	6.75	11.00
	1980/70	I.A.	—	BV	6.75	14.50

Type 3. Rev: Left scale pan points to U in UNA.

KM#	Date	Mintage	VF	XF	Unc	BU
M49b.3	1979	4.508	—	BV	6.75	13.50

Obv: Mexican eagle. Rev: Winged Victory.

KM#	Date	Mintage	VF	XF	Unc	BU
613	1996	—	—	—	—	9.50
	1996	—	—	—	Proof	32.50
	1997	—	—	—	—	11.50
	1997	—	—	—	Proof	32.50
	1998	—	—	—	—	11.50
	1998	—	—	—	Proof	35.00

Type 4. Rev: Left scale pan points between
U and N of UNA.

M49b.4 1979 Inc. Ab. — BV 6.75 13.50

LIBERTAD SERIES

KM#	Date	Mintage	VF	XF	Unc	BU
494.4	1993	1.000	—	BV	BV	12.00
	1993	—	—	—	Proof	34.00
	1994	.400	—	BV	BV	12.00
	1994	.010	—	—	Proof	34.00
	1995	.500	—	BV	BV	11.00
	1995	2,000	—	—	Proof	34.00

31.1000 g, .999 SILVER, 1.0000 oz ASW
Libertad

494.1	1982	1.050	—	BV	BV	12.00
	1983	1.002	—	BV	BV	12.00
	1983	998 pcs.	—	—	Proof	200.00
	1984	1.014	—	BV	BV	12.00
	1985	2.017	—	BV	BV	12.00
	1986	1.699	—	BV	BV	12.00
	1986	.030	—	—	Proof	20.00
	1987	.500	—	BV	BV	38.00
	1987	.012	—	—	Proof	45.00
	1988	1.501	—	BV	BV	35.00
	1988	*8,000	—	—	Proof	Rare
	1989	1.397	—	BV	BV	24.00
	1989	.010	—	—	Proof	39.00

Reeded edge.

494.2	1988	*2,000	—	—	Proof	42.00
	1990	1.200	—	BV	BV	12.00
	1990	.010	—	—	Proof	22.00
	1991	1.651	—	BV	BV	14.00

Mule. Obv: KM#494.3. Rev: KM#494.2.

494.5	1991	.010	—	—	Proof	20.00

2 ONZAS TROY de PLATA

62.2070 g, .999 SILVER, 2.0000 oz ASW
Obv: Mexican eagle. Rev: Winged Victory.

614	1996	—	—	—	—	22.00
	1996	—	—	—	Proof	42.50
	1997	—	—	—	—	22.00
	1997	—	—	—	Proof	42.50
	1998	—	—	—	—	22.00
	1998	—	—	—	Proof	42.50

Obv: Eight dots below eagle's left talons.
Rev: Revised design and lettering.

494.3	1991	Inc. Ab.	—	BV	BV	14.00
	1992	2.458	—	BV	BV	12.00
	1992	.010	—	—	Proof	32.00

5 ONZAS TROY de PLATA

Obv: Seven dots below eagle's left talons,
dull claws on right talon, thick letters.

155.5175 g, .999 SILVER, 5.0000 oz ASW
Obv: Mexican eagle. Rev: Winged Victory.
Illustration reduced. Actual size: 65mm.

KM#	Date	Mintage	VF	XF	Unc	BU
615	1996	—	—	—	—	45.00
	1996	—	—	—	Proof	75.00
	1997	—	—	—	—	45.00
	1997	—	—	—	Proof	75.00
	1998	—	—	—	—	45.00
	1998	—	—	—	Proof	75.00

GOLD BULLION ISSUES
1/20 ONZA ORO PURO
(1/20 Ounce of Pure Gold)

1.7500 g, .900 GOLD, .0500 oz AGW
Obv: Winged Victory. Rev: Calendar stone.

530	1987	—	—	—	BV + 30%
	1988	—	—	—	BV + 30%
	1994	.010	—	—	BV + 30%

1.5551 g, .999 GOLD, .0500 oz AGW
Obv: Winged Victory. Rev: Eagle and snake.

585	1991	.010	—	—	BV + 30%
	1992	.065	—	—	BV + 30%
	1993	.010	—	—	BV + 30%

1/15 ONZA ORO PURO
(1/15 Ounce of Pure Gold)

Obv: Winged Victory above legend.

628	1987	—	—	—	BV + 25%

1/10 ONZA ORO PURO
(1/10 Ounce of Pure Gold)

3.1103 g, .999 GOLD, .1000 oz AGW

541	1991	.010	—	—	BV + 20%
	1992	.051	—	—	BV + 20%
	1993	.010	—	—	BV + 20%

1/4 ONZA ORO PURO
(1/4 Ounce of Pure Gold)

8.6396 g, .900 GOLD, .2500 oz AGW

KM#	Date	Mintage	VF	XF	Unc	BU
487	1981	.313	—	—	BV + 11%	
	1994	2,500	—	—	BV + 11%	

7.7758 g, .999 GOLD, .2500 oz AGW
Obv: Winged Victory above legend.
Rev: Eagle and snake.

590	1991	.010	—	—	BV + 11%
	1992	.028	—	—	BV + 11%
	1993	2,500	—	—	BV + 11%

1/2 ONZA ORO PURO
(1/2 Ounce of Pure Gold)

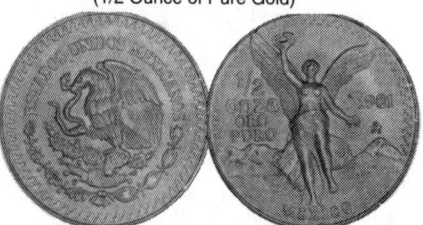

17.2792 g, .900 GOLD, .5000 oz AGW

488	1981	.193	—	—	BV + 8%
	1989	3,500	—	—	Proof 400.00
	1994	2,500	—	—	BV + 8%

15.5517 g, .999 GOLD, .5000 oz AGW
Obv: Winged Victory above legend.
Rev: Eagle and snake.

591	1991	.010	—	—	BV + 8%
	1992	.025	—	—	BV + 8%
	1993	2,500	—	—	BV + 8%

ONZA ORO PURO
(1 Ounce of Pure Gold)

34.5585 g, .900 GOLD, 1.0000 oz AGW

489	1981	.596	—	—	BV + 3%
	1985	—	—	—	BV + 3%
	1988	—	—	—	BV + 3%
	1994	1,000	—	—	BV + 3%

31.1035 g, .999 GOLD, 1.0000 oz AGW
Obv: Winged Victory above legend.
Rev: Eagle and snake.

592	1991	.109	—	—	BV + 3%
	1992	.046	—	—	BV + 3%
	1993	.010	—	—	BV + 3%

(50 PESOS)

41.6666 g, .900 GOLD, 1.2057 oz AGW

KM#	Date	Mintage	VF	XF	Unc	BU
482	1943	.089	—	—	BV	525.00

PLATINUM BULLION ISSUES
1/4 ONZA
(1/4 ounce)

7.7775 g, .999 PLATINUM, .2500 oz APW

| 538 | 1989 | 704 pcs. | — | — | Proof 240.00 |

MEDALLIC ISSUES (M)
(10 PESOS)

8.3333 g, .900 GOLD, .2411 oz AGW
200th Anniversary - Birth of Hidalgo

| M91a | 1953 | — | — | — | BV 135.00 |

Centennial of Constitution

| M123a | 1957 | *.073 | — | — | BV 135.00 |

***NOTE:** Mintage includes #M122a.*

(20 PESOS)

16.6666 g, .900 GOLD, .4823 oz AGW
200th Anniversary - Birth of Hidalgo

| M92a | 1953 | — | — | — | BV 240.00 |

(50 PESOS)

41.6666 g, .900 GOLD, 1.2057 oz AGW
Centennial of Constitution

KM#	Date	Mintage	VF	XF	Unc	BU
M122a	1957					
	Inc. M123a		—	—	BV	575.00

MINT SETS (MS)

KM#	Date	Mintage	Identification	Issue Price	Mkt. Val.
MS1	1977(16)	500	—	—	500.00
MSA2	1977(9)	—	434.1,434.2,442,452, 460 thick date, 460 thin date,472,477.1,484,Type 2 for 3 ring binder	—	85.00
MS2	1978(9)	500	KM434.1,434.2,442,452, 460 open 8, 460 closed 8, 472,477,484,Type 1 flat pack	—	150.00
MS3	1978(9)	—	KM434.1,434.2,442,452, 460 open 8, 460 closed 8, 472,477.2,484,Type 2 for 3 ring binder	—	65.00
MS4	1979(8)	—	KM434.2,442,452 square 9, 452 round 9, 460(2), 472, 477.2,484, Type 1 flat pack	11.00	9.00
MS5	1979(8)	—	KM434.1,434.2,442,452 square 9, 452 round 9, 460,477,484, Type 2 for 3 ring binder	11.00	10.00
MS6	1980(9)	—	KM434.2, 442, 452 square 9, 452 round 9, 460 open 8, 460 closed 8, 477.2, 485-486	4.20	12.00
MS7	1981(9)	—	KM442 open 8, 442 closed 8, 452 rectangular 9, 452 round 9, 460 open 8, 460 closed 8, 477.2, 485,486	—	15.00
MS8	1982(7)	—	KM442,452,460,477,485, 486,490	—	14.00
MS9	1983(11)	—	KM442(2), 452(2), 460(2), 490(1), 491(2), 492(2)	—	14.00
MS10	1983(9)	—	KM442(2),452(2),460(2), 490(1),491(2),492(2) for 3 ring binder	—	12.50
MS11	1984(8)	—	KM485-486,490-491,493, 495(2),496	—	18.00
MS12	1985(12)	—	KM477.2,485,493(2), 495(2),496,502,508,509, 510,512	—	16.00
MS13	1986(7)	—	KM493,495,496,508,512, 525,529	—	18.00
MS14	1985/1986(7)	—	KM493,495-496,502,508 509,512	—	18.50
MS15	1987(9)	—	KM493,495(2),496,502(2), 512, 529(2)	—	35.00
MS16	1988(8)	—	KM493,495a,502,508,512, 529,531,536	—	20.00

NOTE: The 1978 and 1979 sets were issued in 2 varieties of plastic holders, one of which has holes for insertion in an official 3 ring binder which was sold for $3.30.

NOTE: In 1989 The Banco de Mexico began preparing mint sets by year with coins dated from 1970 thru 1997, MSa2 is such a set.

PROOF SETS (PS)

KM#	Date	Mintage	Identification	Issue Price	Mkt. Val.
PS1	1982/1983(8)	998	KM442,452,460,485, 477.2,486,490,494.1	495.00	300.00
PS2	1982/1983(8)	*2	KM460,477.2,485,486, 490,491,492,PnB169 (in white box with Mo. in gold)	—	—
PS3	1982/1983(7)	*23	KM460,477.2,485,486, 490,491,492(in white box with Mo in gold)	—	500.00
PS4	1982/1983(7)	*17	KM460,477.2,485,486, 490,491,492 (in white box)	—	500.00
PS5	1982/1983(7)	*8	KM460,477.2,485,486, 490,491,492 (in white box)	—	500.00
PS6	1983(7)	3	KM460,477.2,485,486, 490,491,492	—	—
PS7	1985/1986(12)	—	KM497a-499a,503-505, 514-515,519,521, 523-524	—	250.00
PS8	1985(4)	—	KM500.2-501.2,506.2, 507.2	—	700.00
PS9	1985(3)	—	KM499a,514,515 (in blue box)	—	60.00
PS10	1985(3)	—	KM503-505 (in blue box)	—	60.00
PS11	1985(2)	—	KM511,513	—	350.00
PS12	1989(3)	3,500	KM488,494,538, Rainbow	730.00	665.00
PS13	1992(5)	5,000	KM494.3,542-545	—	87.50
PS14	1993(5)	5,000	KM494.4,542-545	—	87.50
PS15	1994(5)	5,000	KM494.4,542-545	—	85.00

NOTE: KM#PS2, PS3, PS4 and PS5 are commonly referred to as pattern proof sets.

Bibliography

Boyd, Julian P. (Editor). *The Papers of Thomas Jefferson.* Vol. 7. New Jersey: Princeton University Press, 1953.

Bowers, Q. David. *The History of United States Coinage as Illustrated by the Garrett Collection.* Los Angeles: Bowers & Ruddy Galleries, 1979.

Breen, Walter. *Walter Breen's Complete Encyclopedia of U.S. and Colonial Coins.* New York: F.C.I. Press, Doubleday, 1988.

Bressett, Ken, and Kosoff, A. *Official A.N.A. Grading Standards for United States Coins,* Fourth Edition. Colorado Springs, Colo.: American Numismatic Association, 1991.

Brown, Martin R., and Dunn, John W. *A Guide to the Grading of United States Coins.* Fourth and Fifth Editions. Racine, Wis.: Whitman Publishing Co., 1964 and 1969.

Bullowa, David M. *Numismatic Notes and Monographs No. 83: The Commemorative Coinage of the United States 1892-1938.* New York, N.Y.: American Numismatic Society, 1938.

Evans, George G. *Illustrated History of the United States Mint.* Revised Edition. Philadelphia: George G. Evans, 1892.

Fitzpatrick, John C. (Editor). *The Writings of George Washington.* Vol. 28. Washington: U.S. Government Printing Office, 1938.

Heath, Dr. George. *The Numismatist,* September 1888 and February 1892.

Hepburn, A. Barton. *A History of Currency in the United States.* Revised Edition. New York: Sentry Press, 1967.

Krueger, Kurt R. "Grading: Bestial Pandemonium Unleashed." *The Numismatist,* January 1976. Colorado Springs, Colo.: American Numismatic Association, 1975.

Ruddy, James F. *Photograde.* Wolfeboro, N.H.: Bowers and Merena Galleries Inc., 1983.

Sheldon, William H. *Early American Cents.* New York: Harper & Row. 1949.

Syrett, Harold C. *The Papers of Alexander Hamilton.* Vol. 7. New York: Columbia University Press, 1963.

Taxay, Don. *The U.S. Mint and Coinage: An Illustrated History From 1776 to the Present.* Second Edition. New York: Arco Publishing Co., 1969.

U.S. Congress. Senate. *International Monetary Conference.* 1878. Senate Ex. Doc., 58. 45th Congress, Third Session. Washington, 1879.

U.S. Congress. Senate. *Coinage Laws of the United States 1792 to 1894 with an Appendix of Statistics Relating to Coins and Currency.* Fourth Edition. Washington, D.C.: Government Printing Office, 1894.

Van Allen, Leroy C., and Mallis, A. George. *Comprehensive Catalog and Encyclopedia of U.S. Morgan and Peace Silver Dollars.* New York: F.C.I. Press, 1976.

Willem, John M. *The United States Trade Dollar: America's Only Unwanted, Unhonored Coin.* New York: By the author, 1959; reprint edition, Racine, Wis.: Western Publishing Co., 1965.

Yeoman, R.S. *A Guidebook of United States Coins.* 45th Edition. Racine, Wis.: Western Publishing Co., 1991.